Case Studies in Contemporary Criticism

JONATHAN SWIFT

Gulliver's Travels

Case Studies in Contemporary Criticism

SERIES EDITOR: *Ross C Murfin*

Case Studies in Contemporary Criticism

SERIES EDITOR: Ross C Murfin, *Southern Methodist University*

JONATHAN SWIFT
Gulliver's Travels

Complete, Authoritative Text with
Biographical and Historical Contexts,
Critical History, and Essays from
Five Contemporary Critical Perspectives

EDITED BY

Christopher Fox
University of Notre Dame

Bedford/St. Martin's
BOSTON ◆ NEW YORK

For Bedford/St. Martin's
President: Charles H. Christensen
Editorial Director: Joan E. Feinberg
Managing Editor: Elizabeth M. Schaaf
Developmental Editor: Stephen A. Scipione
Production Editor: Ann Sweeney
Copyeditor: Jane Zanichkowsky
Text design: Sandra Rigney, The Book Department
Cover design: Richard Emery Design, Inc.
Cover art: Details from maps illustrating Gulliver's voyage adapted from Motte's 1726 edition of *Gulliver's Travels*

Library of Congress Catalog Card Number: 92–75897
Copyright © 1995 by Bedford Books *of* St. Martin's Press

Manufactured in the United States of America.

3   2
f   e   d

For information, write: Bedford/St. Martin's, 75 Arlington Street, Boston, MA 02116 (617–399–4000)

ISBN: 0–312–06665–1

Acknowledgment

Terry J. Castle, "Why the Houyhnmnms Don't Write: Swift, Satire, and the Fear of the Text," *Essays in Literature 7* (1980). © Western Illinois University, 1980.

About the Series

Case Studies in Contemporary Criticism provide college students with an entrée into the current critical and theoretical ferment in literary studies. Each volume reprints the complete text of a classic literary work and presents critical essays that approach the work from different theoretical perspectives, together with the editors' introductions to both the literary work and the critics' theoretical perspectives.

The volume editor of each *Case Study* has selected and prepared an authoritative text of the classic work, written an introduction to the work's biographical and historical contexts, and surveyed the critical responses to the work since its initial publication. Thus situated biographically, historically, and critically, the work is examined in five critical essays, each representing a theoretical perspective of importance to contemporary literary studies. These essays, prepared especially for undergraduates by exemplary critics, show theory in praxis; whether written by established scholars or exceptional young critics, they demonstrate how current theoretical approaches can generate compelling readings of great literature.

As series editor, I have prepared introductions, with bibliographies, to the theoretical perspectives represented in the five critical essays. Each introduction presents the principal concepts of a particular theory in their historical context and discusses the major figures and key works that have influenced their formulation. It is my hope that these introductions will reveal to students that good criticism is informed by a set of coherent assumptions, and will encourage them to recognize and examine their own assumptions about literature. Finally, I have compiled a glossary of key terms that recur in these volumes and in the discourse of contemporary theory and criticism. We hope that the *Case Studies in Contemporary Criticism* series will reaffirm the richness of its literary works, even as it introduces invigorating new ways to mine their apparently inexhaustible wealth.

Ross C Murfin
Series Editor
Southern Methodist University

About This Volume

Part One takes as its basis the Herbert Davis edition of *Gulliver's Travels*, itself based largely on George Faulkner's Dublin edition of 1735. With the exception of some slight modernizations in spelling, I have retained original orthography and punctuation, and the illustrations and maps prepared for eighteenth-century editions of Swift's work.

Part Two includes five exemplary critical essays that analyze *Gulliver's Travels* from different contemporary theoretical perspectives: feminist, new historicist, deconstructive, reader response, and psycho-analytical. One of these essays, Terry Castle's, has been published previously. The other four, by Felicity Nussbaum, Carole Fabricant, Michael Conlon, and Carol Barash are new contributions. My own essays, on historical and biographical contexts of Swift's book, and its critical history, introduce each part.

Acknowledgments

This volume has especially benefited from conversation and criticism of the contributors and of my Notre Dame colleagues in the eighteenth century, particularly Seamus Deane, Julia Douthwaite, Thomas Jemielity, and James Walton. Student discussions in a 1994 Notre Dame undergraduate English seminar also improved the work, as did the comments of John Dussinger, Barbara Green, James Woolley, Robert Lambriola, Paul William Child, Thomas Kaska, Sean Kohl, and Geoffrey Fox. At various stages, Julie Costello, Hong Won Suh, and Margaret Stein have worked hard on this project. Laura Sue Fuderer, and David G. Schappert have brought to it the expertise of professional librarians. The work of the series editor, Ross C Murfin, and the wonderful group of editors at Bedford Books, including Stephen A. Scipione, Ann Sweeney, and Jane Zanichkowsky has been exemplary. Each has made this a better book. Finally, I cannot thank enough my secretary, Nila Gerhold, who has worked on this project, with good-natured patience and professionalism, from beginning to end.

Christopher Fox
University of Notre Dame

Contents

ix

Case Studies in Contemporary Criticism

JONATHAN SWIFT

Gulliver's Travels

PART ONE

Gulliver's Travels:
The Complete Text

Introduction:
Biographical and
Historical Contexts

"As to my native country," said Jonathan Swift, "I happened indeed by a perfect accident, to be born here, my mother being left here from returning to her house at Leicester . . . and thus I am a Teague, or an Irishman, or what people please, although the best part of my life was in England" (*Corresp.* 4: 229). The author of *Gulliver's Travels* was born November 30, 1667, in Hoey's Court, a street in a fashionable part of Dublin. Six months earlier, his father, also named Jonathan, had died. This death, the son would later say, "was much lamented on account of his reputation for integrity with a tolerable good understanding" (*Prose Writings* 5: 191). The elder Jonathan Swift had immigrated from England to Ireland around 1660, to take a job at the King's Inns, the center of Dublin's legal establishment. In the summer of 1664, he had married another English immigrant, Abigail Erick, from Leicester. Through his English father, the author of *Gulliver's Travels* was related to the poet and playwright John Dryden. But a family member Swift respected far more was his grandfather Thomas Swift, an Anglican clergyman who had supported Charles I and the Royalist cause during the English Civil War and who had suffered, as a result, under the Puritans (Ehrenpreis 1: 4, 24; Swift, *Prose Writings* 5: 190).

The civil war that led his grandfather into prison in the 1640s also had a profound impact on Swift's native Ireland. Several decades before Swift's birth, the Puritan leader Oliver Cromwell had brought his New

Model Army into Ireland to crush the Royalist cause and the growing Catholic resistance, which had shown itself in the uprising of 1641. In the wake of Cromwell's push, Anglican Royalists, who had maintained support for the Crown, were severely punished, with many of their churches left in ruins (Simms, "Restoration" 433; Woolley 84–86). Irish Catholics suffered a worse fate. Many lost their family estates and were driven into smaller holdings west of the River Shannon, in what was called the "transplantation to Connacht" (Canny 107).

In Swift's lifetime, Irish troubles would flare again during the so-called Glorious Revolution, which brought the Protestant William of Orange to the throne to replace the Catholic James II, who fled to France on Christmas Day in 1688. In 1689, James would sail to Ireland to begin an ill-fated campaign to reclaim the throne. Preparations for war escalated until June 1690, when William arrived in Ireland with a fleet of 300 ships and 15,000 troops. On July 1, William's forces met James's followers, known as Jacobites, at the Battle of the Boyne. There, and later, at Aughrim Hill, the Jacobites would suffer a decisive defeat, and James would go into permanent exile in Louis XIV's France (Simms, "War of the Two Kings" 497–98). William's victory and the subsequent Act of Settlement (1701) secured the Protestant succession in Great Britain, though (Swift believed) with some lasting problems at home and abroad (*Prose Writings* 9: 31).

Abroad, the presence at Versailles of James II and his Catholic son (the "Old" Pretender, James III) heightened tensions between Britain and France and helped contribute to a state of almost continual war.[1] In recounting recent history, the hero of *Gulliver's Travels*, Lemuel Gulliver, can thus speak of "the *Revolution* under the Prince of *Orange;* the long War with *France* entered into by the said Prince, and renewed by his Successor" in which "the greatest Powers of *Christendom* were engaged" — wars, Gulliver adds, that have left about "a Million" dead (226). Some of the most vivid descriptions in *Gulliver's Travels* — of battles with "twenty Thousand killed on each Side; dying Groans, Limbs flying in the Air," of "dead Bodies drop[ping] down in Pieces from the Clouds, to the great Diversion of all the Spectators" (228) — suggest Swift's aversion to such events.

Added to the moral repugnance of war was its economic consequence. "Few of this generation," Swift would write in 1711, "can remember any thing but war and taxes, and they think it is as it should be: whereas 'tis certain we are the most undone people in Europe" (*Journal*

---

[1]Nineteen of the twenty-four years between 1689 and 1713 were spent at war.

To Stella 2: 397). To pay for their wars, King William and his successors increasingly drew on public credit, financed through the new Bank of England. In Part Two of *Gulliver's Travels,* Swift's king of Brobdingnag would ask how any country could afford such "chargeable and extensive Wars" or the new practice of keeping a standing army (133). Part One humorously makes a similar point when the giant, Gulliver, is kept by the emperor of the little people (the Lilliputians) for use against a rival country, Blefuscu. Given the immense cost of maintaining this secret weapon ("above a Million and a half" of the country's "greatest Gold Coin"), it is the treasurer of Lilliput who most wants to get rid of Gulliver (79). The emperor, however, wants to use his giant to reduce "the whole Empire of *Blefuscu* into a Province" to be governed "by a Viceroy" (69).

That this is how England ruled its colonies — including Ireland — adds satiric resonance to the king's request and to Gulliver's response: "I would never," Gulliver says, "be an Instrument of bringing a free and brave People into Slavery" (69). Swift had used similar language several years earlier, in a series of pamphlets published in Dublin condemning English colonial rule. This reminds us of something sometimes forgotten: that Swift's career as a writer was distinctly that of an *Irish* writer. Growing up, he faced his country's deep divisions in religion and politics, as well as its ambiguous relations to England. Internally, Ireland was split by three religious factions at odds with each other. The Roman Catholic population (made up of both Gaelic and "Old English"[2] groups) constituted the vast majority of the roughly three million people. The rest of the population was divided between the Presbyterians (or Dissenters, as they were called), who held strength in the north, and the Anglicans, who made up roughly two thirds of the population of the city of Dublin. As an Anglican priest, and later dean of St. Patrick's Cathedral in Dublin, Swift spent a lifetime defending this latter "minority within a minority" (McMinn, "Swift and Ireland" 38).

Swift would also increasingly support the larger cause of his country against England and what he called its "*contemptuous* Treatment of Ireland*" (*Prose Writings* 9: 20). In an early work, *The Story of An Injured Lady* (1707), Swift argued that it would have probably "been much better" for England if Ireland "had been damned, or burnt, or sunk to the Bottom of the Sea." If even the "smallest Advantage" might result from "any new Oppression" of its Irish subjects, wrote Swift, England would "never disputeth it a Moment" (*Prose Writings* 9: 6–7). As Oliver

---

[2]Established families of Anglo-Catholic descent.

Ferguson notes in his study of Swift and Ireland, the political realities here were harsh:

> Though in title a kingdom, eighteenth-century Ireland was in fact virtually an English colony. Almost all important government and ecclesiastical positions were held by English appointees. In addition, a number of minor posts, pensions, and sinecures held by nonresident Englishmen were a constant drain on the nation's economy. The country had its own parliament, but its powers were so curtailed as to make it little more than a rubber stamp for measures enacted in England. Under the terms of Poynings' Law, an act passed during the reign of Henry VII, the Irish Parliament could not convene without the consent of the King, and it could pass no laws without the approval of the King and the English Privy Council. It was convened . . . by the lord lieutenant, acting on orders from England. In session it could submit "Heads of Bills" to England for approval. There the Privy council could delete, add, or reject as it saw fit. (7–8)

Most important, as Swift saw it, colonial mercantile policies had put Ireland under severe economic hardship. The English government's philosophy here was clear: "[Y]ou shall in all things endeavour to advance and improve the trade of that our kingdom so far as it shall not be a prejudice to this our kingdom of England, which we mean shall not be wronged how much soever the benefit of [Ireland] might be concerned in it" (Cullen 397). To improve Britain's economy, Ireland's trade was severely restricted, particularly through the Woolen Act (1699), which prohibited Ireland from exporting its woolen goods to any place other than designated English ports. This gave England a virtual monopoly over Ireland's chief product. Through these and other acts, Ireland's ability to support itself was systematically strained. In his *Modest Proposal* (1729), Swift argues that the situation is so bad that the only thing left for the Irish to sell is their children — to the butcher. For "I have been assured," Swift's narrator tells us,

> that a young healthy Child, well nursed, is, at a Year old, a most delicious, nourishing, and wholesome Food; whether *Stewed, Roasted, Baked,* or *Boiled;* and, I make no doubt, that it will equally serve in a *Fricasie,* or *Ragoust.* (*Prose Writings* 12: 111)

By the time he wrote this deliberately outrageous pamphlet (responding to what he saw as an outrageous situation) Swift had become an Irish national hero through his published attacks on the ruling government, beginning with a *Proposal For the Universal Use of Irish Manufacture ... Utterly Rejecting and Renouncing Every Thing Wearable that comes from England* (1720) and culminating with the great *Drapier's Letters* of 1724–25, written under the pseudonym "Marcus Brutus, Drapier."[3] The best known of these letters, published October 22, 1724, and addressed *To The Whole People of Ireland*, argued that, "in *Reason*, all *Government* without the Consent of the *Governed*, is the *very Definition of Slavery*." Worse yet, said Swift, those "who have used *Power* to cramp *Liberty*, have gone so far as to resent even the *Liberty* of *Complaining*; although a Man upon the Rack, was never known to be refused the Liberty of *roaring* as loud as he thought fit" (*Prose Writings* 10: 63).

The authorities were not pleased. As with Swift's 1720 *Universal Use of Irish Manufacture*, calling for a general boycott of British goods, the new pamphlet was declared illegal and seditious. The printer, John Harding, was arrested, and a reward of £300 was offered to anyone who would publicly swear to the author's identity. No one did. When a Dublin grand jury refused to pursue the case, the jury was dismissed and another put in its place, with express instructions from Chief Justice Whitshed to bring charges against both printer and author. When that jury refused, Swift wrote a poem about the Latin motto inscribed on Whitshed's coach ("Liberty & my Native Country"):

Libertas & natale solum;
Fine words; I wonder where you stole 'em.
(*Poems* 282)

When we read of Lemuel Gulliver's refusal to bring "a free and brave People into Slavery" or his later accounts of the coercive use of political and colonial force (264), we should read them with this Irish context in mind, as we should Gulliver's opening complaint that "People in Power" are "very watchful over the Press" (28), for Swift's strongest activities on behalf of the Irish were undertaken during the same years he was writing *Gulliver's Travels* (1726). Swift was, then, not simply born in Ireland; he spent most of his life involved in Irish affairs — a fact that, as Carole Fabricant points out in an essay in this volume, profoundly shaped Swift's sense of history and view of the world. In *The Field Day Anthology of Irish Writing* (1991), Andrew Carpenter notes that this also affects Swift's style, which has "a fantastic

---

[3]As with most of Swift's writings, including *Gulliver's Travels*, Swift's name did not appear on the publication.

grotesque side closer to that of the Irish comic tradition than to anything in English literature." Indeed, the "tone of his major work is profoundly un-English . . . full of rough energy and aggression, quite unlike that of even the most energetic of his English contemporaries." Carpenter sees this aggression as coming largely from Swift's "own lack of cultural security" (1: 327), a point still under some debate (Deane, *Short History of Irish Literature* 45).[4] Nonetheless, Swift's Irish life is important to understanding his satiric stance.

We know little of Swift's first years in Ireland, aside from a story (perhaps apocryphal) that he was kidnapped for a time by his Irish nurse (Ehrenpreis 1: 30). We do know that at about age six, with the help of his Uncle Godwin (a lawyer attached to the powerful Ormond family), Swift was sent to the excellent grammar school at Kilkenny, 70 miles southwest of Dublin. Kilkenny College, as it was called, numbered among its students Swift's cousin and friend, Thomas Swift, and the future playwright William Congreve (Simms, "Restoration" 436). Aside from a mention of some happy Saturday afternoons and "charming custards in a blind alley," Swift's memories of his nine years there were not fond. He would later complain about the "Confinement ten hours a day, to nouns and Verbs, the Terror of the Rod, the bloddy Noses and broken Shins" (*Corresp.* 1: 109).

From Kilkenny, Swift and his cousin Thomas moved on to Trinity College, Dublin, where Swift enrolled on April 24, 1682. He was fifteen at the time. Trinity College's curriculum was highly conservative, stressing the study of Aristotelian logic, physics, and metaphysics, along with language and literature. Swift did poorly at the first set of subjects, later claiming that he was

> Sunk over head and ears in matter,
> Nor can of metaphysics smatter. . . .
> And think all notions too abstracted
> Are like the ravings of a cracked head.
> (*Poems* 429)

At language and literature, however (that is, Greek and Latin) he excelled, earning a grade of good, or *bene* (Ehrenpreis 1: 61).

As a student at Trinity, Swift also formed what would be a lifelong friendship with his tutor, St. George Ashe, who was later named profes-

---

[4]Also see Deane's "Swift and the Anglo-Irish Intellect" and Fabricant's *Swift's Landscape*.

sor of mathematics in 1685 and provost of the college in 1692. Ashe was an active member of the Dublin Philosophical Society, founded in 1683 to advance the new science, then pursued in the most progressive centers of learning in Europe. The same decade the Dublin Society was founded, a member of the Royal Society of London, Isaac Newton, demonstrated the laws of gravitation in his *Principia Mathematica, or Mathematical Principles of Natural Philosophy* (1687). The Dublin Society's president in 1684, Sir William Petty, similarly moved in an international scholarly community, having studied medicine in Holland and France. He then taught at Oxford, where he was famous for reviving a hanged woman (Ehrenpreis 1: 81). Petty later used his brilliance in mathematics to build a fortune through a survey of Irish lands confiscated from Catholics. He also wrote *An Essay on Political Arithmetick,* a landmark book in the history of economics that he presented to the Dublin Society on August 25, 1686 (Gunther 12: 195), and a work that Swift would later parody in the savage mathematics of *A Modest Proposal.*

The Dublin Society's interest in the new science showed itself not only in a rage for mathematics, but also in a concern for observation and experiment. In Dublin, Petty conducted experiments on a wide range of improvements, including designs for a new land carriage and a double-bottomed boat. To test the latter, he built a model navy of little ships (not unlike those Lemuel Gulliver would tow away from Blefuscu in Part One of *Gulliver's Travels* [Ehrenpreis 1: 84]). Swift's tutor Ashe pursued similar interests, giving papers to the Dublin Society on the usefulness of mathematics and on the results of his own experiments mixing coal dust and clay and in freezing eggs and urine. Another Dublin Philosophical Society member, Allen Mullen, M.D., liked to inject various substances (including opium and water) into dogs and record the ensuing effects (Hoppen 108–109).

The last experiment also appears in "The Academy of Lagado" in Part Three of *Gulliver's Travels* (172), which satirizes a series of research projects, some actually being pursued (Nicolson and Mohler). Because of this satire, Swift has been often seen as hostile to the new science. This might be too simple an explanation, for Swift also loved to read about various experiments in *The Philosophical Transactions of the Royal Society* (Smith, "Scientific Discourse"; Patey). Swift seems, however, to have been less hopeful than his friend, Ashe, about science's power to improve human life. Part Three of *Gulliver's Travels* appears, instead, to question the whole idea of progress and the mindless pursuit of the new at the expense of the old. Nonetheless, Swift's Lemuel

Gulliver, a surgeon with some university training, does seem to embrace values normally associated with science, among them a belief in the new authority of observation and quantification. Does Swift, however, embrace the views of Gulliver? Swift's attitude toward science is a contested matter. In *Gulliver's Travels,* is he satirizing all science, or simply *bad* science? However we decide that question, it is evident that Swift experienced the new experimental science (some of it perhaps even at first hand) during his years at Trinity College, Dublin, where he stayed from 1682 through 1689, when "The Troubles" connected to the war of the two kings forced him to flee Ireland and sail to England. (*Prose Writings* 5: 193)

   In England, Swift stayed briefly with his mother in Leicester before going to London to become a secretary to Sir William Temple, who would soon move into retirement at Moor Park in Surrey. Temple had enjoyed a distinguished career as a diplomat, serving as the chief negotiator of the Triple Alliance (1668), which brought Britain, Holland, and Sweden together with the aim of restoring a balance of power in Europe. In his work at The Hague, Temple had also met Prince William of Orange, who would later become king of England. Even in retirement, Temple remained an advisor to the king, who consulted him often. In the early 1690s, after King William objected to a bill that called for regular meetings of Parliament, young Jonathan Swift was sent by Temple to plea for the bill's passage. Soon after listening to Swift's arguments, the king vetoed the bill. "This was the first time," Swift later said, that he "had ever any converse with Courts, and he told his friends [that] it was the first incident that helped to cure him of vanity" (*Prose Writings* 5: 194). Lemuel Gulliver's experience with the emperor of Lilliput would similarly leave him with an "imperfect Idea of Courts and Ministers" (68). As Michael McKeon notes, the perils and pitfalls of state service becomes a key theme in *Gulliver's Travels* (341).
   By the time he joined Temple's household as secretary in 1690, Swift had felt the first effects of an ailment he later described as "a giddyness and coldness of Stomach, that almost brought him to his Grave, and . . . pursued him with Intermissions of two or thre[e] years to the end of his Life."[5] What he believed he had contracted by eating too much fruit we now know as Ménière's Syndrome, a disorder first identified in 1861, long after Swift's death. The ailment affects one's middle ear, bringing on vertigo or a loss of balance, nausea, deafness,

---

[5]Swift often employs the third person when speaking about himself.

and tinnitus (disturbing sounds that seem to come from inside one's head). After a major attack, Swift returned to Ireland, he says, "by advice of Physicians, who weakly imagined that his native air might be of some use to recover his Health." But "growing worse," he decided to go back to Moor Park in 1691 (*Prose Writings* 5: 193). From then on, Swift would doctor himself with a regimen of daily exercise, walking, running, riding, swimming, and in bad weather, climbing stairs (Ehrenpreis 2: 2). Despite these precautions, the symptoms would periodically recur, and he would say in old age that

> That old vertigo in his head,
> Will never leave him, till he's dead.
> (*Poems* 487)

This physical condition would also later contribute to myths of Swift's madness.

When he felt more healthy, Swift engaged in another activity confessed in a letter in February 1692:

> there is something in me which must be employ'd, & when I am alone, turns all, for want of practice, into speculation & thought; insomuch that in these seven weeks I have been here, I have writt, & burnt and writt again, upon almost all manner of subjects, more perhaps than any man in England. (*Corresp.* 1: 3–4)

Under Temple's roof, between 1690 and 1691, Swift had already composed his first surviving poem, *An Ode to the King*. A later *Ode to the Athenian Society,* also written in high Pindaric form, would be published in 1693. He would write several other Pindarics and soon afterward abandon the form altogether. He also completed his M.A. at Oxford, to prepare for a career in the church, and left Moor Park to return to Ireland, where he was ordained a priest on January 13, 1695. Thanks to scholars like Louis Landa and Phillip Harth, we know something of Swift's connections to the thought and practice of the Anglican Church. We know very little, however, about Swift's private religious views. George Orwell would later say that in *Gulliver's Travels* at least, Swift's "attitude is in effect the Christian attitude, minus the bribe of the 'next world'" (141). In a 1995 study of Swift's religious thinking, Michael DePorte would not find this statement far from the mark. Swift's first parish in Ireland was in an isolated section up north in Kilroot, an area known as a stronghold of religious dissent. If Swift began his great satire on religious fanaticism, *A Tale of A Tub,* here, it was started "in a place notorious for such zeal" (McMinn, *Life* 8). After a long year, Swift resigned his position at Kilroot and returned to Moor Park in 1696. There he began a major course of reading and took on the immense task of editing Sir William Temple's works — a project that gave Swift his first real glimpse of the world of publishing (Elias 200–201).

At Moor Park Swift also met young Esther Johnson (1681–1728), who later became his beloved "Stella." With her older friend Rebecca Dingley, Esther would eventually follow Swift to Dublin to live out her life. While away from Esther Johnson for several years, Swift kept a detailed record of his daily life, now known as the *Journal To Stella* (1710–1713). He would first call her by that name in print in a series of poems celebrating her birthday, beginning with "Stella's Birthday (1719)," which opens:

> Stella this day is thirty-four,
> (We shan't dispute a year or more:)
> However Stella, be not troubled,
> Although thy size and years are doubled,
> Since first I saw thee at sixteen,
> The brightest virgin on the green.
> So little is thy form declined;
> Made up so largely in the mind.
>
> *(Poems* 187)

The humor and the indirect praise, as well as the anti-Romantic strain, mark (and to some extent mask) the closeness of this relationship. The evening Stella died, Swift wrote that he had lost "the truest, most virtuous, and valuable friend, that I, or perhaps any other person ever was blessed with" (*Prose Writings* 5: 227). As Felicity Nussbaum argues later in this volume, Swift's view of women is highly complex. Our understanding is certainly complicated by Swift's relationship with another young woman, Esther Vanhomrigh (1687–1723), who also followed him to Dublin, some years after Stella. "I was born with violent passions which terminate all in one that unexpressible passion I have for you," the woman he would call "Vanessa" wrote Swift (*Corresp.* 2: 364). Whether Swift reciprocated is a matter for conjecture; by the time of Vanessa's death, they were estranged. Swift's poem about the affair, *Cadenus and Vanessa,* leaves the level of his own involvement a mystery (*Poems* 151).

After Sir William Temple's death in 1699, Swift became chaplain to the earl of Berkeley and then accepted another position in Ireland, this time as vicar of Laracor, twenty miles from Dublin. In 1701, he published his first political pamphlet, *The Contests and Dissensions Between the Nobles and the Commons in Athens and Rome*. Written, like so many of Swift's works, for a specific occasion (in this case, the Tory attempt to impeach some Whig lords) the pamphlet argues the dangers of political factionalism. It also stresses the need for a balance of power between the king and the "people," the executive and the legislative branches of government. For when "the Ballance is broke," says Swift, "Power will never continue long in equal Division between the two" but "will run entirely into one" (*Prose Writings* 1: 197). This concern for balance of power would later show itself in the portrayal of various forms of government in *Gulliver's Travels*. Several of these offer bad examples of what happens when too much power ends up in too few hands; at least one (Brobdingnag) gives a happy instance of a mixed state that manages to balance power for the public good. Swift's sense of the need for such balance, and his support for the Anglican Church, propel most of his early political writing.

In 1702, Swift received a Doctor of Divinity degree from Trinity College, Dublin. Over the next few years, he would also begin a series of trips to London in unofficial attempts to secure special funds, known as the First Fruits, for the Anglican Church of Ireland. These trips brought Swift into contact with the major Whig writers Joseph Addison and Richard Steele, whose serial publications *The Tatler* and *The Spectator* did much to establish popular taste. In London, Swift also renewed his friendship with William Congreve, who had established a major reputation as a dramatist. Swift's own fame would follow with *A Tale of A Tub*, published in 1704 with two other works, *The Battle of the Books*, a mock-heroic skirmish between ancient and modern writers, and *The Mechanical Operation of the Spirit*, a satire on religious fundamentalism.

The *Tale* itself was a triumph, running through ten editions in Swift's lifetime. In an "Apology" added to the 1710 edition, Swift said that he had hoped that "numerous and gross Corruptions in Religion and Learning might furnish Matter" for a satire, and had decided "to proceed in a manner, that should be altogether new, the World having been already too long nauseated with endless Repetitions upon every Subject" (*Prose Writings* 1: 1).

What resulted *was* new and, like a number of Swift's works, a spoof. The *Tale* pretends to be an example of "modern" writing at its finest, composed by an author who dubs himself Secretary of the Universe and who claims to deliver "momentous Truths" (1: 77, 114). In fact, "where I am not understood," he says, "it shall be concluded, that something very useful and profound is couch't underneath" (1: 28).

Wildly imaginative and digressive, the *Tale* includes a chapter advocating the use and improvement of madness in a commonwealth (1: 102–14). In between such digressions one finds a rambling history of Christianity, told in the story of three brothers, Peter, Martin, and Jack, who have been left their father's will. How the will is interpreted, reinterpreted, and twisted over the years to suit current fashion points to Swift's characteristic concern with the written word, its instability and vulnerability, especially when manipulated for the purposes of power. How meaning itself can be distorted and reshaped is a major theme in *Gulliver's Travels*. So is the theme of corruption, especially corruption of the primary meaning of the word, as Terry Castle's essay in this volume demonstrates.

A Tale of A Tub also reveals Swift's talent for parody (impersonating another style or voice). This ventriloquism would become a trademark. Swift's later *Meditation upon a Broomstick* (1704), for example, parodies the style of the scientific meditation, or "meleteticks,"[6] as it was called, popularized by Robert Boyle, a fellow of the Royal Society (Hunter, "*Gulliver* and the Novel" 62–3). Swift's "City Shower" (1710) would parody hackneyed imitations of the Virgilian georgic, a poem that often depicts animals in their natural setting. In Swift's poem the animals are people; the natural setting, the streets of London.

Under the name of "Isaac Bickerstaff," Swift would also parody another form: popular astrology and in particular the writing of a famous astrologer of the time, John Partridge, who had at one point predicted the death of the queen and had also attacked the Anglican Church (Lowe). Swift's astrologer Bickerstaff has his own predictions, the first of which is Partridge's death: for "I have consulted the Star of his Nativity by my own Rules," Bickerstaff says, "and find he will infallibly die upon the 29th of *March* next, about eleven at Night, of a raging Fever" (*Prose Writings* 2: 145). One month later a pamphlet was published bearing the title *The Accomplishment of the First of Mr. Bickerstaff's Predictions, Being An Account of the Death of Mr. Partridge, the Almanack-Maker, upon the 29th*. When the real Partridge wrote to say that he was still around, Bickerstaff published yet another pamphlet, proving invincibly that "Mr. *Partridge* is not alive," and that the individual using Partridge's name in print must be an impostor.

This use of a fictional author, the scrambling of fact and fiction, and the parody of various kinds of writing would all later find their way into *Gulliver's Travels,* which plays with a number of styles and types of lit-

[6]For the larger tradition of meleteticks, see Hunter's *Before Novels* 201–08.

erature, including spiritual autobiography, conversion narrative, travel tale, imaginary voyage, scientific report, and features of what would come to be called the novel.

From 1707 through 1709, Swift returned to London to barter for the First Fruits for the Irish Anglican Church, again without success. He even solicited the Whig Lord Lieutenant of Ireland, Wharton, only to be turned down "with sufficient coldness" (*Prose Writings* 8: 121). In exchange for the First Fruits, the Whigs wanted toleration for Irish Dissenters, something Swift couldn't concede. Swift's conservatism here had Irish roots. As Joseph McMinn explains, "Irish Anglicanism, precisely because it was threatened by Dissent, especially in the north, had to be ultra-conservative. Numerically, as well as politically, it could not entertain toleration" (*Life* 17). At this point, Swift began publishing a series of pamphlets criticizing toleration and outlining his views of the relation of church and state. The most amusing of these is *An Argument Against Abolishing Christianity* (1709). This tract ironically argues that Christianity does not need to be abolished, since it hardly exists anyway. But the Church still serves a valuable social purpose. Where else, he asks, can more men meet more women? "Where more Meetings for Business? Where more Bargains driven of all Sorts? And where so many Conveniences, or Incitements to sleep?" (*Prose Writings* 2: 31).

The year the *Argument* was published, the Whig party resisted a very favorable peace treaty offered by Louis XIV of France. Even old Whigs like Robert Harley were finding themselves increasingly disenchanted with continual war. So was Queen Anne. By 1710, as Swift tells us, she had decided to extricate herself "as soon as possible" from those who had profited by "perpetuating the War," and began dismissing prominent Whig leaders (*Prose Writings* 3: 8). With a delicate coalition led by Robert Harley and the Tory leader, Henry St. John Bolingbroke, a new ministry came to power in a "wave of war-weariness" (Downie, *Jonathan Swift* 154).

On August 31, 1710, Swift again left Dublin for London, this time as the official spokesman for the Anglican Church of Ireland, for yet another attempt to get the First Fruits. Swift had tried unsuccessfully for years to pry a promise from the Whigs; it took the new ministry a matter of days to move on his request. He was introduced to the new lord treasurer, Robert Harley, on October 4. In "less than three weeks," Swift reported, Harley secured the First Fruits from the queen (*Prose Writings* 8: 122). Harley was also one of the first politicians in a new age of print to recognize the power of the press to shape public opinion

(Downie, *Robert Harley* 28). He asked Swift to stay on and become part of "an entirely new scene," which needed a "good pen, to keep up the spirits raised in the people, to assert the principles, and justify the proceedings of the new ministers" (*Prose Writings* 8: 123). For the next two years (1711–13) Swift found himself at the very seat of British power, defending a new ministry that was trying to end a war and negotiate a peace in Europe. To support these ends, Swift published a series of thirty-three essays in a periodical called *The Examiner* and also wrote a larger work, *The Conduct of the Allies* (1711), calculating the costs of war.

His Whig friends were upset, and Swift's switch in party affiliation has remained a point of contention, particularly for later commentators (Lock; Downie). Swift always said he adhered to old Whig principles. How could he support a Tory regime? Was his move prompted by self-interest? or by a change in political beliefs? The first was certainly a factor; Swift was an ambitious man. The second is qualified by several points, not the least of which was the Whigs' support of a war Swift disliked and their lack of support, in his view, for the established church, evidenced among other sins by their failure to fund the First Fruits. Swift would argue too that the very meaning of the terms "Whig" and "Tory" had changed since King William's time.[7] His *Examiner,* No. 15, dated November 6, 1710, states that

> I would be glad to ask a Question about *two Great Men* of the late Ministry, how they came to be *Whigs?* And by what figure of Speech, half a Dozen others, lately put into great Employments, can be called *Tories?* I doubt, whoever would suit the Definition to the Persons, must make it directly contrary to what we understood it at the Time of the Revolution. (*Prose Writings* 3: 15)

Swift believed that he hadn't changed; the Whigs had. He had increasingly come to see the Whig ministry as being controlled by the new money interest, made up of bankers and stockjobbers who were making a killing on the war. At least this is the way he represented the Whigs in writing to support the new ministry. The Whig leadership, he said, had sold out to evil "Persons, whose Principle and Interest it was to corrupt our Manners, blind our Understandings, drain our Wealth, and in Time destroy our Constitution both in Church and State" and "at last" bring

[7]Howard Erskine-Hill also reminds us that in the early decades of the eighteenth century, "Whig and Tory were terms with no precise or stable definition" and that "there was in Swift's time no acceptance of a two-party system resembling twentieth-century Democrats and Republicans in the USA or Conservative and Labour in Britain" (6).

us "to the very Brink of Ruin" (*Prose Writings* 3: 12). Such rhetoric helped sway public opinion away from war and prepare the ground for a peace finally ratified at Utrecht the spring of 1713. On April 3 of that year, Swift wrote Stella: "[N]ow the great Work is in effect done, and I believe it will appear a most excellent Peace for Europe" (*Journal To Stella* 2: 652).

Swift was undoubtedly proud of his efforts here. He did not know that the same ministry he was defending was also conducting secret negotiations in France with the Pretender, James III. Other problems loomed large. Queen Anne's health was failing, and a major rift had developed between the two leaders, Harley and Bolingbroke, both of them Swift's friends.

Swift's contacts with the Tories had meanwhile connected him with other writers, among them the queen's physician, Dr. John Arbuthnot, a man of polymathic learning. Another writer, John Gay, would gain fame for his satire on the Whig first minister, Sir Robert Walpole, in *The Beggar's Opera* (1728). The work of Swift's fellow Irishman Thomas Parnell would spark a later craze for "graveyard poetry." And the young Catholic poet Alexander Pope would become one of Swift's dearest friends. Together this group, known as the Scriblerians, constituted what would be called the "most celebrated collection of clever fellows this country ever saw" (Fox, *Locke and the Scriblerians* 81–3).

Around 1713, the group began meeting regularly to discuss an ambitious program of attack on intellectual pride and folly. The cornerstone of this program was their work *The Memoirs of the Extraordinary Life, Works, and Discoveries of Martinus Scriblerus*. Cast in the form of a pseudobiography of a fictional creation — Martinus Scriblerus, eminent pedant, learned commentator on Pope's *Dunciad*, and noted author of *The Art of Sinking in Poetry* and other published matter — *The Memoirs* satirize what Swift and his friends saw as gross misapplications of the human intellect, above all, the type of mentality that turns "every Trifle into a serious thing" and reduces all to system (*Memoirs* 129). Based on a comment of Pope's, Leslie Stephen and others have suggested that *Gulliver's Travels* may have "originated in Swift's mind in the course of his meditations upon Scriblerus" (Stephen 167). More direct connections between these works, however, have yet to be established.

This was one of the last times Swift would visit with his London friends for years to come. In June 1713, Swift took on a new and prominent role in Dublin as dean of St. Patrick's Cathedral. He would remain dean for thirty-two years, until his death in 1745. In 1714, he made a brief return to London to try to mediate the growing dispute between

Harley and Bolingbroke, which had grown bitter and public. Unsuccessful, Swift shipped six cases of books from London and left for Dublin on May 31, 1714. Two months later, Queen Anne would die days after dismissing Harley, and the entire government Swift had supported would fall with the arrival from Germany of a new king, George I of Hanover.

When Swift returned home, he composed the poem "In Sickness: Written Soon After the Author's Coming to Live in Ireland, Upon the Queen's Death, October 1714," in which he laments his loneliness at leaving his London friends and his physician, John Arbuthnot. This sense of isolation was amplified by illness and a firm belief in his approaching end:

> 'Tis true — then why should I repine,
> To see my life so fast decline?
> But, why obscurely here alone?
> Where I am neither loved nor known.
> My state of health none care to learn . . .
> And, those with whom I now converse,
> Without a tear will tend my hearse.
>   (*Poems* 165)

Swift was mistaken. He would live thirty more years, all but the last few in an active life.

Starting with Stella, who often nursed him back to health, he would also continue to build a wide network of Irish friends. By 1717, he had met Thomas Sheridan, a brilliant Dublin schoolmaster who hailed from Cavan. Though Sheridan was twenty years younger than Swift, the two became close, and often engaged in rhyming contests that involved the exchange of elaborate riddles, jokes, and puns. Such word games (or Pun-ic wars) were much to Swift's liking, and found their way into his published work, adding a playful indeterminacy to the plainest prose. (At the beginning of *Gulliver's Travels,* for example, young Lemuel Gulliver is apprenticed to "my good Master Bates" [Fox 1992]). Another close companion, Patrick Delany, was an excellent teacher and junior fellow at Trinity College, Dublin. Delany and Sheridan's son, Thomas, would later write biographies of Swift.

At about this time, Swift also began taking a series of lengthy trips in Ireland, riding hundreds of miles on horseback through rugged and underpopulated areas, many of them non-English-speaking. As late as

1723, at fifty-six years of age, he rode two hundred miles south to Carbery on the wild coast of western Cork and wrote a Latin poem about the place. Joseph McMinn has explored the possible connections between these solitary journeys and the writing of *Gulliver's Travels* ("Jonathan's Travels"). Probably with the help of his friend Anthony Raymond, Swift also translated a Gaelic poem, *Pléaraca na Ruarcach,* or "The Description of an Irish Feast," which opens:

> O'Rourke's noble fare
> Will ne'er be forgot,
> By those who were there,
> And those who were not.
> (*Poems* 221)

These years also found Swift increasingly involved in Irish affairs. When he first returned to Ireland he swore he would stay out of local politics. But by 1719, Swift complained to his friend Charles Ford that "as the World is now turned, no Cloyster is retired enough to keep Politicks out" (*Corresp.* 2: 330). St. Patrick's Cathedral, located in a section of Dublin known as the Liberties, had a high concentration of parishioners who worked in the woolen industry. It is out of this group that Swift's pseudonym, the Drapier, and his reputation as an Irish patriot would emerge. By the 1720s, he was publishing pamphlets that struck at the very heart of colonial rule and also composing what many regard as his masterpiece, *Gulliver's Travels.*

"I am now writing a History of my Travells," Swift told Charles Ford on April 15, 1721, "which will be a large Volume, and gives Account of Countryes hitherto unknown; but they go on slowly for want of Health and Humor" (*Corresp.* 2: 381). Three years later, in January 1724, Swift would tell Ford that "I have left the Country of Horses, and am in the flying Island, where I shall not stay long, and my two last Journeys will be soon over" (*Corresp.* 3: 5). On August 14, 1725, Swift would report that "I have finished my Travells, and I am now transcribing them; they are admirable Things, and will wonderfully mend the World" (*Corresp.* 3: 87). On September 29 he would write Pope that "I have employed my time . . . in finishing correcting, amending, and Transcribing my Travells, in four parts Compleat . . . and intended for the press when the world shall deserve them, or rather when a Printer shall be found brave enough to venture his Eares" (*Corresp.* 3: 102).

The last statement alludes to the reaction to the recent printing of the *Drapier's Letters,* which had landed his printer in jail. Swift's correspondence with Ford, unpublished until the twentieth century, tells us that *Gulliver's Travels* was composed between 1721 and 1725, during a busy period in Swift's life, and that Part Three, "A Voyage to Laputa," was written *after* Part Four, "A Voyage to the Country of the Houyhnhnms." (The older story about the book's composition, with Part Four often presumed to be written last, had important ramifications for the early criticism of Swift). On Sunday, March 6, 1726, Swift left Ireland for London, carrying the manuscript of the *Travels*. He stayed several months with Pope and Bolingbroke, then returned to Dublin on August 15. His arrival home was a public event, if we believe local newspapers and the report by Thomas Sheridan:

> In his return to Dublin, upon notice that the ship in which he sailed was in the bay, several heads of different corporations, and principal citizens of Dublin, went out to meet him in a great number of wherries engaged for that purpose, in order to welcome him back. He had the pleasure to find his friend Dr. Sheridan, in company with a number of his intimates, at the side of his ship, ready to receive him into their boat, with the agreeable tidings, that [Stella, who had been ill] was past all danger. The boats, adorned with streamers, and colours, in which were many emblematical devices, made a fine appearance; and thus was the Drapier brought to his landing-place in a kind of triumph, where he was received and welcomed on shore by a multitude of his grateful countrymen, by whom he was conducted to his house amid repeated acclamations, of *Long live the Drapier*. The bells were all set a ringing, and bonfires kindled in every street. (Sheridan 260–61)

Several months later, on October 28, 1726, the London publisher Benjamin Motte released *Travels Into Several Remote Nations of the World In Four Parts*, written by one "Lemuel Gulliver, first a surgeon and then a Captain of several Ships."

The book caused a sensation. "Gulliver is in every body's Hands," Arbuthnot wrote Swift a week later, adding that "Gulliver is a happy man that at his age can write such a merry work" (*Corresp*. 3: 179–80). Eleven days later, Pope found *Gulliver* the talk of the town, and congratulated Swift "upon what you call your Couzen's wonderful Book." Some, Pope added, think it "rather too bold, and too general a Satire: but none that I hear of accuse it of particular reflections" (*Corresp*. 3: 181). The next day, November 17, John Gay wrote Swift from London with his own report of the response:

About ten days ago a Book was publish'd here of the Travels of one Gulliver, which hath been the conversation of the whole town ever since: The whole impression sold in a week; and nothing is more diverting than to hear the different opinions people give of it, though all agree in liking it extreamly. 'Tis generally said that you are the Author, but I am told, the Bookseller declares he knows not from what hand it came. From the highest to the lowest it is universally read, from the Cabinet-council to the Nursery. The Politicians . . . agree, that it is free from particular reflections, but that the Satire on general societies of men is too severe. (*Corresp.* 3: 182)

As the comments on the severity of the satire make clear, early readers also found some problems. Arbuthnot would tell Swift, for instance, that he thought Part Three (the satire on science) to be the "lea[st] Brilliant," though this part, Gay would add, "hath its defenders too." Gay would also note that "[a]mong Lady-critics, some have found out that Mr. Gulliver had a particular malice to maids of honour" (*Corresp.* 3: 179, 183).

Interesting here is the extent to which these early responses would be echoed in later criticism, in questions about the political allusions or "reflections" in *Gulliver* (Are they directed at general groups, or at specific people?); about Part Three (How does it fit?); about Gulliver's treatment of women (Is it sexist?); or about the satire on human nature, particularly in Part Four (Is it too severe?). Addressing Swift as "Gulliver" and referring to his "merry work," Arbuthnot raises other questions. What is the connection between the actual author and the fictional one? Are their views identical or different? For example, when the work ends in Gulliver's raging anger at human pride, does this represent Swift's views, or those of a literary character? Is this ultimately a "merry work" or a tragic one? As the critical history of *Gulliver's Travels* suggests, many of these questions are still with us.

Swift was fifty-nine when *Gulliver's Travels* was published. He would continue to write for at least ten more years, and he would publish important political pamphlets including *A Short View of the State of Ireland* (1728) and *A Modest Proposal* (1729), as well as such humorous pieces as *Polite Conversation* (1738) and *Directions to Servants* (published posthumously in 1745). In later life, Swift also produced much poetry, ranging from the wildly scatological "The Lady's Dressing Room" to his superb "Verses on the Death of Dr. Swift" (1731). The latter, written when he was very much alive, imagined what the reaction to his death might be among friends and enemies alike. In 1735 his

Dublin printer, George Faulkner, brought out the first four volumes of Swift's collected works, volume three of which contains a new edition of *Gulliver,* complete with a prefatory letter from Captain Gulliver to his fictional editor, Richard Sympson, complaining about the mistakes in earlier editions, which "have either omitted some material Circumstances, or minced or changed them in such a Manner, that I do hardly know mine own Work" (28). This corrected 1735 edition, probably overseen by Swift, is the basis of the following text.

In the late 1730s, Swift's attacks of deafness and vertigo intensified, and his health gradually worsened. Edward Young would later recall an evening walk with Swift and some others about a mile outside of Dublin. Swift "stopt short," Young says, "as we passed on; but, perceiving that he did not follow us, I went back; and found him fixed as a statue, and earnestly gazing upward at a noble elm, which in its uppermost branches was much withered, and decayed. Pointing at it, he said, 'I shall be like that tree, I shall die at the top'" (Williams 179–80). Swift was still well enough to work on a satire on corruption in the Irish House of Commons, *The Legion Club,* and to enjoy his seventieth birthday in 1737, which was celebrated throughout Dublin. Soon after that, however, he began to fail. In 1742, when Swift was seventy-five, his friends moved to have him declared "of unsound mind and memory." He died on October 19, 1745, and was buried next to Stella in St. Patrick's Cathedral. He left his life savings to found the first mental hospital in Ireland, St. Patrick's Hospital for the Insane. In his own words,

> He gave the little wealth he had,
> To build a house for fools and mad:
> And showed by one satiric touch,
> No nation wanted it so much.
>   (*Poems* 498)

Christopher Fox

WORKS CITED

Canny, Nicholas. *Kingdom and Colony: Ireland in the Atlantic World 1560–1800.* Baltimore: Johns Hopkins UP, 1988.

Carpenter, Andrew. "Jonathan Swift." *The Field Day Anthology of Irish Writing.* Ed. Seamus Deane. Vol. 1. Derry: Field Day Publications, 1991. 327–30. 3 vols.

Cullen, L. M. "Economic Trends, 1660–91." Moody 387–407.

Deane, Seamus. *A Short History of Irish Literature*. London: Hutchinson; Notre Dame, Ind.: U of Notre Dame P, 1986.

———. "Swift and the Anglo-Irish Intellect." *Eighteenth-Century Ireland* 1 (1986):9–22.

DePorte, Michael. "Swift, God, and Power." Forthcoming in *Walking Naboth's Vineyard: New Studies of Swift*. Ed. Christopher Fox and Brenda Tooley. Notre Dame, Ind.: U of Notre Dame P, 1995. 79–97.

Downie, J. A. *Jonathan Swift Political Writer*. London: Routledge, 1984.

———. *Robert Harley and the Press: Propaganda and Public Opinion in the Age of Swift and Defoe*. Cambridge: Cambridge UP, 1979.

Ehrenpreis, Irvin. *Swift; The Man, His Works, and the Age*. 3 vols. Cambridge, Mass.: Harvard UP, 1962–83.

Elias, A. C., Jr. *Swift at Moor Park: Problems in Biography and Criticism*. Philadelphia: U of Pennsylvania P, 1982.

Erskine-Hill, Howard. *Gulliver's Travels*. Cambridge: Cambridge UP, 1993.

Fabricant, Carole. *Swift's Landscape*. Baltimore: Johns Hopkins UP, 1982.

Ferguson, Oliver W. *Jonathan Swift and Ireland*. Urbana: U of Illinois P, 1962.

Fox, Christopher. *Locke and the Scriblerians: Identity and Consciousness in Early Eighteenth-Century Britain*. Berkeley: U of California P, 1988.

———. "The Myth of Narcissus in Swift's *Travels*." *Eighteenth-Century Studies* 20 (1986–87): 17–33; rev. and rpt. in *Reader Entrapment in Eighteenth-Century Literature*. Ed. Carl Kropf. New York: AMS P, 1992. 89–107.

Gunther, R. T. *Early Science in Oxford*. 15 vols. Oxford, 1923–1945; rpt. London: Dawsons of Pall Mall, 1968.

Harth, Phillip. *Swift and Anglican Rationalism: The Religious Background of "A Tale of A Tub."* Chicago: U of Chicago P, 1961.

Hoppen, K. Theodore. *The Common Scientist in the Seventeenth Century. A Study of the Dublin Philosophical Society 1683–1708*. Charlottesville: UP of Virginia, 1970.

Hunter, J. Paul. *Before Novels: The Cultural Contexts of Eighteenth-Century English Fiction*. New York: Norton, 1990.

————. "*Gulliver's Travels* and the Novel." Ed. Frederik N. Smith, *Genres of Gulliver's Travels*. 56–74.

Landa, Louis. *Swift and the Church of Ireland*. Oxford: Clarendon, 1954.

Lock, F. P. *Swift's Tory Politics*. Newark: U of Delaware P, 1983.

Lowe, N. F. "Why Swift Killed Partridge." *Swift Studies* 6 (1991): 70–82.

McKeon, Michael. *The Origins of the English Novel, 1600–1740*. Baltimore: Johns Hopkins UP, 1987.

McMinn, Joseph. *Jonathan Swift: A Literary Life*. New York: St. Martin's P, 1991.

————. "Jonathan's Travels: Swift's Sense of Ireland." *Swift Studies* 7 (1992): 36–53.

————. "Swift and Ireland." *Critical Approaches to Teaching Swift*. Ed. Peter Schakel. New York: AMS P, 1992. 36–51.

Moody, T. W., F. X. Martin, and F. J. Byrne, eds. *Early Modern Ireland, 1534–1691*. Oxford: Clarendon, 1976. Vol. 3 of *A New History of Ireland*. 10 vols. 1976–1984.

Nicolson, Marjorie, and Nora M. Mohler. "The Scientific Background of Swift's Voyage to LaPuta." *Annals of Science* 2 (1937): 299–334.

Orwell, George. "Politics vs. Literature: An Examination of *Gulliver's Travels.*" *Selected Essays*. London: Penguin, 1957. 121–42.

Patey, Douglas Lane. "Swift's Satire on 'Science' and the Structure of *Gulliver's Travels*." *English Literary History* 58 (1991): 809–39.

Sheridan, Thomas. *The Life of the Rev. Dr. Jonathan Swift*. London, 1784; rpt. New York: Garland, 1974.

Simms, J. G. "The Restoration, 1660–85." Moody 420–53.

————. "The War of the Two Kings, 1685–91." Moody 478–508.

Smith, Frederik N., ed. *The Genres of Gulliver's Travels*. Newark: U of Delaware P; London: Associated UP, 1990.

————. "Scientific Discourse: *Gulliver's Travels* and the *Philosophical Transactions*." Smith, *Genres of Gulliver's Travels* 139–62.

Stephen, Leslie. *Swift*. New York: Harper, 1898.

Swift, Jonathan. *The Complete Poems*. Ed. Pat Rogers. London: Penguin, 1983.

————. *The Correspondence of Jonathan Swift*. Ed. Harold Williams, Rev. David Woolley. 5 vols. Oxford: Clarendon, 1963–72.

————. *Journal To Stella*. Ed. Harold Williams. 2 vols. Oxford: Clarendon, 1948.

————. *The Prose Writings of Jonathan Swift*. Ed. Herbert Davis. 14 vols. Oxford: Blackwell, 1939–68.

Swift, Jonathan, et al. *The Memoirs of the Extraordinary Life, Works, and Discoveries of Martinus Scriblerus*. Ed. Charles Kerby-Miller. New Haven: Yale UP, 1950. New York: Russell, 1966.

Williams, Kathleen. *Swift: The Critical Heritage*. London: Routledge, 1970.

Woolley, James, ed. *Jonathan Swift and Thomas Sheridan: The Intelligencer*. Oxford: Clarendon, 1990.

VOLUME III.

Of the Author's

WORKS.

CONTAINING,

TRAVELS

INTO SEVERAL

Remote Nations of the WORLD.

In Four PARTS, viz.

I. A Voyage to LIL-
LIPUT.

II. A Voyage to BROB-
DINGNAG.

III. A Voyage to LA-

PUTA, BALNIBARBI,
LUGGNAGG, GLUBB-
DUBDRIE and JAPAN.

IV. A Voyage to the
COUNTRY of the
HOUYHNHNMS.

By *LEMUEL GULLIVER*, firft a Surgeon,
and then a CAPTAIN of feveral SHIPS.

—— —— *Retroq*;
Vulgus abborret ab his.

In this Impreffion feveral Errors in the *London* and *Dublin*
Editions are correded.

DUBLIN:

Printed by and for GEORGE FAULKNER, Printer
and Bookfeller, in *Effex-Street*, oppofite to the
Bridge. MDCCXXXV.

Gulliver's Travels

ADVERTISEMENT

Mr. Sympson's *Letter to Captain* Gulliver, *prefixed to this Volume, will make a long Advertisement unnecessary. Those Interpolations complained of by the Captain, were made by a Person since deceased, on whose Judgment the Publisher relyed to make any Alterations that might be thought necessary. But, this Person, not rightly comprehending the Scheme of the Author, nor able to imitate his plain simple Style, thought fit among many other Alterations and Insertions, to compliment the Memory of her late Majesty, by saying,* That she governed without a Chief Minister. *We are assured, that the Copy sent to the Bookseller in* London, *was a Transcript of the Original, which Original being in the Possession of a very worthy Gentleman in* London, *and a most intimate Friend of the Authors; after he had bought the Book in Sheets, and compared it with the Originals, bound it up with blank Leaves, and made those Corrections, which the Reader will find in our Edition. For, the same Gentleman did us the Favour to let us transcribe his Corrections.*

A LETTER FROM CAPT. *GULLIVER,*
TO HIS COUSIN *SYMPSON*

I hope you will be ready to own publickly, whenever you shall be called to it, that by your great and frequent Urgency you prevailed on me to publish a very loose and uncorrect Account of my Travels; with

Direction to hire some young Gentlemen of either University to put them in Order, and correct the Style, as my Cousin *Dampier*° did by my Advice, in his Book called, *A Voyage round the World.* But I do not remember I gave you Power to consent, that any thing should be omitted, and much less that any thing should be inserted: Therefore, as to the latter, I do here renounce every thing of that Kind; particularly a Paragraph about her Majesty the late Queen *Anne,* of most pious and glorious Memory; although I did reverence and esteem her more than any of human Species. But you, or your Interpolator, ought to have considered, that as it was not my Inclination, so was it not decent to praise any Animal of our Composition before my Master *Houyhnhnm:* And besides, the Fact was altogether false; for to my Knowledge, being in *England* during some Part of her Majesty's Reign, she did govern by a chief Minister; nay, even by two successively; the first whereof was the Lord of *Godolphin,*° and the second the Lord of *Oxford;*° so that you have made me *say the thing that was not.* Likewise, in the Account of the Academy of Projectors, and several Passages of my Discourse to my Master *Houyhnhnm,* you have either omitted some material Circumstances, or minced or changed them in such a Manner, that I do hardly know mine own Work. When I formerly hinted to you something of this in a Letter, you were pleased to answer, that you were afraid of giving Offence; that People in Power were very watchful over the Press; and apt not only to interpret, but to punish every thing which looked like an *Inuendo* (as I think you called it.) But pray, how could that which I spoke so many Years ago, and at above five Thousand Leagues distance, in another Reign, be applyed to any of the *Yahoos,* who now are said to govern the Herd; especially, at a time when I little thought on or feared the Unhappiness of living under them. Have not I the most Reason to complain, when I see these very *Yahoos* carried by *Houyhnhnms* in a Vehicle, as if these were Brutes, and those the rational Creatures? And, indeed, to avoid so monstrous and detestable a Sight, was one principal Motive of my Retirement hither.

Thus much I thought proper to tell you in Relation to your self, and to the Trust I reposed in you.

I do in the next Place complain of my own great Want of Judgment, in being prevailed upon by the Intreaties and false Reasonings of you

---

Dampier: William Dampier (1652–1715), sailor and author of *A New Voyage Round the World* (1697).   *Godolphin ... Oxford:* Sidney Godolphin (1645–1712) and Robert Harley, Earl of Oxford (1661–1724) were successive Lord High Treasurers of England from 1702–1710 and 1711–1714.

and some others, very much against mine own Opinion, to suffer my Travels to be published. Pray bring to your Mind how often I desired you to consider, when you insisted on the Motive of *publick Good;* that the *Yahoos* were a Species of Animals utterly incapable of Amendment by Precepts or Examples: And so it hath proved; for instead of seeing a full Stop put to all Abuses and Corruptions, at least in this little Island, as I had Reason to expect: Behold, after above six Months Warning, I cannot learn that my Book hath produced one single Effect according to mine Intentions: I desired you would let me know by a Letter, when Party and Faction were extinguished; Judges learned and upright; Pleaders honest and modest, with some Tincture of common Sense; and *Smithfield* ° blazing with Pyramids of Law-Books; the young Nobility's Education entirely changed; the Physicians banished; the Female *Yahoos* abounding in Virtue, Honour, Truth and good Sense: Courts and Levees of great Ministers thoroughly weeded and swept; Wit, Merit and Learning rewarded; all Disgracers of the Press in Prose and Verse, condemned to eat nothing but their own Cotten, and quench their Thirst with their own Ink. These, and a Thousand other Reformations, I firmly counted upon by your Encouragement; as indeed they were plainly deducible from the Precepts delivered in my Book. And, it must be owned, that seven Months were a sufficient Time to correct every Vice and Folly to which *Yahoos* are subject; if their Natures had been capable of the least Disposition to Virtue or Wisdom: Yet so far have you been from answering mine Expectation in any of your Letters; that on the contrary, you are loading our Carrier every Week with Libels, and Keys,° and Reflections, and Memoirs, and Second Parts; wherein I see myself accused of reflecting upon great States-Folk; of degrading human Nature, (for so they have still the Confidence to stile it) and of abusing the Female Sex. I find likewise, that the Writers of those Bundles are not agreed among themselves; for some of them will not allow me to be Author of mine own Travels; and others make me Author of Books to which I am wholly a Stranger.

I find likewise, that your Printer hath been so careless as to confound the Times, and mistake the Dates of my several Voyages and Returns; neither assigning the true Year, or the true Month, or Day of the Month: And I hear the original Manuscript is all destroyed, since the Publication of my Book. Neither have I any Copy left; however, I have sent you some Corrections, which you may insert, if ever there should

Smithfield: Site in London of Bartholomew Fair and various popular entertainments.
Keys: Commentaries.

be a second Edition: And yet I cannot stand to them, but shall leave that Matter to my judicious and candid Readers, to adjust it as they please.

I hear some of our Sea-*Yahoos* find Fault with my Sea-Language, as not proper in many Parts, nor now in Use. I cannot help it. In my first Voyages, while I was young, I was instructed by the oldest Mariners, and learned to speak as they did. But I have since found that the Sea-*Yahoos* are apt, like the Land ones, to become new fangled in their Words; which the latter change every Year; insomuch, as I remember upon each Return to mine own Country, their old Dialect was so altered, that I could hardly understand the new. And I observe, when any *Yahoo* comes from *London* out of Curiosity to visit me at mine own House, we neither of us are able to deliver our Conceptions in a Manner intelligible to the other.

If the Censure of *Yahoos* could any Way affect me, I should have great Reason to complain, that some of them are so bold as to think my Book of Travels a meer Fiction out of mine own Brain; and have gone so far as to drop Hints, that the *Houyhnhnms* and *Yahoos* have no more Existence than the Inhabitants of *Utopia*.

Indeed I must confess, that as to the People of *Lilliput, Brobdingrag,* (for so the Word should have been spelt, and not erroneously *Brobdingnag*) and *Laputa;* I have never yet heard of any *Yahoo* so presumptuous as to dispute their Being, or the Facts I have related concerning them; because the Truth immediately strikes every Reader with Conviction. And, is there less Probability in my Account of the *Houyhnhnms* or *Yahoos,* when it is manifest as to the latter, there are so many Thousands in this City, who only differ from their Brother Brutes in *Houyhnhnmland,* because they use a Sort of *Jabber,* and do not go naked. I wrote for their Amendment, and not their Approbation. The united Praise of the whole Race would be of less Consequence to me, than the neighing of those two degenerate *Houyhnhnms* I keep in my Stable; because, from these, degenerate as they are, I still improve in some Virtues, without any Mixture of Vice.

Do these miserable Animals presume to think that I am so far degenerated as to defend my Veracity; *Yahoo* as I am, it is well known through all *Houyhnhnmland,* that by the Instructions and Example of my illustrious Master, I was able in the Compass of two Years (although I confess with the utmost Difficulty) to remove that infernal Habit of Lying, Shuffling, Deceiving, and Equivocating, so deeply rooted in the very Souls of all my Species; especially the *Europeans.*

I have other Complaints to make upon this vexatious Occasion; but I forbear troubling myself or you any further. I must freely confess, that since my last Return, some corruptions of my Yahoo Nature have revived in me by Conversing with a few of your Species, and particularly those of mine own Family, by an unavoidable Necessity; else I should never have attempted so absurd a Project as that of reforming the *Yahoo* Race in this Kingdom; but, I have now done with all such visionary Schemes for ever.

April 2, 1727.

THE PUBLISHER *TO THE* READER

The Author of these Travels, Mr. *Lemuel Gulliver,* is my antient and intimate Friend; there is likewise some Relation between us by the Mother's Side. About three Years ago Mr. *Gulliver* growing weary of the Concourse of curious People coming to him at his House in *Redriff,*° made a small Purchase of Land, with a convenient House, near *Newark,* in *Nottinghamshire,* his native Country; where he now lives retired, yet in good Esteem among his Neighbours.

Although Mr. *Gulliver* was born in *Nottinghamshire,* where his Father dwelt, yet I have heard him say, his Family came from *Oxfordshire;* to confirm which, I have observed in the Church-Yard at *Banbury,*° in that County, several Tombs and Monuments of the *Gullivers.*

Before he quitted *Redriff,* he left the Custody of the following Papers in my Hands, with the Liberty to dispose of them as I should think fit. I have carefully perused them three Times: The Style is very plain and simple; and the only Fault I find is, that the Author, after the Manner of Travellers, is a little too circumstantial. There is an Air of Truth apparent through the whole; and indeed the Author was so distinguished for his Veracity, that it became a Sort of Proverb among his Neighbours at *Redriff,* when any one affirmed a Thing, to say, it was as true as if Mr. *Gulliver* had spoke it.

By the Advice of several worthy Persons, to whom, with the Author's Permission, I communicated these Papers, I now venture to send them into the World; hoping they may be, at least for some time, a better Entertainment to our young Noblemen, than the common Scribbles of Politicks and Party.

This Volume would have been at least twice as large, if I had not made bold to strike out innumerable Passages relating to the Winds and

---

Redriff: A section of London also known as Rotherhithe.   *Banbury:* An English town famous for its Puritanism.

Tides, as well as to the Variations and Bearings in the several Voyages; together with the minute Descriptions of the Management of the Ship in Storms, in the Style of Sailors: Likewise the Account of the Longitudes and Latitudes; wherein I have Reason to apprehend that Mr. *Gulliver* may be a little dissatisfied: But I was resolved to fit the Work as much as possible to the general Capacity of Readers. However, if my own Ignorance in Sea-Affairs shall have led me to commit some Mistakes, I alone am answerable for them: And if any Traveller hath a Curiosity to see the whole Work at large, as it came from the Hand of the Author, I will be ready to gratify him.

As for any further Particulars relating to the Author, the Reader will receive Satisfaction from the first Pages of the Book.

Richard Sympson.

THE CONTENTS

PART I

PART II

CHAP. I

CHAP. II

CHAP. III

CHAP. IV

CHAP. V

CHAP. VI

CHAP. VII

CHAP. VIII

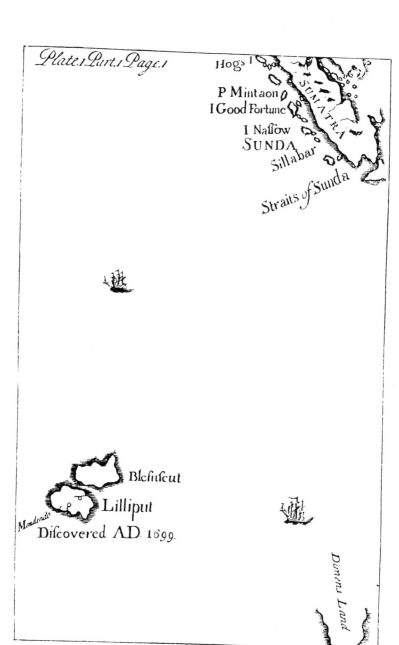

Plate.1 Part.1 Page.1

Hogs I

P Mintaon
I Good Fortune

I Naſſow
SUNDA
Sillabar

SUMATRA

Straits of Sunda

Blefuſcut

Mendendo   Lilliput
Discovered AD. 1699.

Dimens Land

PART I
A Voyage To *Lilliput*

CHAPTER I

The Author giveth some Account of himself and Family; his first In-
ducements to travel. He is shipwrecked, and swims for his Life; gets safe on
shoar in the Country of Lilliput; *is made a Prisoner, and carried up the*
Country.

My Father had a small Estate in *Nottinghamshire;* I was the Third of
five Sons. He sent me to *Emanuel-College* in *Cambridge,* at Fourteen
Years old,° where I resided three Years, and applied my self close to my
Studies: But the Charge of maintaining me (although I had a very
scanty Allowance) being too great for a narrow Fortune; I was bound
Apprentice to Mr. *James Bates,* an eminent Surgeon° in *London,* with
whom I continued four Years; and my Father now and then sending me
small Sums of Money, I laid them out in learning Navigation, and other
Parts of the Mathematicks, useful to those who intend to travel, as I
always believed it would be some time or other my Fortune to do.
When I left Mr. *Bates,* I went down to my Father; where, by the Assistance of him and my Uncle *John,* and some other Relations, I got Forty

Cambridge **[University], at Fourteen Years old:** At that time, a normal age to start
college. Swift entered Trinity College, Dublin, at fifteen.   **Surgeon:** Surgeons were still
associated with the Company of Barber Surgeons and did not have the prestige of licensed
physicians.

Pounds, and a Promise of Thirty Pounds a Year to maintain me at *Leyden*:° There I studied Physick° two Years and seven Months, knowing it would be useful in long Voyages.

Soon after my Return from *Leyden*, I was recommended by my good Master Mr. *Bates*, to be Surgeon to the *Swallow*, Captain *Abraham Pannell* Commander; with whom I continued three Years and a half, making a Voyage or two into the *Levant*,° and some other Parts. When I came back, I resolved to settle in *London*, to which Mr. *Bates*, my Master, encouraged me; and by him I was recommended to several Patients. I took Part of a small House in the *Old Jury*; and being advised to alter my Condition, I married Mrs. *Mary Burton*,° second Daughter to Mr. *Edmond Burton*, Hosier, in *Newgate-street*, with whom I received four Hundred Pounds for a Portion.°

But, my good Master *Bates* dying in two Years after, and I having few Friends, my Business began to fail; for my Conscience would not suffer me to imitate the bad Practice of too many among my Brethren. Having therefore consulted with my Wife, and some of my Acquaintance, I determined to go again to Sea. I was Surgeon successively in two Ships, and made several Voyages, for six Years, to the *East* and *West-Indies*; by which I got some Addition to my Fortune. My Hours of Leisure I spent in reading the best Authors, ancient and modern; being always provided with a good Number of Books; and when I was ashore, in observing the Manners and Dispositions of the People, as well as learning their Language; wherein I had a great Facility by the Strength of my Memory.

The last of these Voyages not proving very fortunate, I grew weary of the Sea, and intended to stay at home with my Wife and Family. I removed from the *Old Jury* to *Fetter-Lane*, and from thence to *Wapping*, hoping to get Business among the Sailors; but it would not turn to account. After three Years Expectation that things would mend, I accepted an advantageous Offer from Captain *William Prichard*, Master of the *Antelope*, who was making a Voyage to the *South-Sea*. We set sail from *Bristol*, May 4th, 1699, and our Voyage at first was very prosperous.

It would not be proper for some Reasons, to trouble the Reader with the Particulars of our Adventures in those Seas: Let it suffice to inform him, that in our Passage from thence to the *East-Indies*, we were

---

Leyden: In the Netherlands; site of the best medical school in eighteenth-century Europe. **Physick:** Medicine. **Levant:** The Near East. **Mrs. Mary Burton:** Women were called "Mrs." regardless of marital state. **Portion:** Dowry.

driven by a violent Storm to the Northwest of *Van Diemen's* Land.° By an Observation, we found ourselves in the Latitude of 30 Degrees 2 Minutes South. Twelve of our Crew were dead by immoderate Labour, and ill Food; the rest were in a very weak Condition. On the fifth of *November,* which was the beginning of Summer in those Parts, the Weather being very hazy, the Seamen spyed a Rock, within half a Cable's length° of the Ship; but the Wind was so strong, that we were driven directly upon it, and immediately split. Six of the Crew, of whom I was one, having let down the Boat into the Sea, made a Shift to get clear of the Ship, and the Rock. We rowed by my Computation, about three Leagues,° till we were able to work no longer, being already spent with Labour while we were in the Ship. We therefore trusted ourselves to the Mercy of the Waves; and in about half an Hour the Boat was overset by a sudden Flurry from the North. What became of my Companions in the Boat, as well as of those who escaped on the Rock, or were left in the Vessel, I cannot tell; but conclude they were all lost. For my own Part, I swam as Fortune directed me, and was pushed forward by Wind and Tide. I often let my Legs drop, and could feel no Bottom: But when I was almost gone, and able to struggle no longer, I found myself within my Depth; and by this Time the Storm was much abated. The Declivity was so small, that I walked near a Mile before I got to the Shore, which I conjectured was about Eight o'Clock in the Evening. I then advanced forward near half a Mile, but could not discover any Sign of Houses or Inhabitants; at least I was in so weak a Condition, that I did not observe them. I was extremely tired, and with that, and the Heat of the Weather, and about half a Pint of Brandy that I drank as I left the Ship, I found my self much inclined to sleep. I lay down on the Grass, which was very short and soft; where I slept sounder than ever I remember to have done in my Life, and as I reckoned, above Nine Hours; for when I awaked, it was just Day-light. I attempted to rise, but was not able to stir: For as I happened to lie on my Back, I found my Arms and Legs were strongly fastened on each Side to the Ground; and my Hair, which was long and thick, tied down in the same Manner. I likewise felt several slender Ligatures across my Body, from my Armpits to my Thighs. I could only look upwards; the Sun began to grow hot, and the Light offended mine Eyes. I heard a confused Noise about me, but in the Posture I lay, could see nothing except the Sky. In a little time I felt

---

Van Diemen's **Land:** Island off the southeastern coast of Australia; in Swift's time, sometimes also a name for Australia itself.   **a Cable's length:** 600 feet.   **three Leagues:** A league is about 3 miles; thus, they rowed roughly 9 miles.

something alive moving on my left Leg, which advancing gently forward over my Breast, came almost up to my Chin; when bending mine Eyes downwards as much as I could, I perceived it to be a human Creature not six Inches high,° with a Bow and Arrow in his Hands, and a Quiver at his Back. In the mean time, I felt at least Forty more of the same Kind (as I conjectured) following the first. I was in the utmost Astonishment, and roared so loud, that they all ran back in a Fright; and some of them, as I was afterwards told, were hurt with the Falls they got by leaping from my Sides upon the Ground. However, they soon returned; and one of them, who ventured so far as to get a full Sight of my Face, lifting up his Hands and Eyes by way of Admiration, cryed out in a shrill, but distinct Voice, *Hekinah Degul:* The others repeated the same Words several times, but I then knew not what they meant. I lay all this while, as the Reader may believe, in great Uneasiness: At length, struggling to get loose, I had the Fortune to break the Strings, and wrench out the Pegs that fastened my left Arm to the Ground; for, by lifting it up to my Face, I discovered the Methods they had taken to bind me; and, at the same time, with a violent Pull, which gave me excessive Pain, I a little loosened the Strings that tied down my Hair on the left Side; so that I was just able to turn my Head about two Inches. But the Creatures ran off a second time, before I could seize them; whereupon there was a great Shout in a very shrill Accent; and after it ceased, I heard one of them cry aloud, *Tolgo Phonac;* when in an Instant I felt above an Hundred Arrows discharged on my left Hand, which pricked me like so many Needles; and besides, they shot another Flight into the Air, as we do Bombs° in *Europe;* whereof many, I suppose, fell on my Body, (though I felt them not) and some on my Face, which I immediately covered with my left Hand. When this Shower of Arrows was over, I fell a groaning with Grief and Pain; and then striving again to get loose, they discharged another Volly larger than the first; and some of them attempted with Spears to stick me in the Sides; but, by good Luck, I had on me a Buff Jerkin,° which they could not pierce. I thought it the most prudent Method to lie still; and my Design was to continue so till Night, when my left Hand being already loose, I could easily free myself: And as for the Inhabitants, I had Reason to believe I might be a Match for the greatest Armies they could bring against me, if they were all of the same Size with him that I saw. But Fortune disposed otherwise of me. When the People observed I was quiet, they

---

a human Creature not six Inches high: The scale in Lilliput is one inch to a normal foot in our world.   **Bombs:** Shells.   **Buff Jerkin:** A heavy leather jacket.

discharged no more Arrows: But by the Noise increasing, I knew their Numbers were greater; and about four Yards from me, over-against my right Ear, I heard a Knocking for above an Hour, like People at work; when turning my Head that Way, as well as the Pegs and Strings would permit me, I saw a Stage erected about a Foot and a half from the Ground, capable of holding four of the Inhabitants, with two or three Ladders to mount it: From whence one of them, who seemed to be a Person of Quality, made me a long Speech, whereof I understood not one Syllable. But I should have mentioned, that before the principal Person began his Oration, he cryed out three times *Langro Dehul san:* (these Words and the former were afterwards repeated and explained to me.) Whereupon immediately about fifty of the Inhabitants came, and cut the Strings that fastened the left side of my Head, which gave me the Liberty of turning it to the right, and of observing the Person and Gesture of him who was to speak. He appeared to be of a middle Age, and taller than any of the other three who attended him; whereof one was a Page, who held up his Train, and seemed to be somewhat longer than my middle Finger; the other two stood one on each side to support him. He acted every part of an Orator; and I could observe many Periods of Threatnings, and others of Promises, Pity, and Kindness. I answered in a few Words, but in the most submissive Manner, lifting up my left Hand and both mine Eyes to the Sun, as calling him for a Witness; and being almost famished with Hunger, having not eaten a Morsel for some Hours before I left the Ship, I found the Demands of Nature so strong upon me, that I could not forbear shewing my Impatience (perhaps against the strict Rules of Decency) by putting my Finger frequently on my Mouth, to signify that I wanted Food. The *Hurgo* (for so they call a great Lord, as I afterwards learnt) understood me very well: He descended from the Stage, and commanded that several Ladders should be applied to my Sides, on which above an hundred of the Inhabitants mounted, and walked towards my Mouth, laden with Baskets full of Meat, which had been provided, and sent thither by the King's Orders upon the first Intelligence he received of me. I observed there was the Flesh of several Animals, but could not distinguish them by the Taste. There were Shoulders, Legs, and Loins shaped like those of Mutton, and very well dressed, but smaller than the Wings of a Lark. I eat them by two or three at a Mouthful; and took three Loaves at a time, about the bigness of Musket Bullets. They supplyed me as fast as they could, shewing a thousand Marks of Wonder and Astonishment at my Bulk and Appetite. I then made another Sign that I wanted Drink. They found by my eating that a small Quantity would not suffice me;

and being a most ingenious People, they slung up with great Dexterity one of their largest Hogsheads;° then rolled it towards my Hand, and beat out the Top; I drank it off at a Draught, which I might well do, for it hardly held half a Pint, and tasted like a small wine of *Burgundy*, but much more delicious. They brought me a second Hogshead, which I drank in the same Manner, and made Signs for more, but they had none to give me. When I had performed these Wonders, they shouted for Joy, and danced upon my Breast, repeating several times as they did at first, *Hekinah Degul*. They made me a Sign that I should throw down the two Hogsheads, but first warned the People below to stand out of the Way, crying aloud, *Borach Mivola;* and when they saw the Vessels in the Air, there was an universal Shout of *Hekinah Degul*. I confess I was often tempted, while they were passing backwards and forwards on my Body, to seize Forty or Fifty of the first that came in my Reach, and dash them against the Ground. But the Remembrance of what I had felt, which probably might not be the worst they could do; and the Promise of Honour I made them, for so I interpreted my submissive Behaviour, soon drove out those Imaginations. Besides, I now considered my self as bound by the Laws of Hospitality to a People who had treated me with so much Expence and Magnificence. However, in my Thoughts I could not sufficiently wonder at the Intrepidity of these diminutive Mortals, who durst venture to mount and walk on my Body, while one of my Hands was at Liberty, without trembling at the very Sight of so prodigious a Creature as I must appear to them. After some time, when they observed that I made no more Demands for Meat, there appeared before me a Person of high Rank from his Imperial Majesty. His Excellency having mounted on the Small of my Right Leg, advanced forwards up to my Face, with about a Dozen of his Retinue; And producing his Credentials under the Signet Royal, which he applied close to mine Eyes, spoke about ten Minutes, without any Signs of Anger, but with a kind of determinate Resolution; often pointing forwards, which, as I afterwards found was towards the Capital City, about half a Mile distant, whither it was agreed by his Majesty in Council that I must be conveyed. I answered in few Words, but to no Purpose, and made a Sign with my Hand that was loose, putting it to the other, (but over his Excellency's Head, for Fear of hurting him or his Train) and then to my own Head and Body, to signify that I desired my Liberty. It appeared that he understood me well enough; for he shook his Head by way of

---

Hogsheads: Large barrels or casks holding anywhere from 100 to 140 gallons.

Disapprobation, and held his Hand in a Posture to shew that I must be carried as a Prisoner. However, he made other Signs to let me understand that I should have Meat and Drink enough, and very good Treatment. Whereupon I once more thought of attempting to break my Bonds; but again, when I felt the Smart of their Arrows upon my Face and Hands, which were all in Blisters, and many of the Darts still sticking in them; and observing likewise that the Number of my Enemies encreased; I gave Tokens to let them know that they might do with me what they pleased. Upon this, the *Hurgo* and his Train withdrew, with much Civility and chearful Countenances. Soon after I heard a general Shout, with frequent Repetitions of the Words, *Peplom Selan,* and I felt great Numbers of the People on my Left Side relaxing the Cords to such a Degree, that I was able to turn upon my Right, and to ease my self with making Water; which I very plentifully did, to the great Astonishment of the People, who conjecturing by my Motions what I was going to do, immediately opened to the right and left on that Side, to avoid the Torrent which fell with such Noise and Violence from me. But before this, they had dawbed my Face and both my Hands with a sort of Ointment very pleasant to the Smell, which in a few Minutes removed all the Smart of their Arrows. These Circumstances, added to the Refreshment I had received by their Victuals and Drink, which were very nourishing, disposed me to sleep. I slept about eight Hours as I was afterwards assured; and it was no Wonder; for the Physicians, by the Emperor's Order, had mingled a sleeping Potion in the Hogsheads of Wine.

It seems that upon the first Moment I was discovered sleeping on the Ground after my Landing, the Emperor had early Notice of it by an Express; and determined in Council that I should be tyed in the Manner I have related (which was done in the Night while I slept) that Plenty of Meat and Drink should be sent me, and a Machine prepared to carry me to the Capital City.

This Resolution perhaps may appear very bold and dangerous, and I am confident would not be imitated by any Prince in *Europe* on the like Occasion; however, in my Opinion it was extremely Prudent as well as Generous. For supposing these People had endeavoured to kill me with their Spears and Arrows while I was asleep; I should certainly have awaked with the first Sense of Smart, which might so far have rouzed my Rage and Strength, as to enable me to break the Strings wherewith I was tyed; after which, as they were not able to make Resistance, so they could expect no Mercy.

These People are most excellent Mathematicians, and arrived to a great Perfection in Mechanicks by the Countenance and Encouragement of the Emperor, who is a renowned Patron of Learning. This Prince hath several Machines fixed on Wheels, for the Carriage of Trees and other great Weights. He often buildeth his largest Men of War, whereof some are Nine Foot long, in the Woods where the Timber grows, and has them carried on these Engines three or four Hundred Yards to the Sea. Five Hundred Carpenters and Engineers were immediately set at work to prepare the greatest Engine they had. It was a Frame of Wood raised three Inches from the Ground, about seven Foot long and four wide, moving upon twenty two Wheels. The Shout I heard, was upon the Arrival of this Engine, which, it seems, set out in four Hours after my Landing. It was brought parallel to me as I lay. But the principal Difficulty was to raise and place me in this Vehicle. Eighty Poles, each of one Foot high, were erected for this Purpose, and very strong Cords of the bigness of Packthread were fastened by Hooks to many Bandages, which the Workmen had girt round my Neck, my Hands, my Body, and my Legs. Nine Hundred of the strongest Men were employed to draw up these Cords by many Pullies fastned on the Poles; and thus in less than three Hours, I was raised and slung into the Engine, and there tyed fast. All this I was told; for while the whole Operation was performing, I lay in a profound Sleep, by the Force of that soporiferous Medicine infused into my Liquor. Fifteen hundred of the Emperor's largest Horses, each about four Inches and a half high, were employed to draw me towards the Metropolis, which, as I said, was half a Mile distant.

About four Hours after we began our Journey, I awaked by a very ridiculous Accident; for the Carriage being stopt a while to adjust something that was out of Order, two or three of the young Natives had the Curiosity to see how I looked when I was asleep; they climbed up into the Engine, and advancing very softly to my Face, one of them, an Officer in the Guards, put the sharp End of his Half-Pike a good way up into my left Nostril, which tickled my Nose like a Straw, and made me sneeze violently: Whereupon they stole off unperceived; and it was three Weeks before I knew the Cause of my awaking so suddenly. We made a long March the remaining Part of the Day, and rested at Night with Five Hundred Guards on each Side of me, half with Torches, and half with Bows and Arrows, ready to shoot me if I should offer to stir. The next Morning at Sun-rise we continued our March, and arrived within two Hundred Yards of the City-Gates about Noon. The Emperor, and all his Court, came out to meet us; but his great Officers would by no means suffer his Majesty to endanger his Person by mounting on my Body.

At the Place where the Carriage stopt, there stood an ancient Temple, esteemed to be the largest in the whole Kingdom; which having been polluted some Years before by an unnatural Murder, was, according to the Zeal of those People, looked upon as Prophane, and therefore had been applied to common Use, and all the Ornaments and Furniture carried away. In this Edifice it was determined I should lodge. The great Gate fronting to the North was about four Foot high, and almost two Foot wide, through which I could easily creep. On each Side of the Gate was a small Window not above six Inches from the Ground: Into that on the Left Side, the King's Smiths conveyed fourscore and eleven Chains, like those that hang to a Lady's Watch in *Europe*, and almost as large, which were locked to my Left Leg with six and thirty Padlocks. Over against this Temple, on the other Side of the great Highway, at twenty Foot Distance, there was a Turret at least five Foot high. Here the Emperor ascended with many principal Lords of his Court, to have an Opportunity of viewing me, as I was told, for I could not see them. It was reckoned that above an hundred thousand Inhabitants came out of the Town upon the same Errand; and in spight of my Guards, I believe there could not be fewer than ten thousand, at several Times, who mounted upon my Body by the Help of Ladders. But a Proclamation was soon issued to forbid it, upon Pain of Death. When the Workmen found it was impossible for me to break loose, they cut all the Strings that bound me; whereupon I rose up with as melancholly a Disposition as ever I had in my Life. But the Noise and Astonishment of the People at seeing me rise and walk, are not to be expressed. The Chains that held my left Leg were about two Yards long, and gave me not only the Liberty of walking backwards and forwards in a Semicircle; but being fixed within four Inches of the Gate, allowed me to creep in, and lie at my full Length in the Temple.

CHAPTER II

The Emperor of Lilliput, *attended by several of the Nobility, comes to see the Author in his Confinement. The Emperor's Person and Habit described. Learned Men appointed to teach the Author their Language. He gains Favour by his mild Disposition. His Pockets are searched, and his Sword and Pistols taken from him.*

When I found myself on my Feet, I looked about me, and must confess I never beheld a more entertaining Prospect. The Country round appeared like a continued Garden; and the inclosed Fields, which were generally Forty Foot square, resembled so many Beds of Flowers. These Fields were intermingled with Woods of half a Stang,° and the tallest Trees, as I could judge, appeared to be seven Foot high. I viewed the Town on my left Hand, which looked like the painted Scene of a City in a Theatre.

I had been for some Hours extremely pressed by the Necessities of Nature; which was no Wonder, it being almost two Days since I had last disburthened myself. I was under great Difficulties between Urgency and Shame. The best Expedient I could think on, was to creep into my House, which I accordingly did; and shutting the Gate after me, I went as far as the Length of my Chain would suffer; and discharged my Body of that uneasy Load. But this was the only Time I was ever guilty of so uncleanly an Action; for which I cannot but hope the candid Reader will give some Allowance, after he hath maturely and impartially considered my Case, and the Distress I was in. From this Time my constant Practice was, as soon as I rose, to perform that Business in open Air, at the full Extent of my Chain; and due Care was taken every Morning before Company came, that the offensive Matter should be carried off in Wheel-barrows, by two Servants appointed for that Purpose. I would not have dwelt so long upon a Circumstance, that perhaps at first Sight may appear not very momentous; if I had not thought it necessary to justify my Character in Point of Cleanliness to the World; which I am told, some of my Maligners have been pleased, upon this and other Occasions, to call in Question.

When this Adventure was at an End, I came back out of my House, having Occasion for fresh Air. The Emperor was already descended from the Tower, and advancing on Horseback towards me, which had like to have cost him dear; for the Beast, although very well trained, yet wholly unused to such a Sight, which appeared as if a Mountain moved before him, reared up on his hinder Feet: But that Prince, who is an excellent Horseman, kept his Seat, until his Attendants ran in, and held the Bridle, while his Majesty had Time to dismount. When he alighted, he surveyed me round with great Admiration, but kept beyond the Length of my Chains. He ordered his Cooks and Butlers, who were already prepared, to give me Victuals and Drink, which they pushed forward in a sort of Vehicles upon Wheels until I could reach them. I took those Vehicles, and soon emptied them all; twenty of them were filled with Meat, and ten with Liquor; each of the former afforded me two or three good Mouthfuls, and I emptied the Liquor of ten Vessels,

Stang: Quarter of an acre.

which was contained in earthen Vials, into one Vehicle, drinking it off
at a Draught; and so I did with the rest. The Empress, and young
Princes of the Blood, of both Sexes, attended by many Ladies, sate at
some Distance in their Chairs; but upon the Accident that happened to
the Emperor's Horse, they alighted, and came near his Person; which I
am now going to describe. He is taller by almost the Breadth of my
Nail, than any of his Court; which alone is enough to strike an Awe into
the Beholders. His Features are strong and masculine, with an *Austrian*
Lip, and arched Nose, his Complexion olive, his Countenance erect, his
Body and Limbs well proportioned, all his Motions graceful, and his
Deportment majestick. He was then past his Prime, being twenty-eight
Years and three Quarters old, of which he had reigned about seven, in
great Felicity, and generally victorious. For the better Convenience of
beholding him, I lay on my Side, so that my Face was parallel to his, and
he stood but three Yards off: However, I have had him since many
Times in my Hand, and therefore cannot be deceived in the Descrip-
tion. His Dress was very plain and simple, the Fashion of it between the
Asiatick and the *European;* but he had on his Head a light Helmet of
Gold, adorned with Jewels, and a Plume on the Crest. He held his
Sword drawn in his Hand, to defend himself, if I should happen to
break loose; it was almost three Inches long, the Hilt and Scabbard were
Gold enriched with Diamonds. His Voice was shrill, but very clear and
articulate, and I could distinctly hear it when I stood up. The Ladies and
Courtiers were all most magnificently clad, so that the Spot they stood
upon seemed to resemble a Petticoat spread on the Ground, embroi-
dered with Figures of Gold and Silver. His Imperial Majesty spoke often
to me, and I returned Answers, but neither of us could understand a
Syllable. There were several of his Priests and Lawyers present (as I conjectured by their Habits) who were commanded to address themselves
to me, and I spoke to them in as many Languages as I had the least
Smattering of, which were *High* and *Low Dutch, Latin, French, Spanish,*
Italian, and *Lingua Franca;* but all to no purpose. After about two
Hours the Court retired, and I was left with a strong Guard, to prevent
the Impertinence, and probably the Malice of the Rabble, who were
very impatient to croud about me as near as they durst; and some of
them had the Impudence to shoot their Arrows at me as I sate on the
Ground by the Door of my House; whereof one very narrowly missed
my left Eye. But the Colonel ordered six of the Ringleaders to be seized,
and thought no Punishment so proper as to deliver them bound into
my Hands, which some of his Soldiers accordingly did, pushing them
forwards with the But-ends of their Pikes into my Reach: I took them

all in my right Hand, put five of them into my Coat-pocket; and as to
the sixth, I made a Countenance as if I would eat him alive. The poor
Man squalled terribly, and the Colonel and his Officers were in much
Pain, especially when they saw me take out my Penknife: But I soon put
them out of Fear; for, looking mildly, and immediately cutting the
Strings he was bound with, I set him gently on the Ground, and away
he ran. I treated the rest in the same Manner, taking them one by one
out of my Pocket; and I observed, both the Soldiers and People were
highly obliged at this Mark of my Clemency, which was represented
very much to my Advantage at Court.

Towards Night I got with some Difficulty into my House, where I
lay on the Ground, and continued to do so about a Fortnight; during
which time the Emperor gave Orders to have a Bed prepared for me. Six
Hundred Beds of the common Measure were brought in Carriages, and
worked up in my House; an Hundred and Fifty of their Beds sown together made up the Breadth and Length, and these were four double,
which however kept me but very indifferently from the Hardness of the
Floor, that was of smooth Stone. By the same Computation they provided me with Sheets, Blankets, and Coverlets, tolerable enough for one
who had been so long enured to Hardships as I.

As the News of my Arrival spread through the Kingdom, it brought
prodigious Numbers of rich, idle, and curious People to see me; so that
the Villages were almost emptied, and great Neglect of Tillage and
Houshold Affairs must have ensued, if his Imperial Majesty had not provided by several Proclamations and Orders of State against this Incon-
veniency. He directed that those, who had already beheld me, should
return home, and not presume to come within fifty Yards of my House,
without Licence from Court; whereby the Secretaries of State got considerable Fees.

In the mean time, the Emperor held frequent Councils to debate
what Course should be taken with me; and I was afterwards assured by
a particular Friend, a Person of great Quality, who was as much in the
Secret as any; that the Court was under many Difficulties concerning
me. They apprehended my breaking loose; that my Diet would be very
expensive, and might cause a Famine. Sometimes they determined to
starve me, or at least to shoot me in the Face and Hands with poisoned
Arrows, which would soon dispatch me: But again they considered, that
the Stench of so large a Carcase might produce a Plague in the Metropolis, and probably spread through the whole Kingdom. In the midst of
these Consultations, several Officers of the Army went to the Door of
the great Council-Chamber; and two of them being admitted, gave an

Account of my Behaviour to the six Criminals above-mentioned; which made so favourable an Impression in the Breast of his Majesty, and the whole Board, in my Behalf, that an Imperial Commission was issued out, obliging all the Villages nine hundred Yards round the City to deliver in every Morning six Beeves,° forty Sheep, and other Victuals for my Sustenance; together with a proportionable Quantity of Bread and Wine, and other Liquors: For the due Payment of which his Majesty gave Assignments upon his Treasury. For this Prince lives chiefly upon his own Demesnes; seldom, except upon great Occasions raising any Subsidies upon his Subjects, who are bound to attend him in his Wars at their own Expence. An Establishment was also made of Six Hundred Persons to be my Domesticks, who had Board-Wages allowed for their Maintenance, and Tents built for them very conveniently on each side of my Door. It was likewise ordered, that three hundred Taylors should make me a Suit of Cloaths after the Fashion of the Country: That, six of his Majesty's greatest Scholars should be employed to instruct me in their Language: And, lastly, that the Emperor's Horses, and those of the Nobility, and Troops of Guards, should be exercised in my Sight, to accustom themselves to me. All these Orders were duly put in Execution; and in about three Weeks I made a great Progress in Learning their Language; during which Time, the Emperor frequently honoured me with his Visits, and was pleased to assist my Masters in teaching me. We began already to converse together in some Sort; and the first Words I learnt, were to express my Desire, that he would please to give me my Liberty; which I every Day repeated on my Knees. His Answer, as I could apprehend, was, that this must be a Work of Time, not to be thought on without the Advice of his Council; and that first I must *Lumos Kelmin pesso desmar lon Emposo; that is, Swear a Peace with him and his Kingdom.* However, that I should be used with all Kindness; and he advised me to acquire by my Patience and discreet Behaviour, the good Opinion of himself and his Subjects. He desired I would not take it ill, if he gave Orders to certain proper Officers to search me; for probably I might carry about me several Weapons, which must needs be dangerous Things, if they answered the Bulk of so prodigious a Person. I said, his Majesty should be satisfied, for I was ready to strip my self, and turn up my Pockets before him. This I delivered, part in Words, and part in Signs. He replied, that by the Laws of the Kingdom, I must be searched by two of his Officers: That he knew this could not be done without my Consent and Assistance; that he had so good an Opinion of

Beeves: Full-grown cattle.

my Generosity and Justice, as to trust their Persons in my Hands: That whatever they took from me should be returned when I left the Country, or paid for at the Rate which I would set upon them. I took up the two Officers in my Hands, put them first into my Coat-Pockets, and then into every other Pocket about me, except my two Fobs, and another secret Pocket which I had no Mind should be searched, wherein I had some little Necessaries of no Consequence to any but my self. In one of my Fobs there was a Silver Watch, and in the other a small Quantity of Gold in a Purse. These Gentlemen, having Pen, Ink, and Paper about them, made an exact Inventory of every thing they saw; and when they had done, desired I would set them down, that they might deliver it to the Emperor. This Inventory I afterwards translated into *English*, and is Word for Word as follows.

Imprimis, In the right Coat-Pocket of the *Great Man Mountain* (for so I interpret the Words *Quinbus Flestrin*) after the strictest Search, we found only one great Piece of coarse Cloth, large enough to be a Foot-Cloth for your Majesty's chief Room of State. In the left Pocket, we saw a huge Silver Chest, with a Cover of the same Metal, which we, the Searchers, were not able to lift. We desired it should be opened; and one of us stepping into it, found himself up to the mid Leg in a sort of Dust, some part whereof flying up to our Faces, set us both a sneezing for several Times together. In his right Waistcoat-Pocket, we found a prodigious Bundle of white thin Substances, folded one over another, about the Bigness of three Men, tied with a strong Cable, and marked with Black Figures; which we humbly conceive to be Writings; every Letter almost half as large as the Palm of our Hands. In the left there was a sort of Engine, from the Back of which were extended twenty long Poles, resembling the Pallisado's before your Majesty's Court; wherewith we conjecture the *Man Mountain* combs his Head; for we did not always trouble him with Questions, because we found it a great Difficulty to make him understand us. In the large Pocket on the right Side of his middle Cover, (so I translate the Word *Ranfu-Lo*, by which they meant my Breeches) we saw a hollow Pillar of Iron, about the Length of a Man, fastened to a strong Piece of Timber, larger than the Pillar; and upon one side of the Pillar were huge Pieces of Iron sticking out, cut into strange Figures; which we know not what to make of. In the left Pocket, another Engine of the same kind. In the smaller Pocket on the right Side, were several round flat Pieces of white and red Metal, of different Bulk: Some of the white, which seemed to be Silver, were so large and heavy, that my Comrade and I could hardly lift them. In the left Pocket were two black Pillars irregularly shaped: we could not, without Difficulty, reach the Top of them as we stood at the Bottom of his Pocket: One of them was covered, and seemed all of a Piece; but at the upper End of the other, there appeared a white round Substance, about twice the bigness of our Heads. Within each of these was inclosed a prodigious Plate of Steel; which, by our Orders, we obliged him to shew us, because we apprehended they might be dangerous Engines.° He took them out of their Cases, and told us, that in his own Country his Practice was to shave his Beard with one of these, and to cut his Meat with the other. There were two Pockets which we could not enter: These he called his Fobs; they were two large Slits cut into the Top of his middle Cover, but squeezed close by the Pressure of his Belly. Out of the right Fob hung a great Silver Chain, with a wonderful kind of Engine at the Bottom. We directed him to draw out whatever was at the End of that Chain; which appeared to be a Globe, half Silver, and half of some transparent Metal: For on the transparent Side we saw certain strange Figures circularly drawn, and thought we could touch them, until we found our Fingers stopped with that lucid Substance. He put this Engine to our Ears, which made an incessant Noise like that of a Water-Mill. And we conjecture it is either some unknown Animal, or the God that he worships: But we are more inclined to the latter Opinion, because he assured us (if we understood him right, for he expressed himself very imperfectly) that he seldom did any Thing without consulting it. He called it his Oracle, and said it pointed out the Time for every Action of his Life. From the left Fob he took out a Net almost large enough for a Fisherman, but contrived to open and shut like a Purse, and served him for the same Use: We found therein several massy Pieces of yellow Metal, which if they be real Gold, must be of immense Value.

Having thus, in Obedience to your Majesty's Commands, diligently searched all his Pockets; we observed a Girdle about his Waist made of the Hyde of some prodigious Animal; from which, on the left Side, hung a Sword of the Length of five Men; and on the right, a Bag or Pouch divided into two Cells; each Cell capable of holding three of your Majesty's Subjects. In one of these Cells were several Globes or Balls of a most ponderous Metal, about the Bigness of our Heads, and required a strong Hand to lift them: The other Cell contained a Heap of certain black Grains, but of no great Bulk or Weight, for we could hold above fifty of them in the Palms of our Hands.

This is an exact Inventory of what we found about the Body of the *Man Mountain;* who used us with great Civility, and due Respect to

Engines: Mechanical contrivances, often of a military nature.

your Majesty's Commission. Signed and Sealed on the fourth Day of the eighty ninth Moon of your Majesty's auspicious Reign.

Clefren Frelock, Marsi Frelock.

When this Inventory was read over to the Emperor, he directed me to deliver up the several Particulars. He first called for my Scymiter, which I took out, Scabbard and all. In the mean time he ordered three thousand of his choicest Troops, who then attended him, to surround me at a Distance, with their Bows and Arrows just ready to discharge: But I did not observe it; for mine Eyes were wholly fixed upon his Majesty. He then desired me to draw my Scymiter, which, although it had got some Rust by the Sea-Water, was in most Parts exceeding bright. I did so, and immediately all the Troops gave a Shout between Terror and Surprize; for the Sun shone clear, and the Reflexion dazzled their Eyes, as I waved the Scymiter to and fro in my Hand. His Majesty, who is a most magnanimous Prince, was less daunted than I could expect; he ordered me to return it into the Scabbard, and cast it on the Ground as gently as I could, about six Foot from the End of my Chain. The next Thing he demanded was one of the hollow Iron Pillars, by which he meant my Pocket-Pistols. I drew it out, and at his Desire, as well as I could, expressed to him the Use of it, and charging it only with Powder, which by the Closeness of my Pouch, happened to escape wetting in the Sea, (an Inconvenience that all prudent Mariners take special Care to provide against) I first cautioned the Emperor not to be afraid; and then I let it off in the Air. The Astonishment here was much greater than at the Sight of my Scymiter. Hundreds fell down as if they had been struck dead; and even the Emperor, although he stood his Ground, could not recover himself in some time. I delivered up both my Pistols in the same Manner as I had done my Scymiter, and then my Pouch of Powder and Bullets; begging him that the former might be kept from Fire; for it would kindle with the smallest Spark, and blow up his Imperial Palace into the Air. I likewise delivered up my Watch, which the Emperor was very curious to see; and commanded two of his tallest Yeomen of the Guards to bear it on a Pole upon their Shoulders, as Dray-men in *England* do a Barrel of Ale. He was amazed at the continual Noise it made, and the Motion of the Minute-hand, which he could easily discern; for their Sight is much more acute than ours: He asked the Opinions of his learned Men about him, which were various and remote, as the Reader may well imagine without my repeating; although indeed I could not very perfectly understand them. I then gave up my Silver and Copper Money, my Purse with nine large Pieces of Gold, and some smaller

ones; my Knife and Razor, my Comb and Silver Snuff-Box, my Handkerchief and Journal Book. My Scymiter, Pistols, and Pouch, were conveyed in Carriages to his Majesty's Stores; but the rest of my Goods
were returned me.

I had, as I before observed, one private Pocket which escaped their
Search, wherein there was a Pair of Spectacles (which I sometimes use
for the Weakness of mine Eyes) a Pocket Perspective,° and several other
little Conveniences; which being of no Consequence to the Emperor, I
did not think my self bound in Honour to discover; and I apprehended
they might be lost or spoiled if I ventured them out of my Possession.

CHAPTER III

*The Author diverts the Emperor and his Nobility of both Sexes, in a
very uncommon Manner. The Diversions of the Court of Lilliput described.
The Author hath his Liberty granted him upon certain Conditions.*

My Gentleness and good Behaviour had gained so far on the Emperor and his Court, and indeed upon the Army and People in general,
that I began to conceive Hopes of getting my Liberty in a short Time. I
took all possible Methods to cultivate this favourable Disposition. The
Natives came by Degrees to be less apprehensive of any Danger from
me. I would sometimes lie down, and let five or six of them dance on
my Hand. And at last the Boys and Girls would venture to come and
play at Hide and Seek in my Hair. I had now made a good Progress in
understanding and speaking their Language. The Emperor had a mind
one Day to entertain me with several of the Country Shows; wherein
they exceed all Nations I have known, both for Dexterity and Magnificence. I was diverted with none so much as that of the Rope-Dancers,
performed upon a slender white Thread, extended about two Foot, and
twelve Inches from the Ground. Upon which, I shall desire Liberty,
with the Reader's Patience, to enlarge a little.

This Diversion is only practised by those Persons, who are Candidates for great Employments, and high Favour, at Court. They are
trained in this Art from their Youth, and are not always of noble Birth,
or liberal Education. When a great Office is vacant, either by Death or
Disgrace, (which often happens) five or six of those Candidates petition
the Emperor to entertain his Majesty and the Court with a Dance on
the Rope; and whoever jumps the highest without falling, succeeds in

Pocket Perspective: A small telescope.

the Office. Very often the chief Ministers themselves are commanded to shew their Skill, and to convince the Emperor that they have not lost their Faculty. *Flimnap,* the Treasurer, is allowed to cut a Caper on the strait Rope, at least an Inch higher than any other Lord in the whole Empire. I have seen him do the Summerset° several times together, upon a Trencher fixed on the Rope, which is no thicker than a common Packthread in *England.* My Friend *Reldresal,* principal Secretary for private Affairs, is, in my Opinion, if I am not partial, the second after the Treasurer; the rest of the great Officers are much upon a Par.

These Diversions are often attended with fatal Accidents, whereof great Numbers are on Record. I my self have seen two or three Candidates break a Limb. But the Danger is much greater, when the Ministers themselves are commanded to shew their Dexterity: For, by contending to excel themselves and their Fellows, they strain so far, that there is hardly one of them who hath not received a Fall; and some of them two or three. I was assured, that a Year or two before my Arrival, *Flimnap* would have infallibly broke his Neck, if one of the *King's Cushions,* that accidentally lay on the Ground, had not weakened the Force of his Fall.

There is likewise another Diversion, which is only shewn before the Emperor and Empress, and first Minister, upon particular Occasions. The Emperor lays on a Table three fine silken Threads° of six Inches long. One is Blue, the other Red, and the third Green. These Threads are proposed as Prizes, for those Persons whom the Emperor hath a mind to distinguish by a peculiar Mark of his Favour. The Ceremony is performed in his Majesty's great Chamber of State; where the Candidates are to undergo a Tryal of Dexterity very different from the former; and such as I have not observed the least Resemblance of in any other Country of the old or the new World. The Emperor holds a Stick in his Hands, both Ends parallel to the Horizon, while the Candidates advancing one by one, sometimes leap over the Stick, sometimes creep under it backwards and forwards several times, according as the Stick is advanced or depressed. Sometimes the Emperor holds one End of the Stick, and his first Minister the other; sometimes the Minister has it entirely to himself. Whoever performs his Part with most Agility, and holds out the longest in *leaping* and *creeping,* is rewarded with the Blue-coloured Silk; the Red is given to the next, and the Green to the third,

---

Summerset: Somersault.   **three fine silken Threads:** Alludes to the honorary ribbons awarded by the king of England for service to the state: blue, for the Order of the Garter; red, for the Order of the Bath; and green, for the Order of the Thistle.

which they all wear girt twice round about the Middle; and you see few great Persons about this Court, who are not adorned with one of these Girdles.

The Horses of the Army, and those of the Royal Stables, having been daily led before me, were no longer shy, but would come up to my very Feet, without starting. The Riders would leap them over my Hand as I held it on the Ground; and one of the Emperor's Huntsmen, upon a large Courser, took my Foot, Shoe and all; which was indeed a prodigious Leap. I had the good Fortune to divert the Emperor one Day, after a very extraordinary Manner. I desired he would order several Sticks of two Foot high, and the Thickness of an ordinary Cane, to be brought me; whereupon his Majesty commanded the Master of his Woods to give Directions accordingly; and the next Morning six Wood-men arrived with as many Carriages, drawn by eight Horses to each. I took nine of these Sticks, and fixing them firmly in the Ground in a Quadrangular Figure, two Foot and a half square; I took four other Sticks, and tyed them parallel at each Corner, about two Foot from the Ground; then I fastened my Handkerchief to the nine Sticks that stood erect; and extended it on all Sides, till it was as tight as the Top of a Drum; and the four parallel Sticks rising about five Inches higher than the Handkerchief, served as Ledges on each Side. When I had finished my Work, I desired the Emperor to a let a Troop of his best Horse, Twenty-four in Number, come and exercise upon this Plain. His Majesty approved of the Proposal, and I took them up one by one in my Hands, ready mounted and armed, with the proper Officers to exercise them. As soon as they got into Order, they divided into two Parties, performed mock Skirmishes, discharged blunt Arrows, drew their Swords, fled and pursued, attacked and retired; and in short discovered the best military Discipline I ever beheld. The parallel Sticks secured them and their Horses from falling over the Stage; and the Emperor was so much delighted, that he ordered this Entertainment to be repeated several Days; and once was pleased to be lifted up, and give the Word of Command; and, with great Difficulty, persuaded even the Empress her self to let me hold her in her close Chair, within two Yards of the Stage, from whence she was able to take a full View of the whole Performance. It was my good Fortune that no ill Accident happened in these Entertainments; only once a fiery Horse that belonged to one of the Captains, pawing with his Hoof struck a Hole in my Handkerchief, and his Foot slipping, he overthrew his Rider and himself; but I immediately relieved them both: For covering the Hole with one Hand, I set down the Troop with the other, in the same Manner as I took them up. The Horse that fell was strained in the left Shoulder, but the Rider got no Hurt; and I repaired my Handkerchief as well as I could: However, I would not trust to the Strength of it any more in such dangerous Enterprizes.

About two or three Days before I was set at Liberty, as I was entertaining the Court with these Kinds of Feats, there arrived an Express to inform his Majesty, that some of his Subjects riding near the Place where I was first taken up, had seen a great black Substance lying on the Ground, very oddly shaped, extending its Edges round as wide as his Majesty's Bedchamber, and rising up in the Middle as high as a Man: That it was no living Creature, as they at first apprehended; for it lay on the Grass without Motion, and some of them had walked round it several Times: That by mounting upon each others Shoulders, they had got to the Top, which was flat and even; and, stamping upon it, they found it was hollow within: That they humbly conceived it might be something belonging to the *Man-Mountain;* and if his Majesty pleased, they would undertake to bring it with only five Horses. I presently knew what they meant; and was glad at Heart to receive this Intelligence. It seems, upon my first reaching the Shore, after our Shipwreck, I was in such Confusion, that before I came to the Place where I went to sleep, my Hat, which I had fastened with a String to my Head while I was rowing, and had stuck on all the Time I was swimming, fell off after I came to Land; the String, as I conjecture, breaking by some Accident which I never observed, but thought my Hat had been lost at Sea. I intreated his Imperial Majesty to give Orders it might be brought to me as soon as possible, describing to him the Use and the Nature of it: And the next Day the Waggoners arrived with it, but not in a very good Condition; they had bored two Holes in the Brim, within an Inch and a half of the Edge, and fastened two Hooks in the Holes; these Hooks were tied by a long Cord to the Harness, and thus my Hat was dragged along for above half an *English* Mile: But the Ground in that Country being extremely smooth and level, it received less Damage than I expected.

Two Days after this Adventure, the Emperor having ordered that Part of his Army, which quarters in and about his Metropolis, to be in a Readiness, took a fancy of diverting himself in a very singular Manner. He desired I would stand like a *Colossus,*° with my Legs as far asunder as

---

Colossus: Statue that stood astride the harbor entrance to Rhodes; one of the ancient Seven Wonders of the World.

I conveniently could. He then commanded his General (who was an old experienced Leader, and a great Patron of mine) to draw up the Troops in close Order, and march them under me; the Foot by Twenty-four in a Breast, and the Horse by Sixteen, with Drums beating, Colours flying, and Pikes advanced. This Body consisted of three Thousand Foot, and a Thousand Horse. His Majesty gave Orders, upon Pain of Death, that every Soldier in his March should observe the strictest Decency, with regard to my Person; which, however, could not prevent some of the younger Officers from turning up their Eyes as they passed under me. And, to confess the Truth, my Breeches were at that Time in so ill a Condition, that they afforded some Opportunities for Laughter and Admiration.

I had sent so many Memorials and Petitions for my Liberty, that his Majesty at length mentioned the Matter first in the Cabinet, and then in a full Council; where it was opposed by none, except *Skyresh Bolgolam*, who was pleased, without any Provocation, to be my mortal Enemy. But it was carried against him by the whole Board, and confirmed by the Emperor. That Minister was *Galbet*, or Admiral of the Realm; very much in his Master's Confidence, and a Person well versed in Affairs, but of a morose and sour Complection. However, he was at length persuaded to comply; but prevailed that the Articles and Conditions upon which I should be set free, and to which I must swear, should be drawn up by himself. These Articles were brought to me by *Skyresh Bolgolam* in Person, attended by two under Secretaries, and several Persons of Distinction. After they were read, I was demanded to swear to the Performance of them; first in the Manner of my own Country, and afterwards in the Method prescribed by their Laws; which was to hold my right Foot in my left Hand, to place the middle Finger of my right Hand on the Crown of my Head, and my Thumb on the Tip of my right Ear. But, because the Reader may perhaps be curious to have some Idea of the Style and Manner of Expression peculiar to that People, as well as to know the Articles upon which I recovered my Liberty; I have made a Translation of the whole Instrument, Word for Word, as near as I was able; which I here offer to the Publick.

GOLBASTO MOMAREN EVLAME GURDILO SHEFIN MULLY ULLY GUE, most Mighty Emperor of *Lilliput*, Delight and Terror of the Universe, whose Dominions extend five Thousand Blustrugs, (about twelve Miles in Circumference) to the Extremities of the Globe: Monarch of all Monarchs: Taller than the Sons of Men; whose Feet press down to the Center, and whose Head strikes against the Sun: At whose Nod the

Princes of the Earth shake their Knees; pleasant as the Spring, comfortable as the Summer, fruitful as Autumn, dreadful as Winter. His most sublime Majesty proposeth to the *Man-Mountain*, lately arrived at our Celestial Dominions, the following Articles, which by a solemn Oath he shall be obliged to perform.

FIRST, The *Man-Mountain* shall not depart from our Dominions, without our Licence under our Great Seal.

SECONDLY, He shall not presume to come into our Metropolis, without our express Order; at which time, the Inhabitants shall have two Hours Warning, to keep within their Doors.

THIRDLY, The said *Man-Mountain* shall confine his Walks to our principal high Roads; and not offer to walk or lie down in a Meadow, or Field of Corn.

FOURTHLY, As he walks the said Roads, he shall take the utmost Care not to trample upon the Bodies of any of our loving Subjects, their Horses, or Carriages; nor take any of our said Subjects into his Hands, without their own Consent.

FIFTHLY, If an Express require extraordinary Dispatch; the *Man-Mountain* shall be obliged to carry in his Pocket the Messenger and Horse, a six Days Journey once in every Moon, and return the said Messenger back (if so required) safe to our Imperial Presence.

SIXTHLY, He shall be our Ally against our Enemies in the Island of *Blefuscu,* and do his utmost to destroy their Fleet, which is now preparing to invade Us.

SEVENTHLY, That the said *Man-Mountain* shall, at his Times of Leisure, be aiding and assisting to our Workmen, in helping to raise certain great Stones, towards covering the Wall of the principal Park, and other our Royal Buildings.

EIGHTHLY, That the said *Man-Mountain* shall, in two Moons Time, deliver in an exact Survey of the Circumference of our Dominions, by a Computation of his own Paces round the Coast.

LASTLY, That upon his solemn Oath to observe all the above Articles, the said *Man-Mountain* shall have a daily Allowance of Meat and Drink, sufficient for the Support of 1728 of our Subjects; with free Access to our Royal Person, and other marks of our Favour. Given at our Palace at *Belfaborac* the Twelfth Day of the Ninety-first Moon of our Reign.

I swore and subscribed to these Articles with great Chearfulness and Content, although some of them were not so honourable as I could have wished; which proceeded wholly from the Malice of *Skyresh Bolgolam* the High Admiral: Whereupon my Chains were immediately unlocked, and I was at full Liberty: The Emperor himself, in Person, did me the Honour to be by at the whole Ceremony. I made my Acknowledgments, by prostrating myself at his Majesty's Feet: But he commanded me to rise; and after many gracious Expressions, which, to avoid the Censure of Vanity, I shall not repeat; he added, that he hoped I should prove a useful Servant, and well deserve all the Favours he had already conferred upon me, or might do for the future.

The Reader may please to observe, that in the last Article for the Recovery of my Liberty, the Emperor stipulates to allow me a Quantity of Meat and Drink, sufficient for the Support of 1728 *Lilliputians.* Some time after, asking a Friend at Court how they came to fix on that determinate Number; he told me, that his Majesty's Mathematicians, having taken the Height of my Body by the Help of a Quadrant, and finding it to exceed theirs in the Proportion of Twelve to One, they concluded from the Similarity of their Bodies, that mine must contain at least 1728 of theirs, and consequently would require as much Food as was necessary to support that Number of *Lilliputians.* By which, the Reader may conceive an Idea of the Ingenuity of that People, as well as the prudent and exact Oeconomy of so great a Prince.

CHAPTER IV

Mildendo, *the Metropolis of* Lilliput, *described, together with the Emperor's Palace. A Conversation between the Author and a principal Secretary, concerning the Affairs of that Empire: The Author's Offers to serve the Emperor in his Wars.*

The first Request I made after I had obtained my Liberty, was, that I might have Licence to see *Mildendo*, the Metropolis; which the Emperor easily granted me, but with a special Charge to do no Hurt, either to the Inhabitants, or their Houses. The People had Notice by Proclamation of my Design to visit the Town. The Wall which encompassed

it, is two Foot and an half high, and at least eleven Inches broad, so that
a Coach and Horses may be driven very safely round it; and it is flanked
with strong Towers at ten Foot Distance. I stept over the great *Western*
Gate, and passed very gently, and sideling through the two principal
Streets, only in my short Waistcoat, for fear of damaging the Roofs and
Eves of the Houses with the Skirts of my Coat. I walked with the utmost
Circumspection, to avoid treading on any Stragglers, who might remain
in the Streets, although the Orders were very strict, that all People
should keep in their Houses, at their own Peril. The Garret Windows
and Tops of Houses were so crowded with Spectators, that I thought in
all my Travels I had not seen a more populous Place. The City is an
exact Square, each Side of the Wall being five Hundred Foot long. The
two great Streets which run cross and divide it into four Quarters, are
five Foot wide. The Lanes and Alleys which I could not enter, but only
viewed them as I passed, are from Twelve to Eighteen Inches. The
Town is capable of holding five Hundred Thousand Souls. The Houses
are from three to five Stories. The Shops and Markets well provided.

The Emperor's Palace is in the Center of the City, where the two
great Streets meet. It is inclosed by a Wall of two Foot high, and Twenty
Foot distant from the Buildings. I had his Majesty's Permission to step
over this Wall; and the Space being so wide between that and the Palace,
I could easily view it on every Side. The outward Court is a Square of
Forty Foot, and includes two other Courts: In the inmost are the Royal
Apartments, which I was very desirous to see, but found it extremely
difficult; for the great Gates, from one Square into another, were but
Eighteen Inches high, and seven Inches wide. Now the Buildings of the
outer Court were at least five Foot high; and it was impossible for me to
stride over them, without infinite Damage to the Pile, although the
Walls were strongly built of hewn Stone, and four Inches thick. At the
same time, the Emperor had a great Desire that I should see the Magnificence of his Palace: But this I was not able to do till three Days after,
which I spent in cutting down with my Knife some of the largest Trees
in the Royal Park, about an Hundred Yards distant from the City. Of
these Trees I made two Stools, each about three Foot high, and strong
enough to bear my Weight. The People having received Notice a second time, I went again through the City to the Palace, with my two
Stools in my Hands. When I came to the Side of the outer Court, I
stood upon one Stool, and took the other in my Hand: This I lifted over
the Roof, and gently set it down on the Space between the first and
second Court, which was eight Foot wide. I then stept over the Buildings very conveniently from one Stool to the other, and drew up the

first after me with a hooked Stick. By this Contrivance I got into the inmost Court; and lying down upon my Side, I applied my Face to the Windows of the middle Stories, which were left open on Purpose, and discovered the most splendid Apartments that can be imagined. There I saw the Empress, and the young Princes in their several Lodgings, with their chief Attendants about them. Her Imperial Majesty was pleased to smile very graciously upon me, and gave me out of the Window her Hand to kiss.

But I shall not anticipate the Reader with farther Descriptions of this Kind, because I reserve them for a greater Work, which is now almost ready for the Press; containing a general Description of this Empire, from its first Erection, through a long Series of Princes, with a particular Account of their Wars and Politicks, Laws, Learning, and Religion; their Plants and Animals, their peculiar Manners and Customs, with other Matters very curious and useful; my chief Design at present being only to relate such Events and Transactions as happened to the Publick, or to my self, during a Residence of about nine Months in that Empire.

One Morning, about a Fortnight after I had obtained my Liberty; *Reldresal,* Principal Secretary (as they style him) of private Affairs, came to my House, attended only by one Servant. He ordered his Coach to wait at a Distance, and desired I would give him an Hour's Audience; which I readily consented to, on Account of his Quality, and Personal Merits, as well as of the many good Offices he had done me during my Sollicitations at Court. I offered to lie down, that he might the more conveniently reach my Ear; but he chose rather to let me hold him in my Hand during our Conversation. He began with Compliments on my Liberty; said, he might pretend to some Merit in it; but, however, added, that if it had not been for the present Situation of things at Court, perhaps I might not have obtained it so soon. For, *said he,* as flourishing a Condition as we appear to be in to Foreigners, we labour under two mighty Evils; a violent Faction at home, and the Danger of an Invasion by a most potent Enemy from abroad. As to the first, you are to understand, that for above seventy Moons past, there have been two struggling Parties in this Empire, under the Names of *Tramecksan,* and *Slamecksan,* from the high and low Heels on their Shoes, by which they distinguish themselves.

It is alleged indeed, that the high Heels are most agreeable to our ancient Constitution: But however this be, his Majesty hath determined to make use of only low Heels in the Administration of the Government, and all Offices in the Gift of the Crown; as you cannot but observe; and particularly, that his Majesty's Imperial Heels are lower at least by a *Drurr* than any of his Court; (*Drurr* is a Measure about the fourteenth Part of an Inch.) The Animosities between these two Parties run so high, that they will neither eat nor drink, nor talk with each other. We compute the *Tramecksan,* or High-Heels, to exceed us in Number; but the Power is wholly on our Side. We apprehend his Imperial Highness, the Heir to the Crown, to have some Tendency towards the High-Heels; at least we can plainly discover one of his Heels higher than the other; which gives him a Hobble in his Gait. Now, in the midst of these intestine Disquiets, we are threatened with an Invasion from the Island of *Blefuscu,* which is the other great Empire of the Universe, almost as large and powerful as this of his Majesty. For as to what we have heard you affirm, that there are other Kingdoms and States in the World, inhabited by human Creatures as large as your self, our Philosophers are in much Doubt; and would rather conjecture that you dropt from the Moon, or one of the Stars; because it is certain, than an hundred Mortals of your Bulk, would, in a short Time, destroy all the Fruits and Cattle of his Majesty's Dominions. Besides, our Histories of six Thousand Moons make no Mention of any other Regions, than the two great Empires of *Lilliput* and *Blefuscu.* Which two mighty Powers have, as I was going to tell you, been engaged in a most obstinate War for six and thirty Moons past. It began upon the following Occasion. It is allowed on all Hands, that the primitive Way of breaking Eggs before we eat them, was upon the larger End: But his present Majesty's Grandfather, while he was a Boy, going to eat an Egg, and breaking it according to the ancient Practice, happened to cut one of his Fingers. Whereupon the Emperor his Father, published an Edict, commanding all his Subjects, upon great Penalties, to break the smaller End of their Eggs. The People so highly resented this Law, that our Histories tell us, there have been six Rebellions raised on that Account; wherein one Emperor lost his Life, and another his Crown.° These civil Commotions were constantly fomented by the Monarchs of *Blefuscu;* and when they were quelled, the Exiles always fled for Refuge to that Empire. It is computed, that eleven Thousand Persons have, at several Times, suffered Death, rather than submit to break their Eggs at the smaller End. Many hundred large Volumes have been published upon this Controversy: But the Books of the *Big-Endians* have been long forbidden, and the whole Party rendred incapable by Law of holding Employments. Dur-

Crown: Alludes to over a century of religious wars during which one king, Charles I, lost his life in 1649, and another, James II, his crown in 1688.

ing the Course of these Troubles, the Emperors of *Blefuscu* did frequently expostulate by their Ambassadors, accusing us of making a Schism in Religion, by offending against a fundamental Doctrine of our great Prophet *Lustrog*, in the fifty-fourth Chapter of the *Brundrecal*, (which is their *Alcoran*.) This, however, is thought to be a meer Strain upon the Text: For the Words are these; *That all true Believers shall break their Eggs at the convenient End:* and which is the convenient End, seems, in my humble Opinion, to be left to every Man's Conscience, or at least in the Power of the chief Magistrate to determine. Now the *Big-Endian* Exiles have found so much Credit in the Emperor of *Blefuscu's* Court; and so much private Assistance and Encouragement from their Party here at home, that a bloody War hath been carried on between the two Empires for six and thirty Moons with various Success; during which Time we have lost Forty Capital Ships, and a much greater Number of smaller Vessels, together with thirty thousand of our best Seamen and Soldiers; and the Damage received by the Enemy is reckoned to be somewhat greater than ours. However, they have now equipped a numerous Fleet, and are just preparing to make a Descent upon us: And his Imperial Majesty, placing great Confidence in your Valour and Strength, hath commanded me to lay this Account of his Affairs before you.

I desired the Secretary to present my humble Duty to the Emperor, and to let him know, that I thought it would not become me, who was a Foreigner, to interfere with Parties; but I was ready, with the Hazard of my Life, to defend his Person and State against all Invaders.

CHAPTER V

The Author *by an extraordinary Stratagem prevents an Invasion. A high Title of Honour is conferred upon him. Ambassadors arrive from the Emperor of* Blefuscu, *and sue for Peace. The Empress's Apartment on fire by an Accident; the* Author *instrumental in saving the rest of the Palace.*

The Empire of *Blefuscu*, is an Island situated to the North North-East Side of *Lilliput*, from whence it is parted only by a Channel of eight Hundred Yards wide. I had not yet seen it, and upon this Notice of an intended Invasion, I avoided appearing on that Side of the Coast, for fear of being discovered by some of the Enemies Ships, who had received no Intelligence of me; all intercourse between the two Empires having been strictly forbidden during the War, upon Pain of Death; and an Embargo laid by our Emperor upon all Vessels whatsoever. I communicated to his Majesty a Project I had formed of seizing the Enemies whole Fleet; which, as our Scouts assured us, lay at Anchor in the Harbour ready to sail with the first fair Wind. I consulted the most experienced Seamen, upon the Depth of the Channel, which they had often plummed; who told me, that in the Middle at high Water it was seventy *Glumgluffs* deep, which is about six Foot of *European* Measure; and the rest of it fifty *Glumgluffs* at most. I walked to the North-East Coast over against *Blefuscu;* where, lying down behind a Hillock, I took out my small Pocket Perspective Glass, and viewed the Enemy's Fleet at Anchor, consisting of about fifty Men of War, and a great Number of Transports: I then came back to my House, and gave Order (for which I had a Warrant) for a great Quantity of the strongest Cable and Bars of Iron. The Cable was about as thick as Packthread, and the Bars of the Length and Size of a Knitting-Needle. I trebled the Cable to make it stronger; and for the same Reason I twisted three of the Iron Bars together, bending the Extremities into a Hook. Having thus fixed fifty Hooks to as many Cables, I went back to the North-East Coast, and putting off my Coat, Shoes, and Stockings, walked into the Sea in my Leathern Jerken, about half an Hour before high Water. I waded with what Haste I could, and swam in the Middle about thirty Yards until I felt the Ground; I arrived at the Fleet in less than half an Hour. The Enemy was so frighted when they saw me, that they leaped out of their Ships, and swam to Shore; where there could not be fewer than thirty thousand Souls. I then took my Tackling, and fastning a Hook to the Hole at the Prow of each, I tyed all the Cords together at the End. While I was thus employed, the Enemy discharged several Thousand Arrows, many of which stuck in my Hands and Face; and besides the excessive Smart, gave me much Disturbance in my Work. My greatest Apprehension was for mine Eyes, which I should have infallibly lost, if I had not suddenly thought of an Expedient. I kept, among other little Necessaries, a Pair of Spectacles in a private Pocket, which, as I observed before, had escaped the Emperor's Searchers. These I took out, and fastened as strongly as I could upon my Nose; and thus armed went on boldly with my Work in spight of the Enemy's Arrows; many of which struck against the Glasses of my Spectacles, but without any other Effect, further than a little to discompose them. I had now fastened all the Hooks, and taking the Knot in my Hand, began to pull; but not a Ship would stir, for they were all too fast held by their Anchors; so that the boldest Part of my Enterprize remained. I therefore let go the Cord, and leaving the Hooks fixed to the Ships, I resolutely cut with my Knife the Cables that fastened the Anchors; receiving above two hundred

Shots in my Face and Hands: Then I took up the knotted End of the Cables to which my Hooks were tyed; and with great Ease drew fifty of the Enemy's largest Men of War after me.

The *Blefuscudians,* who had not the least Imagination of what I intended, were at first confounded with Astonishment. They had seen me cut the Cables, and thought my Design was only to let the Ships run a-drift, or fall foul on each other: But when they perceived the whole Fleet moving in Order, and saw me pulling at the End; they set up such a Scream of Grief and Dispair, that it is almost impossible to describe or conceive. When I had got out of Danger, I stopt a while to pick out the Arrows that stuck in my Hands and Face, and rubbed on some of the same Ointment that was given me at my first Arrival, as I have formerly mentioned. I then took off my Spectacles, and waiting about an Hour until the Tyde was a little fallen, I waded through the Middle with my Cargo, and arrived safe at the Royal Port of *Lilliput.*

The Emperor and his whole Court stood on the Shore, expecting the Issue of this great Adventure. They saw the Ships move forward in a large Half-Moon, but could not discern me, who was up to my Breast in Water. When I advanced to the Middle of the Channel, they were yet more in Pain because I was under Water to my Neck. The Emperor concluded me to be drowned, and that the Enemy's Fleet was approaching in a hostile Manner: But he was soon eased of his Fears; for the Channel growing shallower every Step I made, I came in a short Time within Hearing; and holding up the End of the Cable by which the Fleet was fastened, I cryed in a loud Voice, *Long live the most puissant Emperor of Lilliput!* This great Prince received me at my Landing with all possible Encomiums, and created me a *Nardac* upon the Spot, which is the highest Title of Honour among them.

His Majesty desired I would take some other Opportunity of bringing all the rest of his Enemy's Ships into his Ports. And so unmeasurable is the Ambition of Princes, that he seemed to think of nothing less than reducing the whole Empire of *Blefuscu* into a Province, and governing it by a Viceroy; of destroying the *Big-Endian* Exiles, and compelling that People to break the smaller End of their Eggs; by which he would remain sole Monarch of the whole World. But I endeavoured to divert him from this Design, by many Arguments drawn from the Topicks of Policy as well as Justice: And I plainly protested, that I would never be an Instrument of bringing a free and brave People into Slavery: And when the Matter was debated in Council, the wisest Part of the Ministry were of my Opinion.

This open bold Declaration of mine was so opposite to the Schemes

and Politicks of his Imperial Majesty, that he could never forgive me:
He mentioned it in a very artful Manner at Council, where, I was told,
that some of the wisest appeared, at least by their Silence, to be of my
Opinion; but others, who were my secret Enemies, could not forbear
some Expressions, which by a Side-wind reflected on me. And from this
Time began an Intrigue between his Majesty, and a Junta of Ministers
maliciously bent against me, which broke out in less than two Months,
and had like to have ended in my utter Destruction. Of so little Weight
are the greatest Services to Princes, when put into the Balance with a
Refusal to gratify their Passions.

About three Weeks after this Exploit, there arrived a solemn Em-
bassy from *Blefuscu,* with humble Offers of a Peace; which was soon
concluded upon Conditions very advantageous to our Emperor; wherewith I shall not trouble the Reader. There were six Ambassadors, with a
Train of about five Hundred Persons; and their Entry was very magnificent, suitable to the Grandeur of their Master, and the Importance of
their Business. When their Treaty was finished, wherein I did them several good Offices by the Credit I now had, or at least appeared to have
at Court; their Excellencies, who were privately told how much I had
been their Friend, made me a Visit in Form. They began with many
Compliments upon my Valour and Generosity; invited me to that Kingdom in the Emperor their Master's Name; and desired me to shew them
some Proofs of my prodigious Strength, of which they had heard so
many Wonders; wherein I readily obliged them, but shall not interrupt
the Reader with the Particulars.

When I had for some time entertained their Excellencies to their
infinite Satisfaction and Surprize, I desired they would do me the Honour to present my most humble Respects to the Emperor their Master,
the Renown of whose Virtues had so justly filled the whole World with
Admiration, and whose Royal Person I resolved to attend before I returned to my own Country. Accordingly, the next time I had the Honour to see our Emperor, I desired his general Licence to wait on the
Blefuscudian Monarch, which he was pleased to grant me, as I could
plainly perceive, in a very cold Manner; but could not guess the Reason,
till I had a Whisper from a certain Person, that *Flimnap* and *Bolgolam*
had represented my Intercourse with those Ambassadors, as a Mark of
Disaffection, from which I am sure my Heart was wholly free. And this
was the first time I began to conceive some imperfect Idea of Courts
and Ministers.

It is to be observed, that these Ambassadors spoke to me by an Interpreter; the Languages of both Empires differing as much from each

other as any two in *Europe,* and each Nation priding itself upon the Antiquity, Beauty, and Energy of their own Tongues, with an avowed Contempt for that of their Neighbour: Yet our Emperor standing upon the Advantage he had got by the Seizure of their Fleet, obliged them to deliver their Credentials, and make their Speech in the *Lilliputian* Tongue. And it must be confessed, that from the great Intercourse of Trade and Commerce between both Realms; from the continual Reception of Exiles, which is mutual among them; and from the Custom in each Empire to send their young Nobility and richer Gentry to the other, in order to polish themselves, by seeing the World, and understanding Men and Manners; there are few Persons of Distinction, or Merchants, or Seamen, who dwell in the Maritime Parts, but what can hold Conversation in both Tongues; as I found some Weeks after, when I went to pay my Respects to the Emperor of *Blefuscu,* which in the Midst of great Misfortunes, through the Malice of my Enemies, proved a very happy Adventure to me, as I shall relate in its proper Place.

The Reader may remember, that when I signed those Articles upon which I recovered my Liberty, there were some which I disliked upon Account of their being too servile, neither could any thing but an extreme Necessity have forced me to submit. But being now a *Nardac,* of the highest Rank in that Empire, such Offices were looked upon as below my Dignity; and the Emperor (to do him Justice) never once mentioned them to me. However, it was not long before I had an Opportunity of doing his Majesty, at least, as I then thought, a most signal Service. I was alarmed at Midnight with the Cries of many Hundred People at my Door; by which being suddenly awaked, I was in some Kind of Terror. I heard the Word *Burglum* repeated incessantly; several of the Emperor's Court making their Way through the Croud, intreated me to come immediately to the Palace, where her Imperial Majesty's Apartment was on fire, by the Carelessness of a Maid of Honour, who fell asleep while she was reading a Romance. I got up in an Instant; and Orders being given to clear the Way before me; and it being likewise a Moonshine Night, I made a shift to get to the Palace without trampling on any of the People. I found they had already applied Ladders to the Walls of the Apartment, and were well provided with Buckets, but the Water was at some Distance. These Buckets were about the Size of a large Thimble, and the poor People supplied me with them as fast as they could; but the Flame was so violent, that they did little Good. I might easily have stifled it with my Coat, which I unfortunately left behind me for haste, and came away only in my Leathern Jerkin. The Case seemed wholly desperate and deplorable; and this magnificent Palace would have infallibly been burnt down to the Ground, if, by a Presence of Mind, unusual to me, I had not suddenly thought of an Expedient. I had the Evening before drank plentifully of a most delicious wine, called *Glimigrim,* (the *Blefuscudians* call it *Flunec,* but ours is esteemed the better Sort) which is very diuretick. By the luckiest Chance in the World, I had not discharged myself of any Part of it. The Heat I had contracted by coming very near the Flames, and by my labouring to quench them, made the Wine begin to operate by Urine; which I voided in such a Quantity, and applied so well to the proper Places, that in three Minutes the Fire was wholly extinguished; and the rest of that noble Pile, which had cost so many Ages in erecting, preserved from Destruction.

It was now Day-light, and I returned to my House, without waiting to congratulate with the Emperor; because, although I had done a very eminent Piece of Service, yet I could not tell how his Majesty might resent the Manner by which I had performed it: For, by the fundamental Laws of the Realm, it is Capital in any Person, of what Quality soever, to make water within the Precincts of the Palace. But I was a little comforted by a Message from his Majesty, that he would give Orders to the Grand Justiciary for passing my Pardon in Form; which, however, I could not obtain. And I was privately assured, that the Empress conceiving the greatest Abhorrence of what I had done, removed to the most distant Side of the Court, firmly resolved that those Buildings should never be repaired for her Use; and, in the Presence of her chief Confidents, could not forbear vowing Revenge.

CHAPTER VI

Of the Inhabitants of Lilliput; *their Learning, Laws, and Customs. The Manner of Educating their Children. The Author's Way of living in that Country. His Vindication of a great Lady.*

Although I intend to leave the Description of this Empire to a particular Treatise, yet in the mean time I am content to gratify the curious Reader with some general Ideas. As the common Size of the Natives is somewhat under six Inches, so there is an exact Proportion in all other Animals, as well as Plants and Trees: For Instance, the tallest Horses and Oxen are between four and five Inches in Height, the Sheep an Inch and a half, more or less; their Geese about the Bigness of a Sparrow; and so the several Gradations downwards, till you come to the smallest, which, to my Sight, were almost invisible; but Nature hath adapted the

Eyes of the *Lilliputians* to all Objects proper for their View: They see with great Exactness, but at no great Distance. And to show the Sharpness of their Sight towards Objects that are near, I have been much pleased with observing a Cook pulling a Lark, which was not so large as a common Fly; and a young Girl threading an invisible Needle with invisible Silk. Their tallest Trees are about seven Foot high; I mean some of those in the great Royal Park, the Tops whereof I could but just reach with my Fist clinched. The other Vegetables are in the same Proportion: But this I leave to the Reader's Imagination.

I shall say but little at present of their Learning, which for many Ages hath flourished in all its Branches among them: But their Manner of Writing is very peculiar; being neither from the Left to the Right, like the *Europeans;* nor from the Right to the Left, like the *Arabians;* nor from up to down, like the *Chinese;* nor from down to up, like the *Cascagians;* but aslant from one Corner of the Paper to the other, like Ladies in *England.*

They bury their Dead with their Heads directly downwards; because they hold an Opinion, that in eleven Thousand Moons they are all to rise again; in which Period, the Earth (which they conceive to be flat) will turn upside down, and by this Means they shall, at their Resurrection, be found ready standing on their Feet. The Learned among them confess the Absurdity of this Doctrine; but the Practice still continues, in Compliance to the Vulgar.

There are some Laws and Customs in this Empire very peculiar; and if they were not so directly contrary to those of my own dear Country, I should be tempted to say a little in their Justification. It is only to be wished, that they were as well executed. The first I shall mention, relateth to Informers. All Crimes against the State, are punished here with the utmost Severity; but if the Person accused make his Innocence plainly to appear upon his Tryal, the Accuser is immediately put to an ignominious Death; and out of his Goods or Lands, the innocent Person is quadruply recompensed for the Loss of his Time, for the Danger he underwent, for the Hardship of his Imprisonment, and for all the Charges he hath been at in making his Defence. Or, if that Fund be deficient, it is largely supplyed by the Crown. The Emperor doth also confer on him some publick Mark of his Favour; and Proclamation is made of his Innocence through the whole City.

They look upon Fraud as a greater Crime than Theft, and therefore seldom fail to punish it with Death: For they alledge, that Care and Vigilance, with a very common Understanding, may preserve a Man's Goods from Thieves; but Honesty hath no Fence against superior

Cunning: And since it is necessary that there should be a perpetual Intercourse of buying and selling, and dealing upon Credit; where Fraud is permitted or connived at, or hath no Law to punish it, the honest Dealer is always undone, and the Knave gets the Advantage. I remember when I was once interceeding with the King for a Criminal who had wronged his Master of a great Sum of Money, which he had received by Order, and ran away with; and happening to tell his Majesty, by way of Extenuation, that it was only a Breach of Trust; the Emperor thought it monstrous in me to offer, as a Defence, the greatest Aggravation of the Crime: And truly, I had little to say in Return, farther than the common Answer, that different Nations had different Customs; for, I confess, I was heartily ashamed.

Although we usually call Reward and Punishment, the two Hinges upon which all Government turns; yet I could never observe this Maxim to be put in Practice by any Nation, except that of *Lilliput*. Whoever can there bring sufficient Proof that he hath strictly observed the Laws of his Country for Seventy-three Moons, hath a Claim to certain Privileges, according to his Quality and Condition of Life, with a proportionable Sum of Money out of a Fund appropriated for that Use: He likewise acquires the Title of *Snilpall*, or *Legal*, which is added to his Name, but doth not descend to his Posterity. And these People thought it a prodigious Defect of Policy among us, when I told them that our Laws were enforced only by Penalties, without any Mention of Reward. It is upon this account that the Image of Justice, in their Courts of Judicature, is formed with six Eyes, two before, as many behind, and on each Side one, to signify Circumspection; with a Bag of Gold open in her right Hand, and a Sword sheathed in her left, to shew she is more disposed to reward than to punish.

In chusing Persons for all Employments, they have more Regard to good Morals than to great Abilities: For, since Government is necessary to Mankind, they believe that the common Size of human Understandings, is fitted to some Station or other; and that Providence never intended to make the Management of publick Affairs a Mystery, to be comprehended only by a few Persons of sublime Genius, of which there seldom are three born in an Age: But, they suppose Truth, Justice, Temperance, and the like, to be in every Man's Power; the Practice of which Virtues, assisted by Experience and a good Intention, would qualify any Man for the Service of his Country, except where a Course of Study is required. But they thought the Want of Moral Virtues was so far from being supplied by superior Endowments of the Mind, that Employments could never be put into such dangerous Hands as those of Persons so qualified; and at least, that the Mistakes committed by Ignorance in a virtuous Disposition, would never be of such fatal Consequence to the Publick Weal, as the Practices of a Man, whose Inclinations led him to be corrupt, and had great Abilities to manage, to multiply, and defend his Corruptions.

In like Manner, the Disbelief of a Divine Providence renders a Man uncapable of holding any publick Station: For, since Kings avow themselves to be the Deputies of Providence, the *Lilliputians* think nothing can be more absurd than for a Prince to employ such Men as disown the Authority under which he acteth.

In relating these and the following Laws, I would only be understood to mean the original Institutions, and not the most scandalous Corruptions into which these People are fallen by the degenerate Nature of Man. For as to that infamous Practice of acquiring great Employments by dancing on the Ropes, or Badges of Favour and Distinction by leaping over Sticks, and creeping under them; the Reader is to observe, that they were first introduced by the Grand-father of the Emperor now reigning; and grew to the present Height, by the gradual Increase of Party and Faction.

Ingratitude is among them a capital Crime, as we read it to have been in some other Countries: For they reason thus; that whoever makes ill Returns to his Benefactor, must needs be a common Enemy to the rest of Mankind, from whom he hath received no Obligation; and therefore such a Man is not fit to live.

Their Notions relating to the Duties of Parents and Children differ extremely from ours. For, since the Conjunction of Male and Female is founded upon the great Law of Nature, in order to propagate and continue the Species; the *Lilliputians* will needs have it, that Men and Women are joined together like other Animals, by the Motives of Concupiscence; and that their Tenderness towards their Young, proceedeth from the like natural Principle: For which Reason they will never allow, that a Child is under any Obligation to his Father for begetting him, or to his Mother for bringing him into the World; which, considering the Miseries of human Life, was neither a Benefit in itself, nor intended so by his Parents, whose Thoughts in their Love-encounters were otherwise employed. Upon these, and the like Reasonings, their Opinion is, that Parents are the last of all others to be trusted with the Education of their own Children: And therefore they have in every Town publick Nurseries, where all Parents, except Cottagers and Labourers, are obliged to send their Infants of both Sexes to be reared and educated when they come to the Age of twenty Moons; at which Time they are supposed to have some Rudiments of Docility. These Schools are of several kinds, suited to different Qualities, and to both Sexes. They have certain Professors well skilled in preparing Children for such a Condition of Life as befits the Rank of their Parents, and their own Capacities as well as Inclinations. I shall first say something of the Male Nurseries, and then of the Female.

The Nurseries for Males of Noble or Eminent Birth, are provided with grave and learned Professors, and their several Deputies. The Clothes and Food of the Children are plain and simple. They are bred up in the Principles of Honour, Justice, Courage, Modesty, Clemency, Religion, and Love of their Country: They are always employed in some Business, except in the Times of eating and sleeping, which are very short, and two Hours for Diversions, consisting of bodily Exercises. They are dressed by Men until four Years of Age, and then are obliged to dress themselves, although their Quality be ever so great; and the Women Attendants, who are aged proportionably to ours at fifty, perform only the most menial Offices. They are never suffered to converse with Servants, but go together in small or greater Numbers to take their Diversions, and always in the Presence of a Professor, or one of his Deputies; whereby they avoid those early bad Impressions of Folly and Vice to which our Children are subject. Their Parents are suffered to see them only twice a Year; the Visit is not to last above an Hour; they are allowed to kiss the Child at Meeting and Parting; but a Professor, who always standeth by on those Occasions, will not suffer them to whisper, or use any fondling Expressions, or bring any Presents of Toys, Sweetmeats, and the like.

The Pension from each Family for the Education and Entertainment of a Child, upon Failure of due Payment, is levied by the Emperor's Officers.

The Nurseries for Children of ordinary Gentlemen, Merchants, Traders, and Handicrafts, are managed proportionably after the same Manner; only those designed for Trades, are put out Apprentices at seven Years old; whereas those of Persons of Quality continue in their Exercises until Fifteen, which answers to One and Twenty with us: But the Confinement is gradually lessened for the last three Years.

In the Female Nurseries, the young Girls of Quality are educated much like the Males, only they are dressed by orderly Servants of their own Sex, but always in the Presence of a Professor or Deputy, until they come to dress themselves, which is at five Years old. And if it be found that these Nurses ever presume to entertain the Girls with frightful or foolish Stories, or the common Follies practised by Chamber-Maids among us; they are publickly whipped thrice about the City, imprisoned for a Year, and banished for Life to the most desolate Part of the Country. Thus the young Ladies there are as much ashamed of being Cowards and Fools, as the Men; and despise all personal Ornaments beyond Decency and Cleanliness; neither did I perceive any Difference in their Education, made by their Difference of Sex, only that the Exercises of the Females were not altogether so robust; and that some Rules were given them relating to domestick Life, and a smaller Compass of Learning was enjoyned them: For, their Maxim is, that among People of Quality, a Wife should be always a reasonable and agreeable Companion, because she cannot always be young. When the Girls are twelve Years old, which among them is the marriageable Age, their Parents or Guardians take them home, with great Expressions of Gratitude to the Professors, and seldom without Tears of the young Lady and her Companions.

In the Nurseries of Females of the meaner Sort, the Children are instructed in all Kinds of Works proper for their Sex, and their several Degrees: Those intended for Apprentices are dismissed at seven Years old, the rest are kept to eleven.

The meaner Families who have Children at these Nurseries, are obliged, besides their annual Pension, which is as low as possible, to return to the Steward of the Nursery a small Monthly Share of their Gettings, to be a Portion for the Child; and therefore all Parents are limited in their Expences by the Law. For the *Lilliputians* think nothing can be more unjust, than that People, in Subservience to their own Appetites, should bring Children into the World, and leave the Burthen of supporting them on the Publick. As to Persons of Quality, they give Security to appropriate a certain Sum for each Child, suitable to their Condition; and these Funds are always managed with good Husbandry, and the most exact Justice.

The Cottagers and Labourers keep their Children at home, their Business being only to till and cultivate the Earth; and therefore their Education is of little Consequence to the Publick; but the Old and Diseased among them are supported by Hospitals: For begging is a Trade unknown in this Empire.

And here it may perhaps divert the curious Reader, to give some Account of my Domestick, and my Manner of living in this Country, during a Residence of nine Months and thirteen Days. Having a Head mechanically turned, and being likewise forced by Necessity, I had made for myself a Table and Chair convenient enough, out of the largest Trees in the Royal Park. Two hundred Sempstresses were employed to make me Shirts, and Linnen for my Bed and Table, all of the strongest and coarsest kind they could get; which, however, they were forced to quilt together in several Folds; for the thickest was some Degrees finer than Lawn. Their Linnen is usually three Inches wide, and three Foot make a Piece. The Sempstresses took my Measure as I lay on the Ground, one standing at my Neck, and another at my Mid-Leg, with a strong Cord extended, that each held by the End, while the third measured the Length of the Cord with a Rule of an Inch long. Then they measured my right Thumb, and desired no more; for by a mathematical Computation, that twice round the Thumb is once round the Wrist, and so on to the Neck and the Waist; and by the Help of my old Shirt, which I displayed on the Ground before them for a Pattern, they fitted me exactly. Three hundred Taylors were employed in the same Manner to make me Clothes; but they had another Contrivance for taking my Measure. I kneeled down, and they raised a Ladder from the Ground to my Neck; upon this Ladder one of them mounted, and let fall a Plum-Line from my Collar to the Floor, which just answered the Length of my Coat; but my Waist and Arms I measured myself. When my Cloaths were finished, which was done in my House, (for the largest of theirs would not have been able to hold them) they looked like the Patchwork made by the Ladies in *England*, only that mine were all of a Colour.

I had three hundred Cooks to dress my Victuals, in little convenient Huts built about my House, where they and their Families lived, and prepared me two Dishes a-piece. I took up twenty Waiters in my Hand, and placed them on the Table; an hundred more attended below on the Ground, some with Dishes of Meat, and some with Barrels of Wine, and other Liquors, slung on their Shoulders; all which the Waiters above drew up as I wanted, in a very ingenious Manner, by certain Cords, as we draw the Bucket up a Well in *Europe*. A Dish of their Meat was a good Mouthful, and a Barrel of their Liquor a reasonable Draught. Their Mutton yields to ours, but their Beef is excellent. I have had a Sirloin so large, that I have been forced to make three Bits of it; but this is rare. My Servants were astonished to see me eat it Bones and all, as in our Country we do the Leg of a Lark. Their Geese and Turkeys I usually eat at a Mouthful, and I must confess they far exceed ours. Of their smaller Fowl I could take up twenty or thirty at the End of my Knife.

One Day his Imperial Majesty being informed of my Way of living, desired that himself, and his Royal Consort; with the young Princes of the Blood of both Sexes, might have the Happiness (as he was pleased to call it) of dining with me. They came accordingly, and I placed them upon Chairs of State on my Table, just over against me, with their Guards about them. *Flimnap* the Lord High Treasurer attended there likewise, with his white Staff;° and I observed he often looked on me with a sour Countenance, which I would not seem to regard, but eat more than usual, in Honour to my dear Country, as well as to fill the Court with Admiration. I have some private Reasons to believe, that this Visit from his Majesty gave *Flimnap* an Opportunity of doing me ill Offices to his Master. That Minister had always been my secret Enemy, although he outwardly caressed me more than was usual to the Moroseness of his Nature. He represented to the Emperor the low Condition of his Treasury; that he was forced to take up Money at great Discount; that Exchequer Bills would not circulate under nine *per Cent.* below Par; that I had cost his Majesty above a Million and a half of *Sprugs,* (their greatest Gold Coin, about the Bigness of a Spangle;) and upon the whole, that it would be adviseable in the Emperor to take the first fair Occasion of dismissing me.

I am here obliged to vindicate the Reputation of an excellent Lady, who was an innocent Sufferer upon my Account. The Treasurer took a Fancy to be jealous of his Wife, from the Malice of some evil Tongues, who informed him that her Grace had taken a violent Affection for my Person; and the Court-Scandal ran for some Time that she once came privately to my Lodging. This I solemnly declare to be a most infamous Falsehood, without any Grounds, farther than that her Grace was pleased to treat me with all innocent Marks of Freedom and Friendship. I own she came often to my House, but always publickly, nor ever without three more in the Coach, who were usually her Sister, and young Daughter, and some particular Acquaintance; but this was common to many other Ladies of the Court. And I still appeal to my Servants round, whether they at any Time saw a Coach at my Door without knowing what Persons were in it. On those Occasions, when a Servant had given me Notice, my Custom was to go immediately to the Door; and after paying my Respects, to take up the Coach and two Horses very carefully in my Hands, (for if there were six Horses, the Postillion always unharnessed four) and place them on a Table, where I had fixed a moveable Rim quite round, of five Inches high, to prevent Accidents. And I have often had four Coaches and Horses at once on my Table full of Company, while I sat in my Chair leaning my Face towards them; and

white Staff: The symbol of office of the Lord High Treasurer.

when I was engaged with one Sett, the Coachmen would gently drive the others round my Table. I have passed many an Afternoon very agreeably in these Conversations: But I defy the Treasurer, or his two Informers. (I will name them, and let them make their best of it) *Clustril* and *Drunlo,* to prove that any Person ever came to me *incognito,* except the Secretary *Reldresal,* who was sent by express Command of his Imperial Majesty, as I have before related. I should not have dwelt so long upon this Particular, if it had not been a Point wherein the Reputation of a great Lady is so nearly concerned; to say nothing of my own; although I had the Honour to be a *Nardac,* which the Treasurer himself is not; for all the World knows he is only a *Clumglum,* a Title inferior by one Degree, as that of a Marquess is to a Duke in *England;* yet I allow he preceded me in right of his Post. These false Informations, which I afterwards came to the Knowledge of, by an Accident not proper to mention, made the Treasurer shew his Lady for some Time an ill Countenance, and me a worse: For although he were at last undeceived and reconciled to her, yet I lost all Credit with him; and found my Interest decline very fast with the Emperor himself, who was indeed too much governed by that Favourite.

CHAPTER VII

The Author being informed of a Design to accuse him of High Treason, makes his Escape to Blefuscu. *His Reception there.*

Before I proceed to give an Account of my leaving this Kingdom, it may be proper to inform the Reader of a private Intrigue which had been for two Months forming against me.

I had been hitherto all my Life a Stranger to Courts, for which I was unqualified by the Meanness of my Condition. I had indeed heard and read enough of the Dispositions of great Princes and Ministers; but never expected to have found such terrible Effects of them in so remote a Country, governed, as I thought, by very different Maxims from those in *Europe.*

When I was just preparing to pay my Attendance on the Emperor of *Blefuscu;* a considerable Person at Court (to whom I had been very serviceable at a time when he lay under the highest Displeasure of his Imperial Majesty) came to my House very privately at Night in a close Chair, and without sending his Name, desired Admittance: The Chairmen were dismissed; I put the Chair, with his Lordship in it, into my Coat-Pocket; and giving Orders to a trusty Servant to say I was indisposed and gone to sleep, I fastened the Door of my House, placed the Chair on the Table, according to my usual Custom, and sat down by it. After the common Salutations were over, observing his Lordship's Countenance full of Concern; and enquiring into the Reason, he desired I would hear him with Patience, in a Matter that highly concerned my Honour and my Life. His Speech was to the following Effect, for I took Notes of it as soon as he left me.

You are to know, said he, that several Committees of Council have been lately called in the most private Manner on your Account: And it is but two Days since his Majesty came to a full Resolution.

You are very sensible that *Skyris Bolgolam* (*Galbet,* or High Admiral) hath been your mortal Enemy almost ever since your Arrival. His original Reasons I know not; but his Hatred is much encreased since your great Success against *Blefuscu,* by which his Glory, as Admiral, is obscured. This Lord, in Conjunction with *Flimnap* the High Treasurer, whose Enmity against you is notorious on Account of his Lady; *Limtoc* the General, *Lalcon* the Chamberlain, and *Balmuff* the grand Justiciary, have prepared Articles of Impeachment against you, for Treason, and other capital Crimes.

This Preface made me so impatient, being conscious of my own Merits and Innocence, that I was going to interrupt; when he intreated me to be silent; and thus proceeded.

Out of Gratitude for the Favours you have done me, I procured Information of the whole Proceedings, and a Copy of the Articles, wherein I venture my Head for your Service.

Articles of Impeachment against Quinbus Flestrin,
(*the* Man-Mountain.)

ARTICLE I

Whereas, by a Statute made in the Reign of his Imperial Majesty *Calin Deffar Plune,* it is enacted, That whoever shall make water within the Precincts of the Royal Palace, shall be liable to the Pains and Penalties of High Treason: Notwithstanding, the said *Quinbus Flestrin,* in open Breach of the said Law, under Colour of extinguishing the Fire kindled in the Apartment of his Majesty's most dear Imperial Consort, did maliciously, traitorously, and devilishly, by discharge of his Urine, put out the said Fire kindled in the said Apartment, lying and being within the Precincts of the said Royal Palace; against the Statute in that Case provided, &c. against the Duty, &c.

ARTICLE II

THAT the said *Quinbus Flestrin* having brought the Imperial Fleet of *Blefuscu* into the Royal Port, and being afterwards commanded by his Imperial Majesty to seize all the other Ships of the said Empire of *Blefuscu,* and reduce that Empire to a Province, to be governed by a Vice-Roy from hence; and to destroy and put to death not only all the *Big-Endian Exiles,* but likewise all the People of that Empire, who would not immediately forsake the *Big-Endian* Heresy: He the said *Flestrin,* like a false Traitor against his most Auspicious, Serene, Imperial Majesty, did petition to be excused from the said Service, upon Pretence of Unwillingness to force the Consciences, or destroy the Liberties and Lives of an innocent People.

ARTICLE III

THAT, whereas certain Embassadors arrived from the Court of *Blefuscu* to sue for Peace in his Majesty's Court: He the said *Flestrin* did, like a false Traitor, aid, abet, comfort, and divert the said Embassadors; although he knew them to be Servants to a Prince who was lately an open Enemy to his Imperial Majesty, and in open War against his said Majesty.

ARTICLE IV

THAT the said *Quinbus Flestrin,* contrary to the Duty of a faithful Subject, is now preparing to make a Voyage to the Court and Empire of *Blefuscu,* for which he hath received only verbal Licence from his Imperial Majesty; and under Colour of the said Licence, doth falsely and traitorously intend to take the said Voyage, and thereby to aid, comfort, and abet the Emperor of *Blefuscu,* so late an Enemy, and in open War with his Imperial Majesty aforesaid.

There are some other Articles, but these are the most important, of which I have read you an Abstract.

In the several Debates upon this Impeachment, it must be confessed that his Majesty gave many Marks of his great *Lenity;* often urging the Services you had done him, and endeavouring to extenuate your Crimes. The Treasurer and Admiral insisted that you should be put to the most painful and ignominious Death, by setting Fire on your House at Night; and the General was to attend with Twenty Thousand Men armed with poisoned Arrows, to shoot you on the Face and Hands. Some of your Servants were to have private orders to strew a poisonous Juice on your Shirts and Sheets, which would soon make you tear your own Flesh, and die in the utmost Torture. The General came into the same Opinion; so that for a long time there was a Majority against you. But his Majesty resolving, if possible, to spare your Life, at last brought off the Chamberlain.

Upon this Incident, *Reldresal*, principal Secretary for private Affairs, who always approved himself your true Friend, was commanded by the Emperor to deliver his Opinion, which he accordingly did; and therein justified the good Thoughts you have of him. He allowed your Crimes to be great; but that still there was room for Mercy, the most commendable Virtue in a Prince, and for which his Majesty was so justly celebrated. He said, the Friendship between you and him was so well known to the World, that perhaps the most honourable Board might think him partial: However, in Obedience to the Command he had received, he would freely offer his Sentiments. That if his Majesty, in Consideration of your Services, and pursuant to his own merciful Disposition, would please to spare your Life, and only give order to put out both your Eyes; he humbly conceived, that by this Expedient, Justice might in some measure be satisfied, and all the World would applaud the *Lenity* of the Emperor, as well as the fair and generous Proceedings of those who have the Honour to be his Counsellors. That the Loss of your Eyes would be no Impediment to your bodily Strength, by which you might still be useful to his Majesty. That Blindness is an Addition to Courage, by concealing Dangers from us; that the Fear you had for your Eyes, was the greatest Difficulty in bringing over the Enemy's Fleet; and it would be sufficient for you to see by the Eyes of the Ministers, since the greatest Princes do no more.

This Proposal was received with the utmost Disapprobation by the whole Board. *Bolgolam*, the Admiral, could not preserve his Temper; but rising up in Fury, said, he wondered how the Secretary durst presume to give his Opinion for preserving the Life of a Traytor: That the Services you had performed, were, by all true Reasons of State, the great Aggravation of your Crimes; that you, who were able to extinguish the Fire, by discharge of Urine in her Majesty's Apartment (which he mentioned with Horror) might, at another time, raise an Inundation by the same Means, to drown the whole Palace; and the same Strength which enabled you to bring over the Enemy's Fleet, might serve, upon the first

Discontent, to carry it back: That he had good Reasons to think you were a *Big-Endian* in your Heart; and as Treason begins in the Heart before it appears in Overt-Acts; so he accused you as a Traytor on that Account, and therefore insisted you should be put to death.

The Treasurer was of the same Opinion; he shewed to what Streights his Majesty's Revenue was reduced by the Charge of maintaining you, which would soon grow insupportable: That the Secretary's Expedient of putting out your Eyes, was so far from being a Remedy against this Evil, that it would probably increase it; as it is manifest from the common Practice of blinding some Kind of Fowl, after which they fed the faster, and grew sooner fat: That his sacred Majesty, and the Council, who are your Judges, were in their own Consciences fully convinced of your Guilt; which was a sufficient Argument to condemn you to death, without the *formal Proofs required by the strict Letter of the Law.*

But his Imperial Majesty fully determined against capital Punishment, was graciously pleased to say, that since the Council thought the Loss of your Eyes too easy a Censure, some other may be inflicted hereafter. And your Friend the Secretary humbly desiring to be heard again, in Answer to what the Treasurer had objected concerning the great Charge his Majesty was at in maintaining you; said, that his Excellency, who had the sole Disposal of the Emperor's Revenue, might easily provide against this Evil, by gradually lessening your Establishment; by which, for want of sufficient Food, you would grow weak and faint, and lose your Appetite, and consequently decay and consume in a few Months; neither would the Stench of your Carcass be then so dangerous, when it should become more than half diminished; and immediately upon your Death, five or six thousand of his Majesty's Subjects might, in two or three Days, cut your Flesh from your Bones, take it away by Cart-loads, and bury it in distant Parts to prevent Infection; leaving the Skeleton as a Monument of Admiration to Posterity.

Thus by the great Friendship of the Secretary, the whole Affair was compromised. It was strictly enjoined, that the Project of starving you by Degrees should be kept a Secret; but the Sentence of putting out your Eyes was entered on the Books; none dissenting except *Bolgolam* the Admiral, who being a Creature of the Empress, was perpetually instigated by her Majesty to insist upon your Death; she having born perpetual Malice against you, on Account of that infamous and illegal Method you took to extinguish the Fire in her Apartment.

In three Days your Friend the Secretary will be directed to come to your House, and read before you the Articles of Impeachment; and then to signify the great *Lenity* and Favour of his Majesty and Council; whereby you are only condemned to the Loss of your Eyes, which his Majesty doth not question you will gratefully and humbly submit to; and Twenty of his Majesty's Surgeons will attend, in order to see the Operation well performed, by discharging very sharp pointed Arrows into the Balls of your Eyes, as you lie on the Ground.

I leave to your Prudence what Measures you will take; and to avoid Suspicion, I must immediately return in as private a Manner as I came.

His Lordship did so, and I remained alone, under many Doubts and Perplexities of Mind.

It was a Custom introduced by this Prince and his Ministry, (very different, as I have been assured, from the Practices of former Times) that after the Court had decreed any cruel Execution, either to gratify the Monarch's Resentment, or the Malice of a Favourite; the Emperor always made a Speech to his whole Council, expressing his *great Lenity and Tenderness, as Qualities known and confessed by all the World.* This Speech was immediately published through the Kingdom; nor did any thing terrify the People so much as those Encomiums on his Majesty's Mercy; because it was observed, that the more these Praises were enlarged and insisted on, the more *inhuman* was the Punishment, and the *Sufferer more innocent.* Yet, as to myself, I must confess, having never been designed for a Courtier, either by my Birth or Education, I was so ill a Judge of Things, that I could not discover the *Lenity* and Favour of this Sentence; but conceived it (perhaps erroneously) rather to be rigorous than gentle. I sometimes thought of standing my Tryal; for although I could not deny the Facts alledged in the several Articles, yet I hoped they would admit of some Extenuations. But having in my Life perused many State-Tryals, which I ever observed to terminate as the Judges thought fit to direct; I durst not rely on so dangerous a Decision, in so critical a Juncture, and against such powerful Enemies. Once I was strongly bent upon Resistance: For while I had Liberty, the whole Strength of that Empire could hardly subdue me, and I might easily with Stones pelt the Metropolis to Pieces: But I soon rejected that Project with Horror, by remembering the Oath I had made to the Emperor, the Favours I received from him, and the high Title of *Nardac* he conferred upon me. Neither had I so soon learned the Gratitude of Courtiers, to persuade myself that his Majesty's *present Severities acquitted me of all past Obligations.*

At last I fixed upon a Resolution, for which it is probable I may incur some Censure, and not unjustly; for I confess I owe the preserving mine Eyes, and consequently my Liberty, to my own great Rashness and

Want of Experience: Because if I had then known the Nature of Princes and Ministers, which I have since observed in many other Courts, and their Methods of treating Criminals less obnoxious than myself; I should with great Alacrity and Readiness have submitted to so *easy* a Punishment. But hurried on by the Precipitancy of Youth; and having his Imperial Majesty's Licence to pay my Attendance upon the Emperor of *Blefuscu;* I took this Opportunity, before the three Days were elapsed, to send a Letter to my Friend the Secretary, signifying my Resolution of setting out that Morning for *Blefuscu,* pursuant to the Leave I had got; and without waiting for an Answer, I went to that Side of the Island where our Fleet lay. I seized a large Man of War, tied a Cable to the Prow, and lifting up the Anchors, I stript myself, put my Cloaths (together with my Coverlet, which I carryed under my Arm) into the Vessel; and drawing it after me, between wading and swimming, arrived at the Royal Port of *Blefuscu,* where the People had long expected me: They lent me two Guides to direct me to the Capital City, which is of the same Name; I held them in my Hands until I came within two Hundred Yards of the Gate; and desired them to signify my Arrival to one of the Secretaries, and let him know, I there waited his Majesty's Commands. I had an Answer in about an Hour, that his Majesty, attended by the Royal Family, and great Officers of the Court, was coming out to receive me. I advanced a Hundred Yards; the Emperor, and his Train, alighted from their Horses, the Empress and Ladies from their Coaches; and I did not perceive they were in any Fright or Concern. I lay on the Ground to kiss his Majesty's and the Empress's Hand. I told his Majesty, that I was come according to my Promise, and with the Licence of the Emperor my Master, to have the Honour of seeing so mighty a Monarch, and to offer him any Service in my Power, consistent with my Duty to my own Prince; not mentioning a Word of my Disgrace, because I had hitherto no regular Information of it, and might suppose myself wholly ignorant of any such Design; neither could I reasonably conceive that the Emperor would discover° the Secret while I was out of his Power: Wherein, however, it soon appeared I was deceived.

I shall not trouble the Reader with the particular Account of my Reception at this Court, which was suitable to the Generosity of so great a Prince; nor of the Difficulties I was in for want of a House and Bed, being forced to lie on the Ground, wrapt up in my Coverlet.

---

discover: Uncover, make known.

CHAPTER VIII

The Author, by a lucky Accident, finds Means to leave Blefuscu; *and, after some Difficulties, returns safe to his Native Country.*

Three Days after my Arrival, walking out of Curiosity to the North-East Coast of the Island; I observed, about half a League off, in the Sea, somewhat that looked like a Boat overturned: I pulled off my Shoes and Stockings, and wading two or three Hundred Yards, I found the Object to approach nearer by Force of the Tide; and then plainly saw it to be a real Boat, which I supposed might, by some Tempest, have been driven from a Ship. Whereupon I returned immediately towards the City, and desired his Imperial Majesty to lend me Twenty of the tallest Vessels he had left after the Loss of his Fleet, and three Thousand Seamen under the Command of his Vice-Admiral. This Fleet sailed round, while I went back the shortest Way to the Coast where I first discovered the Boat; I found the Tide had driven it still nearer; the Seamen were all provided with Cordage, which I had beforehand twisted to a sufficient Strength. When the Ships came up, I stript myself, and waded till I came within an Hundred Yards of the Boat; after which I was forced to swim till I got up to it. The Seamen threw me the End of the Cord, which I fastened to a Hole in the forepart of the Boat, and the other End to a Man of War: But I found all my Labour to little Purpose; for being out of my Depth, I was not able to work. In this Necessity, I was forced to swim behind, and push the Boat forwards as often as I could, with one of my Hands; and the Tide favouring me, I advanced so far, that I could just hold up my Chin and feel the Ground. I rested two or three Minutes, and then gave the Boat another Shove, and so on till the Sea was no higher than my Arm-pits. And now the most laborious Part being over, I took out my other Cables which were stowed in one of the Ships, and fastening them first to the Boat, and then to nine of the Vessels which attended me; the Wind being favourable, the Seamen towed, and I shoved till we arrived within forty Yards of the Shore; and waiting till the Tide was out, I got dry to the Boat, and by the Assistance of two Thousand Men, with Ropes and Engines, I made a shift to turn it on its Bottom, and found it was but little damaged.

I shall not trouble the Reader with the Difficulties I was under by the Help of certain Paddles, which cost me ten Days making, to get my Boat to the Royal Port of *Blefuscu;* where a mighty Concourse of People appeared upon my Arrival, full of Wonder at the Sight of so prodigious a Vessel. I told the Emperor, that my good Fortune had thrown this Boat in my Way, to carry me to some Place from whence I might return into my native Country; and begged his Majesty's Orders for getting Materials to fit it up; together with his Licence to depart; which, after some kind Expostulations, he was pleased to grant.

I did very much wonder, in all this Time, not to have heard of any Express relating to me from our Emperor to the Court of *Blefuscu*. But I was afterwards given privately to understand, that his Imperial Majesty, never imagining I had the least Notice of his Designs, believed I was only gone to *Blefuscu* in Performance of my Promise, according to the Licence he had given me, which was well known at our Court; and would return in a few Days when that Ceremony was ended. But he was at last in pain at my long absence; and, after consulting with the Treasurer, and the rest of that Cabal; a Person of Quality was dispatched with the Copy of the Articles against me. This Envoy had Instructions to represent to the Monarch of *Blefuscu*, the great *Lenity* of his Master, who was content to punish me no further than with the Loss of mine Eyes: That I had fled from Justice, and if I did not return in two Hours, I should be deprived of my Title of *Nardac*, and declared a Traitor. The Envoy further added; that in order to maintain the Peace and Amity between both Empires, his Master expected, that his Brother of *Blefuscu* would give Orders to have me sent back to *Lilliput*, bound Hand and Foot, to be punished as a Traitor.

The Emperor of *Blefuscu* having taken three Days to consult, returned an Answer consisting of many Civilities and Excuses. He said, that as for sending me bound, his Brother knew it was impossible; that although I had deprived him of his Fleet, yet he owed great Obligations to me for many good Offices I had done him in making the Peace. That however, both their Majesties would soon be made easy; for I had found a prodigious Vessel on the Shore, able to carry me on the Sea, which he had given order to fit up with my own Assistance and Direction; and he hoped in a few Weeks both Empires would be freed from so insupportable an Incumbrance.

With this Answer the Envoy returned to *Lilliput*, and the Monarch of *Blefuscu* related to me all that had past; offering me at the same time (but under the strictest Confidence) his gracious Protection, if I would continue in his Service; wherein although I believed him sincere, yet I resolved never more to put any Confidence in Princes or Ministers, where I could possibly avoid it; and therefore, with all due Acknowledgments for his favourable Intentions, I humbly begged to be excused. I told him, that since Fortune, whether good or evil, had thrown a Vessel in my Way; I was resolved to venture myself in the Ocean, rather than be an Occasion of Difference between two such mighty Monarchs. Neither did I find the Emperor at all displeased; and I discovered by a certain Accident, that he was very glad of my Resolution, and so were most of his Ministers.

These Considerations moved me to hasten my Departure somewhat sooner than I intended; to which the Court, impatient to have me gone, very readily contributed. Five hundred Workmen were employed to make two Sails to my Boat, according to my Directions, by quilting thirteen fold of their strongest Linnen together. I was at the Pains of making Ropes and Cables, by twisting ten, twenty or thirty of the thickest and strongest of theirs. A great Stone that I happened to find, after a long Search by the Sea-shore, served me for an Anchor. I had the Tallow of three hundred Cows for greasing my Boat, and other Uses. I was at incredible Pains in cutting down some of the largest Timber Trees for Oars and Masts, wherein I was, however, much assisted by his Majesty's Ship-Carpenters, who helped me in smoothing them, after I had done the rough Work.

In about a Month, when all was prepared, I sent to receive his Majesty's Commands, and to take my leave. The Emperor and Royal Family came out of the Palace; I lay down on my Face to kiss his Hand, which he very graciously gave me; so did the Empress, and young Princes of the Blood. His Majesty presented me with fifty Purses of two hundred *Sprugs* a-piece, together with his Picture at full length, which I put immediately into one of my Gloves, to keep it from being hurt. The Ceremonies at my Departure were too many to trouble the Reader with at this time.

I stored the Boat with the Carcasses of an hundred Oxen, and three hundred Sheep, with Bread and Drink proportionable, and as much Meat ready dressed as four hundred Cooks could provide. I took with me six Cows and two Bulls alive, with as many Yews and Rams, intending to carry them into my own Country, and propagate the Breed. And to feed them on board, I had a good Bundle of Hay, and a Bag of Corn. I would gladly have taken a Dozen of the Natives; but this was a thing the Emperor would by no Means permit; and besides a diligent Search into my Pockets, his Majesty engaged my Honour not to carry away any of his Subjects, although with their own Consent and Desire.

Having thus prepared all things as well as I was able; I set sail on the Twenty-fourth Day of *September* 1701, at six in the Morning; and when I had gone about four Leagues to the Northward, the Wind being at South-East; at six in the Evening, I descryed a small Island about half a League to the North West. I advanced forward, and cast Anchor on the Lee-side of the Island, which seemed to be uninhabited. I then took

some Refreshment, and went to my Rest. I slept well, and as I conjecture at least six Hours; for I found the Day broke in two Hours after I
awaked. It was a clear Night; I eat my Breakfast before the Sun was up;
and heaving Anchor, the Wind being favourable, I steered the same
Course that I had done the Day before, wherein I was directed by my
Pocket-Compass. My Intention was to reach, if possible, one of those
Islands, which I had reason to believe lay to the North-East of *Van
Diemen's* Land. I discovered nothing all that Day; but upon the next,
about three in the Afternoon, when I had by my Computation made
Twenty-four Leagues from *Blefuscu*, I descryed a Sail steering to the
South-East; my Course was due East. I hailed her, but could get no
Answer; yet I found I gained upon her, for the Wind slackened. I made
all the Sail I could, and in half an Hour she spyed me, then hung out her
Antient,° and discharged a Gun. It is not easy to express the Joy I was
in upon the unexpected Hope of once more seeing my beloved Country, and the dear Pledges I had left in it. The Ship slackned her Sails, and
I came up with her between five and six in the Evening, *September* 26;
but my Heart leapt within me to see her *English* Colours. I put my
Cows and Sheep into my Coat-Pockets, and got on board with all my
little Cargo of Provisions. The Vessel was an *English* Merchant-man,
returning from *Japan* by the *North* and *South Seas;* the Captain, Mr.
John Biddel of *Deptford,* a very civil Man, and an excellent Sailor. We
were now in the Latitude of 30 Degrees South; there were about fifty
Men in the Ship; and here I met an old Comrade of mine, one *Peter
Williams,* who gave me a good Character to the Captain. This Gentleman treated me with Kindness, and desired I would let him know what
Place I came from last, and whither I was bound; which I did in few
Words; but he thought I was raving, and that the Dangers I underwent
had disturbed my Head; whereupon I took my black Cattle and Sheep
out of my Pocket, which, after great Astonishment, clearly convinced
him of my Veracity. I then shewed him the Gold given me by the Emperor of *Blefuscu,* together with his Majesty's Picture at full Length, and
some other Rarities of that Country. I gave him two Purses of two Hundred *Sprugs* each, and promised, when we arrived in *England,* to make
him a Present of a Cow and a Sheep big with Young.

I shall not trouble the Reader with a particular Account of this Voy-
age, which was very prosperous for the most Part. We arrived in the
Downs on the 13th of *April* 1702. I had only one Misfortune, that the
Rats on board carried away one of my Sheep; I found her Bones in a

Antient: Flag.

Hole, picked clean from the Flesh. The rest of my Cattle I got safe on Shore, and set them a grazing in a Bowling-Green at *Greenwich,* where the Fineness of the Grass made them feed very heartily, although I had always feared the contrary: Neither could I possibly have preserved them in so long a Voyage, if the Captain had not allowed me some of his best Bisket, which rubbed to Powder, and mingled with Water, was their constant Food. The short Time I continued in *England,* I made a considerable Profit by shewing my Cattle to many Persons of Quality, and others: And before I began my second Voyage, I sold them for six Hundred Pounds. Since my last Return, I find the Breed is considerably increased, especially the Sheep; which I hope will prove much to the Advantage of the Woollen Manufacture, by the Fineness of the Fleeces.

I stayed but two Months with my Wife and Family; for my insatiable Desire of seeing foreign Countries would suffer me to continue no longer. I left fifteen Hundred Pounds with my Wife, and fixed her in a good House at *Redriff.* My remaining Stock I carried with me, Part in Money, and Part in Goods, in Hopes to improve my Fortunes. My eldest Uncle, *John,* had left me an Estate in Land, near *Epping,* of about Thirty Pounds a Year; and I had a long Lease of the *Black-Bull* in *Fetter-Lane,* which yielded me as much more: So that I was not in any Danger of leaving my Family upon the Parish. My Son *Johnny,* named so after his Uncle, was at the Grammar School, and a towardly Child. My Daughter *Betty* (who is now well married, and has Children) was then at her Needle-Work. I took Leave of my Wife, and Boy and Girl, with Tears on both Sides; and went on board the *Adventure,* a Merchant-Ship of three Hundred Tons, bound for *Surat,* Captain *John Nicholas* of *Liverpool,* Commander. But my Account of this Voyage must be referred to the second Part of my Travels.

The End of the First Part

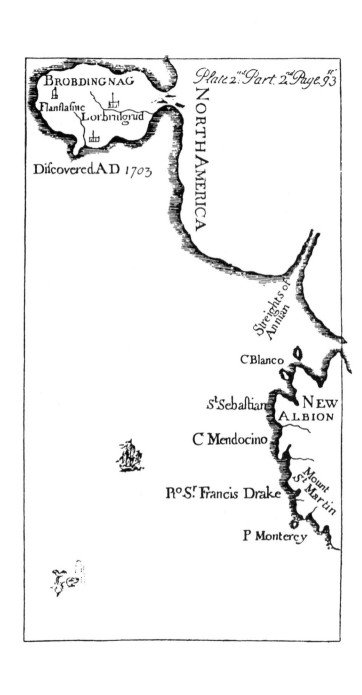

BROBDINGNAG

Flanflasinc
Lorbrulgrud

Discovered A D 1703

NORTH AMERICA

Plate 2.ᵈ Part. 2.ᵈ Page. 93

Streights of Annian

C Blanco

St Sebastian

NEW
ALBION

C Mendocino

Po Sr Francis Drake

Mount St Martin

P Montercy

PART II
A Voyage to *Brobdingnag*

CHAPTER I

A great Storm described. The long Boat sent to fetch Water, the Author goes with it to discover the Country. He is left on Shoar, is seized by one of the Natives, and carried to a Farmer's House. His Reception there, with several Accidents that happened there. A Description of the Inhabitants.

Having been condemned by Nature and Fortune to an active and restless Life; in two Months after my Return, I again left my native Country, and took Shipping in the *Downs* on the 20th Day of *June* 1702, in the *Adventure*, Capt. *John Nicholas*, a *Cornish* Man, Commander, bound for *Surat*. We had a very prosperous Gale till we arrived at the *Cape* of *Good-hope*, where we landed for fresh Water; but discovering a Leak we unshipped our Goods, and wintered there; for the Captain falling sick of an Ague, we could not leave the *Cape* till the End of *March*. We then set sail, and had a good Voyage till we passed the *Streights* of *Madagascar*; but having got Northward of that Island, and to about five Degrees South Latitude, the Winds, which in those Seas are observed to blow a constant equal Gale between the North and West, from the Beginning of *December* to the Beginning of *May*, on the 19th of *April* began to blow with much greater Violence, and more Westerly than usual; continuing so for twenty Days together, during which time we were driven a little to the East of the *Molucca* Islands, and about three Degrees Northward of the Line, as our Captain found by an Observation he took the 2d of *May,* at which time the Wind ceased, and it was a perfect Calm, whereat I was not a little rejoyced. But he being a Man well experienced in the Navigation of those Seas, bid us all prepare against a Storm, which accordingly happened the Day following: For a Southern Wind, called the Southern *Monsoon,* began to set in.

Finding it was like to overblow, we took in our Sprit-sail, and stood by to hand the Fore-sail; but making foul Weather, we looked the Guns were all fast, and handed the Missen. The Ship lay very broad off, so we thought it better spooning before the Sea, than trying or hulling. We reeft the Foresail and set him, we hawled aft the Fore-sheet; the Helm was hard a Weather. The Ship wore bravely. We belay'd the Foredownhall; but the Sail was split, and we hawl'd down the Yard, and got the Sail into the Ship, and unbound all the things clear of it. It was a very fierce Storm; the Sea broke strange and dangerous. We hawl'd off upon the Lanniard of the Wipstaff, and helped the Man at Helm. We would not get down our Top-Mast, but let all stand, because she scudded before the Sea very well, and we knew that the Top-Mast being aloft, the Ship was the wholesomer, and made better way through the Sea, seeing we had Sea room. When the Storm was over, we set Fore-sail and Mainsail, and brought the Ship to. Then we set the Missen, Maintop-Sail and the Foretop-Sail. Our Course was East North-east, the Wind was at South-west. We got the Star-board Tacks aboard, we cast off our Weather-braces and Lifts; we set in the Lee-braces, and hawl'd forward by the Weather-bowlings, and hawl'd them tight, and belayed them, and hawl'd over the Missen Tack to Windward, and kept her full and by as near as she would lye.

During this Storm, which was followed by a strong Wind West South-west, we were carried by my Computation about five hundred Leagues to the East,° so that the oldest Sailor on Board could not tell in what part of the World we were. Our Provisions held out well, our Ship was staunch, and our Crew all in good Health; but we lay in the utmost Distress for Water. We thought it best to hold on the same Course rather than turn more Northerly, which might have brought us to the Northwest Parts of great *Tartary,*° and into the frozen Sea.°

On the 16*th* Day of *June* 1703, a Boy on the Top-mast discovered Land. On the 17*th* we came in full View of a great Island or Continent,

---

about five hundred Leagues to the East: Roughly 1500 miles, which would put Gulliver in then-uncharted waters in the middle of the North Pacific.   ***Tartary:*** Landmass north of Asia and Europe; Siberia.   **frozen Sea:** Arctic Ocean.

(for we knew not whether) on the Southside whereof was a small Neck of Land jutting out into the Sea, and a Creek too shallow to hold a Ship of above one hundred Tuns. We cast Anchor within a League of this Creek, and our Captain sent a dozen of his Men well armed in the Long Boat, with Vessels for Water if any could be found. I desired his leave to go with them, that I might see the Country, and make what Discoveries I could. When we came to Land we saw no River or Spring, nor any Sign of Inhabitants. Our Men therefore wandered on the Shore to find out some fresh Water near the Sea, and I walked alone about a Mile on the other side, where I observed the Country all barren and rocky. I now began to be weary, and seeing nothing to entertain my Curiosity, I returned gently down towards the Creek; and the Sea being full in my View, I saw our Men already got into the Boat, and rowing for Life to the Ship. I was going to hollow° after them, although it had been to little purpose, when I observed a huge Creature walking after them in the Sea, as fast as he could: He waded not much deeper than his Knees, and took prodigious strides: But our Men had the start of him half a League, and the Sea thereabouts being full of sharp pointed Rocks, the Monster was not able to overtake the Boat. This I was afterwards told, for I durst not stay to see the Issue of that Adventure; but ran as fast as I could the Way I first went; and then climbed up a steep Hill, which gave me some Prospect of the Country. I found it fully cultivated; but that which first surprized me was the Length of the Grass, which in those Grounds that seemed to be kept for Hay, was above twenty Foot high.

I fell into a high Road, for so I took it to be, although it served to the Inhabitants only as a foot Path through a Field of Barley. Here I walked on for sometime, but could see little on either Side, it being now near Harvest, and the Corn rising at least forty Foot. I was an Hour walking to the end of this Field; which was fenced in with a Hedge of at least one hundred and twenty Foot high, and the Trees so lofty that I could make no Computation of their Altitude. There was a Stile to pass from this Field into the next: It had four Steps, and a Stone to cross over when you came to the uppermost. It was impossible for me to climb this Stile, because every Step was six Foot high, and the upper Stone above twenty. I was endeavouring to find some Gap in the Hedge; when I discovered one of the Inhabitants in the next Field advancing towards the Stile, of the same Size with him whom I saw in the Sea pursuing our Boat. He appeared as Tall as an ordinary Spire-steeple; and took about ten Yards at every Stride, as near as I could guess. I was struck with the

hollow: Shout.

utmost Fear and Astonishment, and ran to hide my self in the Corn, from whence I saw him at the Top of the Stile, looking back into the next Field on the right Hand; and heard him call in a Voice many Degrees louder than a speaking Trumpet; but the Noise was so High in the Air, that at first I certainly thought it was Thunder. Whereupon seven Monsters like himself came towards him with Reaping-Hooks in their Hands, each Hook about the largeness of six Scythes. These People were not so well clad as the first, whose Servants or Labourers they seemed to be. For, upon some Words he spoke, they went to reap the Corn in the Field where I lay. I kept from them at as great a Distance as I could, but was forced to move with extream Difficulty; for the Stalks of the Corn were sometimes not above a Foot distant, so that I could hardly squeeze my Body betwixt them. However, I made a shift to go forward till I came to a part of the Field where the Corn had been laid by the Rain and Wind: Here it was impossible for me to advance a step; for the Stalks were so interwoven that I could not creep through, and the Beards of the fallen Ears so strong and pointed, that they pierced through my Cloaths into my Flesh. At the same time I heard the Reapers not above an hundred Yards behind me. Being quite dispirited with Toil, and wholly overcome by Grief and Despair, I lay down between two Ridges, and heartily wished I might there end my Days. I bemoaned my desolate Widow, and Fatherless Children: I lamented my own Folly and Wilfulness in attempting a second Voyage against the Advice of all my Friends and Relations. In this terrible Agitation of Mind I could not forbear thinking of *Lilliput,* whose Inhabitants looked upon me as the greatest Prodigy that ever appeared in the World; where I was able to draw an Imperial Fleet in my Hand, and perform those other Actions which will be recorded for ever in the Chronicles of that Empire, while Posterity shall hardly believe them, although attested by Millions. I reflected what a Mortification it must prove to me to appear as inconsiderable in this Nation, as one single *Lilliputian* would be among us. But, this I conceived was to be the least of my Misfortunes: For, as human Creatures are observed to be more Savage and cruel in Proportion to their Bulk; what could I expect but to be a Morsel in the Mouth of the first among these enormous Barbarians who should happen to seize me? Undoubtedly Philosophers are in the Right when they tell us, that nothing is great or little otherwise than by Comparison:° It

nothing is great or little otherwise than by Comparison: Swift's friend George Berkeley (1685–1753) was one philosopher who emphasized the relativity of our judgment of size, in his *Essay Towards a New Theory of Vision* (1709).

might have pleased Fortune to let the *Lilliputians* find some Nation, where the People were as diminutive with respect to them, as they were to me. And who knows but that even this prodigious Race of Mortals might be equally overmatched in some distant Part of the World, whereof we have yet no Discovery?

Scared and confounded as I was, I could not forbear going on with these Reflections; when one of the Reapers approaching within ten Yards of the Ridge where I lay, made me apprehend that with the next Step I should be squashed to Death under his Foot, or cut in two with his Reaping Hook. And therefore when he was again about to move, I screamed as loud as Fear could make me. Whereupon the huge Creature trod short, and looking round about under him for some time, at last espied me as I lay on the Ground. He considered a while with the Caution of one who endeavours to lay hold on a small dangerous Animal in such a Manner that it shall not be able either to scratch or to bite him; as I my self have sometimes done with a *Weasel* in *England*. At length he ventured to take me up behind by the middle between his Fore-finger and Thumb, and brought me within three Yards of his Eyes, that he might behold my Shape more perfectly. I guessed his Meaning; and my good Fortune gave me so much Presence of Mind, that I resolved not to struggle in the least as he held me in the Air above sixty Foot from the Ground; although he grievously pinched my Sides, for fear I should slip through his Fingers. All I ventured was to raise mine Eyes towards the Sun, and place my Hands together in a supplicating Posture, and to speak some Words in an humble melancholy Tone, suitable to the Condition I then was in. For, I apprehended every Moment that he would dash me against the Ground, as we usually do any little hateful Animal which we have a Mind to destroy. But my good Star would have it, that he appeared pleased with my Voice and Gestures, and began to look upon me as a Curiosity; much wondering to hear me pronounce articulate Words, although he could not understand them. In the mean time I was not able to forbear Groaning and shedding Tears, and turning my Head towards my Sides; letting him know, as well as I could, how cruelly I was hurt by the Pressure of his Thumb and Finger. He seemed to apprehend my Meaning; for, lifting up the Lappet° of his Coat, he put me gently into it, and immediately ran along with me to his Master, who was a substantial Farmer, and the same Person I had first seen in the Field.

The Farmer having (as I supposed by their Talk) received such an

Lappet: Lapel.

Account of me as his Servant could give him, took a piece of a small Straw, about the Size of a walking Staff, and therewith lifted up the Lappets of my Coat; which it seems he thought to be some kind of Covering that Nature had given me. He blew my Hairs aside to take a better View of my Face. He called his Hinds° about him, and asked them (as I afterwards learned) whether they had ever seen in the Fields any little Creature that resembled me. He then placed me softly on the Ground upon all four; but I got immediately up, and walked slowly backwards and forwards, to let those People see I had no Intent to run away. They all sate down in a Circle about me, the better to observe my Motions. I pulled off my Hat, and made a low Bow towards the Farmer: I fell on my Knees, and lifted up my Hands and Eyes, and spoke several Words as loud as I could: I took a Purse of Gold out of my Pocket, and humbly presented it to him. He received it on the Palm of his Hand, then applied it close to his Eye, to see what it was, and afterwards turned it several times with the Point of a Pin, (which he took out of his Sleeve,) but could make nothing of it. Whereupon I made a Sign that he should place his Hand on the Ground: I then took the Purse, and opening it, poured all the Gold into his Palm. There were six *Spanish*-Pieces of four Pistoles each, besides twenty or thirty smaller Coins. I saw him wet the Tip of his little Finger upon his Tongue, and take up one of my largest Pieces, and then another; but he seemed to be wholly ignorant what they were. He made me a Sign to put them again into my Purse, and the Purse again into my Pocket; which after offering to him several times, I thought it best to do.

The Farmer by this time was convinced I must be a rational Creature. He spoke often to me, but the Sound of his Voice pierced my Ears like that of a Water-Mill; yet his Words were articulate enough. I answered as loud as I could in several Languages; and he often laid his Ear within two Yards of me, but all in vain, for we were wholly unintelligible to each other. He then sent his Servants to their Work, and taking his Handkerchief out of his Pocket, he doubled and spread it on his Hand, which he placed flat on the Ground with the Palm upwards, making me a Sign to step into it, as I could easily do, for it was not above a Foot in thickness. I thought it my part to obey; and for fear of falling, laid my self at full Length upon the Handkerchief, with the Remainder of which he lapped me up to the Head for further Security; and in this Manner carried me home to his House. There he called his Wife, and shewed me to her; but she screamed and ran back as Women in *England* do at the

Hinds: Farmworkers.

Sight of a Toad or a Spider. However, when she had a while seen my Behaviour, and how well I observed the Signs her Husband made, she was soon reconciled, and by Degrees grew extreamly tender of me.

It was about twelve at Noon, and a Servant brought in Dinner. It was only one substantial Dish of Meat (fit for the plain Condition of an Husband-Man) in a Dish of about four and twenty Foot Diameter. The Company were the Farmer and his Wife, three Children, and an old Grandmother: When they were sat down, the Farmer placed me at some Distance from him on the Table, which was thirty Foot high from the Floor. I was in a terrible Fright, and kept as far as I could from the Edge, for fear of falling. The Wife minced a bit of Meat, then crumbled some Bread on a Trencher, and placed it before me. I made her a low Bow, took out my Knife and Fork, and fell to eat; which gave them exceeding Delight. The Mistress sent her Maid for a small Dram-cup, which held about two Gallons; and filled it with Drink: I took up the Vessel with much difficulty in both Hands, and in a most respectful Manner drank to her Ladyship's Health, expressing the Words as loud as I could in *English;* which made the Company laugh so heartily, that I was almost deafened with the Noise. This Liquour tasted like a small Cyder, and was not unpleasant. Then the Master made me a Sign to come to his Trencher side; but as I walked on the Table, being in great surprize all the time, as the indulgent Reader will easily conceive and excuse, I happened to stumble against a Crust, and fell flat on my Face, but received no hurt. I got up immediately, and observing the good People to be in much Concern, I took my Hat (which I held under my Arm out of good Manners) and waving it over my Head, made three Huzza's, to shew I had got no Mischief by the Fall. But advancing forwards toward my Master (as I shall henceforth call him) his youngest Son who sate next him, an arch Boy of about ten Years old, took me up by the Legs, and held me so high in the Air, that I trembled every Limb; but his Father snatched me from him; and at the same time gave him such a Box on the left Ear, as would have felled an *European* Troop of Horse to the Earth; ordering him to be taken from the Table. But, being afraid the Boy might owe me a Spight; and well remembring how mischievous all Children among us naturally are to Sparrows, Rabbits, young Kittens, and Puppy-Dogs; I fell on my Knees, and pointing to the Boy, made my Master understand, as well as I could, that I desired his Son might be pardoned. The Father complied, and the Lad took his Seat again; whereupon I went to him and kissed his Hand, which my Master took, and made him stroak me gently with it.

In the Midst of Dinner my Mistress's favourite Cat leapt into her

Lap. I heard a Noise behind me like that of a Dozen Stocking-Weavers at work; and turning my Head, I found it proceeded from the Purring of this Animal, who seemed to be three Times larger than an Ox, as I computed by the View of her Head, and one of her Paws, while her Mistress was feeding and stroaking her. The Fierceness of this Creature's Countenance altogether discomposed me; although I stood at the further End of the Table, above fifty Foot off; and although my Mistress held her fast for fear she might give a Spring, and seize me in her Talons. But it happened there was no Danger; for the Cat took not the least Notice of me when my Master placed me within three Yards of her. And as I have been always told, and found true by Experience in my Travels, that flying, or discovering Fear before a fierce Animal, is a certain Way to make it pursue or attack you; so I resolved in this dangerous Juncture to shew no Manner of Concern. I walked with Intrepidity five or six Times before the very Head of the Cat, and came within half a Yard of her; whereupon she drew her self back, as if she were more afraid of me: I had less Apprehension concerning the Dogs, whereof three or four came into the Room, as it is usual in Farmers Houses; one of which was a Mastiff equal in Bulk to four Elephants, and a Greyhound somewhat taller than the Mastiff, but not so large.

When Dinner was almost done, the Nurse came in with a Child of a Year old in her Arms; who immediately spyed me, and began a Squall that you might have heard from *London-Bridge* to *Chelsea;* after the usual Oratory of Infants, to get me for a Play-thing. The Mother out of pure Indulgence took me up, and put me towards the Child, who presently seized me by the Middle, and got my Head in his Mouth, where I roared so loud that the Urchin was frighted, and let me drop; and I should infallibly have broke my Neck, if the Mother had not held her Apron under me. The Nurse to quiet her Babe made use of a Rattle, which was a Kind of hollow Vessel filled with great Stones, and fastned by a Cable to the Child's Waist: But all in vain, so that she was forced to apply the last Remedy by giving it suck. I must confess no Object ever disgusted me so much as the Sight of her monstrous Breast, which I cannot tell what to compare with, so as to give the curious Reader an Idea of its Bulk, Shape and Colour. It stood prominent six Foot, and could not be less than sixteen in Circumference. The Nipple was about half the Bigness of my Head, and the Hue both of that and the Dug so varified with Spots, Pimples and Freckles, that nothing could appear more nauseous: For I had a near Sight of her, she sitting down the more conveniently to give Suck, and I standing on the Table. This made me reflect upon the fair Skins of our *English* Ladies, who appear so beautiful to us, only because they are of our own Size, and their Defects not to be seen but through a magnifying Glass, where we find by Experiment that the smoothest and whitest Skins look rough and coarse, and ill coloured.

I remember when I was at *Lilliput,* the Complexions of those diminutive People appeared to me the fairest in the World: And talking upon this Subject with a Person of Learning there, who was an intimate Friend of mine; he said, that my Face appeared much fairer and smoother when he looked on me from the Ground, than it did upon a nearer View when I took him up in my Hand, and brought him close; which he confessed was at first a very shocking Sight. He said, he could discover great Holes in my Skin; that the Stumps of my Beard were ten Times stronger than the Bristles of a Boar; and my Complexion made up of several Colours altogether disagreeable: Although I must beg Leave to say for my self, that I am as fair as most of my Sex and Country, and very little Sunburnt by all my Travels. On the other Side, discoursing of the Ladies in that Emperor's Court, he used to tell me, one had Freckles, another too wide a Mouth, a third too large a Nose; nothing of which I was able to distinguish. I confess this Reflection was obvious enough; which, however, I could not forbear, lest the Reader might think those vast Creatures were actually deformed: For I must do them Justice to say they are a comely Race of People; and particularly the Features of my Master's Countenance, although he were but a Farmer, when I beheld him from the Height of sixty Foot, appeared very well proportioned.

When Dinner was done, my Master went out to his Labourers; and as I could discover by his Voice and Gesture, gave his Wife a strict Charge to take Care of me. I was very much tired and disposed to sleep, which my Mistress perceiving, she put me on her own Bed, and covered me with a clean white Handkerchief, but larger and coarser than the Main Sail of a Man of War.

I slept about two Hours, and dreamed I was at home with my Wife and Children, which aggravated my Sorrows when I awaked and found my self alone in a vast Room, between two and three Hundred Foot wide, and above two Hundred high; lying in a Bed twenty Yards wide. My Mistress was gone about her houshold Affairs, and had locked me in. The Bed was eight Yards from the Floor. Some natural Necessities required me to get down: I durst not presume to call, and if I had, it would have been in vain with such a Voice as mine at so great a Distance from the Room where I lay, to the Kitchen where the Family kept. While I was under these Circumstances, two Rats crept up the Curtains, and ran smelling backwards and forwards on the Bed: One of them came up almost to my Face; whereupon I rose in a Fright, and drew out my Hanger° to defend my self. These horrible Animals had the Boldness to attack me on both Sides, and one of them held his Fore-feet at my Collar; but I had the good Fortune to rip up his Belly before he could do me any Mischief. He fell down at my Feet; and the other seeing the Fate of his Comrade, made his Escape, but not without one good Wound on the Back, which I gave him as he fled, and made the Blood run trickling from him. After this Exploit I walked gently to and fro on the Bed, to recover my Breath and Loss of Spirits. These Creatures were of the Size of a large Mastiff, but infinitely more nimble and fierce; so that if I had taken off my Belt before I went to sleep, I must have infallibly been torn to Pieces and devoured. I measured the Tail of the dead Rat, and found it to be two Yards long, wanting an Inch; but it went against my Stomach to drag the Carcass off the Bed, where it lay still bleeding; I observed it had yet some Life, but with a strong Slash cross the Neck, I thoroughly dispatched it.

Soon after, my Mistress came into the Room, who seeing me all bloody, ran and took me up in her Hand. I pointed to the dead *Rat,* smiling and making other Signs to shew I was not hurt; whereat she was extremely rejoyced, calling the Maid to take up the dead *Rat* with a Pair of Tongs, and throw it out of the Window. Then she set me on a Table, where I shewed her my Hanger all bloody, and wiping it on the Lappet of my Coat, returned it to the Scabbard. I was pressed to do more than one Thing, which another could not do for me; and therefore endeavoured to make my Mistress understand that I desired to be set down on the Floor; which after she had done, my Bashfulness would not suffer me to express my self farther than by pointing to the Door, and bowing several Times. The good Woman with much Difficulty at last perceived what I would be at; and taking me up again in her Hand, walked into the Garden where she set me down. I went on one Side about two Hundred Yards; and beckoning to her not to look or to follow me, I hid my self between two Leaves of Sorrel, and there discharged the Necessities of Nature.

I hope, the gentle Reader will excuse me for dwelling on these and the like Particulars; which however insignificant they may appear to grovelling vulgar Minds, yet will certainly help a Philosopher to enlarge his Thoughts and Imagination, and apply them to the Benefit of publick as well as private Life; which was my sole Design in presenting this and

---

Hanger: A dagger or short sword.

other Accounts of my Travels to the World; wherein I have been chiefly studious of Truth, without affecting any Ornaments of Learning, or of Style. But the whole Scene of this Voyage made so strong an Impression on my Mind, and is so deeply fixed in my Memory, that in committing it to Paper, I did not omit one material Circumstance: However, upon a strict Review, I blotted out several Passages of less Moment which were in my first Copy, for fear of being censured as tedious and trifling, whereof Travellers are often, perhaps not without Justice, accused.

CHAPTER II

A Description of the Farmer's Daughter. The Author carried to a Market-Town, and then to the Metropolis. The Particulars of his Journey.

My Mistress had a Daughter of nine Years old, a Child of towardly Parts for her Age, very dextrous at her Needle, and skilful in dressing her Baby.° Her Mother and she contrived to fit up the Baby's Cradle for me against Night: The Cradle was put into a small Drawer of a Cabinet, and the Drawer placed upon a hanging Shelf for fear of the *Rats*. This was my Bed all the Time I stayed with those People, although made more convenient by Degrees, as I began to learn their Language, and make my Wants known. This young Girl was so handy, that after I had once or twice pulled off my Cloaths before her, she was able to dress and undress me, although I never gave her that Trouble when she would let me do either my self. She made me seven Shirts, and some other Linnen of as fine Cloth as could be got, which indeed was coarser than Sackcloth; and these she constantly washed for me with her own Hands. She was likewise my School-Mistress to teach me the Language: When I pointed to any thing, she told me the Name of it in her own Tongue, so that in a few Days I was able to call for whatever I had a mind to. She was very good natured, and not above forty Foot high, being little for her Age. She gave me the Name of *Grildrig*, which the Family took up, and afterwards the whole Kingdom. The Word imports what the *Latins* call *Nanunculus*, the *Italians Homunceletino*, and the *English Mannikin*. To her I chiefly owe my Preservation in that Country: We never parted while I was there; I called her my *Glumdalclitch*, or little Nurse: And I should be guilty of great Ingratitude if I omitted this honourable Mention of her Care and Affection towards me, which I heartily wish it lay in my Power to requite as she deserves, instead of

Baby: Doll.

being the innocent but unhappy Instrument of her Disgrace, as I have too much Reason to fear.

It now began to be known and talked of in the Neighbourhood, that my Master had found a strange Animal in the Field, about the Bigness of a *Splacknuck*, but exactly shaped in every Part like a human Creature; which it likewise imitated in all its actions; seemed to speak in a little Language of its own, had already learned several Words of theirs, went erect upon two Legs, was tame and gentle, would come when it was called, do whatever it was bid, had the finest Limbs in the World, and a Complexion fairer than a Nobleman's Daughter of three Years old. Another Farmer who lived hard by, and was a particular Friend of my Master, came on a Visit on Purpose to enquire into the Truth of this Story. I was immediately produced, and placed upon a Table; where I walked as I was commanded, drew my Hanger, put it up again, made my Reverence to my Master's Guest, asked him in his own Language how he did, and told him he was welcome; just as my little Nurse had instructed me. This Man, who was old and dim-sighted, put on his Spectacles to behold me better, at which I could not forbear laughing very heartily; for his Eyes appeared like the Full-Moon shining into a Chamber at two Windows. Our People, who discovered the Cause of my Mirth, bore me Company in Laughing; at which the old Fellow was Fool enough to be angry and out of Countenance. He had the Character of a great Miser; and to my Misfortune he well deserved it by the cursed Advice he gave my Master, to shew me as a Sight upon a Market-Day in the next Town, which was half an Hour's Riding, about two and twenty Miles from our House. I guessed there was some Mischief contriving, when I observed my Master and his Friend whispering long together, sometimes pointing at me; and my Fears made me fancy that I overheard and understood some of their Words. But, the next Morning *Glumdalclitch* my little Nurse told me the whole Matter, which she had cunningly picked out from her Mother. The poor Girl laid me on her Bosom, and fell a weeping with Shame and Grief. She apprehended some Mischief would happen to me from rude vulgar Folks, who might squeeze me to Death, or break one of my Limbs by taking me in their Hands. She had also observed how modest I was in my Nature, how nicely I regarded my Honour; and what an Indignity I should conceive it to be exposed for Money as a publick Spectacle to the meanest of the People. She said, her *Papa* and *Mamma* had promised that *Grildrig* should be hers; but now she found they meant to serve her as they did last Year, when they pretended to give her a Lamb; and yet, as soon as it was fat, sold it to a Butcher. For my own Part, I may truly affirm that

I was less concerned than my Nurse. I had a strong Hope which never left me, that I should one Day recover my Liberty; and as to the Ignominy of being carried about for a Monster,° I considered my self to be a perfect Stranger in the Country; and that such a Misfortune could never be charged upon me as a Reproach if ever I should return to *England;* since the King of *Great Britain* himself, in my Condition, must have undergone the same Distress.

My Master, pursuant to the Advice of his Friend, carried me in a Box the next Market-Day to the neighbouring Town; and took along with him his little Daughter my Nurse upon a Pillion behind him. The Box was close on every Side, with a little Door for me to go in and out, and a few Gimlet-holes to let in Air. The Girl had been so careful to put the Quilt of her Baby's Bed into it, for me to lye down on. However, I was terribly shaken and discomposed in this Journey, although it were but of half an Hour. For the Horse went about forty Foot at every Step; and trotted so high, that the Agitation was equal to the rising and falling of a Ship in a great Storm, but much more frequent: Our Journey was somewhat further than from *London* to St. *Albans.*° My Master alighted at an Inn which he used to frequent; and after consulting a while with the Inn-keeper, and making some necessary Preparations, he hired the *Grultrud,* or Cryer, to give Notice through the Town, of a strange Creature to be seen at the Sign of the Green *Eagle,* not so big as a *Splacnuck,* (an Animal in that Country very finely shaped, about six Foot long) and in every Part of the Body resembling an human Creature; could speak several Words, and perform an Hundred diverting Tricks.

I was placed upon a Table in the largest Room of the Inn, which might be near three Hundred Foot square. My little Nurse stood on a low Stool close to the Table, to take care of me, and direct what I should do. My Master, to avoid a Croud, would suffer only Thirty People at a Time to see me. I walked about on the Table as the Girl commanded; she asked me Questions as far as she knew my Understanding of the Language reached, and I answered them as loud as I could. I turned about several Times to the Company, paid my humble Respects, said they were welcome; and used some other Speeches I had been taught. I took up a Thimble filled with Liquor, which *Glumdalclitch* had given me for a Cup, and drank their Health. I drew out my Hanger, and flourished with it after the Manner of Fencers in *England.* My

---

Monster: A freak.   **from *London* to *St. Albans:*** The distance between London and St. Albans is about 20 miles.

Nurse gave me Part of a Straw, which I exercised as a Pike, having learned the Art in my Youth. I was that Day shewn to twelve Sets of Company; and as often forced to go over again with the same Fopperies, till I was half dead with Weariness and Vexation. For, those who had seen me, made such wonderful Reports, that the People were ready to break down the Doors to come in. My Master for his own Interest would not suffer any one to touch me, except my Nurse; and, to prevent Danger, Benches were set round the Table at such a Distance, as put me out of every Body's Reach. However, an unlucky School-Boy aimed a Hazel Nut directly at my Head, which very narrowly missed me; otherwise, it came with so much Violence, that it would have infallibly knocked out my Brains; for it was almost as large as a small Pumpion:° But I had the Satisfaction to see the young Rogue well beaten, and turned out of the Room.

My Master gave publick Notice, that he would shew me again the next Market-Day: And in the mean time, he prepared a more convenient Vehicle for me, which he had Reason enough to do; for I was so tired with my first Journey, and with entertaining Company eight Hours together, that I could hardly stand upon my Legs, or speak a Word. It was at least three Days before I recovered my Strength; and that I might have no rest at home, all the neighbouring Gentlemen from an Hundred Miles round, hearing of my Fame, came to see me at my Master's own House. There could not be fewer than thirty Persons with their Wives and Children; (for the Country is very populous;) and my Master demanded the Rate of a full Room whenever he shewed me at Home, although it were only to a single Family. So that for some time I had but little Ease every Day of the Week, (except *Wednesday,* which is their Sabbath) although I were not carried to the Town.

My Master finding how profitable I was like to be, resolved to carry me to the most considerable Cities of the Kingdom. Having therefore provided himself with all things necessary for a long Journey, and settled his Affairs at Home; he took Leave of his Wife; and upon the 17*th* of *August* 1703, about two Months after my Arrival, we set out for the Metropolis, situated near the Middle of that Empire, and about three Thousand Miles distance from our House: My Master made his Daughter *Glumdalclitch* ride behind him. She carried me on her Lap in a Box tied about her Waist. The Girl had lined it on all Sides with the softest Cloth she could get, well quilted underneath; furnished it with her Baby's Bed, provided me with Linnen and other Necessaries; and made

Pumpion: Pumpkin.

every thing as convenient as she could. We had no other Company but a Boy of the House, who rode after us with the Luggage.

My Master's Design was to shew me in all the Towns by the Way, and to step out of the Road for Fifty or an Hundred Miles, to any Village or Person of Quality's House where he might expect Custom. We made easy Journies of not above seven or eight Score Miles a Day: For *Glumdalclitch,* on Purpose to spare me, complained she was tired with the trotting of the Horse. She often took me out of my Box at my own Desire, to give me Air, and shew me the Country; but always held me fast by Leading-strings. We passed over five or six Rivers many Degrees broader and deeper than the *Nile* or the *Ganges;* and there was hardly a Rivulet so small as the *Thames* at *London-Bridge.* We were ten Weeks in our Journey; and I was shewn in Eighteen large Towns, besides many Villages and private Families.

On the 26th Day of *October,* we arrived at the Metropolis, called in their Language *Lorbrulgrud,* or *Pride of the Universe.* My Master took a Lodging in the principal Street of the City, not far from the Royal Palace; and put out Bills in the usual Form, containing an exact Description of my Person and Parts. He hired a large Room between three and four Hundred Foot wide. He provided a Table sixty Foot in Diameter, upon which I was to act my Part; and pallisadoed it round three Foot from the Edge, and as many high, to prevent my falling over. I was shewn ten Times a Day to the Wonder and Satisfaction of all People. I could now speak the Language tolerably well; and perfectly understood every Word that was spoken to me. Besides, I had learned their Alphabet, and could make a shift to explain a Sentence here and there; for *Glumdalclitch* had been my Instructer while we were at home, and at leisure Hours during our Journey. She carried a little Book in her Pocket, not much larger than a *Sanson's Atlas;°* it was a common Treatise for the use of young Girls, giving a short Account of their Religion; out of this she taught me my Letters, and interpreted the Words.

CHAPTER III

The Author sent for to Court. The Queen buys him of his Master the Farmer, and presents him to the King. He disputes with his Majesty's great Scholars. An Apartment at Court provided for the Author. He is in high

---

Sanson's Atlas: If about the size of French mapmaker Nicolas Sanson's (1600–1667) popular atlases, the "little Book" would be huge by Gulliver's standards.

Favour with the Queen. He stands up for the Honour of his own Country. His Quarrels with the Queen's Dwarf.

The frequent Labours I underwent every Day, made in a few Weeks a very considerable Change in my Health: The more my Master got by me, the more unsatiable he grew. I had quite lost my Stomach, and was almost reduced to a Skeleton. The Farmer observed it; and concluding I soon must die, resolved to make as good a Hand of me as he could. While he was thus reasoning and resolving with himself; a *Slardral*, or Gentleman Usher, came from Court, commanding my Master to bring me immediately thither for the Diversion of the Queen and her Ladies. Some of the latter had already been to see me; and reported strange Things of my Beauty, Behaviour, and good Sense. Her Majesty and those who attended her, were beyond Measure delighted with my Demeanor. I fell on my Knees, and begged the Honour of kissing her Imperial Foot; but this Gracious Princess held out her little Finger towards me (after I was set on a Table) which I embraced in both my Arms, and put the Tip of it, with the utmost Respect, to my Lip. She made me some general Questions about my Country and my Travels, which I answered as distinctly and in as few Words as I could. She asked, whether I would be content to live at Court. I bowed down to the Board of the Table, and humbly answered, that I was my Master's Slave; but if I were at my own Disposal, I should be proud to devote my Life to her Majesty's Service. She then asked my Master whether he were willing to sell me at a good Price. He, who apprehended I could not live a Month, was ready enough to part with me; and demanded a Thousand Pieces of Gold; which were ordered him on the Spot, each Piece being about the Bigness of eight Hundred Moydores:° But, allowing for the Proportion of all Things between that Country and *Europe,* and the high Price of Gold among them; was hardly so great a Sum as a Thousand Guineas would be in *England.* I then said to the Queen; since I was now her Majesty's most humble Creature and Vassal, I must beg the Favour, that *Glumdalclitch,* who had always tended me with so much Care and Kindness, and understood to do it so well, might be admitted into her Service, and continue to be my Nurse and Instructor. Her Majesty agreed to my Petition; and easily got the Farmer's Consent, who was glad enough to have his Daughter preferred at Court: And the poor Girl herself was not able to hide her Joy. My late Master withdrew, bidding me farewell, and saying he had left me in a good Service; to which I replyed not a Word, only making him a slight Bow.

Moydores: Portuguese gold coins.

The Queen observed my Coldness; and when the Farmer was gone out of the Apartment, asked me the Reason. I made bold to tell her Majesty, that I owed no other Obligation to my late Master, than his not dashing out the Brains of a poor harmless Creature found by Chance in his Field; which Obligation was amply recompenced by the Gain he had made in shewing me through half the Kingdom, and the Price he had now sold me for. That the Life I had since led, was laborious enough to kill an Animal of ten Times my Strength. That my Health was much impaired by the continual Drudgery of entertaining the Rabble every Hour of the Day; and that if my Master had not thought my Life in Danger, her Majesty perhaps would not have got so cheap a Bargain. But as I was out of all fear of being ill treated under the Protection of so great and good an Empress, the Ornament of Nature, the Darling of the World, the Delight of her Subjects, the Phœnix of the Creation; so, I hoped my late Master's Apprehensions would appear to be groundless; for I already found my Spirits to revive by the Influence of her most August Presence.

This was the Sum of my Speech, delivered with great Improprieties and Hesitation; the latter Part was altogether framed in the Style peculiar to that People, whereof I learned some Phrases from *Glumdalclitch*, while she was carrying me to Court.

The Queen giving great Allowance for my Defectiveness in speaking, was however surprised at so much Wit and good Sense in so diminutive an Animal. She took me in her own Hand, and carried me to the King, who was then retired to his Cabinet. His Majesty, a Prince of much Gravity, and austere Countenance, not well observing my Shape at first View, asked the Queen after a cold Manner, how long it was since she grew fond of a *Splacknuck;* for such it seems he took me to be, as I lay upon my Breast in her Majesty's right Hand. But this Princess, who hath an infinite deal of Wit and Humour, set me gently on my Feet upon the Scrutore;° and commanded me to give His Majesty an Account of my self, which I did in a very few Words; and *Glumdalclitch,* who attended at the Cabinet Door, and could not endure I should be out of her Sight, being admitted; confirmed all that had passed from my Arrival at her Father's House.

The King, although he be as learned a Person as any in his Dominions and had been educated in the Study of Philosophy,° and particularly Mathematicks; yet when he observed my Shape exactly, and saw me walk erect, before I began to speak, conceived I might be a piece of

---

Scrutore: Writing table or desk.   **Philosophy:** Natural philosophy, or science.

Clock-work, (which is in that Country arrived to a very great Perfection) contrived by some ingenious Artist.° But, when he heard my Voice, and found what I delivered to be regular and rational, he could not conceal his Astonishment. He was by no means satisfied with the Relation I gave him of the Manner I came into his Kingdom; but thought it a Story concerted between *Glumdalclitch* and her Father, who had taught me a Sett of Words to make me sell at a higher Price. Upon this Imagination he put several other Questions to me, and still received rational Answers, no otherwise defective than by a Foreign Accent, and an imperfect Knowledge in the Language; with some rustick Phrases which I had learned at the Farmer's House, and did not suit the polite Style of a Court.

His Majesty sent for three great Scholars who were then in their weekly waiting (according to the Custom in that Country.) These Gentlemen, after they had a while examined my Shape with much Nicety, were of different Opinions concerning me. They all agreed that I could not be produced according to the regular Laws of Nature; because I was not framed with a Capacity of preserving my Life, either by Swiftness, or climbing of Trees, or digging Holes in the Earth. They observed by my Teeth, which they viewed with great Exactness, that I was a carnivorous Animal; yet most Quadrupeds being an Overmatch for me; and Field-Mice, with some others, too nimble, they could not imagine how I should be able to support my self, unless I fed upon Snails and other Insects; which they offered by many learned Arguments to evince that I could not possibly do. One of them seemed to think that I might be an Embrio, or abortive Birth. But this Opinion was rejected by the other two, who observed my Limbs to be perfect and finished; and that I had lived several Years, as it was manifested from my Beard; the Stumps whereof they plainly discovered through a Magnifying-Glass. They would not allow me to be a Dwarf, because my Littleness was beyond all Degrees of Comparison; for the Queen's favourite Dwarf, the smallest ever known in that Kingdom, was near thirty Foot high. After much Debate, they concluded unanimously that I was only *Relplum Scalcath,* which is interpreted literally *Lusus Naturæ;*° a Determination exactly agreeable to the Modern Philosophy of *Europe:* whose Professors, disdaining the old Evasion of *occult Causes,* whereby the Followers of *Aristotle* endeavour in vain to disguise their Ignorance; have invented this wonderful Solution of all Difficulties, to the unspeakable Advancement of human Knowledge.

---

ingenious Artist: Craftsman.   *Lusus Naturæ:* Latin for "freak of nature."

After this decisive Conclusion, I entreated to be heard a Word or two. I applied my self to the King, and assured His Majesty, that I came from a Country which abounded with several Millions of both Sexes, and of my own Stature; where the Animals, Trees, and Houses were all in Proportion; and where by Consequence I might be as able to defend my self, and to find Sustenance, as any of his Majesty's Subjects could do here; which I took for a full Answer to those Gentlemens Arguments. To this they only replied with a Smile of Contempt; saying, that the Farmer had instructed me very well in my Lesson. The King, who had a much better Understanding, dismissing his learned Men, sent for the Farmer, who by good Fortune was not yet gone out of Town: Having therefore first examined him privately, and then confronted him with me and the young Girl; his Majesty began to think that what we told him might possibly be true. He desired the Queen to order, that a particular Care should be taken of me; and was of Opinion, that *Glumdalclitch* should still continue in her Office of tending me, because he observed we had a great Affection for each other. A convenient Apartment was provided for her at Court; she had a sort of Governess appointed to take care of her Education, a Maid to dress her, and two other Servants for menial Offices; but, the Care of me was wholly appropriated to her self. The Queen commanded her own Cabinet-maker to contrive a Box that might serve me for a Bed-chamber, after the Model that *Glumdalclitch* and I should agree upon. This Man was a most ingenious Artist; and according to my Directions, in three Weeks finished for me a wooden Chamber of sixteen Foot square, and twelve High; with Sash Windows, a Door, and two Closets, like a *London* Bedchamber. The Board that made the Ceiling was to be lifted up and down by two Hinges, to put in a Bed ready furnished by her Majesty's Upholsterer; which *Glumdalclitch* took out every Day to air, made it with her own Hands, and letting it down at Night, locked up the Roof over me. A Nice Workman, who was famous for little Curiosities, undertook to make me two Chairs, with Backs and Frames, of a Substance not unlike Ivory; and two Tables, with a Cabinet to put my Things in. The Room was quilted on all Sides, as well as the Floor and the Ceiling, to prevent any Accident from the Carelessness of those who carried me; and to break the Force of a Jolt when I went in a Coach. I desired a Lock for my Door to prevent Rats and Mice from coming in: The Smith after several Attempts made the smallest that was ever seen among them; for I have known a larger at the Gate of a Gentleman's House in *England*. I made a shift to keep the Key in a Pocket of my own, fearing *Glumdalclitch* might lose it. The Queen likewise ordered the thinnest

Silks that could be gotten, to make me Cloaths; not much thicker than an *English* Blanket, very cumbersome till I was accustomed to them. They were after the Fashion of the Kingdom, partly resembling the *Persian,* and partly the *Chinese;* and are a very grave decent Habit.

The Queen became so fond of my Company, that she could not dine without me. I had a Table placed upon the same at which her Majesty eat, just at her left Elbow; and a Chair to sit on. *Glumdalclitch* stood upon a Stool on the Floor, near my Table, to assist and take Care of me. I had an entire set of Silver Dishes and Plates, and other Necessaries, which in Proportion to those of the Queen, were not much bigger than what I have seen in a *London* Toy-shop, for the Furniture of a Baby-house: These my little Nurse kept in her Pocket, in a Silver Box, and gave me at Meals as I wanted them; always cleaning them her self. No Person dined with the Queen but the two Princesses Royal; the elder sixteen Years old, and the younger at that time thirteen and a Month. Her Majesty used to put a Bit of Meat upon one of my Dishes, out of which I carved for my self; and her Diversion was to see me eat in Miniature. For the Queen (who had indeed but a weak Stomach) took up at one Mouthful, as much as a dozen *English* Farmers could eat at a Meal, which to me was for some time a very nauseous Sight. She would craunch° the Wing of a Lark, Bones and all, between her Teeth, although it were nine Times as large as that of a full grown Turkey; and put a Bit of Bread in her Mouth, as big as two twelve-penny Loaves. She drank out of a golden Cup, above a Hogshead at a Draught. Her Knives were twice as long as a Scythe set strait upon the Handle. The Spoons, Forks, and other Instruments were all in the same Proportion. I remember when *Glumdalclitch* carried me out of Curiosity to see some of the Tables at Court, where ten or a dozen of these enormous Knives and Forks were lifted up together; I thought I had never till then beheld so terrible a Sight.

It is the Custom, that every *Wednesday,* (which as I have before observed, was their Sabbath) the King and Queen, with the Royal Issue of both Sexes, dine together in the Apartment of his Majesty; to whom I was now become a Favourite; and at these Times my little Chair and Table were placed at his left Hand before one of the Salt-sellers. This Prince took a Pleasure in conversing with me; enquiring into the Manners, Religion, Laws, Government, and Learning of *Europe,* wherein I gave him the best Account I was able. His Apprehension was so clear, and his Judgment so exact, that he made very wise Reflexions and Ob-

craunch: Crunch.

servations upon all I said. But, I confess, that after I had been a little too copious in talking of my own beloved Country; of our Trade, and Wars by Sea and Land, of our Schisms in Religion, and Parties in the State; the Prejudices of his Education prevailed so far, that he could not forbear taking me up in his right Hand, and stroaking me gently with the other; after an hearty Fit of laughing, asked me whether I were a *Whig* or a *Tory*. Then turning to his first Minister, who waited behind him with a white Staff, near as tall as the Main-mast of the Royal *Sovereign;* ° he observed, how contemptible a Thing was human Grandeur, which could be mimicked by such diminutive Insects as I: And yet, said he, I dare engage,° those Creatures have their Titles and Distinctions of Honour; they contrive little Nests and Burrows, that they call Houses and Cities; they make a Figure in Dress and Equipage; they love, they fight, they dispute, they cheat, they betray. And thus he continued on, while my Colour came and went several Times, with Indignation to hear our noble Country, the Mistress of Arts and Arms, the Scourge of *France,* the Arbitress of *Europe,* the Seat of Virtue, Piety, Honour and Truth, the Pride and Envy of the World, so contemptuously treated.

But, as I was not in a Condition to resent Injuries, so, upon mature Thoughts, I began to doubt whether I were injured or no. For, after having been accustomed several Months to the Sight and Converse of this People, and observed every Object upon which I cast mine Eyes, to be of proportionable Magnitude; the Horror I had first conceived from their Bulk and Aspect was so far worn off, that if I had then beheld a Company of *English* Lords and Ladies in their Finery and Birth-day Cloaths,° acting their several Parts in the most courtly Manner of Strutting, and Bowing and Prating; to say the Truth, I should have been strongly tempted to laugh as much at them as this King and his Grandees did at me. Neither indeed could I forbear smiling at my self, when the Queen used to place me upon her Hand towards a Looking-Glass, by which both our Persons appeared before me in full View together; and there could nothing be more ridiculous than the Comparison: So that I really began to imagine my self dwindled many Degrees below my usual Size.

Nothing angered and mortified me so much as the Queen's Dwarf, who being of the lowest Stature that was ever in that Country, (for I verily think he was not full Thirty Foot high) became so insolent at

---

Royal *Sovereign*: One of the largest ships in the British navy.   **engage:** Bet.   **Birth-day Cloaths:** Festive clothes worn at court on the sovereign's birthday.

seeing a Creature so much beneath him, that he would always affect to swagger and look big as he passed by me in the Queen's Antichamber, while I was standing on some Table talking with the Lords or Ladies of the Court; and he seldom failed of a smart Word or two upon my Littleness; against which I could only revenge my self by calling him *Brother*, challenging him to wrestle; and such Repartees as are usual in the Mouths of *Court Pages*. One Day at Dinner, this malicious little Cubb was so nettled with something I had said to him, that raising himself upon the Frame of her Majesty's Chair, he took me up by the Middle, as I was sitting down, not thinking any Harm, and let me drop into a large Silver Bowl of Cream; and then ran away as fast as he could. I fell over Head and Ears, and if I had not been a good Swimmer, it might have gone very hard with me; for *Glumdalclitch* in that Instant happened to be at the other End of the Room; and the Queen was in such a Fright, that she wanted Presence of Mind to assist me. But my little Nurse ran to my Relief; and took me out, after I had swallowed above a Quart of Cream. I was put to Bed; however I received no other Damage than the Loss of a Suit of Cloaths, which was utterly spoiled. The Dwarf was soundly whipped, and as a further Punishment, forced to drink up the Bowl of Cream, into which he had thrown me; neither was he ever restored to Favour: For, soon after the Queen bestowed him to a Lady of high Quality; so that I saw him no more, to my very great Satisfaction; for I could not tell to what Extremity such a malicious Urchin might have carried his Resentment.

He had before served me a scurvy Trick, which set the Queen a laughing, although at the same time she were heartily vexed, and would have immediately cashiered him, if I had not been so generous as to intercede. Her Majesty had taken a Marrow-bone upon her Plate; and after knocking out the Marrow, placed the Bone again in the Dish erect as it stood before; the Dwarf watching his Opportunity, while *Glumdalclitch* was gone to the Sideboard, mounted the Stool that she stood on to take care of me at Meals; took me up in both Hands, and squeezing my Legs together, wedged them into the Marrow-bone above my Waist; where I stuck for some time, and made a very ridiculous Figure. I believe it was near a Minute before any one knew what was become of me; for I thought it below me to cry out. But, as Princes seldom get their Meat hot, my Legs were not scalded, only my Stockings and Breeches in a sad Condition. The Dwarf at my Entreaty had no other Punishment than a sound whipping.

I was frequently raillied by the Queen upon Account of my Fearfulness; and she used to ask me whether the People of my Country were as great Cowards as my self. The Occasion was this. The Kingdom is much pestered with Flies in Summer; and these odious Insects, each of them as big as a *Dunstable* Lark, hardly gave me any Rest while I sat at Dinner, with their continual Humming and Buzzing about mine Ears. They would sometimes alight upon my Victuals, and leave their loathsome Excrement or Spawn behind, which to me was very visible, although not to the Natives of that Country, whose large Opticks were not so acute as mine in viewing smaller Objects. Sometimes they would fix upon my Nose or Forehead, where they stung me to the Quick, smelling very offensively; and I could easily trace that viscous Matter, which our Naturalists tell us enables those Creatures to walk with their Feet upwards upon a Ceiling. I had much ado to defend my self against these detestable Animals, and could not forbear starting when they came on my Face. It was the common Practice of the Dwarf to catch a Number of these Insects in his Hand, as School-boys do among us, and let them out suddenly under my Nose, on Purpose to frighten me, and divert the Queen. My Remedy was to cut them in Pieces with my Knife as they flew in the Air; wherein my Dexterity was much admired.

I remember one Morning when *Glumdalclitch* had set me in my Box upon a Window, as she usually did in fair Days to give me Air, (for I durst not venture to let the Box be hung on a Nail out of the Window, as we do with Cages in *England*) after I had lifted up one of my Sashes, and sat down at my Table to eat a Piece of Sweet-Cake for my Breakfast; above twenty Wasps, allured by the Smell, came flying into the Room, humming louder than the Drones of as many Bagpipes. Some of them seized my Cake, and carried it piecemeal away; others flew about my Head and Face, confounding me with the Noise, and putting me in the utmost Terror of their Stings. However I had the Courage to rise and draw my Hanger, and attack them in the Air. I dispatched four of them, but the rest got away, and I presently shut my Window. These Insects were as large as Partridges; I took out their Stings, found them an Inch and a half long, and as sharp as Needles. I carefully preserved them all, and having since shewn them with some other Curiosities in several Parts of *Europe;* upon my Return to *England* I gave three of them to *Gresham College,*° and kept the fourth for my self.

Gresham College: Meeting place of The Royal Society of London, the chief scientific body in England.

CHAPTER IV

The Country described. A Proposal for correcting modern Maps. The King's Palace, and some Account of the Metropolis. The Author's Way of travelling. The chief Temple described.

I now intend to give the Reader a short Description of this Country, as far as I travelled in it, which was not above two thousand Miles round *Lorbrulgrud* the Metropolis. For, the Queen, whom I always attended, never went further when she accompanied the King in his Progresses; and there staid till his Majesty returned from viewing his Frontiers. The whole Extent of this Prince's Dominions reacheth about six thousand Miles in Length, and from three to five in Breadth. From whence I cannot but conclude, that our Geographers of *Europe* are in a great Error, by supposing nothing but Sea between *Japan* and *California;* For it was ever my Opinion, that there must be a Balance of Earth to counterpoise the great Continent of *Tartary;* and therefore they ought to correct their Maps and Charts, by joining this vast Tract of Land to the Northwest Parts of *America;* wherein I shall be ready to lend them my Assistance.

The Kingdom is a Peninsula, terminated to the North-east by a Ridge of Mountains thirty Miles high which are altogether impassable by Reason of the Volcanoes upon the Tops. Neither do the most Learned know what sort of Mortals inhabit beyond those Mountains, or whether they be inhabited at all. On the three other Sides it is bounded by the Ocean. There is not one Sea-port in the whole Kingdom; and those Parts of the Coasts into which the Rivers issue, are so full of pointed Rocks, and the Sea generally so rough, that there is no venturing with the smallest of their Boats; so that these People are wholly excluded from any Commerce with the rest of the World. But the large Rivers are full of Vessels, and abound with excellent Fish; for they seldom get any from the Sea, because the Sea-fish are of the same Size with those in *Europe,* and consequently not worth catching; whereby it is manifest, that Nature in the Production of Plants and Animals of so extraordinary a Bulk, is wholly confined to this Continent; of which I leave the Reasons to be determined by Philosophers.° However, now and then they take a Whale that happens to be dashed against the Rocks, which the common People feed on heartily. These Whales I have known so large that a Man could hardly carry one upon his Shoulders; and sometimes for Curiosity they are brought in Hampers to

Philosophers: Scientists.

Lorbrulgrud: I saw one of them in a Dish at the King's Table, which passed for a Rarity; but I did not observe he was fond of it; for I think indeed the Bigness disgusted him, although I have seen one somewhat larger in *Greenland.*

The Country is well inhabited, for it contains fifty one Cities, near an hundred walled Towns, and a great Number of Villages. To satisfy my curious Reader, it may be sufficient to describe *Lorbrulgrud.* This City stands upon almost two equal Parts on each Side the River that passes through. It contains above eighty thousand Houses. It is in Length three *Glonglungs* (which make about fifty four English Miles) and two and a half in Breadth, as I measured it myself in the Royal Map made by the King's Order, which was laid on the Ground on purpose for me, and extended an hundred Feet; I paced the Diameter and Circumference several times Bare-foot, and computing by the Scale, measured it pretty exactly.

The King's Palace is no regular Edifice, but an Heap of Buildings about seven Miles round: The chief Rooms are generally two hundred and forty Foot high, and broad and long in Proportion. A Coach was allowed to *Glumdalclitch* and me, wherein her Governess frequently took her out to see the Town, or go among the Shops; and I was always of the Party, carried in my Box; although the Girl at my own Desire would often take me out, and hold me in her Hand, that I might more conveniently view the Houses and the People as we passed along the Streets. I reckoned our Coach to be about a Square of *Westminster-Hall,* but not altogether so High; however, I cannot be very exact. One Day the Governess ordered our Coachman to stop at several shops; where the Beggars watching their Opportunity, crouded to the Sides of the Coach, and gave me the most horrible Spectacles that ever an *European* Eye beheld. There was a Woman with a Cancer in her Breast, swelled to a monstrous Size, full of Holes, in two or three of which I could have easily crept, and covered my whole Body. There was a Fellow with a Wen in his Neck, larger than five Woolpacks;° and another with a couple of wooden Legs, each about twenty Foot high. But, the most hateful Sight of all was the Lice crawling on their Cloaths: I could see distinctly the Limbs of these Vermin with my naked Eye, much better than those of an *European* Louse through a Microscope; and their Snouts with which they rooted like Swine. They were the first I had ever beheld; and I should have been curious enough to dissect one of them,

---

Woolpacks: Large bags for carrying fleece or wool.

if I had proper Instruments (which I unluckily left behind me in the Ship) although indeed the Sight was so nauseous, that it perfectly turned my Stomach.

Beside the large Box in which I was usually carried, the Queen ordered a smaller one to be made for me, of about twelve Foot Square, and ten high, for the Convenience of Travelling; because the other was somewhat too large for *Glumdalclitch's* Lap, and cumbersome in the Coach; it was made by the same Artist, whom I directed in the whole Contrivance. This travelling Closet was an exact Square with a Window in the Middle of three of the Squares, and each Window was latticed with Iron Wire on the outside, to prevent Accidents in long Journeys. On the fourth Side, which had no Window, two strong Staples were fixed, through which the Person that carried me, when I had a Mind to be on Horseback, put in a Leathern Belt, and buckled it about his Waist. This was always the Office of some grave trusty Servant in whom I could confide, whether I attended the King and Queen in their Progresses, or were disposed to see the Gardens, or pay a Visit to some great Lady or Minister of State in the Court, when *Glumdalclitch* happened to be out of Order:° For I soon began to be known and esteemed among the greatest Officers,° I suppose more upon Account of their Majesty's Favour, than any Merit of my own. In Journeys, when I was weary of the Coach, a Servant on Horseback would buckle my Box, and place it on a Cushion before him; and there I had a full Prospect of the Country on three Sides from my three Windows. I had in this Closet a Field-Bed and a Hammock hung from the Ceiling, two Chairs and a Table, neatly screwed to the Floor, to prevent being tossed about by the Agitation of the Horse or the Coach. And having been long used to Sea-Voyages, those Motions, although sometimes very violent, did not much discompose me.

Whenever I had a Mind to see the Town, it was always in my Travelling-Closet; which *Glumdalclitch* held in her Lap in a kind of open Sedan, after the Fashion of the Country, borne by four Men, and attended by two others in the Queen's Livery. The People who had often heard of me, were very curious to croud about the Sedan; and the Girl was complaisant enough to make the Bearers stop, and to take me in her Hand that I might be more conveniently seen.

I was very desirous to see the chief Temple, and particularly the Tower belonging to it, which is reckoned the highest in the Kingdom. Accordingly one Day my Nurse carried me thither, but I may truly say I

---

out of Order: Ill.   **greatest Officers:** Those in high office.

came back disappointed; for, the Height is not above three thousand Foot, reckoning from the Ground to the highest Pinnacle top; which allowing for the Difference between the Size of those People, and us in *Europe*, is no great matter for Admiration, nor at all equal in Proportion, (if I rightly remember) to *Salisbury* Steeple.° But, not to detract from a Nation to which during my Life I shall acknowledge myself extremely obliged; it must be allowed, that whatever this famous Tower wants in Height, is amply made up in Beauty and Strength. For the Walls are near an hundred Foot thick, built of hewn Stone, whereof each is about forty Foot square, and adorned on all Sides with Statues of Gods and Emperors cut in Marble larger than the Life, placed in their several Niches. I measured a little Finger which had fallen down from one of these Statues, and lay unperceived among some Rubbish; and found it exactly four Foot and an Inch in Length. *Glumdalclitch* wrapped it up in a Handkerchief, and carried it home in her Pocket to keep among other Trinkets, of which the Girl was very fond, as Children at her Age usually are.

The King's Kitchen is indeed a noble Building, vaulted at Top, and about six hundred Foot high. The great Oven is not so wide by ten Paces as the Cupola at St. *Paul*'s: ° For I measured the latter on purpose after my Return. But if I should describe the Kitchen-grate, the prodigious Pots and Kettles, the Joints of Meat turning on the Spits, with many other Particulars; perhaps I should be hardly believed; at least a severe Critick would be apt to think I enlarged a little, as Travellers are often suspected to do. To avoid which Censure, I fear I have run too much into the other Extream; and that if this Treatise should happen to be translated into the Language of *Brobdingnag*, (which is the general Name of that Kingdom) and transmitted thither; the King and his People would have Reason to complain; that I had done them an Injury by a false and diminutive Representation.

His Majesty seldom keeps above six hundred Horses in his Stables: They are generally from fifty four to sixty Foot high. But, when he goes abroad on solemn Days, he is attended for State by a Militia Guard of five hundred Horse, which indeed I thought was the most splendid Sight that could be ever beheld, till I saw part of his Army in Battalia:° whereof I shall find another Occasion to speak.

Salisbury Steeple: 404 feet high on the human scale, roughly 9/10 of a mile on the Brobdingnagian.   Cupola at *St. Paul*'s: 145 feet in diameter, 365 feet high.   Battalia: In battle order.

CHAPTER V

Several Adventures that happened to the Author. The Execution of a Criminal. The Author shews his Skill in Navigation.

I should have lived happy enough in that Country, if my Littleness had not exposed me to several ridiculous and troublesome Accidents; some of which I shall venture to relate. *Glumdalclitch* often carried me into the Gardens of the Court in my smaller Box, and would sometimes take me out of it and hold me in her Hand, or set me down to walk. I remember, before the Dwarf left the Queen, he followed us one Day into those Gardens; and my Nurse having set me down, he and I being close together, near some Dwarf Apple-trees, I must need shew my Wit by a silly Allusion between him and the Trees, which happens to hold in their Language as it doth in ours. Whereupon, the malicious Rogue watching his Opportunity, when I was walking under one of them, shook it directly over my Head, by which a dozen Apples, each of them near as large as a *Bristol* Barrel, came tumbling about my Ears; one of them hit me on the Back as I chanced to stoop, and knocked me down flat on my Face, but I received no other Hurt; and the Dwarf was pardoned at my Desire, because I had given the Provocation.

Another Day, *Glumdalclitch* left me on a smooth Grass-plot to divert my self while she walked at some Distance with her Governess. In the mean time, there suddenly fell such a violent Shower of Hail, that I was immediately by the Force of it struck to the Ground: And when I was down, the Hail-stones gave me such cruel Bangs all over the Body, as if I had been pelted with Tennis-Balls; however I made a Shift to creep on all four, and shelter my self by lying flat on my Face on the Lee-side of a Border of Lemmon Thyme; but so bruised from Head to Foot, that I could not go abroad in ten Days. Neither is this at all to be wondered at; because Nature in that Country observing the same Proportion through all her Operations, a Hail-stone is near Eighteen Hundred Times as large as one in *Europe;* which I can assert upon Experience, having been so curious to weigh and measure them.

But, a more dangerous Accident happened to me in the same Garden, when my little Nurse, believing she had put me in a secure Place, which I often entreated her to do, that I might enjoy my own Thoughts; and having left my Box at home to avoid the Trouble of carrying it, went to another Part of the Garden with her Governess and some Ladies of her Acquaintance. While she was absent and out of hearing, a small white Spaniel belonging to one of the chief Gardiners, having got by Accident into the Garden, happened to range near the Place where I lay. The Dog following the Scent, came directly up, and taking me in his Mouth, ran strait to his Master, wagging his Tail, and set me gently on the Ground. By good Fortune he had been so well taught, that I was carried between his Teeth without the least Hurt, or even tearing my Cloaths. But, the poor Gardiner, who knew me well, and had a great Kindness for me, was in a terrible Fright. He gently took me up in both his Hands, and asked me how I did; but I was so amazed° and out of Breath, that I could not speak a Word. In a few Minutes I came to my self, and he carried me safe to my little Nurse, who by this time had returned to the Place where she left me, and was in cruel Agonies when I did not appear, nor answer when she called; she severely reprimanded the Gardiner on Account of his Dog. But, the Thing was hushed up, and never known at Court; for the Girl was afraid of the Queen's Anger; and truly as to my self, I thought it would not be for my Reputation that such a Story should go about.

This Accident absolutely determined *Glumdalclitch* never to trust me abroad for the future out of her Sight. I had been long afraid of this Resolution; and therefore concealed from her some little unlucky Adventures that happened in those Times when I was left by my self. Once a Kite° hovering over the Garden, made a Stoop° at me, and if I had not resolutely drawn my Hanger, and run under a thick Espalier,° he would have certainly carried me away in his Talons. Another time, walking to the Top of a fresh Mole-hill, I fell to my Neck in the Hole through which that Animal had cast up the Earth; and coined some Lye not worth remembring, to excuse my self for spoiling my Cloaths. I likewise broke my right Shin against the Shell of a Snail, which I happened to stumble over, as I was walking alone, and thinking on poor *England*.

I cannot tell whether I were more pleased or mortified to observe in those solitary Walks, that the smaller Birds did not appear to be at all afraid of me; but would hop about within a Yard Distance, looking for Worms, and other Food, with as much Indifference and Security as if no Creature at all were near them. I remember, a Thrush had the Confidence to snatch out of my Hand with his Bill, a Piece of Cake that *Glumdalclitch* had just given me for my Breakfast. When I attempted to catch any of these Birds, they would boldly turn against me, endeavouring to pick° my Fingers, which I durst not venture within their Reach; and then they would hop back unconcerned to hunt for Worms or Snails, as they did before. But, one Day I took a thick Cudgel, and

amazed: Dazed.   **Kite:** A bird of prey.   **Stoop:** Swoop.   **Espalier:** Trellis.   **pick:** Peck.

threw it with all my Strength so luckily at a Linnet, that I knocked him down, and seizing him by the Neck with both my Hands, ran with him in Triumph to my Nurse. However, the Bird who had only been stunned, recovering himself, gave me so many Boxes with his Wings on both Sides of my Head and Body, although I held him at Arms Length, and was out of the Reach of his Claws, that I was twenty Times thinking to let him go. But I was soon relieved by one of our Servants, who wrong off the Bird's Neck; and I had him next Day for Dinner by the Queen's Command. This Linnet, as near as I can remember, seemed to be somewhat larger than an *English* Swan.

The Maids of Honour often invited *Glumdalclitch* to their Apartments, and desired she would bring me along with her, on Purpose to have the Pleasure of seeing and touching me. They would often strip me naked from Top to Toe, and lay me at full Length in their Bosoms; wherewith I was much disgusted; because, to say the Truth, a very offensive Smell came from their Skins; which I do not mention or intend to the Disadvantage of those excellent Ladies, for whom I have all Manner of Respect: But, I conceive, that my Sense was more acute in Proportion to my Littleness; and that those illustrious Persons were no more disagreeable to their Lovers, or to each other, than People of the same Quality are with us in *England*. And, after all, I found their natural Smell was much more supportable than when they used Perfumes, under which I immediately swooned away. I cannot forget, that an intimate Friend of mine in *Lilliput* took the Freedom in a warm Day, when I had used a good deal of Exercise, to complain of a strong Smell about me; although I am as little faulty that way as most of my Sex: But I suppose, his Faculty of Smelling was as nice with regard to me, as mine was to that of this People. Upon this Point, I cannot forbear doing Justice to the Queen my Mistress, and *Glumdalclitch* my Nurse; whose Persons were as sweet as those of any Lady in *England*.

That which gave me most Uneasiness among these Maids of Honour, when my Nurse carried me to visit them, was to see them use me without any Manner of Ceremony, like a Creature who had no Sort of Consequence. For, they would strip themselves to the Skin, and put on their Smocks in my Presence, while I was placed on their Toylet° directly before their naked Bodies; which, I am sure, to me was very far from being a tempting Sight, or from giving me any other Motions° than those of Horror and Disgust. Their Skins appeared so coarse and uneven, so variously coloured when I saw them near, with a Mole here

---

Toylet: Dressing table.   **Motions:** Emotions.

and there as broad as a Trencher, and Hairs hanging from it thicker than Pack-threads; to say nothing further concerning the rest of their Persons. Neither did they at all scruple while I was by, to discharge what they had drunk, to the Quantity of at least two Hogsheads, in a Vessel that held above three Tuns. The handsomest among these Maids of Honour, a pleasant frolicksome Girl of sixteen, would sometimes set me astride upon one of her Nipples; with many other Tricks, wherein the Reader will excuse me for not being over particular. But, I was so much displeased, that I entreated *Glumdalclitch* to contrive some excuse for not seeing that young Lady any more.

One Day, a young Gentleman who was Nephew to my Nurse's Governess, came and pressed them both to see an Execution. It was of a Man who had murdered one of that Gentleman's intimate Acquaintance. *Glumdalclitch* was prevailed on to be of the Company, very much against her Inclination, for she was naturally tender hearted: And, as for my self, although I abhorred such Kind of Spectacles; yet my Curiosity tempted me to see something that I thought must be extraordinary. The Malefactor was fixed in a Chair upon a Scaffold erected for the Purpose; and his Head cut off at one Blow with a Sword of about forty Foot long. The Veins and Arteries spouted up such a prodigious Quantity of Blood, and so high in the Air, that the great *Jet d'Eau*° at *Versailles* was not equal for the Time it lasted; and the Head when it fell on the Scaffold Floor, gave such a Bounce, as made me start, although I were at least an *English* Mile distant.

The Queen, who often used to hear me talk of my Sea-Voyages, and took all Occasions to divert me when I was melancholy, asked me whether I understood how to handle a Sail or an Oar; and whether a little Exercise of Rowing might not be convenient for my Health. I answered, that I understood both very well. For although my proper Employment had been to be Surgeon or Doctor to the Ship; yet often upon a Pinch, I was forced to work like a common Mariner. But, I could not see how this could be done in their Country, where the smallest Wherry was equal to a first Rate Man of War among us; and such a Boat as I could manage, would never live in any of their Rivers: Her Majesty said, if I would contrive a Boat, her own Joyner should make it, and she would provide a Place for me to sail in. The Fellow was an ingenious Workman, and by my Instructions in ten Days finished a Pleasure-Boat with all its Tackling, able conveniently to hold eight *Europeans.* When it

---

Jet d'Eau: Water fountains at the palace of Louis XIV, some capable of shooting a jet of 75 feet.

was finished, the Queen was so delighted, that she ran with it in her Lap to the King, who ordered it to be put in a Cistern full of Water, with me in it, by way of Tryal; where I could not manage my two Sculls or little Oars for want of Room. But, the Queen had before contrived another Project. She ordered the Joyner to make a wooden Trough of three Hundred Foot long, fifty broad, and eight deep; which being well pitched to prevent leaking, was placed on the Floor along the Wall, in an outer Room of the Palace. It had a Cock near the Bottom, to let out the Water when it began to grow stale; and two Servants could easily fill it in half an Hour. Here I often used to row for my Diversion, as well as that of the Queen and her Ladies, who thought themselves agreeably entertained with my Skill and Agility. Sometimes I would put up my Sail, and then my Business was only to steer, while the Ladies gave me a Gale with their Fans; and when they were weary, some of the Pages would blow my Sail forward with their Breath, while I shewed my Art by steering Starboard or Larboard as I pleased. When I had done, *Glumdalclitch* always carried back my Boat into her Closet, and hung it on a Nail to dry.

In this Exercise, I once met an Accident which had like to have cost me my Life. For, one of the Pages having put my Boat into the Trough; the Governess who attended *Glumdalclitch,* very officiously lifted me up to place me in the Boat; but I happened to slip through her Fingers, and should have infallibly fallen down forty Foot upon the Floor, if by the luckiest Chance in the World, I had not been stop'd by a Corking-pin° that stuck in the good Gentlewoman's Stomacher;° the Head of the Pin passed between my Shirt and the Waistband of my Breeches; and thus I was held by the Middle in the Air, till *Glumdalclitch* ran to my Relief.

Another time, one of the Servants, whose Office it was to fill my Trough every third Day with fresh Water; was so careless to let a huge Frog (not perceiving it) slip out of his Pail. The Frog lay concealed till I was put into my Boat, but then seeing a resting Place, climbed up, and made it lean so much on one Side, that I was forced to balance it with all my Weight on the other, to prevent overturning. When the Frog was got in, it hopped at once half the Length of the Boat, and then over my Head, backwards and forwards, dawbing my Face and Cloaths with its odious Slime. The Largeness of its Features made it appear the most deformed Animal that can be conceived. However, I desired

---

Corking-pin: Large pin. **Stomacher:** Decorative cloth worn over the bosom and stomach.

Glumdalclitch to let me deal with it alone. I banged it a good while with one of my Sculls, and at last forced it to leap out of the Boat.

But, the greatest Danger I ever underwent in that Kingdom, was from a Monkey, who belonged to one of the Clerks of the Kitchen. *Glumdalclitch* had locked me up in her Closet,° while she went somewhere upon Business, or a Visit. The Weather being very warm, the Closet Window was left open, as well as the Windows and the Door of my bigger Box, in which I usually lived, because of its Largeness and Conveniency. As I sat quietly meditating at my Table, I heard something bounce in at the Closet Window, and skip about from one Side to the other; whereat, although I were much alarmed, yet I ventured to look out, but not stirring from my Seat; and then I saw this frolicksome Animal, frisking and leaping up and down, till at last he came to my Box, which he seemed to view with great Pleasure and Curiosity, peeping in at the Door and every Window. I retreated to the farther Corner of my Room, or Box; but the Monkey looking in at every Side, put me into such a Fright, that I wanted Presence of Mind to conceal my self under the Bed, as I might easily have done. After some time spent in peeping, grinning, and chattering, he at last espyed me; and reaching one of his Paws in at the Door, as a Cat does when she plays with a Mouse, although I often shifted Place to avoid him; he at length seized the Lappet of my Coat (which being made of that Country Silk, was very thick and strong) and dragged me out. He took me up in his right Fore-foot, and held me as a Nurse doth a Child she is going to suckle; just as I have seen the same Sort of Creature do with a Kitten in *Europe*: And when I offered to struggle, he squeezed me so hard, that I thought it more prudent to submit. I have good Reason to believe that he took me for a young one of his own Species, by his often stroaking my Face very gently with his other Paw. In these Diversions he was interrupted by a Noise at the Closet Door, as if some Body were opening it; whereupon he suddenly leaped up to the Window at which he had come in, and thence upon the Leads and Gutters, walking upon three Legs, and holding me in the fourth, till he clambered up to a Roof that was next to ours. I heard *Glumdalclitch* give a Shriek at the Moment he was carrying me out. The poor Girl was almost distracted: That Quarter of the Palace was all in an Uproar; the Servants ran for Ladders; the Monkey was seen by Hundreds in the Court, sitting upon the Ridge of a Building, holding me like a Baby in one of his Fore-Paws, and feeding me with the other, by cramming into my Mouth some Victuals he had

Closet: Small room.

squeezed out of the Bag on one Side of his Chaps, and patting me when I would not eat; whereat many of the Rabble below could not forbear laughing; neither do I think they justly ought to be blamed; for without Question, the Sight was ridiculous enough to every Body but my self. Some of the People threw up Stones, hoping to drive the Monkey down; but this was strictly forbidden, or else very probably my Brains had been dashed out.

The Ladders were now applied, and mounted by several Men; which the Monkey observing, and finding himself almost encompassed; not being able to make Speed enough with his three Legs, let me drop on a Ridge-Tyle, and made his Escape. Here I sat for some time five Hundred Yards from the Ground, expecting every Moment to be blown down by the Wind, or to fall by my own Giddiness, and come tumbling over and over from the Ridge to the Eves. But an honest Lad, one of my Nurse's Footmen, climbed up, and putting me into his Breeches Pocket, brought me down safe.

I was almost choaked with the filthy Stuff the Monkey had crammed down my Throat; but, my dear little Nurse picked it out of my Mouth with a small Needle; and then I fell a vomiting, which gave me great Relief. Yet I was so weak and bruised in the Sides with the Squeezes given me by this odious Animal, that I was forced to keep my Bed a Fortnight. The King, Queen, and all the Court, sent every Day to enquire after my Health; and her Majesty made me several Visits during my Sickness. The Monkey was killed, and an Order made that no such Animal should be kept about the Palace.

When I attended the King after my Recovery, to return him Thanks for his Favours, he was pleased to railly me a good deal upon this Adventure. He asked me what my Thoughts and Speculations were while I lay in the Monkey's Paw; how I liked the Victuals he gave me, his Manner of Feeding; and whether the fresh Air on the Roof had sharpened my Stomach. He desired to know what I would have done upon such an Occasion in my own Country. I told his Majesty, that in *Europe* we had no Monkies, except such as were brought for Curiosities from other Places, and so small, that I could deal with a Dozen of them together, if they presumed to attack me. And as for that monstrous Animal with whom I was so lately engaged, (it was indeed as large as an Elephant) if my Fears had suffered me to think so far as to make Use of my Hanger (looking fiercely, and clapping my Hand upon the Hilt as I spoke) when he poked his Paw into my Chamber, perhaps I should have given him such a Wound, as would have made him glad to withdraw it with more Haste than he put it in. This I delivered in a firm Tone, like a Person who was jealous lest his Courage should be called in Question. However, my Speech produced nothing else besides a loud Laughter; which all the Respect due to his Majesty from those about him, could not make them contain. This made me reflect, how vain an Attempt it is for a Man to endeavour doing himself Honour among those who are out of all Degree of Equality or Comparison with him. And yet I have seen the Moral of my own Behaviour very frequent in *England* since my Return; where a little contemptible Varlet, without the least Title to Birth, Person, Wit, or common Sense, shall presume to look with Importance, and put himself upon a Foot with the greatest Persons of the Kingdom.

I was every Day furnishing the Court with some ridiculous Story; and *Glumdalclitch*, although she loved me to Excess, yet was arch enough to inform the Queen, whenever I committed any Folly that she thought would be diverting to her Majesty. The Girl who had been out of Order, was carried by her Governess to take the Air about an Hour's Distance, or thirty Miles from Town. They alighted out of the Coach near a small Footpath in a Field; and *Glumdalclitch* setting down my travelling Box, I went out of it to walk. There was a Cow-dung in the Path, and I must needs try my Activity by attempting to leap over it. I took a Run, but unfortunately jumped short, and found my self just in the Middle up to my Knees. I waded through with some Difficulty, and one of the Footmen wiped me as clean as he could with his Handkerchief; for I was filthily bemired, and my Nurse confined me to my Box until we returned home; where the Queen was soon informed of what had passed, and the Footmen spread it about the Court; so that all the Mirth, for some Days, was at my Expence.

CHAPTER VI

Several Contrivances of the Author to please the King and Queen. He shews his Skill in Musick. The King enquires into the State of Europe, *which the Author relates to him. The King's Observations thereon.*

I used to attend the King's Levee° once or twice a Week, and had often seen him under the Barber's Hand, which indeed was at first very terrible to behold. For, the Razor was almost twice as long as an ordinary Scythe. His Majesty, according to the Custom of the Country, was only shaved twice a Week. I once prevailed on the Barber to give me

King's Levee: King's morning reception.

some of the Suds or Lather, out of which I picked Forty or Fifty of the strongest Stumps of Hair. I then took a Piece of fine Wood, and cut it like the Back of a Comb, making several Holes in it at equal Distance, with as small a Needle as I could get from *Glumdalclitch*. I fixed in the Stumps so artificially,° scraping and sloping them with my Knife towards the Points, that I made a very tolerable Comb; which was a seasonable Supply, my own being so much broken in the Teeth, that it was almost useless: Neither did I know any Artist in that Country so nice and exact, as would undertake to make me another.

And this puts me in mind of an Amusement wherein I spent many of my leisure Hours. I desired the Queen's Woman to save for me the Combings of her Majesty's Hair, whereof in time I got a good Quantity; and consulting with my Friend the Cabinetmaker, who had received general Orders to do little Jobbs for me; I directed him to make two Chair-frames, no larger than those I had in my Box, and then to bore little Holes with a fine Awl round those Parts where I designed the Backs and Seats; through these Holes I wove the strongest hairs I could pick out, just after the Manner of Cane-chairs in *England*. When they were finished, I made a Present of them to her Majesty, who kept them in her Cabinet, and used to shew them for Curiosities; as indeed they were the Wonder of every one who beheld them. The Queen would have had me sit upon one of these Chairs, but I absolutely refused to obey her; protesting I would rather dye a Thousand Deaths than place a dishonourable Part of my Body on those precious Hairs that once adorned her Majesty's Head. Of these Hairs (as I had always a Mechanical Genius) I likewise made a neat little Purse about five Foot long, with her Majesty's Name decyphered in Gold Letters; which I gave to *Glumdalclitch*, by the Queen's Consent. To say the Truth, it was more for Shew than Use, being not of Strength to bear the Weight of the larger Coins; and therefore she kept nothing in it, but some little Toys that Girls are fond of.

The King, who delighted in Musick, had frequent Consorts° at Court, to which I was sometimes carried, and set in my Box on a Table to hear them: But, the Noise was so great, that I could hardly distinguish the Tunes. I am confident, that all the Drums and Trumpets of a Royal Army, beating and sounding together just at your Ears, could not equal it. My Practice was to have my Box removed from the Places where the Performers sat, as far as I could; then to shut the Doors and

artificially: Artfully.   **Consorts:** Concerts.

Windows of it, and draw the Window-Curtains; after which I found their Musick not disagreeable.

I had learned in my Youth to play a little upon the Spinet; *Glumdalclitch* kept one in her Chamber, and a Master attended twice a Week to teach her: I call it a Spinet, because it somewhat resembled that Instrument, and was play'd upon in the same Manner. A Fancy came into my Head, that I would entertain the King and Queen with an *English* Tune upon this Instrument. But this appeared extremely difficult: For, the Spinet was near sixty Foot long, each Key being almost a Foot wide; so that, with my Arms extended, I could not reach to above five Keys; and to press them down required a good smart stroak with my Fist, which would be too great a Labour, and to no purpose. The Method I contrived was this. I prepared two round Sticks about the Bigness of common Cudgels; they were thicker at one End than the other; and I covered the thicker End with a Piece of a Mouse's Skin, that by rapping on them, I might neither Damage the Tops of the Keys, nor interrupt the Sound. Before the Spinet, a Bench was placed about four Foot below the Keys, and I was put upon the Bench. I ran sideling upon it that way and this, as fast as I could, banging the proper Keys with my two Sticks; and made a shift to play a Jigg to the great Satisfaction of both their Majesties: But, it was the most violent Exercise I ever underwent, and yet I could not strike above sixteen Keys, nor, consequently, play the Bass and Treble together, as other Artists do; which was a great Disadvantage to my Performance.

The King, who as I before observed, was a Prince of excellent Understanding, would frequently order that I should be brought in my Box, and set upon the Table in his Closet. He would then command me to bring one of my Chairs out of the Box, and sit down within three Yards Distance upon the Top of the Cabinet; which brought me almost to a Level with his Face. In this Manner I had several Conversations with him. I one Day took the Freedom to tell his Majesty, that the Contempt he discovered towards *Europe*, and the rest of the World, did not seem answerable to those excellent Qualities of Mind, that he was Master of. That, Reason did not extend itself with the Bulk of the Body: On the contrary, we observed in our Country, that the tallest Persons were usually least provided with it. That among other Animals, Bees and Ants had the Reputation of more Industry, Art, and Sagacity than many of the larger Kinds. And that, as inconsiderable as he took me to be, I hoped I might live to do his Majesty some signal Service. The King heard me with Attention; and began to conceive a much better Opinion of me than he had ever before. He desired I would give him as exact an Account of the Government of *England* as I possibly could; because, as fond as Princes commonly are of their own Customs (for so he conjectured of other Monarchs by my former Discourses) he should be glad to hear of any thing that might deserve Imitation.

Imagine with thy self, courteous Reader, how often I then wished for the Tongue of *Demosthenes* or *Cicero*, that might have enabled me to celebrate the Praise of my own dear native Country in a Style equal to its Merits and Felicity.

I began my Discourse by informing his Majesty, that our Dominions consisted of two Islands, which composed three mighty Kingdoms under one Sovereign, besides our Plantations in *America*. I dwelt long upon the Fertility of our Soil, and the Temperature° of our Climate. I then spoke at large upon the Constitution of an *English* Parliament, partly made up of an illustrious Body called the House of Peers, Persons of the noblest Blood, and of the most ancient and ample Patrimonies. I described that extraordinary Care always taken of their Education in Arts and Arms, to qualify them for being Counsellors born to the King and Kingdom; to have a Share in the Legislature, to be Members of the highest Court of Judicature from whence there could be no Appeal; and to be Champions always ready for the Defence of their Prince and Country by their Valour, Conduct and Fidelity. That these were the Ornament and Bulwark of the Kingdom; worthy Followers of their most renowned Ancestors, whose Honour had been the Reward of their Virtue; from which their Posterity were never once known to degenerate. To these were joined several holy Persons, as part of that Assembly, under the Title of Bishops; whose peculiar Business it is, to take care of Religion, and of those who instruct the People therein. These were searched and sought out through the whole Nation, by the Prince and wisest Counsellors, among such of the Priesthood, as were most deservedly distinguished by the Sanctity of their Lives, and the Depth of their Erudition; who were indeed the spiritual Fathers of the Clergy and the People.

That, the other Part of the Parliament consisted of an Assembly called the House of Commons; who were all principal Gentlemen, *freely* picked and culled out by the People themselves, for their great Abilities, and Love of their Country, to represent the Wisdom of the whole Na-

---

Temperature: Temperateness.

tion. And, these two Bodies make up the most august Assembly in *Europe;* to whom, in Conjunction with the Prince, the whole Legislature is committed.

I then descended to the Courts of Justice, over which the Judges, those venerable Sages and Interpreters of the Law, presided, for determining the disputed Rights and Properties of Men, as well as for the Punishment of Vice, and Protection of Innocence. I mentioned the prudent Management of our Treasury; the Valour and Atchievements of our Forces by Sea and Land. I computed the Number of our People, by reckoning how many Millions there might be of each Religious Sect, or Political Party among us. I did not omit even our Sports and Pastimes, or any other Particular which I thought might redound to the Honour of my Country. And, I finished all with a brief historical Account of Affairs and Events in *England* for about an hundred Years past.

This Conversation was not ended under five Audiences, each of several Hours; and the King heard the whole with great Attention; frequently taking Notes of what I spoke, as well as Memorandums of what Questions he intended to ask me.

When I had put an End to these long Discourses, his Majesty in a sixth Audience consulting his Notes, proposed many Doubts, Queries, and Objections, upon every Article. He asked, what Methods were used to cultivate the Minds and Bodies of our young Nobility; and in what kind of Business they commonly spent the first and teachable Part of their Lives. What Course was taken to supply that Assembly, when any noble Family became extinct. What Qualifications were necessary in those who are to be created new Lords: Whether the Humour of the Prince, a Sum of Money to a Court-Lady, or a Prime Minister; or a Design of strengthening a Party opposite to the publick Interest, ever happened to be Motives in those Advancements. What Share of Knowledge these Lords had in the Laws of their Country, and how they came by it, so as to enable them to decide the Properties of their Fellow-Subjects in the last Resort. Whether they were always so free from Avarice, Partialities, or Want, that a Bribe, or some other sinister View, could have no Place among them. Whether those holy Lords I spoke of, were constantly promoted to that Rank upon Account of their Knowledge in religious Matters, and the Sanctity of their Lives, had never been Compliers with the Times, while they were common Priests; or slavish prostitute Chaplains to some Nobleman, whose Opinions they continued servilely to follow after they were admitted into that Assembly.

He then desired to know, what Arts were practised in electing those whom I called Commoners.° Whether, a Stranger with a strong Purse might not influence the vulgar Voters to chuse him before their own Landlord, or the most considerable Gentleman in the Neighbourhood. How it came to pass, that People were so violently bent upon getting into this Assembly, which I allowed to be a great Trouble and Expence, often to the Ruin of their Families, without any Salary or Pension: Because this appeared such an exalted Strain of Virtue and publick Spirit, that his Majesty seemed to doubt it might possibly not be always sincere: And he desired to know, whether such zealous Gentlemen could have any Views of refunding themselves for the Charges and Trouble they were at, by sacrificing the publick Good to the Designs of a weak and vicious Prince, in Conjunction with a corrupted Ministry. He multiplied his Questions, and sifted° me thoroughly upon every Part of this Head; proposing numberless Enquiries and Objections, which I think it not prudent or convenient to repeat.

Upon what I said in relation to our Courts of Justice, his Majesty desired to be satisfied in several Points: And, this I was the better able to do, having been formerly almost ruined by a long Suit in Chancery, which was decreed for me with Costs. He asked, what Time was usually spent in determining between Right and Wrong; and what Degree of Expence. Whether Advocates and Orators had Liberty to plead in Causes manifestly known to be unjust, vexatious, or oppressive. Whether Party in Religion or Politicks were observed to be of any Weight in the Scale of Justice. Whether those pleading Orators were Persons educated in the general Knowledge of Equity; or only in provincial, national, and other local Customs. Whether they or their Judges had any Part in penning those Laws, which they assumed the Liberty of interpreting and glossing upon at their Pleasure. Whether they had ever at different Times pleaded for and against the same Cause, and cited Precedents to prove contrary Opinions. Whether they were a rich or a poor Corporation. Whether they received any pecuniary Reward for pleading or delivering their Opinions. And particularly whether they were ever admitted as Members in the lower Senate.

He fell next upon the Management of our Treasury; and said, he thought my Memory had failed me, because I computed our Taxes at about five or six Millions a Year; and when I came to mention the Issues,° he found they sometimes amounted to more than double; for, the Notes he had taken were very particular in this Point; because he

---

Commoners: Members of the House of Commons.   **sifted:** Cross-examined.   **Issues:** Expenditures.

hoped, as he told me, that the Knowledge of our Conduct might be useful to him; and he could not be deceived in his Calculations. But, if what I told him were true, he was still at a Loss how a Kingdom could run out of its Estate like a private Person. He asked me, who were our Creditors? and, where we found Money to pay them? He wondered to hear me talk of such chargeable and extensive Wars; that, certainly we must be a quarrelsome People, or live among very bad Neighbours; and that our Generals must needs be richer than our Kings. He asked, what Business we had out of our own Islands, unless upon the Score of Trade or Treaty, or to defend the Coasts with our Fleet. Above all, he was amazed to hear me talk of a mercenary standing Army in the Midst of Peace, and among a free People. He said, if we were governed by our own Consent in the Persons of our Representatives, he could not imagine of whom we were afraid, or against whom we were to fight; and would hear my Opinion, whether a private Man's House might not better be defended by himself, his Children, and Family; than by half a Dozen Rascals picked up at a Venture in the Streets, for small Wages, who might get an Hundred Times more by cutting their Throats.

He laughed at my odd Kind of Arithmetick (as he was pleased to call it) in reckoning the Numbers of our People by a Computation drawn from the several Sects among us in Religion and Politicks. He said, he knew no Reason, why those who entertain Opinions prejudicial to the Publick, should be obliged to change, or should not be obliged to conceal them. And, as it was Tyranny in any Government to require the first, so it was Weakness not to enforce the second: For, a Man may be allowed to keep Poisons in his Closet, but not to vend them about as Cordials.

He observed, that among the Diversions of our Nobility and Gentry, I had mentioned Gaming. He desired to know at what Age this Entertainment was usually taken up, and when it was laid down. How much of their Time it employed; whether it ever went so high as to affect their Fortunes. Whether mean vicious People, by their Dexterity in that Art, might not arrive at great Riches, and sometimes keep our very Nobles in Dependance, as well as habituate them to vile Companions; wholly take them from the Improvement of their Minds, and force them by the Losses they received, to learn and practice that infamous Dexterity upon others.

He was perfectly astonished with the historical Account I gave him of our Affairs during the last Century; protesting it was only an Heap of Conspiracies, Rebellions, Murders, Massacres, Revolutions, Banishments; the very worst Effects that Avarice, Faction, Hypocrisy,

Perfidiousness, Cruelty, Rage, Madness, Hatred, Envy, Lust, Malice, and Ambition could produce.

His Majesty in another Audience, was at the Pains to recapitulate the Sum of all I had spoken; compared the Questions he made, with the Answers I had given; then taking me into his Hands, and stroaking me gently, delivered himself in these Words, which I shall never forget, nor the Manner he spoke them in. My little Friend *Grildrig;* you have made a most admirable Panegyrick upon your Country. You have clearly proved that Ignorance, Idleness, and Vice are the proper Ingredients for qualifying a Legislator. That Laws are best explained, interpreted, and applied by those whose Interest and Abilities lie in perverting, confounding, and eluding them. I observe among you some Lines of an Institution, which in its Original might have been tolerable; but these half erased, and the rest wholly blurred and blotted by Corruptions. It doth not appear from all you have said, how any one Perfection is required towards the Procurement of any one Station among you; much less that Men are ennobled on Account of their Virtue, that Priests are advanced for their Piety or Learning, Soldiers for their Conduct or Valour, Judges for their Integrity, Senators for the Love of their Country, or Counsellors for their Wisdom. As for yourself (continued the King) who have spent the greatest Part of your Life in travelling; I am well disposed to hope you may hitherto have escaped many Vices of your Country. But, by what I have gathered from your own Relation, and the Answers I have with much Pains wringed and extorted from you; I cannot but conclude the Bulk of your Natives, to be the most pernicious Race of little odious Vermin that Nature ever suffered to crawl upon the Surface of the Earth.

CHAPTER VII

The Author's Love of his Country. He makes a Proposal of much Advantage to the King; which is rejected. The King's great Ignorance in Politicks. The Learning of that Country very imperfect and confined. Their Laws, and military Affairs, and Parties in the State.

Nothing but an extreme Love of Truth could have hindered me from concealing this Part of my Story. It was in vain to discover my Resentments, which were always turned into Ridicule: And I was forced to rest with Patience, while my noble and most beloved Country was so injuriously treated. I am heartily sorry as any of my Readers can possibly be, that such an Occasion was given: But this Prince happened to be so curious and inquisitive upon every Particular, that it could not consist either with Gratitude or good Manners to refuse giving him what Satisfaction I was able. Yet thus much I may be allowed to say in my own Vindication; that I artfully eluded many of his Questions; and gave to every Point a more favourable turn by many Degrees than the strictness of Truth would allow. For, I have always born that laudable Partiality to my own Country, which *Dionysius Halicarnassensis* ° with so much Justice recommends to an Historian. I would hide the Frailties and Deformities of my Political Mother, and place her Virtues and Beauties in the most advantageous Light. This was my sincere Endeavour in those many Discourses I had with that Monarch, although it unfortunately failed of Success.

But, great Allowances should be given to a King who lives wholly secluded from the rest of the World, and must therefore be altogether unacquainted with the Manners and Customs that most prevail in other Nations: The want of which Knowledge will ever produce many *Prejudices*, and a certain *Narrowness of Thinking;* from which we and the politer Countries of *Europe* are wholly exempted. And it would be hard indeed, if so remote a Prince's Notions of Virtue and Vice were to be offered as a Standard for all Mankind.

To confirm what I have now said, and further to shew the miserable Effects of a *confined Education;* I shall here insert a Passage which will hardly obtain Belief. In hopes to ingratiate my self farther into his Majesty's Favour, I told him of an Invention discovered between three and four hundred Years ago, to make a certain Powder; into an heap of which the smallest Spark of Fire falling, would kindle the whole in a Moment, although it were as big as a Mountain; and make it all fly up in the Air together, with a Noise and Agitation greater than Thunder. That, a proper Quantity of this Powder rammed into an hollow Tube of Brass or Iron, according to its Bigness, would drive a Ball of Iron or Lead with such Violence and Speed, as nothing was able to sustain its Force. That, the largest Balls thus discharged, would not only Destroy whole Ranks of an Army at once; but batter the strongest Walls to the Ground; sink down Ships with a thousand Men in each, to the Bottom of the Sea; and when linked together by a Chain, would cut through Masts and Rigging; divide Hundreds of Bodies in the Middle, and lay

---

Dionysius Halicarnassensis: A Greek writer who poured praise on Rome's accomplishments.

all Waste before them. That we often put this Powder into large hollow Balls of Iron, and discharged them by an Engine into some City we were besieging; which would rip up the Pavement, tear the Houses to Pieces, burst and throw Splinters on every Side, dashing out the Brains of all who came near. That I knew the Ingredients very well, which were Cheap, and common; I understood the Manner of compounding them, and could direct his Workmen how to make those Tubes of a Size proportionable to all other Things in his Majesty's Kingdom; and the largest need not be above two hundred Foot long; twenty or thirty of which Tubes, charged with the proper Quantity of Powder and Balls, would batter down the Walls of the strongest Town in his Dominions in a few Hours; or destroy the whole Metropolis, if ever it should pretend to dispute his absolute Commands. This I humbly offered to his Majesty, as a small Tribute of Acknowledgment in return of so many Marks that I had received of his Royal Favour and Protection.

The King was struck with Horror at the Description I had given of those terrible Engines, and the Proposal I had made. He was amazed how so impotent and groveling an Insect as I (these were his Expressions) could entertain such inhuman Ideas, and in so familiar a Manner as to appear wholly unmoved at all the Scenes of Blood and Desolation, which I had painted as the common Effects of those destructive Machines; whereof he said, some evil Genius, Enemy to Mankind, must have been the first Contriver. As for himself, he protested, that although few Things delighted him so much as new Discoveries in Art or in Nature; yet he would rather lose Half his Kingdom than be privy to such a Secret; which he commanded me, as I valued my Life, never to mention any more.

A strange Effect of *narrow Principles* and *short Views!* that a Prince possessed of every Quality which procures Veneration, Love and Esteem; of strong Parts, great Wisdom and profound Learning; endued with admirable Talents for Government, and almost adored by his Subjects; should from a *nice unnecessary Scruple,* whereof in *Europe* we can have no Conception, let slip an Opportunity put into his Hands, that would have made him absolute Master of the Lives, the Liberties, and the Fortunes of his People. Neither do I say this with the least Intention to detract from the many Virtues of that excellent King; whose Character I am sensible will on this Account be very much lessened in the Opinion of an *English* Reader: But, I take this Defect among them to have risen from their Ignorance; by not having hitherto reduced *Politicks* into a *Science,* as the more acute Wits of *Europe* have done. For, I remember very well, in a Discourse one Day with the King; when I happened to say, there were several thousand Books among us written upon the *Art of Government;* it gave him (directly contrary to my Intention) a very mean Opinion of our Understandings. He professed both to abominate and despise all *Mystery, Refinement,* and *Intrigue,* either in a Prince or a Minister. He could not tell what I meant by *Secrets of State,* where an Enemy or some Rival Nation were not in the Case. He confined the Knowledge of governing within very *narrow Bounds;* to common Sense and Reason, to Justice and Lenity, to the Speedy Determination of Civil and criminal Causes; with some other obvious Topicks which are not worth considering. And, he gave it for his Opinion; that whoever could make two Ears of Corn, or two Blades of Grass to grow upon a Spot of Ground where only one grew before; would deserve better of Mankind, and do more essential Service to his Country, than the whole Race of Politicians put together.

The Learning of this People is very defective; consisting only in Morality, History, Poetry and Mathematicks; wherein they must be allowed to excel. But, the last of these is wholly applied to what may be useful in Life; to the Improvement of Agriculture and all mechanical Arts; so that among us it would be little esteemed. And as to Ideas, Entities, Abstractions and Transcendentals, I could never drive the least Conception into their Heads.

No Law of that Country must exceed in Words the Number of Letters in their Alphabet; which consists only of two and twenty. But indeed, few of them extend even to that Length. They are expressed in the most plain and simple Terms, wherein those People are not Mercurial enough to discover above one Interpretation. And, to write a Comment upon any Law, is a capital Crime. As to the Decision of civil Causes, or Proceedings against Criminals, their Precedents are so few, that they have little Reason to boast of any extraordinary Skill in either.

They have had the Art of Printing, as well as the *Chinese,* Time out of Mind. But their Libraries are not very large; for that of the King's, which is reckoned the largest, doth not amount to above a thousand Volumes; placed in a Gallery of twelve hundred Foot long; from whence I had Liberty to borrow what Books I pleased. The Queen's Joyner had contrived in one of *Glumdalclitch's* Rooms a Kind of wooden Machine five and twenty Foot high, formed like a standing Ladder; the Steps were each fifty Foot long: It was indeed a moveable Pair of Stairs, the lowest End placed at ten Foot Distance from the Wall of the Chamber. The Book I had a Mind to read was put up leaning against the Wall. I first mounted to the upper Step of the Ladder, and turning my Face towards the Book, began at the Top of the Page, and so walking to the Right and Left about eight or ten Paces according to the Length of the

Lines, till I had gotten a little below the Level of mine Eyes; and then descending gradually till I came to the Bottom: After which I mounted again, and began the other Page in the same Manner, and so turned over the Leaf, which I could easily do with both my Hands, for it was as thick and stiff as a Paste-board, and in the largest Folio's not above eighteen or twenty Foot long.

Their Stile is clear, masculine, and smooth, but not Florid; for they avoid nothing more than multiplying unnecessary Words, or using various Expressions. I have perused many of their Books, especially those in History and Morality. Among the latter I was much diverted with a little old Treatise, which always lay in *Glumdalclitch*'s Bedchamber, and belonged to her Governess, a grave elderly Gentlewoman, who dealt in Writings of Morality and Devotion. The Book treats of the Weakness of Human kind; and is in little Esteem except among Women and the Vulgar. However, I was curious to see what an Author of that Country could say upon such a Subject. This Writer went through all the usual Topicks of *European* Moralists; shewing how diminutive, contemptible, and helpless an Animal was Man in his own Nature; how unable to defend himself from the Inclemencies of the Air, or the Fury of wild Beasts: How much he was excelled by one Creature in Strength, by another in Speed, by a third in Foresight, by a fourth in Industry. He added, that Nature was degenerated in these latter declining Ages of the World, and could now produce only small abortive Births in Comparison of those in ancient Times. He said, it was very reasonable to think, not only that the Species of Men were originally much larger, but also that there must have been Giants in former Ages; which, as it is asserted by History and Tradition, so it hath been confirmed by huge Bones and Sculls casually dug up in several Parts of the Kingdom, far exceeding the common dwindled Race of Man in our Days. He argued, that the very Laws of Nature absolutely required we should have been made in the Beginning, of a Size more large and robust, not so liable to Destruction from every little Accident of a Tile falling from an House, or a Stone cast from the Hand of a Boy, or of being drowned in a little Brook. From this Way of Reasoning the Author drew several moral Applications useful in the Conduct of Life, but needless here to repeat. For my own Part, I could not avoid reflecting, how universally this Talent was spread of drawing Lectures in Morality, or indeed rather Matter of Discontent and repining, from the Quarrels we raise with Nature. And, I believe upon a strict Enquiry, those Quarrels might be shewn as ill-grounded among us, as they are among that People.

As to their military Affairs; they boast that the King's Army consists of an hundred and seventy six thousand Foot, and thirty two thousand Horse: If that may be called an Army which is made up of Tradesmen in the several Cities, and Farmers in the Country, whose Commanders are only the Nobility and Gentry, without Pay or Reward. They are indeed perfect enough in their Exercises; and under very good Discipline, wherein I saw no great merit: For, how should it be otherwise, where every Farmer is under the Command of his own Landlord, and every Citizen under that of the principal Men in his own City, chosen after the Manner of *Venice* by *Ballot?*

I have often seen the Militia of *Lorbrulgrud* drawn out to Exercise in a great Field near the City, of twenty Miles Square. They were in all not above twenty five thousand Foot, and six thousand Horse; but it was impossible for me to compute their Number, considering the Space of Ground they took up. A *Cavalier* mounted on a large Steed might be about Ninety Foot high. I have seen this whole Body of Horse upon the Word of Command draw their Swords at once, and brandish them in the Air. Imagination can Figure nothing so Grand, so surprising and so astonishing. It looked as if ten thousand Flashes of Lightning were darting at the same time from every Quarter of the Sky.

I was curious to know how this Prince, to whose Dominions there is no Access from any other Country, came to think of Armies, or to teach his People the Practice of military Discipline. But I was soon informed, both by Conversation, and Reading their Histories. For, in the Course of many Ages they have been troubled with the same Disease, to which the whole Race of Mankind is Subject; the Nobility often contending for Power, the People for Liberty, and the King for absolute Dominion. All which, however happily tempered by the Laws of that Kingdom, have been sometimes violated by each of the three Parties; and have more than once occasioned Civil Wars, the last whereof was happily put an End to by this Prince's Grandfather in a general Composition; and the Militia then settled with common Consent hath been ever since kept in the strictest Duty.

CHAPTER VIII

The King and Queen make a Progress to the Frontiers. The Author attends them. The Manner in which he leaves the Country very particularly related. He returns to England.

I had always a strong Impulse that I should some time recover my Liberty, although it were impossible to conjecture by what Means, or to form any Project with the least Hope of succeeding. The Ship in which I sailed was the first ever known to be driven within Sight of that Coast; and the King had given strict Orders, that if at any Time another appeared, it should be taken ashore, and with all its Crew and Passengers brought in a Tumbril to *Lorbrulgrud*. He was strongly bent to get me a Woman of my own Size, by whom I might propagate the Breed: But I think I should rather have died than undergone the Disgrace of leaving a Posterity to be kept in Cages like tame Canary Birds; and perhaps in time sold about the Kingdom to Persons of Quality for Curiosities. I was indeed treated with much Kindness; I was the Favourite of a great King and Queen, and the Delight of the whole Court; but it was upon such a Foot as ill became the Dignity of human Kind. I could never forget those domestick Pledges I had left behind me. I wanted to be among People with whom I could converse upon even° Terms; and walk about the Streets and Fields without Fear of being trod to Death like a Frog or young Puppy. But, my Deliverance came sooner than I expected, and in a Manner not very common: The whole Story and Circumstances of which I shall faithfully relate.

I had now been two Years in this Country; and, about the Beginning of the third, *Glumdalclitch* and I attended the King and Queen in Progress to the South Coast of the Kingdom. I was carried as usual in my Travelling-Box, which, as I have already described, was a very convenient Closet of twelve Foot wide. I had ordered a Hammock to be fixed by silken Ropes from the four Corners at the Top; to break the Jolts, when a Servant carried me before him on Horseback, as I sometimes desired; and would often sleep in my Hammock while we were upon the Road. On the Roof of my Closet, set not directly over the Middle of the Hammock, I ordered the Joyner to cut out a Hole of a Foot square to give me Air in hot Weather as I slept; which Hole I shut at pleasure with a Board that drew backwards and forwards through a Groove.

When we came to our Journey's End, the King thought proper to pass a few Days at a Palace he hath near *Flanflasnic*, a City within eighteen *English* Miles of the Sea-side. *Glumdalclitch* and I were much fatigued: I had gotten a small Cold; but the poor Girl was so ill as to be confined to her Chamber. I longed to see the Ocean, which must be the

even: Equal.

only scene of my Escape, if ever it should happen. I pretended to be worse than I really was; and desired leave to take the fresh Air of the Sea, with a Page whom I was very fond of, and who had sometimes been trusted with me. I shall never forget with what Unwillingness *Glumdalclitch* consented; nor the strict Charge she gave the Page to be careful of me; bursting at the same time into a Flood of Tears, as if she had some Foreboding of what was to happen. The Boy took me out in my Box about Half an Hour's Walk from the Palace, towards the Rocks on the Sea-shore. I ordered him to set me down; and lifting up one of my Sashes, cast many a wistful melancholy Look towards the Sea. I found myself not very well; and told the Page that I had a Mind to take a Nap in my Hammock, which I hoped would do me good. I got in, and the Boy shut the Window close down, to keep out the Cold. I soon fell asleep: And all I can conjecture is, that while I slept, the Page thinking no Danger could happen, went among the Rocks to look for Birds Eggs; having before observed him from my Window searching about, and picking up one or two in the Clefts. Be that as it will; I found my self suddenly awaked with a violent Pull upon the Ring which was fastned at the Top of my Box, for the Conveniency of Carriage. I felt the Box raised very high in the Air, and then born forward with prodigious Speed. The first Jolt had like to have shaken me out of my Hammock; but afterwards the Motion was easy enough. I called out several times as loud as I could raise my Voice, but all to no purpose. I looked towards my Windows, and could see nothing but the Clouds and Sky. I heard a Noise just over my Head like the clapping of Wings; and then began to perceive the woful Condition I was in; that some Eagle had got the Ring of my Box in his Beak, with an Intent to let it fall on a Rock, like a Tortoise in a Shell, and then pick out my Body and devour it. For the Sagacity and Smell of this Bird enable him to discover his Quarry at a great Distance, although better concealed than I could be within a two Inch Board.

In a little time I observed the Noise and flutter of Wings to encrease very fast; and my Box was tossed up and down like a Sign-post in a windy Day. I heard several Bangs or Buffets, as I thought, given to the Eagle (for such I am certain it must have been that held the Ring of my Box in his Beak) and then all on a sudden felt my self falling perpendicularly down for above a Minute; but with such incredible Swiftness that I almost lost my Breath. My Fall was stopped by a terrible Squash,° that

Squash: Splash.

sounded louder to mine Ears than the Cataract of *Niagara;* after which I was quite in the Dark for another Minute, and then my Box began to rise so high that I could see Light from the Tops of my Windows. I now perceived that I was fallen into the Sea. My Box, by the Weight of my Body, the Goods that were in, and the broad Plates of Iron fixed for Strength at the four Corners of the Top and Bottom, floated about five Foot deep in Water. I did then, and do now suppose, that the Eagle which flew away with my Box was pursued by two or three others, and forced to let me drop while he was defending himself against the Rest, who hoped to share in the Prey. The Plates of Iron fastned at the Bottom of the Box, (for those were the strongest) preserved the Balance while it fell; and hindred it from being broken on the Surface of the Water. Every Joint of it was well grooved, and the Door did not move on Hinges, but up and down like a Sash; which kept my Closet so tight that very little Water came in. I got with much Difficulty out of my Hammock, having first ventured to draw back the Slip board on the Roof already mentioned, contrived on purpose to let in Air; for want of which I found my self almost stifled.

How often did I then wish my self with my dear *Glumdalclitch,* from whom one single Hour had so far divided me! And I may say with Truth, that in the midst of my own Misfortune, I could not forbear lamenting my poor Nurse, the Grief she would suffer for my Loss, the Displeasure of the Queen, and the Ruin of her Fortune. Perhaps many Travellers have not been under greater Difficulties and Distress than I was at this Juncture; expecting every Moment to see my Box dashed in Pieces, or at least overset by the first violent Blast, or a rising Wave. A Breach in one single Pane of Glass would have been immediate Death: Nor could any thing have preserved the Windows but the strong Lattice Wires placed on the outside against Accidents in Travelling. I saw the Water ooze in at several Crannies, although the Leaks were not considerable; and I endeavoured to stop them as well as I could. I was not able to lift up the Roof of my Closet, which otherwise I certainly should have done, and sat on the Top of it, where I might at least preserve myself from being shut up, as I may call it, in the Hold. Or, if I escaped these Dangers for a Day or two, what could I expect but a miserable Death of Cold and Hunger! I was four Hours under these Circumstances, expecting and indeed wishing every Moment to be my last.

I have already told the Reader, that there were two strong Staples fixed upon the Side of my Box which had no Window, and into which the Servant, who used to carry me on Horseback, would put a Leathern

Belt, and buckle it about his Waist. Being in this disconsolate State, I heard, or at least thought I heard some kind of grating Noise on that Side of my Box where the Staples were fixed; and soon after I began to fancy that the Box was pulled, or towed along in the Sea; for I now and then felt a sort of tugging, which made the Waves rise near the Tops of my Windows, leaving me almost in the Dark. This gave me some faint Hopes of Relief, although I were not able to imagine how it could be brought about. I ventured to unscrew one of my Chairs, which were always fastned to the Floor; and having made a hard shift to screw it down again directly under the Slipping-board that I had lately opened; I mounted on the Chair, and putting my Mouth as near as I could to the Hole, I called for Help in a loud Voice, and in all the Languages I understood. I then fastned my Handkerchief to a Stick I usually carried, and thrusting it up the Hole, waved it several times in the Air; that if any Boat or Ship were near, the Seamen might conjecture some unhappy Mortal to be shut up in the Box.

I found no Effect from all I could do, but plainly perceived my Closet to be moved along; and in the Space of an Hour, or better, that Side of the Box where the Staples were, and had no Window, struck against something that was hard. I apprehended it to be a Rock, and found my self tossed more than ever. I plainly heard a Noise upon the Cover of my Closet, like that of a Cable, and the grating of it as it passed through the Ring. I then found my self hoisted up by Degrees at least three Foot higher than I was before. Whereupon, I again thrust up my Stick and Handkerchief, calling for Help till I was almost hoarse. In return to which, I heard a great Shout repeated three times, giving me such Transports of Joy as are not to be conceived but by those who feel them. I now heard a trampling over my Head; and somebody calling through the Hole with a loud Voice in the *English* Tongue: *If there be any Body below, let them speak.* I answered, I was an *Englishman,* drawn by ill Fortune into the greatest Calamity that ever any Creature underwent; and begged, by all that was moving, to be delivered out of the Dungeon I was in. The Voice replied, I was safe, for my Box was fastned to their Ship; and the Carpenter should immediately come, and saw an Hole in the Cover, large enough to pull me out. I answered, that was needless, and would take up too much Time; for there was no more to be done, but let one of the Crew put his Finger into the Ring, and take the Box out of the Sea into the Ship, and so into the Captain's Cabbin. Some of them upon hearing me talk so wildly, thought I was mad; others laughed; for indeed it never came into my Head, that I was now got among People of my own Stature and Strength. The Carpenter came, and in a few Minutes sawed a Passage about four Foot square; then let down a small Ladder, upon which I mounted, and from thence was taken into the Ship in a very weak Condition.

The Sailors were all in Amazement, and asked me a thousand Questions, which I had no Inclination to answer. I was equally confounded at the Sight of so many Pigmies; for such I took them to be, after having so long accustomed mine Eyes to the monstrous Objects I had left. But the Captain, Mr. *Thomas Wilcocks,* an honest worthy *Shropshire* Man, observing I was ready to faint, took me into his Cabbin, gave me a Cordial to comfort me, and made me *turn in* upon his own Bed; advising me to take a little Rest, of which I had great need. Before I went to sleep I gave him to understand, that I had some valuable Furniture in my Box too good to be lost; a fine Hammock, an handsome Field-Bed, two Chairs, a Table and a Cabinet: That my Closet was hung on all Sides, or rather quilted with Silk and Cotton: That if he would let one of the Crew bring my Closet into his Cabbin, I would open it before him, and shew him my Goods. The Captain hearing me utter these Absurdities, concluded I was raving: However, (I suppose to pacify me) he promised to give Order as I desired; and going upon Deck, sent some of his Men down into my Closet, from whence (as I afterwards found) they drew up all my Goods, and stripped off the Quilting; but the Chairs, Cabinet and Bed-sted being screwed to the Floor, were much damaged by the Ignorance of the Seamen, who tore them up by Force. Then they knocked off some of the Boards for the Use of the Ship; and when they had got all they had a Mind for, let the Hulk drop into the Sea, which by Reason of many Breaches made in the Bottom and Sides, sunk *to rights.* And indeed I was glad not to have been a Spectator of the Havock they made; because I am confident it would have sensibly touched me, by bringing former Passages into my Mind, which I had rather forget.

I slept some Hours, but perpetually disturbed with Dreams of the Place I had left, and the Dangers I had escaped. However, upon waking I found my self much recovered. It was now about eight a Clock at Night, and the Captain ordered Supper immediately, thinking I had already fasted too long. He entertained me with great Kindness, observing me not to look wildly, or talk inconsistently; and when we were left alone, desired I would give him a Relation of my Travels, and by what Accident I came to be set adrift in that monstrous wooden Chest. He said, that about twelve a Clock at Noon, as he was looking through his

Glass, he spied it at a Distance, and thought it was a Sail, which he had a Mind to make; being not much out of his Course, in hopes of buying some Biscuit, his own beginning to fall short. That, upon coming nearer, and finding his Error, he sent out his Long-boat to discover what I was; that his Men came back in a Fright, swearing they had seen a swimming House. That he laughed at their Folly, and went himself in the Boat, ordering his Men to take a strong Cable along with them. That the Weather being calm, he rowed round me several times, observed my Windows, and the Wire Lattices that defended them. That he discovered two Staples upon one Side, which was all of Boards, without any Passage for Light. He then commanded his Men to row up to that Side; and fastning a Cable to one of the Staples, ordered his Men to tow my Chest (as he called it) towards the Ship. When it was there, he gave Directions to fasten another Cable to the Ring fixed in the Cover, and to raise up my Chest with Pullies, which all the Sailors were not able to do above two or three Foot. He said, they saw my Stick and Handkerchief thrust out of the Hole, and concluded, that some unhappy Man must be shut up in the Cavity. I asked whether he or the Crew had seen any prodigious Birds in the Air about the Time he first discovered me: To which he answered, that discoursing this Matter with the Sailors while I was asleep, one of them said he had *observed* three Eagles flying towards the North; but remarked nothing of their being larger than the usual Size; which I suppose must be imputed to the great Height they were at: And he could not guess the Reason of my Question. I then asked the Captain how far he reckoned we might be from Land; he said, by the best Computation he could make, we were at least an hundred Leagues. I assured him, that he must be mistaken by almost half; for I had not left the Country from whence I came, above two Hours before I dropt into the Sea. Whereupon he began again to think that my Brain was disturbed, of which he gave me a Hint, and advised me to go to Bed in a Cabin he had provided. I assured him I was well refreshed with his good Entertainment and Company, and as much in my Senses as ever I was in my Life. He then grew serious, and desired to ask me freely whether I were not troubled in Mind by the Consciousness of some enormous Crime, for which I was punished at the Command of some Prince, by exposing me in that Chest; as great Criminals in other Countries have been forced to Sea in a leaky Vessel without Provisions: For, although he should be sorry to have taken so ill a Man into his Ship, yet he would engage his Word to set me safe on Shore in the first Port where we arrived. He added, that his Suspicions were much increased by some very absurd Speeches I had delivered at first to the Sailors, and afterwards to himself, in relation to my Closet or Chest, as well as by my odd Looks and Behaviour while I was at Supper.

I begged his Patience to hear me tell my Story; which I faithfully did from the last Time I left *England*, to the Moment he first discovered me. And, as Truth always forceth its Way into rational Minds; so, this honest worthy Gentleman, who had some Tincture of Learning, and very good Sense, was immediately convinced of my Candor and Veracity. But, further to confirm all I had said, I entreated him to give Order that my Cabinet should be brought, of which I kept the Key in my Pocket, (for he had already informed me how the Seamen disposed of my Closet) I opened it in his Presence, and shewed him the small Collection of Rarities I made in the Country from whence I had been so strangely delivered. There was the Comb I had contrived out of the Stumps of the King's Beard; and another of the same Materials, but fixed into a paring of her Majesty's Thumb-nail, which served for the Back. There was a Collection of Needles and Pins from a Foot to half a Yard long. Four Wasp-Stings, like Joyners Tacks: Some Combings of the Queen's Hair: A Gold Ring which one Day she made me a Present of in a most obliging Manner, taking it from her little Finger, and throwing it over my Head like a Collar. I desired the Captain would please to accept this Ring in Return of his Civilities; which he absolutely refused. I shewed him a Corn that I had cut off with my own Hand from a Maid of Honour's Toe; it was about the Bigness of a *Kentish* Pippin, and grown so hard, that when I returned to *England,* I got it hollowed into a Cup and set in Silver. Lastly, I desired him to see the Breeches I had then on, which were made of a Mouse's Skin.

I could force nothing on him but a Footman's Tooth, which I observed him to examine with great Curiosity, and found he had a Fancy for it. He received it with abundance of Thanks, more than such a Trifle could deserve. It was drawn by an unskilful Surgeon in a Mistake from one of *Glumdalclitch*'s Men, who was afflicted with the Tooth-ache; but it was as sound as any in his Head. I got it cleaned, and put it into my Cabinet. It was about a Foot long, and four Inches in Diameter.

The Captain was very well satisfied with this plain Relation I had given him; and said, he hoped when we returned to *England,* I would oblige the World by putting it in Paper, and making it publick. My Answer was, that I thought we were already overstocked with Books of Travels: That nothing could now pass which was not extraordinary;

wherein I doubted, some Authors less consulted Truth than their own
Vanity or Interest, or the Diversion of ignorant Readers. That my Story
could contain little besides common Events, without those ornamental
Descriptions of strange Plants, Trees, Birds, and other Animals; or the
barbarous Customs and Idolatry of savage People, with which most
Writers abound. However, I thanked him for his good Opinion, and
promised to take the Matter into my Thoughts.

He said, he wondered at one Thing very much; which was, to hear
me speak so loud; asking me whether the King or Queen of that Country were thick of Hearing. I told him it was what I had been used to for
above two Years past; and that I admired as much at the Voices of him
and his Men, who seemed to me only to whisper, and yet I could hear
them well enough. But, when I spoke in that Country, it was like a Man
talking in the Street to another looking out from the Top of a Steeple,
unless when I was placed on a Table, or held in any Person's Hand. I
told him, I had likewise observed another Thing; that when I first got
into the Ship, and the Sailors stood all about me, I thought they were
the most little contemptible Creatures I had ever beheld. For, indeed,
while I was in that Prince's Country, I could never endure to look in a
Glass after mine Eyes had been accustomed to such prodigious Objects;
because the Comparison gave me so despicable a Conceit of my self.
The Captain said, that while we were at Supper, he observed me to look
at every thing with a Sort of Wonder; and that I often seemed hardly
able to contain my Laughter; which he knew not well how to take, but
imputed it to some Disorder in my Brain. I answered, it was very true;
and I wondered how I could forbear, when I saw his Dishes of the Size
of a Silver Three-pence, a Leg of Pork hardly a Mouthful, a Cup not so
big as a Nutshell: And so I went on, describing the rest of his
Houshold-stuff and Provisions after the same Manner. For although the
Queen had ordered a little Equipage of all Things necessary for me
while I was in her Service; yet my Ideas were wholly taken up with what
I saw on every Side of me; and I winked at my own Littleness, as People
do at their own Faults. The Captain understood my Raillery very well,
and merrily replied with the old *English* Proverb, that he doubted, mine
Eyes were bigger than my Belly; for he did not observe my Stomach so
good, although I had fasted all Day: And continuing in his Mirth, protested he would have gladly given an Hundred Pounds to have seen my
Closet in the Eagle's Bill, and afterwards in its Fall from so great an
Height into the Sea; which would certainly have been a most astonishing Object, worthy to have the Description of it transmitted to future

Ages: And the Comparison of *Phaeton*° was so obvious, that he could not forbear applying it, although I did not much admire the Conceit.°

The Captain having been at *Tonquin,* was in his Return to *England* driven North Eastward to the Latitude of 44 Degrees, and of Longitude 143. But meeting a Trade Wind two Days after I came on board him, we sailed Southward a long Time, and coasting *New-Holland,*° kept our Course West-south-west, and then South-south-west till we doubled the *Cape of Good-hope.* Our Voyage was very prosperous, but I shall not trouble the Reader with a Journal of it. The Captain called in at one or two Ports, and sent in his Long-boat for Provisions and fresh Water; but I never went out of the Ship till we came into the *Downs,* which was on the 3d Day of *June* 1706, about nine Months after my Escape. I offered to leave my Goods in Security for Payment of my Freight; but the Captain protested he would not receive one Farthing. We took kind Leave of each other; and I made him promise he would come to see me at my House in *Redriff.* I hired a Horse and Guide for five Shillings, which I borrowed of the Captain.

As I was on the Road; observing the Littleness of the Houses, the Trees, the Cattle and the People, I began to think my self in *Lilliput.* I was afraid of trampling on every Traveller I met; and often called aloud to have them stand out of the Way; so that I had like to have gotten one or two broken Heads for my Impertinence.

When I came to my own House, for which I was forced to enquire, one of the Servants opening the Door, I bent down to go in (like a Goose under a Gate) for fear of striking my Head. My Wife ran out to embrace me, but I stooped lower than her Knees, thinking she could otherwise never be able to reach my Mouth. My Daughter kneeled to ask my Blessing, but I could not see her till she arose; having been so long used to stand with my Head and Eyes erect to above Sixty Foot; and then I went to take her up with one Hand, by the Waist. I looked down upon the Servants, and one or two Friends who were in the House, as if they had been Pigmies, and I a Giant. I told my wife, she had been too thrifty; for I found she had starved herself and her Daughter to nothing. In short, I behaved my self so unaccountably, that they were all of the Captain's Opinion when he first saw me; and concluded I had lost my Wits. This I mention as an Instance of the great Power of Habit and Prejudice.

Phaeton: Son of Helios who fell into the sea while trying to drive the chariot of the sun: in Swift's time, a tale often used to illustrate the dangers of pride. **Conceit:** Comparison, witty turn of thought. *New-Holland:* Dutch name for Australia.

In a little Time I and my Family and Friends came to a right Understanding: But my Wife protested I should never go to Sea any more; although my evil Destiny so ordered, that she had not Power to hinder me; as the Reader may know hereafter. In the mean Time, I here conclude the second Part of my unfortunate Voyages.

The End of the Second Part

Plate *III*. Part *III*.   Page 190.

Parts Unknown

LAND OF
St James Bay
Robbin I
IESSO
Salmonth
C Canal

C Patience
Strait of the Vries

Companys
Land
Stati I

Sea of Corea
Sanda I
Tupru
Meaco Iedo
JAPON
Osaca Chingo
Nivato
Tedo
Tonsa P
Bungo I
Dimerli Strats
I Tanaxuma

Iob
Toy Pt
Red Pt
Bosho Pt
Barnevelts
Ongdutkig I
South I
Sialo
Glangurn
Maldoneda
I Dewta
Glubdubdrib
Urat
Timal

Laputa

BALNIBARBI
Lagado
Dicovered A.D 1701

I. UGN. AGG
Maldipagdul
Clamrguig

PART III
A Voyage to *Laputa,*
Balnibarbi, Luggnagg,
Glubbdubdrib and Japan

CHAPTER I

The Author sets out on his Third Voyage. Is taken by Pyrates. The Malice of a Dutchman. *His Arrival at an Island. He is received into* Laputa.

I had not been at home above ten Days, when Captain *William Robinson, a Cornish* Man,° Commander of the *Hope-well,* a stout Ship of three Hundred Tuns, came to my House. I had formerly been Surgeon of another Ship where he was Master, and a fourth Part Owner, in a Voyage to the *Levant.* He had always treated me more like a Brother than an inferior Officer; and hearing of my Arrival made me a Visit, as I apprehended only out of Friendship, for nothing passed more than what is usual after long Absence. But repeating his Visits often, expressing his Joy to find me in good Health, asking whether I were now settled for Life, adding that he intended a Voyage to the *East-Indies,* in two Months, at last he plainly invited me, although with some Apologies, to be Surgeon of the Ship. That I should have another Surgeon under me, besides our two Mates; that my Sallary should be double to the usual Pay; and that having experienced my Knowledge in Sea-Affairs

Cornish **Man:** A native of Cornwall, in southwestern England.

to be at least equal to his, he would enter into any Engagement to follow my Advice, as much as if I had Share in the Command.

He said so many other obliging things, and I knew him to be so honest a Man, that I could not reject his Proposal; the Thirst I had of seeing the World, notwithstanding my past Misfortunes, continuing as violent as ever. The only Difficulty that remained, was to persuade my Wife, whose Consent however I at last obtained, by the Prospect of Advantage she proposed to her Children.

We set out the 5th Day of *August*, 1706, and arrived at Fort St. *George*,° the 11th of *April* 1707. We stayed there three Weeks to refresh our Crew, many of whom were sick. From thence we went to *Tonquin*, where the Captain resolved to continue some time; because many of the Goods he intended to buy were not ready, nor could he expect to be dispatched in several Months. Therefore in hopes to defray some of the Charges he must be at, he bought a Sloop, loaded it with several Sorts of Goods, wherewith the *Tonquinese* usually trade to the neighbouring Islands; and putting Fourteen Men on Board, whereof three were of the Country, he appointed me Master of the Sloop, and gave me Power to traffick, while he transacted his Affairs at *Tonquin*.

We had not sailed above three Days, when a great Storm arising, we were driven five Days to the North-North-East, and then to the East; after which we had fair Weather, but still with a pretty strong Gale from the West. Upon the tenth Day we were chased by two Pyrates,° who soon overtook us; for my Sloop was so deep loaden, that she sailed very slow; neither were we in a Condition to defend our selves.

We were boarded about the same Time by both the Pyrates, who entered furiously at the Head of their Men; but finding us all prostrate upon our Faces, (for so I gave Order,) they pinioned us with strong Ropes, and setting a Guard upon us, went to search the Sloop.

I observed among them a *Dutchman*, who seemed to be of some Authority, although he were not Commander of either Ship. He knew us by our Countenances to be *Englishmen*, and jabbering to us in his own Language, swore we should be tyed Back to Back, and thrown into the Sea. I spoke *Dutch* tolerably well; I told him who we were, and begged him in Consideration of our being Christians and Protestants, of neighbouring Countries, in strict Alliance, that he would move the

---

Fort St. *George:* Built by the East India Company on the southeast coast of India, Fort St. George later became the city of Madras.　　**Pyrates:** Pirate ships.

Captains to take some Pity on us. This inflamed his Rage; he repeated his Threatnings, and turning to his Companions, spoke with great Vehemence, in the *Japanese* Language, as I suppose; often using the Word *Christianos.*

The largest of the two Pyrate Ships was commanded by a *Japanese* Captain, who spoke a little *Dutch,* but very imperfectly. He came up to me, and after several Questions, which I answered in great Humility, he said we should not die. I made the Captain a very low Bow, and then turning to the *Dutchman,* said, I was sorry to find more Mercy in a Heathen, than in a Brother Christian. But I had soon Reason to repent those foolish Words; for that malicious Reprobate, having often endeavoured in vain to persuade both the Captains that I might be thrown into the Sea, (which they would not yield to after the Promise made me, that I should not die) however prevailed so far as to have a Punishment inflicted on me, worse in all human Appearance than Death it self. My Men were sent by an equal Division into both the Pyrate-Ships, and my Sloop new manned. As to my self, it was determined that I should be set a-drift, in a small Canoe, with Paddles and a Sail, and four Days Provisions; which last the *Japanese* Captain was so kind to double out of his own Stores, and would permit no Man to search me. I got down into the Canoe, while the *Dutchman* standing upon the Deck, loaded me with all the Curses and injurious Terms his Language could afford.

About an Hour before we saw the Pyrates, I had taken an Observation, and found we were in the Latitude of 46 N. and of Longitude 183. When I was at some Distance from the Pyrates, I discovered by my Pocket-Glass several Islands to the South-East. I set up my Sail, the Wind being fair, with a Design to reach the nearest of those Islands, which I made a Shift to do in about three Hours. It was all rocky; however I got many Birds Eggs; and striking Fire, I kindled some Heath and dry Sea Weed, by which I roasted my Eggs. I eat no other Supper, being resolved to spare my Provisions as much as I could. I passed the Night under the Shelter of a Rock, strowing some Heath under me, and slept pretty well.

The next Day I sailed to another Island, and thence to a third and fourth, sometimes using my Sail, and sometimes my Paddles. But not to trouble the Reader with a particular Account of my Distresses; let it suffice, that on the 5th Day, I arrived at the last Island in my Sight, which lay South-South-East to the former.

This Island was at a greater Distance than I expected, and I did not

reach it in less than five Hours. I encompassed it almost round before
I could find a convenient Place to land in, which was a small Creek,
about three Times the Wideness of my Canoe. I found the Island to be
all rocky, only a little intermingled with Tufts of Grass, and sweet
smelling Herbs. I took out my small Provisions, and after having refreshed myself, I secured the Remainder in a Cave, whereof there were
great Numbers. I gathered Plenty of Eggs upon the Rocks, and got a
Quantity of dry Seaweed, and parched Grass, which I designed to kindle the next Day, and roast my Eggs as well as I could. (For I had
about me my Flint, Steel, Match, and Burning-glass.) I lay all Night in
the Cave where I had lodged my Provisions. My Bed was the same dry
Grass and Sea-weed which I intended for Fewel. I slept very little; for
the Disquiets of my Mind prevailed over my Wearyness, and kept me
awake. I considered how impossible it was to preserve my Life, in so
desolate a Place; and how miserable my End must be. Yet I found my
self so listless and desponding, that I had not the Heart to rise; and
before I could get Spirits enough to creep out of my Cave, the Day was
far advanced. I walked a while among the Rocks, the Sky was perfectly
clear, and the Sun so hot, that I was forced to turn my Face from it:
When all on a Sudden it became obscured, as I thought, in a Manner
very different from what happens by the Interposition of a Cloud. I
turned back, and perceived a vast Opake Body between me and the
Sun, moving forwards towards the Island: It seemed to be about two
Miles high, and hid the Sun six or seven minutes, but I did not observe
the Air to be much colder, or the Sky more darkned, than if I had
stood under the Shade of a Mountain. As it approached nearer over the
Place where I was, it appeared to be a firm Substance, the Bottom flat,
smooth, and shining very bright from the Reflexion of the Sea below.
I stood upon a Height about two Hundred Yards from the Shoar, and
saw this vast Body descending almost to a Parallel with me, at less than
an *English* Mile Distance. I took out my Pocket-Perspective, and could
plainly discover Numbers of People moving up and down the Sides of
it, which appeared to be sloping, but what those People were doing, I
was not able to distinguish.

The natural Love of Life gave me some inward Motions of Joy; and
I was ready to entertain a Hope, that this Adventure might some Way
or other help to deliver me from the desolate Place and Condition I
was in. But, at the same Time, the Reader can hardly conceive my Astonishment, to behold an Island in the Air, inhabited by Men, who
were able (as it should seem) to raise, or sink, or put it into a progressive Motion, as they pleased. But not being, at that Time, in a Dispo-

sition to philosophise upon° this Phænomenon, I rather chose to observe what Course the Island would take; because it seemed for a while to stand still. Yet soon after it advanced nearer; and I could see the Sides of it, encompassed with several Gradations of Galleries and Stairs, at certain Intervals, to descend from one to the other. In the lowest Gallery, I beheld some People fishing with long Angling Rods, and others looking on. I waved my Cap, (for my Hat was long since worn out,) and my Handkerchief towards the Island; and upon its nearer Approach, I called and shouted with the utmost Strength of my Voice; and then looking circumspectly, I beheld a Crowd gathered to that Side which was most in my View. I found by their pointing towards me and to each other, that they plainly discovered me, although they made no Return to my Shouting: But I could see four or five Men running in great Haste up the Stairs to the Top of the Island, who then disappeared. I happened rightly to conjecture, that these were sent for Orders to some Person in Authority upon this Occasion.

The Number of People increased; and in less than Half an Hour, the Island was moved and raised in such a Manner, that the lowest Gallery appeared in a Parallel of less than an Hundred Yards Distance from the Height where I stood. I then put my self into the most supplicating Postures, and spoke in the humblest Accent, but received no Answer. Those who stood nearest over-against me, seemed to be Persons of Distinction, as I supposed by their Habit. They conferred earnestly with each other, looking often upon me. At length one of them called out in a clear, polite, smooth Dialect, not unlike in Sound to the *Italian;* and therefore I returned an Answer in that Language, hoping at least that the Cadence might be more agreeable to his Ears. Although neither of us understood the other, yet my Meaning was easily known, for the People saw the Distress I was in.

They made Signs for me to come down from the Rock, and go towards the Shoar, which I accordingly did; and the flying Island being raised to a convenient Height, the Verge directly over me, a Chain was let down from the lowest Gallery, with a Seat fastned to the Bottom, to which I fixed my self, and was drawn up by Pullies.

CHAPTER II

The Humours and Dispositions of the Laputians *described. An Account of their Learning. Of the King and his Court. The Author's Recep-*

---

philosophise upon: Think scientifically about.

tion there. The Inhabitants subject to Fears and Disquietudes. An Account of the Women.

At my alighting I was surrounded by a Crowd of People, but those who stood nearest seemed to be of better Quality. They beheld me with all the Marks and Circumstances of Wonder; neither indeed was I much in their Debt; having never till then seen a Race of Mortals so singular in their Shapes, Habits, and Countenances. Their Heads were all reclined either to the Right, or the Left; one of their Eyes turned inward, and the other directly up to the Zenith. Their outward Garments were adorned with the Figures of Suns, Moons, and Stars, interwoven with those of Fiddles, Flutes, Harps, Trumpets, Guittars, Harpsicords, and many more Instruments of Musick, unknown to us in *Europe.* I observed here and there many in the Habit of Servants, with a blown Bladder fastned like a Flail to the End of a short Stick, which they carried in their Hands. In each Bladder was a small Quantity of dried Pease, or little Pebbles, (as I was afterwards informed.) With these Bladders they now and then flapped the Mouths and Ears of those who stood near them, of which Practice I could not then conceive the Meaning. It seems, the Minds of these People are so taken up with intense Speculations, that they neither can speak, nor attend to the Discourses of others, without being rouzed by some external Taction° upon the Organs of Speech and Hearing; for which Reason, those Persons who are able to afford it, always keep a *Flapper,* (the Original is *Climenole*) in their Family, as one of their Domesticks; nor ever walk abroad or make Visits without him. And the Business of this Officer is, when two or more Persons are in Company, gently to strike with his Bladder the Mouth of him who is to speak, and the Right Ear of him or them to whom the Speaker addresseth himself. This *Flapper* is likewise employed diligently to attend his Master in his Walks, and upon Occasion to give him a soft Flap on his Eyes; because he is always so wrapped up in Cogitation, that he is in manifest Danger of falling down every Precipice, and bouncing his Head against every Post; and in the Streets, of jostling others, or being jostled himself into the Kennel.°

It was necessary to give the Reader this Information, without which he would be at the same Loss with me, to understand the Proceedings of these People, as they conducted me up the Stairs, to the Top of the Island, and from thence to the Royal Palace. While we were ascending, they forgot several Times what they were about, and left me to my self,

---

Taction: Touch.   **Kennel:** Gutter.

till their Memories were again rouzed by their *Flappers;* for they appeared altogether unmoved by the Sight of my foreign Habit and Countenance, and by the Shouts of the Vulgar, whose Thoughts and Minds were more disengaged.

At last we entered the Palace, and proceeded into the Chamber of Presence; where I saw the King seated on his Throne, attended on each Side by Persons of prime Quality. Before the Throne, was a large Table filled with Globes and Spheres, and Mathematical Instruments of all Kinds. His Majesty took not the least Notice of us, although our Entrance were not without sufficient Noise, by the Concourse of all Persons belonging to the Court. But, he was then deep in a Problem, and we attended at least an Hour, before he could solve it. There stood by him on each Side, a young Page, with Flaps in their Hands; and when they saw he was at Leisure, one of them gently struck his Mouth, and the other his Right Ear; at which he started like one awaked on the sudden, and looking towards me, and the Company I was in, recollected the Occasion of our coming, whereof he had been informed before. He spoke some Words; whereupon immediately a young Man with a Flap came up to my Side, and flapt me gently on the Right Ear; but I made Signs as well as I could, that I had no Occasion for such an Instrument; which as I afterwards found, gave his Majesty and the whole Court a very mean Opinion of my Understanding. The King, as far as I could conjecture, asked me several Questions, and I addressed my self to him in all the Languages I had. When it was found, that I could neither understand nor be understood, I was conducted by his Order to an Apartment in his Palace, (this Prince being distinguished above all his Predecessors for his Hospitality to Strangers,) where two Servants were appointed to attend me. My Dinner was brought, and four Persons of Quality, whom I remembered to have seen very near the King's Person, did me the Honour to dine with me. We had two Courses, of three Dishes each. In the first Course, there was a Shoulder of Mutton, cut into an Æquilateral Triangle; a Piece of Beef into a Rhomboides; and a Pudding into a Cycloid. The second Course was two Ducks, trussed up into the Form of Fiddles; Sausages and Puddings resembling Flutes and Haut-boys,° and a Breast of Veal in the Shape of a Harp. The Servants cut our Bread into Cones, Cylinders, Parallelograms, and several other Mathematical Figures.

While we were at Dinner, I made bold to ask the Names of several Things in their Language; and those noble Persons, by the Assistance of

Haut-boys: Oboes.

their *Flappers,* delighted to give me Answers, hoping to raise my Admiration of their great Abilities, if I could be brought to converse with them. I was soon able to call for Bread, and Drink, or whatever else I wanted.

After Dinner my Company withdrew, and a Person was sent to me by the King's Order, attended by a *Flapper.* He brought with him Pen, Ink, and Paper, and three or four Books; giving me to understand by Signs, that he was sent to teach me the Language. We sat together four Hours, in which Time I wrote down a great Number of Words in Columns, with the Translations over against them. I likewise made a Shift to learn several short Sentences. For my Tutor would order one of my Servants to fetch something, to turn about, to make a Bow, to sit, or stand, or walk, and the like. Then I took down the Sentence in Writing. He shewed me also in one of his Books, the Figures of the Sun, Moon, and Stars, the Zodiack, the Tropics, and Polar Circles, together with the Denominations of many Figures of Planes and Solids. He gave me the Names and Descriptions of all the Musical Instruments, and the general Terms of Art in playing on each of them. After he had left me, I placed all my Words with their Interpretations in alphabetical Order. And thus in a few Days, by the Help of a very faithful Memory, I got some Insight into their Language.

The Word, which I interpret the *Flying* or *Floating Island,* is in the Original *Laputa;* whereof I could never learn the true Etymology. *Lap* in the old obsolete Language signifieth *High,* and *Untuh* a *Governor;* from which they say by Corruption was derived *Laputa* from *Lapuntuh.* But I do not approve of this Derivation, which seems to be a little strained. I ventured to offer to the Learned among them a Conjecture of my own, that *Laputa* was *quasi Lap outed; Lap* signifying properly the dancing of the Sun Beams in the Sea; and *outed* a Wing, which however I shall not obtrude, but submit to the judicious Reader.

Those to whom the King had entrusted me, observing how ill I was clad, ordered a Taylor to come next Morning, and take my Measure for a Suit of Cloths. This Operator did his Office after a different Manner from those of his Trade in *Europe.* He first took my Altitude by a Quadrant, and then with Rule and Compasses, described the Dimensions and Out-Lines of my whole Body; all which he entred upon Paper, and in six Days brought my Cloths very ill made, and quite out of Shape, by happening to mistake a Figure in the Calculation. But my Comfort was, that I observed such Accidents very frequent, and little regarded.

During my Confinement for want of Cloaths, and by an Indisposition that held me some Days longer, I much enlarged my Dictionary; and when I went next to Court, was able to understand many Things the King spoke, and to return him some Kind of Answers. His Majesty had given Orders, that the Island should move North-East and by East, to the vertical Point over *Lagado,* the Metropolis of the whole Kingdom, below upon the firm Earth. It was about Ninety Leagues distant, and our Voyage lasted four Days and an Half. I was not in the least sensible of the progressive Motion made in the Air by the Island. On the second Morning, about Eleven o'Clock, the King himself in Person, attended by his Nobility, Courtiers, and Officers, having prepared all their Musical Instruments, played on them for three Hours without Intermission; so that I was quite stunned with the Noise; neither could I possibly guess the Meaning, till my Tutor informed me. He said, that the People of their Island had their Ears adapted to hear the Musick of the Spheres, which always played at certain Periods; and the Court was now prepared to bear their Part in whatever Instrument they most excelled.

In our Journey towards *Lagado* the Capital City, his Majesty ordered that the Island should stop over certain Towns and Villages, from whence he might receive the Petitions of his Subjects. And to this Purpose, several Packthreads were let down with small Weights at the Bottom. On these Packthreads the People strung their Petitions, which mounted up directly like the Scraps of Paper fastned by School-boys at the End of the String that holds their Kite. Sometimes we received Wine and Victuals from below, which were drawn up by Pullies.

The Knowledge I had in Mathematicks gave me great Assistance in acquiring their Phraseology, which depended much upon that Science and Musick; and in the latter I was not unskilled. Their Ideas are perpetually conversant in Lines and Figures. If they would, for Example, praise the Beauty of a Woman, or any other Animal, they describe it by Rhombs, Circles, Parallelograms, Ellipses, and other Geometrical Terms; or else by Words of Art drawn from Musick, needless here to repeat. I observed in the King's Kitchen all Sorts of Mathematical and Musical Instruments, after the Figures of which they cut up the Joynts that were served to his Majesty's Table.

Their Houses are very ill built, the Walls bevil,° without one right Angle in any Apartment; and this Defect ariseth from the Contempt they bear for practical Geometry; which they despise as vulgar and

bevil: Not at right angles.

mechanick, those Instructions they give being too refined for the Intellectuals° of their Workmen; which occasions perpetual Mistakes. And although they are dextrous enough upon a Piece of Paper in the Management of the Rule, the Pencil, and the Divider, yet in the common Actions and Behaviour of Life, I have not seen a more clumsy, awkward, and unhandy People, nor so slow and perplexed in their Conceptions upon all other Subjects, except those of Mathematicks and Musick. They are very bad Reasoners, and vehemently given to Opposition, unless when they happen to be of the right Opinion, which is seldom their Case. Imagination, Fancy, and Invention, they are wholly Strangers to, nor have any Words in their Language by which those Ideas can be expressed; the whole Compass of their Thoughts and Mind, being shut up within the two forementioned Sciences.

Most of them, and especially those who deal in the Astronomical Part, have great Faith in judicial Astrology,° although they are ashamed to own it publickly. But, what I chiefly admired, and thought altogether unaccountable, was the strong Disposition I observed in them towards News and Politicks; perpetually enquiring into publick Affairs, giving their Judgments in Matters of State; and passionately disputing every Inch of a Party Opinion. I have indeed observed the same Disposition among most of the Mathematicians I have known in *Europe;* although I could never discover the least Analogy between the two Sciences; unless those People suppose, that because the smallest Circle hath as many Degrees as the largest, therefore the Regulation and Management of the World require no more Abilities than the handling and turning of a Globe. But, I rather take this Quality to spring from a very common Infirmity of human Nature, inclining us to be more curious and conceited in Matters where we have least Concern, and for which we are least adapted either by Study or Nature.

These People are under continual Disquietudes, never enjoying a Minute's Peace of Mind; and their Disturbances proceed from Causes which very little affect the rest of Mortals. Their Apprehensions arise from several Changes they dread in the Celestial Bodies. For Instance; that the Earth by the continual Approaches of the Sun towards it, must in Course of Time be absorbed or swallowed up. That the Face of the Sun will by Degrees be encrusted with its own Effluvia, and give no more Light to the World. That, the Earth very narrowly escaped a Brush from the Tail of the last Comet, which would have infallibly reduced it

---

Intellectuals: Minds.   **judicial Astrology:** Predicting the future by the position of the stars.

to Ashes; and that the next, which they have calculated for One and Thirty Years hence, will probably destroy us. For, if in its Perihelion° it should approach within a certain Degree of the Sun, (as by their Calculations they have Reason to dread) it will conceive a Degree of Heat ten Thousand Times more intense than that of red hot glowing Iron; and in its Absence from the Sun, carry a blazing Tail Ten Hundred Thousand and Fourteen Miles long; through which if the Earth should pass at the Distance of one Hundred Thousand Miles from the *Nucleus,* or main Body of the Comet, it must in its Passage be set on Fire, and reduced to Ashes. That the Sun daily spending its Rays without any Nutriment to supply them, will at last be wholly consumed and annihilated; which must be attended with the Destruction of this Earth, and of all the Planets that receive their Light from it.

They are so perpetually alarmed with the Apprehensions of these and the like impending Dangers, that they can neither sleep quietly in their Beds, nor have any Relish for the common Pleasures or Amusements of Life. When they meet an Acquaintance in the Morning, the first Question is about the Sun's Health; how he looked at his Setting and Rising, and what Hopes they have to avoid the Stroak of the approaching Comet. This Conversation they are apt to run into with the same Temper that Boys discover, in delighting to hear terrible Stories of Sprites and Hobgoblins, which they greedily listen to, and dare not go to Bed for fear.

The Women of the Island have Abundance of Vivacity; they contemn their Husbands, and are exceedingly fond of Strangers, whereof there is always a considerable Number from the Continent below, attending at Court, either upon Affairs of the several Towns and Corporations, or their own particular Occasions; but are much despised, because they want the same Endowments. Among these the Ladies chuse their Gallants: But the Vexation is, that they act with too much Ease and Security; for the Husband is always so rapt in Speculation, that the Mistress and Lover may proceed to the greatest Familiarities before his Face, if he be but provided with Paper and Implements, and without his *Flapper* at his Side.

The Wives and Daughters lament their Confinement to the Island, although I think it the most delicious Spot of Ground in the World; and although they live here in the greatest Plenty and Magnificence, and are allowed to do whatever they please: They long to see the World, and take the Diversions of the Metropolis, which they are not allowed to do

---

Perihelion: The point in the orbit when the orbiting body is closest to the sun.

without a particular Licence from the King; and this is not easy to be obtained, because the People of Quality have found by frequent Experience, how hard it is to persuade their Women to return from below. I was told, that a great Court Lady, who had several Children, is married to the prime Minister, the richest Subject in the Kingdom, a very graceful Person, extremely fond of her, and lives in the finest Palace of the Island; went down to *Lagado*, on the Pretence of Health, there hid her self for several Months, till the King sent a Warrant to search for her; and she was found in an obscure Eating-House all in Rags, having pawned her Cloths to maintain an old deformed Footman, who beat her every Day, and in whose Company she was taken much against her Will. And although her Husband received her with all possible Kindness, and without the least Reproach; she soon after contrived to steal down again with all her Jewels, to the same Gallant, and hath not been heard of since.

This may perhaps pass with the Reader rather for an *European* or *English* story, than for one of a Country so remote. But he may please to consider, that the Caprices of Womankind are not limited by any Climate or Nation; and that they are much more uniform than can be easily imagined.

In about a Month's Time I had made a tolerable Proficiency in their Language, and was able to answer most of the King's Questions, when I had the Honour to attend him. His Majesty discovered not the least Curiosity to enquire into the Laws, Government, History, Religion, or Manners of the Countries where I had been; but confined his Questions to the State of Mathematicks, and received the Account I gave him, with great Contempt and Indifference, though often rouzed by his *Flapper* on each Side.

CHAPTER III

A Phænomenon solved by modern Philosophy and Astronomy. The Laputians *great Improvements in the latter. The King's Method of suppressing Insurrections.*

I Desired Leave of this Prince to see the Curiosities of the Island; which he was graciously pleased to grant, and ordered my Tutor to attend me. I chiefly wanted to know to what Cause in Art or in Nature, it

---

philosophical Account: Scientific account.

owed its several Motions; whereof I will now give a philosophical Account° to the Reader.

The flying or floating Island is exactly circular; its Diameter 7837 Yards, or about four Miles and an Half, and consequently contains ten Thousand Acres. It is three Hundred Yards thick. The Bottom, or under Surface, which appears to those who view it from below, is one even regular Plate of Adamant, shooting up to the Height of about two Hundred Yards. Above it lye the several Minerals in their usual Order; and over all is a Coat of rich Mould ten or twelve Foot deep. The Declivity of the upper Surface, from the Circumference to the Center, is the natural Cause why all the Dews and Rains which fall upon the Island, are conveyed in small Rivulets towards the Middle, where they are emptyed into four large Basons, each of about Half a Mile in Circuit, and two Hundred Yards distant from the Center. From these Basons the Water is continually exhaled by the Sun in the Day-time, which effectually prevents their overflowing. Besides, as it is in the Power of the Monarch to raise the Island above the Region of Clouds and Vapours, he can prevent the falling of Dews and Rains whenever he pleases. For the highest Clouds cannot rise above two Miles, as Naturalists agree, at least they were never known to do so in that Country.

At the Center of the Island there is a Chasm about fifty Yards in Diameter, from whence the Astronomers descend into a large Dome, which is therefore called *Flandona Gagnole,* or the *Astronomers Cave;* situated at the Depth of an Hundred Yards beneath the upper Surface of the Adamant. In this Cave are Twenty Lamps continually burning, which from the Reflection of the Adamant cast a strong Light into every Part. The Place is stored with great Variety of Sextants, Quadrants, Telescopes, Astrolabes, and other Astronomical Instruments. But the greatest Curiosity, upon which the Fate of the Island depends, is a Load-stone of a prodigious Size, in Shape resembling a Weaver's Shuttle. It is in Length six Yards, and in the thickest Part at least three Yards over.° This Magnet is sustained by a very strong Axle of Adamant, passing through its Middle, upon which it plays, and is poized so exactly that the weakest Hand can turn it. It is hooped round with an hollow Cylinder of Adamant, four Foot deep, as many thick, and twelve Yards in Diameter, placed horizontally, and supported by Eight Adamantine Feet, each Six Yards high. In the Middle of the Concave Side there is a Groove Twelve Inches deep, in which the Extremities of the Axle are lodged, and turned round as there is Occasion.

three Yards over: Three yards across.

Plate 4. Part 3.

Page 218.

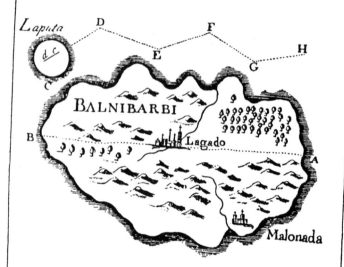

This Stone cannot be moved from its Place by any Force, because the Hoop and its Feet are one continued Piece with that Body of Adamant which constitutes the Bottom of the Island.

By Means of this Load-stone, the Island is made to rise and fall, and move from one Place to another. For, with respect to that Part of the Earth over which the Monarch presides, the Stone is endued at one of its Sides with an attractive Power, and at the other with a repulsive. Upon placing the Magnet erect with its attracting End towards the Earth, the Island descends; but when the repelling Extremity points downwards, the Island mounts directly upwards. When the Position of the Stone is oblique, the Motion of the Island is so too. For in this Magnet the Forces always act in Lines parallel to its Direction.

By this oblique Motion the Island is conveyed to different Parts of the Monarch's Dominions. To explain the Manner of its Progress, let *A B* represent a Line drawn cross the Dominions of *Balnibarbi;* let the Line *c d* represent the Load-stone, of which let *d* be the repelling End, and *c* the attracting End, the Island being over *C;* let the Stone be placed in the Position *c d* with its repelling End downwards; then the Island will be driven upwards obliquely towards *D*. When it is arrived at *D*, let the Stone be turned upon its Axle till its attracting End points towards *E,* and then the Island will be carried obliquely towards *E;* where if the Stone be again turned upon its Axle till it stands in the Position *E F,* with its repelling Point downwards, the Island will rise obliquely towards *F*, where by directing the attracting End towards *G*, the Island may be carried to *G*, and from *G* to *H,* by turning the Stone, so as to make its repelling Extremity point directly downwards. And thus by changing the Situation of the Stone as often as there is Occasion, the Island is made to rise and fall by Turns in an oblique Direction; and by those alternate Risings and Fallings (the Obliquity being not considerable) is conveyed from one Part of the Dominions to the other.

But it must be observed, that this Island cannot move beyond the Extent of the Dominions below; nor can it rise above the Height of four Miles. For which the Astronomers (who have written large Systems concerning the Stone) assign the following Reason: That the Magnetick Virtue does not extend beyond the Distance of four Miles, and that the Mineral which acts upon the Stone in the Bowels of the Earth, and in the Sea about six Leagues distant from the Shoar, is not diffused through the whole Globe, but terminated with the Limits of the King's Dominions: And it was easy from the great Advantage of such a superior Situation, for a Prince to bring under his Obedience whatever Country lay within the Attraction of that Magnet.

When the Stone is put parallel to the Plane of the Horizon, the Island standeth still; for in that Case, the Extremities of it being at equal Distance from the Earth, act with equal Force, the one in drawing downwards, the other in pushing upwards; and consequently no Motion can ensue.

This Load-stone is under the Care of certain Astronomers, who from Time to Time give it such Positions as the Monarch directs. They spend the greatest Part of their Lives in observing the celestial Bodies, which they do by the Assistance of Glasses, far excelling ours in Goodness. For, although their largest Telescopes do not exceed three Feet, they magnify much more than those of a Hundred with us, and shew the Stars with greater Clearness. This Advantage hath enabled them to extend their Discoveries much farther than our Astronomers in *Europe.* They have made a Catalogue of Ten Thousand fixed Stars, whereas the largest of ours do not contain above one third Part of that Number. They have likewise discovered two lesser Stars, or *Satellites,* which revolve about *Mars;*° whereof the innermost is distant from the Center of the primary Planet exactly three of his Diameters, and the outermost five; the former revolves in the Space of ten Hours, and the latter in Twenty-one and an Half; so that the Squares of their periodical Times, are very near in the same Proportion with the Cubes of their Distance from the Center of *Mars;* which evidently shews them to be governed by the same Law of Gravitation, that influences the other heavenly Bodies.

They have observed Ninety-three different Comets, and settled their Periods with great Exactness. If this be true, (and they affirm it with great Confidence) it is much to be wished that their Observations were made publick; whereby the Theory of Comets, which at present is very lame and defective, might be brought to the same Perfection with other Parts of Astronomy.

The King would be the most absolute Prince in the Universe, if he could but prevail on a Ministry to join with him; but these having their Estates below on the Continent, and considering that the Office of a Favourite hath a very uncertain Tenure, would never consent to the enslaving their Country.

If any Town should engage in Rebellion or Mutiny, fall into violent Factions, or refuse to pay the usual Tribute; the King hath two Methods of reducing them to Obedience. The first and the mildest Course is by keeping the Island hovering over such a Town, and the Lands about it;

---

two lesser Stars . . . *Mars:* Mars does have two satellites — Phobos and Deimos — though they were not discovered until 1877, long after Swift's prediction.

whereby he can deprive them of the Benefit of the Sun and the Rain, and consequently afflict the Inhabitants with Dearth and Diseases. And if the Crime deserve it, they are at the same time pelted from above with great Stones, against which they have no Defence, but by creeping into Cellars or Caves, while the Roofs of their Houses are beaten to Pieces. But if they still continue obstinate, or offer to raise Insurrections; he proceeds to the last Remedy, by letting the Island drop directly upon their Heads, which makes a universal Destruction both of Houses and Men. However, this is an Extremity to which the Prince is seldom driven, neither indeed is he willing to put it in Execution; nor dare his Ministers advise him to an Action, which as it would render them odious to the People, so it would be a great Damage to their own Estates that lie all below; for the Island is the King's Demesn.

But there is still indeed a more weighty Reason, why the Kings of this Country have been always averse from executing so terrible an Action, unless upon the utmost Necessity. For if the Town intended to be destroyed should have in it any tall Rocks, as it generally falls out in the larger Cities; a Situation probably chosen at first with a View to prevent such a Catastrophe: Or if it abound in high Spires or Pillars of Stone, a sudden Fall might endanger the Bottom or under Surface of the Island, which although it consist as I have said, of one entire Adamant two hundred Yards thick, might happen to crack by too great a Choque, or burst by approaching too near the Fires from the Houses below; as the Backs both of Iron and Stone will often do in our Chimneys. Of all this the People are well apprized, and understand how far to carry their Obstinacy, where their Liberty or Property is concerned. And the King, when he is highest provoked, and most determined to press a City to Rubbish, orders the Island to descend with great Gentleness, out of a Pretence of Tenderness to his People, but indeed for fear of breaking the Adamantine Bottom; in which Case it is the Opinion of all their Philosophers, that the Load-stone could no longer hold it up, and the whole Mass would fall to the Ground.

By a fundamental Law of this Realm, neither the King nor either of his two elder Sons, are permitted to leave the Island; nor the Queen till she is past Child-bearing.

CHAPTER IV

The Author leaves Laputa, *is conveyed to* Balnibarbi, *arrives at the Metropolis. A Description of the Metropolis and the Country adjoining.*

The Author hospitably received by a great Lord. His Conversation with that Lord.

Although I cannot say that I was ill treated in this Island, yet I must confess I thought my self too much neglected, not without some Degree of Contempt. For neither Prince nor People appeared to be curious in any Part of Knowledge, except Mathematicks and Musick, wherein I was far their inferior, and upon that Account very little regarded.

On the other Side, after having seen all the Curiosities of the Island, I was very desirous to leave it, being heartily weary of those People. They were indeed excellent in two Sciences for which I have great Esteem, and wherein I am not unversed; but at the same time so abstracted and involved in Speculation, that I never met with such disagreeable Companions. I conversed only with Women, Tradesmen, *Flappers,* and Court-Pages, during two Months of my Abode there; by which at last I rendered my self extremely contemptible; yet these were the only People from whom I could ever receive a reasonable Answer.

I had obtained by hard Study a good Degree of Knowledge in their Language: I was weary of being confined to an Island where I received so little Countenance; and resolved to leave it with the first Opportunity.

There was a great Lord at Court, nearly related to the King, and for that Reason alone used with respect. He was universally reckoned the most ignorant and stupid Person among them. He had performed many eminent Services for the Crown, had great natural and acquired Parts, adorned with Integrity and Honour; but so ill an Ear for Musick, that his Detractors reported he had been often known to beat Time in the wrong Place; neither could his Tutors without extreme Difficulty teach him to demonstrate the most easy Proposition in the Mathematicks. He was pleased to shew me many Marks of Favour, often did me the Honour of a Visit, desired to be informed in the Affairs of *Europe,* the Laws and Customs, the Manners and Learning of the several Countries where I had travelled. He listened to me with great Attention, and made very wise Observations on all I spoke. He had two *Flappers* attending him for State, but never made use of them except at Court, and in Visits of Ceremony; and would always command them to withdraw when we were alone together.

I intreated this illustrious Person to intercede in my Behalf with his Majesty for Leave to depart; which he accordingly did, as he was pleased to tell me, with Regret: For, indeed he had made me several Offers very advantageous, which however I refused with Expressions of the highest Acknowledgment.

On the 16th Day of *February,* I took Leave of his Majesty and the Court. The King made me a Present to the Value of about two Hundred Pounds *English;* and my Protector his Kinsman as much more, together with a Letter of Recommendation to a Friend of his in *Lagado,* the Metropolis: The Island being then hovering over a Mountain about two Miles from it, I was let down from the lowest Gallery, in the same Manner as I had been taken up.

The Continent, as far as it is subject to the Monarch of the *Flying Island,* passeth under the general Name of *Balnibarbi;* and the Metropolis, as I said before, is called *Lagado.* I felt some little Satisfaction in finding my self on firm Ground. I walked to the City without any Concern, being clad like one of the Natives, and sufficiently instructed to converse with them. I soon found out the Person's House to whom I was recommended; presented my Letter from his Friend the Grandee in the Island, and was received with much Kindness. This great Lord, whose Name was *Munodi,* ordered me an Apartment in his own House, where I continued during my Stay, and was entertained in a most hospitable Manner.

The next Morning after my Arrival he took me in his Chariot to see the Town, which is about half the Bigness of *London;* but the Houses very strangely built, and most of them out of Repair. The People in the Streets walked fast, looked wild, their Eyes fixed, and were generally in Rags. We passed through one of the Town Gates, and went about three Miles into the Country, where I saw many Labourers working with several Sorts of Tools in the Ground, but was not able to conjecture what they were about; neither did I observe any Expectation either of Corn or Grass, although the Soil appeared to be excellent. I could not forbear admiring at these odd Appearances both in Town and Country; and I made bold to desire my Conductor, that he would be pleased to explain to me what could be meant by so many busy Heads, Hands and Faces, both in the Streets and the Fields, because I did not discover any good Effects they produced; but on the contrary, I never knew a Soil so unhappily cultivated, Houses so ill contrived and so ruinous, or a People whose Countenances and Habit expressed so much Misery and Want.

This Lord *Munodi* was a Person of the first Rank, and had been some Years Governor of *Lagado;* but by a Cabal of Ministers was discharged for Insufficiency. However the King treated him with Tenderness, as a well-meaning Man, but of a low contemptible Understanding.

When I gave that free Censure of the Country and its Inhabitants, he made no further Answer than by telling me, that I had not been long enough among them to form a Judgment; and that the different Nations of the World had different Customs; with other common Topicks to the same Purpose. But when we returned to his Palace, he asked me how I liked the Building, what Absurdities I observed, and what Quarrel I had with the Dress and Looks of his Domesticks. This he might safely do; because every Thing about him was magnificent, regular and polite. I answered, that his Excellency's Prudence, Quality, and Fortune, had exempted him from those Defects which Folly and Beggary had produced in others. He said, if I would go with him to his Country House about Twenty Miles distant, where his Estate lay, there would be more Leisure for this Kind of Conversation. I told his Excellency, that I was entirely at his Disposal; and accordingly we set out next Morning.

During our Journey, he made me observe the several Methods used by Farmers in managing their Lands; which to me were wholly unaccountable: For except in some very few Places, I could not discover one Ear of Corn, or Blade of Grass. But, in three Hours travelling, the Scene was wholly altered; we came into a most beautiful Country; Farmers Houses at small Distances, neatly built, the Fields enclosed, containing Vineyards, Corngrounds and Meadows. Neither do I remember to have seen a more delightful Prospect. His Excellency observed my Countenance to clear up; he told me with a Sigh, that there his Estate began, and would continue the same till we should come to his House. That his Countrymen ridiculed and despised him for managing his Affairs no better, and for setting so ill an Example to the Kingdom; which however was followed by very few, such as were old and wilful, and weak like himself.

We came at length to the House, which was indeed a noble Structure, built according to the best Rules of ancient Architecture. The Fountains, Gardens, Walks, Avenues, and Groves were all disposed with exact Judgment and Taste. I gave due Praises to every Thing I saw, whereof his Excellency took not the least Notice till after Supper; when, there being no third Companion, he told me with a very melancholy Air, that he doubted he must throw down his Houses in Town and Country, to rebuild them after the present Mode; destroy all his Plantations, and cast others into such a Form as modern Usage required; and give the same Directions to all his Tenants, unless he would submit to incur the Censure of Pride, Singularity, Affectation, Ignorance, Caprice; and perhaps encrease his Majesty's Displeasure.

That the Admiration I appeared to be under, would cease or diminish when he had informed me of some Particulars, which probably I never heard of at Court, the People there being too much taken up in their own Speculations, to have Regard to what passed here below.

The Sum of his Discourse was to this Effect. That about Forty Years ago, certain Persons went up to *Laputa,* either upon Business or Diversion; and after five Months Continuance, came back with a very little Smattering in Mathematicks, but full of Volatile Spirits acquired in that Airy Region. That these Persons upon their Return, began to dislike the Management of every Thing below; and fell into Schemes of putting all Arts, Sciences, Languages, and Mechanicks upon a new Foot. To this End they procured a Royal Patent for erecting an Academy of PROJECTORS in *Lagado:* And the Humour prevailed so strongly among the People, that there is not a Town of any Consequence in the Kingdom without such an Academy. In these Colleges, the Professors contrive new Rules and Methods of Agriculture and Building, and new Instruments and Tools for all Trades and Manufactures, whereby, as they undertake, one Man shall do the Work of Ten; a Palace may be built in a Week, of Materials so durable as to last for ever without repairing. All the Fruits of the Earth shall come to Maturity at whatever Season we think fit to chuse, and increase an Hundred Fold more than they do at present; with innumerable other happy Proposals. The only Inconvenience is, that none of these Projects are yet brought to Perfection; and in the mean time, the whole Country lies miserably waste, the Houses in Ruins, and the People without Food or Cloaths. By all which, instead of being discouraged, they are Fifty Times more violently bent upon prosecuting their Schemes, driven equally on by Hope and Despair: That, as for himself, being not of an enterprizing Spirit, he was content to go on in the old Forms; to live in the Houses his Ancestors had built, and act as they did in every Part of Life without Innovation. That, some few other Persons of Quality and Gentry had done the same; but were looked on with an Eye of Contempt and ill Will, as Enemies to Art, ignorant, and ill Commonwealths-men, preferring their own Ease and Sloth before the general Improvement of their Country.

His Lordship added, that he would not by any further Particulars prevent the Pleasure I should certainly take in viewing the grand Academy, whither he was resolved I should go. He only desired me to observe a ruined Building upon the Side of a Mountain about three Miles distant, of which he gave me this Account. That he had a very convenient Mill within Half a Mile of his House, turned by a Current from a large River, and sufficient for his own Family as well as a great Number of his Tenants. That, about seven Years ago, a Club of those Projectors came to him with Proposals to destroy this Mill, and build another on the Side of that Mountain, on the long Ridge whereof a long Canal must be cut for a Repository of Water, to be conveyed up by Pipes and Engines to supply the Mill: Because the Wind and Air upon a Height agitated the Water, and thereby made it fitter for Motion: And because the Water descending down a Declivity would turn the Mill with half the Current of a River whose Course is more upon a Level. He said, that being then not very well with the Court, and pressed by many of his Friends, he complied with the Proposal; and after employing an Hundred Men for two Years, the Work miscarryed, the Projectors went off, laying the Blame intirely upon him; railing at him ever since, and putting others upon the same Experiment, with equal Assurance of Success, as well as equal Disappointment.

In a few Days we came back to Town; and his Excellency, considering the bad Character he had in the Academy, would not go with me himself, but recommended me to a Friend of his to bear me Company thither. My Lord was pleased to represent me as a great Admirer of Projects, and a Person of much Curiosity and easy Belief; which indeed was not without Truth; for I had my self been a Sort of Projector in my younger Days.

CHAPTER V

The Author permitted to see the grand Academy of Lagado. The Academy largely described. The Arts wherein the Professors employ themselves.

This Academy is not an entire single Building, but a Continuation of several Houses on both Sides of a Street; which growing waste, was purchased and applyed to that Use.

I was received very kindly by the Warden, and went for many Days to the Academy. Every Room hath in it one or more Projectors; and I believe I could not be in fewer than five Hundred Rooms.

The first Man I saw was of a meagre Aspect, with sooty Hands and Face, his Hair and Beard long, ragged and singed in several Places. His Clothes, Shirt, and Skin were all of the same Colour. He had been Eight Years upon a Project for extracting Sun-Beams out of Cucumbers, which were to be put into Vials hermetically sealed, and let out to warm the Air in raw inclement Summers. He told me, he did not doubt in Eight Years more, that he should be able to supply the Governors Gardens with Sun-shine at a reasonable Rate; but he complained that his Stock was low, and intreated me to give him something as an Encour-

agement to Ingenuity, especially since this had been a very dear Season
for Cucumbers. I made him a small Present, for my Lord had furnished
me with Money on purpose, because he knew their Practice of begging
from all who go to see them.

I went into another Chamber, but was ready to hasten back, being
almost overcome with a horrible Stink. My Conductor pressed me forward, conjuring me in a Whisper to give no Offence, which would be
highly resented; and therefore I durst not so much as stop my Nose.
The Projector of this Cell was the most ancient Student of the Academy. His Face and Beard were of a pale Yellow; his Hands and Clothes
dawbed over with Filth. When I was presented to him, he gave me a
very close Embrace, (a Compliment I could well have excused). His
Employment from his first coming into the Academy, was an Operation
to reduce human Excrement to its original Food, by separating the several Parts, removing the Tincture which it receives from the Gall, making the Odour exhale, and scumming off the Saliva. He had a weekly
Allowance from the Society, of a Vessel filled with human Ordure,
about the Bigness of a *Bristol* Barrel.

I saw another at work to calcine Ice into Gunpowder; who likewise
shewed me a Treatise he had written concerning the Malleability of Fire,
which he intended to publish.

There was a most ingenious Architect who had contrived a new
Method for building Houses, by beginning at the Roof, and working
downwards to the Foundation; which he justified to me by the like
Practice of those two prudent Insects the Bee and the Spider.

There was a Man born blind, who had several Apprentices in his
own Condition: Their Employment was to mix Colours for Painters,
which their Master taught them to distinguish by feeling and smelling.
It was indeed my Misfortune to find them at that Time not very perfect
in their Lessons; and the Professor himself happened to be generally
mistaken: This Artist is much encouraged and esteemed by the whole
Fraternity.

In another Apartment I was highly pleased with a Projector, who
had found a Device of plowing the Ground with Hogs, to save the
Charges of Plows, Cattle, and Labour. The Method is this: In an Acre
of Ground you bury at six Inches Distance, and eight deep, a Quantity
of Acorns, Dates, Chesnuts, and other Maste° or Vegetables whereof
these Animals are fondest; then you drive six Hundred or more of them
into the Field, where in a few Days they will root up the whole Ground

Maste: Nuts of trees, such as chestnuts, used to feed pigs.

in search of their Food, and make it fit for sowing, at the same time manuring it with their Dung. It is true, upon Experiment they found the Charge and Trouble very great, and they had little or no Crop. However, it is not doubted that this Invention may be capable of great Improvement.

I went into another Room, where the Walls and Ceiling were all hung round with Cobwebs, except a narrow Passage for the Artist to go in and out. At my Entrance he called aloud to me not to disturb his Webs. He lamented the fatal Mistake the World had been so long in of using Silk-Worms, while we had such plenty of domestick Insects, who infinitely excelled the former, because they understood how to weave as well as spin. And he proposed farther, that by employing Spiders, the Charge of dying Silks would be wholly saved; whereof I was fully convinced when he shewed me a vast Number of Flies most beautifully coloured, wherewith he fed his Spiders; assuring us, that the Webs would take a Tincture from them; and as he had them of all Hues, he hoped to fit every Body's Fancy, as soon as he could find proper Food for the Flies, of certain Gums, Oyls, and other glutinous Matter, to give a Strength and Consistence to the Threads.

There was an Astronomer who had undertaken to place a Sun-Dial upon the great Weather-Cock on the Town-House, by adjusting the annual and diurnal Motions of the Earth and Sun, so as to answer and coincide with all accidental Turnings of the Wind.

I was complaining of a small Fit of the Cholick; upon which my Conductor led me into a Room, where a great Physician resided, who was famous for curing that Disease by contrary Operations from the same Instrument. He had a large Pair of Bellows, with a long slender Muzzle of Ivory. This he conveyed eight Inches up the Anus, and drawing in the Wind, he affirmed he could make the Guts as lank as a dried Bladder. But when the Disease was more stubborn and violent, he let in the Muzzle while the Bellows was full of Wind, which he discharged into the Body of the Patient; then withdrew the Instrument to replenish it, clapping his Thumb strongly against the Orifice of the Fundament; and this being repeated three or four Times, the adventitious Wind would rush out, bringing the noxious along with it (like Water put into a Pump) and the Patient recovers. I saw him try both Experiments upon a Dog, but could not discern any Effect from the former. After the latter, the Animal was ready to burst, and made so violent a Discharge, as was very offensive to me and my Companions. The Dog died on the Spot, and we left the Doctor endeavouring to recover him by the same Operation.

I visited many other Apartments, but shall not trouble my Reader with all the Curiosities I observed, being studious of Brevity.

I had hitherto seen only one Side of the Academy, the other being appropriated to the Advancers of speculative Learning; of whom I shall say something when I have mentioned one illustrious Person more, who is called among them *the universal Artist*. He told us, he had been Thirty Years employing his Thoughts for the Improvement of human Life. He had two large Rooms full of wonderful Curiosities, and Fifty Men at work. Some were condensing Air into a dry tangible Substance, by extracting the Nitre, and letting the aqueous or fluid Particles percolate: Others softening Marble for Pillows and Pin-cushions; others petrifying the Hoofs of a living Horse to preserve them from foundring.° The Artist himself was at that Time busy upon two great Designs: The first, to sow Land with Chaff, wherein he affirmed the true seminal Virtue to be contained, as he demonstrated by several Experiments which I was not skilful enough to comprehend. The other was, by a certain Composition of Gums, Minerals, and Vegetables outwardly applied, to prevent the Growth of Wool upon two young Lambs; and he hoped in a reasonable Time to propagate the Breed of naked Sheep all over the Kingdom.

We crossed a Walk to the other Part of the Academy, where, as I have already said, the Projectors in speculative Learning resided.

The first Professor I saw was in a very large Room, with Forty Pupils about him. After Salutation, observing me to look earnestly upon a Frame, which took up the greatest Part of both the Length and Breadth of the Room; he said, perhaps I might wonder to see him employed in a Project for improving speculative Knowledge by practical and mechanical Operations. But the World would soon be sensible of its Usefulness; and he flattered himself, that a more noble exalted Thought never sprang in any other Man's Head. Every one knew how laborious the usual Method is of attaining to Arts and Sciences; whereas by his Contrivance, the most ignorant Person at a reasonable Charge, and with a little bodily Labour, may write Books in Philosophy, Poetry, Politicks, Law, Mathematicks and Theology, without the least Assistance from Genius or Study. He then led me to the Frame, about the Sides whereof all his Pupils stood in Ranks. It was Twenty Foot square, placed in the Middle of the Room. The Superficies was composed of several Bits of Wood, about the Bigness of a Dye,° but some larger than others. They were all linked together by slender Wires. These Bits of Wood

foundring: Going lame.   **Dye:** Small cube; one of a pair of dice.

Plate 5 Part 3.

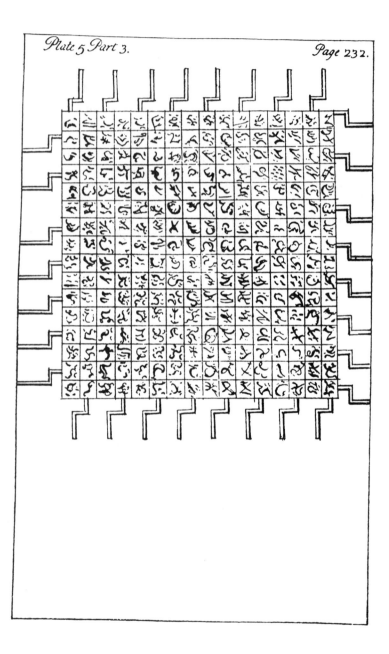

were covered on every Square with Paper pasted on them; and on these Papers were written all the Words of their Language in their several Moods, Tenses, and Declensions, but without any Order. The Professor then desired me to observe, for he was going to set his Engine at work. The Pupils at his Command took each of them hold of an Iron Handle, whereof there were Forty fixed round the Edges of the Frame; and giving them a sudden Turn, the whole Disposition of the Words was entirely changed. He then commanded Six and Thirty of the Lads to read the several Lines softly as they appeared upon the Frame; and where they found three or four Words together that might make Part of a Sentence, they dictated to the four remaining Boys who were Scribes. This Work was repeated three or four Times, and at every Turn the Engine was so contrived, that the Words shifted into new Places, as the square Bits of Wood moved upside down.

Six Hours a-Day the young Students were employed in this Labour; and the Professor shewed me several Volumes in large Folio already collected, of broken Sentences, which he intended to piece together; and out of those rich Materials to give the World a compleat Body of all Arts and Sciences; which however might be still improved, and much expedited, if the Publick would raise a Fund for making and employing five Hundred such Frames in *Lagado,* and oblige the Managers to contribute in common their several Collections.

He assured me, that this Invention had employed all his Thoughts from his Youth; that he had emptyed the whole Vocabulary into his Frame, and made the strictest Computation of the general Proportion there is in Books between the Numbers of Particles, Nouns, and Verbs, and other Parts of Speech.

I made my humblest Acknowledgments to this illustrious Person for his great Communicativeness; and promised if ever I had the good Fortune to return to my native Country, that I would do him Justice, as the sole Inventer of this wonderful Machine; the Form and Contrivance of which I desired Leave to delineate upon Paper as in the Figure here annexed. I told him, although it were the Custom of our Learned in *Europe* to steal Inventions from each other, who had thereby at least this Advantage, that it became a Controversy which was the right Owner; yet I would take such Caution, that he should have the Honour entire without a Rival.

We next went to the School of Languages, where three Professors sat in Consultation upon improving that of their own Country.

The first Project was to shorten Discourse by cutting Polysyllables into one, and leaving out Verbs and Participles; because in Reality all things imaginable are but Nouns.

The other, was a Scheme for entirely abolishing all Words whatsoever: And this was urged as a great Advantage in Point of Health as well as Brevity. For, it is plain, that every Word we speak is in some Degree a Diminution of our Lungs by Corrosion; and consequently contributes to the shortning of our Lives. An Expedient was therefore offered, that since Words are only Names for *Things,* it would be more convenient for all Men to carry about them, such *Things* as were necessary to express the particular Business they are to discourse on. And this Invention would certainly have taken Place, to the great Ease as well as Health of the Subject, if the Women in Conjunction with the Vulgar and Illiterate had not threatned to raise a Rebellion, unless they might be allowed the Liberty to speak with their Tongues, after the Manner of their Forefathers: Such constant irreconcileable Enemies to Science are the common People. However, many of the most Learned and Wise adhere to the new Scheme of expressing themselves by *Things;* which hath only this Inconvenience attending it; that if a Man's Business be very great, and of various Kinds, he must be obliged in Proportion to carry a greater Bundle of *Things* upon his Back, unless he can afford one or two strong Servants to attend him. I have often beheld two of those Sages almost sinking under the Weight of their Packs, like Pedlars among us; who when they met in the Streets would lay down their Loads, open their Sacks, and hold Conversation for an Hour together; then put up their Implements, help each other to resume their Burthens, and take their Leave.

But, for short Conversations a Man may carry Implements in his Pockets and under his Arms, enough to supply him, and in his House he cannot be at a Loss; therefore the Room where Company meet who practice this Art, is full of all *Things* ready at Hand, requisite to furnish Matter for this Kind of artificial Converse.

Another great Advantage proposed by this Invention, was, that it would serve as an universal Language to be understood in all civilized Nations, whose Goods and Utensils are generally of the same Kind, or nearly resembling, so that their Uses might easily be comprehended. And thus, Embassadors would be qualified to treat with foreign Princes or Ministers of State, to whose Tongues they were utter Strangers.

I was at the Mathematical School, where the Master taught his Pupils after a Method scarce imaginable to us in *Europe.* The Proposition and Demonstration were fairly written on a thin Wafer, with Ink composed of a Cephalick Tincture.° This the Student was to swallow upon a fasting Stomach, and for three Days following eat nothing but Bread and Water. As the Wafer digested, the Tincture mounted to his Brain, bearing the Proposition along with it. But the Success hath not hitherto been answerable, partly by some Error in the *Quantum*° or Composition, and partly by the Perverseness of Lads; to whom this Bolus is so nauseous, that they generally steal aside, and discharge it upwards before it can operate; neither have they been yet persuaded to use so long an Abstinence as the Prescription requires.

CHAPTER VI

A further Account of the Academy. The Author proposeth some Improvements, which are honourably received.

In the School of political Projectors I was but ill entertained; the Professors appearing in my Judgment wholly out of their Senses; which is a Scene that never fails to make me melancholy. These unhappy People were proposing Schemes for persuading Monarchs to chuse Favourites upon the Score of their Wisdom, Capacity and Virtue; of teaching Ministers to consult the publick Good; of rewarding Merit, great Abilities, and eminent Services; of instructing Princes to know their true Interest, by placing it on the same Foundation with that of their People: Of chusing for Employments Persons qualified to exercise them; with many other wild impossible Chimæras, that never entered before into the Heart of Man to conceive; and confirmed in me the old Observation, that there is nothing so extravagant and irrational which some Philosophers have not maintained for Truth.

But, however I shall so far do Justice to this Part of the Academy, as to acknowledge that all of them were not so visionary. There was a most ingenious Doctor who seemed to be perfectly versed in the whole Nature and System of Government. This illustrious Person had very usefully employed his Studies in finding out effectual Remedies for all Diseases and Corruptions, to which the several Kinds of publick Administration are subject by the Vices or Infirmities of those who govern, as well as by the Licentiousness of those who are to obey. For Instance: Whereas all Writers and Reasoners have agreed, that there is a strict universal Resemblance between the natural and the political Body; can there be any thing more evident, than that the Health of both must be

---

Cephalick Tincture: Medicine for the head. **Quantum:** Quantity.

preserved, and the Diseases cured by the same Prescriptions? It is allowed, that Senates and great Councils are often troubled with redun-
dant, ebullient, and other peccant Humours;° with many Diseases of
the Head, and more of the Heart; with strong Convulsions, with grievous Contractions of the Nerves and Sinews in both Hands, but especially the Right: With Spleen, Flatus, Vertigoes and Deliriums; with
scrophulous Tumours full of fœtid purulent Matter; with sower frothy
Ructations;° with Canine Appetites and Crudeness of Digestion; besides many others needless to mention. This Doctor therefore proposed, that upon the meeting of a Senate, certain Physicians should
attend at the three first Days of their sitting, and at the Close of each
Day's Debate, feel the Pulses of every Senator; after which having
maturely considered, and consulted upon the Nature of the several
Maladies, and the Methods of Cure; they should on the fourth Day
return to the Senate-House, attended by their Apothecaries stored
with proper Medicines; and before the Members sat, administer to
each of them Lenitives,° Aperitives,° Abstersives,° Corrosives,° Restringents,° Palliatives, Laxatives, Cephalalgicks,° Ictericks,° Apophlegmaticks,° Acousticks,° as their several Cases required; and according as
these Medicines should operate, repeat, alter, or omit them at the next
Meeting.

　This Project could not be of any great Expence to the Publick; and
might in my poor Opinion, be of much Use for the Dispatch of Business in those Countries where Senates have any Share in the legislative
Power; beget Unanimity, shorten Debates, open a few Mouths which
are now closed, and close many more which are now open; curb the
Petulancy of the Young, and correct the Positiveness of the Old; rouze
the Stupid, and damp the Pert.

　Again; Because it is a general Complaint that the Favourites of
Princes are troubled with short and weak Memories; the same Doctor
proposed, that whoever attended a first Minister, after having told his
Business with the utmost Brevity, and in the plainest Words; should at

---

peccant Humours: The old humoral theory of medicine held that health was a balance of
four humors (black bile, yellow bile, blood, and phlegm) that flowed through the body.
Disease resulted when one humor became excessive and morbid ("peccant"); hence, the
need for various forms of evacuation and bloodletting to restore the necessary balance.
Ructations: Belches.　Lenitives: Painkillers.　Aperitives: Laxatives.　Abstersives:
Purgatives.　Corrosives: Harsh medicines.　Restringents: Medicines that inhibit
bowel movement.　Cephalalgicks: Medicines for headaches.　Ictericks: Remedies for
jaundice.　Apophlegmaticks: Drugs that combat phlegm (or stupidity).　Acousticks:
Medicines for deafness.

his Departure give the said Minister a Tweak by the Nose, or a Kick in
the Belly, or tread on his Corns, or lug him thrice by both Ears, or run
a Pin into his Breech, or pinch his Arm black and blue; to prevent Forgetfulness: And at every Levee Day repeat the same Operation, till the
Business were done or absolutely refused.

He likewise directed, that every Senator in the great Council of a
Nation, after he had delivered his Opinion, and argued in the Defence
of it, should be obliged to give his Vote directly contrary; because if that
were done, the Result would infallibly terminate in the Good of the
Publick.

When Parties in a State are violent, he offered a wonderful Contrivance to reconcile them. The Method is this. You take an Hundred
Leaders of each Party; you dispose them into Couples of such whose
Heads are nearest of a Size; then let two nice Operators saw off the
Occiput° of each Couple at the same Time, in such a Manner that the
Brain may be equally divided. Let the *Occiputs* thus cut off be inter-
changed, applying each to the Head of his opposite Party-man. It seems
indeed to be a Work that requireth some Exactness; but the Professor
assured us, that if it were dextrously performed, the Cure would be infallible. For he argued thus; that the two half Brains being left to debate
the Matter between themselves within the Space of one Scull, would
soon come to a good Understanding, and produce that Moderation as
well as Regularity of Thinking, so much to be wished for in the Heads
of those, who imagine they came into the World only to watch and
govern its Motion: And as to the Difference of Brains in Quantity or
Quality, among those who are Directors in Faction; the Doctor assured
us from his own Knowledge, that it was a perfect Trifle.

I heard a very warm Debate between two Professors, about the most
commodious and effectual Ways and Means of raising Money without
grieving the Subject. The first affirmed, the justest Method would be to
lay a certain Tax upon Vices and Folly; and the Sum fixed upon every
Man, to be rated after the fairest Manner by a Jury of his Neighbours.
The second was of an Opinion directly contrary; to tax those Qualities
of Body and Mind for which Men chiefly value themselves; the Rate to
be more or less according to the Degrees of excelling; the Decision
whereof should be left entirely to their own Breast. The highest Tax was
upon Men, who are the greatest Favourites of the other Sex; and the
Assessments according to the Number and Natures of the Favours they

Occiput: Back of the head.

have received; for which they are allowed to be their own Vouchers. Wit, Valour, and Politeness were likewise proposed to be largely taxed, and collected in the same Manner, by every Person giving his own Word for the Quantum of what he possessed. But, as to Honour, Justice, Wisdom and Learning, they should not be taxed at all; because, they are Qualifications of so singular a Kind, that no Man will either allow them in his Neighbour, or value them in himself.

The Women were proposed to be taxed according to their Beauty and Skill in Dressing; wherein they had the same Privilege with the Men, to be determined by their own Judgment. But Constancy, Chastity, good Sense, and good Nature were not rated, because they would not bear the Charge of Collecting.

To keep Senators in the Interest of the Crown, it was proposed that the Members should raffle for Employments; every Man first taking an Oath, and giving Security that he would vote for the Court, whether he won or no; after which the Losers had in their Turn the Liberty of raffling upon the next Vacancy. Thus, Hope and Expectation would be kept alive; none would complain of broken Promises, but impute their Disappointments wholly to Fortune, whose Shoulders are broader and stronger than those of a Ministry.

Another Professor shewed me a larger Paper of Instructions for discovering Plots and Conspiracies against the Government. He advised great Statesmen to examine into the Dyet of all suspected Persons; their Times of eating; upon which Side they lay in Bed; with which Hand they wiped their Posteriors; to take a strict View of their Excrements, and from the Colour, the Odour, the Taste, the Consistence, the Crudeness, or Maturity of Digestion, form a Judgment of their Thoughts and Designs: Because Men are never so serious, thoughtful, and intent, as when they are at Stool; which he found by frequent Experiment: For in such Conjunctures,° when he used merely as a Trial° to consider which was the best Way of murdering the King, his Ordure would have a Tincture of Green; but quite different when he thought only of raising an Insurrection, or burning the Metropolis.

The whole Discourse was written with great Acuteness, containing many Observations both curious and useful for Politicians, but as I conceived not altogether compleat. This I ventured to tell the Author, and offered if he pleased to supply him with some Additions. He received

---

in such Conjunctures: In such surroundings.   **as a Trial:** As an experiment.

my Proposition with more Compliance than is usual among Writers, especially those of the Projecting Species; professing he would be glad to receive farther Information.

I told him, that in the Kingdom of *Tribnia*, by the Natives called *Langden*, where I had long sojourned, the Bulk of the People consisted wholly of Discoverers, Witnesses, Informers, Accusers, Prosecutors, Evidences,° Swearers; together with their several subservient and subaltern Instruments; all under the Colours, the Conduct, and pay of Ministers and their Deputies. The Plots in that Kingdom are usually the Workmanship of those Persons who desire to raise their own Characters of profound Politicians; to restore new Vigour to a crazy Administration; to stifle or divert general Discontents; to fill their Coffers with Forfeitures; and raise or sink the Opinion of publick Credit, as either shall best answer their private Advantage. It is first agreed and settled among them, what suspected Persons shall be accused of a Plot: Then, effectual Care is taken to secure all their Letters and other Papers, and put the Owners in Chains. These Papers are delivered to a Set of Artists very dextrous in finding out the mysterious Meanings of Words, Syllables and Letters. For Instance, they can decypher a Close-stool to signify a Privy-Council; a Flock of Geese, a Senate; a lame Dog, an Invader; the Plague, a standing Army; a Buzard, a Minister; the Gout, a High Priest; a Gibbet, a Secretary of State; a Chamber pot, a Committee of Grandees; a Sieve, a Court Lady; a Broom, a Revolution; a Mouse-trap, an Employment; a bottomless Pit, the Treasury; a Sink,° a C — t; a Cap and Bells, a Favourite; a broken Reed, a Court of Justice; an empty Tun, a General; a running Sore, the Administration.

When this Method fails, they have two others more effectual; which the Learned among them call Acrosticks, and Anagrams. *First,* they can decypher all initial Letters into political Meanings: Thus, *N,* shall signify a Plot; *B,* a Regiment of Horse; *L,* a Fleet at Sea. Or, *secondly,* by transposing the Letters of the Alphabet, in any suspected Paper, they can lay open the deepest Designs of a discontented Party. So for Example, if I should say in a Letter to a Friend, *Our Brother* Tom *has just got the Piles;* a Man of Skill in this Art would discover how the same Letters which compose that Sentence, may be analysed into the following Words; *Resist, —— a Plot is brought home —— The Tour.* And this is the Anagrammatick Method.

Evidences: Witnesses.   **a Sink:** A cesspool.

The Professor made me great Acknowledgments for communicating these Observations, and promised to make honourable mention of me in his Treatise.

I saw nothing in this Country that could invite me to a longer Continuance; and began to think of returning home to *England*.

CHAPTER VII

The Author leaves Lagado, *arrives at* Maldonada. *No Ship ready. He takes a short Voyage to* Glubbdubdrib. *His Reception by the Governor.*

The Continent of which this Kingdom is a part, extends itself, as I have Reason to believe, Eastward to that unknown Tract of *America*, Westward of *California*, and North to the Pacifick Ocean, which is not above an hundred and fifty Miles from *Lagado;* where there is a good Port and much Commerce with the great Island of *Luggnagg*, situated to the North-West about 29 Degrees North Latitude, and 140 Longitude. This Island of *Luggnagg* stands South Eastwards of *Japan*, about an hundred Leagues distant. There is a strict Alliance between the *Japanese* Emperor and the King of *Luggnagg*, which affords frequent Opportunities of sailing from one Island to the other. I determined therefore to direct my Course this Way, in order to my Return to *Europe*. I hired two Mules with a Guide to shew me the Way, and carry my small Baggage. I took leave of my noble Proctector, who had shewn me so much Favour, and made me a generous Present at my Departure.

My Journey was without any Accident or Adventure worth relating. When I arrived at the Port of *Maldonada*, (for so it is called) there was no Ship in the Harbour bound for *Luggnagg*, nor like to be in some Time. The Town is about as large as *Portsmouth*. I soon fell into some Acquaintance, and was very hospitably received. A Gentleman of Distinction said to me, that since the Ships bound for *Luggnagg* could not be ready in less than a Month, it might be no disagreeable Amusement for me to take a Trip to the little Island of *Glubbdubdrib*, about five Leagues off to the South-West. He offered himself and a Friend to accompany me, and that I should be provided with a small convenient Barque for the Voyage.

GLUBBDUBDRIB, as nearly as I can interpret the Word, signifies the Island of *Sorcerers* or *Magicians*. It is about one third as large as the Isle of *Wight*, and extreamly fruitful: It is governed by the Head of a certain Tribe, who are all Magicians. This Tribe marries only among each other; and the eldest in Succession is Prince or Governor. He hath a noble Palace, and a Park of about three thousand Acres, surrounded by a Wall of hewn Stone twenty Foot high. In this Park are several small Inclosures for Cattle, Corn and Gardening.

The Governor and his Family are served and attended by Domesticks of a Kind somewhat unusual. By his Skill in Necromancy, he hath Power of calling whom he pleaseth from the Dead, and commanding their Service for twenty four Hours, but no longer; nor can he call the same Persons up again in less than three Months, except upon very extraordinary Occasions.

When we arrived at the Island, which was about Eleven in the Morning, one of the Gentlemen who accompanied me, went to the Governor, and desired Admittance for a Stranger, who came on purpose to have the Honour of attending on his Highness. This was immediately granted, and we all three entered the Gate of the Palace between two Rows of Guards, armed and dressed after a very antick° Manner, and something in their Countenances that made my Flesh creep with a Horror I cannot express. We passed through several Apartments between Servants of the same Sort, ranked on each Side as before, till we came to the Chamber of Presence, where after three profound Obeysances, and a few general Questions, we were permitted to sit on three Stools near the lowest Step of his Highness's Throne. He understood the Language of *Balnibarbi,* although it were different from that of his Island. He desired me to give him some Account of my Travels; and to let me see that I should be treated without Ceremony, he dismissed all his Attendants with a Turn of his Finger, at which to my great Astonishment they vanished in an Instant, like Visions in a Dream, when we awake on a sudden. I could not recover myself in some Time, till the Governor assured me that I should receive no Hurt; and observing my two Companions to be under no Concern, who had been often entertained in the same Manner, I began to take Courage; and related to his Highness a short History of my several Adventures, yet not without some Hesitation, and frequently looking behind me to the Place where I had seen those domestick Spectres. I had the Honour to dine with the Governor, where a new Set of Ghosts served up the Meat, and waited at Table. I now observed myself to be less terrified than I had been in the Morning. I stayed till Sun-set, but humbly desired his Highness to excuse me for not accepting his Invitation of lodging in the Palace. My

antick: Ancient; strange.

two Friends and I lay at a private House in the Town adjoining, which is the Capital of this little Island; and the next Morning we returned to pay our Duty to the Governor, as he was pleased to command us.

After this Manner we continued in the Island for ten Days, most Part of every Day with the Governor, and at Night in our Lodging. I soon grew so familiarized to the Sight of Spirits, that after the third or fourth Time they gave me no Emotion at all; or if I had any Apprehensions left, my Curiosity prevailed over them. For his Highness the Governor ordered me to call up whatever Persons I would chuse to name, and in whatever Numbers among all the Dead from the Beginning of the World to the present Time, and command them to answer any Questions I should think fit to ask; with this Condition, that my Questions must be confined within the Compass of the Times they lived in. And one Thing I might depend upon, that they would certainly tell me Truth; for Lying was a Talent of no Use in the lower World.

I made my humble Acknowledgments to his Highness for so great a Favour. We were in a Chamber, from whence there was a fair Prospect into the Park. And because my first Inclination was to be entertained with Scenes of Pomp and Magnificence, I desired to see *Alexander* the Great, at the Head of his Army just after the Battle of *Arbela;* which upon a Motion of the Governor's Finger immediately appeared in a large Field under the Window, where we stood. *Alexander* was called up into the Room: It was with great Difficulty that I understood his *Greek,* and had but little of my own. He assured me upon his Honour that he was not poisoned, but dyed of a Fever by excessive Drinking.

Next I saw *Hannibal* passing the *Alps,* who told me he had not a Drop of Vinegar in his Camp.

I saw *Cæsar* and *Pompey* at the Head of their Troops just ready to engage. I saw the former in his last great Triumph. I desired that the Senate of *Rome* might appear before me in one large Chamber, and a modern Representative, in Counterview, in another. The first seemed to be an Assembly of Heroes and Demy-Gods; the other a Knot of Pedlars, Pick-pockets, Highwaymen and Bullies.

The Governor at my Request gave the Sign for *Cæsar* and *Brutus* to advance towards us. I was struck with a profound Veneration at the Sight of *Brutus;* and could easily discover the most consummate Virtue, the greatest Intrepidity, and Firmness of Mind, the truest Love of his Country, and general Benevolence for Mankind in every Lineament of his Countenance. I observed with much Pleasure, that these two Persons were in good Intelligence with each other; and *Cæsar* freely confessed to me, that the greatest Actions of his own Life were not equal by many Degrees to the Glory of taking it away. I had the Honour to have much Conversation with *Brutus;*° and was told that his Ancestor *Junius,*° *Socrates,*° *Epaminondas,*° *Cato* the Younger,° Sir *Thomas More*° and himself, were perpetually together: A *Sextumvirate* to which all the Ages of the World cannot add a Seventh.

It would be tedious to trouble the Reader with relating what vast Numbers of illustrious Persons were called up, to gratify that insatiable Desire I had to see the World in every Period of Antiquity placed before me. I chiefly fed mine Eyes with beholding the Destroyers of Tyrants and Usurpers, and the Restorers of Liberty to oppressed and injured Nations. But it is impossible to express the Satisfaction I received in my own Mind, after such a Manner as to make it a suitable Entertainment to the Reader.

CHAPTER VIII

A further Account of Glubbdubdrib. *Antient and Modern History corrected.*

Having a Desire to see those Antients, who were most renowned for Wit and Learning, I set apart one Day on purpose. I proposed that *Homer* and *Aristotle* might appear at the Head of all their Commentators; but these were so numerous, that some Hundreds were forced to attend in the Court and outward Rooms of the Palace. I knew and could distinguish those two Heroes at first Sight, not only from the Croud, but from each other. *Homer* was the taller and comelier Person of the two, walked very erect for one of his Age, and his Eyes were the most quick and piercing I ever beheld. *Aristotle* stooped much, and made use of a Staff. His Visage was meager, his Hair lank and thin, and his Voice hollow. I soon discovered, that both of them were perfect Strangers to the rest of the Company, and had never seen or heard of

---

Brutus: Brutus (85–42 B.C.), leader of a conspiracy to assassinate Julius Caesar in 44 B.C. *Junius:* Lucius Junius Brutus overthrew the king of Rome in 509 B.C. and subsequently served as a Roman consul. *Socrates:* Socrates (469–399 B.C.), Athenian philosopher and teacher of Plato. *Epaminondas:* Epaminondas (c. 410–362 B.C.), Theban general and politician. *Cato* the Younger: Cato the Younger (95–46 B.C.), defended the Roman Republic against Julius Caesar. Sir *Thomas More:* Sir Thomas More (1478–1535), author of *Utopia,* executed for failing to acknowledge Henry VIII as head of the English church.

them before. And I had a Whisper from a Ghost, who shall be nameless, that these Commentators always kept in the most distant Quarters from their Principals in the lower World, through a Consciousness of Shame and Guilt, because they had so horribly misrepresented the Meaning of those Authors to Posterity. I introduced *Didymus* and *Eustathius*° to *Homer,* and prevailed on him to treat them better than perhaps they deserved; for he soon found they wanted a Genius to enter into the Spirit of a Poet. But *Aristotle* was out of all Patience with the Account I gave him of *Scotus*° and *Ramus,*° as I presented them to him; and he asked them whether the rest of the Tribe were as great Dunces as themselves.

I then desired the Governor to call up *Descartes*° and *Gassendi,*° with whom I prevailed to explain their Systems to *Aristotle.* This great Philosopher freely acknowledged his own Mistakes in Natural Philosophy, because he proceeded in many things upon Conjecture, as all Men must do; and he found, that *Gassendi,* who had made the Doctrine of *Epicurus* as palatable as he could, and the *Vortices* of *Descartes,* were equally exploded. He predicted the same Fate to *Attraction,*° whereof the present Learned are such Zealous Asserters. He said, that new Systems of Nature were but new Fashions, which would vary in every Age; and even those who pretend to demonstrate them from Mathematical Principles, would flourish but a short Period of Time, and be out of Vogue when that was determined.

I spent five Days in conversing with many others of the antient Learned. I saw most of the first *Roman* Emperors. I prevailed on the Governor to call up *Eliogabalus's*° Cooks to dress us a Dinner; but they could not shew us much of their Skill, for want of Materials. A *Helot*° of *Agesilaus*° made us a Dish of *Spartan* Broth, but I was not able to get down a second *Spoonful.*

The two Gentlemen who conducted me to the Island were pressed

---

Didymus and **Eustathius:** Didymus (c. 65 B.C.–A.D. 10) and Eustathius (died c. 1194) wrote extensive commentaries on Homer.   **Scotus:** Duns Scotus (c. 1265–c. 1308), scholastic commentator on Aristotle; source of the word "dunce."   **Ramus:** Pierre la Ramée (1515–72), well-known opponent of Aristotle.   **Descartes:** René Descartes (1596–1650), famous French philosopher, scientist, and mathematician, who opposed Aristotle's system and proposed his own, which held in part that the heavenly spheres were carried around in "vortices" or whirlpools of material particles.   **Gassendi:** Pierre Gassendi (1592–1655), who opposed both Aristotle and Descartes and revived the ancient atomic physics of Epicurus (342–270 B.C.).   **Attraction:** Gravitation, a theory of which had recently been proposed by Isaac Newton.   **Eliogabalus:** Heliogabalus, emperor of Rome, 218–22, known for his extravagance and luxury.   **Helot:** A Spartan slave. **Agesilaus:** Agesilaus II (440–360 B.C.) was king of Sparta during its rise to power.

by their private Affairs to return in three Days, which I employed in
seeing some of the modern Dead, who had made the greatest Figure for
two or three Hundred Years past in our own and other Countries of
Europe; and having been always a great Admirer of old illustrious Families, I desired the Governor would call up a Dozen or two of Kings with
their Ancestors in order, for eight or nine Generations. But my Disappointment was grievous and unexpected. For, instead of a long Train
with Royal Diadems, I saw in one Family two Fidlers, three spruce
Courtiers, and an *Italian* Prelate. In another, a Barber, an Abbot, and
two Cardinals. I have too great a Veneration for crowned Heads to
dwell any longer on so nice a Subject: But as to Counts, Marquesses,
Dukes, Earls, and the like, I was not so scrupulous. And I confess it was
not without some Pleasure that I found my self able to trace the particular Features, by which certain Families are distinguished up to their
Originals. I could plainly discover from whence one Family derives a
long Chin; why a second hath abounded with Knaves for two Generations, and Fools for two more; why a third happened to be crack-
brained, and a fourth to be Sharpers. Whence it came, what *Polydore
Virgil*° says of a certain great House, *Nec Vir fortis, nec Fœmina Casta.*°
How Cruelty, Falshood, and Cowardice grew to be Characteristicks by
which certain Families are distinguished as much as by their Coat of
Arms. Who first brought the Pox° into a noble House, which hath lin-
eally descended in scrophulous Tumours to their Posterity. Neither
could I wonder at all this, when I saw such an Interruption of Lineages
by Pages, Lacqueys, Valets, Coachmen, Gamesters, Fidlers, Players,
Captains, and Pick-pockets.

I was chiefly disgusted with modern History. For having strictly examined all the Persons of greatest Name in the Courts of Princes for an
Hundred Years past, I found how the World had been misled by prostitute Writers, to ascribe the greatest Exploits in War to Cowards, the
wisest Counsel to Fools, Sincerity to Flatterers, *Roman* Virtue to Be-
trayers of their Country, Piety to Atheists, Chastity to Sodomites, Truth
to Informers. How many innocent and excellent Persons had been condemned to Death or Banishment, by the practising of great Ministers
upon the Corruption of Judges, and the Malice of Factions. How many
Villains had been exalted to the highest Places of Trust, Power, Dignity,
and Profit: How great a Share in the Motions and Events of Courts,

---

Polydore Virgil: (1470–1555), an Italian who became an English archdeacon and wrote
a multivolume history of England.   *Nec Vir fortis, nec Fœmina Casta:* "Not a man was
brave, nor a woman chaste."   *Pox:* Syphilis.

Councils, and Senates might be challenged by Bawds, Whores, Pimps, Parasites, and Buffoons: How low an Opinion I had of human Wisdom and Integrity, when I was truly informed of the Springs and Motives of great Enterprizes and Revolutions in the World, and of the contemptible Accidents to which they owed their Success.

Here I discovered the Roguery and Ignorance of those who pretend to write *Anecdotes,* or secret History; who send so many Kings to their Graves with a Cup of Poison; will repeat the Discourse between a Prince and chief Minister, where no Witness was by; unlock the Thoughts and Cabinets of Embassadors and Secretaries of State; and have the perpetual Misfortune to be mistaken. Here I discovered the true Causes of many great Events that have surprized the World: How a Whore can govern the Back-stairs, the Back-stairs a Council, and the Council a Senate. A General confessed in my Presence, that he got a Victory purely by the Force of Cowardice and ill Conduct: And an Admiral, that for want of proper Intelligence, he beat the Enemy to whom he intended to betray the Fleet. Three Kings protested to me, that in their whole Reigns they did never once prefer any Person of Merit, unless by Mistake or Treachery of some Minister in whom they confided: Neither would they do it if they were to live again; and they shewed with great Strength of Reason, that the Royal Throne could not be supported without Corruption; because, that positive, confident, restive Temper, which Virtue infused into Man, was a perpetual Clog to publick Business.

I had the Curiosity to enquire in a particular Manner, by what Method great Numbers had procured to themselves high Titles of Honour, and prodigious Estates; and I confined my Enquiry to a very modern Period: However, without grating upon present Times, because I would be sure to give no Offence even to Foreigners, (for I hope the Reader need not be told that I do not in the least intend my own Country in what I say upon this Occasion) a great Number of Persons concerned were called up, and upon a very slight Examination, discovered such a Scene of Infamy, that I cannot reflect upon it without some Seriousness. Perjury, Oppression, Subornation,° Fraud, Pandarism,° and the like *Infirmities* were amongst the most excusable Arts they had to mention; and for these I gave, as it was reasonable, due Allowance. But when some confessed, they owed their Greatness and Wealth to Sodomy or Incest; others to the prostituting of their own Wives and

Subornation: Corruption, often through bribery.   **Pandarism:** Pimping.

Daughters; others to the betraying their Country or their Prince; some to poisoning, more to the perverting of Justice in order to destroy the Innocent: I hope I may be pardoned if these Discoveries inclined me a little to abate of that profound Veneration which I am naturally apt to pay to Persons of high Rank, who ought to be treated with the utmost Respect due to their sublime Dignity, by us their Inferiors.

I had often read of some great Services done to Princes and States, and desired to see the Persons by whom those Services were performed. Upon Enquiry I was told, that their Names were to be found on no Record, except a few of them whom History hath represented as the vilest Rogues and Traitors. As to the rest, I had never once heard of them. They all appeared with dejected Looks, and in the meanest Habit; most of them telling me they died in Poverty and Disgrace, and the rest on a Scaffold or a Gibbet.°

Among others there was one Person whose Case appeared a little singular. He had a Youth about Eighteen Years old standing by his Side. He told me, he had for many Years been Commander of a Ship; and in the Sea Fight at *Actium*,° had the good Fortune to break through the Enemy's great Line of Battle, sink three of their Capital Ships, and take a fourth, which was the sole Cause of *Antony*'s Flight, and of the Victory that ensued: That the Youth standing by him, his only Son, was killed in the Action. He added, that upon the Confidence of some Merit, the War being at an End, he went to *Rome,* and solicited at the Court of *Augustus* to be preferred to a greater Ship, whose Commander had been killed; but without any regard to his Pretensions, it was given to a Boy who had never seen the Sea, the Son of a *Libertina,* who waited on one of the Emperor's Mistresses. Returning back to his own Vessel, he was charged with Neglect of Duty, and the Ship given to a favourite Page of *Publicola* the Vice-Admiral; whereupon he retired to a poor Farm, at a great Distance from *Rome,* and there ended his Life. I was so curious to know the Truth of this Story, that I desired *Agrippa*° might be called, who was Admiral in that Fight. He appeared, and confirmed the whole Account, but with much more Advantage to the Captain, whose Modesty had extenuated or concealed a great Part of his Merit.

I was surprized to find Corruption grown so high and so quick in that Empire, by the Force of Luxury so lately introduced; which made

---

on a Scaffold or a Gibbet: That is, executed.   *Actium:* Sea battle in 31 B.C. between Mark Antony and Octavius Caesar at the end of which Antony fled with Cleopatra. *Agrippa:* Agrippa (63–12 B.C.), Octavius Caesar's admiral at the Battle of Actium.

me less wonder at many parallel Cases in other Countries, where Vices of all Kinds have reigned so much longer, and where the whole Praise as well as Pillage hath been engrossed by the chief Commander, who perhaps had the least Title to either.

As every Person called up made exactly the same Appearance he had done in the World, it gave me melancholy Reflections to observe how much the Race of human Kind was degenerate among us, within these Hundred Years past. How the Pox under all its Consequences and Denominations had altered every Lineament of an *English* Countenance; shortened the Size of Bodies, unbraced the Nerves, relaxed the Sinews and Muscles, introduced a sallow Complexion, and rendered the Flesh loose and *rancid*.

I descended so low as to desire that some *English* Yeomen of the old Stamp, might be summoned to appear; once so famous for the Simplicity of their Manners, Dyet and Dress; for Justice in their Dealings; for their true Spirit of Liberty; for their Valour and Love of their Country. Neither could I be wholly unmoved after comparing the Living with the Dead, when I considered how all these pure native Virtues were prostituted for a Piece of Money by their Grand-children; who in selling their Votes, and managing at Elections have acquired every Vice and Corruption that can possibly be learned in a Court.

CHAPTER IX

The Author's Return to Maldonada. *Sails to the Kingdom of* Luggnagg. *The Author confined. He is sent for to Court. The Manner of his Admittance. The King's great Lenity to his Subjects.*

The Day of our Departure being come, I took leave of his Highness the Governor of *Glubbdubdribb,* and returned with my two Companions to *Maldonada,* where after a Fortnight's waiting, a Ship was ready to sail for *Luggnagg.* The two Gentlemen and some others were so generous and kind as to furnish me with Provisions, and see me on Board. I was a Month in this Voyage. We had one violent Storm, and were under a Necessity of steering Westward to get into the Trade-Wind, which holds for above sixty Leagues. On the 21st of *April,* 1708, we sailed in the River of *Clumegnig,* which is a Seaport Town, at the South-East Point of *Luggnagg.* We cast Anchor within a League of the Town, and made a Signal for a Pilot. Two of them came on Board in less than half an Hour, by whom we were guided between certain Shoals and Rocks, which are very dangerous in the Passage, to a large Basin, where a Fleet may ride in Safety within a Cable's Length of the Town-Wall.

Some of our Sailors, whether out of Treachery or Inadvertence, had informed the Pilots that I was a Stranger and a great Traveller, whereof these gave Notice to a Custom-House Officer, by whom I was examined very strictly upon my landing. This Officer spoke to me in the Language of *Balnibarbi*, which by the Force of much Commerce is generally understood in that Town, especially by Seamen, and those employed in the Customs. I gave him a short Account of some Particulars, and made my Story as plausible and consistent as I could; but I thought it necessary to disguise my Country, and call my self a *Hollander*; because my Intentions were for *Japan*,° and I knew the *Dutch* were the only *Europeans* permitted to enter into that Kingdom. I therefore told the Officer, that having been shipwrecked on the Coast of *Balnibarbi*, and cast on a Rock, I was received up into *Laputa*, or the flying Island (of which he had often heard) and was now endeavouring to get to *Japan*, from whence I might find a Convenience of returning to my own Country. The Officer said, I must be confined till he could receive Orders from Court, for which he would write immediately, and hoped to receive an Answer in a Fortnight. I was carried to a convenient Lodging, with a Centry placed at the Door; however I had the Liberty of a large Garden, and was treated with Humanity enough, being maintained all the Time at the King's Charge. I was visited by several Persons, chiefly out of Curiosity, because it was reported I came from Countries very remote, of which they had never heard.

I hired a young Man who came in the same Ship to be an Interpreter; he was a Native of *Luggnagg*, but had lived some Years at *Maldonada*, and was a perfect Master of both Languages. By his Assistance I was able to hold a Conversation with those that came to visit me; but this consisted only of their Questions and my Answers.

The Dispatch came from Court about the Time we expected. It contained a Warrant for conducting me and my Retinue to *Traldragdubb* or *Trildrogdrib*, (for it is pronounced both Ways as near as I can remember) by a Party of Ten Horse. All my Retinue was that poor Lad for an Interpreter, whom I persuaded into my Service. At my humble Request we had each of us a Mule to ride on. A Messenger was dispatched half a Day's Journey before us, to give the King Notice of my

---

Japan: In response to missionary activities of Spain and other Christian countries, Japan closed its ports in 1638 to all Europeans except the Dutch, who were restricted to the island of Deshima near Nagasaki.

Approach, and to desire that his Majesty would please to appoint a Day and Hour, when it would be his gracious Pleasure that I might have the Honour to *lick the Dust before his Footstool*. This is the Court Style, and I found it to be more than Matter of Form: For upon my Admittance two Days after my Arrival, I was commanded to crawl upon my Belly, and lick the Floor as I advanced; but on account of my being a Stranger, Care was taken to have it so clean that the Dust was not offensive. However, this was a peculiar Grace, not allowed to any but Persons of the highest Rank, when they desire an Admittance: Nay, sometimes the Floor is strewed with Dust on purpose, when the Person to be admitted happens to have powerful Enemies at Court: And I have seen a great Lord with his Mouth so crammed, that when he had crept to the proper Distance from the Throne, he was not able to speak a Word. Neither is there any Remedy, because it is capital for those who receive an Audience to spit or wipe their Mouths in his Majesty's Presence. There is indeed another Custom, which I cannot altogether approve of. When the King hath a Mind to put any of his Nobles to Death in a gentle indulgent Manner; he commands to have the Floor strowed with a certain brown Powder, of a deadly Composition, which being licked up infallibly kills him in twenty-four Hours. But in Justice to this Prince's great Clemency, and the Care he hath of his Subjects Lives, (wherein it were much to be wished that the Monarchs of *Europe* would imitate him) it must be mentioned for his Honour, that strict Orders are given to have the infected Parts of the Floor well washed after every such Execution; which if his Domesticks neglect, they are in Danger of incurring his Royal Displeasure. I my self heard him give Directions, that one of his Pages should be whipt, whose Turn it was to give Notice about washing the Floor after an Execution, but maliciously had omitted it; by which Neglect a young Lord of great Hopes coming to an Audience, was unfortunately poisoned, although the King at that Time had no Design against his Life. But this good Prince was so gracious, as to forgive the Page his Whipping, upon Promise that he would do so no more, without special Orders.

To return from this Digression; when I had crept within four Yards of the Throne, I raised my self gently upon my Knees, and then striking my Forehead seven Times against the Ground, I pronounced the following Words, as they had been taught me the Night before, *Ickpling Gloffthrobb Squutserumm blhiop Mlashnalt Zwin tnodbalkguffh Slhiophad Gurdlubh Asht.* This is the Compliment established by the Laws of the Land for all Persons admitted to the King's Presence. It may be rendered into *English* thus: *May your cœlestial Majesty out-live the Sun, eleven Moons and an half.* To this the King returned some Answer, which although I could not understand, yet I replied as I had been directed; *Fluft drin Yalerick Dwuldum prastrad mirplush,* which properly signifies, *My Tongue is in the Mouth of my Friend;* and by this Expression was meant that I desired leave to bring my Interpreter; whereupon the young Man already mentioned was accordingly introduced; by whose Intervention I answered as many Questions as his Majesty could put in above an Hour. I spoke in the *Balnibarbian* Tongue, and my Interpreter delivered my Meaning in that of *Luggnagg.*

The King was much delighted with my Company, and ordered his *Bliffmarklub* or High Chamberlain to appoint a Lodging in the Court for me and my Interpreter, with a daily Allowance for my Table, and a large Purse of Gold for my common Expences.

I stayed three Months in this Country out of perfect Obedience to his Majesty, who was pleased highly to favour me, and made me very honourable Offers. But I thought it more consistent with Prudence and Justice to pass the Remainder of my Days with my Wife and Family.

CHAPTER X

The Luggnuggians *commended. A particular Description of the* Struldbrugs, *with many Conversations between the Author and some eminent Persons upon that Subject.*

The *Luggnuggians* are a polite and generous People, and although they are not without some Share of that Pride which is peculiar to all *Eastern* Countries, yet they shew themselves courteous to Strangers, especially such who are countenanced by the Court. I had many Acquaintance among Persons of the best Fashion, and being always attended by my Interpreter, the Conversation we had was not disagreeable.

One Day in much good Company, I was asked by a Person of Quality, whether I had seen any of their *Struldbrugs* or *Immortals.* I said I had not; and desired he would explain to me what he meant by such an Appellation, applyed to a mortal Creature. He told me, that sometimes, although very rarely, a Child happened to be born in a Family with a red circular Spot in the Forehead, directly over the left Eye-brow, which was an infallible Mark that it should never dye. The Spot, as he described it, was about the Compass of a Silver Threepence, but in the Course of

Time grew larger, and changed its Colour; for at Twelve Years old it became green, so continued till Five and Twenty, then turned to a deep blue; at Five and Forty it grew coal black, and as large as an *English* Shilling; but never admitted any farther Alteration. He said these Births were so rare, that he did not believe there could be above Eleven Hundred *Struldbruggs* of both Sexes in the whole Kingdom, of which he computed about Fifty in the Metropolis, and among the rest a young Girl born about three Years ago. That, these Productions were not peculiar to any Family, but a meer Effect of Chance; and the Children of the *Struldbruggs* themselves, were equally mortal with the rest of the People.

I freely own myself to have been struck with inexpressible Delight upon hearing this Account: And the Person who gave it me happening to understand the *Balnibarbian* Language, which I spoke very well, I could not forbear breaking out into Expressions perhaps a little too extravagant. I cryed out as in a Rapture; Happy Nation, where every Child hath at least a Chance for being immortal! Happy People who enjoy so many living Examples of antient Virtue, and have Masters ready to instruct them in the Wisdom of all former Ages! But, happiest beyond all Comparison are those excellent *Struldbruggs*, who being born exempt from that universal Calamity of human Nature, have their Minds free and disingaged, without the Weight and Depression of Spirits caused by the continual Apprehension of Death. I discovered my Admiration that I had not observed any of these illustrious Persons at Court; the black Spot on the Forehead, being so remarkable a Distinction, that I could not have easily overlooked it: And it was impossible that his Majesty, a most judicious Prince, should not provide himself with a good Number of such wise and able Counsellors. Yet perhaps the Virtue of those Reverend Sages was too strict for the corrupt and libertine Manners of a Court. And we often find by Experience, that young Men are too opinionative and volatile to be guided by the sober Dictates of their Seniors. However, since the King was pleased to allow me Access to his Royal Person, I was resolved upon the very first Occasion to deliver my Opinion to him on this Matter freely, and at large by the Help of my Interpreter; and whether he would please to take my Advice or no, yet in one Thing I was determined, that his Majesty having frequently offered me an Establishment in this Country, I would with great Thankfulness accept the Favour, and pass my Life here in the Conversation of those superiour Beings the *Struldbruggs*, if they would please to admit me.

The Gentleman to whom I addressed my Discourse, because (as I have already observed) he spoke the Language of *Balnibarbi*, said to me with a Sort of a Smile, which usually ariseth from Pity to the Ignorant, that he was glad of any Occasion to keep me among them, and desired my Permission to explain to the Company what I had spoke. He did so; and they talked together for some time in their own Language, whereof I understood not a Syllable, neither could I observe by their Countenances what Impression my Discourse had made on them. After a short Silence, the same Person told me, that his Friends and mine (so he thought fit to express himself) were very much pleased with the judicious Remarks I had made on the great Happiness and Advantages of immortal Life; and they were desirous to know in a particular Manner, what Scheme of Living I should have formed to myself, if it had fallen to my Lot to have been born a *Struldbrugg*.

I answered, it was easy to be eloquent on so copious and delightful a Subject, especially to me who have been often apt to amuse myself with Visions of what I should do if I were a King, a General, or a great Lord: And upon this very Case I had frequently run over the whole System how I should employ myself, and pass the Time if I were sure to live for ever.

That, if it had been my good Fortune to come into the World a *Struldbrugg*; as soon as I could discover my own Happiness by understanding the Difference between Life and Death, I would first resolve by all Arts and Methods whatsoever to procure myself Riches: In the Pursuit of which, by Thrift and Management, I might reasonably expect in about two Hundred Years, to be the wealthiest man in the Kingdom. In the second Place, I would from my earliest Youth apply myself to the Study of Arts and Sciences, by which I should arrive in time to excel all others in Learning. Lastly, I would carefully record every Action and Event of Consequence that happened in the Publick,° impartially draw the Characters of the several Successions of Princes, and great Ministers of State; with my own Observations on every Point. I would exactly set down the several Changes in Customs, Language, Fashion of Dress, Dyet and Diversions. By all which Acquirements, I should be a living Treasury of Knowledge and Wisdom, and certainly become the Oracle of the Nation.

I would never marry after Threescore, but live in an hospitable Manner, yet still on the saving Side. I would entertain myself in forming and directing the Minds of hopeful young Men, by convincing them from my own Remembrance, Experience and Observation, fortified by numerous Examples, of the Usefulness of Virtue in publick and private

Publick: State.

Life. But, my choise and constant Companions should be a Sett of my own immortal Brotherhood, among whom I would elect a Dozen from the most ancient down to my own Contemporaries. Where any of these wanted Fortunes, I would provide them with convenient Lodges round my own Estate, and have some of them always at my Table, only mingling a few of the most valuable among you Mortals, whom Length of Time would harden me to lose with little or no Reluctance, and treat your Posterity after the same Manner; just as a Man diverts himself with the annual Succession of Pinks and Tulips in his Garden, without regretting the Loss of those which withered the preceding Year.

These *Struldbruggs* and I would mutually communicate our Observations and Memorials through the Course of Time; remark the several Gradations by which Corruption steals into the World, and oppose it in every Step, by giving perpetual Warning and Instruction to Mankind; which, added to the strong Influence of our own Example, would probably prevent that continual degeneracy of human Nature, so justly complained of in all Ages.

Add to all this, the Pleasure of seeing the various Revolutions of States and Empires; the Changes in the lower and upper World;° antient Cities in Ruins, and obscure Villages become the Seats of Kings. Famous Rivers lessening into shallow Brooks; the Ocean leaving one Coast dry, and overwhelming another: The Discovery of many Countries yet unknown. Barbarity overrunning the politest Nations, and the most barbarous becoming civilized. I should then see the Discovery of the *Longitude,* the *perpetual Motion,* the *universal Medicine,* and many other great Inventions brought to the utmost Perfection.

What wonderful Discoveries should we make in Astronomy, by outliving and confirming our own Predictions; by observing the Progress and Returns of Comets, with the Changes of Motion in the Sun, Moon and Stars.

I enlarged upon many other Topicks, which the natural Desire of endless Life and sublunary Happiness could easily furnish me with. When I had ended, and the Sum of my Discourse had been interpreted as before, to the rest of the Company, there was a good Deal of Talk among them in the Language of the Country, not without some Laughter at my Expence. At last the same Gentleman who had been my Interpreter, said, he was desired by the rest to set me right in a few Mistakes, which I had fallen into through the common Imbecility of

---

lower and upper World: Earth and heavens.

human Nature, and upon that Allowance was less answerable for them. That, this Breed of *Struldbruggs* was peculiar to their Country, for there were no such People either in *Balnibarbi* or *Japan,* where he had the Honour to be Embassador from his Majesty, and found the Natives in both those Kingdoms very hard to believe that the Fact was possible; and it appeared from my Astonishment when he first mentioned the Matter to me, that I received it as a Thing wholly new, and scarcely to be credited. That in the two Kingdoms above-mentioned, where during his Residence he had conversed very much, he observed long Life to be the universal Desire and Wish of Mankind. That, whoever had one Foot in the Grave, was sure to hold back the other as strongly as he could. That the oldest had still Hopes of living one Day longer, and looked on Death as the greatest Evil, from which Nature always prompted him to retreat; only in this Island of *Luggnagg,* the Appetite for living was not so eager, from the continual Example of the *Struldbruggs* before their Eyes.

That the System of Living contrived by me was unreasonable and unjust, because it supposed a Perpetuity of Youth, Health, and Vigour, which no Man could be so foolish to hope, however extravagant he might be in his Wishes. That, the Question therefore was not whether a Man would chuse to be always in the Prime of Youth, attended with Prosperity and Health; but how he would pass a perpetual Life under all the usual Disadvantages which old Age brings along with it. For although few Men will avow their Desires of being immortal upon such hard Conditions, yet in the two Kingdoms beforementioned of *Balnibarbi* and *Japan,* he observed that every Man desired to put off Death for sometime longer, let it approach ever so late; and he rarely heard of any Man who died willingly, except he were incited by the Extremity of Grief or Torture. And he appealed to me whether in those Countries I had travelled as well as my own, I had not observed the same general Disposition.

After this Preface, he gave me a particular Account of the *Struldbruggs* among them. He said they commonly acted like Mortals, till about Thirty Years old, after which by Degrees they grew melancholy and dejected, increasing in both till they came to Fourscore. This he learned from their own Confession; for otherwise there not being above two or three of that Species born in an Age, they were too few to form a general Observation by. When they came to Fourscore Years, which is reckoned the Extremity of living in this Country, they had not only all the Follies and Infirmities of other old Men, but many more which arose from the dreadful Prospect of never dying. They were not only opinionative, peevish, covetous, morose, vain, talkative; but uncapable of Friendship, and dead to all natural Affection, which never descended below their Grand-children. Envy and impotent Desires, are their prevailing Passions. But those Objects against which their Envy seems principally directed, are the Vices of the younger Sort, and the Deaths of the old. By reflecting on the former, they find themselves cut off from all Possibility of Pleasure; and whenever they see a Funeral, they lament and repine that others are gone to an Harbour of Rest, to which they themselves never can hope to arrive. They have no Remembrance of any thing but what they learned and observed in their Youth and middle Age, and even that is very imperfect: And for the Truth or Particulars of any Fact, it is safer to depend on common Traditions than upon their best Recollections. The least miserable among them, appear to be those who turn to Dotage, and entirely lose their Memories; these meet with more Pity and Assistance, because they want many bad Qualities which abound in others.

If a *Struldbrugg* happen to marry one of his own Kind, the Marriage is dissolved of Course by the Courtesy of the Kingdom, as soon as the younger of the two comes to be Fourscore. For the Law thinks it a reasonable Indulgence, that those who are condemned without any Fault of their own to a perpetual Continuance in the World, should not have their Misery doubled by the Load of a Wife.

As soon as they have compleated the Term of Eighty Years, they are looked on as dead in Law; their Heirs immediately succeed to their Estates, only a small Pittance is reserved for their Support; and the poor ones are maintained at the publick Charge. After that Period they are held incapable of any Employment of Trust or Profit; they cannot purchase Lands, or take Leases, neither are they allowed to be Witnesses in any Cause, either Civil or Criminal, not even for the Decision of Meers° and Bounds.

At Ninety they lose their Teeth and Hair; they have at that Age no Distinction of Taste, but eat and drink whatever they can get, without Relish or Appetite. The Diseases they were subject to, still continue without encreasing or diminishing. In talking they forget the common Appellation of Things, and the Names of Persons, even of those who are their nearest Friends and Relations. For the same Reason they never can amuse themselves with reading, because their Memory will not serve to carry them from the Beginning of a Sentence to the End; and by this

Meers: Landmarks or boundaries.

Defect they are deprived of the only Entertainment whereof they might otherwise be capable.

The Language of this Country being always upon the Flux, the *Struldbruggs* of one Age do not understand those of another; neither are they able after two Hundred Years to hold any Conversation (farther than by a few general Words) with their Neighbours the Mortals; and thus they lye under the Disadvantage of living like Foreigners in their own Country.

This was the Account given me of the *Struldbruggs*, as near as I can remember. I afterwards saw five or six of different Ages, the youngest not above two Hundred Years old, who were brought to me at several Times by some of my Friends; but although they were told that I was a great Traveller, and had seen all the World, they had not the least Curiosity to ask me a Question; only desired I would give them *Slumskudask*, or a Token of Remembrance; which is a modest Way of begging, to avoid the Law that strictly forbids it, because they are provided for by the Publick, although indeed with a very scanty Allowance.

They are despised and hated by all Sorts of People: When one of them is born, it is reckoned ominous, and their Birth is recorded very particularly; so that you may know their Age by consulting the Registry, which however hath not been kept above a Thousand Years past, or at least hath been destroyed by Time or publick Disturbances. But the usual Way of computing how old they are, is, by asking them what Kings or great Persons they can remember, and then consulting History; for infallibly the last Prince in their Mind did not begin his Reign after they were Fourscore Years old.

They were the most mortifying Sight I ever beheld; and the Women more horrible than the Men. Besides the usual Deformities in extreme old Age, they acquired an additional Ghastliness in Proportion to their Number of Years, which is not to be described; and among half a Dozen I soon distinguished which was the eldest, although there were not above a Century or two between them.

The Reader will easily believe, that from what I had heard and seen, my keen Appetite for Perpetuity of Life was much abated. I grew heartily ashamed of the pleasing Visions I had formed; and thought no Tyrant could invent a Death into which I would not run with Pleasure from such a Life. The King heard of all that had passed between me and my Friends upon this Occasion, and raillied me very pleasantly; wishing I would send a Couple of *Struldbruggs* to my own Country, to arm our People against the Fear of Death; but this it seems is forbidden by the fundamental Laws of the Kingdom; or else I should have been well content with the Trouble and Expence of transporting them.

I could not but agree, that the Laws of this Kingdom relating to the *Struldbruggs*, were founded upon the strongest Reasons, and such as any other Country would be under the Necessity of enacting in the like Circumstances. Otherwise, as Avarice is the necessary Consequent of old Age, those Immortals would in time become Proprietors of the whole Nation, and engross the Civil Power; which, for want of Abilities to manage, must end in the Ruin of the Publick.

CHAPTER XI

The Author leaves Luggnagg *and sails to* Japan. *From thence he returns in a* Dutch *Ship to* Amsterdam, *and from* Amsterdam *to* England.

I thought this Account of the *Struldbruggs* might be some Entertainment to the Reader, because it seems to be a little out of the common Way; at least, I do not remember to have met the like in any Book of Travels that hath come to my Hands: And if I am deceived, my Excuse must be, that it is necessary for Travellers, who describe the same Country, very often to agree in dwelling on the same Particulars, without deserving the Censure of having borrowed or transcribed from those who wrote before them.

There is indeed a perpetual Commerce between this Kingdom and the great Empire of *Japan;* and it is very probable that the *Japanese* Authors may have given some Account of the *Struldbruggs;* but my Stay in *Japan* was so short, and I was so entirely a Stranger to the Language, that I was not qualified to make any Enquiries. But I hope the *Dutch* upon this Notice will be curious and able enough to supply my Defects.

His Majesty having often pressed me to accept some Employment in his Court, and finding me absolutely determined to return to my Native Country; was pleased to give me his Licence to depart; and honoured me with a Letter of Recommendation under his own Hand to the Emperor of *Japan.* He likewise presented me with four Hundred forty-four large Pieces of Gold (this Nation delighting in even Numbers) and a red Diamond which I sold in *England* for Eleven Hundred Pounds.

On the 6th Day of *May,* 1709, I took a solemn Leave of his Majesty, and all my Friends. This Prince was so gracious as to order a Guard to conduct me to *Glanguenstald,* which is a Royal Port to the *South-West*

Part of the Island. In six Days I found a Vessel ready to carry me to
Japan; and spent fifteen Days in the Voyage. We landed at a small Port-
Town called *Xamoschi,* situated on the *South-East* Part of *Japan.* The
Town lies on the *Western* Part, where there is a narrow Streight, leading
Northward into a long Arm of the Sea, upon the *North-West* Part of
which *Yedo*° the Metropolis stands. At landing I shewed the Custom-
House Officers my Letter from the King of *Luggnagg* to his Imperial
Majesty: They knew the Seal perfectly well; it was as broad as the Palm
of my Hand. The Impression was, *A King lifting up a lame Beggar from
the Earth.* The Magistrates of the Town hearing of my Letter, received
me as a publick Minister; they provided me with Carriages and Servants,
and bore my Charges to *Yedo,* where I was admitted to an Audience,
and delivered my Letter; which was opened with great Ceremony, and
explained to the Emperor by an Interpreter, who gave me Notice of
his Majesty's Order, that I should signify my Request; and whatever
it were, it should be granted for the sake of his Royal Brother of
Luggnagg. This Interpreter was a Person employed to transact Affairs
with the *Hollanders:* He soon conjectured by my Countenance that I
was an *European,* and therefore repeated his Majesty's Commands in
Low-Dutch,° which he spoke perfectly well. I answered, (as I had before
determined) that I was a *Dutch* Merchant, shipwrecked in a very remote
Country, from whence I travelled by Sea and Land to *Luggnagg,* and
then took Shipping for *Japan,* where I knew my Countrymen often
traded, and with some of these I hoped to get an Opportunity of returning into *Europe:* I therefore most humbly entreated his Royal Favour to
give Order, that I should be conducted in Safety to *Nangasac.* To this I
added another Petition, that for the sake of my Patron the King of
Luggnagg, his Majesty would condescend to excuse my performing the
Ceremony imposed on my Countrymen, of *trampling upon the Crucifix;*° because I had been thrown into his Kingdom by my Misfortunes,
without any Intention of trading. When this latter Petition was inter-

Yedo: Toyko.   *Low-Dutch:* Dutch, as opposed to what was called "High Dutch," or
German.   *Trampling upon the crucifix:* This passage alludes to European tales about
the Japanese Inquisition's ritual of *Yefumi,* described in several early travel books, including Herman Moll's 1712 *Atlas Geographus.* We learn here that "none suspected to be a
Christian is suffered to enter any Part of the Empire before he has trampled on a Crucifix,
as a testimony that he is no Christian; and that the *Dutch,* when ask'd, If they are Christians? reply, they are *Hollanders*" (820). For more information, see John A. Dussinger,
"Gulliver in Japan: Another Possible Source," *Notes and Queries* 39, December 1992:
464–67.

preted to the Emperor, he seemed a little surprised; and said, he believed I was the first of my Countrymen who ever made any Scruple in this Point; and that he began to doubt whether I were a real *Hollander* or no; but rather suspected I must be a CHRISTIAN. However, for the Reasons I had offered, but chiefly to gratify the King of *Luggnagg,* by an uncommon Mark of his Favour, he would comply with the *singularity* of my Humour; but the Affair must be managed with Dexterity, and his Officers should be commanded to let me pass as it were by Forgetfulness. For he assured me, that if the Secret should be discovered by my Countrymen, the *Dutch,* they would cut my throat in the Voyage. I returned my Thanks by the Interpreter for so unusual a Favour; and some Troops being at that Time on their March to *Nangasac,* the Commanding Officer had Orders to convey me safe thither, with particular Instructions about the Business of the *Crucifix.*

On the 9th Day of *June,* 1709, I arrived at *Nangasac,* after a very long and troublesome Journey. I soon fell into Company of some *Dutch* Sailors belonging to the *Amboyna* of *Amsterdam,* a stout Ship of 450 Tuns. I had lived long in *Holland,* pursuing my Studies at *Leyden,* and I spoke *Dutch* well: The Seamen soon knew from whence I came last; they were curious to enquire into my Voyages and Course of Life. I made up a Story as short and probable as I could, but concealed the greatest Part. I knew many Persons in *Holland;* I was able to invent Names for my Parents, whom I pretended to be obscure People in the Province of *Guelderland.* I would have given the Captain (one *Theodorus Vangrult*) what he pleased to ask for my Voyage to *Holland;* but, understanding I was a Surgeon, he was contented to take half the usual Rate, on Condition that I would serve him in the Way of my Calling. Before we took Shipping, I was often asked by some of the Crew, whether I had performed the Ceremony abovementioned? I evaded the Question by general Answers, that I had satisfied the Emperor and Court in all Particulars. However, a malicious Rogue of a Skipper° went to an Officer, and pointing to me, told him, I had not yet *trampled on the Crucifix:* But the other, who had received Instructions to let me pass, gave the Rascal twenty Strokes on the Shoulders with a Bamboo; after which I was no more troubled with such Questions.

Nothing happened worth mentioning in this Voyage. We sailed with a fair Wind to the *Cape of Good Hope,* where we staid only to take in fresh Water. On the 6th of *April* we arrived safe at *Amsterdam,* having lost only three Men by Sickness in the Voyage, and a fourth who fell

Skipper: Seaman.

from the Fore-mast into the Sea, not far from the Coast of *Guinea*. From *Amsterdam* I soon after set sail for *England* in a small Vessel belonging to that City.

On the 10th of *April*, 1710, we put in at the *Downs*. I landed the next Morning, and saw once more my Native Country after an Absence of five Years and six Months compleat. I went strait to *Redriff*, whither I arrived the same Day at two in the Afternoon, and found my Wife and Family in good Health.

The End of the Third Part

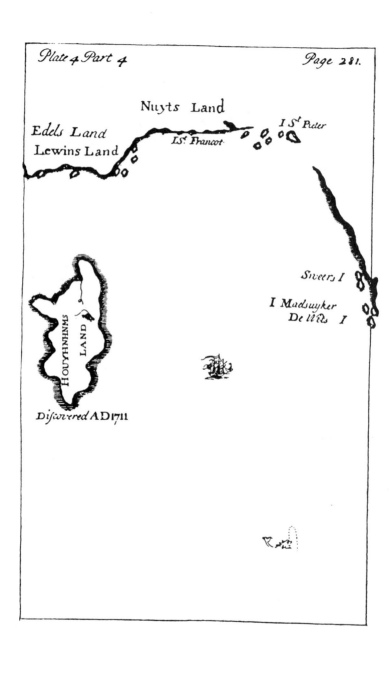

Plate 4 Part 4

Page 281.

Nuyts Land

Edels Land
Lewins Land

I S.t Francot

I S.t Pieter

HOUYHNHNMS LAND

Discovered A D 1711

Sweers I

I Madsuyker
De Wits I

PART IV

A Voyage to the Country of the Houyhnhnms

CHAPTER I

The Author sets out as Captain of a Ship. His Men conspire against him, confine him a long Time to his Cabbin, set him on Shore in an un-known Land. He travels up into the Country. The Yahoos, *a strange Sort of Animal, described. The Author meets two* Houyhnhnms.

I continued at home with my Wife and Children about five Months in a very happy Condition, if I could have learned the Lesson of know-ing when I was well. I left my poor Wife big with Child, and accepted an advantageous Offer made me to be Captain of the *Adventure,* a stout Merchant-man of 350 Tuns: For I understood Navigation well, and being grown weary of a Surgeon's Employment at Sea, which however I could exercise upon Occasion, I took a skilful young Man of that Call-ing, one *Robert Purefoy,* into my Ship. We set sail from *Portsmouth* upon the 7th Day of *September,* 1710; on the 14th we met with Captain *Po-cock* of *Bristol,* at *Tenariff,* who was going to the Bay of *Campeachy,*° to cut Logwood. On the 16th he was parted from us by a Storm: I heard since my Return, that his Ship foundered, and none escaped, but one Cabbin-Boy. He was an honest Man, and a good Sailor, but a little too positive in his own Opinions, which was the Cause of his Destruction,

Campeachy: Campeche, in Mexico's Yucatán Peninsula.

as it hath been of several others. For if he had followed my Advice, he might at this Time have been safe at home with his Family as well as my self.

I had several Men died in my Ship of *Calentures,*° so that I was forced to get Recruits out of *Barbadoes,* and the *Leeward Islands,* where I touched by the Direction of the Merchants who employed me; which I had soon too much Cause to repent; for I found afterwards that most of them had been Buccaneers. I had fifty Hands on Board; and my Orders were, that I should trade with the *Indians* in the *South-Sea,* and make what Discoveries I could. These Rogues whom I had picked up, debauched my other Men, and they all formed a Conspiracy to seize the Ship and secure me; which they did one Morning, rushing into my Cabbin, and binding me Hand and Foot, threatening to throw me overboard, if I offered to stir. I told them, I was their Prisoner, and would submit. This they made me swear to do, and then unbound me, only fastening one of my Legs with a Chain near my Bed; and placed a Centry at my Door with his Piece charged, who was commanded to shoot me dead if I attempted my Liberty. They sent me down Victuals and Drink, and took the Government of the Ship to themselves. Their Design was to turn Pirates, and plunder the *Spaniards,* which they could not do, till they got more Men. But first they resolved to sell the Goods in the Ship, and then go to *Madagascar* for Recruits, several among them having died since my Confinement. They sailed many Weeks, and traded with the *Indians;* but I knew not what Course they took, being kept close Prisoner in my Cabbin, and expecting nothing less than to be murdered, as they often threatened me.

Upon the 9th Day of *May,* 1711, one *James Welch* came down to my Cabbin; and said he had Orders from the Captain to set me ashore. I expostulated with him, but in vain; neither would he so much as tell me who their new Captain was. They forced me into the Long-boat, letting me put on my best Suit of Cloaths, which were as good as new, and a small Bundle of Linnen, but no Arms except my Hanger; and they were so civil as not to search my Pockets, into which I conveyed what Money I had, with some other little Necessaries. They rowed about a League; and then set me down on a Strand. I desired them to tell me what Country it was: They all swore, they knew no more than my self, but said, that the Captain (as they called him) was resolved, after they had sold the Lading, to get rid of me in the first Place where they discovered Land. They pushed off immediately, advising me to make haste, for fear of being overtaken by the Tide; and bade me farewell.

Calentures: Tropical fever.

In this desolate Condition I advanced forward, and soon got upon firm Ground, where I sat down on a Bank to rest my self, and consider what I had best to do. When I was a little refreshed, I went up into the Country, resolving to deliver my self to the first Savages I should meet; and purchase my Life from them by some Bracelets, Glass Rings, and other Toys, which Sailors usually provide themselves with in those Voyages, and whereof I had some about me: The Land was divided by long Rows of Trees, not regularly planted, but naturally growing; there was great Plenty of Grass, and several Fields of Oats. I walked very circumspectly for fear of being surprised, or suddenly shot with an Arrow from behind, or on either Side. I fell into a beaten Road, where I saw many Tracks of human Feet, and some of Cows, but most of Horses. At last I beheld several Animals in a Field, and one or two of the same Kind sitting in Trees. Their Shape was very singular, and deformed, which a little discomposed me, so that I lay down behind a Thicket to observe them better. Some of them coming forward near the Place where I lay, gave me an Opportunity of distinctly marking their Form. Their Heads and Breasts were covered with a thick Hair, some frizzled and others lank; they had Beards like Goats, and a Long Ridge of Hair down their Backs, and the fore Parts of their Legs and Feet; but the rest of their Bodies were bare, so that I might see their Skins, which were of a brown Buff Colour. They had no Tails, nor any Hair at all on their Buttocks, except about the *Anus;* which, I presume Nature had placed there to defend them as they sat on the Ground; for this Posture they used, as well as lying down, and often stood on their hind Feet. They climbed high Trees, as nimbly as a Squirrel, for they had strong extended Claws before and behind, terminating in sharp Points, and hooked. They would often spring, and bound, and leap with prodigious Agility. The Females were not so large as the Males; they had long lank Hair on their Heads, and only a Sort of Down on the rest of their Bodies, except about the *Anus,* and *Pudenda.* Their Dugs° hung between their fore Feet, and often reached almost to the Ground as they walked. The Hair of both Sexes was of several Colours, brown, red, black and yellow. Upon the whole, I never beheld in all my Travels so disagreeable an Animal, or one against which I naturally conceived so strong an Antipathy. So that thinking I had seen enough, full of Contempt and Aversion, I got up and pursued the beaten Road, hoping it might direct me to the Cabbin° of some *Indian.* I had not gone far when I met one of these Creatures full in my Way, and coming up directly to me. The ugly

Dugs: Breasts.　　**Cabbin:** Hut.

Monster, when he saw me, distorted several Ways every Feature of his
Visage, and stared as at an Object he had never seen before; then approaching nearer, lifted up his fore Paw, whether out of Curiosity or
Mischief, I could not tell: But I drew my Hanger, and gave him a good
Blow with the flat Side of it; for I durst not strike him with the Edge,
fearing the Inhabitants might be provoked against me, if they should
come to know, that I had killed or maimed any of their Cattle. When
the Beast felt the Smart, he drew back, and roared so loud, that a Herd
of at least forty came flocking about me from the next Field, howling
and making odious Faces; but I ran to the Body of a Tree, and leaning my
Back against it, kept them off, by waving my Hanger. Several of this cursed
Brood getting hold of the Branches behind, leaped up into the Tree, from
whence they began to discharge their Excrements on my Head: However,
I escaped pretty well, by sticking close to the Stem of the Tree, but was
almost stifled with the Filth, which fell about me on every Side.

In the Midst of this Distress, I observed them all to run away on a
sudden as fast as they could; at which I ventured to leave the Tree, and
pursue the Road, wondering what it was that could put them into this
Fright. But looking on my Left-Hand, I saw a Horse walking softly in
the Field; which my Persecutors having sooner discovered, was the
Cause of their Flight. The Horse started a little when he came near me,
but soon recovering himself, looked full in my Face with manifest Tokens of Wonder: He viewed my Hands and Feet, walking round me
several times. I would have pursued my Journey, but he placed himself
directly in the Way, yet looking with a very mild Aspect, never offering
the least Violence. We stood gazing at each other for some time; at last
I took the Boldness, to reach my Hand towards his Neck, with a Design
to stroak it; using the common Style and Whistle of Jockies when they
are going to handle a strange Horse. But, this Animal seeming to receive my Civilities with Disdain, shook his Head, and bent his Brows,
softly raising up his Left Fore-Foot to remove my Hand. Then he
neighed three or four times, but in so different a Cadence, that I almost
began to think he was speaking to himself in some Language of his own.

While He and I were thus employed, another Horse came up; who
applying himself to the first in a very formal Manner, they gently struck
each others Right Hoof before, neighing several times by Turns, and
varying the Sound, which seemed to be almost articulate. They went
some Paces off, as if it were to confer together, walking Side by Side,
backward and forward, like Persons deliberating upon some Affair of
Weight; but often turning their Eyes towards me, as it were to watch
that I might not escape. I was amazed to see such Actions and Behav-

iour in Brute Beasts; and concluded with myself, that if the Inhabitants of this Country were endued with a proportionable Degree of Reason, they must needs be the wisest People upon Earth. This Thought gave me so much Comfort, that I resolved to go forward until I could discover some House or Village, or meet with any of the Natives; leaving the two Horses to discourse together as they pleased. But the first, who was a Dapple-Grey, observing me to steal off, neighed after me in so expressive a Tone, that I fancied myself to understand what he meant; whereupon I turned back, and came near him, to expect his farther Commands; but concealing my Fear as much as I could; for I began to be in some Pain, how this Adventure might terminate: and the Reader will easily believe I did not much like my present Situation.

The two Horses came up close to me, looking with great Earnestness upon my Face and Hands. The grey Steed rubbed my Hat all round with his Right Fore-hoof, and discomposed it so much, that I was forced to adjust it better, by taking it off, and settling it again; whereat both he and his Companion (who was a brown Bay) appeared to be much surprized; the latter felt the Lappet of my Coat, and finding it to hang loose about me, they both looked with new Signs of Wonder. He stroked my Right Hand, seeming to admire the Softness, and Colour; but he squeezed it so hard between his Hoof and his Pastern, that I was forced to roar; after which they both touched me with all possible Tenderness. They were under great Perplexity about my Shoes and Stockings, which they felt very often, neighing to each other, and using various Gestures, not unlike those of a Philosopher,° when he would attempt to solve some new and difficult Phænomenon.

Upon the whole, the Behaviour of these Animals was so orderly and rational, so acute and judicious, that I at last concluded, they must needs be Magicians, who had thus metamorphosed themselves upon some Design; and seeing a Stranger in the Way, were resolved to divert themselves with him; or perhaps were really amazed at the Sight of a Man so very different in Habit, Feature and Complexion from those who might probably live in so remote a Climate. Upon the Strength of this Reasoning, I ventured to address them in the following Manner: Gentlemen, if you be Conjurers, as I have good Cause to believe, you can understand any Language; therefore I make bold to let your Worships know, that I am a poor distressed *Englishman*, driven by his Misfortunes upon your Coast; and I entreat one of you, to let me ride upon his Back, as if he were a real Horse, to some House or Village, where I

Philosopher: Scientist.

can be relieved. In return of which Favour, I will make you a Present of this Knife and Bracelet, (taking them out of my Pocket.) The two Creatures stood silent while I spoke, seeming to listen with great Attention; and when I had ended, they neighed frequently towards each other, as if they were engaged in serious Conversation. I plainly observed, that their Language expressed the Passions very well, and the Words might with little Pains be resolved into an Alphabet more easily than the *Chinese*.

I could frequently distinguish the Word *Yahoo*, which was repeated by each of them several times; and although it were impossible for me to conjecture what it meant, yet while the two Horses were busy in Conversation, I endeavoured to practice this Word upon my Tongue; and as soon as they were silent, I boldly pronounced *Yahoo* in a loud Voice, imitating, at the same time, as near as I could, the Neighing of a Horse; at which they were both visibly surprized, and the Grey repeated the same Word twice, as if he meant to teach me the right Accent, wherein I spoke after him as well as I could, and found myself perceivably to improve every time, although very far from any Degree of Perfection. Then the Bay tried me with a second Word, much harder to be pronounced; but reducing it to the *English Orthography,* may be spelt thus, *Houyhnhnm.* I did not succeed in this so well as the former, but after two or three farther Trials, I had better Fortune; and they both appeared amazed at my Capacity.

After some farther Discourse, which I then conjectured might relate to me, the two Friends took their Leaves, with the same Compliment of striking each other's Hoof; and the Grey made me Signs that I should walk before him; wherein I thought it prudent to comply, till I could find a better Director. When I offered to slacken my Pace, he would cry *Hhuun, Hhuun;* I guessed his Meaning, and gave him to understand, as well as I could, that I was weary, and not able to walk faster; upon which, he would stand a while to let me rest.

CHAPTER II

The Author conducted by a Houyhnhnm *to his House. The House described. The Author's Reception. The Food of the* Houyhnhnms. *The Author in Distress for want of Meat, is at last relieved. His Manner of feeding in that Country.*

Having travelled about three Miles, we came to a long Kind of Building, made of Timber, stuck in the Ground, and wattled a-cross;

the Roof was low, and covered with Straw. I now began to be a little comforted; and took out some Toys, which Travellers usually carry for Presents to the Savage *Indians* of *America* and other Parts, in hopes the People of the House would be thereby encouraged to receive me kindly. The Horse made me a Sign to go in first; it was a large Room with a smooth Clay Floor, and a Rack and Manger extending the whole Length on one Side. There were three Nags, and two Mares, not eating, but some of them sitting down upon their Hams, which I very much wondered at; but wondered more to see the rest employed in domestick Business: The last seemed but ordinary Cattle; however this confirmed my first Opinion, that a People who could so far civilize brute Animals, must needs excel in Wisdom all the Nations of the World. The Grey came in just after, and thereby prevented any ill Treatment, which the others might have given me. He neighed to them several times in a Style of Authority, and received Answers.

Beyond this Room there were three others, reaching the Length of the House, to which you passed through three Doors, opposite to each other, in the Manner of a Vista:° We went through the second Room towards the third; here the Grey walked in first, beckoning me to attend: I waited in the second Room, and got ready my Presents, for the Master and Mistress of the House: They were two Knives, three Bracelets of false Pearl, a small Looking Glass and a Bead Necklace. The Horse neighed three or four Times, and I waited to hear some Answers in a human Voice, but I heard no other Returns than in the same Dialect, only one or two a little shriller than his. I began to think that this House must belong to some Person of great Note among them, because there appeared so much ceremony before I could gain Admittance. But, that a Man of Quality should be served all by Horses, was beyond my Comprehension. I feared my Brain was disturbed by my Sufferings and Misfortunes: I roused my self, and looked about me in the Room where I was left alone; this was furnished as the first, only after a more elegant Manner. I rubbed mine Eyes often, but the same Objects still occurred. I pinched my Arms and Sides, to awake my self, hoping I might be in a Dream. I then absolutely concluded, that all these Appearances could be nothing else but Necromancy and Magick. But I had no Time to pursue these Reflections; for the Grey Horse came to the Door, and made me a Sign to follow him into the third Room; where I saw a very comely Mare, together with a Colt and Fole, sitting

Vista: Open corridor.

on their Haunches, upon Mats of Straw, not unartfully made, and perfectly neat and clean.

The Mare soon after my Entrance, rose from her Mat, and coming
up close, after having nicely observed my Hands and Face, gave me a
most contemptuous Look; then turning to the Horse, I heard the Word
Yahoo often repeated betwixt them; the meaning of which Word I could
not then comprehend, although it were the first I had learned to pronounce; but I was soon better informed, to my everlasting Mortification: For the Horse beckoning to me with his Head, and repeating the
Word *Hhuun, Hhuun,* as he did upon the Road, which I understood
was to attend him, led me out into a kind of Court, where was another
Building at some Distance from the House. Here we entered, and I saw
three of those detestable Creatures, which I first met after my landing,
feeding upon Roots, and the Flesh of some Animals, which I afterwards
found to be that of Asses and Dogs, and now and then a Cow dead by
Accident or Disease. They were all tied by the Neck with strong Wyths,
fastened to a Beam; they held their Food between the Claws of their
fore Feet, and tore it with their Teeth.

The Master Horse ordered a Sorrel Nag, one of his Servants, to
untie the largest of these Animals, and take him into the Yard. The Beast
and I were brought close together; and our Countenances diligently
compared, both by Master and Servant, who thereupon repeated several
Times the Word *Yahoo.* My Horror and Astonishment are not to be
described, when I observed, in this abominable Animal, a perfect
human Figure; the Face of it indeed was flat and broad, the Nose depressed, the Lips large, and the Mouth wide: But these Differences are
common to all savage Nations, where the Lineaments of the Countenance are distorted by the Natives suffering their Infants to lie grovelling on the Earth, or by carrying them on their Backs, nuzzling with
their Face against the Mother's Shoulders. The Fore-feet of the *Yahoo*
differed from my Hands in nothing else, but the Length of the Nails,
the Coarseness and Brownness of the Palms, and the Hairiness on the
Backs. There was the same Resemblance between our Feet, with the
same Differences, which I knew very well, although the Horses did not,
because of my Shoes and Stockings; the same in every Part of our Bodies, except as to Hairiness and Colour, which I have already described.

The great Difficulty that seemed to stick with the two Horses, was,
to see the rest of my Body so very different from that of a *Yahoo,* for
which I was obliged to my Cloaths, whereof they had no Conception:
The Sorrel Nag offered me a Root, which he held (after their Manner,
as we shall describe in its proper Place) between his Hoof and Pastern;

I took it in my Hand, and having smelt it, returned it to him again as civilly as I could. He brought out of the *Yahoo*'s Kennel a Piece of Ass's Flesh, but it smelt so offensively that I turned from it with loathing; he then threw it to the *Yahoo*, by whom it was greedily devoured. He afterwards shewed me a Wisp of Hay, and a Fettlock full of Oats; but I shook my Head, to signify, that neither of these were Food for me. And indeed, I now apprehended, that I must absolutely starve, if I did not get to some of my own Species: For as to those filthy *Yahoos*, although there were few greater Lovers of Mankind, at that time, than myself; yet I confess I never saw any sensitive Being so detestable on all Accounts; and the more I came near them, the more hateful they grew, while I stayed in that Country. This the Master Horse observed by my Behaviour, and therefore sent the *Yahoo* back to his Kennel. He then put his Forehoof to his Mouth, at which I was much surprized, although he did it with Ease, and with a Motion that appear'd perfectly natural; and made other Signs to know what I would eat; but I could not return him such an Answer as he was able to apprehend; and if he had understood me I did not see how it was possible to contrive any way for finding myself Nourishment. While we were thus engaged, I observed a Cow passing by; whereupon I pointed to her, and expressed a Desire to let me go and milk her. This had its Effect; for he led me back into the House, and ordered a Mare-servant to open a Room, where a good Store of Milk lay in Earthen and Wooden Vessels, after a very orderly and cleanly Manner. She gave me a large Bowl full, of which I drank very heartily, and found myself well refreshed.

About Noon I saw coming towards the House a Kind of Vehicle, drawn like a Sledge by four *Yahoos*. There was in it an old Steed, who seemed to be of Quality; he alighted with his Hind-feet forward, having by Accident got a Hurt in his Left Fore-foot. He came to dine with our Horse, who received him with great Civility. They dined in the best Room, and had Oats boiled in Milk for the second Course, which the old Horse eat warm, but the rest cold. Their Mangers were placed circular in the Middle of the Room, and divided into several Partitions, round which they sat on their Haunches upon Bosses of Straw. In the Middle was a large Rack with Angles answering to every Partition of the Manger. So that each Horse and Mare eat their own Hay, and their own Mash of Oats and Milk, with much Decency and Regularity. The Behaviour of the young Colt and Fole appeared very modest; and that of the Master and Mistress extremely chearful and complaisant° to their

complaisant: Polite.

Guest. The Grey ordered me to stand by him; and much Discourse passed between him and his Friend concerning me, as I found by the Stranger's often looking on me, and the frequent Repetition of the Word *Yahoo*.

I happened to wear my Gloves; which the Master Grey observing, seemed perplexed; discovering Signs of Wonder what I had done to my Fore-feet; he put his Hoof three or four times to them, as if he would signify, that I should reduce them to their former Shape, which I presently did, pulling off both my Gloves, and putting them into my Pocket. This occasioned farther Talk, and I saw the Company was pleased with my Behaviour, whereof I soon found the good Effects. I was ordered to speak the few Words I understood; and while they were at Dinner, the Master taught me the Names for Oats, Milk, Fire, Water, and some others; which I could readily pronounce after him; having from my Youth a great Facility in learning Languages.

When Dinner was done, the Master Horse took me aside, and by Signs and Words made me understand the Concern he was in, that I had nothing to eat. Oats in their Tongue are called *Hlunnh*. This Word I pronounced two or three times; for although I had refused them at first, yet upon second Thoughts, I considered that I could contrive to make of them a Kind of Bread, which might be sufficient with Milk to keep me alive, till I could make my Escape to some other Country, and to Creatures of my own Species. The Horse immediately ordered a white Mare-servant of his Family to bring me a good Quantity of Oats in a Sort of wooden Tray. These I heated before the Fire as well as I could, and rubbed them till the Husks came off, which I made a shift to winnow from the Grain; I ground and beat them between two Stones, then took Water, and made them into a Paste or Cake, which I toasted at the Fire, and eat warm with Milk. It was at first a very insipid Diet, although common enough in many Parts of *Europe*, but grew tolerable by Time; and having been often reduced to hard Fare in my Life, this was not the first Experiment I had made how easily Nature is satisfied. And I cannot but observe, that I never had one Hour's Sickness, while I staid in this Island. It is true, I sometimes made a shift to catch a Rabbet, or Bird, by Springes made of *Yahoos* Hairs; and I often gathered wholesome Herbs, which I boiled, or eat as Salades with my Bread; and now and then, for a Rarity, I made a little Butter, and drank the Whey. I was at first at a great Loss for Salt; but Custom soon reconciled the Want of it; and I am confident that the frequent Use of Salt among us is an Effect of Luxury, and was first introduced only as a Provocative to Drink; except where it is necessary for preserving of Flesh in long

Voyages, or in Places remote from great Markets. For we observe no Animal to be fond of it but Man: And as to myself, when I left this Country, it was a great while before I could endure the Taste of it in any thing that I eat.

This is enough to say upon the Subject of my Dyet, wherewith other Travellers fill their Books, as if the Readers were personally concerned, whether we fare well or ill. However, it was necessary to mention this Matter, lest the World should think it impossible that I could find Sustenance for three Years in such a Country, and among such Inhabitants.

When it grew towards Evening, the Master Horse ordered a Place for me to lodge in; it was but Six Yards from the House, and separated from the Stable of the *Yahoos*. Here I got some Straw, and covering myself with my own Cloaths, slept very sound. But I was in a short time better accommodated, as the Reader shall know hereafter, when I come to treat more particularly about my Way of living.

CHAPTER III

The Author studious to learn the Language, the Houyhnhnm *his Master assists in teaching him. The Language described. Several* Houyhnhnms *of Quality come out of Curiosity to see the Author. He gives his Master a short Account of his Voyage.*

My principal Endeavour was to learn the Language, which my Master (for so I shall henceforth call him) and his Children, and every Servant of his House were desirous to teach me. For they looked upon it as a Prodigy, that a brute Animal should discover such Marks of a rational Creature. I pointed to every thing, and enquired the Name of it, which I wrote down in my *Journal Book* when I was alone, and corrected my bad Accent, by desiring those of the Family to pronounce it often. In this Employment, a Sorrel Nag, one of the under Servants, was very ready to assist me.

In speaking, they pronounce through the Nose and Throat, and their Language approaches nearest to the *High Dutch* or *German,* of any I know in *Europe;* but is much more graceful and significant. The Emperor *Charles* V. made almost the same Observation when he said, That if he were to speak to his Horse, it should be in *High Dutch.*

The Curiosity and Impatience of my Master were so great, that he spent many Hours of his Leisure to instruct me. He was convinced (as he afterwards told me) that I must be a *Yahoo,* but my Teachableness, Civility and Cleanliness astonished him; which were Qualities altogether

so opposite to those Animals. He was most perplexed about my
Cloaths, reasoning sometimes with himself, whether they were a Part of
my Body; for I never pulled them off till the Family were asleep, and got
them on before they waked in the Morning. My Master was eager to
learn from whence I came; how I acquired those Appearances of Reason, which I discovered° in all my Actions; and to know my Story from
my own Mouth, which he hoped he should soon do by the great Proficiency I made in learning and pronouncing their Words and Sentences.
To help my Memory, I formed all I learned into the *English* Alphabet,
and writ the Words down with the Translations. This last, after some
time, I ventured to do in my Master's Presence. It cost me much Trouble to explain to him what I was doing; for the Inhabitants have not the
least Idea of Books or Literature.

In about ten Weeks time I was able to understand most of his Questions; and in three Months could give him some tolerable Answers. He
was extremely curious to know from what Part of the Country I came,
and how I was taught to imitate a rational Creature; because the *Yahoos*,
(whom he saw I exactly resembled in my Head, Hands and Face, that
were only visible,) with some Appearance of Cunning, and the strongest
Disposition to Mischief, were observed to be the most unteachable of
all Brutes. I answered; that I came over the Sea, from a far Place, with
many others of my own Kind, in a great hollow Vessel made of the
Bodies of Trees: That, my Companions forced me to land on this Coast,
and then left me to shift for myself. It was with some Difficulty, and by
the Help of many Signs, that I brought him to understand me. He replied, That I must needs be mistaken, or that I *said the thing which was
not*. (For they have no Word in their Language to express Lying or
Falshood.) He knew it was impossible that there could be a Country
beyond the Sea, or that a Parcel of Brutes could move a wooden Vessel
whither they pleased upon Water. He was sure no *Houyhnhnm* alive
could make such a Vessel, or would trust *Yahoos* to manage it.

The Word *Houyhnhnm,* in their Tongue, signifies a *Horse;* and in its
Etymology, *the Perfection of Nature*. I told my Master, that I was at a
Loss for Expression, but would improve as fast as I could; and hoped in
a short time I should be able to tell him Wonders: He was pleased to
direct his own Mare, his Colt and Fole, and the Servants of the Family
to take all Opportunities of instructing me; and every Day for two or
three Hours, he was at the same Pains himself: Several Horses and
Mares of Quality in the Neighbourhood came often to our House,

discovered: Displayed, exhibited.

upon the Report spread of a wonderful *Yahoo*, that could speak like a *Houyhnhnm*, and seemed in his Words and Actions to discover some Glimmerings of Reason. These delighted to converse with me; they put many Questions, and received such Answers, as I was able to return. By all which Advantages, I made so great a Progress, that in five Months from my Arrival, I understood whatever was spoke, and could express myself tolerably well.

The *Houyhnhnms* who came to visit my Master, out of a Design of seeing and talking with me, could hardly believe me to be a right *Yahoo*, because my Body had a different Covering from others of my Kind. They were astonished to observe me without the usual Hair or Skin, except on my Head, Face and Hands: But I discovered that Secret to my Master, upon an Accident, which happened about a Fortnight before.

I have already told the Reader, that every Night when the Family were gone to Bed, it was my Custom to strip and cover myself with my Cloaths: It happened one Morning early, that my Master sent for me, by the Sorrel Nag, who was his Valet; when he came, I was fast asleep, my Cloaths fallen off on one Side, and my Shirt above my Waste. I awaked at the Noise he made, and observed him to deliver his Message in some Disorder; after which he went to my Master, and in a great Fright gave him a very confused Account of what he had seen: This I presently discovered; for going as soon as I was dressed, to pay my Attendance upon his Honour, he asked me the Meaning of what his Servant had reported; that I was not the same Thing when I slept as I appeared to be at other times; that his Valet assured him, some Part of me was white, some yellow, at least not so white, and some brown.

I had hitherto concealed the Secret of my Dress, in order to distinguish myself as much as possible, from that cursed Race of *Yahoos;* but now I found it in vain to do so any longer. Besides, I considered that my Cloaths and Shoes would soon wear out, which already were in a declining Condition, and must be supplied by some Contrivance from the Hides of *Yahoos,* or other Brutes; whereby the whole Secret would be known. I therefore told my Master, that in the Country from whence I came, those of my Kind always covered their Bodies with the Hairs of certain Animals prepared by Art, as well for Decency, as to avoid Inclemencies of Air both hot and cold; of which, as to my own Person I would give him immediate Conviction, if he pleased to command me; only desiring his Excuse, if I did not expose those Parts that Nature taught us to conceal. He said, my Discourse was all very strange, but especially the last Part; for he could not understand why Nature should

teach us to conceal what Nature had given. That neither himself nor
Family were ashamed of any Parts of their Bodies; but however I might
do as I pleased. Whereupon I first unbuttoned my Coat, and pulled it
off. I did the same with my Wastecoat; I drew off my Shoes, Stockings
and Breeches. I let my Shirt down to my Waste, and drew up the
Bottom, fastening it like a Girdle about my Middle to hide my Naked-
ness.

My Master observed the whole Performance with great Signs of
Curiosity and Admiration. He took up all my Cloaths in his Pastern,
one Piece after another, and examined them diligently; he then
stroaked my Body very gently, and looked round me several Times;
after which he said, it was plain I must be a perfect *Yahoo;* but that I
differed very much from the rest of my Species, in the Whiteness, and
Smoothness of my Skin, my want of Hair in several Parts of my Body,
the Shape and Shortness of my Claws behind and before, and my Affectation of walking continually on my two hinder Feet. He desired to
see no more; and gave me leave to put on my Cloaths again, for I was
shuddering with Cold.

I expressed my Uneasiness at his giving me so often the Appellation
of *Yahoo,* an odious Animal, for which I had so utter an Hatred and
Contempt. I begged he would forbear applying that Word to me, and
take the same Order in his Family, and among his Friends whom he
suffered to see me. I requested likewise, that the Secret of my having a
false Covering to my Body might be known to none but himself, at least
as long as my present Cloathing should last: For as to what the Sorrel
Nag his Valet had observed, his Honour might command him to conceal it.

All this my Master very graciously consented to; and thus the Secret
was kept till my Cloaths began to wear out, which I was forced to supply
by several Contrivances, that shall hereafter be mentioned. In the mean
Time, he desired I would go on with my utmost Diligence to learn their
Language, because he was more astonished at my Capacity for Speech
and Reason, than at the Figure of my Body, whether it were covered or
no; adding, that he waited with some Impatience to hear the Wonders
which I promised to tell him.

From thenceforward he doubled the Pains he had been at to instruct me; he brought me into all Company, and made them treat me
with Civility, because, as he told them privately, this would put me into
good Humour, and make me more diverting.

Every Day when I waited on him, beside the Trouble he was at in
teaching, he would ask me several Questions concerning my self, which

I answered as well as I could; and by those Means he had already received some general Ideas, although very imperfect. It would be tedious to relate the several Steps, by which I advanced to a more regular Conversation: But the first Account I gave of my self in any Order and Length, was to this Purpose:

That, I came from a very far Country, as I already had attempted to tell him, with about fifty more of my own Species; that we travelled upon the Seas, in a great hollow Vessel made of Wood, and larger than his Honour's House. I described the Ship to him in the best Terms I could; and explained by the Help of my Handkerchief displayed, how it was driven forward by the Wind. That, upon a Quarrel among us, I was set on Shoar on this Coast, where I walked forward without knowing whither, till he delivered me from the Persecution of those execrable *Yahoos.* He asked me, Who made the Ship, and how it was possible that the *Houyhnhnms* of my Country would leave it to the Management of Brutes? My Answer was, that I durst proceed no farther in my Relation, unless he would give me his Word and Honour that he would not be offended; and then I would tell him the Wonders I had so often promised. He agreed; and I went on by assuring him, that the Ship was made by Creatures like myself, who in all the Countries I had travelled, as well as in my own, were the only governing, rational Animals; and that upon my Arrival hither, I was as much astonished to see the *Houyhnhnms* act like rational Beings, as he or his Friends could be in finding some Marks of Reason in a Creature he was pleased to call a *Yahoo;* to which I owned my Resemblance in every Part, but could not account for their degenerate and brutal Nature. I said farther, That if good Fortune ever restored me to my native Country, to relate my Travels hither, as I resolved to do; every Body would believe that I *said the Thing which was not;* that I invented the Story out of my own Head: And with all possible Respect to Himself, his Family, and Friends, and under his Promise of not being offended, our Countrymen would hardly think it probable, that a *Houyhnhnm* should be the presiding Creature of a Nation, and a *Yahoo* the Brute.

CHAPTER IV

The Houyhnhnms *Notion of Truth and Falshood. The Author's Discourse disapproved by his Master. The Author gives a more particular Account of himself, and the Accidents of his Voyage.*

My Master heard me with great Appearances of Uneasiness in his

Countenance; because *Doubting* or *not believing*, are so little known in this Country, that the Inhabitants cannot tell how to behave themselves under such Circumstances. And I remember in frequent Discourses with my Master concerning the Nature of Manhood,° in other Parts of the World; having Occasion to talk of *Lying*, and *false Representation*, it was with much Difficulty that he comprehended what I meant; although he had otherwise a most acute Judgment. For he argued thus; That the Use of Speech was to make us understand one another, and to receive Information of Facts; now if any one *said the Thing which was not*, these Ends were defeated; because I cannot properly be said to understand him; and I am so far from receiving Information, that he leaves me worse than in Ignorance; for I am led to believe a Thing *Black* when it is *White*, and *Short* when it is *Long*. And these were all the Notions he had concerning that Faculty of *Lying*, so perfectly well understood, and so universally practised among human Creatures.

To return from this Digression; when I asserted that the *Yahoos* were the only governing Animals in my Country, which my Master said was altogether past his Conception, he desired to know, whether we had *Houyhnhnms* among us, and what was their Employment: I told him, we had great Numbers; that in Summer they grazed in the Fields, and in Winter were kept in Houses, with Hay and Oats, where *Yahoo*-Servants were employed to rub their Skins smooth, comb their Manes, pick their Feet, serve them with Food, and make their Beds. I understand you well, said my Master; it is now very plain from all you have spoken, that whatever Share of Reason the *Yahoos* pretend to, the *Houyhnhnms* are your Masters; I heartily wish our *Yahoos* would be so tractable. I begged his Honour would please to excuse me from proceeding any farther, because I was very certain that the Account he expected from me would be highly displeasing. But he insisted in commanding me to let him know the best and the worst: I told him he should be obeyed. I owned, that the *Houyhnhnms* among us, whom we called *Horses*, were the most generous and comely Animal we had; that they excelled in Strength and Swiftness; and when they belonged to Persons of Quality, employed in Travelling, Racing, and drawing Chariots, they were treated with much Kindness and Care, till they fell into Diseases, or became foundered in the Feet; but then they were sold, and used to all kind of Drudgery till they died; after which their Skins were stripped and sold for what they were worth, and their Bodies left to be

Nature of Manhood: Human nature.

devoured by Dogs and Birds of Prey. But the common Race of Horses had not so good Fortune, being kept by Farmers and Carriers, and other mean People, who put them to greater Labour, and feed them worse. I described as well as I could, our Way of Riding; the Shape and Use of a Bridle, a Saddle, a Spur, and a Whip; of Harness and Wheels. I added, that we fastened Plates of a certain hard Substance called *Iron* at the Bottom of their Feet, to preserve their Hoofs from being broken by the Stony Ways on which we often travelled.

My Master, after some Expressions of great Indignation, wondered how we dared to venture upon a *Houyhnhnm's* Back; for he was sure, that the weakest Servant in his House would be able to shake off the strongest *Yahoo;* or by lying down, and rolling upon his Back, squeeze the Brute to Death. I answered, That our Horses were trained up from three or four Years old to the several Uses we intended them for; That if any of them proved intolerably vicious, they were employed for Carriages; that they were severely beaten while they were young for any mischievous Tricks: That the Males, designed for the common Use of Riding or Draught, were generally *castrated* about two Years after their Birth, to take down their Spirits, and make them more tame and gentle: That they were indeed sensible of Rewards and Punishments; but his Honour would please to consider, that they had not the least Tincture of Reason any more than the *Yahoos* in this Country.

It put me to the Pains of many Circumlocutions to give my Master a right Idea of what I spoke; for their Language doth not abound in Variety of Words, because their Wants and Passions are fewer than among us. But it is impossible to express his noble Resentment at our savage Treatment of the *Houyhnhnm* Race; particularly after I had explained the Manner and Use of *Castrating* Horses among us, to hinder them from propagating their Kind, and to render them more servile. He said, if it were possible there could be any Country where *Yahoos* alone were endued with Reason, they certainly must be the governing Animal, because Reason will in Time always prevail against Brutal Strength. But, considering the Frame of our Bodies, and especially of mine, he thought no Creature of equal Bulk was so ill-contrived, for employing that Reason in the common Offices of Life; whereupon he desired to know whether those among whom I lived, resembled me or the *Yahoos* of his Country. I assured him, that I was as well shaped as most of my Age; but the younger and the Females were much more soft and tender, and the Skins of the latter generally as white as Milk. He said, I differed indeed from other *Yahoos,* being much more cleanly, and not altogether so deformed; but in point of real Advantage, he thought I differed for the worse. That my Nails were of no Use either to my fore or hinder Feet: As to my fore Feet, he could not properly call them by that Name, for he never observed me to walk upon them; that they were too soft to bear the Ground; that I generally went with them uncovered, neither was the Covering I sometimes wore on them, of the same Shape, or so strong as that on my Feet behind. That I could not walk with any Security; for if either of my hinder Feet slipped, I must inevitably fall. He then began to find fault with other Parts of my Body; the Flatness of my Face, the Prominence of my Nose, mine Eyes placed directly in Front, so that I could not look on either Side without turning my Head: That I was not able to feed my self, without lifting one of my fore Feet to my Mouth: And therefore Nature had placed those Joints to answer that Necessity. He knew not what could be the Use of those several Clefts and Divisions in my Feet behind; that these were too soft to bear the Hardness and Sharpness of Stones without a Covering made from the Skin of some other Brute; that my whole Body wanted a Fence against Heat and Cold, which I was forced to put on and off every Day with Tediousness and Trouble. And lastly, that he observed every Animal in this Country naturally to abhor the *Yahoos*, whom the Weaker avoided, and the Stronger drove from them. So that supposing us to have the Gift of Reason, he could not see how it were possible to cure that natural Antipathy which every Creature discovered against us; nor consequently, how we could tame and render them serviceable. However, he would (as he said) debate the Matter no farther, because he was more desirous to know my own Story, the Country, where I was born, and the several Actions and Events of my Life before I came hither.

I assured him, how extreamly desirous I was that he should be satisfied in every Point; but I doubted much, whether it would be possible for me to explain my self on several Subjects whereof his Honour could have no Conception, because I saw nothing in his Country to which I could resemble them. That however, I would do my best, and strive to express my self by Similitudes, humbly desiring his Assistance when I wanted proper Words; which he was pleased to promise me.

I said, my Birth was of honest Parents, in an Island called *England,* which was remote from this Country, as many Days Journey as the strongest of his Honour's Servants could travel in the Annual Course of the Sun. That I was bred a Surgeon, whose Trade it is to cure Wounds and Hurts in the Body, got by Accident or Violence. That my Country was governed by a Female Man, whom we called a *Queen.* That I left it to get Riches, whereby I might maintain my self and Family when I should return. That in my last Voyage, I was Commander of the Ship and had about fifty *Yahoos* under me, many of which died at Sea, and I was forced to supply them by others picked out from several Nations. That our Ship was twice in Danger of being sunk; the first Time by a great Storm, and the second, by striking against a Rock. Here my Master interposed, by asking me, How I could persuade Strangers out of different Countries to venture with me, after the Losses I had sustained, and the Hazards I had run. I said, they were Fellows of desperate Fortunes, forced to fly from the Places of their Birth, on Account of their Poverty or their Crimes. Some were undone by Law-suits; others spent all they had in Drinking, Whoring and Gaming; others fled for Treason; many for Murder, Theft, Poysoning, Robbery, Perjury, Forgery, Coining false Money; for committing Rapes or Sodomy; for flying from their Colours,° or deserting to the Enemy; and most of them had broken Prison. None of these durst return to their native Countries for fear of being hanged, or of starving in a Jail; and therefore were under a Necessity of seeking a Livelihood in other Places.

During this Discourse, my Master was pleased often to interrupt me. I had made Use of many Circumlocutions in describing to him the Nature of the several Crimes, for which most of our Crew had been forced to fly their Country. This Labour took up several Days Conversation before he was able to comprehend me. He was wholly at a Loss to know what could be the Use or Necessity of practising those Vices. To clear up which I endeavoured to give him some Ideas of the Desire of Power and Riches; of the terrible Effects of Lust, Intemperance, Malice, and Envy. All this I was forced to define and describe by putting of Cases, and making Suppositions. After which, like one whose Imagination was struck with something never seen or heard of before, he would lift up his Eyes with Amazement and Indignation. Power, Government, War, Law, Punishment, and a Thousand other Things had no Terms, wherein that Language could express them; which made the Difficulty almost insuperable to give my Master any Conception of what I meant: But being of an excellent Understanding, much improved by Contemplation and Converse, he at last arrived at a competent Knowledge of what human Nature in our Parts of the World is capable to perform; and desired I would give him some particular Account of that Land, which we call *Europe,* especially, of my own Country.

flying from their Colours: Deserting.

CHAPTER V

The Author at his Master's Commands informs him of the State of
England. *The Causes of War among the Princes of* Europe. *The Author*
begins to explain the English *Constitution.*

The Reader may please to observe, that the following Extract of
many Conversations I had with my Master, contains a Summary of the
most material Points, which were discoursed at several times for above
two Years; his Honour often desiring fuller Satisfaction as I farther improved in the *Houyhnhnm* Tongue. I laid before him, as well as I could,
the whole State of *Europe;* I discoursed of Trade and Manufactures, of
Arts and Sciences; and the Answers I gave to all the Questions he made,
as they arose upon several Subjects, were a Fund of Conversation not to
be exhausted. But I shall here only set down the Substance of what
passed between us concerning my own Country, reducing it into Order
as well as I can, without any Regard to Time or other Circumstances,
while I strictly adhere to Truth. My only Concern is, that I shall hardly
be able to do Justice to my Master's Arguments and Expressions, which
must needs suffer by my Want of Capacity, as well as by a Translation
into our barbarous *English.*

In Obedience therefore to his Honour's Commands, I related to
him the *Revolution°* under the Prince of *Orange;* the long War with
France entered into by the said Prince, and renewed by his Successor
the present Queen; wherein the greatest Powers of *Christendom* were
engaged, and which still continued: I computed at his Request, that
about a Million of *Yahoos* might have been killed in the whole Progress
of it; and perhaps a Hundred or more Cities taken, and five times as
many Ships burnt or sunk.

He asked me what were the usual Causes or Motives that made one
Country go to War with another. I answered, they were innumerable;
but I should only mention a few of the chief. Sometimes the Ambition
of Princes, who never think they have Land or People enough to govern: Sometimes the Corruption of Ministers, who engage their Master
in a War in order to stifle or divert the Clamour of the Subjects against
their evil Administration. Difference in Opinions hath cost many Millions of Lives: For Instance, whether *Flesh* be *Bread,* or *Bread* be *Flesh:*
Whether the Juice of a certain *Berry* be *Blood* or *Wine:* Whether *Whis-*
tling be a Vice or a Virtue: Whether it be better to *kiss a Post,* or throw

Revolution: The revolution of 1688, when William of Orange replaced James II as the
British king.

it into the Fire: What is the best Colour for a *Coat*, whether *Black*, *White*, *Red* or *Grey*; and whether it should be *long* or *short*, *narrow* or *wide*, *dirty* or *clean*; with many more. Neither are any Wars so furious and bloody, or of so long Continuance, as those occasioned by Difference in Opinion, especially if it be in things indifferent.

Sometimes the Quarrel between two Princes is to decide which of them shall dispossess a Third of his Dominions, where neither of them pretend to any Right. Sometimes one Prince quarrelleth with another, for fear the other should quarrel with him. Sometimes a War is entered upon, because the Enemy is too *strong*, and sometimes because he is too *weak*. Sometimes our Neighbours *want* the *Things* which we *have*, or *have* the Things which we want; and we both fight, till they take ours or give us theirs. It is a very justifiable Cause of War to invade a Country after the People have been wasted by Famine, destroyed by Pestilence, or embroiled by Factions amongst themselves. It is justifiable to enter into a War against our nearest Ally, when one of his Towns lies convenient for us, or a Territory of Land, that would render our Dominions round and compact. If a Prince send Forces into a Nation, where the People are poor and ignorant, he may lawfully put half of them to Death, and make Slaves of the rest, in order to civilize and reduce° them from their barbarous Way of Living. It is a very kingly, honourable, and frequent Practice, when one Prince desires the Assistance of another to secure him against an Invasion, that the Assistant, when he hath driven out the Invader, should seize on the Dominions himself, and kill, imprison or banish the Prince he came to relieve. Allyance by Blood or Marriage, is a sufficient Cause of War between Princes; and the nearer the Kindred is, the greater is their Disposition to quarrel: *Poor* Nations are *hungry*, and *rich* Nations are *proud*; and Pride and Hunger will ever be at Variance. For these Reasons, the Trade of a *Soldier* is held the most honourable of all others: Because a *Soldier* is a *Yahoo* hired to kill in cold Blood as many of his own Species, who have never offended him, as possibly he can.

There is likewise a Kind of beggarly Princes in *Europe*, not able to make War by themselves, who hire out their Troops to richer Nations for so much a Day to each Man; of which they keep three Fourths to themselves, and it is the best Part of their Maintenance; such are those in many *Northern* Parts of *Europe*.

What you have told me, (said my Master) upon the Subject of War, doth indeed discover most admirably the Effects of that Reason you

reduce: Convert.

pretend to: However, it is happy that the *Shame* is greater than the *Danger;* and that Nature hath left you utterly uncapable of doing much Mischief: For your Mouths lying flat with your Faces, you can hardly bite each other to any Purpose, unless by Consent. Then, as to the Claws upon your Feet before and behind, they are so short and tender, that one of our *Yahoos* would drive a Dozen of yours before him. And therefore in recounting the Numbers of those who have been killed in Battle, I cannot but think that you have *said the Thing which is not.*

I could not forbear shaking my Head and smiling a little at his Ignorance. And, being no Stranger to the Art of War, I gave him a Description of Cannons, Culverins,° Muskets, Carabines,° Pistols, Bullets, Powder, Swords, Bayonets, Sieges, Retreats, Attacks, Undermines,° Countermines,° Bombardments, Seafights; Ships sunk with a Thousand Men; twenty Thousand killed on each Side; dying Groans, Limbs flying in the Air: Smoak, Noise, Confusion, trampling to Death under Horses Feet: Flight, Pursuit, Victory; Fields strewed with Carcases left for Food to Dogs, and Wolves, and Birds of Prey; Plundering, Stripping, Ravishing, Burning and Destroying. And, to set forth the Valour of my own dear Countrymen, I assured him, that I had seen them blow up a Hundred Enemies at once in a Siege, and as many in a Ship; and beheld the dead Bodies drop down in Pieces from the Clouds, to the great Diversion of all the Spectators.

I was going on to more Particulars, when my Master commanded me Silence. He said, whoever understood the Nature of *Yahoos* might easily believe it possible for so vile an Animal, to be capable of every Action I had named, if their Strength and Cunning equalled their Malice. But, as my Discourse had increased his Abhorrence of the whole Species, so he found it gave him a Disturbance in his Mind, to which he was wholly a Stranger before. He thought his Ears being used to such abominable Words, might by Degrees admit them with less Detestation. That, although he hated the *Yahoos* of this Country, yet he no more blamed them for their odious Qualities, than he did a *Gnnayh* (a Bird of Prey) for its Cruelty, or a sharp Stone for cutting his Hoof. But, when a Creature pretending to Reason, could be capable of such Enormities, he dreaded lest the Corruption of that Faculty might be worse than Brutality itself. He seemed therefore confident, that instead of Reason, we were only possessed of some Quality fitted to increase our

---

Culverins: Large cannons.   **Carabines:** Short firearms.   **Undermines:** Mines placed under the walls of a fortress.   **Countermines:** Mines placed by defenders of a fortress to intercept attackers.

natural Vices; as the Reflection from a troubled Stream returns the Image of an ill-shapen Body, not only *larger*, but more *distorted*.

He added, That he had heard too much upon the Subject of War, both in this, and some former Discourses. There was another Point which a little perplexed him at present. I had said, that some of our Crew left their Country on Account of being ruined by *Law:* That I had already explained the Meaning of the Word; but he was at a Loss how it should come to pass, that the *Law* which was intended for *every* Man's Preservation, should be any Man's Ruin. Therefore he desired to be farther satisfied what I meant by *Law*, and the Dispensers thereof, according to the present Practice in my own Country: Because he thought, Nature and Reason were sufficient Guides for a reasonable Animal, as we pretended to be, in shewing us what we ought to do, and what to avoid.

I assured his Honour, that *Law* was a Science wherein I had not much conversed, further than by employing Advocates, in vain, upon some Injustices that had been done me. However, I would give him all the Satisfaction I was able.

I said there was a Society of Men among us, bred up from their Youth in the Art of proving by Words multiplied for the Purpose, that *White* is *Black,* and *Black* is *White,* according as they are paid. To this Society all the rest of the People are Slaves.

For Example. If my Neighbour hath a mind to my *Cow,* he hires a Lawyer to prove that he ought to have my *Cow* from me. I must then hire another to defend my Right; it being against all Rules of *Law* that any Man should be allowed to speak for himself. Now in this Case, I who am the true Owner lie under two great Disadvantages. First, my Lawyer being practiced almost from his Cradle in defending Falshood; is quite out of his Element when he would be an Advocate for Justice, which as an Office unnatural, he always attempts with great Awkwardness, if not with Ill-will. The second Disadvantage is, that my Lawyer must proceed with great Caution: Or else he will be reprimanded by the Judges, and abhorred by his Brethren, as one who would lessen the Practice of the Law. And therefore I have but two Methods to preserve my *Cow.* The first is, to gain over my Adversary's Lawyer with a double Fee; who will then betray his Client, by insinuating that he hath Justice on his Side. The second Way is for my Lawyer to make my Cause appear as unjust as he can; by allowing the *Cow* to belong to my Adversary; and this if it be skilfully done, will certainly bespeak the Favour of the Bench.

Now, your Honour is to know, that these Judges are Persons appointed to decide all Controversies of Property, as well as for the Tryal of Criminals; and picked out from the most dextrous Lawyers who are grown old or lazy: And having been byassed all their Lives against Truth and Equity, are under such a fatal Necessity of favouring Fraud, Perjury and Oppression; that I have known some of them to have refused a large Bribe from the Side where Justice lay, rather than injure the *Faculty*,° by doing any thing unbecoming their Nature or their Office.

It is a Maxim among these Lawyers, that whatever hath been done before, may legally be done again: And therefore they take special Care to record all the Decisions formerly made against common Justice and the general Reason of Mankind. These, under the Name of *Precedents*, they produce as Authorities to justify the most iniquitous Opinions; and the Judges never fail of decreeing accordingly.

In pleading, they studiously avoid entering into the *Merits* of the Cause; but are loud, violent and tedious in dwelling upon all *Circumstances* which are not to the Purpose. For Instance, in the Case already mentioned: They never desire to know what Claim or Title my Adversary hath to my *Cow*; but whether the said *Cow* were Red or Black; her Horns long or short; whether the Field I graze her in be round or square; whether she were milked at home or abroad; what Diseases she is subject to, and the like. After which they consult *Precedents*, adjourn the Cause, from Time to Time, and in Ten, Twenty, or Thirty Years come to an Issue.

It is likewise to be observed, that this Society hath a peculiar Cant and Jargon of their own, that no other Mortal can understand, and wherein all their Laws are written, which they take special Care to multiply; whereby they have wholly confounded the very Essence of Truth and Falshood, of Right and Wrong; so that it will take Thirty Years to decide whether the Field, left me by my Ancestors for six Generations, belong to me, or to a Stranger three Hundred Miles off.

In the Tryal of Persons accused for Crimes against the State, the Method is much more short and commendable: The Judge first sends to sound the Disposition of those in Power; after which he can easily hang or save the Criminal, strictly preserving all the Forms of Law.

Here my Master interposing, said it was a Pity, that Creatures endowed with such prodigious Abilities of Mind as these Lawyers, by the Description I gave of them must certainly be, were not rather encouraged to be Instructors of others in Wisdom and Knowledge. In Answer to which, I assured his Honour, that in all Points out of their own Trade, they were usually the most ignorant and stupid Generation°

Faculty: Profession.   **Generation:** Species.

among us, the most despicable in common Conversation, avowed Enemies to all Knowledge and Learning; and equally disposed to pervert the general Reason of Mankind, in every other Subject of Discourse, as in that of their own Profession.

CHAPTER VI

A Continuation of the State of England, *under Queen* Anne. *The Character of a first Minister in the Courts of* Europe.

My Master was yet wholly at a Loss to understand what Motives could incite this Race of Lawyers to perplex, disquiet, and weary themselves by engaging in a Confederacy of Injustice, merely for the Sake of injuring their Fellow-Animals; neither could he comprehend what I meant in saying they did it for *Hire.* Whereupon I was at much Pains to describe to him the Use of *Money,* the Materials it was made of, and the Value of the Metals: That when a *Yahoo* had got a great Store of this precious Substance, he was able to purchase whatever he had a mind to; the finest Cloathing, the noblest Houses, great Tracts of Land, the most costly Meats and Drinks; and have his Choice of the most beautiful Females. Therefore since *Money* alone, was able to perform all these Feats, our *Yahoos* thought, they could never have enough of it to spend or to save, as they found themselves inclined from their natural Bent either to Profusion or Avarice. That, the rich Man enjoyed the Fruit of the poor Man's Labour, and the latter were a Thousand to One in Proportion to the former. That the Bulk of our People was forced to live miserably, by labouring every Day for small Wages to make a few live plentifully. I enlarged myself much on these and many other Particulars to the same Purpose: But his Honour was still to seek:° For he went upon a Supposition that all Animals had a Title to their Share in the Productions of the Earth; and especially those who presided over the rest. Therefore he desired I would let him know, what these costly Meats were, and how any of us happened to want them. Whereupon I enumerated as many Sorts as came into my Head, with the various Methods of dressing them, which could not be done without sending Vessels by Sea to every Part of the World, as well for Liquors to drink, as for Sauces, and innumerable other Conveniencies. I assured him, that this whole Globe of Earth must be at least three Times gone round, before one of our better Female *Yahoos* could get her Breakfast, or a Cup to put it in. He said,

still to seek: Unable to understand.

That must needs be a miserable Country which cannot furnish Food for its own Inhabitants. But what he chiefly wondered at, was how such vast Tracts of Ground as I described, should be wholly without *Fresh water,* and the People put to the Necessity of sending over the Sea for Drink. I replied, that *England* (the dear Place of my Nativity) was computed to produce three Times the Quantity of Food, more than its Inhabitants are able to consume, as well as Liquors extracted from Grain, or pressed out of the Fruit of certain Trees, which made excellent Drink; and the same Proportion in every other Convenience of Life. But, in order to feed the Luxury and Intemperance of the Males, and the Vanity of the Females, we sent away the greatest Part of our necessary Things to other Countries, from whence in Return we brought the Materials of Diseases, Folly, and Vice, to spend among ourselves. Hence it follows of Necessity, that vast Numbers of our People are compelled to seek their Livelihood by Begging, Robbing, Stealing, Cheating, Pimping, Forswearing, Flattering, Suborning, Forging, Gaming, Lying, Fawning, Hectoring, Voting, Scribling, Stargazing, Poysoning, Whoring, Canting, Libelling, Free-thinking, and the like Occupations: Every one of which Terms, I was at much Pains to make him understand.

That, *Wine* was not imported among us from foreign Countries, to supply the Want of Water or other Drinks, but because it was a Sort of Liquid which made us merry, by putting us out of our Senses; diverted all melancholy Thoughts, begat wild extravagant Imaginations in the Brain, raised our Hopes, and banished our Fears; suspended every Office of Reason for a Time, and deprived us of the Use of our Limbs, untill we fell into a profound Sleep; although it must be confessed, that we always awaked sick and dispirited; and that the Use of this Liquor filled us with Diseases, which made our Lives uncomfortable and short.

But beside all this, the Bulk of our People supported themselves by furnishing the Necessities or Conveniencies of Life to the Rich, and to each other. For Instance, when I am at home and dressed as I ought to be, I carry on my Body the Workmanship of an Hundred Tradesmen; the Building and Furniture of my House employ as many more; and five Times the Number to adorn my Wife.

I was going on to tell him of another Sort of People, who get their Livelihood by attending the Sick; having upon some Occasions informed his Honour that many of my Crew had died of Diseases. But here it was with the utmost Difficulty, that I brought him to apprehend what I meant. He could easily conceive, that a *Houyhnhnm* grew weak and heavy a few Days before his Death; or by some Accident might hurt a Limb. But that Nature, who worketh all things to Perfection, should suffer any Pains to breed in our Bodies, he thought impossible; and desired to know the Reason of so unaccountable an Evil. I told him, we fed on a Thousand Things which operated contrary to each other; that we eat when we were not hungry, and drank without the Provocation of Thirst: That we sat whole Nights drinking strong Liquors without eating a Bit; which disposed us to Sloth, enflamed our Bodies, and precipitated or prevented Digestion. That, prostitute Female *Yahoos* acquired a certain Malady, which bred Rottenness in the Bones of those, who fell into their Embraces: That this and many other Diseases, were propagated from Father to Son; so that great Numbers come into the World with complicated Maladies upon them: That, it would be endless to give him a Catalogue of all Diseases incident to human Bodies; for they could not be fewer than five or six Hundred, spread over every Limb, and Joynt: In short, every Part, external and intestine, having Diseases appropriated to each. To remedy which, there was a Sort of People bred up among us, in the Profession or Pretence of curing the Sick. And because I had some Skill in the Faculty, I would in Gratitude to his Honour, let him know the whole Mystery and Method by which they proceed.

Their Fundamental is, that all Diseases arise from *Repletion;* from whence they conclude, that a great *Evacuation* of the Body is necessary, either through the natural Passage, or upwards at the Mouth. Their next Business is, from Herbs, Minerals, Gums, Oyls, Shells, Salts, Juices, Sea-weed, Excrements, Barks of Trees, Serpents, Toads, Frogs, Spiders, dead Mens Flesh and Bones, Birds, Beasts and Fishes, to form a Composition for Smell and Taste the most abominable, nauseous and detestable, that they can possibly contrive, which the Stomach immediately rejects with Loathing: And this they call a *Vomit.*° Or else from the same Store-house, with some other poysonous Additions, they command us to take in at the Orifice *above* or *below,* (just as the Physician then happens to be disposed) a Medicine equally annoying and disgustful to the Bowels; which relaxing the Belly, drives down all before it: And this they call a *Purge,* or a *Clyster.*° For Nature (as the Physicians alledge) having intended the superior anterior Orifice only for the *Intromission* of Solids and Liquids, and the inferior Posterior for Ejection; these Artists ingeniously considering that in all Diseases Nature is forced out of her Seat; therefore to replace her in it, the Body must be treated in a Manner directly contrary, by interchanging the Use of each Orifice;

Vomit: Drug prescribed to induce vomiting; an emetic.   ***Clyster:*** Enema.

forcing Solids and Liquids in at the *Anus*, and making Evacuations at the Mouth.

But, besides real Diseases, we are subject to many that are only imaginary, for which the Physicians have invented imaginary Cures; these have their several Names, and so have the Drugs that are proper for them; and with these our Female *Yahoos* are always infested.

One great Excellency in this Tribe is their Skill at *Prognosticks*, wherein they seldom fail; their Predictions in real Diseases, when they rise to any Degree of Malignity, generally portending *Death*, which is always in their Power, when Recovery is not: And therefore, upon any unexpected Signs of Amendment, after they have pronounced their Sentence, rather than be accused as false Prophets, they know how to approve their Sagacity to the World by a seasonable Dose.

They are likewise of special Use to Husbands and Wives, who are grown weary of their Mates; to eldest Sons, to great Ministers of State, and often to Princes.

I had formerly upon Occasion discoursed with my Master upon the Nature of *Government* in general, and particularly of our own *excellent Constitution*, deservedly the Wonder and Envy of the whole World. But having here accidentally mentioned a *Minister of State;* he commanded me some Time after to inform him, what Species of *Yahoo* I particularly meant by that Appellation.

I told him, that a *First* or *Chief Minister of State*, whom I intended to describe, was a Creature wholly exempt from Joy and Grief, Love and Hatred, Pity and Anger; at least makes use of no other Passions but a violent Desire of Wealth, Power, and Titles: That he applies his Words to all Uses, except to the Indication of his Mind; That he never tells a *Truth*, but with an Intent that you should take it for a *Lye;* nor a *Lye*, but with a Design that you should take it for a *Truth;* That those he speaks worst of behind their Backs, are in the surest way to Preferment; and whenever he begins to praise you to others or to your self, you are from that Day forlorn.° The worst Mark you can receive is a *Promise*, especially when it is confirmed with an Oath; after which every wise Man retires, and gives over all Hopes.

There are three Methods by which a Man may rise to be Chief Minister: The first is, by knowing how with Prudence to dispose of a Wife, a Daughter, or a Sister: The second, by betraying or undermining his Predecessor: And the third is, by a *furious Zeal* in publick Assemblies against the Corruptions of the Court. But a wise Prince would rather

forlorn: Lost, doomed.

chuse to employ those who practise the last of these Methods; because such Zealots prove always the most obsequious and subservient to the Will and Passions of their Master. That, these *Ministers* having all Employments at their Disposal, preserve themselves in Power by bribing the Majority of a Senate or great Council; and at last by an Expedient called an *Act of Indemnity* (whereof I described the Nature to him) they secure themselves from After-reckonings, and retire from the Publick, laden with the Spoils of the Nation.

The Palace of a *Chief Minister,* is a Seminary to breed up others in his own Trade: The Pages, Lacquies, and Porter, by imitating their Master, become *Ministers of State* in their several Districts, and learn to excel in the three principal *Ingredients,* of *Insolence, Lying,* and *Bribery.* Accordingly, they have a *Subaltern* Court paid to them by Persons of the best Rank; and sometimes by the Force of Dexterity and Impudence, arrive through several Gradations to be Successors to their Lord.

He is usually governed by a decayed Wench, or favourite Footman, who are the Tunnels through which all Graces are conveyed, and may properly be called, *in the last Resort,* the Governors of the Kingdom.

One Day, my Master, having heard me mention the *Nobility* of my Country, was pleased to make me a Compliment which I could not pretend to deserve: That, he was sure, I must have been born of some Noble Family, because I far exceeded in Shape, Colour, and Cleanliness, all the *Yahoos* of his Nation, although I seemed to fail in Strength, and Agility, which must be imputed to my different Way of Living from those other Brutes; and besides, I was not only endowed with the Faculty of Speech, but likewise with some Rudiments of Reason, to a Degree, that with all his Acquaintance I passed for a Prodigy.

He made me observe, that among the *Houyhnhnms,* the *White,* the *Sorrel,* and the *Iron-grey,* were not so exactly shaped as the *Bay,* the *Dapple-grey,* and the *Black;* nor born with equal Talents of Mind, or a Capacity to improve them; and therefore continued always in the Condition of Servants, without ever aspiring to match out of their own Race, which in that Country would be reckoned monstrous and unnatural.

I made his Honour my most humble Acknowledgements for the good Opinion he was pleased to conceive of me; but assured him at the same Time, that my Birth was of the lower Sort, having been born of plain, honest Parents, who were just able to give me a tolerable Education: That, *Nobility* among us was altogether a different Thing from the Idea he had of it; That, our young *Noblemen* are bred from their Childhood in Idleness and Luxury; that, as soon as Years will permit, they consume their Vigour, and contract odious Diseases among lewd Females; and when their Fortunes are almost ruined, they marry some Woman of mean Birth, disagreeable Person, and unsound Constitution, merely for the sake of Money, whom they hate and despise. That, the Productions of such Marriages are generally scrophulous, rickety or deformed Children; by which Means the Family seldom continues above three Generations, unless the Wife take Care to provide a healthy Father among her Neighbours, or Domesticks, in order to improve and continue the Breed. That, a weak diseased Body, a meager Countenance, and sallow Complexion, are the true Marks of *noble Blood;* and a healthy robust Appearance is so disgraceful in a Man of Quality, that the World concludes his real Father to have been a Groom or a Coachman. The Imperfections of his Mind run parallel with those of his Body; being a Composition of Spleen, Dulness, Ignorance, Caprice, Sensuality and Pride.

Without the Consent of this illustrious Body, no Law can be enacted, repealed, or altered: And these Nobles have likewise the Decision of all our Possessions without Appeal.

CHAPTER VII

The Author's great Love of his Native Country. His Master's Observations upon the Constitution and Administration of England, as described by the Author, with parallel Cases and Comparisons. His Master's Observations upon human Nature.

The Reader may be disposed to wonder how I could prevail on my self to give so free a Representation of my own Species, among a Race of Mortals who were already too apt to conceive the vilest Opinion of Human Kind, from that entire Congruity betwixt me and their *Yahoos.* But I must freely confess, that the many Virtues of those excellent *Quadrupeds* placed in opposite View to human Corruptions, had so far opened mine Eyes, and enlarged my Understanding, that I began to view the Actions and Passions of Man in a very different Light; and to think the Honour of my own Kind not worth managing;° which, besides, it was impossible for me to do before a Person of so acute a Judgment as my Master, who daily convinced me of a thousand Faults in my self, whereof I had not the least Perception before, and which with us would never be numbered even among human Infirmities. I had likewise learned from his Example an utter Detestation of all Falsehood or

managing: Sparing from censure.

Disguise; and *Truth* appeared so amiable to me, that I determined upon sacrificing every thing to it.

Let me deal so candidly with the Reader, as to confess, that there was yet a much stronger Motive for the Freedom I took in my Representation of Things. I had not been a Year in this Country, before I contracted such a Love and Veneration for the Inhabitants, that I entered on a firm Resolution never to return to human Kind, but to pass the rest of my Life among these admirable *Houyhnhnms* in the Contemplation and Practice of every Virtue; where I could have no Example or Incitement to Vice. But it was decreed by Fortune, my perpetual Enemy, that so great a Felicity should not fall to my Share. However, it is now some Comfort to reflect, that in what I said of my Countrymen, I *extenuated* their Faults as much as I durst before so strict an Examiner; and upon every Article, gave as *favourable* a Turn as the Matter would bear. For, indeed, who is there alive that will not be swayed by his Byass and Partiality to the Place of his Birth?

I have related the Substance of several Conversations I had with my Master, during the greatest Part of the Time I had the Honour to be in his Service; but have indeed for Brevity sake omitted much more than is here set down.

When I had answered all his Questions, and his Curiosity seemed to be fully satisfied; he sent for me one Morning early, and commanding me to sit down at some Distance, (an Honour which he had never before conferred upon me) He said, he had been very seriously considering my whole Story, as far as it related both to my self and my Country: That, he looked upon us as a Sort of Animals to whose Share, by what Accident he could not conjecture, some small Pittance of *Reason* had fallen, whereof we made no other Use than by its Assistance to aggravate our *natural* Corruptions, and to acquire new ones which Nature had not given us. That, we disarmed our selves of the few Abilities she had bestowed; had been very successful in multiplying our original Wants, and seemed to spend our whole Lives in vain Endeavours to supply them by our own Inventions. That, as to my self, it was manifest I had neither the Strength or Agility of a common *Yahoo;* that I walked infirmly on my hinder Feet; had found out a Contrivance to make my Claws of no Use or Defence, and to remove the Hair from my Chin, which was intended as a Shelter from the Sun and the Weather. Lastly, That I could neither run with Speed, nor climb Trees like my *Brethren* (as he called them) the *Yahoos* in this Country.

That, our Institutions of *Government* and *Law* were plainly owing to our gross Defects in *Reason*, and by consequence, in *Virtue;* because

Reason alone is sufficient to govern a *Rational* Creature; which was therefore a Character we had no Pretence to challenge, even from the Account I had given of my own People; although he manifestly perceived, that in order to favour them, I had concealed many Particulars, and often *said the Thing which was not.*

He was the more confirmed in this Opinion, because he observed, that as I agreed in every Feature of my Body with other *Yahoos,* except where it was to my real Disadvantage in point of Strength, Speed and Activity, the Shortness of my Claws, and some other Particulars where Nature had no Part; so, from the Representation I had given him of our Lives, our Manners, and our Actions, he found as near a Resemblance in the Disposition of our Minds. He said, the *Yahoos* were known to hate one another more than they did any different Species of Animals; and the Reason usually assigned, was, the Odiousness of their own Shapes, which all could see in the rest, but not in themselves. He had therefore begun to think it not unwise in us to *cover* our Bodies, and by that Invention, conceal many of our Deformities from each other, which would else be hardly supportable. But, he now found he had been mistaken; and that the Dissentions of those Brutes in his Country were owing to the same Cause with ours, as I had described them. For, if (said he) you throw among five *Yahoos* as much Food as would be sufficient for fifty, they will, instead of eating peaceably, fall together by the Ears, each single one impatient to *have all to it self;* and therefore a Servant was usually employed to stand by while they were feeding abroad, and those kept at home were tied at a Distance from each other. That, if a Cow died of Age or Accident, before a *Houynhnhnm* could secure it for his own *Yahoos,* those in the Neighbourhood would come in Herds to seize it, and then would ensue such a Battle as I had described, with terrible Wounds made by their Claws on both Sides, although they seldom were able to kill one another, for want of such convenient Instruments of Death as we had invented. At other Times the like Battles have been fought between the *Yahoos* of several Neighbourhoods without any visible Cause: Those of one District watching all Opportunities to surprise the next before they are prepared. But if they find their Project hath miscarried, they return home, and for want of Enemies, engage in what I call a *Civil War* among themselves.

That, in some Fields of his Country, there are certain *shining Stones* of several Colours, whereof the *Yahoos* are violently fond; and when Part of these *Stones* are fixed in the Earth, as it sometimes happeneth, they will dig with their Claws for whole Days to get them out, and carry them away, and hide them by Heaps in their Kennels; but still looking round with great Caution, for fear their Comrades should find out their Treasure. My Master said, he could never discover the Reason of this unnatural Appetite, or how these *Stones* could be of any Use to a *Yahoo;* but now he believed it might proceed from the same Principle of *Avarice,* which I had ascribed to Mankind. That he had once, by way of Experiment, privately removed a Heap of these *Stones* from the Place where one of his *Yahoos* had buried it: Whereupon, the sordid Animal missing his Treasure, by his loud lamenting brought the whole Herd to the Place, there miserably howled, then fell to biting and tearing the rest; began to pine away, would neither eat nor sleep, nor work, till he ordered a Servant privately to convey the *Stones* into the same Hole, and hide them as before; which when his *Yahoo* had found, he presently recovered his Spirits and good Humour; but took Care to remove them to a better hiding Place; and hath ever since been a very serviceable Brute.

My Master farther assured me, which I also observed my self; That in the Fields where these *shining Stones* abound, the fiercest and most frequent Battles are fought, occasioned by perpetual Inroads of the neighbouring *Yahoos.*

He said, it was common when two *Yahoos* discovered such a *Stone* in a Field, and were contending which of them should be the Proprietor, a third would take the Advantage, and carry it away from them both; which my Master would needs contend to have some Resemblance with our *Suits at Law;* wherein I thought it for our Credit not to undeceive him; since the Decision he mentioned was much more equitable than many Decrees among us: Because the Plaintiff and Defendant there lost nothing beside the *Stone* they contended for; whereas our *Courts of Equity,* would never have dismissed the Cause while either of them had any thing left.

My Master continuing his Discourse, said, There was nothing that rendered the *Yahoos* more odious, than their undistinguishing Appetite to devour every thing that came in their Way, whether Herbs, Roots, Berries, corrupted Flesh of Animals, or all mingled together: And it was peculiar in their Temper, that they were fonder of what they could get by Rapine or Stealth at a greater Distance, than much better Food provided for them at home. If their Prey held out, they would eat till they were ready to burst, after which Nature had pointed out to them a certain *Root* that gave them a general Evacuation.

There was also another Kind of *Root* very *juicy,* but something rare and difficult to be found, which the *Yahoos* sought for with much Eagerness, and would suck it with great Delight: It produced the same

Effects that Wine hath upon us. It would make them sometimes hug, and sometimes tear one another; they would howl and grin, and chatter, and reel, and tumble, and then fall asleep in the Mud.

I did indeed observe, that the *Yahoos* were the only Animals in this Country subject to any Diseases; which however, were much fewer than Horses have among us, and contracted not by any ill Treatment they meet with, but by the Nastiness and Greediness of that sordid Brute. Neither has their Language any more than a general Appellation for those Maladies; which is borrowed from the Name of the Beast, and called *Hnea Yahoo,* or the *Yahoo's-Evil;* and the Cure prescribed is a Mixture of *their own Dung* and *Urine,* forcibly put down the *Yahoo*'s Throat. This I have since often known to have been taken with Success: And do here freely recommend it to my Countrymen, for the publick Good, as an admirable Specifick against all Diseases produced by Repletion.

As to Learning, Government, Arts, Manufactures, and the like; my Master confessed he could find little or no Resemblance between the *Yahoos* of that Country and those in ours. For, he only meant to observe what Parity there was in our Natures. He had heard indeed some curious *Houyhnhnms* observe, that in most Herds there was a Sort of ruling *Yahoo,* (as among us there is generally some leading or principal Stag in a Park) who was always more *deformed* in Body, and *mischievous in Disposition,* than any of the rest. That, this *Leader* had usually a Favourite as *like himself* as he could get, whose Employment was to *lick his Master's Feet and Posteriors, and drive the Female* Yahoos *to his Kennel;* for which he was now and then rewarded with a Piece of Ass's Flesh. This *Favourite* is hated by the whole Herd; and therefore to protect himself, keeps always *near the Person of his Leader.* He usually continues in Office till a worse can be found; but the very Moment he is discarded, his Successor, at the Head of all the *Yahoos* in that District, Young and Old, Male and Female, come in a Body, and discharge their Excrements upon him from Head to Foot. But how far this might be applicable to our *Courts* and *Favourites,* and *Ministers of State,* my Master said I could best determine.

I durst make no Return to this malicious Insinuation, which debased human Understanding below the Sagacity of a common *Hound,* who hath Judgment enough to distinguish and follow the Cry of the *ablest Dog in the Pack,* without being ever mistaken.

My Master told me, there were some Qualities remarkable in the *Yahoos,* which he had not observed me to mention, or at least very slightly, in the Accounts I had given him of human Kind. He said, those Animals, like other Brutes, had their Females in common; but in this they differed, that the She-*Yahoo* would admit the Male, while she was pregnant; and that the Hees would quarrel and fight with the Females as fiercely as with each other. Both which Practices were such Degrees of infamous Brutality, that no other sensitive Creature ever arrived at.

Another Thing he wondered at in the *Yahoos*, was their strange Disposition to Nastiness and Dirt; whereas there appears to be a natural Love of Cleanliness in all other Animals. As to the two former Accusations, I was glad to let them pass without any Reply, because I had not a Word to offer upon them in Defence of my Species, which otherwise I certainly had done from my own Inclinations. But I could have easily vindicated human Kind from the Imputation of Singularity upon the last Article, if there had been any *Swine* in that Country, (as unluckily for me there were not) which although it may be a *sweeter Quadruped* than a *Yahoo*, cannot I humbly conceive in Justice pretend to more Cleanliness; so his Honour himself must have owned, if he had seen their filthy Way of feeding, and their Custom of wallowing and sleeping in the Mud.

My Master likewise mentioned another Quality, which his Servants had discovered in several *Yahoos*, and to him was wholly unaccountable. He said, a Fancy would sometimes take a *Yahoo*, to retire into a Corner, to lie down and howl, and groan, and spurn away all that came near him, although he were young and fat, and wanted neither Food nor Water; nor did the Servants imagine what could possibly ail him. And the only Remedy they found was to set him to hard Work, after which he would infallibly come to himself. To this I was silent out of Partiality to my own Kind; yet here I could plainly discover the true Seeds of *Spleen*,° which only seizeth on the *Lazy*, the *Luxurious*, and the *Rich*; who, if they were forced to undergo the *same Regimen*, I would undertake for the Cure.

His Honour had farther observed, that a Female *Yahoo* would often stand behind a Bank or a Bush, to gaze on the young Males passing by, and then appear, and hide, using many antick Gestures and Grimaces; at which time it was observed, that she had a most *offensive Smell;* and when any of the Males advanced, would slowly retire, looking often back, and with a counterfeit Shew of Fear, run off into some convenient Place where she knew the Male would follow her.

Spleen: Melancholy and depression; in the eighteenth century, a fashionable malady often associated with the idle and the rich.

At other times, if a Female Stranger came among them, three or four of her own Sex would get about her, and stare and chatter, and grin, and smell her all over; and then turn off with Gestures that seemed to express Contempt and Disdain.

Perhaps my Master might refine a little° in these Speculations, which he had drawn from what he observed himself, or had been told him by others: However, I could not reflect without some Amazement, and much Sorrow, that the Rudiments of *Lewdness, Coquetry, Censure,* and *Scandal,* should have Place by Instinct in Womankind.

I expected every Moment, that my Master would accuse the *Yahoos* of those unnatural Appetites in both Sexes, so common among us. But Nature it seems hath not been so expert a Schoolmistress; and these politer Pleasures are entirely the Productions of Art and Reason, on our Side of the Globe.

CHAPTER VIII

The Author relateth several Particulars of the Yahoos. *The great Virtues of the* Houyhnhnms. *The Education and Exercise of their Youth. Their general Assembly.*

As I ought to have understood human Nature much better than I supposed it possible for my Master to do, so it was easy to apply the Character he gave of the *Yahoos* to myself and my Countrymen; and I believed I could yet make farther Discoveries from my own Observation. I therefore often begged his Honour to let me go among the Herds of *Yahoos* in the Neighbourhood; to which he always very graciously consented, being perfectly convinced that the Hatred I bore those Brutes would never suffer me to be corrupted by them; and his Honour ordered one of his Servants, a strong Sorrel Nag, very honest and good-natured, to be my Guard; without whose Protection I durst not undertake such Adventures. For I have already told the Reader how much I was pestered by those odious Animals upon my first Arrival. I afterwards failed very narrowly three or four times of falling into their Clutches, when I happened to stray at any Distance without my Hanger. And I have Reason to believe, they had some Imagination that I was of their own Species, which I often assisted myself, by stripping up my Sleeves, and shewing my naked Arms and Breast in their Sight, when my Protector was with me: At which times they would approach as near

might refine a little: May be a bit over ingenious.

as they durst, and imitate my Actions after the Manner of Monkeys, but ever with great Signs of Hatred; as a tame *Jack Daw*° with Cap and Stockings, is always persecuted by the wild ones, when he happens to be got among them.

They are prodigiously nimble from their Infancy; however, I once caught a young Male of three Years old, and endeavoured by all Marks of Tenderness to make it quiet; but the little Imp fell a squalling, and scratching, and biting with such Violence, that I was forced to let it go; and it was high time, for a whole Troop of old ones came about us at the Noise; but finding the Cub was safe, (for away it ran) and my Sorrel Nag being by, they durst not venture near us. I observed the young Animal's Flesh to smell very rank, and the Stink was somewhat between a *Weasel* and a *Fox,* but much more disagreeable. I forgot another Circumstance, (and perhaps I might have the Reader's Pardon, if it were wholly omitted) that while I held the odious Vermin in my Hands, it voided its filthy Excrements of a yellow liquid Substance, all over my Cloaths; but by good Fortune there was a small Brook hard by, where I washed myself as clean as I could; although I durst not come into my Master's Presence, until I were sufficiently aired.

By what I could discover, the *Yahoos* appear to be the most unteachable of all Animals, their Capacities never reaching higher than to draw or carry Burthens. Yet I am of Opinion, this Defect ariseth chiefly from a perverse, restive Disposition. For they are cunning, malicious, treacherous and revengeful. They are strong and hardy, but of a cowardly Spirit, and by Consequence insolent, abject, and cruel. It is observed, that the *Red-haired* of both Sexes are more libidinous and mischievous than the rest, whom yet they much exceed in Strength and Activity.

The *Houyhnhnms* keep the *Yahoos* for present Use in Huts not far from the House; but the rest are sent abroad to certain Fields, where they dig up Roots, eat several Kinds of Herbs, and search about for Carrion, or sometimes catch *Weasels* and *Luhimuhs* (a Sort of *wild Rat*) which they greedily devour. Nature hath taught them to dig deep Holes with their Nails on the Side of a rising Ground, wherein they lie by themselves; only the Kennels° of the Females are larger, sufficient to hold two or three Cubs.

They swim from their Infancy like Frogs, and are able to continue long under Water, where they often take Fish, which the Females carry

---

Jack Daw: A common black or gray Eurasian bird, related to but smaller than the crow.
Kennels: Lairs, holes.

home to their Young. And upon this Occasion, I hope the Reader will pardon my relating an odd Adventure.

Being one Day abroad with my Protector the Sorrel Nag, and the Weather exceeding hot, I entreated him to let me bathe in a River that was near. He consented, and I immediately stripped myself stark naked, and went down softly° into the Stream. It happened that a young Female *Yahoo* standing behind a Bank, saw the whole Proceeding; and inflamed by Desire, as the Nag and I conjectured, came running with all Speed, and leaped into the Water within five Yards of the Place where I bathed. I was never in my Life so terribly frighted; the Nag was grazing at some Distance, not suspecting any Harm: She embraced me after a most fulsome Manner; I roared as loud as I could, and the Nag came galloping towards me, whereupon she quitted her Grasp, with the utmost Reluctancy, and leaped upon the opposite Bank, where she stood gazing and howling all the time I was putting on my Cloaths.

This was Matter of Diversion to my Master and his Family, as well as of Mortification to my self. For now I could no longer deny, that I was a real *Yahoo*, in every Limb and Feature, since the Females had a natural Propensity to me as one of their own Species: Neither was the Hair of this Brute of a Red Colour, (which might have been some Excuse for an Appetite a little irregular) but black as a Sloe, and her Countenance did not make an Appearance altogether so hideous as the rest of the Kind; for, I think, she could not be above Eleven Years old.

Having already lived three Years in this Country, the Reader I suppose will expect, that I should, like other Travellers, give him some Account of the Manners and Customs of its Inhabitants, which it was indeed my principal Study to learn.

As these noble *Houyhnhnms* are endowed by Nature with a general Disposition to all Virtues, and have no Conceptions or Ideas of what is evil in a rational Creature; so their grand Maxim is, to cultivate *Reason*, and to be wholly governed by it. Neither is *Reason* among them a Point problematical as with us, where Men can argue with Plausibility on both Sides of a Question; but strikes you with immediate Conviction; as it must needs do where it is not mingled, obscured, or discoloured by Passion and Interest. I remember it was with extreme Difficulty that I could bring my Master to understand the Meaning of the Word *Opinion,* or how a Point could be disputable; because *Reason* taught us to affirm or deny only where we are certain; and beyond our Knowledge we cannot do either. So that Controversies, Wranglings, Disputes, and

softly: Slowly.

Positiveness in false or dubious Propositions, are Evils unknown among the *Houyhnhnms.* In the like Manner when I used to explain to him our several Systems of *Natural Philosophy,* he would laugh that a Creature pretending to *Reason,* should value itself upon the Knowledge of other Peoples Conjectures, and in Things, where that Knowledge, if it were certain, could be of no Use. Wherein he agreed entirely with the Sentiments of *Socrates,* as *Plato* delivers them;° which I mention as the highest Honour I can do that Prince of Philosophers. I have often since reflected what Destruction such a Doctrine would make in the Libraries of *Europe;* and how many Paths to Fame would be then shut up in the Learned World.

Friendship and *Benevolence* are the two principal Virtues among the *Houyhnhnms;* and these not confined to particular Objects, but universal to the whole Race. For, a Stranger from the remotest Part, is equally treated with the nearest Neighbour, and where-ever he goes, looks upon himself as at home. They preserve *Decency* and *Civility* in the highest Degrees, but are altogether ignorant of *Ceremony.* They have no Fondness° for their Colts or Foles; but the Care they take in educating them proceedeth entirely from the Dictates of *Reason.* And, I observed my Master to shew the same Affection to his Neighbour's Issue that he had for his own. They will have it that *Nature* teaches them to love the whole Species, and it is *Reason* only that maketh a Distinction of Persons, where there is a superior Degree of Virtue.

When the Matron *Houyhnhnms* have produced one of each Sex, they no longer accompany with their Consorts, except they lose one of their Issue by some Casualty, which very seldom happens: But in such a Case they meet again; or when the like Accident befalls a Person, whose Wife is past bearing, some other Couple bestows on him one of their own Colts, and then go together a second Time, until the Mother be pregnant. This Caution is necessary to prevent the Country from being overburthened with Numbers. But the Race of inferior *Houyhnhnms* bred up to be Servants is not so strictly limited upon this Article; these are allowed to produce three of each Sex, to be Domesticks in the Noble Families.

In their Marriages they are exactly careful to chuse such Colours as will not make any disagreeable Mixture in the Breed. *Strength* is chiefly valued in the Male, and *Comeliness* in the Female; not upon the Account

---

Sentiments of *Socrates* . . . them: In Plato's *Apology,* Socrates argues that ethics is a far more important subject than the study of external nature; that, as Pope would later say, "The proper study of mankind is Man" (*Essay On Man,* ep. 2.1, line 2). **Fondness:** Foolish affection, doting.

of *Love,* but to preserve the Race from degenerating: For, where a Female happens to excel in *Strength,* a Consort is chosen with regard to *Comeliness.* Courtship, Love, Presents, Joyntures, Settlements, have no Place in their Thoughts; or Terms whereby to express them in their Language. The young Couple meet and are joined, merely because it is the Determination of their Parents and Friends: It is what they see done every Day; and they look upon it as one of the necessary Actions in a reasonable Being. But the Violation of Marriage, or any other Unchastity, was never heard of: And the married Pair pass their Lives with the same Friendship, and mutual Benevolence that they bear to all others of the same Species, who come in their Way; without Jealousy, Fondness, Quarrelling, or Discontent.

In educating the Youth of both Sexes, their Method is admirable, and highly deserveth our Imitation. These are not suffered to taste a Grain of *Oats,* except upon certain Days, till Eighteen Years old; nor *Milk,* but very rarely; and in Summer they graze two Hours in the Morning, and as many in the Evening, which° their Parents likewise observe; but the Servants are not allowed above half that Time; and a great Part of their Grass is brought home, which they eat at the most convenient Hours, when they can be best spared from Work.

Temperance, Industry, Exercise and *Cleanliness,* are the Lessons equally enjoyned to the young ones of both Sexes: And my Master thought it monstrous in us to give the Females a different Kind of Education from the Males, except in some Articles of Domestick Management; whereby, as he truly observed, one Half of our Natives were good for nothing but bringing Children into the World: And to trust the Care of their Children to such useless Animals, he said was yet a greater Instance of Brutality.

But the *Houyhnhnms* train up their Youth to Strength, Speed, and Hardiness, by exercising them in running Races up and down steep Hills, or over hard stony Grounds; and when they are all in a Sweat, they are ordered to leap over Head and Ears into a Pond or a River. Four times a Year the Youth of certain Districts meet to shew their Proficiency in Running, and Leaping, and other Feats of Strength or Agility; where the Victor is rewarded with a Song made in his or her Praise. On this Festival the Servants drive a Herd of *Yahoos* into the Field, laden with Hay, and Oats, and Milk for a Repast to the *Houyhnhnms;* after which, these Brutes are immediately driven back again, for fear of being noisome to the Assembly.

which: A rule which.

Every fourth Year, at the *Vernal Equinox,* there is a Representative Council of the whole Nation, which meets in a Plain about twenty Miles from our House, and continueth about five or six Days. Here they inquire into the State and Condition of the several Districts; whether they abound or be deficient in Hay or Oats, or Cows or *Yahoos?* And whereever there is any Want (which is but seldom) it is immediately supplied by unanimous Consent and Contribution. Here likewise the Regulation of Children is settled: As for instance, if a *Houyhnhnm* hath two Males, he changeth one of them with another who hath two Females: And when a Child hath been lost by any Casualty, where the Mother is past Breeding, it is determined what Family shall breed another to supply the Loss.

CHAPTER IX

A grand Debate at the General Assembly of the Houyhnhnms; *and how it was determined. The Learning of the* Houyhnhnms. *Their Buildings. Their Manner of Burials. The Defectiveness of their Language.*

One of these Grand Assemblies was held in my time, about three Months before my Departure, whither my Master went as the Representative of our District. In this Council was resumed their old Debate, and indeed, the only Debate that ever happened in their Country; whereof my Master after his Return gave me a very particular Account.

The Question to be debated was, Whether the *Yahoos* should be exterminated from the Face of the Earth. One of the *Members* for the Affirmative offered several Arguments of great Strength and Weight; alledging, That, as the *Yahoos* were the most filthy, noisome, and deformed Animal which Nature ever produced, so they were the most restive and indocible,° mischievous and malicious: They would privately suck the Teats of the *Houyhnhnms* Cows; kill and devour their Cats, trample down their Oats and Grass, if they were not continually watched; and commit a Thousand other Extravagancies. He took Notice of a general Tradition, that *Yahoos* had not been always in their Country: But, that many Ages ago, two of these Brutes appeared together upon a Mountain; whether produced by the Heat of the Sun upon corrupted Mud and Slime, or from the Ooze and Froth of the Sea, was never known. That these *Yahoos* engendered, and their Brood in a short time grew so numerous as to over-run and infest the whole Nation. That the *Houyhnhnms* to get rid of this Evil, made a general Hunt-

indocible: Unteachable.

ing, and at last inclosed the whole Herd; and destroying the Older, every *Houyhnhnm* kept two young Ones in a Kennel, and brought them to such a Degree of Tameness, as an Animal so savage by Nature can be capable of acquiring; using them for Draught and Carriage. That, there seemed to be much Truth in this Tradition, and that those Creatures could not be *Ylnhniamshy* (or *Aborigines* of the Land) because of the violent Hatred the *Houyhnhnms* as well as all other Animals, bore them; which although their evil Disposition sufficiently deserved, could never have arrived at so high a Degree, if they had been *Aborigines*, or else they would have long since been rooted out. That, the Inhabitants taking a Fancy to use the Service of the *Yahoos*, had very imprudently neglected to cultivate the Breed of *Asses*, which were a comely Animal, easily kept, more tame and orderly, without any offensive Smell, strong enough for Labour, although they yield to the other in Agility of Body; and if their Braying be no agreeable Sound, it is far preferable to the horrible Howlings of the *Yahoos*.

Several others declared their Sentiments to the same Purpose; when my Master proposed an Expedient to the Assembly, whereof he had indeed borrowed the Hint from me. He approved of the Tradition, mentioned by the *Honourable Member*, who spoke before; and affirmed, that the two *Yahoos* said to be first seen among them, had been driven thither over the Sea; that coming to Land, and being forsaken by their Companions, they retired to the Mountains, and degenerating by Degrees, became in Process of Time, much more savage than those of their own Species in the Country from whence these two Originals came. The Reason of his Assertion was, that he had now in his Possession, a certain wonderful *Yahoo*, (meaning myself) which most of them had heard of, and many of them had seen. He then related to them, how he first found me; that, my Body was all covered with an artificial Composure° of the Skins and Hairs of other Animals: That, I spoke in a Language of my own, and had thoroughly learned theirs: That, I had related to him the Accidents which brought me thither: That, when he saw me without my Covering, I was an exact *Yahoo* in every Part, only of a whiter Colour, less hairy, and with shorter Claws. He added, how I had endeavoured to persuade him, that in my own and other Countries the *Yahoos* acted as the governing, rational Animal, and held the *Houyhnhnms* in Servitude: That, he observed in me all the Qualities of a *Yahoo*, only a little more civilized by some Tincture of Reason; which however was in a Degree as far inferior to the *Houyhnhnm* Race, as the

---

Composure: Composition.

Yahoos of their Country were to me: That, among other things, I mentioned a Custom we had of *castrating Houyhnhnms* when they were young, in order to render them tame; that the Operation was easy and safe; that it was no Shame to learn Wisdom from Brutes, as Industry is taught by the Ant, and Building by the Swallow. (For so I translate the Word *Lyhannh,* although it be a much larger Fowl.) That, this Invention might be practiced upon the younger *Yahoos* here, which, besides rendering them tractable and fitter for Use, would in an Age put an End to the whole Species without destroying Life. That, in the mean time the *Houyhnhnms* should be *exhorted* to cultivate the Breed of Asses, which, as they are in all respects more valuable Brutes; so they have this Advantage, to be fit for Service at five Years old, which the others are not till Twelve.

This was all my Master thought fit to tell me at that Time, of what passed in the Grand Council. But he was pleased to conceal one Particular, which related personally to myself, whereof I soon felt the unhappy Effect, as the Reader will know in its proper Place, and from whence I date all the succeeding Misfortunes of my Life.

The *Houyhnhnms* have no Letters, and consequently, their Knowledge is all traditional. But there happening few Events of any Moment among a People so well united, naturally disposed to every Virtue, wholly governed by Reason, and cut off from all Commerce with other Nations; the historical Part is easily preserved without burthening their Memories. I have already observed, that they are subject to no Diseases, and therefore can have no Need of Physicians. However, they have excellent Medicines composed of Herbs, to cure accidental Bruises and Cuts in the Pastern or Frog of the Foot by sharp Stones, as well as other Maims and Hurts in the several Parts of the Body.

They calculate the Year by the Revolution of the Sun and the Moon, but use no Subdivisions into Weeks. They are well enough acquainted with the Motions of those two Luminaries, and understand the Nature of *Eclipses;* and this is the utmost Progress of their *Astronomy.*

In *Poetry* they must be allowed to excel all other Mortals; wherein the Justness of their Similes, and the Minuteness, as well as Exactness of their Descriptions, are indeed inimitable. Their Verses abound very much in both of these; and usually contain either some exalted Notions of Friendship and Benevolence, or the Praises of those who were Victors in Races, and other bodily Exercises. Their Buildings, although very rude and simple, are not inconvenient, but well contrived to defend them from all Injuries of Cold and Heat. They have a Kind of Tree, which at Forty Years old loosens in the Root, and falls with the first

Storm; it grows very strait, and being pointed like Stakes with a sharp Stone, (for the *Houyhnhnms* know not the Use of Iron) they stick them erect in the Ground about ten Inches asunder, and then weave in Oatstraw, or sometimes Wattles betwixt them. The Roof is made after the same Manner, and so are the Doors.

The *Houyhnhnms* use the hollow Part between the Pastern and the Hoof of their Fore-feet, as we do our Hands, and this with greater Dexterity, than I could at first imagine. I have seen a white Mare of our Family thread a Needle (which I lent her on Purpose) with that Joynt. They milk their Cows, reap their Oats, and do all the Work which requires Hands, in the same Manner. They have a Kind of hard Flints, which by grinding against other Stones, they form into Instruments, that serve instead of Wedges, Axes, and Hammers. With Tools made of these Flints, they likewise cut their Hay, and reap their Oats, which there groweth naturally in several Fields: The *Yahoos* draw home the Sheaves in Carriages, and the Servants tread them in certain covered Hutts, to get out the Grain, which is kept in Stores. They make a rude Kind of earthen and wooden Vessels, and bake the former in the Sun.

If they can avoid Casualties, they die only of old Age, and are buried in the obscurest Places that can be found, their Friends and Relations expressing neither Joy nor Grief at their Departure; nor does the dying Person discover the least Regret that he is leaving the World, any more than if he were upon returning home from a Visit to one of his Neighbours: I remember, my Master having once made an Appointment with a Friend and his Family to come to his House upon some Affair of Importance; on the Day fixed, the Mistress and her two Children came very late; she made two Excuses, first for her Husband, who, as she said, happened that very Morning to *Lhnuwnh.* The Word is strongly expressive in their Language, but not easily rendered into *English;* it signifies, *to retire to his first Mother.* Her Excuse for not coming sooner, was, that her Husband dying late in the Morning, she was a good while consulting her Servants about a convenient Place where his Body should be laid; and I observed she behaved herself at our House, as chearfully as the rest: She died about three Months after.

They live generally to Seventy or Seventy-five Years, very seldom to Fourscore: Some Weeks before their Death they feel a gradual Decay, but without Pain. During this time they are much visited by their Friends, because they cannot go abroad with their usual Ease and Satisfaction. However, about ten Days before their Death, which they seldom fail in computing, they return the Visits that have been made them by those who are nearest in the Neighbourhood, being carried in a convenient Sledge drawn by *Yahoos;* which Vehicle they use, not only upon this Occasion, but when they grow old, upon long Journeys, or when they are lamed by any Accident. And therefore when the dying *Houyhnhnms* return those Visits, they take a solemn Leave of their Friends, as if they were going to some remote Part of the Country, where they designed to pass the rest of their Lives.

I know not whether it may be worth observing, that the *Houyhnhnms* have no Word in their Language to express any thing that is *evil*, except what they borrow from the Deformities or ill Qualities of the *Yahoos*. Thus they denote the Folly of a Servant, an Omission of a Child, a Stone that cuts their Feet, a Continuance of foul or unseasonable Weather, and the like, by adding to each the Epithet of *Yahoo*. For Instance, *Hhnm Yahoo, Whnaholm Yahoo, Ynlhmnawihlma Yahoo,* and an ill contrived House, *Ynholmhnmrohlnw Yahoo.*

I could with great Pleasure enlarge farther upon the Manners and Virtues of this excellent People; but intending in a short time to publish a Volume by itself expressly upon that Subject, I refer the Reader thither. And in the mean time, proceed to relate my own sad Catastrophe.

CHAPTER X

The Author's Oeconomy and happy Life among the Houyhnhnms. *His great Improvement in Virtue, by conversing with them. Their Conversations. The Author hath Notice given him by his Master that he must depart from the Country. He falls into a Swoon for Grief, but submits. He contrives and finishes a Canoo, by the Help of a Fellow-Servant, and puts to Sea at a Venture.*

I had settled my little Oeconomy to my own Heart's Content. My Master had ordered a Room to be made for me after their Manner, about six Yards from the House; the Sides and Floors of which I plaistered with Clay, and covered with Rush-mats of my own contriving: I had beaten Hemp, which there grows wild, and made of it a Sort of Ticking: This I filled with the Feathers of several Birds I had taken with Springes made of *Yahoos* Hairs; and were excellent Food. I had worked two Chairs with my Knife, the Sorrel Nag helping me in the grosser and more laborious Part. When my Cloaths were worn to Rags, I made my self others with the Skins of Rabbets, and of a certain beautiful Animal about the same Size, called *Nnuhnoh,* the Skin of which is covered with a fine Down. Of these I likewise made very tolerable Stockings. I soaled my Shoes with Wood which I cut from a Tree, and fitted to the upper Leather, and when this was worn out, I supplied it with the Skins of *Yahoos,* dried in the Sun. I often got Honey out of hollow Trees, which I mingled with Water, or eat it with my Bread. No Man could more verify the Truth of these two Maxims, *That, Nature is very easily satisfied;* and, *That, Necessity is the Mother of Invention.* I enjoyed perfect Health of Body, and Tranquility of Mind; I did not feel the Treachery or Inconstancy of a Friend, nor the Injuries of a secret or open Enemy. I had no Occasion of bribing, flattering or pimping, to procure the Favour of any great Man, or of his Minion. I wanted no Fence against Fraud or Oppression: Here was neither Physician to destroy my Body, nor Lawyer to ruin my Fortune: No Informer to watch my Words and Actions, or forge Accusations against me for Hire: Here were no Gibers, Censurers, Backbiters, Pickpockets, Highwaymen, House-breakers, Attorneys, Bawds, Buffoons, Gamesters, Politicians, Wits, Spleneticks, tedious Talkers, Controvertists,° Ravishers, Murderers, Robbers, Virtuoso's;° no Leaders or Followers of Party and Faction; no Encouragers to Vice, by Seducement or Examples: No Dungeon, Axes, Gibbets, Whipping-posts, or Pillories; No cheating Shopkeepers or Mechanicks:° No Pride, Vanity or Affectation: No Fops, Bullies, Drunkards, strolling Whores, or Poxes: No ranting, lewd, expensive Wives: No stupid, proud Pedants: No importunate, over-bearing, quarrelsome, noisy, roaring, empty, conceited, swearing Companions: No Scoundrels raised from the Dust upon the Merit of their Vices; or Nobility thrown into it on account of their Virtues: No Lords, Fidlers, Judges or Dancing-masters.

I had the Favour of being admitted to several *Houyhnhnms,* who came to visit or dine with my Master; where his Honour graciously suffered me to wait in the Room, and listen to their Discourse. Both he and his Company would often descend to ask me Questions, and receive my Answers. I had also sometimes the Honour of attending my Master in his Visits to others. I never presumed to speak, except in answer to a Question; and then I did it with inward Regret, because it was a Loss of so much Time for improving my self: But I was infinitely delighted with the Station of an humble Auditor in such Conversations, where nothing passed but what was useful, expressed in the fewest and most significant Words: Where (as I have already said) the greatest *Decency* was observed, without the least Degree of Ceremony; where no Person spoke without being pleased himself, and pleasing his Compan-

---

Controvertists: Those who engage in controversy.   **Virtuoso's:** Scientists, or dabblers in science.   **Mechanicks:** Manual laborers.

ions: Where there was no Interruption, Tediousness, Heat, or Difference of Sentiments. They have a Notion, That when People are met together, a short Silence doth much improve Conversation: This I found to be true; for during those little Intermissions of Talk, new Ideas would arise in their Minds, which very much enlivened the Discourse. Their Subjects are generally on Friendship and Benevolence; on Order and Oeconomy; sometimes upon the visible Operations of Nature, or ancient Traditions; upon the Bounds and Limits of Virtue; upon the unerring Rules of Reason; or upon some Determinations, to be taken at the next great Assembly; and often upon the various Excellencies of *Poetry*. I may add, without Vanity, that my Presence often gave them sufficient Matter for Discourse, because it afforded my Master an Occasion of letting his Friends into the History of me and my Country, upon which they were all pleased to discant in a Manner not very advantageous to human Kind; and for that Reason I shall not repeat what they said: Only I may be allowed to observe, That his Honour, to my great Admiration, appeared to understand the Nature of *Yahoos* much better than my self. He went through all our Vices and Follies, and discovered many which I had never mentioned to him; by only supposing what Qualities a *Yahoo* of their Country, with a small Proportion of Reason, might be capable of exerting: And concluded, with too much Probability, how vile as well as miserable such a Creature must be.

I freely confess, that all the little Knowledge I have of any Value, was acquired by the Lectures I received from my Master, and from hearing the Discourses of him and his Friends; to which I should be prouder to listen, than to dictate to the greatest and wisest Assembly in *Europe*. I admired the Strength, Comeliness and Speed of the Inhabitants; and such a Constellation of Virtues in such amiable Persons produced in me the highest Veneration. At first, indeed, I did not feel that natural Awe which the *Yahoos* and all other Animals bear towards them; but it grew upon me by Degrees, much sooner than I imagined, and was mingled with a respectful Love and Gratitude, that they would condescend to distinguish me from the rest of my Species.

When I thought of my Family, my Friends, my Countrymen, or human Race in general, I considered them as they really were, *Yahoos* in Shape and Disposition, perhaps a little more civilized, and qualified with the Gift of Speech; but making no other Use of Reason, than to improve and multiply those Vices, whereof their Brethren in this Country had only the Share that Nature allotted them. When I happened to behold the Reflection of my own Form in a Lake or Fountain, I turned away my Face in Horror and detestation of my self; and could better endure the Sight of a common *Yahoo,* than of my own Person. By conversing with the *Houyhnhnms,* and looking upon them with Delight, I fell to imitate their Gait and Gesture, which is now grown into a Habit; and my Friends often tell me in a blunt Way, that *I trot like a Horse;* which, however, I take for a great Compliment: Neither shall I disown, that in speaking I am apt to fall into the Voice and manner of the *Houyhnhnms,* and hear my self ridiculed on that Account without the least Mortification.

In the Midst of this Happiness, when I looked upon my self to be fully settled for Life, my Master sent for me one Morning a little earlier than his usual Hour. I observed by his Countenance that he was in some Perplexity, and at a Loss how to begin what he had to speak. After a short Silence, he told me, he did not know how I would take what he was going to say: That, in the last general Assembly, when the Affair of the *Yahoos* was entered upon, the Representatives had taken Offence at his keeping a *Yahoo* (meaning my self) in his Family more like a *Houyhnhnm* than a Brute Animal. That, he was known frequently to converse with me, as if he could receive some Advantage or Pleasure in my Company: That, such a Practice was not agreeable to Reason or Nature, nor a thing ever heard of before among them. The Assembly did therefore *exhort* him, either to employ me like the rest of my Species, or command me to swim back to the Place from whence I came. That, the first of these Expedients was utterly rejected by all the *Houyhnhnms,* who had ever seen me at his House or their own: For, they alledged, That because I had some Rudiments of Reason, added to the natural Pravity° of those Animals, it was to be feared, I might be able to seduce them into the woody and mountainous Parts of the Country, and bring them in Troops by Night to destroy the *Houyhnhnms* Cattle, as being naturally of the ravenous Kind, and averse from Labour.

My Master added, That he was daily pressed by the *Houyhnhnms* of the Neighbourhood to have the Assembly's *Exhortation* executed, which he could not put off much longer. He doubted,° it would be impossible for me to swim to another Country; and therefore wished I would contrive some Sort of Vehicle resembling those I had described to him, that might carry me on the Sea; in which Work I should have the Assistance of his own Servants, as well as those of his Neighbours. He concluded, that for his own Part he could have been content to keep me in his Service as long as I lived; because he found I had cured myself

Pravity: Depravity.   **doubted:** Feared.

of some bad Habits and Dispositions, by endeavouring, as far as my inferior Nature was capable, to imitate the *Houyhnhnms.*

I should here observe to the Reader, that a Decree of the general Assembly in this Country, is expressed by the Word *Hnhloayn,* which signifies an *Exhortation;* as near as I can render it: For they have no Conception how a rational Creature can be *compelled,* but only advised, or *exhorted;* because no Person can disobey Reason, without giving up his Claim to be a rational Creature.

I was struck with the utmost Grief and Despair at my Master's Discourse; and being unable to support the Agonies I was under, I fell into a Swoon at his Feet: When I came to myself, he told me, that he concluded I had been dead. (For these People are subject to no such Imbecillities of Nature.) I answered, in a faint Voice, that Death would have been too great an Happiness; that although I could not blame the Assembly's *Exhortation,* or the Urgency of his Friends; yet in my weak and corrupt Judgment, I thought it might consist with Reason to have been less rigorous. That, I could not swim a League, and probably the nearest Land to theirs might be distant above an Hundred: That, many Materials, necessary for making a small Vessel to carry me off, were wholly wanting in this Country, which however, I would attempt in Obedience and Gratitude to his Honour, although I concluded the thing to be impossible, and therefore looked on myself as already devoted to Destruction. That, the certain Prospect of an unnatural Death, was the least of my Evils: For, supposing I should escape with Life by some strange Adventure, how could I think with Temper,° of passing my Days among *Yahoos,* and relapsing into my old Corruptions, for want of Examples to lead and keep me within the Paths of Virtue. That, I knew too well upon what solid Reasons all the Determinations of the wise *Houyhnhnms* were founded, not to be shaken by Arguments of mine, a miserable *Yahoo;* and therefore after presenting him with my humble Thanks for the Offer of his Servants Assistance in making a Vessel, and desiring a reasonable Time for so difficult a Work, I told him, I would endeavour to preserve a wretched Being; and, if ever I returned to *England,* was not without Hopes of being useful to my own Species, by celebrating the Praises of the renowned *Houyhnhnms,* and proposing their Virtues to the Imitation of Mankind.

My Master in a few Words made me a very gracious Reply, allowed me the Space of two *Months* to finish my Boat; and ordered the Sorrel Nag, my Fellow-Servant, (for so at this Distance I may presume to call

with Temper: Without losing one's composure.

him) to follow my Instructions, because I told my Master, that his Help would be sufficient, and I knew he had a Tenderness for me.

In his Company my first Business was to go to that Part of the Coast, where my rebellious Crew had ordered me to be set on Shore. I got upon a Height, and looking on every Side into the Sea, fancied I saw a small Island, towards the *North-East:* I took out my Pocket-glass, and could then clearly distinguish it about five Leagues off, as I computed; but it appeared to the Sorrel Nag to be only a blue Cloud: For, as he had no Conception of any Country beside his own, so he could not be as expert in distinguishing remote Objects at Sea, as we who so much converse in that Element.

After I had discovered this Island, I considered no farther; but resolved, it should, if possible, be the first Place of my Banishment, leaving the Consequence to Fortune.

I returned home, and consulting with the Sorrel Nag, we went into a Copse at some Distance, where I with my Knife, and he with a sharp Flint fastened very artificially,° after their Manner, to a wooden Handle, cut down several Oak Wattles° about the Thickness of a Walking-staff, and some larger Pieces. But I shall not trouble the Reader with a particular Description of my own Mechanicks: Let it suffice to say, that in six Weeks time, with the Help of the Sorrel Nag, who performed the Parts that required most Labour, I finished a Sort of *Indian* Canoo, but much larger, covering it with the Skins of *Yahoos,* well stitched together, with hempen Threads of my own making. My Sail was likewise composed of the Skins of the same Animal; but I made use of the youngest I could get, the older being too tough and thick; and I likewise provided myself with four Paddles. I laid in a Stock of boiled Flesh, of Rabbets and Fowls; and took with me two Vessels, one filled with Milk, and the other with Water.

I tried my Canoo in a large Pond near my Master's House, and then corrected in it what was amiss; stopping all the Chinks with *Yahoos* Tallow, till I found it stanch,° and able to bear me, and my Freight. And when it was as compleat as I could possibly make it, I had it drawn on a Carriage very gently by *Yahoos,* to the Sea-side, under the Conduct of the Sorrel Nag, and another Servant.

When all was ready, and the Day came for my Departure, I took Leave of my Master and Lady, and the whole Family, mine Eyes flowing with Tears, and my Heart quite sunk with Grief. But his Honour, out of Curiosity, and perhaps (if I may speak it without Vanity) partly out of

---

artificially: Artfully.   **Wattles:** Sticks.   **stanch:** Watertight.

Kindness, was determined to see me in my Canoe; and got several of his neighbouring Friends to accompany him. I was forced to wait above an Hour for the Tide, and then observing the Wind very fortunately bearing towards the Island, to which I intended to steer my Course, I took a second Leave of my Master: But as I was going to prostrate myself to kiss his Hoof, he did me the Honour to raise it gently to my Mouth. I am not ignorant how much I have been censured for mentioning this last Particular. Detractors are pleased to think it improbable, that so illustrious a Person should descend to give so great a Mark of Distinction to a Creature so inferior as I. Neither have I forgot, how apt some Travellers are to boast of extraordinary Favours they have received. But, if these Censurers were better acquainted with the noble and courteous Disposition of the *Houyhnhnms*, they would soon change their Opinion.

I paid my Respects to the rest of the *Houyhnhnms* in his Honour's Company; then getting into my Canoe, I pushed off from Shore.

CHAPTER XI

The Author's dangerous Voyage. He arrives at New-Holland, *hoping to settle there. Is wounded with an Arrow by one of the Natives. Is seized and carried by Force into a* Portugueze *Ship. The great Civilities of the Captain. The Author arrives at* England.

I began this desperate Voyage on *February* 15, 171–, at 9 o'Clock in the Morning. The Wind was very favourable; however, I made use at first only of my Paddles; but considering I should soon be weary, and that the Wind might probably chop about, I ventured to set up my little Sail; and thus, with the Help of the Tide, I went at the Rate of a League and a Half an Hour, as near as I could guess. My Master and his Friends continued on the Shoar, till I was almost out of Sight; and I often heard the Sorrel Nag (who always loved me) crying out, *Hnuy illa nyha maiah Yahoo,* Take Care of thy self, gentle *Yahoo.*

My Design was, if possible, to discover some small Island uninhabited, yet sufficient by my Labour to furnish me with Necessaries of Life, which I would have thought a greater Happiness than to be first Minister in the politest Court of *Europe;* so horrible was the Idea I conceived of returning to live in the Society and under the Government of *Yahoos.* For in such a Solitude as I desired, I could at least enjoy my own Thoughts, and reflect with Delight on the Virtues of those inimitable *Houyhnhnms*, without any Opportunity of degenerating into the Vices and Corruptions of my own Species.

The Reader may remember what I related when my Crew conspired against me, and confined me to my Cabbin. How I continued there several Weeks, without knowing what Course we took; and when I was put ashore in the Long-boat, how the Sailors told me with Oaths, whether true or false, that they knew not in what Part of the World we were. However, I did then believe us to be about ten Degrees *Southward* of the *Cape of Good Hope,* or about 45 Degrees *Southern* Latitude, as I gathered from some general Words I overheard among them, being I supposed to the *South-East* in their intended Voyage to *Madagascar.* And although this were but little better than Conjecture, yet I resolved to steer my Course *Eastward,* hoping to reach the *South-West* Coast of *New-Holland,* and perhaps some such Island as I desired, lying *Westward* of it. The Wind was full *West,* and by six in the Evening I computed I had gone *Eastward* at least eighteen Leagues; when I spied a very small Island about half a League off, which I soon reached. It was nothing but a Rock with one Creek, naturally arched by the Force of Tempests. Here I put in my Canoo, and climbing a Part of the Rock, I could plainly discover Land to the *East,* extending from *South* to *North.* I lay all Night in my Canoo; and repeating my Voyage early in the Morning, I arrived in seven Hours to the *South-East* Point of *New-Holland.* This confirmed me in the Opinion I have long entertained, that the *Maps* and *Charts* place this Country at least three Degrees more to the *East* than it really is; which Thought I communicated many Years ago to my worthy Friend Mr. *Herman Moll,*° and gave him my Reasons for it, although he hath rather chosen to follow other Authors.°

I saw no Inhabitants in the Place where I landed; and being unarmed, I was afraid of venturing far into the Country. I found some Shell-Fish on the Shore, and eat them raw, not daring to kindle a Fire, for fear of being discovered by the Natives. I continued three Days feeding on Oysters and Limpits, to save my own Provisions; and I fortunately found a Brook of excellent Water, which gave me great Relief.

On the fourth Day, venturing out early a little too far, I saw twenty or thirty Natives upon a Height, not above five hundred Yards from me. They were stark naked, Men, Women and Children round a Fire, as I could discover by the Smoke. One of them spied me, and gave Notice to the rest; five of them advanced towards me, leaving the Women and Children at the Fire. I made what haste I could to the Shore, and getting into my Canoo, shoved off: The Savages observing me retreat, ran

---

Herman Moll: Author of *A New and Correct Map of the Whole World* (1719). **Authors:** Authorities.

after me; and before I could get far enough into the Sea, discharged an Arrow, which wounded me deeply on the Inside of my left Knee (I shall carry the Mark to my Grave). I apprehended the Arrow might be poisoned; and paddling out of the Reach of their Darts (being a calm Day) I made a shift to suck the Wound, and dress it as well as I could.

I was at a Loss what to do, for I durst not return to the same Landing-place, but stood to° the *North,* and was forced to paddle; for the Wind, although very gentle, was against me, blowing *North-West.* As I was looking about for a secure Landing-place, I saw a Sail to the *North North-East,* which appearing every Minute more visible, I was in some Doubt, whether I should wait for them or no; but at last my Detestation of the *Yahoo* Race prevailed; and turning my Canoo, I sailed and paddled together to the *South,* and got into the same Creek from whence I set out in the Morning; choosing rather to trust my self among these *Barbarians,* than live with *European Yahoos.* I drew up my Canoo as close as I could to the Shore, and hid my self behind a Stone by the little Brook, which, as I have already said, was excellent Water.

The Ship came within half a League of this Creek, and sent out her Long-Boat with Vessels to take in fresh Water (for the Place it seems was very well known) but I did not observe it until the Boat was almost on Shore; and it was too late to seek another Hiding-Place. The Seamen at their landing observed my Canoo, and rummaging it all over, easily conjectured that the Owner could not be far off. Four of them well armed searched every Cranny and Lurking-hole, till at last they found me flat on my Face behind the Stone. They gazed a while in Admiration at my strange uncouth Dress; my Coat made of Skins, my wooden-soaled Shoes, and my furred Stockings; from whence, however, they concluded I was not a Native of the Place, who all go naked. One of the Seamen in *Portugueze* bid me rise, and asked who I was. I understood that Language very well, and getting upon my Feet, said, I was a poor *Yahoo,* banished from the *Houyhnhnms,* and desired they would please to let me depart. They admired to hear me answer them in their own Tongue, and saw by my Complection I must be an European; but were at a Loss to know what I meant by *Yahoos* and *Houyhnhnms,* and at the same Time fell a laughing at my strange Tone in speaking, which resembled the Neighing of a Horse. I trembled all the while betwixt Fear and Hatred: I again desired Leave to depart, and was gently moving to my Canoo; but they laid hold on me, desiring to know what Country I was of? whence I came? with many other Questions. I told them, I was born

stood to: Steered towards.

in *England,* from whence I came about five Years ago, and then their
Country and ours were at Peace. I therefore hoped they would not treat
me as an Enemy, since I meant them no Harm, but was a poor *Yahoo,*
seeking some desolate Place where to pass the Remainder of his unfortunate Life.

When they began to talk, I thought I never heard or saw any thing
so unnatural; for it appeared to me as monstrous as if a Dog or a Cow
should speak in *England,* or a *Yahoo* in *Houyhnhnm-Land.* The honest
Portuguese were equally amazed at my strange Dress, and the odd
Manner of delivering my Words, which however they understood very
well. They spoke to me with great Humanity, and said they were sure
their Captain would carry me *gratis* to *Lisbon,* from whence I might
return to my own Country; that two of the Seamen would go back to
the Ship, to inform the Captain of what they had seen, and receive his
Orders; in the mean Time, unless I would give my solemn Oath not to
fly, they would secure me by Force. I thought it best to comply with
their Proposal. They were very curious to know my Story, but I gave
them very little Satisfaction; and they all conjectured, that my
Mixfortunes had impaired my Reason. In two Hours the Boat, which
went loaden with Vessels of Water, returned with the Captain's Commands to fetch me on Board. I fell on my Knees to preserve my Liberty;
but all was in vain, and the Men having tied me with Cords, heaved me
into the Boat, from whence I was taken into the Ship, and from thence
into the Captain's Cabbin.

His Name was *Pedro de Mendez;* he was a very courteous and generous Person; he entreated me to give some Account of my self, and desired to know what I would eat or drink; said, I should be used as well
as himself, and spoke so many obliging Things, that I wondered to find
such Civilities from a *Yahoo.* However, I remained silent and sullen; I
was ready to faint at the very Smell of him and his Men. At last I desired
something to eat out of my own Canoo; but he ordered me a Chicken
and some excellent Wine, and then directed that I should be put to Bed
in a very clean Cabbin. I would not undress my self, but lay on the
Bed-cloaths; and in half an Hour stole out, when I thought the Crew
was at Dinner; and getting to the Side of the Ship, was going to leap
into the Sea, and swim for my Life, rather than continue among *Yahoos.*
But one of the Seamen prevented me, and having informed the Captain,
I was chained to my Cabbin.

After Dinner *Don Pedro* came to me, and desired to know my Reason for so desperate an Attempt; assured me he only meant to do me all
the Service he was able; and spoke so very movingly, that at last I de-

scended to treat him like an Animal which had some little Portion of Reason. I gave him a very short Relation of my Voyage; of the Conspiracy against me by my own Men; of the Country where they set me on Shore, and of my five Years Residence there. All which he looked upon as if it were a Dream or a Vision; whereat I took great Offence: For I had quite forgot the Faculty of Lying, so peculiar to *Yahoos* in all Countries where they preside, and consequently the Disposition of suspecting Truth in others of their own Species. I asked him, Whether it were the Custom of his Country to *say the Thing that was not?* I assured him I had almost forgot what he meant by Falshood; and if I had lived a thousand Years in *Houyhnhnmland,* I should never have heard a Lie from the meanest Servant. That I was altogether indifferent whether he believed me or no; but however, in return for his Favours, I would give so much Allowance to the Corruption of his Nature, as to answer any Objection he would please to make; and he might easily discover the Truth.

The Captain, a wise Man, after many Endeavours to catch me tripping in some Part of my Story, at last began to have a better Opinion of my Veracity. But he added, that since I professed so inviolable an Attachment to Truth, I must give him my Word of Honour to bear him Company in this Voyage without attempting any thing against my Life; or else he would continue me a Prisoner till we arrived at *Lisbon.* I gave him the Promise he required; but at the same time protested that I would suffer the greatest Hardships rather than return to live among *Yahoos.*

Our Voyage passed without any considerable Accident. In Gratitude to the Captain I sometimes sate with him at his earnest Request, and strove to conceal my Antipathy against human Kind, although it often broke out; which he suffered to pass without Observation. But the greatest Part of the Day, I confined myself to my Cabbin, to avoid seeing any of the Crew. The Captain had often intreated me to strip myself of my savage Dress, and offered to lend me the best Suit of Cloaths he had. This I would not be prevailed on to accept, abhorring to cover myself with any thing that had been on the Back of a *Yahoo.* I only desired he would lend me two clean Shirts, which having been washed since he wore them, I believed would not so much defile me. These I changed every second Day, and washed them myself.

We arrived at *Lisbon, Nov.* 5, 1715. At our landing, the Captain forced me to cover myself with his Cloak, to prevent the Rabble from crouding about me. I was conveyed to his own House; and at my earnest Request, he led me up to the highest Room backwards.° I conjured him to

backwards: At the rear of the house.

conceal from all Persons what I had told him of the *Houyhnhnms;* because the least Hint of such a Story would not only draw Numbers of People to see me, but probably put me in Danger of being imprisoned, or burnt by the *Inquisition.* The Captain persuaded me to accept a Suit of Cloaths newly made; but I would not suffer the Taylor to take my Measure; however, Don *Pedro* being almost of my Size, they fitted me well enough. He accoutred me with other Necessaries all new, which I aired for Twenty-four Hours before I would use them.

The Captain had no Wife, nor above three Servants, none of which were suffered to attend at Meals; and his whole Deportment was so obliging, added to very good *human* Understanding, that I really began to tolerate his Company. He gained so far upon me, that I ventured to look out of the back Window. By Degrees I was brought into another Room, from whence I peeped into the Street, but drew my Head back in a Fright. In a Week's Time he seduced me down to the Door. I found my Terror gradually lessened, but my Hatred and Contempt seemed to increase. I was at last bold enough to walk the Street in his Company, but kept my Nose well stopped with Rue,° or sometimes with Tobacco.

In ten Days, Don *Pedro,* to whom I had given some Account of my domestick Affairs, put it upon me as a Point of Honour and Conscience, that I ought to return to my native Country, and live at home with my Wife and Children. He told me, there was an *English* Ship in the Port just ready to sail, and he would furnish me with all things necessary. It would be tedious to repeat his Arguments, and my Contradictions. He said, it was altogether impossible to find such a solitary Island as I had desired to live in; but I might command in my own House, and pass my time in a Manner as recluse as I pleased.

I complied at last, finding I could not do better. I left *Lisbon* the 24th Day of *November,* in an *English* Merchant-man, but who was the Master I never inquired. Don *Pedro* accompanied me to the Ship, and lent me Twenty Pounds. He took kind Leave of me, and embraced me at parting; which I bore as well as I could. During this last Voyage I had no Commerce with the Master, or any of his Men; but pretending I was sick kept close in my Cabbin. On the Fifth of *December,* 1715, we cast Anchor in the *Downs* about Nine in the Morning, and at Three in the Afternoon I got safe to my House at *Redriff.*

My Wife and Family received me with great Surprize and Joy, because they concluded me certainly dead; but I must freely confess, the

Rue: A strong-scented herb.

Sight of them filled me only with Hatred, Disgust and Contempt; and the more, by reflecting on the near Alliance I had to them. For, although since my unfortunate Exile from the *Houyhnhnm* Country, I had compelled myself to tolerate the Sight of *Yahoos,* and to converse with Don *Pedro de Mendez;* yet my Memory and Imaginations were perpetually filled with the Virtues and Ideas of those exalted *Houyhnhnms.* And when I began to consider, that by copulating with one of the *Yahoo*-Species, I had become a Parent of more; it struck me with the utmost Shame, Confusion and Horror.

As soon as I entered the House, my Wife took me in her Arms, and kissed me; at which, having not been used to the Touch of that odious Animal for so many Years, I fell in a Swoon for almost an Hour. At the Time I am writing, it is five Years since my last Return to *England:* During the first Year I could not endure my Wife or Children in my Presence, the very Smell of them was intolerable; much less could I suffer them to eat in the same Room. To this Hour they dare not presume to touch my Bread, or drink out of the same Cup; neither was I ever able to let one of them take me by the Hand. The first Money I laid out was to buy two young Stone-Horses,° which I keep in a good Stable, and next to them the Groom is my greatest Favourite; for I feel my Spirits revived by the Smell he contracts in the Stable. My Horses understand me tolerably well; I converse with them at least four Hours every Day. They are Strangers to Bridle or Saddle; they live in great Amity with me, and Friendship to each other.

CHAPTER XII

The Author's Veracity. His Design in publishing this Work. His Censure of those Travellers who swerve from the Truth. The Author clears himself from any sinister Ends in writing. An Objection answered. The Method of planting Colonies. His Native Country commended. The Right of the Crown to those Countries described by the Author, is justified. The Difficulty of conquering them. The Author takes his last Leave of the Reader; proposeth his Manner of Living for the future; gives good Advice, and concludeth.

Thus, gentle Reader, I have given thee a faithful History of my Travels for Sixteen Years, and above Seven Months; wherein I have not been so studious of Ornament as of Truth. I could perhaps like others have

Stone-Horses: Stallions.

astonished thee with strange improbable Tales; but I rather chose to relate plain Matter of Fact in the simplest Manner and Style; because my principal Design was to inform, and not to amuse thee.

It is easy for us who travel into remote Countries, which are seldom visited by *Englishmen* or other *Europeans,* to form Descriptions of wonderful Animals both at Sea and Land. Whereas, a Traveller's chief Aim should be to make Men wiser and better, and to improve their Minds by the bad, as well as good Example of what they deliver concerning foreign Places.

I could heartily wish a Law were enacted, that every Traveller, before he were permitted to publish his Voyages, should be obliged to make Oath before the *Lord High Chancellor,* that all he intended to print was absolutely true to the best of his Knowledge; for then the World would no longer be deceived as it usually is, while some Writers, to make their Works pass the better upon the Publick, impose the grossest Falsities on the unwary Reader. I have perused several Books of Travels with great Delight in my younger Days; but, having since gone over most Parts of the Globe, and been able to contradict many fabulous Accounts from my own Observation; it hath given me a great Disgust against this Part of Reading, and some Indignation to see the Credulity of Mankind so impudently abused. Therefore since my Acquaintance were pleased to think my poor Endeavours might not be unacceptable to my Country; I imposed on myself as a Maxim, never to be swerved from, that I would *strictly adhere to Truth;* neither indeed can I be ever under the least Temptation to vary from it, while I retain in my Mind the Lectures and Example of my noble Master, and the other illustrious *Houyhnhnms,* of whom I had so long the Honour to be an humble Hearer.

> —— *Nec si miserum Fortuna Sinonem*
> *Finxit, vanum etiam, mendacemque improba finget.*°

I know very well, how little Reputation is to be got by Writings which require neither Genius nor Learning, nor indeed any other Talent, except a good Memory, or an exact *Journal.* I know likewise, that Writers of Travels, like *Dictionary*-Makers, are sunk into Oblivion by the Weight and Bulk of those who come last, and therefore lie uppermost. And it is highly probable, that such Travellers who shall hereafter

---

Nec si miserum . . . finget: "Nor, if cruel fortune has made Sinon miserable, shall she also make him false and deceitful." These lines, from book 2 of Virgil's *Aeneid* (lines 79–80), are the words of Sinon, who convinced the Trojans to bring the wooden horse inside the walls of their city. Sinon is perhaps the archetypal liar.

visit the Countries described in this Work of mine, may by detecting my Errors, (if there be any) and adding many new Discoveries of their own, jostle me out of Vogue, and stand in my Place; making the World forget that ever I was an Author. This indeed would be too great a Mortification if I wrote for Fame: But, as my sole Intention was the PUBLICK GOOD, I cannot be altogether disappointed. For, who can read of the Virtues I have mentioned in the glorious *Houyhnhnms*, without being ashamed of his own Vices, when he considers himself as the reasoning, governing Animal of his Country? I shall say nothing of those remote Nations where *Yahoos* preside; amongst which the least corrupted are the *Brobdingnagians,* whose wise Maxims in Morality and Government, it would be our Happiness to observe. But I forbear descanting further, and rather leave the judicious Reader to his own Remarks and Applications.

I am not a little pleased that this Work of mine can possibly meet with no Censurers: For what Objections can be made against a Writer who relates only plain Facts that happened in such distant Countries, where we have not the least Interest with respect either to Trade or Negotiations? I have carefully avoided every Fault with which common Writers of Travels are often too justly charged. Besides, I meddle not the least with any *Party,* but write without Passion, Prejudice, or Ill-will against any Man or Number of Men whatsoever. I write for the noblest End, to inform and instruct Mankind, over whom I may, without Breach of Modesty, pretend to some Superiority, from the Advantages I received by conversing so long among the most accomplished *Houyhnhnms.* I write without any View towards Profit or Praise. I never suffer a Word to pass that may look like Reflection, or possibly give the least Offence even to those who are most ready to take it. So that, I hope, I may with Justice pronounce myself an Author perfectly blameless; against whom the Tribes of Answerers, Considerers, Observers, Reflecters, Detecters, Remarkers, will never be able to find Matter for exercising their Talents.

I confess, it was whispered to me, that I was bound in Duty as a Subject of *England,* to have given in a Memorial to a Secretary of State, at my first coming over; because, whatever Lands are discovered by a Subject, belong to the Crown. But I doubt, whether our Conquests in the Countries I treat of, would be as easy as those of *Ferdinando Cortez*° over the naked *Americans.* The *Lilliputians* I think, are hardly worth

Ferdinando Cortez: The Spaniard Hernando Cortés (1485–1547), who conquered Mexico in slightly over two years.

the Charge of a Fleet and Army to reduce them; and I question whether it might be prudent or safe to attempt the *Brobdingnagians:* Or, whether an *English* Army would be much at their Ease with the Flying Island over their Heads. The *Houyhnhnms,* indeed, appear not to be so well prepared for War, a Science to which they are perfect Strangers, and especially against missive Weapons.° However, supposing myself to be a Minister of State, I could never give my Advice for invading them. Their Prudence, Unanimity, Unacquaintedness with Fear, and their Love of their Country would amply supply all Defects in the military Art. Imagine twenty Thousand of them breaking into the Midst of an *European* Army, confounding the Ranks, overturning the Carriages, battering the Warriors Faces into Mummy,° by terrible Yerks° from their hinder Hoofs: For they would well deserve the Character given to *Augustus; Recalcitrat undique tutus.*° But instead of Proposals for conquering that magnanimous Nation, I rather wish they were in a Capacity or Disposition to send a sufficient Number of their Inhabitants for civilizing *Europe;* by teaching us the first Principles of Honour, Justice, Truth, Temperance, publick Spirit, Fortitude, Chastity, Friendship, Benevolence, and Fidelity. The *Names* of all which Virtues are still retained among us in most Languages, and are to be met with in modern as well as ancient Authors; which I am able to assert from my own small Reading.

But, I had another Reason which made me less forward to enlarge his Majesty's Dominions by my Discoveries: To say the Truth, I had conceived a few Scruples with relation to the distributive Justice of Princes upon those Occasions. For Instance, A Crew of Pyrates are driven by a Storm they know not whither; at length a Boy discovers Land from the Top-mast; they go on Shore to rob and plunder; they see an harmless People, are entertained with Kindness, they give the Country a new Name, they take formal Possession of it for the King, they set up a rotten Plank or a Stone for a Memorial, they murder two or three Dozen of the Natives, bring away a Couple more by Force for a Sample, return home, and get their Pardon. Here commences a new Dominion acquired with a Title by *Divine Right.* Ships are sent with the first Opportunity; the Natives driven out or destroyed, their Princes tortured to discover their Gold; a free Licence given to all Acts of Inhumanity and Lust; the Earth reeking with the Blood of its Inhabitants: And this execrable Crew of Butchers employed in so pious an Expedition, is a *modern Colony* sent to convert and civilize an idolatrous and barbarous People.

---

missive Weapons: Missiles.   **Mummy:** Pulp.   **Yerks:** Kicks.   ***Recalcitrat undique tutus:*** "[H]e kicks backwards, protected on each side" (Horace, *Satires* 2.1, line 20).

But this Description, I confess, doth by no means affect the *British* Nation, who may be an Example to the whole World for their Wisdom, Care, and Justice in planting Colonies; their liberal Endowments for the Advancement of Religion and Learning; their Choice of devout and able Pastors to propagate *Christianity;* their Caution in stocking their Provinces with People of sober Lives and Conversations from this the Mother Kingdom; their strict Regard to the Distribution of Justice, in supplying the Civil Administration through all their Colonies with Officers of the greatest Abilities, utter Strangers to Corruption: And to crown all, by sending the most vigilant and virtuous Governors, who have no other Views than the Happiness of the People over whom they preside, and the Honour of the King their Master.

But, as those Countries which I have described do not appear to have a Desire of being conquered, and enslaved, murdered or driven out by Colonies; nor abound either in Gold, Silver, Sugar or Tobacco; I did humbly conceive they were by no Means proper Objects of our Zeal, our Valour, or our Interest. However, if those whom it more concerns, think fit to be of another Opinion, I am ready to depose, when I shall be lawfully called, That no *European* did ever visit these Countries before me. I mean, if the Inhabitants ought to be believed.

But, as to the Formality of taking Possession in my Sovereign's Name, it never came once into my Thoughts; and if it had, yet as my Affairs then stood, I should perhaps in point of Prudence and Self-Preservation, have put it off to a better Opportunity.

Having thus answered the *only* Objection that can be raised against me as a Traveller; I here take a final Leave of my Courteous Readers, and return to enjoy my own Speculations in my little Garden at *Redriff;* to apply those excellent Lessons of Virtue which I learned among the *Houyhnhnms;* to instruct the *Yahoos* of my own Family as far as I shall find them docible° Animals; to behold my Figure often in a Glass, and thus if possible habituate my self by Time to tolerate the Sight of a human Creature: To lament the Brutality of *Houyhnhnms* in my own Country, but always treat their Persons with Respect, for the Sake of my noble Master, his Family, his Friends, and the whole *Houyhnhnm* Race, whom these of ours have the Honour to resemble in all their Lineaments, however their Intellectuals° came to degenerate.

I began last Week to permit my Wife to sit at Dinner with me, at the farthest End of a long Table; and to answer (but with the utmost Brevity) the few Questions I asked her. Yet the Smell of a *Yahoo* continuing

docible: Teachable.   **Intellectuals:** Minds.

very offensive, I always keep my Nose well stopt with Rue, Lavender, or Tobacco-Leaves. And although it be hard for a Man late in Life to remove old Habits; I am not altogether out of Hopes in some Time to suffer a Neighbour *Yahoo* in my Company, without the Apprehensions I am yet under of his Teeth or his Claws.

My Reconcilement to the *Yahoo*-kind in general might not be so difficult, if they would be content with those Vices and Follies only which Nature hath entitled them to. I am not in the least provoked at the Sight of a Lawyer, a Pick-pocket, a Colonel, a Fool, a Lord, a Gamester, a Politician, a Whoremunger, a Physician, an Evidence,° a Suborner, an Attorney, a Traytor, or the like: This is all according to the due Course of Things: But, when I behold a Lump of Deformity, and Diseases both in Body and Mind, smitten with *Pride,* it immediately breaks all the Measures of my Patience; neither shall I be ever able to comprehend how such an Animal and such a Vice could tally together. The wise and virtuous *Houyhnhnms,* who abound in all Excellencies that can adorn a rational Creature, have no Name for this Vice in their Language, which hath no Terms to express any thing that is evil, except those whereby they describe the detestable Qualities of their *Yahoos;* among which they were not able to distinguish this of Pride, for want of thoroughly understanding Human Nature, as it sheweth it self in other Countries, where that Animal presides. But I, who had more Experience, could plainly observe some Rudiments of it among the wild *Yahoos.*

But the *Houyhnhnms,* who live under the Government of Reason, are no more proud of the good Qualities they possess, than I should be for not wanting a Leg or an Arm, which no Man in his Wits would boast of, although he must be miserable without them. I dwell the longer upon this Subject from the Desire I have to make the Society of an *English Yahoo* by any Means not insupportable; and therefore I here intreat those who have any Tincture of this absurd Vice, that they will not presume to appear in my Sight.

FINIS.

---

an Evidence: A witness.

PART TWO

Gulliver's Travels:
A Case Study in
Contemporary Criticism

A Critical History of
Gulliver's Travels

Soon after the publication of *Gulliver's Travels* in 1726, John Gay invited Swift to return to London, "where you will have the pleasure of a variety of commentators, to explain the difficult passages to you" (*Corresp.* 3: 184). Since that time, commentary on Swift's book has not been lacking. Even the most hostile contemporary critics acknowledged the work's popularity. "Here is a book come out," wrote Lady Mary Wortley Montagu, "that all our people of taste run mad about." "Great Eloquence" has been employed, she wrote, to prove that human beings are "Beasts" (Williams, *Critical Heritage* 65). Samuel Johnson, otherwise no fan of *Gulliver,* found it "a production so new and strange that it filled the reader with a mingled emotion of merriment and amazement" (2: 203). *The European Magazine* later reported that the book had "a liveliness of description and a simplicity of narrative" that made it "equally interesting to persons of both sexes, and of all ages. It instantly became the only subject of conversation; everybody wondered, everybody admired, and everybody sought for meanings that were never intended" ("Character of Swift" 331).

The last complaint was lodged by Lemuel Gulliver himself, in the "Prefatory Letter from Captain Gulliver to His Cousin Sympson," which Swift added to the Faulkner edition, printed in Dublin in 1735. Here Gulliver laments the numerous errors that had plagued earlier editions and the scandalous interpretations that had been given of *Gulliver.*

The situation was so bad, in fact, that he could hardly recognize his own work. Worst of all, critics had flooded the market with "Libels, and Keys, and Reflections, and Memoirs . . . wherein I see myself accused of reflecting upon great States-Folk; of degrading human Nature" and "of abusing the Female Sex" (29).

Given Swift's reputation as a political writer, the first charge is understandable and one he probably would have welcomed. As Bertrand Goldgar has noted, "whether Swift wished it or not, his book was received almost at once as a decidedly political document and was both understood and used as a contribution to the political journalism of the opposition" to the Whigs and their prime minister, Sir Robert Walpole, sometimes connected with Flimnap in Lilliput (50). Early readers found parallels, too, between Lilliput and England and Blefuscu and France, and between the Low Heels and the Whigs and the High Heels and the Tories. Despite these identifications, early readers found little direct satire of specific statesfolk (Harth 540). Swift's larger attack on the policies pursued by the Whigs was, however, exploited and amplified in such opposition newspapers as *Fog's Weekly Journal* (Goldgar 60–61). Politics would also play a part in later Whig interpretations of Swift.

Early readers were more direct in leveling the other two charges of which Gulliver complains: that his book had satirized women and degraded human nature. Both charges are still debated today. The first appears in Jonathan Smedley's *Gulliveriana* (1728), where Smedley argues that Gulliver "gets nothing Abroad but a mortal Hatred to his wedded Wife, whom he leaves, in Breach of his matrimonial Vow, and runs away with a Mare" (Williams, *Critical Heritage* 91). Alexander Pope would play off the same charge in a humorous poem, "Mary Gulliver to Captain Lemuel Gulliver," which claims to give *her* side of the story:

> Not touch me! never Neighbour call'd me Slut!
> Was *Flimnap's* Dame more sweet in *Lilliput?*
> I've no red Hair to breathe an odious Fume;
> At least thy Consort's cleaner than thy *Groom.*
> Why then that dirty Stable-boy thy Care?
> What mean those Visits to the *Sorrel Mare?*
>
> (277)

As to the other charge — that the book's satire on mankind is too severe — even Swift's friend, Bolingbroke, was said to have disapproved, describing *Gulliver* as "a design of evil consequence to depreciate human nature" (*Corresp.* 3: 183). The anonymous *A Letter From a*

Clergyman to His Friend, With An Account of the Travels of Capt. Lemuel Gulliver (1726) later exclaims that the treatment of "humane Nature" in Part Four "is so monstrously absurd and unjust," it is "with the utmost Pain" that "a generous Mind must indure the Recital" (7). A year later, in his *Critical and Philosophic Enquiry Into the Causes of Prodigies and Miracles* (1727), William Warburton would ask, "[W]here is the sense of a general Satire, if the whole Species be degenerated?" As Warburton saw it, Swift's book was part of a tradition of works by a "Sect of Anti Moralists" who paint "*human Nature*" as "*base, cowardly, envious,* and *a Lover of its self*" (Williams, *Critical Heritage* 71–72).

Swift's book had clearly touched a nerve in ways that made it a key text in the eighteenth-century discussion of the nature of human nature. This discussion raised the question of whether we are basically benevolent or selfish, whether we are social animals or beasts of prey. Seventeenth-century thinkers such as Thomas Hobbes had found the latter to be the case. Hobbes stated in *Leviathan* that, stripped to its core, all human pursuit is "a perpetuall and restlesse desire of Power after power, that ceaseth onely in Death" (161). Without external constraints, human selfishness would prevail. In his *Maxims* (1665), La Rochefoucauld had also argued that there was an inbred selfishness at the bottom of all human acts. Even "in the adversity of our best friends," he said, "we find something that doth not displease us." Swift would later illustrate this maxim in his "Verses on the Death of Dr. Swift":

> Dear honest Ned is in the gout,
> Lies racked with pain, and you without:
> How patiently you hear him groan!
> How glad the case is not your own!
> (*Poems* 486)

When attacked for such views, La Rochefoucauld had replied that he was only saying what the Church had been saying for centuries. However capable of redemption, humankind is flawed, subject to selfishness, irrationality, and the original sin of pride. Swift largely agreed, asserting that

> As Rochefoucauld his maxims drew
> From nature, I believe 'em true:
> They argue no corrupted mind
> In him; the fault is in mankind.
> (*Poems* 485)

As a Christian and a moralist, Swift inherited a tradition in which pride was regarded as the chief human fault and a "main cause of psychological distortion," of "prejudice, misperception, misunderstanding, and worse, delusion, in one's thinking about oneself and everything else" (Keener 79). As a satirist, Swift delighted in puncturing inflated claims to purely altruistic acts (Fox, "Myth of Narcissus" 30). Frederick Keener points out that when Gulliver announces that he has fled "the corruption of fellow surgeons in London," he becomes one of a number of eighteenth-century heroes who "present themselves as extraordinarily selfless in motivation." But, Keener adds, "as quickly as these motives" are announced, the reader is set "thinking about the origins of such professions" (79).

Swift tied such ideas directly to *Gulliver* in several letters to Pope, telling him on September 29, 1725 that "the chief end I propose to my self in all my labors is to vex the world rather than divert it." Indeed, he claims, "I have got Materials Towards a Treatis proving the falsity of that Definition *animal rationale;* and to show it should be only *rationis capax.* Upon this great foundation of Misanthropy (though not Timons manner) The Whole building of my Travels is erected" (*Corresp.* 3: 103). Timon of Athens, the subject of works by Lucian and Shakespeare, was the archetypal hater of humankind. In this letter, Swift differentiates his position from Timon's by arguing that he doesn't hate specific people; he just doesn't expect very much from them. Man is not a rational animal (*animal rationale*), but only an animal capable of reason (*rationis capax*). In another letter Swift would tell Pope and his friends that "after all that I do not hate Mankind, it is vous autres [you others] who hate them because you would have them reasonable Animals, and are Angry for being disappointed. I have always rejected that Definition and made another of my own. . . . This I say, because you are so hardy as to tell me of your Intentions to write Maxims in Opposition to Rochfoucault who is my Favorite" (*Corresp.* 3: 118).

As this last statement implies, Swift's appreciation for La Rochefoucauld was not always shared by others, particularly those who were beginning to entertain newer views of human nature. The earl of Shaftesbury, for one, had argued that, far from being a selfish and fallen race, mankind is largely benevolent; perhaps the only fall we have experienced is the *belief* that we have fallen. Such ideas would later be developed by writers such as Jean-Jacques Rousseau, who would argue that not people but the institutions that surround them are basically corrupt. In Swift's century this new belief in human benevolence began to carry the day, as did a new stress on the prime importance of the individual.

This brought with it a corresponding redefinition of *pride*. During the eighteenth century, this first medieval sin became the main modern virtue, the cornerstone of a new individualism. "[N]othing," wrote David Hume in 1740, "is more useful to us in the conduct of life, than a due degree of pride" (596).

This context may help us understand the reaction to *Gulliver's Travels* that set in soon after its publication and lasted long afterward — particularly the storm over Part Four. T. O. Wedel reminds us that by 1726 the "dignity of human nature [was] already on everyone's lips" (439). The subject reappears several decades later in the first full-length critical consideration of *Gulliver,* the earl of Orrery's *Remarks On the Life And Writings of Dr. Jonathan Swift* (1752). This popular work proclaims "the voyage to the *Houyhnhnms*" to be "a real insult upon mankind" (121). In the "last part of his imaginary travels," Orrery contends, "Swift has indulged a misanthropy that is intolerable. The representation which he has given us of human nature, must terrify, and even debase the mind of the reader who views it" (117). Orrery, who had known Swift late in the latter's life, traces Part Four to nothing short of a pathological "misanthropy of his disposition" that caused the author of *Gulliver's Travels* "to ridicule human nature itself" (41).

In linking Part Four to Swift's disposition, Orrery invented a form of psychobiographical critique that flourishes still. When for instance Swift portrayed the Struldbruggs, we learn that he "probably felt in himself the effects of approaching age, and tacitly dreaded that period of life, in which he might become a representative of those *miserable immortals*" (116). "In painting Yahoos he becomes one himself" (120). While making such claims, Orrery is led to ask how the "same mind, that is capable of exerting the greatest virtue" can here degenerate "into the greatest vice" (86–87).

These statements brought a sharp response from Swift's old friend, Patrick Delany. In *Observations Upon Lord Orrery's Remarks* (1754), Delany asserts that Swift's character has been viciously misrepresented by a person who hardly knew him, and only then *"in the decline of life"* (3). Far from being a misanthrope, says Delany, Swift managed "to do more charities, in a greater variety of ways . . . than perhaps any other man of his fortune in the world" (5–6). But although Delany disliked the attack on Swift's character, he nonetheless agreed with Orrery's "judicious observations" upon *Gulliver,* which "leave little, very material or important, to any that comes after" him (95). (To judge by subsequent criticism, these words were prophetic. More than one Swift scholar has wondered what the critical history would have been like without Orrery's book.)

Delany also agrees with Orrery's degenerate hypothesis about the composition of *Gulliver*. When Swift wrote the book, he was "a good deal past that period of life, from whence ARISTOTLE dates the decline of human abilities" (96). This decline is evident in the fourth voyage. As satire, the Yahoos don't work. That "magnifying-glass, which enlarges all the deform features into monstrous dimentions, defeats its own purpose: for no man will ever know his own likeness in it" (117). Swift's Houyhnhnms fare little better. They show "the utter inability even of the noblest structure of inferior animals, to answer the purposes" of human life. Swift "places them in houses, which they could not build; and feeds them with corn, which they could neither sow nor reap, nor save. He gives them cows, which they could not milk, and deposits that milk in vessels, which they could not make." As an ideal, they fail (113–14).

Soon after Orrery's and Delany's works appeared, Swift's cousin, Deane Swift (1707–1783), tried to answer both in his *Essay Upon the Life, Writings, and Character of Jonathan Swift* (2nd ed., 1755). *Gulliver's Travels*, he wrote, is "a direct, plain and bitter satire against the innumerable follies and corruptions in law, politicks, learning, morals and religion." The first two parts are "intirely political," and satirize "the wars of *Europe* and the factions of WHIG and TORY." The third ridicules "the vain pretensions of chymists, mathematicians, projectors, and the rest of that speculative tribe, who spend their time in aerial studies." The fourth part is justified, for man is more vile than any Yahoo or beast (Williams, *Critical Heritage* 139, 140, 143–44).

John Hawkesworth also replied to Orrery and others in a new edition of Swift's works published in 1755. Where Orrery "*has not* found *the appearance of a fault*," we are told, "*he has laboured hard to* make *one*" (1: vii). Orrery has distorted Swift's real character, which was neither misanthropic nor sexist. Far from being a statement of Swift's hatred of humanity, *Gulliver's Travels* is finally a simple attack on the original sin. "To mortify pride," which "produces not only the most ridiculous follies, but the most extensive calamity, appears to have been one general view of the author in every part of these *Travels*" (1, pt. 2:286).

By the 1750s, however, Hawkesworth's was the minority view. What might well have been regarded earlier as "an acceptable way of underlining the deficiencies of human nature and the need for Christian redemption" was now increasingly seen to reveal Swift's misanthropy (Tippett 22). People used to compliment Swift on "his abominable

Yahoo story" and his knowledge of human nature, says Harriet Byron in Samuel Richardson's *Sir Charles Grandison* (1754). "But I hope," she adds, "that the character of human nature . . . is not to be taken from the overflowings of such dirty imaginations" (Williams, *Critical Heritage* 105). Swift "degrades humanity" in ways that are "irreligious" and "undefensible," claimed W. H. Dilworth in 1758 (Williams, *Critical Heritage* 176). He has "blasphemed a nature little lower than that of angels," adds Edward Young, who concludes a lament on Swift with a quotation from John Milton:

> O *Gulliver!* . . . How have thy *Houyhnhnms* thrown thy judgment from its seat; and laid thy imagination in the mire? In what ordure hast thou dipt thy pencil? What a monster hast thou made of the **Human Face Divine?**
>
> (Williams, *Critical Heritage* 179)

In his *Conjectures on Original Composition* (1759), Young extends Orrery's psychobiographical critique and finds Jonathan Swift and the embittered Lemuel Gulliver at the end of Part Four to be one and the same person.

So does James Beattie in 1778. Like Gulliver, Swift "wallows in nastiness and brutality." This "tale represents human nature itself as the object of contempt and abhorrence" (Williams, *Critical Heritage* 195–97). In 1781, James Harris similarly asserts the benevolence of human nature. "MISANTHROPY is so dangerous a thing," he says, "that I esteem the last part of *Swift's Gulliver*" to be "a worse Book to peruse, than those which we forbid, as the most flagitious and obscene" (Williams, *Critical Heritage* 208). Though it contains little comment on *Gulliver*, Samuel Johnson's *Life* treats the same theme, asking what could have caused Swift's imagination to dwell on "disease, deformity, and filth," ideas "from which almost every other mind shrinks with disgust" (3: 62).

The author of *Gulliver's Travels* did have supporters in the late eighteenth century, among them Thomas Sheridan, who mounted a massive rebuttal of earlier critics' charges in his *Life of Jonathan Swift* (1784). Swift's reputation, Sheridan says, has been harmed by his participation in politics. The Whigs have "always entertained an implacable hatred to Swift, as the great champion of the other side" (v). His memory has also been damaged by Orrery, whose envy led him to downplay Swift's talent and destroy his character. Orrery's strictures were later mimicked by others like Young, Johnson, and Harris, who willfully misrepresented the writer and his work (518).

All their criticisms are predicated, Sheridan adds, on a belief in Swift's misanthropy that is "chiefly founded upon his supposed satyr on human nature, in the picture he has drawn of the Yahoos" (502). However, the whole story of "the Houyhnhnms and Yahoos, far from being intended as a debasement of human nature, if rightly understood, is evidently designed to shew in what the true dignity . . . of man's nature consists" (503). In the first three parts Swift "has given various views of the different vices, follies, and absurdities of mankind, not without some mixture of good qualities, of virtue and wisdom, though in a small proportion to the others, as they are to be found in life." In the last part, however,

> . . . he meant to exhibit two new portraits; one, of pure unmixed vice; the other, of perfect unadulterated virtue. . . . he cloaths the one with the body of a man; the other, with that of a horse. Between these two he divides the qualities of the human mind, taking away the rational soul from the Yahoo, and transferring it to the Houyhnhnm. (503–04)

In this scheme, the Yahoo is an imaginary being who "has no resemblance to man, but in the make of its body, and the vicious propensities of its nature" (504). The Yahoo does not reason; it lacks speech, and it moves on all fours rather than walking erect. Given these differences, how could the Yahoos have been taken as representing humans "by almost all who have read Gulliver" (504) and as satirizing human nature itself?

We cannot blame readers for reaching this conclusion, Sheridan concludes, when critics such as Harris and Young have led them astray. To Young's Miltonic lament on *Gulliver,* Sheridan adds his own lament on Young, complete with a quotation from Shakespeare:

> O Doctor Younge, how has thy prejudice thrown thy judgment from its seat, and let thy imagination hurry thee beyond all bounds of common sense! In what black composition of spleen and envy hast thou dipt thy pen! What a monstrous character hast thou given of
> *One of the noblest men*
> *That ever lived in the tide of times.* (512)

Later defenses of Swift and Part Four were put forward by the political activist William Godwin and by George-Monck Berkeley, the grandson of Swift's friend the Irish philosopher George Berkeley. In *Literary Relics* (1789), George-Monck Berkeley argues that "the History of the Yahoos can by no means be considered as offering any insult to our nature. It only paints mankind in that state to which habits of vice must necessarily sink them" (Williams, *Critical Heritage* 247). In his *Enquirer* (1797), Godwin agrees with this assessment and adds his own: in the Houyhnhnms and the Yahoos, Swift has done no more than "exhibit two different descriptions of men, in their highest improvement and lowest degradation." No work, Godwin adds, "breathes more strongly a generous indignation against vice, and an ardent love of every thing that is excellent and honourable to the human heart" (Clubb 219).

As Godwin's statements indicate, the response to Part Four was not always negative. As early as 1727, the first French translator of *Gulliver*, Desfontaines, found the "voyage to the country of rational horses" the "boldest of the book's inventions" and "the one in which Swift's art and wit are most brilliant" (Williams, *Critical Heritage* 81). Nevertheless, it is fair to say that in Swift's century the earlier voyages were better received. Even Swift's satire on science in Part Three had admirers, though it generally received less attention than the other parts did. Throughout the age, Parts One and Two were widely praised.

Swift's style was especially acclaimed. Lord Monboddo echoed others in arguing that the "author, in English," who has "excelled the most" in the simple style "is Dr. Swift, in his *Gulliver's Travels;* of which the narrative is wonderfully plain and simple, . . . and circumstantial . . . and the character of an English sailor is finely kept up in it." "I will venture to say," Monboddo adds, "that those monstrous lies so narrated, have more the air of probability than many a true story unskilfully told." Because of this, Swift's travels "imposed upon many when they were first published" (Williams, *Critical Heritage* 192).

Monboddo alludes here to the various reports of Gulliver sightings and the wild stories circulating around the time of the book's publication. A companion of Swift's friend Dr. Arbuthnot, for instance, reported that he had fallen "in company with a Master of a ship, who told him that he was very well acquainted with Gulliver, but that the printer had Mistaken, that he liv[e]d in Wapping" and not in Redriff. Arbuthnot would add that "I lent the Book to an old Gentleman, who went immediately to his Map to search for Lilly putt" (*Corresp.* 3: 180). As Monboddo suggests, the verisimilitude, or illusive "realism," of the work was attributed to Swift's use of circumstantial detail. In Richard Sympson's opening letter, for instance, the reader learns that Gulliver's lineage can probably be traced back to Oxfordshire, where gravestones in St. Mary's-Banbury bear the family name (31). A visit to the same graveyard in Banbury today shows this to be the case. Several stones marked "Gulliver" are still faintly legible (Wagner 121).

Swift's simple style and use of detail to make the fantastic seem real would also be noted by nineteenth-century commentators, from Sir Walter Scott, who in 1814 said that "the fiction of the imagination is received by the reader as if it were truth" (Williams, *Critical Heritage* 293–94, 299), to Sir Leslie Stephen, who in 1882 noted the "charming plausibility of every incident, throughout the two first parts" (171).

Reaction to the book in this era was not always sympathetic, however. Scott himself changes tack when it comes to Part Four, which he finds "beyond contest, the basest and most unworthy part of the work." Even a moral purpose, he argues, will not justify the outline of mankind given in the fourth voyage. Allowances nonetheless should "be made for the soured and disgusted state of Swift's mind, which doubtless was even then influenced by the first impressions of that incipient mental disease which, in his case, was marked by universal misanthropy" (Williams, *Critical Heritage* 290, 312–13).

In Scott's account, madness joins misanthropy in producing the horrors of Part Four. But even madness is no excuse for Swift's work, argues Whig critic Francis Jeffrey in the September 1816 *Edinburgh Review*. The author of *Gulliver's Travels,* writes Jeffrey, had no right to "pretend to complain of men in general" after he had broken the hearts of several "amiable women" (such as Stella and Vanessa) and openly deserted and libeled the Whigs. For Jeffrey, the latter sin was especially unforgivable. Indeed, "whatever may be" Swift's "merits as a writer, we do not hesitate to say, that he was despicable as a politician, and hateful as a man." Swift's chief talent (we learn) was libel; his main goal, the vilification of mankind. Both are seen in *Gulliver's Travels:* "Disregarding all the laws of polished hostility," Swift "uses, at one and the same moment, his sword and his poisoned dagger — his hands and his teeth, and his envenomed breath, — and does not even scruple . . . to imitate his own Yahoos, by discharging on his unhappy victims a shower of filth, from which neither courage nor dexterity can afford any protection" (Williams, *Critical Heritage* 316, 318).

In 1818, William Hazlitt came to Swift's defense. Jeffrey, Hazlitt says, "does not seem to have forgotten the party politics of Swift." "I do not carry my political resentments so far back," Hazlitt adds, and "can at this time of day forgive Swift for having been a Tory" (Williams, *Critical Heritage* 329). Among Swift's works, *Gulliver* is a monument:

"Whether the excellence of *Gulliver's Travels* is in the conception or the execution, is of little consequence; the power is somewhere, and it is a power that has moved the world." Swift's object is not (as some have said) to degrade mankind but, rather, "to strip empty pride and grandeur of the imposing air which external circumstances throw around them." In order to do this, Swift "enlarges or diminishes the scale, as he wishes to show the insignificance or the grossness of our overweening self-love." Swift puts things in perspective and cuts humanity down to size. Where, Hazlitt concludes, is "the harm, the misanthropy, the immoral and degrading tendency of this?" (328, 329).

In *Satire and Satirists* (1855), James Hannay agrees. Swift wrote for the Tory party, "so of course the Whigs assail him" (132). Blinded by party prejudice and Orrery's *Remarks*, Jeffrey and others have, in Hannay's view, failed to see Swift at all. His reputation has been harmed too by the controversy over Stella and Vanessa and the supposed misanthropy of his satire. To call Swift's satire "misanthropy," however, is simply to miss the point: "His offenses are not against the instinctive feelings of the heart itself, but rather against society; against a body existing with certain codes of mutual flattery and compromise, concealments, and polite hypocrisies, and servilities, and cowardices" (147).

Thomas Babington Macaulay and William Makepeace Thackeray saw it differently. Writing in the same *Edinburgh Review* that had published Jeffrey's attack, Macaulay characterized the author of *Gulliver's Travels* as "the apostate politician, the ribald priest, the perjured lover, — a heart burning with hatred against the whole human race, — a mind richly stored with images from the dung-hill and the lazar-house" (Berwick 56). Thackeray's *Lectures on the English Humourists* (1853) went further. Part Four of *Gulliver* is "only a consequence" of the nastiness that comes before (153–54). "What fever was boiling in him," asks Thackeray, that Swift "should see all the world bloodshot?" (154). If the fourth voyage has a moral, it must be "horrible, shameful, unmanly, blasphemous," states Thackeray, issuing this cautionary advice:

> Some of this audience mayn't have read the last part of Gulliver, and to such I would recall the advice of the venerable Mr. Punch to persons about to marry, and say "Don't." When Gulliver first lands among the Yahoos, the naked howling wretches clamber up trees and assault him, and he describes himself as "almost stifled with the filth which fell about him." The reader of the fourth part of "Gulliver's Travels" is like the hero himself in this instance. It is

Yahoo language: a monster gibbering shrieks, and gnashing impre-
cations against mankind — tearing down all shreds of modesty,
past all sense of manliness and shame; filthy in word, filthy in
thought, furious, raging, obscene.(153)

In the October 1853 issue of *Blackwood's*, John Eagles accused
Thackeray of some unfairness here, and he lamented the larger Victorian response to Swift: "Oh, this at once bold and squeamish age! —
bold to do bad things, and to cry out against them . . . but delighting in
dressing up an imaginary monster and ticketing it with the name of Jonathan Swift, dead a century and a half ago!" (Berwick 96). Responding
to Thackeray in the *British Quarterly Review*, David Mason also defended Swift against the charge of sexism: "Those who in the present
day, both in this country and in America, maintain the intellectual
equality of the two sexes, and the right of women to as full and varied
an education, and as free a social use of their powers, as is allowed to
men, may claim Swift as a pioneer in their cause." Swift's view of the
equality of the sexes "explains much both in his conduct as a man and
in his habits as a writer" (Berwick 90).

Interesting here is the extent to which Swift's "conduct as a man"
and "habits as a writer" were regarded in the same light. Few eigh-
teenth- and nineteenth-century critics attempted to distinguish between
the man and his work. The same is true of such late-nineteenth-century
critics as Edmund Gosse, for whom *Gulliver* reveals "a brain not wholly
under control" (Voigt 8), or Sir Leslie Stephen, who finds Swift's "revolting images" indicative "of a diseased condition of his mind, perhaps
of actual mental decay" (178).

The year Stephen made this statement, J. C. Bucknill published a
medical paper, "Dean Swift's Disease" (1882), arguing that Swift suffered not from madness but from a physical condition first identified by
Prosper Ménière in 1861. Despite both this discovery and earlier work
by Dr. W. R. Wilde (1849) showing Swift to be sane years after *Gulliver*
was published, the myth of his madness would persist, and would continue to influence interpretations of the book into the current century.
The larger biographical strain in Swift criticism would also last, though
it would be modified by modern psychological approaches and by various formal and poststructural developments.

Despite the biographical bent of much nineteenth-century criticism,
there were attempts to explore the literary history surrounding Swift's
book. From Sir Walter Scott on, this most often involved a search for

historical analogues and sources. Sir Leslie Stephen was already working a well-ploughed field when he found *Gulliver*'s form to be "derived from some of the imaginary travels of which Lucian's *True History* — itself a burlesque of some early travellers' tales — is the first example" (172). (In his *True History*, Lucian of Samosata [c. 115–200] recounts a voyage to the island of the moon and parodies earlier classical writers who gave "so-called histories of their travels describing all the huge monsters, and savage tribes, and extraordinary ways of life they had come across in foreign parts." All these, Lucian says, are lies, "but no one could deny" that they make good stories [*Satirical Sketches* 249].) In addition to connecting *Gulliver* to Lucian and to Rabelais, Stephen cites parallels in stories about ideal commonwealths such as Thomas More's *Utopia*, in animal fables such as "Reynard the Fox," and in conversion narratives such as John Bunyan's *Pilgrim's Progress* (172–73). Stephen also joins earlier commentators in connecting *Gulliver* with a more recent version of the conversion form, Defoe's *Robinson Crusoe* (169).

By the early twentieth century, source study had become the rage. The source study par excellence was produced by William A. Eddy, who adds to the Swift-Lucian connection, finding parallels between Lucian's *Dialogues of the Dead* and Gulliver's interviews with departed spirits in Glubbdubdrib (164–65). Eddy links the play on perspective in Parts One and Two with George Berkeley's *New Theory of Vision* (1709). He also connects *Gulliver* to the larger tradition of the imaginary voyage and to such earlier figures as Cyrano de Bergerac (1620–1655), the author of a modern-day voyage to the moon (61–64, 65). The ties between *Gulliver* and the traditions of imaginary and actual travel literature would be extended in later studies by R. W. Frantz (1934), Willard Bonner (1934), and P. B. Gove (1941), along with more recent work by Jenny Mezciems (1982) and Percy Adams (1962, 1983).

In the first half of the century, the search for sources would also occupy students of Swift's politics. In a 1919 address to the British Academy, Sir Charles Firth found *Gulliver* to contain a hidden history of early eighteenth-century British politics, starting with the reign of Queen Anne (1702–14). In the *Travels*, Firth suggested, "many figures which seem to be imaginary are meant to depict real personages," or are at least "drawn from them" (237). This is particularly true of Part One, which alludes not only to parties (Low Heels and High Heels/Whigs and Tories) but to specific politicians. Prime Minister Flimnap, Firth argued, is "obviously designed to represent [Sir Robert] Walpole," Skyresh Bolgolam, the earl of Nottingham (242–43, 244). Firth's influential arguments would be repeated and refined by others, including

Arthur Case, who, writing in 1945, saw parallels between Gulliver's movement in Part One and the career paths of Oxford and Bolingbroke, the leaders Swift had served. Like Bolingbroke, for instance, Gulliver negotiates a peace between two warring nations (Lilliput and Blefuscu/Britain and France) only to find himself suffering impeachment and exile (70).

This view of *Gulliver* as a consistent political allegory was later challenged. Phillip Harth (1975–76) would suggest that the happenings in Lilliput — "a war, a treaty of peace, the jealousies and machinations of politicians, as well as charges of treason" — could happen anywhere, anytime (542). In *The Politics of "Gulliver's Travels"* (1980), F. P. Lock concurs. The search for sources, Lock concludes, is a wild goose chase that misses the larger point of Swift's satire, which is general rather than specific (121–122). Alan Downie in some ways agrees, at least about the often fanciful identifications of historical characters in Part One. "In most cases," Downie says, "the hints at characterization" there "are vague, and often contradictory." But Downie also argues for the particularity of Swift's satire, especially in Gulliver's discussions with the king of Brobdingnag in Part Two, which are loaded with complaints about new Whig practices, among them the maintenance of a standing army and the public debt ("Political Characterization" 115, 118). Downie asserts, however, that Swift's method of political satire relies on allusion and analogy rather than on any consistent allegory. As he points out elsewhere, "the evidence for a sustained political allegory is strained and raises more questions than it attempts to solve." Nonetheless, certain allusions are there ("Political Significance" 15). Arguing that one of the strengths of Swift's satire is its specificity, Simon Varey would note that when the king of Brobdingnag says your "Generals must needs be richer than [y]our Kings" (131), he "has never heard of Marlborough"; but Swift's eighteenth-century readers would certainly have recognized the allusion here to Britain's greatest general, who had won the Battle of Blenheim (1704) and made a fortune in the process (41, 50).

Twentieth-century scholars would explore other sources of Swift's satire in early modern scientific writings. Most notable was the work of Marjorie Hope Nicolson. Her essay (with Nora Mohler) "The Scientific Background of Swift's *Voyage to Laputa*" (1937) examined the relations between Part Three and *The Philosophical Transactions of the Royal Society*. The *Transactions*, Nicolson and Mohler argued, are the "specific source of Swift's Laputans, his projectors of the Grand Academy of

Lagado, and his Flying Island" (117). Various experiments described in Part Three parallel actual experiments reported in the *Transactions:* Stephen Hales's work, for instance, on the long-range effects of sunbeams, or that of Nehemiah Grew, who studied reproduction in plants. In satirizing such projects in the Academy of Lagado, Swift often "carries a real experiment only one step further — and the added step carries us over the precipice of nonsense" ("Scientific Background" 139, 148–49). So Swift shows us one scientist attempting to extract sunbeams from cucumbers and another throwing away seeds and planting what's left, on the theory that that is where "the true seminal virtue" is found (Davis 281). In other studies, Nicolson links Swift's floating island to eighteenth-century ideas about flight and magnetics, the latter interest evident in the orbicular loadstone shown to various visitors by Royal Society scientists (*Voyages to the Moon* 192–193). Nicolson's study "The Microscope and the English Imagination" traces the early modern interest in that recent invention and shows that *Gulliver* "would not be what it is had Swift not looked through a microscope — perhaps the one he bought for Stella — and felt the fascination and repulsion of grossly magnified nature." In Brobdingnag, Gulliver becomes a kind of human microscope. Swift's book, then, illustrates "the extent to which the new instrument affected the *technique* of an artist" (*Science and Imagination* 157, 193).

Nicolson's work would be amplified by the later studies of Potter (1941), Passmann (1988), Smith (1990), and Patey (1991). Elsewhere, Clive T. Probyn (1974) would study Part Three's satire of those searching for mechanical means to manipulate language and link that satire to universal language schemes put forward by various members of the Royal Society, most notably John Wilkins (1614–1672). J. M. Treadwell (1975) would show that the word *projector* was initially associated with financial speculators, and Louis Landa (1979) would demonstrate the importance of economics to Part Four. Other scholarship would connect *Gulliver* to more popular forms of science. In "Sights and Monsters and Gulliver's *Voyage to Brobdingnag*" (1957), Aline Mackenzie Taylor showed that Gulliver's experience as a human specimen in Part Two (publicly, on exhibition, privately, with the king's scientists) parallels that of freaks in eighteenth-century Europe, including a famous German dwarf who was carried about in a box. Dennis Todd has recently explored the same theme in "The Hairy Maid at the Harpsichord" (1992). The stress in Part Two on gazing, staring, and spectacle is certainly also evident elsewhere in a work that features perhaps the first "bespectacled hero" in literature and that uses the word "*observe*" (or variations thereof) at least 140 times (Rogers, "Gulliver's Glasses" 179, 184). David Oakleaf points out that Swift is also interested in the distortion inherent in observation, even with the latest scientific instruments (the grotesque magnifications of the microscope, for example, evident in Gulliver's closeup view of Brobdingnagian breasts) ("Distortions of the Observing Eye" 166).

Students of Swift and science have become increasingly self-conscious about the value of source study itself, as have others. It is one thing to find a source, another to say exactly what that source means. In his 1990 investigation of the relations between Swift's *Travels* and *The Philosophical Transactions,* Frederik Smith, for instance, is careful to state that he is not interested in finding a specific source, but in isolating a certain style *Gulliver* shares with other scientific discourse: in this case, the "style and approach one can identify broadly with the new science" that emerged in the late seventeenth century and that emphasized "a cautious, neutralized observation of phenomena." The "accoutrements of this scientific prose," Smith adds, "are maps, diagrams, measurements, lists, the accumulation of empirical evidence, and . . . the plain style advocated by the Royal Society. *Gulliver's Travels* has all of these" (*Scientific Discourse* 145).

The use of source study in interpreting the *Travels* has remained a question in twentieth-century scholarship, particularly in debates over the so-called history of ideas, in controversies about the ending of *Gulliver,* and in discussions of concerns raised by the New Criticism. The history of ideas is most closely associated with A. O. Lovejoy, who set out to analyze the climate of ideas in which works of philosophy, literature, and art were produced. This often involved tracing a master theme or "unit idea" through a number of different texts.

The shifting conception of pride interested Lovejoy. In a 1920 essay, "The Pride of the Yahoo," Lucius Elder had quoted Gulliver's characterization of the Yahoo as "a Lump of Deformity . . . smitten with *Pride*" (266) and argued that the Yahoos are examples of human irrationality, the horses, models of reason. Swift, Elder suggested, shared with other Enlightenment thinkers an overriding belief in "the supremacy of true Reason" (210). A year later, Lovejoy would test that assumption. When writers of Swift's age referred to pride it "is not primarily," he said, "the pride of the individual human creature . . . but the generic pride of man as such" (63). This pride is most often connected with an overreliance on reason itself. We must be very careful then, Lovejoy added, not "to exaggerate the rationalism" of the age, for influential authors "in the early and mid-eighteenth century made a great point of reducing man's claims to 'reason' to a minimum" (68).

Modifying this approach in 1926, T. O. Wedel would note an emerging optimism about human reason at the time *Gulliver* appeared but demonstrate Swift's resistance to that same movement. In "assaulting man's pride in reason," Swift "was attacking the new optimism at its very root" (444). Swift's antirationalism here would have been well understood by earlier writers such as Blaise Pascal, who spoke of the twofold nature of mankind as a mixture of extremes, reason and passion, angel and brute (435). On this reading, neither Yahoos nor Houyhnhnms truly represent mankind because mankind is an amalgam of both. As a man, Gulliver "cannot attain to the rational felicity of the Houyhnhnms." To do so would be inhuman. It would be equally inhuman to stoop to the level of the Yahoos. Swift's main thesis is in the contrast between the two: "Gulliver, occupying a position between the two, part beast, part reason, is Swift's allegorical picture of the dual nature of man" (443). Gulliver, then, is neither rational animal nor irrational beast; he is, as Swift told Pope in 1725, an animal capable of reason.

This argument was influential. During the next three decades, the Houyhnhnms would increasingly be seen as objects of satire rather than ideals to emulate. The misanthropic Gulliver would also be gradually separated from the historical Swift. This latter shift was helped along by David Nichol Smith's 1935 edition of Swift's letters to Charles Ford, which included new information about the composition of *Gulliver*, showing the fourth voyage to have been completed before Swift finished the third (xxxviii–xl). This fact alone, George Sherburn would say in 1938, challenged "romantic conceptions of Swift's 'deepening gloom'" ("Methods in Books about Swift" 640).

In "The Final Comedy of Lemuel Gulliver" (1941), John F. Ross would complete the separation between hero and author, arguing that "Gulliver in the last voyage is not Swift" (74). By dwelling on Gulliver's severe attack on "the Yahoo nature of man," critics have missed the point that the book is a comic masterpiece and that much of the comedy comes at Gulliver's expense. "Swift," Ross argued, "may not be a comic figure, but Gulliver decidedly is" (71). On this view, Swift's book might be more aptly titled *Gullible's Travels*, as we watch a simple-minded character respond to the complexities of experience and often miss the point. This is the figure who sees little people where he should see small minds and who defends his innocence in an affair with a Lilliputian lady while ignoring the one fact that would have cleared them both immediately: the difference in their sizes. This is the character who offers the

king of Brobdingnag gunpowder and then finds the king's humane response a "strange effect of *narrow Principles* and *short Views*" (134).
Finally, this is the figure who gets comically taken into the
Houyhnhnms' ways and world: "The horses have no room for anything
between Houyhnhnm and Yahoo, and Gulliver takes over this too simple attitude" (84–85). Ross concludes that we "may leave Lemuel in
amiable discourse in the stable, inhaling the grateful odor of horse. But
Swift is not with him." Though "indignant at the Yahoo in man," Swift
can also smile "at the absurdity of the view that can see *only* the Yahoo
in man" (89). That is the true comedy of the last voyage.

Part Four had taken on new importance. Kathleen Williams's approach to *Gulliver* in the 1950s suggests how far Part Four had come
from earlier estimates. Far from the outburst of a misanthrope, the
fourth voyage, she says, is a genuine "summing up of all" Swift's work
that asserts an abiding belief in "the dual nature of man" (*Swift* 177,
207). Swift disliked rationalists and so-called Deists, and registered this
dislike in depicting the Houyhnhnms, who are "remote, unsympathetic,
and in the end profoundly unsatisfying" (190). The horses "lack human
warmth because they lack passions and affections." The Yahoos are also
"inhuman because they have nothing but bodily senses and passions,
and are altogether lacking in reason" (192). The middle way, that "curious mixture of reason and passion," is man, who "lies outside
Houyhnhnm standards of judgment" (196). Not only do the
Houyhnhnms fail to understand Gulliver, Gulliver fails to understand
himself. He buys into the horses' viewpoint, which is absolute. However, as "Pascal believed, and as Swift demonstrates in the story of
Gulliver, any one-sided account of the nature of man, any scheme that
denies the paradoxical reality in favor of simplicity, will lead to disas-
trous practical results, to pride or despair or cynicism" (208).

This last movement was the theme of key essays by Ernest Lee
Tuveson and Samuel Holt Monk. For Tuveson, the real butt of Swift's
satire is not simply the rational horses, but Gulliver himself, who gets
"carried away by the idea that men should be like the Houyhnhnms"
and who "falls into despair and an absurd infatuation for an impossible
ideal" ("The Dean as Satirist" 374). More recent work would take up
this thesis and explore the psychological and medical implications of
Gulliver's obsession (Fox 1986–87, 1993). In Tuveson's reading,
Gulliver's "preoccupation with the unattainable ideal" blinds him to
"the possible one," suggested by, among other things, the presence of
the humane Captain Pedro de Mendez (374). As a failed idealist,

Gulliver shows that we create our own heavens to create our own hells. Our ideas of perfection can make us feel hopelessly imperfect, even drive us insane.

So Samuel Holt Monk would argue in "The Pride of Lemuel Gulliver" (1955). Suggesting that *Gulliver's Travels* shows "an awareness of man's tragic insufficiency," Monk contends that the work is also "a great comic masterpiece" (70). The humor comes from Gulliver himself, who "is NOT Jonathan Swift" (72). Gulliver "in the frenzy of his mad misanthropy has been too facilely identified with Swift." This has made us miss the comedy in the book and take the horses as "Swift's ideal for man" and the Yahoos as his view "of what men are" (76). Neither of these interpretations, Monk believes, is correct. *Gulliver* shows us a man driven to madness by an illusive faith in the life of reason. "From the moment that the banished Gulliver despairingly sets sail from Houyhnhnmland, his pride, his misanthropy, his madness are apparent. Deluded by his worship of pure reason, he commits the error of the Houyhnhnms in equating human beings with the Yahoos" (78).

Not everyone would agree. In a 1958 reappraisal, George Sherburn would stress the serious nature of Gulliver's vision and suggest that, unattainable though their reason may be, the Houyhnhnms do represent an ideal. The horse was Swift's favorite animal. He admired its "control, composure, affection, and intelligence" and depicted it in his characterization of the Houyhnhnms (93). Gulliver, finally, is not unlike St. Paul on the road to Damascus, struck by a vision of perfection that alienates him from his former life and delivers a shock from which he cannot easily recover.

R. S. Crane would later join Sherburn and deliver a searching critique of the history of ideas. Crane accuses recent critics of taking a hypothetical framework, "the Christian humanist view" of the duality of human nature, and imposing it on Swift's text. This approach ignores the possibility of "other traditions of thought about human nature" that Swift may have also used (238), including that found in logic texts he studied at Trinity College, Dublin. In those texts, the standard definition of man as rational animal (*Homo est animale rationale*) also included, as an example of an irrational animal, the horse. *Gulliver* gives us a world "in which horses appeared where logicians had put men, and men where logicians had put horses" (248). The reason for this inversion is suggested in the letters to Pope in 1725, in which Swift vows to "vex the world" and demonstrate the "Falsity of that Definition *animal rationale*." *Gulliver's Travels*, in Crane's view, is far from being what

Arbuthnot called a merry work. Rather, it is shock therapy, written to show how utterly far we are from the ideal. Elsewhere, in "The Fifth Voyage of Lemuel Gulliver" (1962) and his *Swift and the Satirist's Art* (1963), Crane's fellow Chicago critic, Edward Rosenheim, would also endorse that view.

Reviewing Swift scholarship from 1945 to 1965, Ricardo Quintana lamented the critical "tendency to forget the first three voyages and to concentrate almost exclusively on the final one." The world had lost track of Swift's Big and Small Endians and had replaced them with the debate between "the Hard and Soft Expositors" ("A Modest Appraisal" 352). James L. Clifford would later lay out the terms of this debate. The "hard" approach to *Gulliver*, he said, is "an interpretation which stresses the shock and difficulty of the work, with almost tragic overtones." The "soft" approach, by contrast, finds comedy in the work, en route to a "middle-ground interpretation" (33, 35). The chief point of the hard school, according to Clifford, is that Swift is no compromiser. His "norms are rigorous and ascetic." Swift "accepted the orthodox Christian position. Man is fallen and corrupt; he is, for the most part, ruled by selfishness and bestiality. But God has also placed in man a small core of reason — too little to do much to improve his condition — but enough to show him the falsity of too much pride" (40). The soft school sees the fourth voyage as "a comic satire on man's foolish pride and his gullibility in taking too seriously all impossible and unattractive ideals" (40). Pedro de Mendez, rather than the rational horse, here represents a reachable human ideal.

"Of course," Clifford admits, "the 'hard' and 'soft' antithesis is much too pat and narrow to cover all the recent approaches to the fourth book of *Gulliver's Travels*" (38). There is, for example, the approach using biblical themes by Roland Frye (1954), the religious interpretation of Martin Kallich (1970), or the myth criticism of scholars such as Dick Taylor, Jr. (1962). Other critics, "while not strictly 'soft,'" Clifford suggests, "could be called 'spongy' or 'mushy,' or even 'soggy'" (38–39). Some, like Swift's biographer Irvin Ehrenpreis, had moved from a soft to a harder position. This can be seen if we compare Ehrenpreis's earlier work with his later essay, "The Meaning of Gulliver's Last Voyage" (1962). In the 1962 essay, Ehrenpreis turned to Crane's question of defining the kind of animal man is and put Part Four in the larger context of the eighteenth-century dispute over human identity. A central figure in that discussion was the British philosopher John Locke; Swift was aware of the debate over Locke's theory of personal identity (Fox, *Locke and the Scriblerians* 19–20, 77–78). In

Lemuel Gulliver's Mirror for Man (1968), W. B. Carnochan would explore Swift's uses of Lockean epistemology in constructing the narrative "consciousness" that we call "Gulliver." Later scholars such as Everett Zimmerman (1983), Michael DePorte (1988), J. Paul Hunter (1990), and Christopher Fox (1993) would pursue that line of inquiry.

Concluding his analysis of the hard and soft dispute, Clifford marveled at Swift's genius in confounding his readers and in producing a work that enlisted a whole group of great scholars on both sides of the question (47). In a later attempt to resolve the issue, Milton P. Foster brought the contending voices together in a *Casebook on Gulliver among the Houyhnhnms* (1961). Despite such efforts, Richard Rodino would remind us thirty years later that the hard and soft debate is "still going strong" (1055).

The Battle of the Hard and Soft Expositors originated in the same period that witnessed the rise of the New Criticism. In 1938, Herbert Davis complained that earlier work had not sufficiently studied Swift's art. Is it the "prerogative of the scholar," he asked, "to begin first with . . . the biographical and historical and technical study, and only then afterwards to go on to the reading of the book, to what we may perhaps call the literary . . . study of it? Could we not rather more frequently begin there, and make use of the other studies only as aids to full understanding and interpretation?" (278). At the time, Davis was engaged in editing what many considered the authoritative edition of Swift's prose. Davis's call for closer attention to "the reading of the book" would be heeded by a generation of New Critics who dominated the literary scene well into the 1970s.

A key figure in New Critical approaches to Swift was Ricardo Quintana, whose 1948 "Situational Satire: A Commentary on the Method of Swift" marked a move away from his *Mind and Art of Jonathan Swift* (1936). The earlier book had analyzed relations between Swift's mind and art, life and work. By 1948, Quintana wanted to separate the two and argue for the *impersonality* of a work of art. A literary work is not (as the nineteenth century believed) an expression of self, but an escape from self. In *Gulliver's Travels,* Quintana argues, Jonathan Swift is as much outside the text as we are. What *is* present is a fictional self, or persona, in this case Lemuel Gulliver, who like other literary characters inhabits his own world, independent of the author. That world is the text. The text is an autonomous world of its own, a "complex structure" with its own unity and set of internal relations, which it is the critic's job to trace ("Situational Satire" 132). Pursuing those ends, New Critical studies (as Donald Mell notes) were often "resolutely rhetorical and formal in approach, shunning earlier biographical considerations and playing down historical backgrounds and contexts" (70). These formal and rhetorical dimensions would be explored in such works as Martin Price's *Swift's Rhetorical Art* (1953) and William B. Ewald's *The Masks of Jonathan Swift* (1954).

Much of the New Criticism was concerned with Swift's use of irony and impersonation. Harold Kelling, for example, would in 1952 examine the ironic import of Gulliver's partial point of view. Later, in *The Power of Satire* (1960), Robert C. Elliott would explore the formal relations governing the work vis-à-vis the controlling device of a satiric speaker, Lemuel Gulliver, who is himself satirized in the course of the narrative (184–222). Maynard Mack would similarly study the place of Swift's "assumed identity, Gulliver" in the larger satiric design. "Through Gulliver," writes Mack,

> Swift is able to deliver the most powerful indictment of man's inhumanity ever written in prose, and at the same time to distinguish his own realistic view of man's nature from the misanthropy of which he has sometimes been accused. While Gulliver is still naïve, mainly in the first two voyages, satire can be uttered through him, he himself remaining unaware of it. Later, when he begins to fall into misanthropy, still more corrosive satire can be uttered by him. But in the end, satire is uttered of him, and we see his mistake. For we discover . . . that all through the fourth voyage Gulliver is represented as becoming more and more like a horse. . . . To suppose, as many careless critics have done, that Swift is recommending this as an *ideal* for man is the consequence of the fatal error mentioned earlier — of identifying the author of an Augustan work with its *persona*. (113–14)

In a 1963 critique, Irvin Ehrenpreis found some problems with the New Critical approach. In positing the existence of persona and in stressing the impersonality of art, New Critics were able to rescue eighteenth-century writers from old romantic clichés. Since the work of art was an expression not of the writer's personality, but of a separate fictional character, it was easy to argue, for instance, that the utterances of the misanthropic Gulliver were not those of Jonathan Swift. But the cost of this approach, Ehrenpreis claimed, was to separate the author entirely from his work and world ("Personae" 26, 29–30).

Later, Claude Rawson would also challenge formalistic assumptions about Swift, including that of the existence of a separate speaker, or persona, in Swift's first-person narratives. In "A Reading of a *Modest*

Proposal," Rawson would show that Swift's own attitudes were (sometimes frighteningly) close to those of his narrator. Rawson also had real difficulty seeing a separate persona at work in *Gulliver's Travels.* In 1968, Frank Brady asked whether Gulliver has "a consistent character, or even what can be called a 'character' at all" (1). In his essay "Gulliver and the Gentle Reader" and in his later book by that name, Rawson would answer no to both questions. We cannot, Rawson believes, "take Gulliver as a novel-character who suffers a tragic alienation, and for whom therefore we feel pity or some kind of contempt, largely because we do not . . . think of him as a 'character' at all in more than a very attenuated sense: the emphasis is so preponderantly on what can be shown through him (including what he says and thinks) than on his person in its own right, that we are never allowed to accustom ourselves to him as a real personality despite all the rudimentary local colour about his early career, family life and professional doings." Rawson would also take on another formalist assumption, arguing that in looking for an overarching unity in Swift's work and thought, New Critics had missed the savage energy of Swift's prose, often unleashed on the unwary reader with little warning, giving "a curious precariousness to the reader's grasp of what is going on." Indeed, the "tense hovering" in *Gulliver* "between laughter and something else, the structural indefiniteness of genre and the incessantly shifting status and function of the parodic element, the ironic twists and counter twists, and the endless flickering uncertainties of local effect suggest that one of Swift's most active satiric weapons is *bewilderment*" ("Gulliver and the Gentle Reader" 54, 67, 79–80).

Rawson's emphasis on the disjunctive, temporal nature of the reading experience would be echoed by subsequent reader-response critics who would explore the creative relationship between interpreter and text. Scholars such as Robert Uphaus (1979), Frederik Smith (1984), Brean Hammond (1988), and Janet Aikins (1990) have attempted to chart a reader's path through *Gulliver,* and have found it full of turns and twists and ambiguities. So has Michael J. Conlon in his reader-response essay in this volume. In stressing that meaning lies only in the *interaction* between the reader and the text, such criticism has challenged the older, formalistic assumption that the text is an autonomous world-in-itself. The emphasis in Rawson and other reader-response critics on the discontinuity — the local and interruptive qualities — in *Gulliver's Travels* has also raised questions about the New Critical search for an underlying unity in the work.

A similar critique has come from another direction, in many ways anticipated by Edward Said's 1969 essay, "Swift's Tory Anarchy." Mentioning *Gulliver* but working predominantly out of Swift's *Tale of A Tub,* Said saw Swift's real subject to be the act of writing itself. Said also took exception to various formalist attempts to find a larger unity in Swift's work and life. Rather than viewing Swift simply "as an Anglican divine whose life can be described as a sequence of events over a period of time," argued Said, we do Swift "a greater service if we accept the discontinuities he experienced in the way he experienced them: as either actual or imminent losses of tradition, heritage, position, history, losses located at the center of his disjointed verbal production" (65).

In *Swift's Landscape* (1982), Carole Fabricant largely agreed. As she saw it, Said's comments (and Rawson's, on Swift's "anarchic proclivities") suggest reasons "why Swift cannot be looked at in traditional terms." The traditional approach "has tended to produce narrowly formalistic analyses that examine Swift's verbal structures in a vacuum, divorced from the mind and personality that created them, as well as from the soil that fertilized them" (7–8). Fabricant's own interest here is in the soil that fertilized Swift's imagination, in his experience as an *Irish* writer, a fact that had often been ignored. Her work, along with that of scholars such as Oliver Ferguson (1962), Andrew Carpenter, and Seamus Deane, has given impetus to further study of the material and cultural forces and the Anglo-Irish colonial experience that shaped Swift's world (Tooley and Fox, "Swift and Irish Studies").

Even among these critics, there have been different views of how that experience shaped *Gulliver's Travels.* Fabricant reads the book through Swift's experience as a colonized being, as does Clement Hawes (1991). In works ranging from *Place, Personality and the Irish Writer* (1977) to his recent introduction to Swift in *The Field Day Anthology of Irish Writing* (1991), Andrew Carpenter stresses the ambiguity of Swift's Anglo-Irish position — a position that produces a simultaneous sense of more than one reality, that curious double vision in *Gulliver* that "operates outrageously on the reader's sensibilities" (*Place* 186). In related essays, Seamus Deane sees Gulliver's traveling as part of the larger colonial enterprise (1986, 1995). Gulliver's wandering has been connected by Patrick Reilly with Swift's own sense as a displaced person (1982); by Joseph McMinn, with Swift's travels among native Irish people and between two shores (1992); by Michael McKeon, with the economic realities of Swift's experience as a dispossessed son, caught between an old aristocratic ideal of service and the failure of that same system to reward him (1987).

The relation between language and authority has also interested scholars who have extended Said's suggestion that Swift's real subject is the act of writing. A good example of such an approach is Terry Castle's 1980 essay "Why the Houyhnhnms Don't Write," reprinted in this volume. Grant Holly (1979), Neil Saccamano (1984), Clive T. Probyn (1985, 1992), Louise K. Barnett (1990), Richard Rodino (1991), and Peter Wagner (1992) have joined Castle in exploring Swift's satire upon the text and the conventions of writing itself. Much of this work has focused on *Gulliver*'s intertextuality, its use of other texts (the opening letters, for instance, from Gulliver and from editor Richard Sympson to the reader) to give an "illusory sense" of reality to the text (Probyn, "Starting" 20). This approach also explores *Gulliver*'s generic instability and its parody of various kinds of writing, where Swift shows that his text is "made up of other texts" (Probyn, "Starting" 20). In *The Genres of "Gulliver's Travels"* (1990), Frederik Smith points out, for example, that Swift's book "alludes on its first page" to the pirate and author William Dampier and the genre of the travel book, and then "proceeds to scramble" various genres together ("Afterword" 246). As Smith and others demonstrate, *Gulliver* can be read many different ways: as a picaresque tale, an imaginary voyage, an exemplary history, a novel, a children's book, an allegory, a spiritual biography or conversion story, an anatomy, a work of science fiction, a travel book, a scientific text, a philosophical treatise, a political satire, a Menippean satire, a narrative satire, a romance. Because of *Gulliver*'s Virgilian echoes and its "attention to the cultivation of the land, and to food," Margaret Anne Doody would add "georgic" to this list ("Insects, Vermin, and Horses" 151). "One would be sorely misled," Smith concludes, if one were to assume that any one genre could be a trustworthy guide through Swift's book ("Afterword" 250–51).

If a work such as *Gulliver* shows linguistic and generic instability, what happens when that text goes out into the world? By "engaging in the Trade of a Writer," wrote Swift under the guise of the Drapier, "I have drawn upon my self the Displeasure of the Government" (*Prose Writings* 10: 81). As Swift learned in the Drapier affair (1724–25), the "graphic act," in Deborah Wyrick's words, "engenders . . . danger" (xvi). In a recent critique, "The Battle of the Ancients and (Post) Moderns" (1991), Carole Fabricant raises the issue of "how to acknowledge the importance of discourse and textuality" in Swift "without losing sight of the historical forces and power relations" that informed "how and what language" meant in his society (256–57). Recalling Edward Said's comment that what Swift "is doing above all is *writing* in a world of power" ("Swift as Intellectual" 87), Fabricant argues that the "Swift-ian subject exists and speaks through the printed word but cannot be reduced simply to a 'writing subject' or 'textual self' since (among other things) it expresses itself from a position, however provisional, of morally committed action and exists in a world that is pervasively and inescapably political" (260).

The link between language and power in *Gulliver* has been explored by others, including Timothy Reiss, who finds in Houyhnhnm dis-course a satire on the underlying Cartesian belief in scientific rationality that has dominated Western thought. The Houyhnhnms and Cartesians come together in believing that "there *is* no other true and rational knowledge but what they themselves can express" ("Gulliver's Critique of Euclid" 346). This last connection has also been drawn by feminist scholars, including Felicity Nussbaum in this volume. In a related essay, Laura Brown has studied the disjunctive relationship between Swift's anticolonialist and antifeminist discourse, and the curious dynamic that results (433). In *The Brink of All We Hate: English Satires on Women, 1660–1750* (1984), Nussbaum elsewhere has positioned Swift's work in relation to traditions of antifeminist writing. Ellen Pollak (1985) has countered earlier criticisms of Swift's misogyny with a study of the emergence of the "myth of passive womanhood," a myth Swift disliked. (Pollak's book grew out of an earlier and important 1977–78 debate in *Signs* with Susan Gubar.) More recently, Margaret Anne Doody (1988) has explored Swift's relations with women writers ("Swift among the Women").

Other feminist work has brought new historical and psychoanalyti-cal perspectives to bear on Swift's work. Susan Bruce (1988), for in-stance, has examined the connections between the flying island and fe-male anatomy, gynecology, and power, and Ruth Salvaggio has found Gulliver's urination in Part One to be a phallic extension of male desire. In Part Two, the situation is reversed: "Since each of Gulliver's caretak-ers makes him into an object of her desire (the daughter's doll, the queen's pet), his predicament in Brobdingnag is one of submission to the feminine, a position which he must inevitably accept — for when he is alienated from this maternal comfort, his world becomes a dangerous place." In Lilliput, Swift had placed "no tiny blonde in this King Kong's hands." To "the extent that Swift did have a choice," we hear, "he chose to deal with women as large and overpowering rather than small and submissive" (425, 426).

In extending the psychoanalytical approach of theorists such as Lacan while resisting the patriarchal implications of Freudian theory,

Salvaggio and others have modified an interpretive tradition that has occupied students of *Gulliver* for much of the twentieth century. In a 1926 paper, "Gulliver Phantasies," delivered to the New York Society for Clinical Psychiatry and published in English in 1928, Sándor Ferenczi argued that Gulliver's role as a urinary fireman in Lilliput is obviously a compensation for Swift's sexual inadequacy, his failure to perform. (In subsequent essays, David Oakleaf [1982] and Christopher Fox [1993] have shown the same scene to be a staple of psychiatric literature of Swift's time.) In "Neurotic Traits of Jonathan Swift as Revealed by *Gulliver's Travels:* A Minor Contribution to the Problem of Psychosexual Infantilism and Cocrophilia" (1942), Dr. Benjamin Karpman found the work to be a symptom of Swift's own failed psychosexual development. The most detailed study of this, however, is Dr. Phyllis Greenacre's *Swift and Carroll: A Psychoanalytic Study of Two Lives* (1955), which explores the work as, among other things, a masturbatory fantasy (115).

Norman O. Brown's 1959 essay, "The Excremental Vision," sought to correct this kind of criticism. "If the duty of criticism toward Jonathan Swift is to judge him insane, criticism should be turned over to the psychoanalysts," who have "shown that they can be counted on to issue a medical certificate of insanity against genius," he exclaimed. But why not use a "different method for the application of psychoanalysis to Swift," namely, not to search his work for symptoms of insanity, but to appreciate Swift's "insight into the universal neurosis of mankind"? Then "psychoanalysis becomes a method not for explaining away but for explicating Swift" (34, 37). More recently, Hermann Real and Heinz Vienken have extended this critique. To judge by such works as John Traugott's "The Yahoo in the Doll's House" (1984) and recent feminist studies, later psychoanalytic interpreters have taken such criticism to heart. In her contribution to this volume, Carol Barash uses Brown's "Excremental Vision" as her starting point, and draws on Lacan to argue that Gulliver's rejection of the body is bound up with his response to the female body, its rewards and its threats. Elsewhere, Carol Houlihan Flynn (1990) has explored the implications of the body for a larger understanding of Swift's work.

Swift's book then, has had, as John Gay said "a variety of commentators." Arguing that "grasping the larger meanings of *Gulliver's Travels* must include acknowledging the various meanings" such "readers have generated," Richard Rodino called several years ago for "a full history of the critical reception" of *Gulliver* (1056). This survey of interpretation over a 270-year span has not aimed at such exhaustiveness. Nevertheless, it has I hope been broad enough to suggest the fascination the book has had for readers, and the range and richness of their response.

Christopher Fox

WORKS CITED

Adams, Percy G. *Travel Literature and the Evolution of the Novel.* Lexington: U of Kentucky P, 1983.

———. *Travelers and Travel Liars, 1660–1800.* Berkeley: U of California P, 1962.

Aikins, Janet E. "Reading 'With Conviction': Trial by Satire." Smith 203–29.

Barnett, Louise K. "Deconstructing *Gulliver's Travels:* Modern Readers and the Problematic of Genre." Smith 230–45.

Berwick, Donald M. *The Reputation of Jonathan Swift 1781–1882.* 1941. New York: Haskell House, 1965.

Bonner, Willard Hallam. *Captain William Dampier, Buccaneer-Author.* Stanford: Stanford UP, 1934.

Brady, Frank, ed. *Twentieth-Century Interpretations of "Gulliver's Travels": A Collection of Critical Essays.* Englewood Cliffs, NJ: Prentice, 1968.

Brown, Laura. "Reading Race and Gender: Jonathan Swift." *Eighteenth-Century Studies* 23 (1990): 424–43.

Brown, Norman O. "The Excremental Vision." Tuveson 31–54.

Bruce, Susan. "The Flying Island and Female Anatomy: Gynaecology and Power in *Gulliver's Travels.*" *Genders* 2 (1988): 60–76.

Bucknill, J. C. "Dean Swift's Disease." *Brain: A Journal of Neurology* 4 (1882): 493–506.

Carnochan, W. B. *Lemuel Gulliver's Mirror for Man.* Berkeley: U of California P, 1968.

Carpenter, Andrew. "Double Vision in Anglo-Irish Literature." *Place, Personality and the Irish Writer.* Ed. Andrew Carpenter. New York: Barnes and Noble, 1977. 173–89.

———. "Jonathan Swift." *The Field Day Anthology of Irish Writing.* Ed. Seamus Deane. 3 vols. Derry: Field Day Publications, 1991. 1: 327–30.

Case, Arthur E. *Four Essays on "Gulliver's Travels."* Princeton: Princeton UP, 1945.

Castle, Terry J. "Why the Houyhnhnms Don't Write: Swift, Satire, and Fear of the Text." *Essays in Literature* 7 (1980): 31–44.

"Character of Jonathan Swift, D.D., Dean of Saint Patrick's, Dublin." *The European Magazine, and London Review* 18 (Nov. 1790): 329–35.

Clifford, James L. "Gulliver's Fourth Voyage: 'Hard' and 'Soft' Schools of Interpretation." *Quick Springs of Sense: Studies in the Eighteenth Century.* Ed. Larry Champion. Athens: U of Georgia P, 1974. 33–49.

Clubb, Merrell D. "The Criticism of Gulliver's 'Voyage to the Houyhnhnms,' 1726–1914." *Stanford Studies in Language and Literature.* Ed. Hardin Craig. Stanford: Stanford UP, 1941. 203–32.

Crane, R. S. "The Houyhnhnms, the Yahoos, and the History of Ideas." *Reason and Imagination: Studies in the History of Ideas, 1600–1800.* Ed. J. A. Mazzeo. New York: Columbia UP, 1962. 231–53.

Davis, Herbert. "Recent Studies of Swift: A Survey." *University of Toronto Quarterly* 7 (1938): 273–88.

Deane, Seamus. "Swift and the Anglo-Irish Intellect." *Eighteenth-Century Ireland* 1 (1986): 9–22.

———. "Swift: Virtue, Travel and the Enlightenment." *Walking Naboth's Vineyard: New Studies of Swift.* Ed. Christopher Fox and Brenda Tooley. Notre Dame, IN: U of Notre Dame P, 1995. 17–39

Delany, Patrick. *Observations Upon Lord Orrery's Remarks On The Life And Writings of Dr. Jonathan Swift.* Dublin, 1754.

DePorte, Michael. "Teaching the Third Voyage." *Approaches to Teaching Swift's "Gulliver's Travels."* Ed. Edward J. Rielly. New York: MLA, 1988. 57–62.

Doody, Margaret Anne. "Insects, Vermin, and Horses: *Gulliver's Travels* and Virgil's *Georgics.*" *Augustan Studies.* Ed. Douglas Lane Patey and Timothy Keegan. Newark: U of Delaware P, 1985. 147–74.

———. "Swift among the Women." *Yearbook of English Studies* 18 (1988): 68–92.

Downie, J. A. "Political Characterization in *Gulliver's Travels.*" *Yearbook of English Studies* 7 (1977): 108–20.

———. "The Political Significance of *Gulliver's Travels.*" *Swift and His Contexts.* Ed. John Irwin Fischer, Hermann J. Real, and James Woolley. New York: AMS P, 1989. 1–19.

Eddy, William A. *"Gulliver's Travels": A Critical Study.* Princeton, 1923. Gloucester, MA: Peter Smith, 1963.

Ehrenpreis, Irvin. "The Meaning of Gulliver's Last Voyage." Tuveson 123–42.

———. "Personae." *Restoration and Eighteenth-Century Literature: Essays in Honor of Alan Dugald McKillop.* Ed. Carroll Camden. Chicago: U of Chicago P, 1963. 25–37.

Elder, Lucius W. "The Pride of the Yahoo." *Modern Language Notes* 35 (1920): 206–11.

Elliott, Robert C. *The Power of Satire: Magic, Ritual, Art.* Princeton: Princeton UP, 1960.

Ewald, William B. *The Masks of Jonathan Swift.* Oxford: Basil Blackwell, 1954.

Fabricant, Carole. "The Battle of the Ancients and (Post)Moderns: Rethinking Swift through Contemporary Perspectives." *The Eighteenth Century: Theory and Interpretation* 32 (1991): 256–73.

———. *Swift's Landscape.* Baltimore: Johns Hopkins UP, 1982.

Ferenczi, Sándor. "Gulliver Phantasies." *International Journal of Psychoanalysis* 9 (1928): 283–300.

Ferguson, Oliver. *Jonathan Swift and Ireland.* Urbana: U of Illinois P, 1962.

Firth, Charles H. "The Political Significance of *Gulliver's Travels.*" *Proceedings of the British Academy* 9 (1919–20): 237–59.

Flynn, Carol Houlihan. *The Body in Swift and Defoe.* Cambridge: Cambridge UP, 1990.

Foster, Milton P. *A Casebook on Gulliver among the Houyhnhnms.* New York: Crowell, 1961.

Fox, Christopher. *Locke and the Scriblerians: Identity and Consciousness in Early Eighteenth-Century Britain.* Berkeley: U of California P, 1988.

———. "The Myth of Narcissus in Swift's *Travels.*" *Eighteenth-Century Studies* 20 (1986–87): 17–33.

———. "Of Logic and Lycanthropy: Gulliver and the Faculties of the Mind." *Literature and Medicine during the Eighteenth Century.* Ed. Roy Porter and Marie Mulvey Roberts. London: Routledge, 1993. 101–17.

———. "Sexuality and the Body." *Approaches to Teaching Swift's "Gulliver's Travels."* Ed. Edward J. Rielly. New York: MLA, 1988. 69–74.

Frantz, R. W. *The English Traveller and the Movement of Ideas, 1660–1732.* Lincoln, 1934. Lincoln: U of Nebraska P, 1967.

Frye, Roland M. "Swift's Yahoo and the Christian Symbols for Sin." *Journal of the History of Ideas* 15 (1954): 201–17.

Goldgar, Bertrand A. *Walpole and the Wits: The Relation of Politics to Literature, 1722–1742.* Lincoln: U of Nebraska P, 1976.

Gove, Philip Babcock. *The Imaginary Voyage in Prose Fiction . . . with an annotated check list of 215 imaginary voyages from 1700 to 1800.* New York: Columbia UP, 1941.

Greenacre, Phyllis. *Swift and Carroll: A Psychoanalytic Study of Two Lives.* New York: International Universities P, 1955.

Gubar, Susan. "The Female Monster in Augustan Satire." *Signs: Journal of Women in Culture and Society* 3 (1977–1978): 380–94.

———. "Reply to Pollak." *Signs: Journal of Women in Culture and Society* 3 (1977–78): 732–33.

Hammond, Brean. *Gulliver's Travels.* Philadelphia: Open University P, 1988.

Hannay, James. *Satire and Satirists.* New York: Redfield, 1855.

Harth, Phillip. "The Problem of Political Allegory in *Gulliver's Travels.*" *Modern Philology* 73, pt. 2 (1975–76): 540–47.

Hawes, Clement. "Three Times round the Globe: Gulliver and Colonial Discourse." *Cultural Critique* 18 (1991): 187–214.

Hawkesworth, John. *Life of Swift. The Works of Jonathan Swift.* 12 vols. London, 1766. 1: 1–71.

Hobbes, Thomas. *Leviathan.* Ed. C. B. Macpherson. Harmondsworth: Penguin, 1968.

Holly, Grant. "Travel and Translation: Textuality in *Gulliver's Travels.*" *Criticism* 21 (1979): 134–52.

Hume, David. *A Treatise of Human Nature.* Ed. L. A. Selby-Bigge, rev. P. H. Nidditch, 2nd ed. Oxford: Clarendon, 1978.

Hunter, J. Paul. "*Gulliver's Travels* and the Novel." Smith 56–74.

Johnson, Samuel. *Life of Swift. Lives of the English Poets.* 3 vols. Ed. George Birkbeck Hill. Oxford: Clarendon, 1905. 3: 1–74.

Kallich, Martin. *The Other End of the Egg: Religious Satire in "Gulliver's Travels."* Bridgeport, CT: Conference on British Studies at the U of Bridgeport, 1970.

Karpman, Benjamin. "Neurotic Traits of Jonathan Swift as Revealed in *Gulliver's Travels*: A Minor Contribution to the Problem of Psychosexual Infantilism and Cocrophilia." *Psychoanalytic Review* 29 (1942): 26–45.

Keener, Frederick. "The Rub of Self-Love." *The Chain of Becoming.* New York: Columbia UP, 1983. 55–85.

Kelling, Harold D. "*Gulliver's Travels*: A Comedy of Humours." *University of Toronto Quarterly* 21 (1952): 362–75.

Landa, Louis. "The Dismal Science in Houyhnhnmland." *Novel* 13 (1979): 38–49.

A Letter From a Clergyman to His Friend, With An Account of the Travels of Capt. Lemuel Gulliver: To Which is Added, The True Reasons Why a Certain Doctor Was Made a Dean. London, 1726. Los Angeles: William Andrews Clark Memorial Library, 1970.

Lock, F. P. *The Politics of "Gulliver's Travels."* Oxford: Clarendon, 1980.

Lovejoy, Arthur O. "'Pride' in Eighteenth-Century Thought." *Essays in the History of Ideas*. New York: Capricorn Books, 1960. 62–68.

Lucian of Samosata. *Satirical Sketches*. Trans. Paul Turner. Bloomington: Indiana UP, 1990.

Mack, Maynard. "Gulliver's Travels." Tuveson 111–14.

McKeon, Michael. *The Origins of the English Novel, 1600–1740*. Baltimore: Johns Hopkins UP, 1987.

McMinn, Joseph. "Jonathan's Travels: Swift's Sense of Ireland." *Swift Studies* 7 (1992): 36–53.

Mell, Donald. "Recent Work in *Gulliver*." *The Journal of Irish Literature* 20 (1991): 70–73.

Mezciems, Jenny. "'Tis Not to Divert the Reader': Moral and Literary Determinants in Some Early Travel Narratives." *Prose Studies* 5 (1982): 1–19.

Monk, Samuel Holt. "The Pride of Lemuel Gulliver." Brady 70–79.

Nicolson, Marjorie Hope. "The Microscope and the English Imagination." *Science and Imagination*. Ithaca: Great Seal Books, 1956. 155–234.

Nicolson, Marjorie Hope, and Nora M. Mohler. "The Scientific Background of Swift's *Voyage to Laputa*." *Science and Imagination* 110–54.

———. *Voyages to the Moon*. New York: Macmillan, 1948.

Nussbaum, Felicity. *The Brink of All We Hate: English Satires on Women, 1660–1750*. Lexington: U of Kentucky P, 1984.

Oakleaf, David. "Gulliver's Melancholy Dream of Power." *Transactions of the Samuel Johnson Society of the Northwest*. Ed. R. H. Carrie. 13 (1982): 48–59.

———. "*Trompe l'Oeil*: Gulliver and the Distortions of the Observing Eye." *University of Toronto Quarterly* 53 (1983–84): 166–80.

Orrery, John, Earl of. *Remarks On the Life and Writings of Dr. Jonathan Swift, Dean of St. Patrick's Dublin*. 3rd ed. London, 1752.

Passmann, D. F. "Mud and Slime: Some Implications of the Yahoos' Genealogy and the History of an Idea." *The British Journal for Eighteenth-Century Studies* 2 (1988): 1–17.

Patey, Douglas Lane. "Swift's Satire on 'Science' and the Structure of *Gulliver's Travels.*" *English Literary History* 58 (1991): 809–39.

Pollak, Ellen. "Comment on Susan Gubar's 'The Female Monster in Augustan Satire.'" *Signs: Journal of Women in Culture and Society* 3 (1977–78): 728–32.

———. *The Poetics of Sexual Myth: Gender and Ideology in the Verse of Swift and Pope.* Chicago: U of Chicago P, 1985.

———. "Swift among the Feminists." Schakel 65–75.

Pope, Alexander. *Minor Poems.* Ed. Norman Ault and John Butt. London: Methuen, 1964.

Potter, George R. "Swift and Natural Science." *Philological Quarterly* 20 (1941): 97–118.

Price, Martin. *Swift's Rhetorical Art: A Study in Structure and Meaning.* New Haven: Yale UP, 1953.

Probyn, Clive T. "Haranging upon Texts: Swift and the Idea of the Book." *Proceedings of the First Münster Symposium on Jonathan Swift.* Ed. Hermann J. Real and Heinz J. Vienken. Munich: Wilhelm Fink, 1985. 187–97.

———. "Starting from the Margins: Teaching Swift in the Light of Poststructuralist Theories of Reading and Writing." Schakel 19–35.

———. "Swift and Linguistics: The Context behind Lagado and around the Fourth Voyage." *Neophilogus* 58 (1974): 425–39.

Quintana, Ricardo. *The Mind and Art of Jonathan Swift.* London: Oxford UP, 1936.

———. "A Modest Appraisal: Swift Scholarship and Criticism, 1945–65." *Fair Liberty Was All His Cry: A Tercentenary Tribute to Jonathan Swift, 1667–1745.* Ed. A. Norman Jeffares. London: Macmillan, 1967. 342–55.

———. "Situational Satire: A Commentary on the Method of Swift." *University of Toronto Quarterly* 17 (1947–48): 130–36.

Rawson, Claude J. "Gulliver and the Gentle Reader." *Imagined Worlds: Essays on Some English Novels and Novelists in Honor of John Butt.* Ed. Maynard Mack and Ian Gregor. London: Methuen, 1968. 51–90.

———. *Gulliver and the Gentle Reader: Studies in Swift and Our Time.* London: Routledge, 1973.

———. "A Reading of *A Modest Proposal.*" *Augustan Worlds.* Ed. J. C. Hilson et al. Leicester: Leicester UP, 1978. 29–50.

Real, Hermann J., and Heinz J. Vienken. "Psychoanalytic Criticism and Swift: The History of a Failure." *Eighteenth-Century Ireland* 1 (1986): 127–41.

Reilly, Patrick. "The Displaced Person." *Jonathan Swift: The Brave Desponder.* Carbondale: Southern Illinois UP, 1982. 174–209.

Reiss, Timothy J. "Gulliver's Critique of Euclid." *The Discourse of Modernism.* Ithaca: Cornell UP, 1982. 328–50.

Rodino, Richard. " 'Splendide Mendax': Authors, Characters, and Readers in *Gulliver's Travels.*" *PMLA* 106 (1991): 1054–70.

Rogers, Pat. "Gulliver's Glasses." *The Art of Jonathan Swift.* Ed. Clive T. Probyn. London: Vision, 1978. 179–88.

Rosenheim, Edward W. "The Fifth Voyage of Lemuel Gulliver." *Modern Philology* 60 (1962): 103–19.

———. *Swift and the Satirist's Art.* Chicago: U of Chicago P, 1963.

Ross, John F. "The Final Comedy of Lemuel Gulliver." Tuveson 71–89.

Saccamano, Neil. "Authority and Publication: The Works of Swift." *The Eighteenth Century: Theory of Interpretation* 25 (1984): 241–62.

Said, Edward. "Swift as Intellectual." *The World, the Text, and the Critic.* Cambridge, MA: Harvard UP, 1983. 72–89.

———. "Swift's Tory Anarchy." *The World, the Text, and the Critic.* Cambridge, MA: Harvard UP, 1983. 54–71.

Salvaggio, Ruth. "Swift and Psychoanalysis, Language and Woman." *Women's Studies* 15 (1988): 417–34.

Schakel, Peter J. *Critical Approaches to Teaching Swift.* Ed. Peter J. Schakel. New York: AMS P, 1992.

Sherburn, George. "Errors Concerning the Houyhnhnms." *Modern Philology* 56 (1958): 92–97.

———. "Methods in Books about Swift." *Studies in Philology* 35 (1938): 635–56.

Sheridan, Thomas. *The Life of the Rev. Dr. Jonathan Swift.* London, 1775. New York: Garland, 1974.

Smith, Frederik N. "Afterword: Style, Swift's Reader, and the Genres of *Gulliver's Travels.*" Smith 246–59.

———. "The Danger of Reading Swift: The Double Binds of *Gulliver's Travels.*" *Studies in the Literary Imagination* 17 (1984): 35–47.

——, ed. *The Genres of "Gulliver's Travels."* Newark: U of Delaware P, 1990.

——. "Scientific Discourse: *Gulliver's Travels* and *The Philosophical Transactions.*" Smith 139–62.

Stephen, Leslie. *Swift*. New York: Harper, 1898.

Swift, Jonathan. *The Complete Poems*. Ed. Pat Rogers. London: Penguin, 1983.

——. *The Correspondence of Jonathan Swift*. 5 vols. Ed. Harold Williams. Oxford: Clarendon, 1963–65.

——. *The Letters of Jonathan Swift to Charles Ford*. Ed. David Nichol Smith. Oxford: Clarendon, 1935.

——. *The Prose Works of Jonathan Swift*. Ed. Herbert Davis, et al. 14 vols. Oxford: Blackwell, 1939–68.

Taylor, Aline Mackenzie. "Sights and Monsters and Gulliver's *Voyage to Brobdingnag.*" *Tulane Studies in English* 7 (1957): 29–82.

Taylor, Dick, Jr. "Gulliver's Pleasing Visions: Self-Deception as a Major Theme in *Gulliver's Travels.*" *Tulane Studies in English* 12 (1962): 7–61.

Thackeray, William Makepeace. *The Lectures on the English Humourists of the Eighteenth Century*. Vol. 11 of *The Works*, 26 vols. London, 1910–11; rpt. New York: AMS Press, 1968.

Tippett, Brian. *An Introduction to the Variety of Criticism: "Gulliver's Travels."* Atlantic Highlands, NJ: Humanities P International, 1989.

Todd, Dennis. "The Hairy Maid at the Harpsichord: Some Speculations on the Meaning of *Gulliver's Travels.*" *Texas Studies in Literature and Language* 34 (1992): 239–83.

Tooley, Brenda, and Christopher Fox. "Swift and Irish Studies." *Walking Naboth's Vineyard: New Studies of Swift*. Ed. Christopher Fox and Brenda Tooley. Notre Dame, IN: U of Notre Dame P, 1995. 1–16.

Traugott, John. "The Yahoo in the Doll's House: *Gulliver's Travels* the Children's Classic." *English Satire and the Satiric Tradition*. Ed. Claude Rawson. Oxford: Basil Blackwell, 1984. 127–50.

Treadwell, J. M. "Jonathan Swift: The Satirist as Projector." *Texas Studies in Literature and Language* 17 (1975): 439–60.

Tuveson, Ernest Lee, ed. *Swift: A Collection of Critical Essays*. Englewood Cliffs, NJ: Prentice, 1964.

——. "Swift: The Dean as Satirist." *University of Toronto Quarterly* 22 (1953): 368–75.

Uphaus, Robert W. "Swift and the Problematic Nature of Meaning." *The Impossible Observer.* Lexington: U of Kentucky P, 1979. 9–27.

Varey, Simon. "Exemplary History and the Political Satire of *Gulliver's Travels.*" Smith 39–55.

Voigt, Milton. *Swift and the Twentieth Century.* Detroit: Wayne State UP, 1964.

Wagner, Peter. "Swift's Great Palimpsest: Intertextuality and Travel Literature in *Gulliver's Travels.*" *Dispositio* 17 (1992): 107–32.

Wedel, T. O. "On the Philosophical Background of *Gulliver's Travels.*" *Studies in Philology* 23 (1926): 434–50.

Wilde, William Robert Wills. *The Closing Years of Dean Swift's Life.* Dublin: Hodges and Smith, 1849.

Williams, Kathleen. *Jonathan Swift and the Age of Compromise.* Lawrence: U of Kansas P, 1958.

———. *Swift: The Critical Heritage.* London: Routledge, 1970.

Wyrick, Deborah Baker. *Jonathan Swift and the Vested Word.* Chapel Hill: U of North Carolina P, 1988.

Zimmerman, Everett. *Swift's Narrative Satires: Author and Authority.* Ithaca: Cornell UP, 1983.

Feminist Criticism
and
Gulliver's Travels

WHAT IS FEMINIST CRITICISM?

Feminist criticism comes in many forms, and feminist critics have a variety of goals. Some are interested in rediscovering the works of women writers overlooked by a masculine-dominated culture. Others have revisited books by male authors and reviewed them from a woman's point of view to understand how they both reflect and shape the attitudes that have held women back.

Since the early 1970s three strains of feminist criticism have emerged, strains that can be categorized as French, American, and British. These categories should not be allowed to obscure either the global implications of the women's movement or the fact that interests and ideas have been shared by feminists from France, Great Britain, and the United States. British and American feminists have examined similar problems while writing about many of the same writers and works, and American feminists have recently become more receptive to French theories about femininity and writing. Historically speaking, however, French, American, and British feminists have examined similar problems from somewhat different perspectives.

French feminists have tended to focus their attention on language, analyzing the ways in which meaning is produced. They have concluded that language as we commonly think of it is a decidedly male realm. Drawing on the ideas of the psychoanalytic philosopher Jacques Lacan, French feminists remind us that language is a realm of public discourse. A child enters the linguistic realm just as it comes to grasp its separateness from its mother, just about the time that boys identify with their father, the family representative of culture. The language learned reflects a binary logic that opposes such terms as active/passive, masculine/feminine, sun/moon, father/mother, head/heart, son/daughter, intelligent/sensitive, brother/sister, form/matter, phallus/vagina, reason/emotion. Because this logic tends to group with masculinity such qualities as light, thought, and activity, French feminists have said that the structure of language is phallocentric: it privileges the phallus and, more generally, masculinity by associating them with things and values more appreciated by the (masculine-dominated) culture. Moreover, French feminists believe, "masculine desire dominates speech and posits woman as an idealized fantasy-fulfillment for the incurable emotional lack caused by separation from the mother" (Jones 83).

In the view of French feminists, language is associated with separation from the mother. Its distinctions represent the world from the male point of view, and it systematically forces women to choose: either they can imagine and represent themselves as men imagine and represent them (in which case they may speak, but will speak as men) or they can choose "silence," becoming in the process "the invisible and unheard sex" (Jones 83).

But some influential French feminists have argued that language only *seems* to give women such a narrow range of choices. There is another possibility, namely that women can develop a *feminine* language. In various ways, early French feminists such as Annie Leclerc, Xavière Gauthier, and Marguerite Duras have suggested that there is something that may be called *l'écriture féminine:* women's writing. Recently, Julia Kristeva has said that feminine language is "semiotic," not "symbolic." Rather than rigidly opposing and ranking elements of reality, rather than symbolizing one thing but not another in terms of a third, feminine language is rhythmic and unifying. If from the male perspective it seems fluid to the point of being chaotic, that is a fault of the male perspective.

According to Kristeva, feminine language is derived from the pre-oedipal period of fusion between mother and child. Associated with the maternal, feminine language is not only a threat to culture, which is patriarchal, but also a medium through which women may be creative in new ways. But Kristeva has paired her central, liberating claim — that truly feminist innovation in all fields requires an understanding of the relation between maternity and feminine creation — with a warning. A feminist language that refuses to participate in "masculine" discourse, that places its future entirely in a feminine, semiotic discourse, risks being politically marginalized by men. That is to say, it risks being relegated to the outskirts (pun intended) of what is considered socially and politically significant.

Kristeva, who associates feminine writing with the female body, is joined in her views by other leading French feminists. Hélène Cixous, for instance, also posits an essential connection between the woman's body, whose sexual pleasure has been repressed and denied expression, and women's writing. "Write your self. Your body must be heard," Cixous urges; once they learn to write their bodies, women will not only realize their sexuality but enter history and move toward a future based on a "feminine" economy of giving rather than the "masculine" economy of hoarding (Cixous 250). For Luce Irigaray, women's sexual pleasure (*jouissance)* cannot be expressed by the dominant, ordered, "logical," masculine language. She explores the connection between women's sexuality and women's language through the following analogy: as women's *jouissance* is more multiple than men's unitary, phallic pleasure ("woman has sex organs just about everywhere"), so "feminine" language is more diffusive than its "masculine" counterpart. ("That is undoubtedly the reason . . . her language . . . goes off in all directions and . . . he is unable to discern the coherence," Irigaray writes [101–03].)

Cixous's and Irigaray's emphasis on feminine writing as an expression of the female body has drawn criticism from other French feminists. Many argue that an emphasis on the body either reduces "the feminine" to a biological essence or elevates it in a way that shifts the valuation of masculine and feminine but retains the binary categories. For Christine Fauré, Irigaray's celebration of women's difference fails to address the issue of masculine dominance, and a Marxist-feminist, Catherine Clément, has warned that "poetic" descriptions of what constitutes the feminine will not challenge that dominance in the realm of production. The boys will still make the toys, and decide who gets to use them. In her effort to redefine women as political rather than as sexual beings, Monique Wittig has called for the abolition of sexual categories that Cixous and Irigaray retain and revalue as they celebrate women's writing.

American feminist critics have shared with French critics both an interest in and a cautious distrust of the concept of feminine writing. Annette Kolodny, for instance, has worried that the "richness and variety of women's writing" will be missed if we see in it only its "feminine mode" or "style" ("Some Notes" 78). And yet Kolodny herself proceeds, in the same essay, to point out that women *have* had their own style, which includes reflexive constructions ("she found herself crying") and particular, recurring themes (clothing and self-fashioning are two that Kolodny mentions; other American feminists have focused on madness, disease, and the demonic).

Interested as they have become in the "French" subject of feminine style, American feminist critics began by analyzing literary texts rather than philosophizing abstractly about language. Many reviewed the great works by male writers, embarking on a revisionist rereading of literary tradition. These critics examined the portrayals of women characters, exposing the patriarchal ideology implicit in such works and showing how clearly this tradition of systematic masculine dominance is inscribed in our literary tradition. Kate Millett, Carolyn Heilbrun, and Judith Fetterley, among many others, created this model for American feminist criticism, a model that Elaine Showalter came to call "the feminist critique" of "male-constructed literary history" ("Poetics" 125).

Meanwhile another group of critics including Sandra Gilbert, Susan Gubar, Patricia Meyer Spacks, and Showalter herself created a somewhat different model. Whereas feminists writing "feminist critique" have analyzed works by men, practitioners of what Showalter used to refer to as "gynocriticism" have studied the writings of those women who, against all odds, produced what she calls "a literature of their own." In *The Female Imagination* (1975), Spacks examines the female literary tradition to find out how great women writers across the ages have felt, perceived themselves, and imagined reality. Gilbert and Gubar, in *The Madwoman in the Attic* (1979), concern themselves with well-known women writers of the nineteenth century, but they too find that general concerns, images, and themes recur, because the authors that they treat wrote "in a culture whose fundamental definitions of literary authority are both overtly and covertly patriarchal" (45).

If one of the purposes of gynocriticism is to (re)study well-known women authors, another is to rediscover women's history and culture, particularly women's communities that have nurtured female creativity. Still another related purpose is to discover neglected or forgotten women writers and thus to forge an alternative literary tradition, a canon that better represents the female perspective by better representing the literary works that have been written by women. Showalter, in *A Literature of Their Own* (1977), admirably began to fulfill this purpose, providing a remarkably comprehensive overview of women's writing through three of its phases. She defines these as the "Feminine, Feminist, and Female" phases, phases during which women first imitated a masculine tradition (1840–80), then protested against its standards and values (1880–1920), and finally advocated their own autonomous, female perspective (1920 to the present).

With the recovery of a body of women's texts, attention has returned to a question raised in 1978 by Lillian Robinson: Doesn't American feminist criticism need to formulate a theory of its own practice? Won't reliance on theoretical assumptions, categories, and strategies developed by men and associated with nonfeminist schools of thought prevent feminism from being accepted as equivalent to these other critical discourses? Not all American feminists believe that a special or unifying theory of feminist practice is urgently needed; Showalter's historical approach to women's culture allows a feminist critic to use theories based on nonfeminist disciplines. Kolodny has advocated a "playful pluralism" that encompasses a variety of critical schools and methods. But Jane Marcus and others have responded that if feminists adopt too wide a range of approaches, they may relax the tensions between feminists and the educational establishment necessary for political activism.

The question of whether feminism weakens or fortifies itself by emphasizing its separateness — and by developing unity through separateness — is one of several areas of debate within American feminism. Another area of disagreement touched on earlier, between feminists who stress universal feminine attributes (the feminine imagination, feminine writing) and those who focus on the political conditions experienced by certain groups of women at certain times in history, parallels a larger distinction between American feminist critics and their British counterparts.

While it has been customary to refer to an Anglo-American tradition of feminist criticism, British feminists tend to distinguish themselves from what they see as an American overemphasis on texts linking women across boundaries and decades and an underemphasis on popular art and culture. They regard their own critical practice as more political than that of American feminists, whom they have often faulted for being uninterested in historical detail. They would join such American critics as Myra Jehlen to suggest that a continuing preoccupation with women writers might create the danger of placing women's texts outside the history that conditions them.

In the view of British feminists, the American opposition to male stereotypes that denigrate women has often led to counterstereotypes of feminine virtue that ignore real differences of race, class, and culture among women. In addition, they argue that American celebrations of individual heroines falsely suggest that powerful individuals may be immune to repressive conditions and may even imply that *any* individual can go through life unconditioned by the culture and ideology in which she or he lives.

Similarly, the American endeavor to recover women's history — for example, by emphasizing that women developed their own strategies to gain power within their sphere — is seen by British feminists like Judith Newton and Deborah Rosenfelt as an endeavor that "mystifies" male oppression, disguising it as something that has created for women a special world of opportunities. More important from the British standpoint, the universalizing and "essentializing" tendencies in both American practice and French theory disguise women's oppression by highlighting sexual difference, suggesting that a dominant system is impervious to political change. By contrast, British feminist theory emphasizes an engagement with historical process in order to promote social change.

In the essay that follows, Felicity A. Nussbaum begins her feminist reading of *Gulliver's Travels* by discussing Swift's antifeminism, pointing out that *Gulliver's Travels* has, from the beginning, been judged a misogynist work. And for good reason, Nussbaum points out. "The vivid scenes of rabid antagonism toward women are among the most memorable in the book, and much of the comedy is at woman's expense." Swift is undeniably explicit in "cataloging [his] contempt" for women.

It might seem that such a text would readily lend itself to a feminist reading in general, and feminist critique in particular. Such is not the case, however, according to Nussbaum. Indeed, "*Gulliver's Travels* seems to resist a feminist reading," Nussbaum writes, "in part because Gulliver's own rhetorical ambiguity makes locating the exact satiric intention difficult." That is to say, since Gulliver is himself the object of the text's satire, how are we to know what readers are meant to think of his antifeminism?

At this point, Nussbaum sidesteps the question of whether *Gulliver's Travels* is — or its author was — misogynist or antifeminist, focusing instead on gender as a category in literature and the way in which cultural attitudes are expressed through gender. From her perspective, misogyny is not in the nature of any one writer or text but, rather, a "cluster of discourses circulating within the culture." Gender relations are "thoroughly embedded within semiotic and cultural codes," which in turn define the consciousness of the individual and hence "the ways in which we imagine and represent reality."

Nussbaum is particularly interested in Gulliver's consciousness. A feminized and victimized consciousness on one hand (it is capable of "disrupting traditional gender relations and positing new alternatives during the course of the *Travels*"), it is, on the other, one that fails to "rise above" its "provincial" training far enough to "articulate these possibilities." The result, according to Nussbaum, is its "utter rejection of the female in Part Four."

As the foregoing suggests, Nussbaum distinguishes between the construction of female gender in Parts One and Two on one hand and that in Parts Three and Four on the other. In One and Two, woman is associated with concepts like *mother* and *nation;* thus patriotism informs attitudes of male subjection to the female gender. But "if maternity is the dominant trope of Parts One and Two, the whore prevails in Part Three." There, Nussbaum argues, "the floating island Laputa is sexual rather than maternal in its association with the Spanish *la puta,* the whore." In Part Four, the nation Gulliver visits epitomizes masculine reason, while the servant class, the Yahoos, are feminized in their slatternly Otherness.

Finally, however, Nussbaum returns as she must to the doubleness of gender construction in *Gulliver's Travels;* the Houyhnhnms, after all, are objectionable in many ways, and to the extent that they are culturally constitutive of maleness, *Gulliver's Travels* is not entirely antifeminist. Indeed, as Nussbaum implies, it may ultimately be more racist (anti-Other) than antifeminist; antifeminism, in other words, may just be the code through which a whole culture's racism is expressed. "Throughout the text," Nussbaum suggests, "Gulliver's sexuality becomes a subject of contention when he is the object of aggressive 'native' women. . . . Sexual union with Other women troubles Gulliver, not because of his loyal attachment to his wife . . . or from any moral scruples, but because union with the Other would resolve his repulsion into attraction and into identity with them." Such relations would force him to acknowledge the Yahoo element in himself that he so pointedly professes to abhor.

Rather than serving as an example of feminist critique, Nussbaum's essay offers more nearly what has been called British *cultural* critique, for it calls into question certain feminist assumptions, including the

French/gynocritical one that "women's strategies of knowing are *inherently* different from men's." Nussbaum argues instead that the extent to which their ways of knowing differ is largely a function of class, race, and nationality, not of any innate gender-based characteristic.

Ross C Murfin

FEMINIST CRITICISM: A SELECTED BIBLIOGRAPHY

French Feminist Theories

Beauvoir, Simone de. *The Second Sex.* 1953. Trans. and ed. H. M. Parshley. New York: Bantam, 1961.

Cixous, Hélène. "The Laugh of the Medusa." Trans. Keith Cohen and Paula Cohen. *Signs* 1 (1976): 875–94.

Cixous, Hélène, and Catherine Clément. *The Newly Born Woman.* Trans. Betsy Wing. Minneapolis: U of Minnesota P, 1986.

French Feminist Theory. Special issue, *Signs* 7.1 (1981).

Irigaray, Luce. *This Sex Which Is Not One.* Trans. Catherine Porter. Ithaca: Cornell UP, 1985.

Jones, Ann Rosalind. "Inscribing Femininity: French Theories of the Feminine." *Making a Difference: Feminist Literary Criticism.* Ed. Gayle Greene and Coppélia Kahn. London: Methuen, 1985. 80–112.

Kristeva, Julia. *Desire in Language: A Semiotic Approach to Literature and Art.* Ed. Leon S. Roudiez. Trans. Thomas Gora, Alice Jardine, and Roudiez. New York: Columbia UP, 1980.

Marks, Elaine, and Isabelle de Courtivron, eds. *New French Feminisms: An Anthology.* Amherst: U of Massachusetts P, 1980.

Moi, Toril, ed. *French Feminist Thought: A Reader.* Oxford: Basil Blackwell, 1987.

British and American Feminist Theories

Belsey, Catherine, and Jane Moore, eds. *The Feminist Reader: Essays in Gender and the Politics of Literary Criticism.* New York: Basil Blackwell, 1989.

Benhabib, Seyla, and Drucilla Cornell, eds. *Feminism as Critique: On the Politics of Gender.* Minneapolis: U of Minnesota P, 1987.

de Lauretis, Teresa, ed. *Feminist Studies/Critical Studies*. Bloomington: Indiana UP, 1986.

Feminist Readings: French Texts/American Contexts. Special issue, *Yale French Studies* 62 (1982). Essays by Jardine and Spivak.

Fuss, Diana. *Essentially Speaking: Feminism, Nature and Difference*. New York: Routledge, 1989.

Herndl, Diana Price, and Robyn Warhol, eds. *Feminisms: An Anthology of Literary Theory and Criticism*. New Brunswick, NJ: Rutgers UP, 1991.

Keohane, Nannerl O., Michelle Z. Rosaldo, and Barbara C. Gelpi, eds. *Feminist Theory: A Critique of Ideology*. Chicago: U of Chicago P, 1982.

Kolodny, Annette. "Dancing through the Minefield: Some Observations on the Theory, Practice, and Politics of a Feminist Literary Criticism." Showalter, *New Feminist Criticism* 144–67.

———. "Some Notes on Defining a 'Feminist Literary Criticism.'" *Critical Inquiry* 2 (1975): 78.

Lovell, Terry, ed. *British Feminist Thought: A Reader*. Oxford: Basil Blackwell, 1990.

Malson, Micheline, et al., eds. *Feminist Theory in Practice and Process*. Chicago: U of Chicago P, 1986.

Rich, Adrienne. *On Lies, Secrets, and Silence: Selected Prose, 1966–1979*. New York: Norton, 1979.

Showalter, Elaine, ed. *The New Feminist Criticism: Essays on Women, Literature, and Theory*. New York: Pantheon, 1985.

———. "Toward a Feminist Poetics " Showalter, *New Feminist Criticism* 125–43.

Spacks, Patricia Ann Meyer. *The Female Imagination*. New York: Knopf, 1975.

The Feminist Critique

Fetterley, Judith. *The Resisting Reader: A Feminist Approach to American Fiction*. Bloomington: Indiana UP, 1978.

Greer, Germaine. *The Female Eunuch*. New York: McGraw, 1971.

Millett, Kate. *Sexual Politics*. Garden City: Doubleday, 1970.

Robinson, Lillian S. *Sex, Class, and Culture*. 1978. New York: Methuen, 1986.

Wittig, Monique. *Les Guérillères*. Trans. David Le Vay. 1969. New York: Avon, 1973.

Woolf, Virginia. *A Room of One's Own*. New York: Harcourt, 1929.

Women's Writing and Creativity

Abel, Elizabeth, ed. *Writing and Sexual Difference*. Chicago: U of Chicago P, 1982.

Abel, Elizabeth, Marianne Hirsch, and Elizabeth Langland, eds. *The Voyage In: Fictions of Female Development*. Hanover: UP of New England, 1983.

Auerbach, Nina. *Communities of Women: An Idea in Fiction*. Cambridge, MA: Harvard UP, 1978.

Gilbert, Sandra M., and Susan Gubar. *The Madwoman in the Attic: The Woman Writer and the Nineteenth-Century Literary Imagination*. New Haven: Yale UP, 1979.

Jacobus, Mary, ed. *Women Writing and Writing about Women*. New York: Barnes, 1979.

Miller, Nancy K., ed. *The Poetics of Gender*. New York: Columbia UP, 1986.

Newton, Judith Lowder. *Women, Power and Subversion: Social Strategies in British Fiction, 1778–1860*. Athens: U of Georgia P, 1981.

Poovey, Mary. *The Proper Lady and the Woman Writer: Ideology as Style in the Works of Mary Wollstonecraft, Mary Shelley, and Jane Austen*. Chicago: U of Chicago P, 1984.

Showalter, Elaine. *A Literature of Their Own: British Women Novelists from Brontë to Lessing*. Princeton: Princeton UP, 1977.

Marxist and Class Analysis

Barrett, Michèle. *Women's Oppression Today: Problems in Marxist Feminist Analysis*. London: Verso, 1980.

Delphy, Christine. *Close to Home: A Materialist Analysis of Women's Oppression*. Trans. and ed. Diana Leonard. Amherst: U of Massachusetts P, 1984.

Haraway, Donna J. *Simians, Cyborgs, and Women: The Reinvention of Nature*. New York: Routledge, 1991.

Hartsock, Nancy C. M. *Money, Sex, and Power: Toward a Feminist Historical Materialism*. Boston: Northeastern UP, 1985.

Kaplan, Cora. *Sea Changes: Culture and Feminism*. London: Verso, 1986.

Mitchell, Juliet. *Woman's Estate*. New York: Pantheon, 1971.

Newton, Judith, and Deborah Rosenfelt, eds. *Feminist Criticism and*

Social Change: Sex, Class and Race in Literature and Culture.
New York: Methuen, 1985.

Sargent, Lydia, ed. *Women and Revolution: A Discussion of the Unhappy Marriage of Marxism and Feminism.* Montreal: Black Rose, 1981.

Spivak, Gayatri Chakravorty. *In Other Worlds: Essays in Cultural Politics.* New York: Methuen, 1987.

Women's History/Women's Studies

Bridenthal, Renate, and Claudia Koonz, eds. *Becoming Visible: Women in European History.* Boston: Houghton, 1977.

Farnham, Christie, ed. *The Impact of Feminist Research in the Academy.* Bloomington: Indiana UP, 1987.

Kelly, Joan. *Women, History and Theory.* Chicago: U of Chicago P, 1984.

McConnell-Ginet, Sally, et al., eds. *Woman and Language in Literature and Society.* New York: Praeger, 1980.

Mitchell, Juliet, and Ann Oakley, eds. *The Rights and Wrongs of Women.* London: Penguin, 1976.

Newton, Judith L., et al., eds. *Sex and Class in Women's History.* London: Routledge, 1983.

Riley, Denise. *"Am I That Name?": Feminism and the Category of "Women" in History.* Minneapolis: U of Minnesota P, 1988.

Rowbotham, Sheila. *Woman's Consciousness, Man's World.* Harmondsworth: Penguin, 1973.

Scott, Joan Wallach. *Gender and the Politics of History.* New York: Columbia UP, 1988.

Smith-Rosenberg, Carroll. *Disorderly Conduct: Visions of Gender in Victorian America.* New York: Knopf, 1985.

Feminism and Sexualities

Butler, Judith. *Gender Trouble: Feminism and the Subversion of Identity.* New York: Routledge, 1990.

Fuss, Diana, ed. *Inside/Out: Lesbian Theories, Gay Theories.* New York: Routledge, 1991.

The Lesbian Issue. Special issue, *Signs* 9 (Summer 1984).

Martin, Biddy, and Chandra Talpade Mohanty. "Feminist Politics: What's Home Got to Do with It?" *Life/Lines: Theorizing*

Women's Autobiography. Ed. Bella Brodski and Celeste Schenck. Ithaca: Cornell UP, 1988.

Snitow, Ann, Christine Stansell, and Sharon Thompson, eds. *Powers of Desire: The Politics of Sexuality.* New York: Monthly Review Press, 1983.

Vance, Carole S., ed. *Pleasure and Danger: Exploring Female Sexuality.* Boston: Routledge, 1984.

Feminism, Race, and Nationality

Christian, Barbara. *Black Feminist Criticism: Perspectives on Black Women Writers.* New York: Pergamon, 1985.

Collins, Patricia Hill. *Black Feminist Thought: Knowledge, Consciousness, and the Politics of Empowerment.* Boston: Unwin Hyman, 1990.

hooks, bell. *Ain't I a Woman? Black Women and Feminism.* Boston: South End, 1981.

Mohanty, Chandra Talpade, Ann Russo, and Lourdes Torres, eds. *Third World Women and the Politics of Feminism.* Bloomington: Indiana UP, 1991.

Moraga, Cherrie, and Gloria Anzaldua. *This Bridge Called My Back: Writings by Radical Women of Color.* New York: Kitchen Table, 1981.

Schipper, Mineke, ed. *Unheard Words: Women and Literature in Africa, the Arab World, Asia, the Caribbean, and Latin America.* London: Allison, 1985.

Trinh, T. Minh-ha. *Woman, Native, Other: Writing Postcoloniality and Feminism.* Bloomington: Indiana UP, 1989.

Feminism and Other Critical Approaches

Armstrong, Nancy, ed. *Literature as Women's History I.* Special issue, *Genre* 19–20 (1986–87).

Benstock, Shari. *Textualizing the Feminine: On the Limits of Genre.* Norman: U of Oklahoma P, 1991.

Chodorow, Nancy. *The Reproduction of Mothering: Psychoanalysis and the Sociology of Gender.* Berkeley: U of California P, 1978.

Diamond, Irene, and Lee Quinby, eds. *Feminism and Foucault: Reflections on Resistance.* Boston: Northeastern UP, 1988.

Elliot, Patricia. *From Mastery to Analysis: Theories of Gender in Psychoanalytic Criticism.* Ithaca: Cornell UP, 1990.

Felman, Shoshana, ed. *Literature and Psychoanalysis: The Question of Reading: Otherwise.* Baltimore: Johns Hopkins UP, 1982.

———. "Women and Madness: The Critical Fallacy." *Diacritics* 5 (1975): 2–10.

Feminist Studies 14 (1988). Special issue on feminism and deconstruction.

Gallop, Jane. *The Daughter's Seduction: Feminism and Psychoanalysis.* Ithaca: Cornell UP, 1982.

Keller, Evelyn Fox. *Reflections on Gender and Science.* New Haven: Yale UP, 1985.

Meese, Elizabeth, and Alice Parker, eds. *The Difference Within: Feminism and Critical Theory.* Amsterdam: John Benjamins, 1989.

Nicholson, Linda J., ed. *Feminism/Postmodernism.* New York: Routledge, 1990.

Penley, Constance, ed. *Feminism and Film Theory.* New York: Routledge, 1988.

Weedon, Chris. *Feminist Practice and Poststructuralist Theory.* New York: Basil Blackwell, 1987.

Feminist Approaches to Swift

Brown, Laura. "Reading Race and Gender: Jonathan Swift." *Eighteenth-Century Studies* 23 (1990): 425–43.

Bruce, Susan. "The Flying Island and Female Anatomy: Gynaecology and Power in *Gulliver's Travels.*" *Genders* 2 (1988): 60–76.

Flynn, Carol Houlihan. *The Body in Swift and Defoe.* Cambridge: Cambridge UP, 1990.

Nussbaum, Felicity A. *The Brink of All We Hate: English Satires on Women, 1660–1750.* Lexington: U of Kentucky P, 1984.

Pollak, Ellen. *The Poetics of Sexual Myth: Gender and Ideology in the Verse of Swift and Pope.* Chicago: U of Chicago P, 1985.

Rees, Christine. "Gay, Swift, and the Nymphs of Drury-Lane." *Essays in Criticism* 23 (1973): 1–21.

Rogers, Katharine M. *The Troublesome Helpmate: A History of Misogyny in Literature.* Seattle: U of Washington P, 1966.

A FEMINIST PERSPECTIVE

FELICITY A. NUSSBAUM

Gulliver's Malice:
Gender and the Satiric Stance

Among Lady-critics, some have found that Mr. Gulliver had a
particular malice to maids of honour.
                    –JOHN GAY TO JONATHAN SWIFT, 17 NOVEMBER 1726

I

Many early readers of *Gulliver's Travels* judged it to be an antifeminist book, a judgment that Swift flaunted by incorporating it
into the 1735 edition. That edition carried a prefatory letter dated
1727 from Captain Gulliver to his Cousin Sympson that remarks on
the book's reception: "I see myself accused of reflecting upon great
States-Folk; of degrading human Nature, . . . and of abusing the Female Sex" (29). Many readers had, of course, anticipated the antifeminism in *Gulliver's Travels* because of Swift's earlier writings.
George Faulkner had cautioned about Swift's poetry that "the Ladies
may resent certain satyrical Touches against the mistaken Conduct in
some of the fair Sex" (Faulkner 2: i–ii), and Richardson's Pamela
complains of the "*unmanly* Contempt, with which a certain celebrated Genius treats our Sex in general, in most of his Pieces that I
have seen" (*Pamela* 4: 367). In the person of Lemuel Gulliver, Swift
teases Henrietta Howard on 28 November 1726 "to beg you would
continue your goodness to me by reconcileing me to the Maids of
Honour whom they say I have most grievously offended. I am so
stupid as not to find out how I have disobliged them: Is there any
harm in a young Ladys reading of romances?" (*Corresp.* 3: 190).
Readers of *Gulliver's Travels* cannot fail to remember the offensive
smell oozing from the naked bodies of the Brobdingnagian maids of
honor, the huge flabby dugs of the Yahoo women, Gulliver's revulsion at seeing his wife upon his final homecoming, and his terror at
the explicitly sexual advances of various women who pursue him during his travels. The vivid scenes of rabid antagonism toward women
are among the most memorable in the book, and much of the com-

edy is at woman's expense.[1] In short, Swift's satires against women have long marked him as part of the lingering misogynist tradition from Juvenal and Ovid that was revitalized in the seventeenth century by Robert Gould, Richard Ames, Lord Rochester, and Dryden.[2]

Gulliver's Travels seems to resist a feminist reading, however, in part because Gulliver's own rhetorical ambiguity makes locating the exact satiric intention difficult. Gulliver is an unreliable narrator who is himself implicated in the satire on all humanity. While women and the effeminate are frequently the object of satiric attack, the extent to which *Gulliver's Travels* is antifeminist remains contested. In fact, even among feminists Swift's misogyny has not been universally assumed. Laura Brown has acutely pointed out that feminist readings of Swift have occasionally reversed themselves on identical evidence, a measure of the interpretive difficulty one faces when confronted with his writings.[3] Similarly, much has been made of Swift's propensity to create double-edged satire against women, exhibiting both its pathos and its comedy.[4]

One might draw, for example, on the positive example of Swift's dear friend Stella (Esther Johnson), who nurtures and sustains him, in contradiction to the disreputable women of "The Progress of Beauty" (1719) and "A Beautiful Young Nymph Going to Bed" (1731). In "To Stella, Visiting me in my Sickness" (1720), Swift praises Stella's integrity:

> The World shall in its Atoms end,
> E'er *Stella* can deceive a Friend.
> By Honour seated in her Breast,
> She still determines what is best:
> What Indignation in her Mind
> Against Enslavers of Mankind! (57–62; *Poems* 2: 725)

In counterpoint to these adulatory sentiments, "The Progress of Beauty" darkly condemns Celia's evolution from nymph to rotting whore:

> Yet as she wasts, she grows discreet,
> Till Midnight never shows her Head;

---

[1] These touchstone passages are among those regularly expurgated in children's versions of *Gulliver's Travels*. See Smedman.

[2] See, for example, Nussbaum, *Brink of All We Hate*; Pollak; and Rogers.

[3] Brown has also significantly linked protofeminist and imperialist strategies.

[4] See Aden. Christine Rees contends that Swift becomes "more preoccupied with confirming or destroying pre-existing images of the sex, whether created by literature, by social expectations, or by the woman concerned" (7).

So rotting Celia stroles the Street
When sober Folks are all a-bed. (101–04; *Poems* 1: 229)

Similarly, "A Beautiful Young Nymph" expresses disgust for women: "*Corinna* in the Morning dizen'd, / Who sees, will spew; who smells, be poison'd" (73–74; *Poems* 2: 583). Though Swift is capable of praising women, few authors are more explicit in cataloging their contempt for members of the sex.

In determining the extent of Swift's misogyny, how is one to interpret the undecipherable coded words Swift uses in *Journal to Stella* to convey personal and political gossip: "Farewell deelest Md Md FW FW FW Me Me Me lele" (16 May 1713; 2: 669)? Is it an intimate little language that allows Swift to explore the nature of his love for Esther Johnson (Stella) while he playfully includes Rebecca Dingley in his address? Or is it a means of inverting reality in order to infantilize and control women, whose emotional power he fears? In a less veiled mode, Swift measures Stella's capacity for reason when he writes to his friend Charles Ford, "I would have him and you know that I hate Yahoos of both Sexes, and that Stella and Madame de Villette are onely tolerable at best, for want of Houyhnhnms" (19 Jan. 1723–24; *Corresp.* 3: 4). Stella would seem to be the exception to Swift's attitude toward women, yet she is "onely tolerable at best."

Swift's intriguing relationships with Stella, Vanessa (Esther Vanhomrigh), and Rebecca Dingley tempt the feminist critic into reconciling these contradictions and explaining Swift's apparent misogyny through biographical readings of his works. Is it mere accident, for example, that the cluster of scatological poems from 1727 to 1733 and the publication of *Gulliver's Travels* coincided so closely with his beloved Stella's death in 1728? In Swift's own autobiographical account, the "Family of Swift," he recounts his motherless state and the doting attention of his nurse. His orphaned relationship to England, occasioned by his being born in Ireland and taken to England at an early age, as well as his sense of later being exiled to Ireland when Queen Anne refused to appoint him to a high church post, certainly contributed to his ambivalence toward the nation and its sovereign. If England is Swift's political mother in this narrative, and Ireland may be imagined as his loving if sometimes excessively doting nurse, then how is the fact that Swift apparently never married connected to his attitude toward literal, surrogate, and political mothers? These are fascinating questions, yet this sort of biographical criticism poses serious problems and has limitations that give us pause.

Since misogyny means "hatred for women," it implies an agent of that hatred and a personally motivated vendetta against the female sex. Postmodern theories of subjectivity, however, suggest that the author is less an autonomous coherent identity whose motivations can be accurately tracked than a rough-hewn subjectivity where conflicting discourses intersect. As a result, "misogyny" as a manifestation of individual psychology against women has, I think, begun to lose its explanatory effect when set in the context of feminist cultural criticism. For our purposes, we may redefine *misogyny* as a cluster of discourses circulating within the culture directed against all women everywhere, and as a set of codes to be taken up for various aims at different moments in history. Shifting from a premise of individual animosity to an antifeminist domain of discourse within specific cultures and histories releases the reader from the need to determine the author's "intention" and makes possible instead the analysis of gender as a category constitutive of cultural meanings. Feminist criticism need not mean resorting to a reductive approach that would simply label Swift misogynist or not.

Certainly feminist criticism in its current stage is multivocal and diverse in its ends. Its various approaches include traditional historical and new critical readings, psychoanalysis, Marxism, deconstruction, new historicism, and cultural critique, all of which may be brought to bear on eighteenth-century texts. Feminist criticism is unified, however, in thinking of gender as a crucial "constitutive element of social relationships based on perceived differences between the sexes" and as "a primary way of signifying relationships of power" (Scott 42). In other words, gender relations are thoroughly embedded within semiotic and cultural codes that define the ways in which we imagine and represent reality. Further, feminist analysis engages in transforming these codes rather than simply adding onto existing knowledge or relegating gender and sexuality to the margins. The point for some feminists is to emphasize the way in which women's strategies of knowing are *inherently* different from men's or, for other feminists, the way they are *constructed* as essentially different. One difficulty with positing a feminist way of knowing is that such an understanding cannot be assumed to be equally and identically available to all women throughout history and across cultures, since women's experiences and memories vary widely. The heterogeneity of class, race, nation, and sexuality among women makes any uniform epistemology suspect — and difficult to attain. The question then becomes, What are the terms through which any feminist criticism can be unified without allowing it to mutate into a master theory that will engage in the very practices it contests? How can the binary

oppositions, the contradictions and variations among women, be articulated so that they do not simply cancel each other out and empty feminism of its capacity to encourage social change?

Cultural materialist feminism, with its emphasis on the catalytic
power of the contradictions that emanate from opposing concepts, identities, and ways of knowing, continues to strive toward recognizing differences among women in theory and practice. It also analyzes the representations and material effects of those differences. Chela Sandoval, for
example, has argued in behalf of an "oppositional consciousness" that
refuses to smooth over contradictions among women in the interests of
achieving apparent unity. Such an approach acknowledges and articulates
the asymmetries of women's histories and cultural situations while engaging in collective activity. What then can feminist theory informed by
cultural critique bring to the study of literary historical texts?

For our purposes, we may attempt first to distinguish between the
kinds of ambiguities that produce creative confrontation, empowerment, and agency for feminist critics of *Gulliver's Travels* and alterna-
tively to distinguish those that set up antagonisms that impede the use
of these enabling concepts. I will argue that Gulliver's consciousness,
because of its complexity and alterity, its feminization and victimization,
could be imagined as disrupting traditional gender relations and positing new alternatives during the course of the *Travels*. Yet Gulliver, with
his provincial nature, fails to rise above the context at hand to articulate
these possibilities, and his utter rejection of the female in Part Four reinforces and perpetuates traditional male/female hierarchies. Gulliver's
fluid subjectivity, his status as satirist or satiric object, is finally a subjectivity gone askew. His identity becomes rigidly fixed at the conclusion,
and in its inflexibility becomes synonymous with racial arrogance, delusion, and an isolated individualism. In response to this failed promise,
however, the feminist critic finds grounds for resistant readings in noting that Gulliver himself is a gendered object of satire, and his antifeminist sentiments may be among those mocked.

II

Gender relations shift throughout the four parts of *Gulliver's Travels* as Gulliver defines the meanings of the sexes in the countries he visits.
In the first two parts, the voyages to Lilliput and Brobdingnag, the female body becomes a substitute for the nation and the concept of
woman a metaphor for mother country. The nation is at once a female

man and a repulsed nursing mother. In Part Three the floating island Laputa is sexual rather than maternal in its association with the Spanish *la puta*, the whore. Finally, in Part Four the nation Gulliver visits is the epitome of masculine reason while the servant class, the Yahoos, are feminized in their slatternly otherness. Gulliver clearly does not display the libertinism and sexual appetite of Lovelace, Mr. B, or even Tom Jones and, unlike many colonial adventurers, sexual conquest does not drive his narrative. Rather than seeking the sexual possession or military conquering of the satirized body of woman, Gulliver settles for quiet misanthropy and conjugal visits to domestic horses.

In Lilliput, Gulliver is the Great Man-Mountain who is demasculinized when his captors take away his scimitar, scabbard, and pocket pistols and confine him to specific boundaries. The privileged status he enjoys when he assists the empress in viewing an entertainment is compromised by the elaborate rules of confinement governing his life as a Lilliputian subject. Gulliver's gendering includes his own consciousness of himself as subject to a nation that he represents metaphorically as a mother. Gulliver patriotically intones to Brobdingnag's king:

> For, I have always borne that laudable Partiality to my own Country, which *Dionysius Halicarnassensis* with so much Justice recommends to an Historian. I would hide the Frailties and Deformities of my Political Mother, and place her Virtues and Beauties in the most advantageous Light. (133)

His protestations in defense of England are followed by sympathetic accounts of her achievements at war in an apparent attempt to hide her deformities.

In the best-known incident in Part One, gender also figures significantly when a careless maid of honor, typically female in her reading tastes, "fell asleep while she was reading a Romance" (69) and caused the fire in the empress's apartment. No longer pinioned, Gulliver gleefully urinates on the fire, a masculine marking of territory that relieves him but brings the empress to accuse him of an assault on the nation. His misplaced assistance to the female sovereign leads to his expulsion from the country. We are expected to believe that the empress's extreme response to Gulliver's deed and her demanding his punishment derive in part from her being a female man, a woman who unnaturally usurps political authority. After all, Gulliver's political discussions in the nations he visits take place exclusively with the kings and emperors, not with their consorts. In short, the satire in Part One is not simply directed against women but also redounds against Gulliver himself as a politically naive and inept giant whose masculine authority comically seems to be in jeopardy.

The nursing breast of the political mother, especially in the first two parts, is desired and reviled simultaneously. In *Gulliver's Travels* both the sexual and maternal functions of the breast seem operative when, for example, Gulliver is set astride the nipple of the maid of honor and when he fears he will be swallowed up in the cancerous holes of the Brobdingnagian beggar woman's breast. The preoccupation with the breast and its functions in *Gulliver's Travels* is indicative of a larger cultural obsession. Ruth Perry has carefully defined a shift in the eighteenth century away from the breast's sexuality to its maternity, as giving one's children out to be wetnursed became increasingly unfashionable for the middle and upper classes. The breast, she argues, is the "site of [woman's] sexual definition and dependence and of the struggle between men over her sexual uses" (233).[5] This shift could also be described as an increasing separation between the functions to be performed by different bodies in a division of labor among women. From this perspective, it is not so much that the wife and nursing mother's breast is designated as maternal but that the sexual breast must be found elsewhere and is displaced onto non-European women and European women of the working class. The breast is material evidence of woman's traumatizing power, and it is particularly troublesome on the body of the Other woman or even in the animal kingdom.

A case in point is the potential threat of the Brobdingnagian monkey to infantilize Gulliver and nurse him: "He took me up in his right Fore-foot, and held me as a Nurse doth a Child she is going to suckle" (123). The monkey's attempts to feed Gulliver with his own victuals lead Gulliver to choke and vomit. In this terrifying connection of the monkey to the monstrous mother giving suck, animal and female are collapsed into the same entity in spite of the monkey's maleness. The case of the Brobdingnagian nurse, the breast, usually associated with a mixture of nurture and sexual desire, is equally the occasion for Gulliver's repulsion at woman's body:

> I must confess no Object ever disgusted me so much as the Sight of her monstrous Breast, which I cannot tell what to compare with, so as to give the curious Reader an Idea of its Bulk, Shape and Colour. It stood prominent six Foot, and could not be less than sixteen in Circumference. The Nipple was about half the Big-

[5]Also, Barbara Gelpi in her study of Shelley reads similar evidence to argue that maternity is eroticized at the turn of the eighteenth century.

ness of my Head, and the Hue both of that and the Dug so varified with Spots, Pimples, and Freckles, that nothing could appear
more nauseous. . . . This made me reflect upon the fair Skins of
our *English* Ladies, who appear so beautiful to us, only because
they are of our own Size, and their Defects not to be seen but
through a magnifying Glass. . . . (98–99)

Although he quickly counters that the Brobdingnagians are not deformed but comely and well proportioned, and that he too would look
repulsive magnified many times, Gulliver implies that all women are the
same if you scrutinize them under a magnifying glass: coarse, disgust-
ing, smelly. On the other hand, he deflects the satire when he concedes
that it is his *perspective* that leads to this view, not the reality. But the
satiric damage is done. The effect of his insistence that women are both
horrid and not is to leave the reader with the ineradicable image of
monstrous pimpled breasts. Gulliver's visceral disgust remains with the
reader, and his caveat that their deformity was only in the scale of perception quickly fades.

The boundaries are precariously undefined between Gulliver and
woman, between man and animal. In Brobdingnag women are even
more central to the narrative than in Lilliput, in part perhaps because of
their imposing size. Glumdalclitch, the nine-year-old daughter of
Gulliver's mistress, names him, teaches him the language from "a common Treatise for the use of young Girls" (105), and acts as a surrogate
mother. Infantilized, petted, and made a public spectacle, Gulliver becomes a feminized commodity, a profitable object. The queen mocks
his womanly cowardice, and the maids of honor threaten the "humanity" he is so ready to relinquish by the end of Part Four:

The Maids of Honour often invited *Glumdalclitch* to their Apartments . . . on Purpose to have the Pleasure of seeing and touching
me. They would often strip me naked from Top to Toe, and lay
me at full Length in their Bosoms; wherewith I was much disgusted; because, to say the Truth, a very offensive Smell came
from their Skins; which I do not mention or intend to the Disadvantage of those excellent Ladies, for whom I have all Manner of
Respect . . . like a Creature who had no Sort of Consequence.
For, they would strip themselves to the Skin, and put on their
Smocks in my Presence, while I was placed on their Toylet directly
before their naked Bodies. (120)

Gulliver's nausea signals his desire to distance himself from the female
body in all its material presence. Gulliver flees impending sexuality and

propagation when the king insists seeking "a Woman of my own Size, by whom I might propagate the Breed" (138). The active pursuit of his sexuality would result in the propagation of a whole species of curiosities to be marketed around the country.

If maternity is the dominant trope of Parts One and Two, the whore prevails in Part Three. Laputa's restless women flaunt their sexual transgressions in the faces of husbands who are so engaged in speculation that they fail to notice. At the Academy of Lagado Gulliver learns that "Constancy, Chastity, good Sense, and good Nature were not rated [taxed], because they would not bear the Charge of Collecting" (180). In Glubbdubdrib Gulliver discovers that the world has "been misled by prostitute Writers," and he is especially offended to learn that the leaders govern by sodomy, incest, and prostituting their own wives and daughters (187). Politics is dominated by the intrigue and illegitimate power associated with whoring: "[A] Whore can govern the Back-stairs, the Back-stairs a Council, and the Council a Senate" (188). The women long to escape from the flying island to Lagado below. The Laputans attempt to maintain control over the female body even as that attempt is frustrated by the women's flagrant exercise of sexual license.[6]

The Laputan men are rational to excess and, as a result, are bad reasoners. This is particularly remarkable since women (with whom Gulliver identifies in this part) were largely excluded from political participation because of their alleged irrationality. The double edge of the satire on women is evident in Gulliver's complaint about Balnibarbi:

> I conversed only with Women, Tradesmen, *Flappers*, and Court-Pages, during two Months of my Abode there; by which at last I rendered my self extremely contemptible; yet these were the only People from whom I could ever receive a reasonable Answer. (166)

It is the women, the vulgar, and the illiterate who, after all, threatened to rebel against the scheme to carry a bundle of *things* as equivalents to the *words* they might have occasion to include in conversation. Gulliver identifies himself with the female and other disempowered Laputans in attempting to gain understanding of this country, since they are paradoxically among those who provide answers that correspond with his notion of rationality.

Throughout the text Gulliver's sexuality becomes a subject of con-

---

[6]Susan Bruce argues that Laputa's rising and falling resembles descriptions of the uterus in midwifery manuals and is emblematic of the failure of science to control women.

tention when he is the object of aggressive "native" women. Accusations of uncontrolled sexual licentiousness in Other women and descriptions of women who throw themselves at the feet of European adventurers as a means of excusing adultery and polygamy among male travelers are common in travel narratives from Tahiti to the New World.[7] Gulliver, for example, is accused of infidelity with the wife of Flimnap (the analogue to Prime Minister Robert Walpole), who possesses "a violent Affection for my Person" (77). The passionate attachment of the women to Gulliver emphasizes his global heterosexual attractiveness and indicates his uncontestable masculinity even in the face of his victimization by the queen ("a Female Man"), giant women, or rational masculine horselike beings. Sexual union with Other women troubles Gulliver, not because of his loyal attachment to his wife (whom he married because he was "advised to alter my Condition") or from any moral scruples, but because union with the Other would resolve his repulsion into attraction and into identity with them. In short, he would have to acknowledge his own feminization and his affinities not only with Yahoos in general, but with the *female* Yahoo, who rests at the bottom of the scale. Lascivious and antagonistic toward other females, she exemplifies the worst characteristics of women everywhere:

> [A] Female *Yahoo* would often stand behind a Bank or a Bush, to gaze on the young Males passing by, and then appear, and hide, using many antick Gestures and Grimaces; at which time it was observed, that she had a most *offensive Smell;* and when any of the Males advanced, would slowly retire, looking often back, and with a counterfeit Shew of Fear, run off into some convenient Place where she knew the Male would follow her.
>
> At other times, if a Female Stranger came among them, three or four of her own Sex would get about her, and stare and chatter, and grin, and smell her all over; and then turn off with Gestures that seemed to express Contempt and Disdain.
>
> Perhaps my Master might refine a little in these Speculations, which he had drawn from what he observed himself, or had been told him by others: However, I could not reflect without some Amazement, and much Sorrow, that the Rudiments of *Lewdness, Coquetry, Censure,* and *Scandal,* should have Place by Instinct in Womankind. (239–240)

In fact, when Gulliver himself finally becomes attracted to a creature on his travels, it is an animal of another species. He mentions "a very

[7]See, for example, my essay "The Other Woman."

comely Mare, together with a Colt and Fole, sitting on their Haunches, upon Mats of Straw, not unartfully made, and perfectly neat and clean" (211–12), but the mare's response to him, comically, is one of contempt, and there follows a crucial moment when they *name* him a Yahoo:

> The Mare soon after my Entrance, rose from her Mat, and coming up close, after having nicely observed my Hands and Face, gave me a most contemptuous Look; then turning to the Horse, I heard the Word *Yahoo* often repeated betwixt them; the meaning of which Word I could not then comprehend, although it were the first I had learned to pronounce; but I was soon better informed, to my everlasting Mortification. (212)

Gulliver's sexual attraction to the Houyhnhnm Other, then, signals his own becoming an Other to the Other — his becoming a Yahoo in the mind of his object of sexual desire — and paradoxically his feminization, since the Houyhnhnms of both sexes are figured as rational and masculine: "For now I could no longer deny, that I was a real *Yahoo*, in every Limb and Feature, since the Females had a natural Propensity to me as one of their own Species" (242). Here the threat of female sexuality in its troubling capacity to transform things seems to be realized. Nothing exceeds his terror when a young female Yahoo,

> inflamed by Desire, . . . came running with all Speed, and leaped into the Water within five Yards of the Place where I bathed. I was never in my Life so terribly frighted; . . . She embraced me after a most fulsome Manner; I roared as loud as I could, and the Nag came galloping towards me, whereupon she quitted her Grasp . . . [and] stood gazing and howling all the time I was putting on my Cloaths. (242)

If, as John Barrell has written, by the mid-eighteenth century masculinity means having intercourse rather than resisting it, Gulliver's refusal to take sexual license, even with a Yahoo, effeminates him. The threat continues when, returning home to his wife, he faces the identity he had hoped to abandon, since "by copulating with one of the *Yahoo*-Species, I had become a Parent of more; it struck me with the utmost Shame, Confusion and Horror" (261). His masculinity is in jeopardy when all of humanity, represented in his wife and children, would seem to be equivalent to being female and having a sexual nature. Gulliver both resembles the Yahoos and does not resemble them in his failure to be attracted to the women of their species.

Part Four is a rejection not only of the Yahoo woman's sexuality but of Englishwomen's sexuality. This is made explicit in a series of poems by Pope (and perhaps Gay as well), including Mary Gulliver's comic lament voicing her resentment to Captain Lemuel Gulliver upon his return to England that her sexual competition includes Flimnap's Lilliputian wife and a sorrel mare:

> Welcome, thrice welcome to thy native Place!
> — What, touch me not? what, shun a Wife's Embrace?
> Have I for this thy tedious Absence born,
> And wak'd and wish'd whole Nights for thy Return?
> In five long Years I took no second Spouse;
> What *Redriff* Wife so long hath kept her Vows? (1–6)

Although Gulliver is clearly feminized here as a Yahoo, he is also a *male* Yahoo, and thus becomes the object of the female Other's desire, a condition he was able to escape in the preceding parts by reasserting his racial difference. Pope's poem is also explicit in its racism:

> *Biddel*, like thee, might farthest *India* rove;
> He chang'd his Country, but retain'd his Love.
> There's Captain *Pennel*, absent half his Life,
> Comes back, and is the kinder to his Wife.
> Yet *Pennell's* Wife is brown, compar'd to me;
> And Mistress *Biddel* sure is Fifty three. (19–24)

This poem comments on a persistent and insidious strategy in *Gulliver's Travels* that denigrates the women Gulliver encounters by comparing them to Englishwomen throughout the work. For example, when Gulliver describes the Lilliputians' penmanship, he compares it to an Englishwoman's slanted scrawl as a sign of their mutual inferiority and of the Lilliputians' feminization. In Part Two a Brobdingnagian woman's reaction is satirized by comparing it to the obvious emotional excesses of Englishwomen. The first reaction of the farmer's wife is to shriek at the sight of Gulliver as if he were a monstrous spider: "[B]ut she screamed and ran back as Women in *England* do at the Sight of a Toad or a Spider" (96–97).

Similarly, the smells of the maids of honor are compared to those of English females; and when the wife of the Laputan prime minister pawns her clothes in order to run away with a deformed footman, Gulliver takes the opportunity to remark on the commonality of women's sexual licentiousness across cultures:

> This may perhaps pass with the Reader rather for an *European*
> or *English* Story, than for one of a Country so remote. But he

may please to consider, that the Caprices of Womankind are not
limited by any Climate or Nation; and that they are much more
uniform than can be easily imagined. (160)

By the conclusion of *Gulliver's Travels*, Englishwomen too are drawn
into the morass; Gulliver can no longer compare them favorably to the
Other women (such as the Yahoos) he encounters, and he does not
single out the Houyhnhnm females for praise. The differences between
Englishwomen and Lilliputian or Brobdingnagian women, between
Queen Anne and the queen of Lilliput, between his wife and a Yahoo
are collapsed into generalized contempt for the whole female sex.

Gulliver's Travels implies that women's characteristics transcend
time and place, and cross-gendered "traits" are a sign of the Other.
While Gulliver in the end proffers an argument against colonialism,
his reassertion of masculine privilege denigrates Englishwomen and
Other women in his alignment with the rational Houyhnhnms who,
despite being of both sexes, are gendered male. Gulliver seeks to escape the feminization located metaphorically in the Yahoos, but he is
also the object of satire in both his feminization and his masculine
posturing.

III

Clearly, Gulliver depicts women as beings who, like the Laputan
women, are capable of reason (*rationis capax*) but are not reasonable
creatures. While the satirist Mary Wollstonecraft, writing later in the
century, did not address Swift directly in her polemical *A Vindication of
the Rights of Woman* (1792), she recognized that Enlightenment philosophers excluded eighteenth-century women from the highest
reaches of rational thinking. In the *Vindication* she launches a direct
attack at antifeminist satirists in order to attain a position largely inac-
cessible to eighteenth-century women: a reasoned public and political
stance. Her argument moves confidently along a certain trajectory to
clear away the history of antifeminism by answering its satiric attacks,
attacking women herself, and acknowledging that women's situation
does not allow them to hold a wide general view. Wollstonecraft uses
satire to define a revolutionary position for "woman" as perpetrator
rather than object of satire. In short, in empowering satire's objects and
widening their field of vision, Wollstonecraft usurps for women the
room for the comprehensive understanding that allows people to see

the relationships between things. These arguments make it possible for her, by taking the satirist's stance, to satirize woman herself and to enact her own prescription that women should relinquish the trivial and take possession of the whole.

Wollstonecraft cannily joins, and then disrupts, the satiric fraternity in order to locate a place to stand as a feminist. Antifeminist satire, Wollstonecraft radically insists, can be redefined to be useful to women though it often has the pernicious effect of reinforcing the worst female instincts. Wollstonecraft enters the logic of antifeminist satire to conclude that women deserve its assaults:

> In the most trifling danger they [women] cling to their support, with parasitical tenacity, piteously demanding succor; and their *natural* protector extends his arm, or lifts up his voice, to guard the lovely trembler — from what? Perhaps the frown of an old cow, or the jump of a mouse; a rat would be a serious danger. (153)

She writes, "After surveying the history of woman, I cannot help agreeing with the severest satirist, considering the sex as the weakest as well as the most oppressed half of the species" (119).

But finally Wollstonecraft steps outside antifeminist satire to argue strongly against Milton and Pope, Rousseau and Dr. Gregory, John Fordyce and Lord Chesterfield, as well as the less likely targets of Hester Thrale, Madame de Genlis, and Madame de Staël. Her point is to clear away a vast forest of antifeminist dogma in order to achieve, for herself and thus implicitly for all women, a rational superior view that recognizes and exposes male domination of women. A feminist deployment of hatred for women's culturally ascribed characteristics becomes her innovative satiric strategy.

Yet Wollstonecraft's feminism is bound by racial and class restrictions. In the terms of the *Vindication* the satiric position she defines is uninhabitable by the Egyptian, the Turk, or the African slave of either sex. Wollstonecraft charges servants and slaves, like Englishwomen, with being naturally fond of dress, pleasure, and sway over others. Further, in the logic of her argument on polygamy, African women are "of a hotter constitution" (164) than African men, and more sexualized than Europeans of either sex. In short, Wollstonecraft's argument in favor of monogamous marriage, European culture, and bourgeois values is constructed at the expense of the Other.

If eighteenth-century feminism sometimes colludes in racism, it also serves as an example of the uses that a female satirist can make of anti-feminist satire. The unorthodox, if temporary, alliance of feminist with misogynist cultural codes may be used to organize them, elaborate upon them, and co-opt them in order to articulate the previously unpresentable. For Wollstonecraft, women's hatred of Woman is, paradoxically, the seed of feminism. Wollstonecraft encourages women to make something of the rubble of antifeminist satire so that they may amend its narratives and write other vindications. Where a contemporary feminist politics of satire differs from Wollstonecraft's is in its recognition that it must be provisional in the face of history and culture, and that it must make alignments with other oppressed groups in constructing a collective satiric practice. Recognizing the impossibility of locating a privileged standpoint that grants a full vision of the social structure, Chela Sandoval calls this feminist attitude a "*tactical subjectivity* with the capacity to recenter depending upon the kinds of oppression to be confronted" (14). A feminist politics of satire acknowledges its interested position in adopting a theoretical stance that is wide enough to encompass a collective whole.

In *Gulliver's Travels* the traveling category of the female connects to revenge, hysteria, licentiousness, and the physically repugnant in the early parts, and it is increasingly associated with Gulliver himself and thus the human race. Gulliver's longing to possess the Houyhnhnms' rationality is also a longing to command the essence of masculinity, to escape the feminine, and to eschew the sexual. The vacillating and elastic relation of Gulliver to the feminine and to sexuality is, I think, one of the difficulties that a feminist approach to *Gulliver's Travels* must face. Gulliver's flexible consciousness appeals to the feminist because of its occasional alignment with women, but the slippery nature of its satiric object limits that appeal. Avoiding any potential alliance with others (except perhaps with the asexual Don Pedro), Gulliver's satiric identity cannot be easily categorized as male or female, yet he refuses to confront contradiction so that the insufficiency of either gender (as it has been construed) might become the catalyst for new alignments. Gulliver's psychic "world-travelling,"[8] his shifting of identities, stops at the dead end of his mad acrimony against the human race, and in particular against the women of that race. A feminist reading counters Gulliver's reinforcement of traditional hierarchies to make him, at least in his expressed disgust for women, unequivocally the object of *its* sat-

---

[8]Maria Lugones offers the concept as a cross-racial feminist strategy.

ire, while at the same time it galvanizes Gulliver's alignment with the oppressed and makes possible reading against the grain.

WORKS CITED

Aden, John. "Corinna and the Sterner Muse of Swift." *English Language Notes* 4 (1966): 23–31.

Barrell, John. "'The Dangerous Goddess': Masculinity, Prestige, and the Aesthetic in Early Eighteenth-Century Britain." *Cultural Critique* 12 (1989): 101–31.

Brown, Laura. "Reading Race and Gender: Jonathan Swift." *Eighteenth-Century Studies* 23 (1990): 425–43.

Bruce, Susan. "The Flying Island and Female Anatomy: Gynaecology and Power in *Gulliver's Travels*." *Genders* 2 (1988): 60–76.

Faulkner, George. *The Works of Jonathan Swift, D.D., D.S.P.D. in 4 vols.* Dublin, 1735.

Gelpi, Barbara Charlesworth. *Shelley's Goddess: Maternity, Language, Subjectivity.* New York: Oxford UP, 1992.

Lugones, Maria. "Playfulness, 'World'-Travelling, and Loving Perception." *Hypatia: A Journal of Feminist Philosophy* 2.2 (1987): 3–19.

Nussbaum, Felicity A. *The Brink of All We Hate: English Satires on Women, 1660–1750.* Lexington: U of Kentucky P, 1984.

———. "The Other Woman: Polygamy, Pamela, and the Prerogative of Empire." *Women, "Race," and Writing in the Early Modern Period.* Ed. Margo Hendricks and Patricia Parker. New York: Routledge, 1994.

Perry, Ruth. "Colonizing the Breast: Sexuality and Maternity in Eighteenth-Century England." *Journal of the History of Sexuality* 2.2 (1991): 204–34.

Pollak, Ellen. *The Poetics of Sexual Myth: Gender and Ideology in the Verse of Swift and Pope.* Chicago: U of Chicago P, 1985.

Pope, Alexander. "Mary Gulliver to Captain Lemuel Gulliver." *Minor Poems.* Ed. Norman Ault and John Butt. London: Methuen, 1954. 276–79. Vol. 6 of *The Poetical Works of Alexander Pope.* The Twickenham Edition. Gen. ed. John Butt. 11 vols. 1939–69.

Rees, Christine. "Gay, Swift, and the Nymphs of Drury-Lane." *Essays in Criticism* 23 (1973): 1–21.

Richardson, Samuel. *Pamela; Or, Virtue Rewarded.* Oxford: Basil Blackwell, 1931. Vol 4 of *The Novels of Samuel Richardson.* Shakespeare Head Edition. 18 vols. 1929–31.

Rogers, Katharine M. *The Troublesome Helpmate: A History of Misogyny in Literature*. Seattle: U of Washington P, 1966.

Sandoval, Chela. "U.S. Third World Feminism: The Theory and Method of Oppositional Consciousness in the Postmodern World." *Genders* 10 (1991): 1–24.

Scott, Joan Wallach. "Gender: A Useful Category of Historical Analysis." *Gender and the Politics of History*. New York: Columbia UP, 1988. 28–50.

Smedman, Sarah. "Like Me, Like Me Not: *Gulliver's Travels* as Children's Book." *The Genres of Gulliver's Travels*. Ed. Frederik N. Smith. Newark: U of Delaware P, 1990. 75–100.

Swift, Jonathan. *The Correspondence of Jonathan Swift*. 5 vols. Ed. Harold Williams. Oxford: Clarendon, 1963–65.

———. *Journal to Stella*. 2 vols. Ed. Harold Williams. Oxford: Clarendon, 1948.

———. *The Poems of Jonathan Swift*. 2nd ed., rev. 3 vols. Ed. Harold Williams. Oxford: Clarendon, 1958.

———. *The Prose Works of Jonathan Swift*. 14 vols. Ed. Herbert Davis. Oxford: Basil Blackwell, 1939–68.

Wollstonecraft, Mary. *A Vindication of the Rights of Woman*. 1792. Ed. Miriam Brody Kramnick. Harmondsworth: Penguin, 1975.

The New Historicism
and
Gulliver's Travels

WHAT IS THE NEW HISTORICISM?

The new historicism is, first of all, *new:* one of the most recent developments in contemporary theory, it is still evolving. Enough of its contours have come into focus for us to realize that it exists and deserves a name, but any definition of the new historicism is bound to be somewhat fuzzy, like a partially developed photographic image. Some individual critics that we may label new historicist may also be deconstructors, or feminists, or Marxists. Some would deny that the others are even writing the new kind of historical criticism.

All of them, though, share the conviction that, somewhere along the way, something important was lost from literary studies: historical consciousness. Poems and novels came to be seen in isolation, as urnlike objects of precious beauty. The new historicists, whatever their differences and however defined, want us to see that even the most urnlike poems are caught in a web of historical conditions, relationships, and influences. In an essay on "The Historical Necessity for — and Difficulties with — New Historical Analysis in Introductory Literature Courses" (1987), Brook Thomas suggests that discussions of Keats's "Ode on a Grecian Urn" might begin with questions such as the following: Where would Keats have seen such an urn? How did a Grecian urn end up in a museum in England? Some very important historical and

political realities, Thomas suggests, lie behind and inform Keats's definitions of art, truth, beauty, the past, and timelessness. They are realities
that psychoanalytic and reader-response critics, formalists and feminists
and deconstructors, might conceivably overlook.

Although a number of influential critics working between 1920 and
1950 wrote about literature from a psychoanalytic perspective, the majority of critics took what might generally be referred to as the historical
approach. With the advent of the New Criticism, or formalism, however, historically oriented critics almost seemed to disappear from the
face of the earth. Jerome McGann writes: "A text-only approach has
been so vigorously promoted during the last thirty-five years that most
historical critics have been driven from the field, and have raised the flag
of their surrender by yielding the title 'critic' to the victor, and accepting the title 'scholar' for themselves" (*Inflections* 17). Of course, the
title "victor" has been vied for by a new kind of psychoanalytic critic, by
reader-response critics, by so-called deconstructors, and by feminists
since the New Critics of the 1950s lost it during the following decade.
But historical scholars have not been in the field, seriously competing to
become a dominant critical influence.

At least they haven't until quite recently. In the late 1970s and early
1980s new historicism first began to be practiced and articulated in the
ground breaking work of Louis Montrose and Stephen Greenblatt.
Through their work and that of others, new historicism transformed the
field of Renaissance Studies, and later began to influence other fields as
well. By 1984, Herbert Lindenberger could write: "It comes as something of a surprise to find that history is making a powerful comeback"
(16). E. D. Hirsch, Jr. has also suggested that it is time to turn back to
history and to historical criticism: "Far from being naive, historically
based criticism is the newest and most valuable kind . . . for our students
(and our culture) at the present time" (197). McGann obviously agrees.
In *Historical Studies and Literary Criticism* (1985), he speaks approv-
ingly of recent attempts to make sociohistorical subjects and methods
central to literary studies once again.

As the word *sociohistorical* suggests, the new historicism is not the
same as the historical criticism practiced forty years ago. For one thing,
it is informed by recent critical theory: by psychoanalytic criticism,
reader-response criticism, feminist criticism, and perhaps especially by
deconstruction. The new historicist critics are less fact- and event-
oriented than historical critics used to be, perhaps because they have
come to wonder whether the truth about what really happened can ever

be purely and objectively known. They are less likely to see history as linear and progressive, as something developing toward the present.

As the word "sociohistorical" also suggests, the new historicists view history as a social science and the social sciences as being properly historical. McGann most often alludes to sociology when discussing the future of literary studies. "A sociological poetics must be recognized not only as relevant to the analysis of poetry, but in fact as central to the analysis" (*Inflections* 62). Lindenberger cites anthropology as particularly useful in the new historical analysis of literature, especially anthropology as practiced by Victor Turner and Clifford Geertz. Geertz, who has related theatrical traditions in nineteenth-century Bali to forms of political organization that developed during the same period, has influenced some of the most important critics writing the new kind of historical criticism. Due in large part to Geertz's influence, new historicists such as Stephen Greenblatt have asserted that literature is not a sphere apart or distinct from the history that is relevant to it. That is what old historical criticism tended to do, to present history as information you needed to know before you could fully appreciate the separate world of art. Thus the new historicists have discarded old distinctions between literature, history, and the social sciences, while blurring other boundaries. They have erased the line dividing historical and literary materials, showing that the production of one of Shakespeare's plays was a political act and that the coronation of Elizabeth I was carried out with the same care for staging and symbol lavished on a work of dramatic art.

In addition to breaking down barriers that separate literature and history, history and the social sciences, new historicists have reminded us that it is treacherously difficult to reconstruct the past as it really was — rather than as we have been conditioned by our own place and time to believe that it was. And they know that the job is utterly impossible for anyone who is unaware of the difficulty and of the nature of his or her own historical vantage point. "Historical criticism can no longer make any part of [its] sweeping picture unselfconsciously, or treat any of its details in an untheorized way," McGann wrote in 1985 (*Historical Studies* 11). *Unselfconsciously* and *untheorized* are key words here; when the new historicist critics of literature describe a historical change, they are highly conscious of, and even likely to discuss, the *theory* of historical change that informs their account. They know that the changes they happen to see and describe are the ones that their theory of change allows or helps them to see and describe. And they know, too, that their theory of change is historically determined. They seek to minimize the distortion inherent in their perceptions and representations by admitting that they see through preconceived notions; in other words, they learn and reveal the color of the lenses in the glasses that they wear.

All three of the critics whose recent writings on the so-called back-to-history movement have been quoted thus far — Hirsch, Lindenberger, and McGann — mention the name of the late Michel Foucault. As much an archaeologist as a historian and as much a philosopher as either, Foucault in his writings brought together incidents and phenomena from areas of inquiry and orders of life that we normally regard as unconnected. As much as anyone, he encouraged the new historicist critic of literature to redefine the boundaries of historical inquiry.

Foucault's views of history were influenced by Friedrich Nietzsche's concept of a *wirkliche* ("real" or "true") history that is neither melioristic nor metaphysical. Foucault, like Nietzsche, didn't understand history as development, as a forward movement toward the present. Neither did he view history as an abstraction, idea, or ideal, as something that began "In the beginning" and that will come to THE END, a moment of definite closure, a Day of Judgment. In his own words, Foucault "abandoned [the old history's] attempts to understand events in terms of . . . some great evolutionary process" (*Discipline and Punish* 129). He warned new historians to be aware of the fact that investigators are themselves "situated." It is difficult, he reminded them, to see present cultural practices critically from within them, and on account of the same cultural practices, it is almost impossible to enter bygone ages. In *Discipline and Punish: The Birth of the Prison* (1975), Foucault admitted that his own interest in the past was fueled by a passion to write the history of the present.

Like Marx, Foucault saw history in terms of power, but his view of power owed more perhaps to Nietzsche than to Marx. Foucault seldom viewed power as a repressive force. Certainly, he did not view it as a tool of conspiracy used by one specific individual or institution against another. Rather, power represents a whole complex of forces; it is that which produces what happens. Thus, even a tyrannical aristocrat does not simply wield power, because he is formed and empowered by discourses and practices that constitute power. Viewed by Foucault, power is "positive and productive," not "repressive" and "prohibitive" (Smart 63). Furthermore, no historical event, according to Foucault, has a single cause; rather, it is intricately connected with a vast web of economic, social, and political factors.

A brief sketch of one of Foucault's major works may help clarify some of his ideas. *Discipline and Punish* begins with a shocking but accurate description of the public drawing and quartering of a Frenchman who had botched his attempt to assassinate King Louis XV. Foucault proceeds, then, by describing rules governing the daily life of modern Parisian felons. What happened to torture, to punishment as public spectacle? he asks. What complex network of forces made it disappear? In working toward a picture of this "power," Foucault turns up many interesting puzzle pieces, such as that in the early revolutionary years of the nineteenth century, crowds would sometimes identify with the prisoner and treat the executioner as if *he* were the guilty party. But Foucault sets forth a related reason for keeping prisoners alive, moving punishment indoors, and changing discipline from physical torture into mental rehabilitation: colonization. In this historical period, people were needed to establish colonies and trade, and prisoners could be used for that purpose. Also, because these were politically unsettled times, governments needed infiltrators and informers. Who better to fill those roles than prisoners pardoned or released early for showing a willingness to be rehabilitated? As for rehabilitation itself, Foucault compares it to the old form of punishment, which began with a torturer extracting a confession. In more modern, "reasonable" times, psychologists probe the minds of prisoners with a scientific rigor that Foucault sees as a different kind of torture, a kind that our modern perspective does not allow us to see as such.

Thus, a change took place, but perhaps not so great a change as we generally assume. It may have been for the better or for the worse; the point is that agents of power didn't make the change because mankind is evolving and, therefore, more prone to perform good-hearted deeds. Rather, different objectives arose, including those of a new class of doctors and scientists bent on studying aberrant examples of the human mind.

Foucault's type of analysis has recently been practiced by a number of literary critics at the vanguard of the back-to-history movement. One of these critics, Stephen Greenblatt, has written on Renaissance changes in the development of both literary characters and real people. Like Foucault, he is careful to point out that any one change is connected with a host of others, no one of which may simply be identified as the cause or the effect. Greenblatt, like Foucault, insists on interpreting literary devices as if they were continuous with other representational devices in a culture; he turns, therefore, to scholars in other fields in order to better understand the workings of literature. "We wall off literary symbolism from the symbolic structures operative elsewhere," he writes, "as if art alone were a human creation, as if humans themselves were not, in Clifford Geertz's phrase, cultural artifacts." Following Geertz, Greenblatt sets out to practice what he calls "anthropological or cultural criticism." Anthropological literary criticism, he continues, addresses itself "to the interpretive constructions the members of a society apply to their experience," since a work of literature is itself an interpretive construction, "part of the system of signs that constitutes a given culture." He suggests that criticism must never interpret the past without at least being "conscious of its own status as interpretation" (4).

Not all of the critics trying to lead students of literature back to history are as "Foucauldian" as Greenblatt. Some of these new historicists owe more to Marx than to Foucault. Others, like Jerome McGann, have followed the lead of Soviet critic M. M. Bakhtin, who was less likely than Marx to emphasize social class as a determining factor. (Bakhtin was more interested in the way that one language or style is the parody of an older one.) Still other new historicists, like Brook Thomas, have clearly been more influenced by Walter Benjamin, best known for essays such as "Theses on the Philosophy of History" and "The Work of Art in the Age of Mechanical Reproduction."

Moreover, there are other reasons not to declare that Foucault has been the central influence on the new historicism. Some new historicist critics would argue that Foucault critiqued old-style historicism to such an extent that he ended up being antihistorical or, at least, nonhistorical. As for his commitment to a radical remapping of relations of power and influence, cause and effect, in the view of some critics, Foucault consequently adopted too cavalier an attitude toward chronology and facts. In the minds of other critics, identifying and labeling a single master or central influence goes against the very grain of the new historicism. Practitioners of the new historicism have sought to decenter the study of literature and move toward the point where literary studies overlap with anthropological and sociological studies. They have also struggled to see history from a decentered perspective, both by recognizing that their own cultural and historical position may not afford the best understanding of other cultures and times and by realizing that events seldom have any single or central cause. At this point, then, it is appropriate to pause and suggest that Foucault shouldn't be seen as *the* cause of the new historicism, but as one of several powerful, interactive influences.

It is equally useful to suggest that the debate over the sources of the movement, the differences of opinion about Foucault, and even my own need to assert his importance may be historically contingent; that is to say, they may all result from the very *newness* of the new historicism itself. New intellectual movements often cannot be summed up or represented by a key figure, any more than they can easily be summed up or represented by an introduction or a single essay. They respond to disparate influences and almost inevitably include thinkers who represent a wide range of backgrounds. Like movements that are disintegrating, new movements embrace a broad spectrum of opinions and positions.

But just as differences within a new school of criticism cannot be overlooked, neither should they be exaggerated, since it is the similarity among a number of different approaches that makes us aware of a new movement under way. Greenblatt, Hirsch, McGann, and Thomas all started with the assumption that works of literature are simultaneously influenced by and influencing reality, broadly defined. Thus, whatever their disagreements, they share a belief in referentiality — a belief that literature refers to and is referred to by things outside itself — that is fainter in the works of formalist, poststructuralist, and even reader-response critics. They believe with Greenblatt that the "central concerns" of criticism "should prevent it from permanently sealing off one type of discourse from another or decisively separating works of art from the minds and lives of their creators and their audiences" (5).

McGann, in his introduction to *Historical Studies and Literary Criticism*, turns referentiality into a rallying cry:

> What will not be found in these essays . . . is the assumption, so common in text-centered studies of every type, that literary works are self-enclosed verbal constructs, or looped intertextual fields of autonomous signifiers and signifieds. In these essays, the question of referentiality is once again brought to the fore. (3)

In "Keats and the Historical Method in Literary Criticism," he outlines a program for those who have rallied to the cry. These procedures, which he claims are "practical derivatives of the Bakhtin school," assume that historicist critics, who must be interested in a work's point of origin and in its point of reception, will understand the former by studying biography and bibliography. After mastering these details, the critic must then consider the expressed intentions of the author, because, if printed, these intentions have also modified the developing history of the work. Next, the new historicist must learn the history of the work's reception, as that body of opinion has become part of the platform on which we are situated when we study the book. Finally, McGann urges the new historicist critic to point toward the future, toward his or her *own* audience, defining for its members the aims and limits of the critical project and injecting the analysis with a degree of self-consciousness that alone can give it credibility (*Inflections* 62).

In the essay that follows, Carole Fabricant begins by reminding us that *Gulliver's Travels* is a narrative containing historical narratives, by Gulliver, about his own past and that of his native country. The histories he tells, which often have a strong fictional element, are said to vary according to "occasion, audience, desired effect"; they are, moreover, to a great extent a function of the surrounding culture's mode of narrative production. For example, when Gulliver finds himself in the oral culture of the Houyhnhnms, his narratives differ from those he tells in the print culture of Glubbdubdrib.

Fabricant continues by arguing that Swift's "lifelong preoccupation with history" caused him to explore, in various writings, questions about the reliability of all historical accounts. Each culture represented in *Gulliver's Travels* is interested in and engaged in debates about antiquity. (Are the Yahoos aboriginal, the Houyhnhnms wonder, or did two of them emerge relatively recently from the muddy slime?) The historical narratives produced to answer such questions are, Gulliver learns, far from the truth about what happened in the past.

When historical narratives have to be communicated from one culture or language to another, problems in truth-telling are only compounded, as we implicitly learn while Gulliver struggles first to understand the languages of those whose histories he hears and later to translate their narrations into a "barbarous English" unlikely to do justice to the original. To complicate matters further, history involves not only treacherous cross-cultural and cross-linguistic translation but also translation across expanses of time, during which whole paradigms of thought and understanding change and evolve.

Fabricant continually grounds Swift's positions on history in his own historical position, writing that "the intertwined problems of historical knowledge and translation" were of particular interest to Swift, "a poet who wished to render into English not only standard classical authors but also Gaelic writers." In addition, it was a matter of great concern that "the history of his native [Ireland] was regularly told by those who couldn't speak its language or read the chronicles on which their narratives were based." Throughout his life, Swift, like Gulliver, was a kind of intermediary. An Irishman from an oral culture writing largely for an English print culture, he served "in effect as translator between alien (and alienated) communities separated not only by national and cultural differences, but by class divisions as well."

Fabricant's historical meditation on Swift's historical meditations may be said to be new historicist for a number of reasons, including its suggestion that all history has a fictive content; that that content flows from the ideologies, power relationships, and modes of production prevalent in the culture that gives rise to it; and that what is told is a function not only of the medium in which it is told but also of the audience expected to consume it. In some ways, though, Fabricant's status as a new historicist is best revealed by the way in which she represents *Gulliver's Travels*, that is, as a kind of proto-new historicist text: "A work that functions through . . . contradictory claims," it "regularly calls attention to its own status as history while it continually undermines all simplistic notions of unmediated historical truth. It vindicates its claims to credibility by citing the archetypal liar, Sinon."

It is also a text that, in Fabricant's view, continually reminds readers that their interpretations of it are historically determined. Its "invocations to the reader prompt us, as late twentieth-century readers, to reflect on how and where *we* stand in relation to Gulliver's narrative, and how we too are inevitably part of the process whereby the narrative is reshaped, adapted to modern ways of seeing and speaking, in our attempt to recover its 'original' contexts or to reconstruct its 'intended' meaning."

The admission that our interpretations of historical texts are translations that make their subjects make sense in modern terms is, of course, an implicit admission that the new historicist who sees Swift as a kind of proto-new historicist may be seeing what is visible only from our own historical vantage point. That admission, however, does not destroy the validity of what Fabricant is doing; it serves, rather, as the kind of friendly warning that ultimately enhances credibility. Like *Gulliver's Travels*, it reminds us of the dangers of equating any single, time-bound version of history with timeless truth. In so doing, it increases our willingness to entertain its version seriously.

Fabricant's essay has a great deal more to suggest than any introduction can or should adumbrate — about the instability of generic boundaries, for instance, and even about the instability of humanity's view of itself during the period in which Swift wrote. Suffice it to say here that, like all good new historicist analyses, it affords an entirely new view of a text, its author, and its period by decentering or destabilizing old categories of thought. Boundaries between history, literature, politics, anthropology, and literary criticism (not to mention between historical, structuralist, and poststructuralist literary criticism) are crossed and re-crossed as the critic builds up her description of a colonialist/anti-colonialist Gulliver; of an English Irishman, Swift, who was and was not Gulliver; and, finally, of a text that is neither novel nor history nor travelogue nor prisoner's diary nor fairy tale nor satire nor anthropological field study but, rather, all of these things at once.

Ross C Murfin

THE NEW HISTORICISM:
A SELECTED BIBLIOGRAPHY

The New Historicism: Further Reading

Graff, Gerald, and Gerald Gibbons, eds. *Criticism in the University.* Evanston: Northwestern UP, 1985. This volume, which contains Hirsch's essay, "Back to History," in the section entitled "Pedagogy and Polemics," also includes sections devoted to the historical backgrounds of academic criticism; the influence of Marxism, feminism, and critical theory in general on the new historicism; and varieties of "cultural criticism."

Hirsch, E. D., Jr. "Back to History." Graff and Gibbons 189–97.

History and . . . Special issue, *New Literary History* 21 (1990). See especially the essays by Carolyn Porter, Rena Fraden, Clifford Geertz, and Renato Rosaldo.

Howard, Jean. "The New Historicism in Renaissance Studies." *English Literary Renaissance* 16 (1986): 13–43.

Lindenberger, Herbert. *The History in Literature: On Value, Genre, Institutions.* New York: Columbia UP, 1990.

———. "Toward a New History in Literary Study." *Profession: Selected Articles from the Bulletins of the Association of Departments of English and the Association of the Departments of Foreign Languages.* New York: MLA, 1984. 16–23.

Liu, Alan. "The Power of Formalism: The New Historicism." *English Literary History* 56 (1989): 721–71.

McGann, Jerome. *The Beauty of Inflections: Literary Investigations in Historical Method and Theory.* Oxford: Clarendon-Oxford UP, 1985.

———. *Historical Studies and Literary Criticism.* Madison: U of Wisconsin P, 1985. See especially the introduction and the essays in the following sections: "Historical Methods and Literary Interpretations" and "Biographical Contexts and the Critical Object."

Montrose, Louis Adrian. "Renaissance Literary Studies and the Subject of History." *English Literary Renaissance* 16 (1986): 5–12.

Morris, Wesley. *Toward a New Historicism*. Princeton: Princeton UP, 1972.

Thomas, Brook. "The Historical Necessity for — and Difficulties with — New Historical Analysis in Introductory Literature Courses." *College English* 49 (1987): 509–22.

———. *The New Historicism and Other Old-Fashioned Topics*. Princeton: Princeton UP, 1991.

———. "Walter Benn Michaels and the New Historicism: Where's the Difference?" *Boundary 2* 18 (1991): 118–59.

Veeser, Harold, ed. *The New Historicism*. New York: Routledge, 1989.

Wayne, Don E. "Power, Politics, and the Shakespearean Text: Recent Criticism in England and the United States." *Shakespeare Reproduced: The Text in History and Ideology*. Ed. Jean Howard and Marion O'Conner. New York: Methuen, 1987. 47–67.

The New Historicism: Influential Examples

New Historicism has taken its present form less through the elaboration of basic theoretical postulates and more through certain influential examples. The works listed represent some of the most important contributions guiding research in this area.

American Literary History. A journal devoted to new historicist and cultural criticism; the first issue was Spring 1989. New York: Oxford UP.

Brown, Gillian. *Domestic Individualism: Imagining Self in Nineteenth-Century America*. Berkeley: U of California P, 1990.

Dollimore, Jonathan. *Radical Tragedy: Religion, Ideology and Power in the Drama of Shakespeare and His Contemporaries*. Brighton, Eng.: Harvester, 1984.

Dollimore, Jonathan, and Alan Sinfield, eds. *Political Shakespeare: New Essays in Cultural Materialism*. Manchester, Eng.: Manchester UP, 1985. See especially the essays by Dollimore, Greenblatt, and Tennenhouse.

Goldberg, Jonathan. *James I and the Politics of Literature*. Baltimore: Johns Hopkins UP, 1983.

Greenblatt, Stephen. *Renaissance Self-Fashioning from More to Shakespeare*. Chicago: U of Chicago P, 1980. See ch. 1 and the chapter on *Othello* entitled "The Improvisation of Power."

———. *Shakespearean Negotiations: The Circulation of Social Energy in Renaissance England*. Berkeley: U of California P, 1985. See especially "The Circulation of Social Energy" and "Invisible Bullets: Renaissance Authority and Its Subversion, *Henry IV* and *Henry V*."

Marcus, Leah. *Puzzling Shakespeare: Local Reading and Its Discontents*. Berkeley: U of California P, 1988.

Michaels, Walter Benn. *The Gold Standard and the Logic of Naturalism: American Literature at the Turn of the Century*. Berkeley: U of California P, 1987.

Montrose, Louis Adrian. " 'Shaping Fantasies': Figurations of Gender and Power in Elizabethan Culture." *Representations* 2 (1983): 61–94. One of the most influential early new historicist essays.

Mullaney, Steven. *The Place of the Stage: License, Play, and Power in Renaissance England*. Chicago: U of Chicago P, 1987.

Representations. This quarterly journal, printed by the University of California Press, regularly publishes new historicist studies and cultural criticism.

Sinfield, Alan. *Literature, Politics, and Culture in Postwar Britain*. Berkeley: U of California P, 1989.

Tennenhouse, Leonard. *Power on Display: The Politics of Shakespeare's Genres*. New York and London: Methuen, 1986.

Foucault and His Influence

As I point out in the introduction to the new historicism, some new historicists would question the "privileging" of Foucault implicit in this section heading ("Foucault and His Influence") and the following one ("Other Writers and Works"). They might cite the greater importance of one of these other writers or point out that to cite a central influence or a definitive cause runs against the very spirit of the movement.

Dreyfus, Hubert L. and Paul Rabinow. *Michel Foucault: Beyond Structuralism and Hermeneutics*. Chicago: U of Chicago P, 1983.

Foucault, Michel. *The Archaeology of Knowledge*. Trans. A. M. Sheridan Smith. New York: Harper, 1972.

———. *Discipline and Punish*. Trans. Alan Sheridan. New York: Pantheon, 1978.

———. *The History of Sexuality*, vol. 1. Trans. Robert Hurley. New York: Pantheon, 1978.

———. *Language, Counter-Memory, Practice.* Ed. Donald F. Bouchard. Trans. Bouchard and Sherry Simon. Ithaca: Cornell UP, 1977.

———. *The Order of Things: An Archaeology of the Human Sciences.* New York: Vintage, 1973.

———. *Politics, Philosophy, Culture.* Ed. Lawrence D. Kritzman. Trans. Alan Sheridan et al. New York: Routledge, 1988.

———. *Power/Knowledge.* Ed. Colin Gordon. Trans. Colin Gordon et al. New York: Pantheon, 1980.

———. *Technologies of the Self.* Ed. Luther H. Martin, Huck Gutman, and Patrick H. Hutton. Amherst: U of Massachusetts P, 1988.

Sheridan, Alan, *Michel Foucault: The Will to Truth.* New York: Tavistock, 1980.

Smart, Barry. *Michel Foucault.* New York: Ellis Horwood and Tavistock, 1985.

Other Writers and Works of Interest to New Historicist Critics

Bakhtin, M. M. *The Dialogic Imagination: Four Essays.* Ed. Michael Holquist. Trans. Caryl Emerson. Austin: U of Texas P, 1981. Bakhtin wrote many influential studies on subjects as varied as Dostoyevsky, Rabelais, and formalist criticism. But this book, in part due to Holquist's helpful introduction, is probably the best place to begin reading Bakhtin.

Benjamin, Walter. "The Work of Art in the Age of Mechanical Reproduction." [1936] *Illuminations.* Trans. Harry Zohn. New York: Schocken, 1969.

Fried, Michael. *Absorption and Theatricality: Painting and Beholder in the Works of Diderot.* Berkeley: U of California P, 1980.

Geertz, Clifford. *The Interpretation of Cultures.* New York: Basic, 1973.

———. *Negara: The Theatre State in Nineteenth-Century Bali.* Princeton: Princeton UP, 1980.

Goffman, Erving. *Frame Analysis.* New York: Harper, 1974.

Jameson, Fredric. *The Political Unconscious.* Ithaca: Cornell UP, 1981.

Koselleck, Reinhart. *Futures Past.* Trans. Keith Tribe. Cambridge: MIT P, 1985.

Said, Edward. *Orientalism.* New York: Columbia UP, 1978.

New Historicist Approaches to Swift and *Gulliver's Travels*

Bellamy, Liz. *Jonathan Swift's "Gulliver's Travels."* New York: St. Martin's, 1992.

Brown, Laura. "Reading Race and Gender: Jonathan Swift." *Eighteenth-Century Studies* 23 (1990): 424–43.

Deane, Seamus. "Swift and the Anglo-Irish Intellect." *Eighteenth-Century Ireland* (1986): 9–22.

Fabricant, Carole. "The Battle of the Ancients and (Post) Moderns: Rethinking Swift through Contemporary Perspectives." *The Eighteenth Century* 32 (1991): 256–73.

———. Swift's Landscape. Baltimore: Johns Hopkins UP, 1982.

McKeon, Michael. "Parables of the younger son (I): Swift and the Containment of Desire." *The Origins of the English Novel, 1600–1740*. Baltimore: Johns Hopkins UP, 1987. 338–56.

Said, Edward. "Swift as Intellectual." *The World, the Text, and the Critic.* Cambridge, MA: Harvard UP, 1983. 72–89.

A NEW HISTORICIST PERSPECTIVE

CAROLE FABRICANT

History, Narrativity, and Swift's Project to "Mend the World"

Among the many roles that Gulliver performs in *Gulliver's Travels* is that of historian: producer of a series of interlocking narratives about past and present, his own as well as those of the various lands he visits during his four voyages. The work is literally history, or "his story," conveying an account of events that supposedly occurred in the course of Gulliver's wanderings. But within this overall narrative frame, Gulliver is continually telling and retelling — sometimes shortening or suppressing, at other times enlarging and embellishing, on occasion explicitly fictionalizing — the story of his own life and adventures, as well as that of his native country, for the benefit of those he meets on his journeys. To the king of Brobdingnag, for example, he relates details both of his personal experiences since arriving on the island and of aspects of English society, concluding with "a brief historical Account of Affairs and Events in *England* for about an hundred Years past" (129).

To Captain John Biddel, who saves him after his departure from Blefuscu, Gulliver tells his story "in few Words" (88), whereas he expounds upon his travels at great length to Captain Thomas Wilcocks, his savior after leaving Brobdingnag, "begg[ing the captain's] Patience to hear me tell my Story; which I faithfully did from the last Time I left *England,* to the Moment he first discovered me" (144). The third voyage begins with Gulliver's (hi)storytelling temporarily silenced by a monarch who "discovered not the least Curiosity to enquire into the Laws, Government, History, Religion, or Manners of the Countries where [he] had been" (160), and ends with Gulliver's constructing a fictive history for himself ("I answered . . . that I was a *Dutch* Merchant, shipwrecked in a very remote Country") in response to his auditor's own history as a non-European "employed to transact Affairs with the *Hollanders*" (201). In the land of the Houyhnhnms, confronted with a genuinely receptive audience who "waited with some Impatience to hear the Wonders which [he] promised to tell" (218), Gulliver comes into his own as storyteller-historian, gradually revealing to his hosts everything they want to know (and much that they'd rather not know) about the social and political practices of Europeans.

The range of stories Gulliver tells about himself and his country, within the larger narrative that he presents to us, the readers of his book, suggests the multiplicity of contextual factors — occasion, audience, desired effect, and so on — that contribute to the changing shape of narratives about the past and the present. Also contributing to this variability are the stories' different modes of production and dissemination, reflective of the differences between oral, textual, and print cultures: between the Lilliputian world of written memorials, proclamations, and treaties, demanding frequent acts of reading and interpretation; the world of the Brobdingnagians, who "have had the Art of Printing, as well as the *Chinese,* Time out of Mind" but whose "Libraries are not very large" and who "avoid nothing more than multiplying unnecessary words" (135, 136); the verbally spare, pretextual world of the Houyhnhnms, who "have not the least Idea of Books or Literature" (216); and the print world of the author of the *Travels,* who continually calls attention to his work's status as a published text in competition with numerous other such texts for the attention of a reading public in a society "already overstocked with Books of Travels" (144).

The conflict between an oral and a print culture is registered in many texts contemporary with Swift's, for example, Pope's *Dunciad. Gulliver* thus participates in early eighteenth-century symbolic and ideological struggles between a traditional cultural elite accustomed to exercising a monopoly over the word and its "authorized" meaning, and a middle class with access to modern forms of technology that enabled the dispersion of the word to wider areas of society, thereby exposing it to multiple readings and interpretations. The contradictions surrounding Gulliver's relationship to oral and textual forms of transmission — his eager embrace of the task of reading and interpreting Lilliputian texts, his fervent defense of the Houyhnhnms' lack of textuality, his authorship (albeit ambivalent) of a travel book — underscore the ambiguities inherent in a historical situation in which a writer such as Swift had inextricable ties to both worlds, attracted to the values of a traditional classical culture but necessarily dependent upon the printed word for his very identity as a satirist and political polemicist. For Swift, moreover, the conflict had a very special resonance in terms of the clash between English and Irish culture, between a "civilized" colonial power buttressed by various linguistic and political structures and a "primitive" society functioning largely through oral traditions.

As simultaneously a historical narrative and a series of reflections on the historicity of narratives, *Gulliver* tests the kinds of evidence invoked to support particular claims of veracity (eye witness testimony, written accounts, archaeological remains, oral traditions, and memory are all weighed in this regard at various points in the text), the role the narrator's language plays in determining the shape and content of his narration, and the extent to which present and future concerns affect one's presentation of the past. As one who demonstrated a lifelong preoccupation with history and who produced a large body of writings intended "to set future ages right in their judgment" about aspects of their past (*Prose Works* 7: xxxiv), Swift explored these questions in a number of different contexts and genres throughout his writing career. The *Travels* afforded him the opportunity to carry on this exploration in a freer, more imaginative way than in other texts, where literal truth and factuality were of greater concern. The fabulous nature of the *Travels* was particularly well suited to reflections about the kinds of stories different societies invent to establish their origins and national integrity. Such reflections would have had special relevance to contemporary disputes over the antiquity and authenticity of Irish history, with inevitable implications for English history. As Swift's friend Anthony Raymond, vicar of Trim, argued in *A Short Preliminary Discourse to the History of Ireland* (published a year before the *Travels* and sent to Swift for commentary), "It is to be confessed, that the *Irish*, like other Nations, have fallen into Relations fabulous or uncertain, but then at the same Time we must allow, the Greeks, the Romans, the Germans, the French, the

Scotch and English, are, at least, equally liable to the same Accusation; and perhaps we might affirm, that the Contention about Antiquity is the most ancient and universal Controversy in the World" (4–5).

Conjectures about origins and antiquity recur in the *Travels:* the Brobdingnagian king speculates that "there must have been Giants in former Ages; which, as it is asserted by History and Tradition, so it hath been confirmed by huge Bones and Sculls casually dug up in several Parts of the Kingdom" (136), while the Houyhnhnms in their Grand Assembly reject the notion that the Yahoos are "*Aborigines* of the land" and cite a "Tradition" according to which "many Ages ago, two of these Brutes appeared together upon a Mountain; whether produced by the Heat of the Sun upon corrupted Mud and Slime, or from the Ooze and Froth of the Sea, was never known" (246, 245). Inventing and listening to a variety of fables put forward as modes of historical explanation, Gulliver, the "Splendide Mendax" represented in the engraved frontispiece to Faulkner's 1735 edition, manages to convey truths by lying and provokes his readers, not only to reflect upon the past, but to reflect as well upon the specific ways in which they choose to imagine the past.

Imagining the past certainly seems more achievable than acquiring absolute knowledge of it, judging from Gulliver's voyage to Glubbdubdrib, where he discovers "how the World had been misled by prostitute Writers" of modern history (187) and comes to the realization that only shades called up from the other world would "tell [him] Truth" about what happened in the past (184). Even when he has the unprecedented opportunity to converse with the dead, however, Gulliver finds direct access to historical truth blocked when, after his encounter with Alexander the Great, Gulliver discovers "it was with great Difficulty that I understood his *Greek,* and had but little of my own" (184). This difficulty spotlights the problems surrounding the communication of historical knowledge across different cultures and language systems, and implies the crucial role of translation (with all the impurities and ambiguities it entails) in the historiographic endeavor. In the land of the Houyhnhnms Gulliver is put to "the Pains of many Circumlocutions to give [his] Master a right Idea of what [he] spoke" (221). His assiduous endeavors to learn the equine language are themselves stages of a translation process in which, he says, "I formed all I learned into the *English* Alphabet, and writ the Words down with the Translations" (216). Eventually the procedure must be reversed by a Gulliver intent on communicating his travel experiences to the public but apprehensive that "I shall hardly be able to do Justice to my Master's Arguments and Expressions, which must needs suffer by my

Want of Capacity, as well as by a Translation into our barbarous *English*" (224).

Other sections of the *Travels* stress Gulliver's reliance on translators to comprehend what his foreign hosts are telling him and to communicate his thoughts to them. In Luggnagg, for example, he is "always attended by [his] Interpreter" (193), and the entire discussion about the Struldbruggs takes place in the Luggnaggians' language, which is then translated into the Balnibarbian tongue (presumably understood by Gulliver), who in turn translates it into English that is then edited by Sympson for the benefit of Gulliver's readers. That this highly mediated linguistic transaction functions in many ways as a model for how historical knowledge is (or fails to be) passed on from one generation to the next becomes clear when we learn that "the Language of [Luggnagg] being always upon the Flux, the *Struldbruggs* of one Age do not understand those of another; neither are they able after two Hundred Years to hold any Conversation (farther than by a few general Words) with their Neighbours the Mortals" (199), a highly problematic situation accentuated by Gulliver's observation to his "Cousin Sympson" that, because of his countrymen's tendency to "change [their words] every Year," he finds that "when any *Yahoo* comes from *London* out of Curiosity to visit me at mine own House, we neither of us are able to deliver our Conceptions in a Manner intelligible to the other" (30).

The intertwined problems of historical knowledge and translation would have had particular significance for Swift, since the history of his native country was regularly told by those who couldn't speak its language or read the chronicles on which their narratives were based. Geoffrey Keating's *The General History of Ireland,* written in Irish in the early seventeenth century and translated into English while *Gulliver* was being composed (Raymond was himself engaged in producing such a translation, though he never finished it), served to highlight these problems. As Keating scornfully noted, previous histories of Ireland by English or Anglo-Irish writers "ha[ve] no other Authority than the bare Relation of Persons, who . . . were ignorant of the Transactions of that Kingdom, by Reason of their Unskilfulness in the [Irish] Language, and by Consequence must unavoidably be mistaken, and impose Falshoods upon the World" (xix–xx). Less than a decade after the appearance of the *Travels,* Francis, bishop of Down and Connor, published *A Defence of the Antient Historians,* explaining in the preface that the timing of his project was especially appropriate given that "the [Irish] Natives have of late translated many of their old Fragments into *English* Verse and Prose" (v). His request to be shown relevant historical manuscripts in

Irish, however, coupled with his admission that he doesn't "pretend . . . to understand much of the Language" (xiv), highlights a hermeneutic problem that his *Defence* can only reveal, not resolve.

Swift's sensitivity to the crucial role of translation in a wide range of social and cultural transactions was enhanced by his own dual (and borderline) position in society as a youth growing up in a bilingual community (late-seventeenth-century Dublin) and almost certainly cared for by an Irish-speaking nursemaid, though later receiving a British Anglican education; as a man often associated with the Protestant Ascendancy who nevertheless (according to his friend Thomas Sheridan) enjoyed the conversation of "ev'ry Irish Teague he spies" after "learn[ing] their Irish Tongue to gabble" ("Appendix to the Trifles to the Dean of St. Patricks" 28, 32; *Poems* 3: 1040); as a poet who wished to render into English not only standard classical authors but also Gaelic writers such as Aodh Mac Gabhran (Hugh MacGauran), whose *Pléaraca na Ruarcach*, in a version popularized by the famous Irish harpist Turlough Carolan, was recreated by Swift in his ballad *The Description of an Irish Feast;* and as one who urged the learning and widespread use of English by the Irish populace while he himself continued to incorporate native Irish colloquialisms and dialect into his own verse.

In much of his political writing and in many of his activities Swift (like his creation, Gulliver) served as intermediary and in effect as translator between alien (and alienated) communities separated not only by national and cultural differences, but by class divisions as well. He became the speaker of a kind of "language of accommodation" that made educated English speech accessible to groups on the lower rungs of the social ladder. Swift ordered that his *Drapier's Letters,* whose effectiveness depended on their reaching as wide an audience as possible, be sold "at the lowest Rate" so as not to exclude the poor, and expressed the hope that the tracts would be "read to [those who couldn't read English] by others" (*Prose Works* 10: 3). In the *Travels,* problems related to verbal communication likewise register class as well as cultural divisions. Thus, although Gulliver provides "rational answers" to the questions put to him by the king of Brobdingnag, communication between the two is less than perfect because Gulliver was taught the Brobdingnagian language in a rural laborer's household, where he picked up "some rustick Phrases . . . [that] did not suit the polite Style of a Court" (110). The unbridgeable gap between the ruling-class Houyhnhnms and the subjugated Yahoos is registered in their total lack of verbal communication. In a society whose hierarchic order depends on the maintenance of this communication gap, it is hardly surprising that the representatives at the Grand Assembly feel threatened, not so much by the mere circumstance that the Houyhnhnm Master "keep[s] a *Yahoo* [Gulliver] in his Family" as by the fact that the Master is "known frequently to converse with [him]" (252).

Conversation can thus function as a means of breaking down (class and species) barriers even as it also highlights the problems of trying to communicate in language that differs from place to place and that keeps changing within the same place over time. Gulliver shows interest in carrying on a conversation (however restricted and one-sided) not only with those he meets in his travels, but with his audience too. His frequent addresses to the "gentle" or "curious" reader serve as reminders that stories depend not only on tellers but on auditors as well, who in this case are shown to influence the shape of Gulliver's narrative by (for example) affecting his choices about what to include and what to omit so as to avoid boredom and incredulity while stimulating interest. These invocations to the reader prompt us, as late-twentieth-century readers, to reflect on how and where *we* stand in relation to Gulliver's narrative, and how we too are inevitably part of the process whereby the narrative is reshaped, adapted to new ways of seeing and speaking, in our attempt to recover its "original" contexts or to reconstruct its "intended" meaning.

Gulliver is, then, a text that regularly calls attention to its own status as history while it continually undermines all simplistic notions of unmediated historical truth. It vindicates its claims to credibility by citing the archetypal liar, Sinon (262), while insisting that "the Truth immediately strikes every Reader with Conviction" (30), a statement that, however ironic, does point to the way in which *Gulliver* often forces its unwary audience to acknowledge the validity of its insights into human behavior. How exactly should we characterize a work that functions through these kinds of contradictory claims? As one way of approaching this question, we might note that the confusion evidenced by readers in Swift's day, some of whom reported encounters with Gulliver or rushed to their maps to locate the places described in the four voyages, anticipated the widely divergent interpretations of the work and its relation to historical reality over the past two centuries — for instance, the many critical pieces assigning the *Travels* to different literary genres.[1]

One doesn't have to turn to poststructuralist theory — though it might be useful to recall Derrida's argument that although "every text

[1] A recent collection of essays edited by Frederik N. Smith illustrates my point. See *The Genres of "Gulliver's Travels."*

participates in one or several genres . . . yet such participation never amounts to belonging" (65) — in order to make a case for the *Travels'* resistance to clear-cut categorization along these lines. Recognition and authorial exploitation of generic ambiguity and instability were amply demonstrated in the late seventeenth and early eighteenth centuries in the diversity of literary experimentation occurring during the period, especially around that most hybridized form of writing, the novel. This is one of the many forms of which it may be said that the *Travels* participate but do not belong. As J. Paul Hunter has recently argued, "the novel would not have succeeded so well without the fading of borders" (344). The early novel's close links to a variety of both fictional and nonfictional types of writing contributed to the production of texts capable of exploiting the special authority of both truth and invention to achieve specific aesthetic and/or ideological aims.

Travel narratives in particular, which Swift explicitly invokes as source, model, and foil for his work, functioned at this time to throw into bold relief the rich potential that existed for generic crossover and ambiguity, encompassing as they did texts covering the spectrum from wholly invented tales to quasi-factual and "real-life" voyages to exotic lands (see Adams). Swift exploits this potential by invoking the authority of well-known recorded explorations such as "Cousin" William Dampier's *A Voyage round the World* (28) and insisting that he "write[s] for the noblest End, to inform and instruct Mankind" (263) while at the same time attacking the "many fabulous accounts" of other travelers, who "impose the grossest Falsities on the unwary Reader" (262). The absence of clear generic boundaries allowed Swift to construct a highly fanciful tale of six-inch pygmies, flying islands, and talking horses while at the same time including obvious references to aspects of English society that would have been immediately recognizable to his contemporary readers, and while assuring the latter (not without some justification) that "I have given thee a faithful History of my Travels . . . wherein I have not been so studious of Ornament as of Truth" (261).

In other crucial ways as well, *Gulliver* both points to and enacts the collapse of clear-cut boundaries. If it is difficult to classify the *Travels* generically, it is no easier to characterize Gulliver, as is evident by the responses to him both within the framework of the text and beyond, in the world of Swift criticism. The diverse and conflicting critical views of Gulliver over the past two and a half centuries — as novelistic character, satiric persona, moralist, misanthrope, tragic hero, comic target, and so on — are in a sense an extension of the perplexity Gulliver evokes from the various inhabitants of the lands he visits during his voyages. In many ways the work functions through a series of endeavors to define Gulliver and assign him to a recognizable category, as exemplified by the Brobdingnagian king's conjecture that he "might be a piece of Clockwork" (107–108); the Brobdingnagian scholars' conclusion, after a careful examination, that he is "*Relplum Scalcath* . . . interpreted literally *Lusus Naturae*" (108); and the persistent queries and physical inspections by the Houyhnhnms, who first take him for a Yahoo and later conclude that he does indeed differ somewhat from "other" Yahoos, but "in point of real Advantage . . . differed for the worse" (221, 222). To appreciate the full significance of this probing of Gulliver's nature we need to locate the *Travels* in a larger framework of contemporary texts and social practices that similarly challenged long-standing notions about human identity and tested the fluctuating boundaries between self and not-self, savage and civilized being, the human and the non- (or barely) human. If, as many critics have maintained, the *Travels* may be seen as a satiric reflection on the nature of man, we need to keep in mind that, at the time of its composition, there was no longer a clear consensus about this nature, and that the very concept of *man* was less a fixed standard of measurement than a site of inquiry and often controversy.

Fascination with the often ambiguous boundaries of human nature, and intense curiosity about those borderline cases that hinted at the potential for collapse of these boundaries altogether, were expressed in the popular culture of Swift's day, where fairs and outdoor entertainments regularly featured monster shows and exhibitions of a variety of prodigies and freaks, including giants, dwarfs, and hairy "wild" men resembling beasts (see Todd). In the *Travels* Swift obviously exploits the visual aspects as well as the psychological and epistemological implications of these diversions, both in his portrayal of the unfamiliar creatures Gulliver encounters and in his descriptions of Gulliver's own reduction to an object of public display, "carried about for a Monster," shown as an attraction on market days, and made to "perform an Hundred diverting Tricks" for the amusement of crowds of spectators (103). Even where Gulliver is generically identical to the inhabitants of his host country, differing only in size, his equivocal status is an issue, as when, for example, the Brobdingnagian monkey "held [Gulliver] as a Nurse doth a Child she is going to suckle," presumably because "he took [Gulliver] for a young one of his own Species" (123).

Variations on this species confusion may be found throughout the geographical and quasi-scientific texts of the period, which abound in descriptions of pygmies, cannibals, and a host of other inhabitants of exotic climes, not to mention weird creatures of the deep. Thomas Glover, for example, in a late-seventeenth-century account published by the Royal Society, described at some length his dramatic encounter with "a very strange Fish or rather Monster" in the Rapahannock River in Virginia,

> a most prodigious Creature, much resembling a man, only somewhat larger, standing right up in the water with his head, neck, shoulders, breast, and waste, to the cubits of his arms, above water; his skin was tawny, much like that of an *Indian;* the figure of his head was pyramidal, and slick, without hair; his eyes large and black, and so were his eye-brows; his mouth very wide, with a broad, black streak on the upper lip, which turned upwards at each end like mustachoes; . . . his neck, shoulders, arms, breast and wast, were like unto the neck, arms, shoulders, breast and wast of a man; . . . he seemed to stand with his eyes fixed on me for some time, and afterward dived down . . . (625)[2]

Although the creature is finally revealed as possessing an appendage "which exactly resembled the tayl of a fish with a broad fane at the end of it" (625–26), the effect of this disclosure is less to dispel the mystery by providing a clear definition of the creature than it is to intensify our sense of unease at the visual testimony to blurred lines of separation and unstable identities. The eyeball-to-eyeball encounter records a situation in which each party is in turn inspector and inspected, in which the "ingenious Chirurgion" Glover is no more able than is the ship's surgeon Gulliver to maintain a position of ontological or epistemological superiority vis-à-vis other creatures he meets in the world, since they are capable at any moment of turning the spotlight on *him* as an object of surveillance and inquiry.

The ambiguity and confusion surrounding the whole question of identity would have had a particular resonance for Swift as part of a class (the Anglo-Irish) ambivalent about its own national identity and subject to shifting and arbitrary definitions, as noted in Swift's bitterly facetious question, "Am I a *Free-man* in *England,* and do I become a *Slave* in six Hours, by crossing the Channel?" (*Prose Works* 10: 31). The peculiar character of the political struggle between England and Ireland in Swift's lifetime, in which the colonizers and the colonized were, on the one hand, closely related as to physical appearance, language, and

---

[2]I wish to thank my student Aaron Walden for directing my attention to this passage, which is included in an appendix to his edition of Aphra Behn's *The Widow Ranter: Or The History of Bacon in Virginia* (New York: Garland, 1993).

culture, while on the other hand strenuously differentiated as a means of denying Ireland's claim to equality with England under British law, provided suggestive material for the definitional anxieties and absurdities depicted in the *Travels*. We might recall that Gulliver's sense of profound revulsion at the sight of the Yahoos is directly proportionate to the degree to which, as he himself comes to recognize, the two resemble one another ("My Horror and Astonishment are not to be described, when I observed, in this abominable Animal, a perfect human Figure" [212]).

For over six years prior to the publication of the *Travels*, Swift's writing career had been taken up primarily with producing political tracts defending the cause of Irish nationalism and attacking not only England's policies toward Ireland but also the attitudes that helped shape them. Indeed, Swift interrupted the composition of the *Travels* in order to join the protests against Wood's halfpence by writing his most famous and effective anticolonialist pieces, *The Drapier's Letters*. What particularly distinguished Swift's writings in this regard from others that similarly espoused the so-called Irish interest was their treatment not only of political and economic issues, but also of broader psychological and ideological ones, including the myths of racial Otherness that served to legitimize assumptions of moral superiority and hence assertions of political dominance. Thus in the persona of the Drapier addressing "the Whole People of Ireland," Swift observes that the English "look upon us as a Sort of *Savage Irish,* whom our Ancestors conquered several Hundred Years ago: And if I should describe the *Britons* to you, as they were in *Caesar's* Time, when they *painted their Bodies, or cloathed themselves with the Skins of Beasts,* I should act full as reasonably as they do" (*Prose Works* 10: 64).[3] In his subsequent *Letter to Lord Chancellor Middleton*, Swift exposes the fiction of Otherness, and its links to colonialist conquest, even more emphatically:

> As to *Ireland*, [the English] know little more than they do of *Mexico;* further than that it is a Country subject to the King of *England*, full of Boggs, inhabited by wild *Irish Papists;* who are kept in Awe by mercenary Troops sent from thence. . . . I have seen the grossest Suppositions pass upon them; that the *wild Irish* were taken in Toyls; but that, in some Time, they would grow so tame,

---

[3]Note here the subtle but telling slippage in pronoun referents from "us" (Irish) to "our" (English), which points to the ambiguity of Swift's sense of identity, his straddling of the line between those falsely stereotyped as "savages" and those self-deludedly considered "civilized."

as to eat out of your Hands: . . . And, upon the Arrival of an *Irish-man* to a Country Town, I have known Crouds coming about him, and wondering to see him look so much better than themselves. (*Prose Works* 10: 103)

It is difficult to read the final image without recalling Gulliver in Brobdingnag, displayed in country towns on market days for crowds of curiosity seekers — difficult, indeed, to read the entire passage without remarking its implications for the world of confused generic boundaries, and the unsettling questions they generate about human identity, which we have observed to be a central motif of the *Travels*.

Passages such as these serve to spotlight what is really at stake in asking the question: What is man? They underscore the fact that any answers the question is likely to produce belong to a concretely historical arena where the endeavor to draw boundaries between the human and the non- (or sub-) human inevitably serves to rationalize a political system rooted in power relationships of mastery and subordination. Thus it is in the early parts of Gulliver's sojourns, when he appears most alien and most resistant to the known categories of his hosts, that he is treated worst and kept in closest confinement. Only after he learns to converse in the local language and becomes a more familiar sight do his living conditions improve. Yet even then, the fact that he continues to be defined as Other, and that that difference (as Tzvetan Todorov has argued in relation to Columbus's attitude toward the Indians in the New World [42–43]) is invariably equated with inferiority, means that Gulliver will remain in a subordinate position no matter how much he ingratiates himself with his hosts. As he laments toward the end of his stay in Brobdingnag, "I was the Favourite of a great King and Queen, and the Delight of the whole Court; but it was upon such a Foot as ill became the Dignity of human Kind" (138).

Thus, if at various points in the work Gulliver is John Bull, the chauvinistic Englishman voyaging to foreign lands, where he is eager to "celebrate the Praise of my own dear native Country in a Style equal to its Merits and Felicity" (128), at other points he more nearly approximates the role of displaced Irishman, perennially adrift on hostile waters — like Ireland itself, characterized in Swift's verse as a "Poor floating Isle, tost on ill Fortune's Waves" (Horace, *Book I, Ode XIV* 1; 3: 770) — and finding himself on alien ground where he is alternately an object of ridicule, a prisoner, and a condemned man: someone robbed of the ability to speak his own language and define himself in his own terms. The Struldbruggs, who "lye under the Disadvantage of living like Foreigners in their own Country" (199), offer a haunting image of those who, like Swift's compatriots, live in a land governed by others, and suggest Swift's own abiding sense of being "a stranger in a strange land" ("Swift To Alexander Pope," Aug. 11, 1729; *Corresp.* 3: 341). Repeatedly finding himself in a state of subjection while continually insisting upon his desire for "liberty," and enmeshed in his narration's alternating rhythms of contraction and expansion, confinement and liberation, Gulliver embodies both the plight and the struggle of the Irish patriot, whose cry on behalf of "fair LIBERTY" (*Verses on the Death of Dr. Swift*, 347; *Poems* 2: 566) is heard throughout Swift's political tracts of the 1720s.

As historian too, Gulliver alternates between colonialist and anticolonialist narratives, between accounts trumpeting the military conquests of imperial England — "twenty or thirty of [these] Tubes, charged with the proper Quantity of Powder and Balls, would batter down the Walls of the strongest Town in his [majesty's] Dominions . . . if ever it should pretend to dispute his absolute Commands" (134) — and descriptions exposing the corruption and brutality that make colonial settlements possible:

> Ships are sent with the first Opportunity; the Natives driven out or destroyed, their Princes tortured to discover their Gold; a free Licence given to all Acts of Inhumanity and Lust; the Earth reeking with the Blood of its Inhabitants: And this execrable Crew of Butchers employed in so pious an Expedition, is a *modern Colony* sent to convert and civilize an idolatrous and barbarous People. (264)

Interestingly, the main anticolonialist narrative in the *Travels* — an allusion to Ireland's successful resistance against England in the affair of Wood's halfpence, portrayed in the Lindalinians' rebellion against royal tyranny, which "broke entirely the King's Measures and . . . forced [him] to give the Town their own Conditions" (310 [Davis ed.]) — was omitted from all editions of the *Travels* published in Swift's lifetime out of fear of government reprisals (indeed, it wasn't restored until 150 years after Swift's death). This suggests that there are some stories about history that can't be told (at least not in print), stories doomed to be silenced by the very mechanisms of oppression that they were designed to expose.

If Gulliver is depicted throughout much of the *Travels* in a series of anticolonialist gestures, such as eagerly embracing the customs and language of the alien cultures he comes in contact with rather than attempting to impose his own putatively more advanced and civilized ones, and refusing to formally claim these lands for the British crown (263, 265), he is also shown to be implicated in colonialist forms of behavior: for example, he uses the skins of Yahoos as a cover for his canoe (254) and he brings back booty from his travels abroad, including gold from Blefuscu (88) and a "small Collection of Rarities" from Brobdingnag (144). Moreover, by publishing his story he reveals his complicity in a system of printed words and published books that functions through what might be thought of as colonialist acts of subsumption and appropriation. This system in effect asserts its superiority over other modes of linguistic production not only by refining and ordering the raw materials out of which it constructs its narratives, but also by commodifying and selling other lands and their inhabitants as cultural artifacts, enacting on a textual level what European nations were doing in carrying on the slave trade and in plundering treasures from abroad. In depicting these contradictory aspects of Gulliver's role, the text prevents the reader from embracing the illusion of an easy, uncomplicated solution to the problems it reveals. While Gulliver's final nay-saying does point to the possibility of genuine resistance, the combined forces of satiric subversion and societal containment render this resistance alternately comic and assimilable into existing structures.

As author of the *Travels,* Swift was himself, of course, vulnerable to these forces of linguistic appropriation. His various strategies for undermining the authority of the *Travels* as a published text making at least tacit claims to accuracy and completeness may therefore be understood, not simply as a satiric technique or a protodeconstructive gesture, but as an act of resistance against such co-optation, as a means of sabotaging the inherently imperialist project of enclosing the Other within one's own discursive structures and claiming to deliver the final word on foreign beings and cultures. Gulliver's complaints that his editor has "either omitted some material Circumstances, or minced or changed them in such a Manner, that [he] hardly know[s his] own Work" (28) and his statement that "the original Manuscript is all destroyed, since the Publication of [his] Book" (29), combined with Swift's exploitation of the picaresque form to shape (and unshape) his narrative, help create a text whose authenticity and coherence are repeatedly called into question, a text noteworthy for its provisional, fragmentary, and open (hence implicitly nonauthoritarian and noncolonizing) character.

But, one might ask, open — and opening up — to what? Simply to more stories and linguistic constructs? Has Gulliver in effect been voyaging on a sea of "endless and inescapable textuality" that demonstrates "the interchangeability of the world and the book" (Holly 139)? If so, what does it matter if the stories Gulliver tells are ones of enslavement or liberation, since they don't refer to anything except their own narrativity and don't have any consequences beyond themselves? It is true (as this essay has been emphasizing) that history in the *Travels* is inseparable from acts of interpretation and translation and is dependent on a series of verbal and textual mediations. The scheme hatched at the Academy of Lagado "for entirely abolishing all Words whatsoever" (176) underscores the absurdity as well as the futility of attempts to circumvent language. On the other hand, schemes for circumventing reality by cutting language loose from all referential moorings are similarly exposed as pointless and inane. We may recall the print machine on which arbitrarily juxtaposed words are continuously rotated via forty iron handles fixed around the edges of the frame, "at every Turn . . . the Words shift[ing] into new Places," producing an ever-growing number of "Volumes in large Folio" that the Lagadian professor hopes will eventually encompass the "compleat Body of all Arts and Sciences" (175): an image of world as text clearly (and effectively) designed to evoke laughter.

It isn't simply that Swift employed a "discourse of experimentalism," one presupposing "a precise referent and a precise signified . . . which is certainly representative of a more or less readily definable reality" (Reiss 334). (For one thing, this observation ignores the ways in which Swift's writings problematize the act of representation.) Even more, it is that Swift embraced a language of moral and political activism, meaning that for him, words are largely what is left over after a call to action has either been heeded (in which case the words have been rendered basically obsolete though continuing to function as the commemoration of an achieved success) or ignored (in which case the words remain as mocking testaments to failure). Gulliver's disappointment that "instead of seeing a full Stop put to all Abuses and Corruptions . . . Behold, after above six Months Warning, I cannot learn that my Book hath produced one single Effect according to mine Intentions" (29) is a comic version of a sentiment that echoes, in considerably more somber tones, throughout Swift's political tracts. Referring to one of the latter, for example, Swift observes, "It seems it had little effect, and I suppose this [one] will have not much more. But, the heart of this People is waxed gross, and their Ears are dull of hearing, and their eyes they have closed" (*Prose Works* 12: 75).

The issue is perhaps less a question of referentiality than of contextuality, of what it means to be a member of a particular language-producing and -consuming community existing at a particular moment in history. Interestingly, Gulliver draws a parallel between writers of travels, producers of potentially ceaseless textuality, and dictionary makers, language stabilizers committed to linking specific signifiers with fixed signifieds; to both are ascribed the same fate of being "sunk into Oblivion by the Weight and Bulk of those who come last, and therefore lie uppermost" (262). To the extent that any kind of printed material escapes historical contextualization and becomes reified as a body of language or literature (whether in a post- *or* a prestructuralist manner), it can indeed be seen as part of a seemingly endless (and in itself largely meaningless) proliferation and displacement of words and authors. A relevant perspective on this matter is provided by the satiric (indeed, rather Swiftian) subversion of the Young Hegelians' penchant for linguistic abstraction in *The German Ideology*. Noting the failure of philosophers "to realise that neither thoughts nor language in themselves form a realm of their own, that they are only *manifestations* of actual life," Marx and Engels proceed to show how the philosophers have created the very problem — that of bridging the gap between words and world — they then must set about solving: specifically, in Marx and Engels' mock-romance, through a quasi-religious quest by the knights-errant, Don Quixote and Sancho Panza, to find a magical word "that would possess the miraculous power of leading from the realm of language and thought to actual life" (504). These two knights-errant would no doubt have felt right at home among the speculative projectors in the Academy of Lagado, equally comfortable with the wielders of autonomous theories and the dabblers in autonomous words.

By contrast, Swift avoids recreating the problem that would necessitate such a quest. Although (as the third voyage makes clear) he rejects a simplistic correlation between word and thing, he at the same time provides his readers with ample opportunities for contextualizing the narrative, for connecting it to a world that often was only too much with them. He accomplishes this through, for instance, his descriptions of the physically repellent beggars crowding around Gulliver's coach in Brobdingnag (115) and of the "many Labourers" and people "generally in Rags" (167) Gulliver encounters in his travels through Lagado (the portrayal of which bears striking similarities to accounts of Ireland's impoverished landscape in Swift's political tracts), as well as through passages where Gulliver assumes the role of patriotic Briton extolling the virtues of England's war machinery and recounting her "successful" military campaigns. The different responses to the latter given in the text, ranging from the Brobdingnagian king's disgust at "how so impotent and groveling an Insect as [Gulliver] . . . could entertain such inhuman Ideas, and in so familiar a Manner as to appear wholly unmoved at all the Scenes of Blood and Desolation" (134) to Gulliver's exuberant testimony that he "had seen [his countrymen] blow up a Hundred Enemies at once in a Siege, and as many in a Ship; and beheld the dead Bodies drop down in Pieces from the Clouds, to the great Diversion of all the Spectators" (226), present us as readers with a range of interpretive choices that possess inescapably ethical and ideological dimensions — that, like our responses to the descriptions of blighted landscapes and poverty-stricken people, concretely situate us in the world, clarifying our relationship to the material conditions of life through the ways in which we acknowledge, deny, consume, (re)produce, aestheticize, or historically transform them. If, as Marx argues in his *Grundrisse,* "consumption completes the act of production by giving the finishing touch to the product as such, by dissolving the latter, by breaking up its independent material form" (27), the realization of Swift's text can only come about through the readers' labor in the real world. And because "consumption is directly also production" (24), our mode of consuming Gulliver's historical narratives will help determine the way in which we produce our own narratives — the way, in the final analysis, we make our own history.

In announcing the completion of the *Travels* to his friend Charles Ford in the summer of 1725, Swift declared, "they are admirable Things, and will wonderfully mend the World" (Aug. 14, 1725; *Corresp.* 3: 87). We of course laugh at this prediction — as Swift himself no doubt did, recognizing its patent absurdity. As I see it, for Swift the only thing more absurd than the expectation that one could readily "mend the world" through one's writings would have been the notion that there isn't a world "out there" (indeed, right here) in need of mending, or that in the final analysis there could be any other purpose for writing "his/story" than to *change* a world that, thanks to the Grub Street hacks, the "modest proposers," the almanac-makers, and (not least) the Modern critics who populate Swift's satires, was already being textualized to death.

WORKS CITED

Adams, Percy G. *Travel Literature and the Evolution of the Novel.* Lexington: U of Kentucky P, 1983.
Derrida, Jacques. "The Law of Genre." Trans. Avital Ronell. *On Nar-*

rative. Ed. W. J. T. Mitchell. Chicago: U of Chicago P, 1981. 51–77.

Francis, Bishop of Down and Connor. *A Defence of the Antient Historians: With a Particular Application of it to the History of Ireland*. Dublin, 1734.

Glover, Thomas. "An Account of Virginia." *Philosophical Transactions: Giving Some Accompt of the Present Undertakings, Studies and Labours of the Ingenious in any Considerable Parts of the World*. Vol. XI. London: Royal Society, 1676. 623ff.

Holly, Grant. "Travel and Translation: Textuality in *Gulliver's Travels*." *Criticism* 21 (1979): 134–52.

Hunter, J. Paul. *Before Novels: The Cultural Contexts of Eighteenth-Century English Fiction*. New York: Norton, 1990.

Keating, Geoffrey. *The General History of Ireland*. Trans. Dermod O'Connor. London, 1732.

Marx, Karl. *Marx's Grundrisse*. Ed. David McLellan. London: Macmillan, 1980.

Marx, Karl, and Friedrich Engels. *The German Ideology*. Ed. S. Ryazanskaya. Moscow: Progress, 1964.

Raymond, Anthony. *A Short Preliminary Discourse to the History of Ireland*. London, 1725.

Reiss, Timothy J. *The Discourse of Modernism*. Ithaca: Cornell UP, 1982.

Smith, Frederik N., ed. *The Genres of "Gulliver's Travels."* Newark: U of Delaware P, 1990.

Swift, Jonathan. *The Correspondence of Jonathan Swift*. 5 vols. Ed. Harold Williams. Oxford: Clarendon, 1963–65.

———. *The Poems of Jonathan Swift*. 3 vols. Ed. Harold Williams. Oxford: Clarendon, 1958.

———. *The Prose Works of Jonathan Swift*. 14 vols. Ed. Herbert Davis et al. Oxford: Basil Blackwell, 1939–68.

Todd, Dennis. "The Hairy Maid at the Harpsichord: Some Speculations on the Meaning of *Gulliver's Travels*." *Texas Studies in Literature and Language* 34 (1992): 239–83.

Todorov, Tzvetan. *The Conquest of America: The Question of the Other*. Trans. Richard Howard. New York: Harper, 1984.

Deconstruction
and
Gulliver's Travels

WHAT IS DECONSTRUCTION?

Deconstruction has a reputation for being the most complex and forbidding of contemporary critical approaches to literature, but in fact almost all of us have, at one time, either deconstructed a text or badly wanted to deconstruct one. Sometimes when we hear a lecturer effectively marshal evidence to show that a book means primarily one thing, we long to interrupt and ask what he or she would make of other, conveniently overlooked passages, passages that seem to contradict the lecturer's thesis. Sometimes, after reading a provocative critical article that *almost* convinces us that a familiar work means the opposite of what we assume it meant, we may wish to make an equally convincing case of our former reading of the text. We may not think that the poem or novel in question better supports our interpretation, but we may recognize that the text can be used to support *both* readings. And sometimes we simply want to make that point: texts can be used to support seemingly irreconcilable positions.

To reach this conclusion is to feel the deconstructive itch. J. Hillis Miller, the preeminent American deconstructor, puts it this way: "Deconstruction is not a dismantling of the structure of a text, but a demonstration that it has already dismantled itself. Its apparently solid ground is no rock but thin air"("Stevens' Rock" 341). To deconstruct a text isn't to show that all the high old themes aren't there to be found in it. Rather, it is to show that a text — not unlike DNA with its double helix — can have intertwined, opposite "discourses" — strands of narrative, threads of meaning.

Ultimately, of course, deconstruction refers to a larger and more complex enterprise than the practice of demonstrating that a text means contradictory things. The term refers to a way of reading texts practiced by critics who have been influenced by the writings of the French philosopher Jacques Derrida. It is important to gain some understanding of Derrida's project and of the historical backgrounds of his work before reading the deconstruction that follows, let alone attempting to deconstruct a text. But it is important, too, to approach deconstruction with anything but a scholar's sober and almost worshipful respect for knowledge and truth. Deconstruction offers a playful alternative to traditional scholarship, a confidently adversarial alternative, and deserves to be approached in the spirit that animates it.

Derrida, a philosopher of language who coined the term "deconstruction," argues that we tend to think and express our thoughts in terms of opposites. Something is black but not white, masculine and therefore not feminine, a cause rather than an effect, and so forth. These mutually exclusive pairs or dichotomies are too numerous to list but would include beginning/end, conscious/unconscious, presence/absence, speech/writing, and construction/destruction (the last being the opposition that Derrida's word *deconstruction* tries to contain and subvert). If we think hard about these dichotomies, Derrida suggests, we will realize that they are not simply oppositions; they are also hierarchies in miniature. In other words, they contain one term that our culture views as being superior and one term viewed as negative or inferior. Sometimes the superior term seems only subtly superior (*speech, masculine, cause*), whereas sometimes we know immediately which term is culturally preferable (*presence* and *beginning* and *consciousness* are easy choices). But the hierarchy always exists.

Of particular interest to Derrida, perhaps because it involves the language in which all the other dichotomies are expressed, is the hierarchical opposition speech/writing. Derrida argues that the "privileging" of speech, that is, the tendency to regard speech in positive terms and writing in negative terms, cannot be disentangled from the privileging of presence. (Postcards are written by absent friends; we read Plato because he cannot speak from beyond the grave.) Furthermore, according to Derrida, the tendency to privilege both speech and presence is part of

the Western tradition of *logocentrism*, the belief that in some ideal beginning were creative *spoken* words, words such as "Let there be light,"
spoken by an ideal, *present* God. According to logocentric tradition,
these words can now only be represented in unoriginal speech or writing
(such as the written phrase in quotation marks above). Derrida doesn't
seek to reverse the hierarchized opposition between speech and writing,
or presence and absence, or early and late, for to do so would be to fall
into a trap of perpetuating the same forms of thought and expression
that he seeks to deconstruct. Rather, his goal is to erase the boundary
between oppositions such as speech and writing, and to do so in such a way
as to throw the order and values implied by the opposition into question.

Returning to the theories of Ferdinand de Saussure, who invented
the modern science of linguistics, Derrida reminds us that the association of speech with present, obvious, and ideal meaning and writing
with absent, merely pictured, and therefore less reliable meaning is suspect, to say the least. As Saussure demonstrated, words are *not* the
things they name and, indeed, they are only arbitrarily associated with
those things. Neither spoken nor written words have present, positive,
identifiable attributes themselves; they have meaning only by virtue of
their difference from other words (*red, read, reed*). In a sense, meanings
emerge from the gaps or spaces between them. Take *read* as an example. To know whether it is the present or past tense of the verb —
whether it rhymes with *red* or *reed* — we need to see it in relation to
some other word (for example, *yesterday*).

Because the meanings of words lie in the differences between them
and in the differences between them and the things they name, Derrida
suggests that all language is constituted by *différance*, a word he has
coined that puns on two French words meaning "to differ" and "to
defer": words are the deferred presences of the things they "mean," and
their meaning is grounded in difference. Derrida, by the way, changes
the *e* in the French word *différence* to an *a* in his neologism *différance;*
the change, which can be seen in writing but cannot be heard in spoken
French, is itself a playful, witty challenge to the notion that writing is
inferior or "fallen" speech.

In *De la grammatologie* [*Of Grammatology*] (1967) and *Dissemination* (1972), Derrida begins to redefine writing by deconstructing some
old definitions. In *Dissemination*, he traces logocentrism back to Plato,
who in the *Phaedrus* has Socrates condemn writing and who, in all the
great dialogues, powerfully postulates that metaphysical longing for
origins and ideals that permeates Western thought. "What Derrida does

in his reading of Plato," Barbara Johnson points out, "is to unfold dimensions of Plato's *text* that work against the grain of (Plato's own) Platonism" (xxiv). Remember: that is what deconstruction does according to Miller; it shows a text dismantling itself.

In *Of Grammatology*, Derrida turns to the *Confessions* of Jean-Jacques Rousseau and exposes a grain running against the grain. Rousseau, another great Western idealist and believer in innocent, noble origins, on one hand condemned writing as mere representation, a corruption of the more natural, childlike, direct, and therefore undevious speech. On the other hand, Rousseau admitted his own tendency to lose self-presence and blurt out exactly the wrong thing in public. He confesses that, by writing at a distance from his audience, he often expressed himself better: "If I were present, one would never know what I was worth," Rousseau admitted (Derrida, *Of Grammatology* 142). Thus, writing is a *supplement* to speech that is at the same time *necessary*. Barbara Johnson, sounding like Derrida, puts it this way: "Recourse to writing . . . is necessary to recapture a presence whose lack has not been preceded by any fullness" (Derrida, *Dissemination* xii). Thus, Derrida shows that one strand of Rousseau's discourse made writing seem a secondary, even treacherous supplement, while another made it seem necessary to communication.

Have Derrida's deconstructions of *Confessions* and the *Phaedrus* explained these texts, interpreted them, opened them up and shown us what they mean? Not in any traditional sense. Derrida would say that anyone attempting to find a single, correct meaning in a text is simply imprisoned by that structure of thought that would oppose two readings and declare one to be right and not wrong, correct rather than incorrect. In fact, any work of literature that we interpret defies the laws of Western logic, the laws of opposition and noncontradiction. In the views of poststructuralist critics, texts don't say "A and not B." They say "A and not-A," as do texts written by literary critics, who are also involved in producing creative writing.

Miller has written that the purpose of deconstruction is to show "the existence in literature of structures of language which contradict the law of non-contradiction." Why find the grain that runs against the grain? To restore what Miller has called "the strangeness of literature," to reveal the "capacity of each work to surprise the reader," to demonstrate that "literature continually exceeds any formula or theory with which the critic is prepared to encompass it" (Miller, *Fiction* 5).

Although its ultimate aim may be to critique Western idealism and logic, deconstruction began as a response to structuralism and to formalism, another structure-oriented theory of reading. (Deconstruction, which is really only one kind of a poststructuralist criticism, is sometimes referred to as poststructuralist criticism, or even as poststructuralism.)

Structuralism, Robert Scholes tells us, may now be seen as a reaction to modernist alienation and despair (3). Using Saussure's theory as Derrida was to do later, European structuralists attempted to create a *semiology*, or science of signs, that would give humankind at once a scientific and a holistic way of studying the world and its human inhabitants. Roland Barthes, a structuralist who later shifted toward poststructuralism, hoped to recover literary language from the isolation in which it had been studied and to show that the laws that govern it govern all signs, from road signs to articles of clothing. Claude Lévi-Strauss, a structural anthropologist who studied everything from village structure to the structure of myths, found in myths what he called *mythemes*, or building blocks, such as basic plot elements. Recognizing that the same mythemes occur in similar myths from different cultures, he suggested that all myths may be elements of one great myth being written by the collective human mind.

Derrida could not accept the notion that structuralist thought might someday explain the laws governing human signification and thus provide the key to understanding the form and meaning of everything from an African village to a Greek myth to Rousseau's *Confessions*. In his view, the scientific search by structural anthropologists for what unifies humankind amounts to a new version of the old search for the lost ideal, whether that ideal be Plato's bright realm of the Idea or the Paradise of Genesis or Rousseau's unspoiled Nature. As for the structuralist belief that texts have "centers" of meaning, in Derrida's view that derives from the logocentric belief that there is a reading of the text that accords with "the book as seen by God." Jonathan Culler, who thus translates a difficult phrase from Derrida's *L'Écriture et la différence* [*Writing* and Difference] (1967) in his book *Structuralist Poetics* (1975), goes on to explain what Derrida objects to in structuralist literary criticism:

> [When] one speaks of the structure of a literary work, one does so from a certain vantage point: one starts with notions of the meaning or effects of a poem and tries to identify the structures responsible for those effects. Possible configurations or patterns that make no contribution are rejected as irrelevant. That is to say, an

intuitive understanding of the poem functions as the "centre" . . . :
it is both a starting point and a limiting principle. (244)

For these reasons, Derrida and his poststructuralist followers reject the
very notion of "linguistic competence" introduced by Noam Chomsky,
a structural linguist. The idea that there is a competent reading "gives a
privileged status to a particular set of rules of reading, . . . granting pre-
eminence to certain conventions and excluding from the realm of language all the truly creative and productive violations of those rules"
(Culler, *Structuralist Poetics* 241).

Poststructuralism calls into question assumptions made about literature
by formalist, as well as by structuralist, critics. Formalism, or the New Criticism as it was once commonly called, assumes a work of literature to be a
freestanding, self-contained object, its meanings found in the complex network of relations that constitute its parts (images, sounds, rhythms, allusions, and so on). To be sure, deconstruction is somewhat like formalism
in several ways. Both the formalist and the deconstructor focus on the literary text; neither is likely to interpret a poem or a novel by relating it to
events in the author's life, letters, historical period, or even culture. And
formalists, long before deconstructors, discovered counterpatterns of
meaning in the same text. Formalists find ambiguity and irony, deconstructors find contradiction and undecidability.

Undecidability, as Paul de Man came to define it, is a complex notion easily misunderstood. There is a tendency to assume it refers to
readers who, when forced to decide between two or more equally plausible and conflicting readings motivated by the same text, throw up
their hands and decide that the choice can't be made. But undecidability in fact debunks this whole notion of reading as a decision-making
process carried out on texts by readers. To say we are forced to choose
or decide — or that we are unable to do so — is to locate the problem
of undecidability falsely outside ourselves, and to make it reside within
a text to which we come as an Other. The poststructuralist concept of
undecidability, we might say, deconstructs the either/or type distinction or opposition that structuralists and formalists have made between
reader and text. It entails what de Man calls the "mutual obliteration"
not only of propositions apparently opposed but also of the subject/
object relation. Undecidability is thus rather different from ambiguity,
as understood by formalists. Formalists believe a complete understanding of a literary work is possible, an understanding in which even the
ambiguities will fulfill a definite, meaningful function. Deconstructors
confront the apparently limitless possibilities for the production of

meaning that develop when the language of the critic enters the language of the text. They cannot accept the formalist view that a work of literary art has organic unity (therefore, structuralists would say, a "center"), if only we could find it. The formalist critic ultimately makes sense of ambiguity; undecidability, by contrast, is never reduced, let alone resolved, by deconstructive reading.

Poststructuralists break with formalists, too, over an issue they have debated with structuralists. The issue involves metaphor and metonymy, two terms for different kinds of rhetorical *tropes,* or figures of speech. *Metonymy* refers to a figure that is chosen to stand for something that it is commonly associated with, or with which it happens to be contiguous or juxtaposed. When said to a waitress, "I'll have the cold plate today" is a metonymic figure of speech for "I'll eat the cold food you're serving today." We refer to the food we want as a plate simply because plates are what food happens to be served on and because everyone understands that by *plate* we mean food. A *metaphor*, on the other hand, is a figure of speech that involves a special, intrinsic, nonarbitrary relationship with what it represents. When you say you are blue, if you believe that there is an intrinsic, timeless likeness between that color and melancholy feeling — a likeness that just doesn't exist between sadness and yellow — then you are using the word *blue* metaphorically.

Although both formalists and structuralists make much of the difference between metaphor and metonymy, Derrida, Miller, and de Man have contended with the distinction deconstructively. They have questioned not only the distinction but also, and perhaps especially, the privilege we grant to metaphor, which we tend to view as the positive and superior figure of speech. De Man, in *Allegories of Reading* (1979), analyzes a passage from Proust's *Swann's Way*, arguing that it is about the nondistinction between metaphor and metonymy — and that it makes its claim metonymically. In *Fiction and Repetition: Seven English Novels* (1982), Miller connects the belief in metaphorical correspondences with other metaphysical beliefs, such as those in origins, endings, transcendence, and underlying truths. Isn't it likely, deconstructors keep implicitly asking, that every metaphor was once a metonym, but that we have simply forgotten what arbitrary juxtaposition or contiguity gave rise to the association that now seems mysteriously special?

The hypothesis that what we call metaphors are really old metonyms may perhaps be made clearer by the following example. We used the word *Watergate* as a metonym to refer to a political scandal that began in the Watergate building complex. Recently, we have used part of the building's name (*gate*) to refer to more recent scandals (*Irangate*). However, already there are people who use and "understand" these terms who are unaware that Watergate is the name of a building. In the future, isn't it possible that *gate,* which began as part of a simple metonym, will seem like the perfect metaphor for scandal — a word that suggests corruption and wrongdoing with a strange and inexplicable rightness?

This is how deconstruction works: by showing that what was prior and privileged in the old hierarchy (for instance, metaphor and speech) can just as easily seem secondary, the deconstructor causes the formerly privileged term to exchange properties with the formerly devalued one. Causes become effects and (d)evolutions become origins, but the result is neither the destruction of the old order or hierarchy nor the construction of a new one. It is, rather, *deconstruction.* In Robert Scholes's words, "If either cause or effect can occupy the position of an origin, then origin is no longer originary; it loses its metaphorical privilege" (88).

Once deconstructed, literal and figurative can exchange properties, so that the prioritizing between them is erased: all words, even dog and cat, are understood to be figures. It's just that we have used some of them so long that we have forgotten how arbitrary and metonymic they are. And, just as literal and figurative can exchange properties, criticism can exchange properties with literature, in the process coming to be seen not merely as a supplement — the second, negative, and inferior term in the binary opposition creative writing/literary criticism — but rather as an equally creative form of work. Would we write if there were not critics — intelligent readers motivated and able to make sense of what is written? Who, then, depends on whom?

"It is not difficult to see the attractions" of deconstructive reading, Jonathan Culler has commented. "Given that there is no ultimate or absolute justification for any system or for the interpretations from it," the critic is free to value "the activity of interpretation itself, . . . rather than any results which might be obtained" (*Structuralist Poetics* 248). Not everyone, however, has so readily seen the attractions of deconstruction. Two eminent critics, M. H. Abrams and Wayne Booth, have observed that a deconstructive reading "is plainly and simply parasitical" on what Abrams calls "the obvious or univocal meaning" (Abrams 457–58). In other words, there would be no deconstructors if critics did not already exist who can see and show central and definite meanings in texts. Miller responded in an essay entitled "The Critic as Host," in which he not only deconstructed the oppositional hierarchy (host/parasite), but also the two terms themselves, showing that each derives from two definitions meaning nearly opposite things. *Host* means "hospitable welcomer" and "military horde." *Parasite* originally had a positive connotation; in Greek, *parasitos* meant "beside the grain" and referred to a friendly guest. Finally, Miller suggests, the words *parasite* and *host* are inseparable, depending on one another for their meaning in a given work, much as do hosts and parasites, authors and critics, structuralists and poststructuralists.

In the essay that follows, Terry J. Castle reminds us that the Houyhnhnms have no system of writing. She also reminds us that we may have difficulty interpreting that absence in a work that seems to be involved, as often as not, in satirizing the often satirical-seeming narrator. Is the Houyhnhnms' lack of writing a defect, as defective Gulliver suggests? Or is it the opposite of one?

Rather than answering that question immediately, Castle brings up structural anthropologist Claude Lévi-Strauss's study of the Nambikwara, a people with no written language. She recounts Lévi-Strauss's account, in *Tristes Tropiques*, of how a Nambikwara chief who saw him writing consequently used meaningless scribbles to mystify and even threaten his baffled tribesmen. Castle also recounts how Jacques Derrida later found, in Lévi-Strauss's account, the myth so prevalent in Western culture, namely, that writing is secondary, fallen, inauthentic, and corrupted, and therefore highly dangerous.

Castle then suggests that a version of that myth operates in Swift's literary works. Indeed, *Gulliver's Travels* is, according to this reading, "a complex meditation on the problematic nature of writing and the possible corruption implied by the Text." One of the objects of Swift's satire is language in general; in particular, though, Swift's "linguistic satire" is directed at writing. (It is thus even more "grammophobic" than it is "linguaphobic," as Castle puts it, offering a "critique of textuality" by presenting "the written artifact," again and again, as an unstable and therefore unreliable object.)

Before turning to *Gulliver's Travels* for examples, Castle discusses Swift's *A Tale of a Tub*. She focuses in particular on the way in which "the gap between speech and text" is "fantasized in [its] symbolic fictions" and used to dramatize the "breakdown of meaning." She shows that, in the process of critiquing textuality, Swift's text inevitably becomes *self-critique*, a necessarily double and even duplicitous thing whose judgment that speech is prior and superior to writing is opposed and contradicted by the fact that this judgment is itself written. Castle thus deconstructs *A Tale* even as she uses Swift's text to exemplify the speech/writing opposition that deconstructors from Derrida on have found in all Western texts.

When she turns her attention to *Gulliver's Travels*, she begins by pointing out that the Lilliputians are compulsive writers. Not only do they organize their lives around significant texts, but these texts also propagate mistakes and injustice. The Brobdingnagians, by contrast, "in proportion to their greater magnanimity as a people, denigrate and restrict the influence of the text." As for Part Three, a "satire of the text" underlies Swift's satire of the Academy of Projectors. In Laputa, "writing itself becomes the mark of an intrinsic intellectual and moral degeneracy"; Laputan society therefore stands in stark contrast to the text-free Houyhnhnms of Part Four.

From what has gone before (both in *Gulliver's Travels* and in Castle's analysis of it), we may be ready to conclude that, indeed, writing is bad and the Houyhnhnms are right not to write. But right/wrong, like reading/writing, is an opposition that begins to break down in a work like *Gulliver's Travels* and this kind of deconstructive analysis of it. Castle writes: "Swift queers the pleasant resolution of the grammaphobic situation (the escape to a Platonic utopia) . . . by one simple and ludicrous transformation. The residents in Utopia are not human." Thus, she suggests, writing for humans may be at once evil and inevitable.

But "this extension of the grammaphobic argument places the reader in an impossible position," Castle writes. "Swift leaves us in Part Four with confirmation of a logical tautology: because we are human, we are open to dehumanization." In the process, of course, Castle leaves us with a whole network of deconstructed oppositions — oppositions between humanity, humaneness, and humanism on one hand, and terms we think of as their opposites on the other.

Ross C Murfin

DECONSTRUCTION: A SELECTED BIBLIOGRAPHY

Deconstruction, Poststructuralism, and Structuralism: Introduction, Guides, and Surveys

Arac, Jonathan, Wlad Godzich, and Wallace Martin, eds. *The Yale Critics: Deconstruction in America*. Minneapolis: U of Minnesota P, 1983. See especially the essays by Bové, Godzich, Pease, and Corngold.

Berman, Art. *From the New Criticism to Deconstruction: The Reception of Structuralism and Post-Structuralism*. Urbana: U of Illinois P, 1988.

Butler, Christopher. *Interpretation, Deconstruction, and Ideology: An Introduction to Some Current Issues in Literary Theory*. Oxford: Oxford UP, 1984.

Cain, William E. "Deconstruction in America: The Recent Literary Criticism of J. Hillis Miller." *College English* 41 (1979): 367–82.

Culler, Jonathan. *On Deconstruction: Theory and Criticism After Structuralism*. Ithaca: Cornell UP, 1982.

———. *Structuralist Poetics: Structuralism, Linguistics and the Study of Literature*. Ithaca: Cornell UP, 1975. See especially ch. 10.

Esch, Deborah. "Deconstruction." *Redrawing the Boundaries: The Transformation of English and American Literary Studies*. Ed. Stephen Greenblatt and Giles Gunn. New York: MLA, 1992. 374–91.

Gasché, Rodolphe. "Deconstruction as Criticism." *Glyph* 6 (1979): 177–215.

Jay, Gregory. *America the Scrivener: Deconstruction and the Subject of Literary History*. Ithaca: Cornell UP, 1990.

Jefferson, Ann. "Structuralism and Post Structuralism." *Modern Literary Theory: A Comparative Introduction*. Ed. Ann Jefferson and David Robey. Totowa, NJ: Barnes, 1982. 84–112.

Leitch, Vincent B. *American Literary Criticism from the Thirties to the Eighties*. New York: Columbia UP, 1988. See especially ch. 10 ("Deconstructive Criticism").

———. *Deconstructive Criticism: An Advanced Introduction and Survey*. New York: Columbia UP, 1983.

Lentricchia, Frank. *After the New Criticism*. Chicago: U of Chicago P, 1980.

Melville, Stephen W. *Philosophy Beside Itself: On Deconstruction and Modernism*. Theory and History of Literature 27. Minneapolis: U of Minnesota P, 1986.

Norris, Christopher. *Deconstruction and the Interests of Theory*. Oklahoma Project for Discourse and Theory 4. Norman: U of Oklahoma P, 1989.

———. *Deconstruction: Theory and Practice*. London: Methuen, 1982. Rev. ed. London: Routledge, 1991.

Raval, Suresh. *Metacriticism*. Athens: U of Georgia P, 1981.

Scholes, Robert. *Structuralism in Literature: An Introduction*. New Haven: Yale UP, 1974.

Sturrock, John. *Structuralism and Since.* New York: Oxford UP, 1979.

Selected Works by Jacques Derrida and Paul de Man

de Man, Paul. *Allegories of Reading.* New Haven: Yale UP, 1979. See especially ch. 1 ("Semiology and Rhetoric").

———. *Blindness and Insight.* New York: Oxford UP, 1971. Minneapolis: U of Minnesota P, 1983. The 1983 edition contains important essays not included in the original edition.

———. *The Resistance to Theory.* Minneapolis: U of Minnesota P, 1986.

Derrida, Jacques. *Acts of Literature.* Ed. Derek Attridge. New York: Routledge, 1992. Includes a helpful editor's introduction on Derrida and literature.

———. *Dissemination.* 1972. Trans. Barbara Johnson. Chicago: U of Chicago P, 1981. See especially the concise, incisive "Translator's Introduction," which provides a useful point of entry into this work and others by Derrida.

———. *Margins of Philosophy.* Trans. Alan Bass. Chicago: U of Chicago P, 1982.

———. *Of Grammatology.* Trans. Gayatri C. Spivak. Baltimore: Johns Hopkins UP, 1976. Trans. of *De la Grammatologie.* 1967.

———. *The Post Card: From Socrates to Freud and Beyond.* Trans. with intro. Alan Bass. Chicago: U of Chicago P, 1987.

———. *Writing and Difference.* 1967. Trans. Alan Bass. Chicago: U of Chicago P, 1978.

Essays in Deconstruction and Poststructuralism

Barthes, Roland. *S/Z.* Trans. Richard Miller. New York: Hill, 1974. In this influential work, Barthes turns from a structuralist to a poststructuralist approach.

Bloom, Harold, et al., eds. *Deconstruction and Criticism.* New York: Seabury, 1979. Includes essays by Bloom, de Man, Derrida, Miller, and Hartman.

Chase, Cynthia. *Decomposing Figures.* Baltimore: Johns Hopkins UP, 1986.

Harari, Josué, ed. *Textual Strategies: Perspectives in Post-Structuralist Criticism.* Ithaca: Cornell UP, 1979.

Johnson, Barbara. *The Critical Difference: Essays in the Contemporary Rhetoric of Reading*. Baltimore: Johns Hopkins UP, 1981.

———. *A World of Difference*. Baltimore: Johns Hopkins UP, 1987.

Krupnick, Mark, ed. *Displacement: Derrida and After*. Bloomington: Indiana UP, 1983.

Miller, J. Hillis. *Ariadne's Thread: Story Lines*. New Haven: Yale UP, 1992. See especially the discussion of "anastomosis" in Joyce, 156–64.

———. *The Ethics of Reading: Kant, de Man, Eliot, Trollope, James, and Benjamin*. New York: Columbia UP, 1987.

———. *Fiction and Repetition: Seven English Novels*. Cambridge, MA: Harvard UP, 1982.

———. *Hawthorne and History, Defacing it*. Oxford: Basil Blackwell, 1991. Contains a bibliography of Miller's work from 1955–1990.

———. "Stevens' Rock and Criticism as Cure." *Georgia Review* 30 (1976): 5–31, 330–48.

Ulmer, Gregory L. *Applied Grammatology*. Baltimore: Johns Hopkins UP, 1985.

Deconstructionist Approaches to Swift and *Gulliver's Travels*

Holly, Grant. "Travel and Translation: Textuality in *Gulliver's Travels*." *Criticism* 21 (1979): 134–52.

Pollak, Ellen. *The Poetics of Sexual Myth: Gender and Ideology in the Verse of Swift and Pope*. Chicago: U of Chicago P, 1985.

Probyn, Clive T. "Starting from the Margins: Teaching Swift in the Light of Poststructuralist Theories of Reading and Writing." *Critical Approaches to Teaching Swift*. Ed. Peter J. Schakel. New York: AMS P, 1992. 19–35.

Rodino, Richard. " 'Splendide Mendax': Authors, Characters, and Readers in *Gulliver's Travels*." *PMLA* 106 (1991): 1054–70.

Wyrick, Deborah Baker. *Jonathan Swift and the Vested Word*. Chapel Hill: U of North Carolina P, 1988.

Other Work Referred to in "What Is Deconstruction?"

Abrams, M. H. "Rationality and the Imagination in Cultural History." *Critical Inquiry* 2 (1976): 447–64.

A DECONSTRUCTIONIST PERSPECTIVE

TERRY CASTLE

Why the Houyhnhnms Don't Write: Swift, Satire, and the Fear of the Text

The Houyhnhnms have no system of writing. When Gulliver transcribes Houyhnhnm words into English in his "Master's Presence," the horse is puzzled. "It cost me much Trouble to explain to him what I was doing; for the Inhabitants have not the least Idea of Books or Literature" (216). This absence is not due, as one might expect, to the fact that the Houyhnhnms are hoofed creatures. In chapter IX, two paragraphs after noting again their lack of "Letters," Gulliver is careful to tell us that the Houyhnhnms can "do all the Work which requires Hands" (248), including the threading of needles. Clearly a point is being made here. As on so many occasions in *Gulliver's Travels*, however, we may feel it is an enigmatic one. Is the Houyhnhnms' lack of writing, as Gulliver's chapter note suggests, part of a "Defectiveness of their Language" (245)? But Swift has severely undermined our sense of Gulliver's reliability by this point in Part Four: does the satirist really intend to present the absence of script as good? Is it a necessary feature of the Houyhnhnms' ideal community? Grammaphobia, or fear of the written word, is at least potential within the Swiftian text.

The Nambikwara have no system of writing. In *Tristes Tropiques* — a record, like *Gulliver's Travels*, of voyages to strange lands — Lévi-Strauss presents us with a transformation of the scene between Gulliver and his master. When the Nambikwara chief first sees the anthropologist making field notes, he, too, is puzzled. Unlike the dispassionate Houyhnhnm however, the chief immediately demands pencil and paper and begins to imitate this act of writing. Subsequently, he uses the scribbles he has made to mystify his fellow tribesmen: he threatens them with his own version of the anthropologist's magic. Lévi-Strauss, because he is a scientist and not a satirist, can make an explicit comment on all of this; he explicates the parable. It reminds us, he says, of the sinister ease with which writing can be alienated from its ostensible signification. Because of its incontrovertible presence as object, its semantic function may be co-opted by a sociological one. The written artifact, utterly voided of meaning, nevertheless retains an oppressive, disruptive effect on the human community. Writing "had been borrowed as a symbol. . . . It had

not been a question of acquiring knowledge, of remembering and understanding, but rather of increasing the authenticity and prestige of one
individual — a function — at the expense of others." The Nambikwara
fall into the world of writing: with the discovery of the text in its most
arbitrary and superstitious form, a kind of tyranny is instituted and natural personal relations are subverted. For the anthropologist, writing is
thus always a pernicious addition to culture, precisely because its
significatory function is so quickly betrayed by circumstance: "[T]he
primary function of written communication is to facilitate slavery"
(335–36). Grammaphobia is more than potential in Lévi-Strauss's text.

The juxtaposition I have made is not an innocent one. Its consequences for Swift may be drawn out by the following digression. Com-
menting on the Lévi-Strauss anecdote in *Of Grammatology*, the French
theorist of writing Jacques Derrida isolates in the anthropologist's assumptions a central myth of the written word. Lévi-Strauss's remarks
epitomize for him the "classical ideology" of language in Western culture. Briefly, Derrida suggests that "from Plato to Rousseau to Hegel"
an arbitrary relation has been enforced between speech and writing. In
our mythic formulation, speech is primary and writing is secondary. We
impute to speech a natural priority and purity: we identify it as the mode
of signification appropriate to "natural man." Writing, by contrast, is
traditionally imagined as an imitation of speech, as a belated development, as an unnatural superimposition upon the primal and exquisite
purity of oral communication. The ideological separation soon modulates (following upon Plato) into a moral drama, a Fall: if speech pre-
serves a pure relation between Nature and Word, writing interrupts,
compromises, corrupts this relation. The medium of writing itself, because of its impoverished material status, breaches Nature and Word
and lays open a ground for falsehood. The Text, as Devil, is "the Father
of Lies." As such, it makes itself available in turn as an instrument of
corrupt individuals. Thus the fantasy persists that writing is "the dangerous supplement," the shoddy, distracting copy of original truth.
Writing "takes on the status of a tragic fatality come to prey upon natural innocence" (168).

The operation of this myth of writing in Lévi-Strauss is patent: a
pure (oral) society is disrupted by the intervention of writing, a writing,
moreover, that points up, pathetically, its own radical shoddiness, its
inauthenticity as signifier. I would like to claim that a similar myth may
be seen working in Swift. Part Four of *Gulliver's Travels* is, in one reading, a complex meditation on the problematic nature of writing and the

possible corruption implied by the Text. But the theme reappears often in Swift's work. At these moments his obsessive apprehension of the philosophical and sociological dilemmas posed by writing suggests that he is influenced by a mythic structure of the kind Derrida describes. Swift, as we will see, confronts the fallen Text in a number of works, and this text itself becomes, with varying degrees of explicitness, a satiric subject par excellence.

Swift, like Lévi-Strauss in *Tristes Tropiques*, makes the ideological assumption of a radical break between speech and writing. This point has played no part, really, in classic commentaries on Swift's work — those, for instance, of Ehrenpreis, Harth, Monk, Landa, and others.[1] Indeed, Swift criticism has in general tended to leave aside both the question of the satirist's view of his own medium and the problem of the written artifact that his text raises. In a well-known description of the rationalist utopia of Part Four of *Gulliver's Travels*, Samuel H. Monk itemizes every feature of Houyhnhnm life except the one an anthropologist would be the first to notice: that the horses have an exclusively oral culture. The omission here is typical of general inattention to the question of the written word. Even in recent critical discussions that have focused on Swift's view of language, however, the mythic split — the fall of speech into writing — has been presupposed but unacknowledged. Commentators on Swift's linguistic satire have tended to confine themselves to remarks of an unspecific kind, for instance, that the abuse of words satirized by Swift is linked to a larger satire of other kinds of abuse: political, religious, and the like. Thus William Koon writes, in an essay on the language in *A Tale of A Tub*, that "the *Tale's* corrupt language marks corrupt religion and learning as well as the fallen nature of man" (28). And again, "man's sinful nature reveals itself in words as well as in thoughts and deeds" (33).

---

[1]Phillip Harth confines his description of the satire on interpretation in *A Tale of A Tub* to a theological issue: the perverse effect of "zeal" (located in the interpreter) on scriptural exegesis. Yet the "zealous" exegete, Swift's own marred text suggests, is one who, among other things, exploits material flaws associated with textuality: lacunae, ellipses, visible obscurities, and cruxes. It is difficult to escape the conclusion that for Swift the difficulty of interpretation derives as much from problematic elements in the object of interpretation itself, the written artifact, as from the deficiencies of interpreters. See in particular chapter 2, "Reason and Revelation." Irvin Ehrenpreis's classic essay on Part Four of *Gulliver's Travels*, while eloquently particularizing the dilemma Swift's reader faces (to emulate the virtuous Houyhnhnms is to deny one's own humanity), likewise leaves out the "grammatological" dimension of this dilemma: it is impossible for Gulliver (and us) to imitate the purity of Houyhnhnm existence because it is impossible to unlearn the use of ciphers, and thus avoid, as they do, implication in a world of textuality.

However true these remarks, they tend to ignore the special force Swift applies in the *Tale* and elsewhere to a critique of textuality per se. The corrupt words are, in fact, written words. Speech retains all its natural priority in Swift. His fear, his satiric energy, is aroused by the blotted, besmeared copy of speech, by the perverse materiality of the printed page — by an "excremental" vision of the script. The fallen nature of man is revealed most profoundly not in the fact that he speaks (Adam spoke with God in the Garden), but in the fact that he writes. Thus one must particularize the anxious element underlying Swift's work not simply as linguaphobic but as grammaphobic: his is an exemplary examination of the paradoxes that obtain when words thicken, squirm, and breed before our eyes. Let us approach the enigma of the Houyhnhnms' missing script by placing it in a larger context. All of Swift's satiric pieces, to a greater or lesser extent, reflect upon the problematic status of the written word. The mode of reflection varies. Swift's revelation of the fallen nature of writing is primarily philosophic in *A Tale of A Tub;* sociological implications are drawn out in some of the smaller satires; and finally, *Gulliver's Travels* is regulated by an inclusive fiction of the text.

A Tale of A Tub, the most extensive early satire, is, one might claim, Swift's prototypical (and perhaps most complicated) diagnosis of the problem at the heart of the text. A duplicity, or doubleness, informs Swift's revelation: the *Tale* is simultaneously a history and an embodiment of the corruption potential in the scriptory. It is at once a hallucination of Text and a hallucinatory text. This doubleness has, of course, been noted by commentators. Just as the three brothers puzzle over a text (their father's will) in the embedded history in the *Tale,* so Swift's readers must themselves enact a similar problematic process of textual interpretation as they confront the dark mysteries of his framing text — the prefaces, digressions, notes, addenda. We are made the mad interpreters of Swift's text; it invites us to engage in a *folie de texte* and replicate the process that is described anecdotally in the embedded parable of Peter and the rest. More critics than Wotton have fallen into Swift's trap. This formal complementary quality in the work is usually explained in relation to Swift's explicit satiric project noted in the Apology, the twofold exposure of "gross corruptions in Religion and Learning" (*PW* 1: 1). Interpretation of text is the theme that conjoins Swift's satire of religious abuse in the allegorical portion of the *Tale* with his satire on pedagogic abuse, exemplified in the Modern editor's insane critical apparatus.

The theme of interpretation, however, suggests a deep structure in the Swiftian satire. The problem of meaning, raised everywhere on the surface of the *Tale*, points, it would seem, to an underlying, consistent fantasy of the Text itself. On the most profound level (the level of dream?), Swift's satire is motivated by a vision, potentially fearful, of the written artifact as a radically unstable object. This latent myth of the text conditions both the convoluted satiric strategy of a *Tale* and the passionate intensity with which this strategy is put into effect. But how might one specify the prototypical, anxious Text imagined in the *Tale*? How does the written word reveal itself to Swift (and to us) as a corrupt mode of signification? Swift's underlying critique of writing depends first of all, as I have already intimated by my own digression to the Derridean analysis, upon an intuition of its compromised relation to speech. The model in Swift is, in the most general application, Platonic: the written object is a material rendering of something ideal, the pure world of speech. Writing is a copy of a preexisting, naturalized realm of discourse; for the satirist of the text, its very materiality attests to its corruptness; and the copy, in this case, exemplifies a process of degeneration. The solidification of speech into writing is, to use a Derridean concept, a scandal; to use a Swiftian, a scatology.

Swift suggests much of this, of course, in the elaborate bibliographic boondoggle with which the *Tale* begins. We learn in the Apology prefixing the satire that the original version of the Modern's manuscript has been lost, and that the primary text that we read is, after all, that "surreptitious Copy," "with many alterations," feared by the "Bookseller" (*PW* 1: 17) in his own subsequent preface. This would appear to explain why the present manuscript is a pocked transcript, one disrupted at all points by obscurities, typographical ellipses, holes. Yet, the Apology blithely admits, the author's missing original itself also held "Chasms," though indeed, "not so many" (*PW* 1: 9) as the received text. At this point an absurdity has intervened in Swift's potted history of the text. This last information hints subtly at an epistemological equivalence among all the texts; each is equally impure, even the version that is described, oxymoronically, as the "Original Copy" (*PW* 1: 9). Each is impure in regard to the world of spoken discourse, which maintains here an assumed priority. What has been lost in the process of transmission described in the Apology is not an originally pure manuscript (no such thing exists), but truth itself, specifically located in the voice, the words of a human speaker.

The *Tale* fictionalizes this loss most obviously in the mystery attached to the Modern's identity and whereabouts. Again in the Apology, Swift alludes to the rumor (though he discounts it) that the author of the manuscript we read is dead. In any case, the Modern cannot be consulted directly regarding the cruxes in his text; the authority of his voice — the voice of authorial intention — is absent. The point here would seem to be that the Text cannot, ultimately, be referred to the spoken discourse it purports to mirror: the point of contact between speech and writing is breached by accident, by history, by that very plunge into materiality that the written word represents. Symbolically, a death, a disappearance, takes place in the transition from the oral to the written mode. In the embedded allegory death literally intervenes between speech and text: the appearance of the disputed will in the world is here functionally dependent upon the death of an authorial *voice*, the father. The will (an archetypal version of Text) is thus compromised, de-natured, separated from truth at its moment of origin. It is a deathly, parasitic artifact; it feeds off an original, living form of discourse, and replaces it in the world. The Text falls into the world precisely as the voice, traumatically, leaves it; its frustrating, marred surface attests to its belated, unnatural, and ultimately dehumanized status.

The gap between speech and text fantasized in the symbolic fictions of a *Tale* produces anxiety because it occasions, necessarily, the breakdown of meaning. It brings about a hermeneutic catastrophe. The privileged, single meaning is abrogated by that death which mediates between the worlds of discourse and transcription. Because it cannot be referred back to the truth of the voice, the text's signification is unverifiable; its truth is always indeterminate. Once at large in the world, Swift suggests, the paradigmatic manuscript resolves immediately into an independent, free-floating structure of possible meanings — it constitutes its own infinitely expansive ideology. Yet this is the hermeneutic nightmare at the heart of the *Tale*, the source of the satirist's motivating phobia. Separated from the natural constraints of the voice, the text makes itself available for arbitrary, creative interpretation. Confronting, for instance, one of the famous hiatuses in Swift's own manuscript — the "*Hic multa desiderantur*" ("here much is left to be desired"; *PW* 1: 107) — the reader can only conjecture what might fill the ellipsis. The text has lost its voice in the most radical way possible. Hence, like the three brothers of the allegory who encounter the "*altum silentium*" ("deep silence"; *PW* 1: 51) of their father's will and fill the void as they wish, we are invited by the Modern's text to turn imaginists, to become creative readers. Noting his desire that "every Prince in Christendom" assign to seven scholars the task of writing "seven ample Commentaries" on the *Tale*, the Modern asserts that "whatever Difference may be found in their several Conjectures, they will all, without the least Distortion, be manifestly deducible from the Text" (*PW* 1: 117–18). No reading is disallowed by the pocked and whorish text.

It is worth noting in passing how close are Swift's insights regarding the problematic nature of textuality to certain discoveries formalized in modern linguistics and extended in contemporary structuralist literary theory. By raising questions about the interpretative process and the peculiar epistemological complexities that afflict any reader's relations to a text, Swift's work anticipates the concerns, in particular, of Continental theorists such as Barthes and Kristeva. (The parallel likewise refutes the notion that it is only modernist texts of the twentieth century that expose the semantic variability of the literary sign.) To cite just one point of convergence: Swift's allusion to the "Anagrammatick Method" of reading employed by Peter when he looks for the word "SHOULDER" (*PW* 1: 50) in the will suggests that it is possible to read the orthographic marks that make up the text in a nonsequential order. This graphemic way of reading, Swift knows, is not conventional; yet he also suspects, rightly, that there is nothing in the physical nature of the text per se to forbid it. Interpretation of a given text is based on arbitrary reading conventions — ways of arranging, conceptually, its visible marks — and these conventions may conceivably be broached by the innovative reader. Obviously deformed texts, those filled with typographical transpositions, shock us because they remind us precisely that the way we look at the text is arbitrary, and that we might, indeed, modify the process ourselves. Because its actual structure is always indeterminate, Swift seems to say, any text allows convention-free reading; any text might even be said to encourage such madness. The linguist Saussure, whose theory of signs underlies recent structuralist work on literary hermeneutics, made the same discovery in the early part of this century while studying anagrams in *De Rerum Natura*.[2] After positing the presence of anagrams of "Aphrodite" in the opening lines of the Lucretian text, Saussure was forced to admit that he could not prove the anagrams had been intentionally placed there; the appeal to authority, the voice of

---

[2]For a discussion of Saussure's work on anagrams, see Culler (106). The "Anagrammatick Method" of interpretation recurs in Part Three of *Gulliver's Travels*, of course, when the Tribnian experts decipher "*Our Brother Tom has just got the Piles*" as "*Resist; a Plot is brought Home, The Tour.*" Arthur Case identifies in this passage a satire on the Jacobites, who were alleged to use anagrammatic codes, and Bolingbroke, who went by the alias "M. La Tour" while in France (91–92). Swift's political satire here does not exclude his satire on the malleable text; rather, as so often happens in his works, two targets are struck in a single satiric economy.

the author, was impossible. Moreover, the linguist was left with the realization that just as the truth of his anagrammatic interpretation was indeterminate, so all textual exegesis might be equally indeterminate, shaped only by the desire of the interpreter. Writing, because of its hermeneutic instability, easily accommodates its own exploitation. Saussure was so disturbed by the hallucinatory text, the unconstrained text, that he never published his anagrammatic research. Swift attempts to protect himself from the same discovery by enclosing it within the context of satire, of derision. Yet the fantasy of the mercurial text persists.

The critique of writing implied at the deepest level of *A Tale of A Tub* enforces finally in that work a powerful and revealing troping of the text. The manuscript, with its spots and holes and blurs, becomes a demonic and ghastly material presence. It is a monster. Characteristically, Swift figures its monstrosity by way of an image of fertility. The Text, for the satirist, is womb-like (might we say female?): it gives birth, in a process at once out of control and horrifying, to replicas of itself. The Modern's own text, with its offshoots and appendages, is our primary model of the oppressive text; it invites commentary, it seeks to generate new texts. It afflicts us with its apparatus — what Swift catalogues in another context as the innumerable, useless "Prefaces, Epistles, Advertisements, Introductions, Prolegomena's, Apparatus's, To-the-Reader's" (*PW* 1: 81). But Swift shows everywhere, in explicit comment, the sickening ease with which any text may reproduce itself. Later we learn, for instance, that texts inspire in their readers "Scholiastick Midwifry" and that the readers deliver them "of Meanings" that, the Modern notes by the by, "the Authors themselves, perhaps, never conceived." Written words, he continues, are like seed that "will multiply far beyond either the Hopes or Imagination of the Sower" (*PW* 1: 118). Human agency is thus excluded from the grotesque process of textual multiplication: the "immense Bales of Paper" (*PW* 1: 21) that threaten ultimately to subsume Nature itself begin to write themselves. The monstrous text Swift imagines is a mindless entity, a mere automaton, endlessly replicating. The world is "nauseated," says the satirist in his Apology, "by endless Repetitions on every Subject" (*PW* 1: 1).

The grotesque text troped in *A Tale of A Tub* may be redefined in Derridean fashion, summarily, as the guilty text. The text of *A Tale* itself exemplifies guilt: its status as truth is compromised by its corrupt physical nature. Yet it is also guilty in the way that it compels us to construct our own guilty texts. It breeds us, its exegetes, as we read. One might argue at this point, however, that Swift may not necessarily mean to identify every version of Text as potentially corrupt. Do not texts remain somewhere that are in some fashion privileged? Can we not separate good texts from bad texts? Certain commonplace assumptions about satire — particularly, that it implicitly recommends to us an unstated, yet realizable mode of behavior — may mislead here. Viewed superficially, the satire on the evil text in *A Tale of A Tub* might indeed seem to predicate by indirection a good text. If the Modern's manuscript is a negative model of written discourse, it must be possible to extrapolate from it a positive model. Yet in the dysphoric world of writing imagined in Swiftian satire, the innocent text ultimately does not, indeed cannot, exist. So extreme is the anxiety surrounding the Text in the *Tale* that one is forced to conclude that the positive model invoked, paradoxically, is no writing at all. This would seem to be the import of Swift's obsessive returning, throughout the work, to the problem of biblical interpretation. (The traumatic seventeenth-century discovery of the historical corruption of biblical texts underlies Swift's work just as profoundly as it does a work such as Dryden's *Religio Laici*.) No text is privileged in regard to truth; no text is scriptural. Swift would not have been surprised, one suspects, by the notorious "Wicked Bible" printed in Leipzig in 1631, which, due to a typographical error, gave the Seventh Commandment as "Thou shalt commit adultery." Such gross and shocking aberrations merely confirm once again, on the basic level of typography, the theme of the satire. Given its inescapable material status, every writing is a site for corruption, no matter what authority — natural, divine, or archetypal — we may wishfully invest in it. Because they constitute an earthly text, the Scriptures themselves pathetically and paradoxically make up part of the fallen world of writing. Is Swift's fiction of the text, then, a kind of blasphemy? Swift does not state so baldly that God's text itself is corrupt, but at the same time, the possibility is implicit everywhere in his satire. The text is to be feared, whatever its ostensible provenance.

I have dwelled at considerable length on *A Tale of A Tub* because it isolates powerfully the essential features of Swift's fantasy of the text. Its energy, I have tried to suggest, derives from what one might call an underlying phobic response to writing. That vision or hallucination of a fearful gap between speech and writing compels the satire, gives it an anxious, obsessive force. Turning to Swift's other satiric works, however (even those that might not seem at first glance to share an equal fascination with textuality) one finds, I think, evidence of the same theme, variants and elaborations of the same textual fiction.

Many of Swift's satiric pieces play off notions of the grotesquely physical text, the intrusive text, of that arrogant and monstrous text intimated by the *Tale*. *The Battle of the Books*, of course, depends upon the phantasmagoric troping of the text already seen in the earlier work. Swift's satire here, like Pope's in the *Dunciad*, is marked by a compelling sense of the materiality of the written artifact and of the pressure it exerts upon Nature. At the most reductive level, the satire hints, no book is free from these oppressive or guilty qualities. In the bookseller's preface to the reader, for instance, Swift makes his characteristic schism between author and book, voice and text, and thus solidifies writing — as an *entity* — before our eyes:

> I must warn the Reader, to beware of applying to Persons what is here meant, only of Books in the most literal Sense. So, when Virgil is mentioned, we are not to understand the Person of a famous Poet, call'd by that Name, but only certain Sheets of Paper, bound up in Leather, containing in Print, the Works of the said Poet, and so of the rest. (*PW* 1: 139)

Yet the Ancient text, once solidified in such a way as an artifact, is ready to breed a secondary text: the Modern text. The Ancient text itself supplies the necessary condition for the Battle: a world of violence is instituted with this primary materialization of the Word. Swift's overt purpose in his piece is to vindicate the works of the Ancients as against those of the Moderns, but one may wonder how much this conscious project is complicated, even undermined, by the implicit fantasy of the text. In some sense, Virgil is responsible for Dryden: the primary text initiates the chain of replication. And both primary and secondary texts share the same compromised physical status in the end; both are equally present as sites for corruption. (This equivalence is suggested symbolically, perhaps, in the mystery surrounding the outcome of the Battle.) The Goddess Criticism, part of Swift's fantastical mock-heroic machinery, must be seen, finally, as his inclusive model of the hallucinatory Text. She, an archetypal transmogrification of every text existing in the world,

> gathered up her Person into an Octavo Compass: her Body grew white and arid, and split into pieces with Driness; the thick turned into Pastboard, and the thin into Paper, upon which, her Parents and Children, artfully Strowed a Black Juice, or Decoction of Gall and Soot, in Form of Letters; her Head, and Voice, and Spleen, kept their primitive Form, and that which before, was a Cover of Skin, did still continue so. In which Guise, she march'd on. (*PW* 1: 155)

Even Virgil's writings, one must conclude, do not escape the universal reduction of text into paper and "black juice." In such a vision we contemplate the central image of Swiftian grammaphobia.

In works such as the *Bickerstaff Papers*, *A Modest Proposal*, the *Complete Collection of Genteel and Ingenious Conversation*, the satire of the text is given an analogous sociological expansion. Swift's vision of the physical corruptness of writing (and likewise the condition of its hermeneutic guilt) modulates here into a vision of its social guilt. All the discoveries made about the text in *A Tale of A Tub* still apply, but the satirist's emphasis shifts to a consideration of its social effect. The intuitive leap made in these and similar works is easier to observe than to explicate, but one might brief it as follows. Just as writing is itself a dehumanized mode, physical yet mindless, separated at its moment of origin from the truth of the voice, so it works to enforce a larger pattern of dehumanization in society. Writing clogs the world: it mediates negatively between persons, imposes itself as object, as visible obstruction. The text Swift fears is not only materially corrupt, it is hypnotic, fetishistic. As we focus upon the impressive yet false image of truth that it presents, we lose contact with human reality. While we read we cannot listen — the naturalized relations of the voice, of human connection, are breached. With the distraction of the text, moral chaos is made possible.

Thus, for instance, in the instructive pieces on conversation Swift shows the text literally intruding upon the world of human relationships. Simon Wagstaff invites his readers to consult his book while entering into conversation; his text subsumes the voice directly, mediates the spontaneous oral interchange between persons. He recommends

> the following Treatise, to be carried about as a Pocket Companion, by all Gentlemen and Ladies, when they are going to visit, or dine, or drink Tea; or, where they happen to pass the Evening without Cards . . . desiring they would read their several Parts in their Chairs or Coaches, to prepare themselves for every Kind of Conversation, that can probably happen. (*Satires*, *PW* 4: 105)

But if the intrusive text is ludicrous and comical here (and likewise in the Bickerstaff pieces) in *A Modest Proposal* it is less so. Swift's greatest short satire models for us that dehumanized script which encourages the dehumanization of the reader: its rhetoric is indeed hypnotic. Swift's irony devastates precisely because it exploits our conventional, even superstitious assumption about texts: that they are authoritative signs. We imbue the text with authority because it is a text: we fall immediately under its sinister mimetic spell. Yet, the satirist warns, absorption in this dehumanized surface enforces our own dehumanization. To accept the premise of *A Modest Proposal* — the utility of cannibalism — is to divest ourselves, of course, of a conventionally moral sense of things. The satire shocks and liberates because it points up how easily the text distracts us, co-opts us, separates us from human connections. Yet this effect, as I have tried to show, depends upon those assumptions about the written artifact seen elsewhere in Swift. Writing avails itself as an instrument of social evil because its own nature is essentially evil to begin with. Thus the Swiftian critique of Text, primarily framed upon philosophical issues in the early satiric pieces, quickly takes on here a crucial and profound pragmatic force. The epistemological exposé of writing resolves into moral exposé as well.

The themes Swift associates with writing — its fallen aspect, its hermeneutic indeterminacy, and physical and moral degeneracy — all reappear, finally, within the fictional context of *Gulliver's Travels*. One might even be tempted to claim that satire of the written word is an underlying principle of organization in that work. No matter how other perspectives shift throughout the book (most notoriously our view of the narrator himself), a critique of the written word seems to remain a constant. It works as a symbolic reference point against which other elements of the satire may be aligned.

Texts exert a different pressure on each of the societies Gulliver visits, inviting the hypothesis that this pressure is a Swiftian index to the nature of each place. In Part One, for instance, when Swift satirizes the pettiness and pomposity of the Lilliputians he shows us that their society is preeminently text-oriented. The Lilliputians are compulsive writers. They organize their lives around significant texts: published "Edicts" (such as the one that initiates the Big- and Little-Endian controversy), the "Proclamations" and "Orders of State" of their prince, treaties (which do not hold), and "Articles" of behavior like those presented to Gulliver on his arrival. The Lilliputians tend to formalize all their experience, silly as it is, as text. Yet this process of textualizing is, as elsewhere in Swift, a suspect one. Witness the distortion that creeps in as the Lilliputians set out to describe, in scientific discourse, the contents of Gulliver's pocket. Likewise, Gulliver's plight in Part One worsens precisely as texts intervene. The palace fire (the event that initiates Gulliver's fall from favor) starts because of the "Carelessness of a Maid of Honour, who fell asleep while she was reading a Romance" (69). The Englishman's fate is sealed by the "Articles of Impeachment" ordered against him by corrupt Lilliputians. The text, the satirist suggests, disrupts both the physical and social order of things; it is the primary cause of Lilliputian error and the primary tool of their injustice. The Lilliputians are condemned by the intimacy they share with it.

The Brobdingnagians, in proportion to their greater magnanimity as a people, denigrate and restrict the influence of the text. Gulliver notes that they have printing, "[b]ut their Libraries are not very large." Similarly, "they avoid nothing more than multiplying unnecessary Words" (135, 136), and they institute laws — arbitrarily but as best they can — against the process of interpretation itself:

> No Law of that Country must exceed in Words the Number of Letters in their Alphabet; which consists only of two and twenty. But indeed, few of them extend even to that Length. They are expressed in the most plain and simple Terms, wherein those People are not Mercurial enough to discover above one Interpretation. And, to write a Comment upon any Law, is a capital Crime. (135)

Gulliver comments that as a result Brobdingnagian learning is very "confined," but the joke is on him. We predicate Swift's satire on his narrator on a preexisting satire of the text. Thus, when Gulliver's own pettiness is exposed in this book by the Brobdingnagian king, we find the king analogizing England and its inhabitants to a corrupted text: "I observe among you some Lines of an Institution, which in its Original might have been tolerable; but these half erased, and the rest wholly blurred and blotted by Corruptions" (132). The immediate focus of Swiftian satire shifts, of course, between Parts One and Two, but its underlying assumption remains the same: the "little odious Vermin," whether a Lilliputian or Gulliver himself, has pen in hand.

In Part Three, the satire of the text underlies Swift's satire on the Academy of Projectors. Laputan writing is perhaps the most nightmarish in *Gulliver's Travels*. Among the various ridiculous inventions that Gulliver finds in Laputa, for example, is that implement "for improving speculative Knowledge by practical and mechanical Operations" (173), the text-breeding machine. With this device, "the most ignorant Person may write Books in Philosophy, Poetry, Politicks, Law, Mathematicks and Theology, without the least Assistance from Genius or Study." The invention generates arbitrary assortments of letters by mechanical rearrangement of bits of wood and paper, on which are written "all the Words of their Language in their several Moods, Tenses, and Declensions, but without any Order" (173). As in *A Tale of A Tub*, writing is figured as a nonintellectual process; it is automatic, mindless replication:

The Pupils at his Command took each of them hold of an Iron Handle, whereof there were Forty fixed round the Edges of the Frame; and giving them a sudden Turn, the whole Disposition of the Words was entirely changed. He then commanded Six and Thirty of the Lads to read the several Lines softly as they appeared upon the Frame; and where they found three or four Words together that might make Part of a Sentence, they dictated to the four remaining Boys who were Scribes. (175)

Already the texts created thus are many; "several Volumes" exist of "broken Sentences," and the inventor of the machine intends more. With the prospect of five hundred such devices in operation, the number of "rich Materials" still to be produced is incalculable (175). Swift here discovers, then, an appropriate physical model for meaningless, inhuman and infinitely reproducing writing. The text factory is the central locus for grammaphobia in Part Three, but one might note, too, the satirist's exposure again of the "Anagrammatick Method" (181) in the section on political projectors and his dismissal of "Commentary" (185) and interpretation in the episode in which Gulliver calls back the ancient writers from the dead. At all points in the Laputan scenes, even more so perhaps than in Lilliput, the reader encounters a world replete with writing, a world controlled by a technology of the text. In both societies, however, writing itself becomes the mark of an intrinsic intellectual and moral degeneracy.

And here we come back, of course, to the horses. As Gulliver has already told us, "their Knowledge is all traditional" (247). Unlike any other society in *Gulliver's Travels*, the Houyhnhnms have not taken the catastrophic fall into a world of letters. Their complete ignorance of books suggests an improvement even upon the relatively text-free Brobdingnagians.

The situation is not without paradox, however. The pattern of grammaphobia in *Gulliver's Travels* conditions the appalling problem that confronts the reader in Part Four. Houyhnhnm society is indeed pure to the extent that it is free from textuality. It is a naturalized society. The Houyhnhnms are bound by a community of the voice; they are bound by a language of pure sound, the neigh. This is the sense in which Houyhnhnm society qualifies (as some critics, in particular Reichert, would like to see it) as a Swiftian version of the Platonic utopia. The secondary mode of signification is absent, along with its attendant corruption. No demonic texts here, getting in the way of the spoken discourse.

Swift queers the pleasant resolution of the grammaphobic situation (the escape to a Platonic utopia), however, by one simple and ludicrous transformation. The residents in Utopia are not human. By virtue of the essential difference between Houyhnhnm and human, the naturalized society is not, and can never be, our own. Gulliver tries to imitate the gait and speech of the horses, but, most significantly, he is never able to stop writing. Already fallen, he cannot emulate the Houyhnhnms in this crucial respect. (Indeed, Swift hints everywhere of Gulliver's inescapable resemblance to the Yahoos, who, with their enthusiastic and decorative shit-smearing seem, anthropologically speaking, on the way to the discovery of a script.)[3] Thus the satirist's examination of textuality takes its most damning turn. The Houyhnhnms may be textless — and thus admirable — but they are not men and women. For humankind, Swift suggests, the text is *inevitable*. It is already here. The evil text and human presence constitute an inseparable unit in the world.

This extension of the grammaphobic argument places the reader in an impossible position. Swift leaves us in Part Four with confirmation of a logical tautology: because we are human, we are open to dehumanization. Indeed, we already possess the necessary tool. He infects us everywhere with the malignancy of the text, and then says there is nothing we can do about it. Attempted return to the innocence of the Houyhnhnm is doomed to be an incomplete gesture. Meanwhile, the Yahoos drop excrement upon us from the trees. They inscribe our very bodies with a text.

Gulliver's Travels ends, then, with a final implosion of the Swiftian fear of the text. It suspends with paradox, with the extralogical confirmation of grammaphobia. Such anxiety is wholly appropriate to, and might be said to define, Swiftian satire; but on some level it also defines the author himself. In his own career, Swift lived out the identical paradox of the text figured in Part Four.[4] How, after all, can the writer not write? I have deliberately confined myself in this essay to the mythology of writing revealed in Swift's satiric pieces, yet there is, biographically speaking, another side to the issue. The serious works on language

---

[3]Frank Brady makes a point of the Yahoos' approach to human behavior, and hence their transformation into satiric targets, in a note in his introduction to the collection *Twentieth Century Interpretations*: "Strictly speaking, the Yahoos are satirized only to the extent they are assimilated to human beings. As Bergson pointed out, animal behavior in itself is never comic" (10).

[4]Carnochan has suggested that Swift's satire modulates finally into "self-satire," an illustration of the satirist's own "self-critical ways." A general paradox arises in that the greater "satire on man" always points back to Swift himself. Carnochan writes of Gulliver that "he embodies all Swift's doubts about his motives and his literary vocation" (92). Under this notion of vocation we may place our own topic: the paradoxical implication of the writer himself in the corrupt world of writing.

reform — the *Proposal for Correcting the English Tongue* and others — suggest that at moments Swift did believe, or attempt to believe, in a resurrected text. The *Proposal*, for instance, argues that it is possible to reestablish a connection between writing and speech. Swift wishes here that the gap might be bridged nostalgically, that we might go back to the purity of speech when we write. The story, perhaps apocryphal, of Swift reading his works aloud to his servant in order to ensure their comprehensibility works mythically: Swift here resurrects his own text by referring it to the human element of the voice. Obviously, Swift calls attention at times to a hope that his own plain style, free of "Corruptions," will be a model for a new, purified English prose (6).

Still, one may wonder, rightly I think, what the force of such wishing is compared with the intensity and reductiveness of the vision presented in Swiftian satire. My own inclination, as should be apparent, has been to associate Swift's myth of the text — and the world of satire itself — with unconscious forces, with underlying traumatized modes of perception. Placed next to *A Tale of A Tub* and the rest, the pieces on language reform look suspiciously like a kind of reaction-formation; they respond, it would seem, to a prior, deeply anxious experience of textuality. It appears questionable whether Swift himself ever succeeded in domesticating, in the *Proposal* or elsewhere, that hallucinatory material for which his satires everywhere provide the evidence.

And finally, it is the hallucinatory perception in Swift that remains with us, not his programmatic effort to resurrect the text. If Part Four of *Gulliver's Travels* shows that we, unlike Houyhnhnms, cannot be free of writing, Swift's satires show what a problematic supplement this is. Swift powerfully isolates for us the radical indeterminacy of the very texts we allow to influence our lives. The critique is not always logical; it is impelled by an energy that may remind us of the anxiety dream. But its force is not undermined thereby. Particularizing Swift's vision of the text in Derridean fashion, as a myth — as I have tried to here — suggests how one might begin to analyze it,[5] but even this leaves its emotional impact unexplained. Swift's greatest works make up together a *Tale* of a Text; and it is with this compelling text itself that we, readers and writers all, ultimately fall.

---

[5]Since this essay's original publication in 1980, work has been done on Swift's concerns here, including studies by Ellen Pollak (1985), Deborah Baker Wyrick (1988), and Ann Cline Kelly (1988). For a review of some of the broader questions involved, see also Carole Fabricant's 1991 essay, "The Battle of the Ancients and the (Post) Moderns."

WORKS CITED

Brady, Frank. Introduction. *Twentieth-Century Interpretations of "Gulliver's Travels."* Ed. Brady. Englewood Cliffs: Prentice, 1968. 1–11.

Carnochan, W. B. *Lemuel Gulliver's Mirror for Man.* Berkeley: U of California P, 1968.

Case, Arthur E. *Four Essays on "Gulliver's Travels."* Princeton, NJ: Princeton UP, 1958.

Culler, Jonathan. *Saussure.* Glasgow: Collins, 1976.

Derrida, Jacques. *Of Grammatology.* Trans. Gayatri Chakravorty Spivak. Baltimore: Johns Hopkins UP, 1976.

Ehrenpreis, Irvin. "The Meaning of Gulliver's Last Voyage." *Review of English Literature* 3 (1962): 18–38.

Fabricant, Carole. "The Battle of the Ancients and the (Post) Moderns: Rethinking Swift through Contemporary Perspectives." *The Eighteenth Century* 32 (1991): 256–73.

Harth, Phillip. *Swift and Anglican Rationalism.* Chicago: U of Chicago P, 1961.

Kelly, Ann Cline. *Swift and the English Language.* Philadelphia: U of Pennsylvania P, 1988.

Koon, William. "Swift on Language: An Approach to *A Tale of A Tub.*" *Style* 10 (1976): 28–40.

Landa, Louis A. *Swift and the Church of Ireland.* Oxford: Clarendon, 1954.

Lévi-Strauss, Claude. *Tristes Tropiques.* Trans. John Weightman and Doreen Weightman. New York: Antheneum, 1974.

Monk, Samuel H. "The Pride of Lemuel Gulliver." *Sewanee Review* 63 (1955): 48–71.

Pollak, Ellen. *The Poetics of Sexual Myth: Gender and Ideology in the Verse of Swift and Pope.* Chicago: U of Chicago P, 1985.

Reichert, John F. "Plato, Swift, and the Houyhnhnms." *Philological Quarterly* 47 (1968): 179–92.

Swift, Jonathan. *A Proposal for Correcting the English Tongue.* Ed. Herbert Davis, et al. Oxford: Basil Blackwell, 1939–68. Vol. 4 of *The Prose Works.* 14 vols.

———. *The Prose Works of Jonathan Swift.* Ed. Herbert Davis, et al. 14 vols. Oxford: Basil Blackwell, 1939–68.

Wyrick, Deborah Baker. *Jonathan Swift and the Vested Word.* Chapel Hill: U of North Carolina P, 1988.

Reader-Response Criticism
and
Gulliver's Travels

WHAT IS READER-RESPONSE CRITICISM?

Students are routinely asked in English courses for their reactions to texts they are reading. Sometimes there are so many different reactions that we may wonder whether everyone has read the same text. And some students respond so idiosyncratically to what they read that we say their responses are "totally off the wall."

Reader-response critics are interested in the variety of our responses. Reader-response criticism raises theoretical questions about whether our responses to a work are the same as its meanings, whether a work can have as many meanings as we have responses to it, and whether some responses are more valid than, or superior to, others. It asks us to pose the following questions: What have we internalized that helps us determine what is and what isn't "off the wall"? In other words, what is the wall, and what standards help us to define it?

Reader-response criticism also provides models that are useful in answering such questions. Adena Rosmarin has suggested that a work can be likened to an incomplete work of sculpture: to see it fully, we *must* complete it imaginatively, taking care to do so in a way that responsibly takes into account what is there. An introduction to several other models of reader-response theory will allow you to understand better the reader-oriented essay that follows as well as to see a variety of ways in which, as a reader-response critic, you might respond to literary works.

Reader-response criticism, which emerged during the 1970s, focuses on what texts do to, or in, the mind of the reader, rather than regarding a text as something with properties exclusively its own. A poem, Louise M. Rosenblatt wrote as early as 1969, "is what the reader lives through under the guidance of the text and experiences as relevant to the text." Rosenblatt knew her definition would be difficult for many to accept: "The idea that a *poem* presupposes a *reader* actively involved with a *text*," she wrote, "is particularly shocking to those seeking to emphasize the objectivity of their interpretations" (127).

Rosenblatt is implicitly referring to the formalists, the old "New Critics," when she speaks of supposedly objective interpreters shocked by the notion that readers help make poems. Formalists preferred to discuss "the poem itself," the "concrete work of art," the "real poem." And they refused to describe what a work of literature makes a reader "live through." In fact, in *The Verbal Icon* (1954), William K. Wimsatt and Monroe C. Beardsley defined as fallacious the very notion that a reader's response is part of the meaning of a literary work:

> The Affective Fallacy is a confusion between the poem and its *results* (what it *is* and what it *does*). . . . It begins by trying to derive the standards of criticism from the psychological effects of a poem and ends in impressionism and relativism. The outcome . . . is that the poem itself, as an object of specifically critical judgment, tends to disappear. (21)

Reader-response critics take issue with their formalist predecessors. Stanley Fish, author of a highly influential article entitled "Literature in the Reader: Affective Stylistics" (1970), argues that any school of criticism that would see a work of literature as an object, that would claim to describe what it *is* and never what it *does*, is guilty of misconstruing what literature and reading really are. Literature exists when it is read, Fish suggests, and its force is an affective force. Furthermore, reading is a temporal process. Formalists assume it is a spatial one as they step back and survey the literary work as if it were an object spread out before them. They may find elegant patterns in the texts they examine and reexamine, but they fail to take into account that the work is quite different to a reader who is turning the pages and being moved, or affected, by lines that appear and disappear as the reader reads.

In a discussion of the effect that a sentence penned by the seventeenth-century physician Thomas Browne has on a reader reading, Fish pauses to say this about his analysis and also, by extension, about the overall critical strategy he has largely developed: "Whatever is persuasive and illuminating about [it] . . . is the result of my substituting for one question — what does this sentence mean? — another, more operational question — what does this sentence do?" He then quotes a line from John Milton's *Paradise Lost,* a line that refers to Satan and the other fallen angels: "Nor did they not perceive their evil plight." Whereas more traditional critics might say that the "meaning" of the line is "They did perceive their evil plight," Fish relates the uncertain movement of the reader's mind *to* that half-satisfying interpretation. Furthermore, he declares that "the reader's inability to tell whether or not 'they' do perceive and his involuntary question . . . are part of the line's *meaning,* even though they take place in the mind, not on the page" (*Text* 26).

This stress on what pages *do* to minds pervades the writings of most, if not all, reader-response critics. Wolfgang Iser, author of *The Implied Reader* (1974) and *The Act of Reading: A Theory of Aesthetic Response* (1978), finds texts to be full of "gaps," and these gaps, or "blanks," as he sometimes calls them, powerfully affect the reader. The reader is forced to explain them, to connect what the gaps separate, literally to create in his or her mind a poem or novel or play that isn't *in* the text but that the text incites. Stephen Booth, who greatly influenced Fish, equally emphasizes what words, sentences, and passages "do." He stresses in his analyses the "reading experience that results" from a "multiplicity of organizations" in, say, a Shakespeare sonnet (*Essay* ix). Sometimes these organizations don't make complete sense, and sometimes they even seem curiously contradictory. But that is precisely what interests reader-response critics, who, unlike formalists, are at least as interested in fragmentary, inconclusive, and even unfinished texts as in polished, unified works. For it is the reader's struggle to *make sense* of a challenging work that reader-response critics seek to describe.

In *Self-Consuming Artifacts: The Experience of Seventeenth-Century Literature* (1972), Fish reveals his preference for literature that makes readers work at making meaning. He contrasts two kinds of literary presentation. By the phrase "rhetorical presentation," he describes literature that reflects and reinforces opinions that readers already hold; by "dialectical presentation," he refers to works that prod and provoke. A dialectical text, rather than presenting an opinion as if it were truth, challenges readers to discover truths on their own. Such a text may not even have the kind of symmetry that formalist critics seek. Instead of offering a "single, sustained argument," a dialectical text, or self-consuming artifact, may be "so arranged that to enter into the spirit and assumptions of any one of [its] . . . units is implicitly to reject the spirit and assumptions of the unit immediately preceding" (*Artifacts* 9). Such a text needs a reader-response critic to elucidate its workings. Another kind of critic is likely to try to explain why the units are unified and coherent, not why such units are contradicting and "consuming" their predecessors. The reader-response critic proceeds by describing the reader's way of dealing with the sudden twists and turns that character-ize the dialectical text, making the reader return to earlier passages and see them in an entirely new light.

"The value of such a procedure," Fish has written, "is predicated on the idea of meaning as *an event*," not as something "located (presumed to be embedded) *in* the utterance" or "verbal object as a thing in itself" (*Text* 28). By redefining meaning as an event, the reader-response critic once again locates meaning in time: the reader's time. A text exists and signifies while it is being read, and what it signifies or means will de-pend, to no small extent, on *when* it is read. (*Paradise Lost* had some meanings for a seventeenth-century Puritan that it would not have for a twentieth-century atheist.)

With the redefinition of literature as something that only exists meaningfully in the mind of the reader, with the redefinition of the lit-erary work as a catalyst of mental events, comes a concurrent redefini-tion of the reader. No longer is the reader the passive recipient of those ideas that an author has planted in a text. "The reader is *active*," Rosenblatt insists (123). Fish begins "Literature in the Reader" with a similar observation: "If at this moment someone were to ask, 'what are you doing,' you might reply, 'I am reading,' and thereby acknowledge that reading is . . . something *you do*" (*Text* 22). In "How To Recognize a Poem When You See One," he is even more provocative: "Interpret-ers do not decode poems: they make them" (*Text* 327). Iser, in focusing critical interest on the gaps in texts, on what is not expressed, similarly redefines the reader as an active maker. In an essay entitled "Interaction between Text and Reader," he argues that what is missing from a narra-tive causes the reader to fill in the blanks creatively.

Iser's title implies a cooperation between reader and text that is also implied by Rosenblatt's definition of a poem as "what the reader lives through under the guidance of the text." Indeed, Rosenblatt borrowed the term "transactional" to describe the dynamics of the reading pro-cess, which in her view involves interdependent texts and readers inter-acting. The view that texts and readers make poems together, though, is not shared by *all* interpreters generally thought of as reader-response critics. Steven Mailloux has divided reader-response critics into several categories, one of which he labels "subjective." Subjective critics, like David Bleich (or Norman Holland after his conversion by Bleich), assume what Mailloux call the "absolute priority of individual selves as creators of texts" (*Conventions* 31). In other words, these critics do not see the reader's response as one "guided" by the text but rather as one motivated by deep-seated, personal psychological needs. What they find in texts is, in Holland's phrase, their own "identity theme." Holland has argued that as readers we use "the literary work to symbolize and finally to replicate ourselves. We work out through the text our own characteristic patterns of desire" ("UNITY" 816).

Subjective critics, as you may already have guessed, often find themselves confronted with the following question: If all interpretation is a function of private, psychological identity, then why have so many readers interpreted, say, Shakespeare's *Hamlet* in the same way? Different subjective critics have answered the question differently. Holland simply has said that common identity themes exist, such as that involving an oedipal fantasy. Fish, who went through a subjectivist stage, has provided a different answer. In "Interpreting the *Variorum*," he argues that the "stability of interpretation among readers" is a function of shared "interpretive strategies." These strategies, which "exist prior to the act of reading and therefore determine the shape of what is read," are held in common by "interpretive communities" such as the one comprised by American college students reading a novel as a class assignment (*Text* 167, 171).

As I have suggested in the paragraph above, reader-response criticism is not a monolithic school of thought, as is assumed by some detractors who like to talk about the "School of Fish." Several of the critics mentioned thus far have, over time, adopted different versions of reader-response criticism. I have hinted at Holland's growing subjectivism as well as the evolution of Fish's own thought. Fish, having at first viewed meaning as the cooperative production of readers and texts, went on to become a subjectivist, and very nearly a "deconstructor" ready to suggest that all criticism is imaginative creation, fiction about literature, or *metafiction*. In developing the notion of interpretive communities, however, Fish has become more of a social, structuralist, reader-response critic; currently, he is engaged in studying reading communities and their interpretive conventions in order to understand the conditions that give rise to a work's intelligibility.

In spite of the gaps between reader-response critics and even between the assumptions that they have held at various stages of their respective careers, all try to answer similar questions and to use similar strategies to describe the reader's response to a given text. One question these critics are commonly asked has already been discussed: Why do individual readers come up with such similar interpretations if meaning is not embedded *in* the work itself? Other recurring, troubling questions include the following interrelated ones: Just who *is* the reader? (Or, to place the emphasis differently, Just who is *the* reader?) Aren't you reader-response critics just talking about your own idiosyncratic responses when you describe what a line from *Paradise Lost* "does" in and to "the reader's" mind? What about my responses? What if they're different? Will you be willing to say that all responses are equally valid?

Fish defines "the reader" in this way: "*the* reader is the *informed* reader." The informed reader is someone who is "sufficiently experienced as a reader to have internalized the properties of literary discourses, including everything from the most local of devices (figures of speech, etc.) to whole genres." And, of course, the informed reader is in full possession of the "semantic knowledge" (knowledge of idioms, for instance) assumed by the text (*Artifacts* 406).

Other reader-response critics use terms besides "the *informed* reader" to define "*the* reader," and these other terms mean slightly different things. Wayne Booth uses the phrase "the implied reader" to mean the reader "created by the work." (Only "by agreeing to play the role of this created audience," Susan Suleiman explains, "can an actual reader correctly understand and appreciate the work" [8].) Gerard Genette and Gerald Prince prefer to speak of "the narratee, . . . the necessary counterpart of a given narrator, that is, the person or figure who receives a narrative" (Suleiman 13). Like Booth, Iser employs the term "the implied reader," but he also uses "the educated reader" when he refers to what Fish calls the "informed" or "intended" reader. Thus, with different terms, each critic denies the claim that reader-response criticism might lead people to think that there are as many correct interpretations of a work as there are readers to read it.

As Mailloux has shown, reader-response critics share not only questions, answers, concepts, and terms for those concepts but also strategies of reading. Two of the basic "moves," as he calls them, are to show that a work gives readers something to do, and to describe what the reader does by way of response. And there are more complex moves as well. For instance, a reader-response critic might typically (1) cite direct references to reading in the text, in order to justify the focus on reading and show that the inside of the text is continuous with what the reader is doing; (2) show how other nonreading situations in the text nonetheless mirror the situation the reader is in ("Fish shows how in *Paradise Lost* Michael's teaching of Adam in Book XI resembles Milton's teaching of the reader throughout the poem"); and (3) show, therefore, that the reader's response is, or is perfectly analogous to, the topic of the story. For Stephen Booth, *Hamlet* is the tragic story of "an audience that cannot make up its mind." In the view of Roger Easson, Blake's *Jerusalem* "may be read as a poem about the experience of reading *Jerusalem*" (Mailloux, "Learning" 103).

In the first section of the essay that follows, Michael J. Conlon discusses the word *performance,* particularly its use by reader-response critics. Going back to Rosenblatt, who in her attacks on New Criticism, or formalism, urged English teachers to think of reading as a performing art and of their student readers as performers, Conlon moves forward via the ideas of Fish and Tompkins to the recent writings of Marie Maclean, who argues that each reading of a printed text is "a type of individual performance in which text and reader cooperate."

Conlon pauses to admit that Swift wouldn't have thought much of reader-response criticism in its more extreme, subjectivist forms. "The emphasis in [his] writing on reading as an activity governed by rules," plus his belief that an "implicit contract" governs the author-reader relationship, clash with the views of those who would see "the reader's response as a performance inspired exclusively by personal desires and needs, or what Norman Holland calls the reader's 'identity theme.'" Nonetheless, Conlon goes on to suggest, Swift would have accepted "the idea of a creative and judicious interaction of reader and text."

In the second section of his essay, Conlon turns to Swift's use of the words *perform* and *performance* in *Gulliver's Travels.* What he discovers is that, when they are not being used in their "more familiar social and theatrical contexts," they are used to refer to the "measurable behavior of machines, devices, animals, and persons." When used this way, they are used alongside words such as *operation* and *production,* words forming the emerging vocabulary of an increasingly scientific and technical society. Swift often combines the subjects of science and spectacle in such a way as to allow *perform* and *performance* to refer to theatrical and mechanistic behavior simultaneously. He connects science and spectacle, Conlon suggests, in order to satirically characterize the "bad science" of the so-called New Scientists of England as mere show, as grandiose speculation that often ultimately explains nothing.

The intricacies of Conlon's unfolding argument cannot be summarized here. But it may be helpful to keep in mind a point he raises early on and returns to late in the essay, namely, that in the classical and neo-classical periods a connection was made between travel, education, and science, and that for Swift the travel narrator was in many ways similar to the speculative New Scientist. Like the scientist, the traveler documenting heretofore unvisited lands is an authority whose truthfulness is not easily called into question, one who presents "facts" that his audience cannot easily verify themselves and who determines in advance what is valuable and worthy of notice. The bad scientist, moreover, like Gulliver the travelogue author, wants to do more than merely observe and describe: he wants his performance, in Gulliver's words, to convert, reform, and improve.

In Swift's view, then, *performance* can refer to a harmful act that a person or machine perpetrates on someone. When Gulliver's travelogue performance fails to have its intended effect on others, it turns around and hurts its author. As Gulliver "witnesses his book's failure to make any difference in the six months after its publication," he becomes "a misanthrope in Timon's manner." Performative storytelling ultimately leads him "to look upon himself with loathing, . . . to prefer the company of horses . . . , [and] to despair of the possibility of civilized life." Through Gulliver's "Letter to His Cousin Sympson" and the piece entitled "The Publisher to the Reader," Swift warns us against those who write and publish with too much affective intention and design.

Gulliver's failed travelogue, however, is not the same as Swift's *Gulliver's Travels,* and Gulliver's attitude toward his "dramatized reader" (conveyed at first through flattering terms of endearment but characterized ultimately by scornful disdain) is entirely different from the relationship between *Gulliver's Travels* and its "implied reader." Unlike Gulliver's dramatized reader, Swift's implied reader does not move through a world of clear cues and choices but, rather, through one characterized by "vexations, questions, apprehensions, duplicities, and doubts." In concluding, Conlon refers to the behavior of the reader implied by Swift's text as "a performance of understanding." That performance involves traveling an uncertain path through "devices of complication and indirection" such as "irony, parody, oxymoron, and paradox."

Thus, Conlon concludes, *Gulliver's Travels* is a performance, not in the sense of being a passionate spectacle but in a sense recently developed by reader-response critics. It is a text that sends us on a quest through a landscape in which all directions are provisional, in which all signposts point in several directions. The mission it gives us to perform — and subtly helps us to perform — is that of actively acquiring self-knowledge through reading.

Ross C Murfin

READER-RESPONSE CRITICISM: A SELECTED BIBLIOGRAPHY

Some Introductions to Reader-Response Criticism

Fish, Stanley E. "Literature in the Reader: Affective Stylistics." *New Literary History* 2 (1970): 123–62. Rpt. in *Is There a Text in This Class?* 21–67 and in Primeau 154–79.

Freund, Elizabeth. *The Return of the Reader: Reader-Response Criticism.* London: Methuen, 1987.

Holland, Norman N. "UNITY IDENTITY TEXT SELF." *PMLA* 90 (1975): 813–22.

Holub, Robert C. *Reception Theory: A Critical Introduction.* New York: Methuen, 1984.

Mailloux, Steven. "Learning to Read: Interpretation and Reader-Response Criticism." *Studies in the Literary Imagination* 12 (1979): 93–108.

———. "Reader-Response Criticism?" *Genre* 10 (1977): 413–31.

Rosenblatt, Louise M. "Towards a Transactional Theory of Reading." *Journal of Reading Behavior* 1 (1969): 31–47. Rpt. in Primeau 121–46.

Suleiman, Susan R. "Introduction: Varieties of Audience-Oriented Criticism." Suleiman and Crosman 3–45.

Tompkins, Jane P. "An Introduction to Reader-Response Criticism." Tompkins ix–xxiv.

Reader-Response Criticism in Anthologies and Collections

Garvin, Harry R., ed. *Theories of Reading, Looking, and Listening.* Lewisburg: Bucknell UP, 1981. See the essays by Cain and Rosenblatt.

Leitch, Vincent B. *American Literary Criticism from the Thirties to the Eighties.* New York: Columbia UP, 1988.

Primeau, Ronald, ed. *Influx: Essays on Literary Influence.* Port Washington: Kennikat, 1977. See the essays by Fish, Holland, and Rosenblatt.

Suleiman, Susan R., and Inge Crosman, eds. *The Reader in the Text: Essays on Audience and Interpretation.* Princeton: Princeton UP, 1980. See especially the essays by Culler, Iser, and Todorov.

Tompkins, Jane P., ed. *Reader-Response Criticism: From Formalism to Post-Structuralism.* Baltimore: Johns Hopkins UP, 1980. See especially the essays by Bleich, Fish, Holland, Prince, and Tompkins.

Reader-Response Criticism: Some Major Works

Bleich, David. *Subjective Criticism.* Baltimore: Johns Hopkins UP, 1978.

Booth, Stephen. *An Essay on Shakespeare's Sonnets.* New Haven: Yale UP, 1969.

Eco, Umberto. *The Role of the Reader.* Bloomington: Indiana UP, 1979.

Fish, Stanley Eugene. *Doing What Comes Naturally: Change, Rhetoric, and the Practice of Theory in Literary and Legal Studies.* Durham: Duke UP, 1989.

———. *Is There a Text in This Class? The Authority of Interpretive Communities.* Cambridge: Harvard UP, 1980. In this volume are collected most of Fish's most influential essays, including "Literature in the Reader: Affective Stylistics," "What It's Like to Read *L'Allegro* and *Il Penseroso*," "Interpreting the *Variorum*," "Is There a Text in This Class?" "How to Recognize a Poem When You See One," and "What Makes an Interpretation Acceptable?"

———. *Self-Consuming Artifacts: The Experience of Seventeenth-Century Literature.* Berkeley: U of California P, 1972.

———. *Surprised by Sin: The Reader in Paradise Lost.* 2nd ed. Berkeley: U of California P, 1971.

Holland, Norman N. *5 Readers Reading.* New Haven: Yale UP, 1975.

Iser, Wolfgang. *The Act of Reading: A Theory of Aesthetic Response.* Baltimore: Johns Hopkins UP, 1980.

———. *The Implied Reader: Patterns of Communication in Prose Fiction from Bunyan to Beckett.* Baltimore: Johns Hopkins UP, 1974.

Jauss, Hans Robert. *Toward an Aesthetic of Reception.* Trans. Timothy Bahti. Intro. Paul de Man. Minneapolis, U of Minnesota P, 1982.

Mailloux, Steven. *Interpretive Conventions: The Reader in the Study of American Fiction.* Ithaca: Cornell UP, 1982.

———. *Rhetorical Power.* Ithaca: Cornell UP, 1989.

Messent, Peter. *New Readings of the American Novel: Narrative Theory and Its Application.* New York: St. Martin's, 1990.

Prince, Gerald. *Narratology.* New York: Mouton, 1982.

Rabinowitz, Peter. *Before Reading: Narrative Conventions and the Politics of Interpretation.* Ithaca: Cornell UP, 1987.

Radway, Janice A. *Reading the Romance: Women, Patriarchy, and Popular Literature.* Chapel Hill: U of North Carolina P, 1984.

Rosenblatt, Louise M. *The Reader, the Text, the Poem: The Transactional Theory of the Literary Work.* Carbondale, IL: Southern Illinois UP, 1978.

Steig, Michael. *Stories of Reading: Subjectivity and Literary Understanding.* Baltimore: Johns Hopkins UP, 1989.

Exemplary Short Readings of Major Texts

Anderson, Howard. "*Tristram Shandy* and the Reader's Imagination." *PMLA* 86 (1971): 966–73.

Berger, Carole. "The Rake and the Reader in Jane Austen's Novels." *Studies in English Literature, 1500–1900* 15 (1975): 531–44.

Booth, Stephen. "On the Value of *Hamlet*." *Reinterpretations of English Drama: Selected Papers from the English Institute.* Ed. Norman Rabkin. New York: Columbia UP, 1969. 137–76.

Easson, Robert R. "William Blake and His Reader in *Jerusalem*." *Blake's Sublime Allegory.* Ed. Stuart Curran and Joseph A. Wittreich. Madison: U of Wisconsin P, 1973. 309–27.

Kirk, Carey H. "*Moby-Dick:* The Challenge of Response." *Papers on Language and Literature* 13 (1977): 383–90.

Leverenz, David. "Mrs. Hawthorne's Headache: Reading *The Scarlet Letter*." *The Scarlet Letter: A Case Study in Contemporary Criticism.* Ed. Ross C Murfin. Boston: Bedford–St. Martin's, 1991. 263–74.

Lowe-Evans, Mary. "Reading with a 'Nicer Eye': Responding to *Frankenstein*." *Mary Shelley, Frankenstein.* Ed. Johanna M. Smith. Case Studies in Contemporary Criticism Series. Ed. Ross C Murfin. Boston: Bedford–St. Martin's, 1992. 215–29.

Rosmarin, Adena. "Darkening the Reader: Reader-Response Criticism and *Heart of Darkness*." *Heart of Darkness: A Case Study in Contemporary Criticism.* Ed. Ross C Murfin. Boston: Bedford–St. Martin's, 1989. 148–69.

Reader-Oriented Approaches to Swift and *Gulliver's Travels*

Aikins, Janet E. "Reading 'with Conviction': Trial by Satire." *The Genres of "Gulliver's Travels."* Ed. Frederik N. Smith. Newark: U of Delaware P, 1990. 203–29.

Fox, Christopher. "The Myth of Narcissus in Swift's *Travels*." *Eighteenth-Century Studies* 20 (1986–87): 17–33; rpt. in *Reader Entrapment in Eighteenth-Century Literature*. Ed. Carl R. Kropf. New York: AMS P, 1992. 89–107.

Hammond, Brean. *Gulliver's Travels*. Philadelphia: Milton Keynes for Open UP, 1988.

McCrea, Brian. "Surprised by Swift: Entrapment and Escape in *A Tale of A Tub*." *Papers on Language and Literature* 18 (1982): 234–44.

Rawson, Claude J. *Gulliver and the Gentle Reader: Studies in Swift and Our Time*. London: Routledge, 1973.

Rodino, Richard H. "Varieties of Vexatious Experience in Swift and Others." *Papers on Language and Literature* 18 (1982): 325–47.

Smith, Frederik N. "The Danger of Reading Swift: The Double Binds of *Gulliver's Travels*." *Studies in the Literary Imagination* 17 (1984): 35–47; rpt. in *Reader Entrapment in Eighteenth-Century Literature*. Ed. Carl R. Kropf. New York: AMS P, 1992. 109–130.

Uphaus, Robert W. "*Gulliver's Travels, A Modest Proposal,* and the Problematic Nature of Meaning." *Papers on Language and Literature* 10 (1974): 268–278.

Other Work Referred to in "What Is Reader-Response Criticism?"

Wimsatt, William K., and Monroe C. Beardsley. *The Verbal Icon*. Lexington: U of Kentucky P, 1954. See especially the discussion of "The Affective Fallacy," with which reader-response critics have so sharply disagreed.

A READER-RESPONSE PERSPECTIVE

MICHAEL J. CONLON

Performance as Response in
Swift's *Gulliver's Travels*

I

The word *performance* has attracted considerable attention in recent critical writing. John Kronik, the editor of *PMLA,* introducing an issue of the journal devoted exclusively to *performance,* points out how the word has changed in meaning from *event* to *critical category* (425). *Performance* also holds particular significance for reader-response critics. In her introduction to *Reader-Response Criticism: From Formalism to Post-Structuralism* (1980), Jane P. Tompkins locates the earliest phases of this movement in I. A. Richards's work in the 1920s on "emotional response" and in the subsequent work of D. W. Harding and Louise Rosenblatt (x). Rosenblatt, writing in 1966 against the tendency of New Critics to treat "any literary work as an object . . . whose parts can be analyzed without reference . . . to the observer or reader" (1001), urges teachers of English to think of reading as a "Performing Art" and student-readers as performers:

> In the *teaching* of literature, then, we are basically helping our students to learn to perform in response to a text. In this respect we are perhaps closer to the voice teacher . . . than we are to the teacher of history or botany. The reader performs the poem or the novel, as the violinist performs the sonata. But the instrument on which the reader plays, and from which he evokes the work, is — himself. (1000)

Stanley Fish's influential 1970 article "Literature in the Reader: Affective Stylistics" also calls attention away from what the text means and directs it toward how the reader performs. The world of the text is a "world made up of words, constructed in large part by the reader himself as he performs grammatical actions" (34) and makes interpretive decisions and revisions in the process of negotiating each sentence of the text. More recently, Marie Maclean, in *Narrative as Performance* (1988), describes "each reading" of a printed text as "a type of individual performance in which text and reader cooperate" (10).

The emphasis in Jonathan Swift's writing on reading as an activity governed by rules and by an implicit contract between author and reader[1] causes concern for critics who see the reader's response as a performance inspired exclusively by personal desires and needs, or what Norman Holland calls the reader's "identity theme."[2] Nevertheless, Swift does make performance one of the principal subjects of *Gulliver's Travels* (1726). He satirizes the New Scientists and Virtuosi of his age by showing a series of ironic connections between performances in the sciences and performances on stages and in texts. Swift also extends this satire on performance in the sciences to the performances of travel writers like Lemuel Gulliver — set on converting his readers and mending the world.

After pointing out these different targets of Swift's satire in *Gulliver's Travels,* I shall argue that while Swift would reject a subjectivist version of how readers perform, he would accept the idea of a creative and judicious interaction of reader and text. Through the contrast between Gulliver's single-minded "dramatized" reader (frequently addressed as his "Gentle" reader) and the "implied" or actual reader of the text, Swift identifies exemplary response in his implied reader with a *performance of understanding* that exceeds the various ritual, mechanical, and theatrical performances Swift satirizes over the course of Gulliver's narrative. A performance of understanding occurs whenever the reader and text act creatively on each other to produce a more subtle perception of the double meanings of Gulliver's final misanthropy.

II

The terms *performance* and *perform* occur in some twenty different contexts in Gulliver's narrative. On the one hand, Gulliver applies the word *performance* to the measurable behavior of machines, devices, animals, and persons. Together with *performance,* he uses words such as *operation, production, contrivance, observation, information, description,* and *demonstration*. All of these words, Frederik N. Smith points out, characterize the language of the so-called New Science in the eighteenth century, and they appear repeatedly in the pages of the *Philosoph-*

---

[1] Judith C. Mueller explains the idea of a "reading contract" in Swift's writing and discusses this in relation to modern theories of reading in her unpublished dissertation. See especially her introduction.

[2] Holland explains his theory of interpretation as a function of identity in his 1975 article "UNITY IDENTITY TEXT SELF."

ical Transactions of the Royal Society ("Scientific Discourse" 145). On the other hand, Gulliver uses *performance* in its more familiar social and theatrical contexts in characterizing entertainments, diversions, rituals, and various kinds of prescribed or conventionalized activities and ceremonies like Gulliver's reading in Lilliput of the "Articles and Conditions of his Liberty." Critics have long recognized Swift's parody of Royal Society scientific jargon, and most readers notice the theatrical images and metaphors in Gulliver's narrative. What may not be so apparent are the ironic connections Swift makes between *performance* as science and *performance* as theater. I turn now to a discussion of this material and the context it provides for understanding Swift's idea of the reader's response, a subject I return to in Part III of this essay.

Seventeen years ago Hugh Kenner began a discussion of "objectivity" in the novel by describing Lemuel Gulliver's mind as "busy in an idle way, like [the mind] of a Royal Society virtuoso." Gulliver tells us "only the things an observer would have experienced," based on the "discrete report of the senses," and he tells them "in the order in which he would have experienced them" (4). Gulliver's empirical "method," Kenner notes, "resembles the method of the stage, where we see what we see and nothing more" (5). A striking example of this convergence of the empirical and the theatrical occurs in Gulliver's description of his first hour in Lilliput:

> [A]bout four yards from me, over-against my right Ear, I heard a Knocking for above an Hour, like People at work; when turning my Head that Way, as well as the Pegs and Strings would permit me, I saw a Stage erected about a Foot and a half from the Ground, capable of holding four of the Inhabitants, with two or three Ladders to mount it: From whence one of them, who seemed to be a Person of Quality, made me a long Speech, whereof I understood not one Syllable. . . . He appeared to be of a middle Age, and taller than any of the other three who attended him; whereof one was a Page, who held his Train, and seemed to be somewhat longer than my middle Finger; the other two stood one on each side to support him. He acted every part of an Orator; and I could observe many Periods of Threatnings, and others of Promises, Pity, and Kindness. I answered in a few Words, but in the most submissive Manner lifting up my left Hand and both mine Eyes to the Sun, as calling him for a Witness; and being almost famished with Hunger, having not eaten a Morsel for some Hours before I left the Ship, I found the Demands of Nature so strong upon me, that I could not forbear shewing my Impatience

(perhaps against the strict Rules of Decency) by putting my Finger frequently on my Mouth, to signify that I wanted food. (43)

Gulliver takes his readers in this passage from what he hears and sees to what he feels: hunger. And he does so in the deadpan manner and detached tone of an encyclopedist. He expresses no awareness of the quality of his experience and the absurd prospect it presents to the reader of a man lying on the ground, fixed faceup like a specimen by pinions and packthreads, kissing his finger in front of hundreds of little people. Remarkably, Gulliver's principal concern, other than hunger, involves a question of etiquette. The Lilliputians, for their part, turn the occasion into theater, erecting a stage at the side of Gulliver's skull and sending forth an orator. Kenner's original insight into the resemblance between Gulliver's empirical method and the "method of the stage" ignores the ironic incongruity of that resemblance so evident in this particular scene. Gulliver's flatly empirical form of description clashes with the theatrical content of his experience. This view of Gulliver at the outset of his story as both spectator and spectacle provides Swift's readers with an important context for subsequent ironic connections he will make between scientific/technical performances and theatrical/rhetorical performances in Gulliver's visits to Lilliput and Brobdingnag.

As spectator in Lilliput, in a city that reminds him of the "painted Scene of a City in a Theatre" (48), Gulliver witnesses diversions, entertainments, and performances of various kinds, including a "Ceremony . . . performed in his Majesty's great chamber of State" by "Candidates" who display their "Agility" at "*leaping*" over and "*creeping*" under a stick (56). Swift repeatedly calls our attention to the parallels between the Lilliputians' fastidious devotion to the performance of rituals and military exercises and their "great perfection in Mechanicks," mathematics, and logistics. Gulliver remarks at length, for example, on the extraordinary "performance" of his hosts in constructing an "Engine" to move his sleeping body from the shore to the capital city. Once "lodge[d]" inside an "ancient Temple," he finds himself an object of wonder and "Astonishment" to the people — indeed, a spectacle — and he learns, too, that his freedom in Lilliput will depend on how well he performs the tasks listed in the "Articles and Conditions of his Liberty." As the Lilliputians read the Articles, Gulliver "swear[s] to the Performance of them" by performing an absurd ritual: "I was demanded . . . to hold my right Foot in my left Hand, to place the middle Finger of my right Hand on the Crown of my Head, and my Thumb on the Tip of my

right Ear" (59). As this ritual makes clear, Gulliver's identity throughout his stay in Lilliput resembles Thomas Hobbes's idea of the public
person as actor: his "words and actions" are "owned by those whom
[he] represent[s]" (105).

Entertainments and diversions similar to those Gulliver encounters
in Lilliput occur in his voyage to Brobdingnag. His first master carries
Gulliver about as a "public Spectacle." He hires a "Cryer, to give Notice
through the Town, of a strange Creature to be seen at the Sign of the
Green *Eagle*, not so big as a *Splacnuck*, . . . and in every Part of the Body
resembling an human Creature; could speak several Words, and perform an Hundred diverting Tricks" (103). The historical context of this
episode shows once again a connection between scientific and theatrical
ideas of performance. "Gulliver's public exhibition by the farmer," as
Aline Mackenzie Taylor pointed out some thirty-five years ago, reflects
the "universal craze for 'monsters' and curiosities which sustained the
English showmen and their rarities, both animal and human" (29).[3]
More to my point, Taylor's citations show a working connection between the interests of the London showmen and the Royal Society Virtuosi. Indeed, the London shows functioned simultaneously as sources
of public diversion and as handy storehouses of scientific curiosities and
specimens, and it is to the "scientific curiosity of members" of the Royal
Society that "we owe many of the fragmentary records of popular spectacles that have come down to us" (29).

Swift makes a similar connection between science and spectacle in
Gulliver's story by making Gulliver himself the subject of intense scientific examination and philosophical speculation shortly after he leaves
the farmer and his life as a sideshow freak. When the farmer sells
Gulliver to the royal court of Brobdingnag the king immediately assumes that Gulliver is a "piece of Clockwork" — an instrument the age
identified with high performance and superhuman perfection. But the
king's scholars, "after much debate," determine that Gulliver is only
"*Lusus Naturae*," or a freak of nature. In reporting this episode,
Gulliver characterizes the "Determination" of the king's scholars as follows:

> [This is] a Determination exactly agreeable to the Modern Philos-
> ophy of *Europe:* whose Professors, disdaining the old Evasion of

[3]Dennis Todd expands on Taylor's research on the significance of the shows and
diversions of London. He develops a reading of *Gulliver's Travels* that centers on the
"exhibitions of prodigies and monsters." See Todd, "The Hairy Maid at the Harpsichord."

occult Causes, whereby the Followers of *Aristotle* endeavour in vain to disguise their Ignorance; have invented this wonderful Solution of all Difficulties, to the unspeakable Advancement of human Knowledge. (108)

Swift satirizes the New Scientists here by putting in the mouths of the "three great Scholars" a kind of nonexplanation. While Swift was not, Douglas Patey points out, predisposed simply to dismiss science, he did take issue with *bad* science, and he often found, as he does in this episode, the "new scientists . . . as guilty as the old of using insignificant speech to frame explanations that do not explain" (814). The examination of Gulliver as a freak of nature also reenacts the earlier display of Gulliver as performer and freak by the farmer. Even the naming of Gulliver as *lusus,* meaning *sport* or *freak,* calls to mind the related name *ludius,* meaning *stage-player* or *performer.* These repeated connections between scientific demonstration and carnival performance in Part Two anticipate the most dramatic example in *Gulliver's Travels* of Swift's satire on the New Scientists: Gulliver's voyage in Part Three to Laputa.

In Gulliver's description of the flying island of Laputa and its operations, Swift creates an elaborate parody, complete with diagram and measurements, of the scientific reports that appeared in the pages of the *Philosophical Transactions of the Royal Society.*[4] Swift associates his flying island not only with Royal Society writings, but also with flying islands familiar to seventeenth-century theater audiences. I have in mind plays such as William Strode's satire, entitled *The Floating Island,* performed at Oxford in 1636. Gulliver actually calls Laputa the *Floating Island* (156). And Gulliver's descriptions of Laputa owe something to another seventeenth-century performance: Ben Jonson's masque *The Fortunate Isles and Their Union,* which includes an account of a flying castle inhabited by Rosicrucians (members of a secret order devoted to the study of religious mysticism) who busy themselves with impossible projects.[5]

Viewed in the context of theater, the flying island of Laputa would also have reminded Swift's readers of the writings of virtuosi and scientists who describe the natural world as a stage for countless wonders and spectacles, many of them susceptible of scientific control. Simon Schaffer, in his "Natural Philosophy and Public Spectacle in the Eighteenth

[4]Marjorie Nicolson and Nora Mohler provide an important historical context for Swift's parody of scientific papers. See "The Scientific Background of Swift's Voyage to Laputa."

[5]Sidney Gottlieb identifies these allusions in his "The Emblematic Background of Swift's Flying Island."

Century," shows how scientists and assorted virtuosi "could use their control over [the] active powers [of nature] to construct a *theatre* with all the appeal and all the dangers that implied" (14). As the Laputans could play God through their control of the island, so could the New Scientists through their experiments. Control in the natural order, moreover, inevitably leads to the kinds of arbitrary and despotic controls in the social order that Swift illustrates through Laputa's abuses of the people of Balnibarbi.

Life on Laputa combines the performance of precise mathematical equations with daily, ritual performances by the Laputans on musical instruments. The point of Swift's satire here depends in part on the traditional distinction between the sciences of demonstration and the so-called low sciences. "From Aristotle's time until the seventeenth century, mathematics — in particular geometry — was the paradigm of demonstrative science. Other subjects . . . might be assimilated to the methods of geometry, most notably . . . some parts of physics, and . . . the theoretical part of music" (Patey 817). Swift, however, shows the new scientists of Laputa combining mathematics, not with the theoretical part of music, but with *musica practica*. In effect, they combine science and showmanship in a manner reminiscent of the accounts of the public performances of eighteenth-century astronomers and electrical philosophers (Schaffer 6). Just as the island itself absurdly combines the operations of a military weapon, a scientific instrument, and a theatrical event, Laputan knowledge combines a genius for mathematical demonstration and an obsessive attachment to musical performance. Indeed, as Gulliver emphasizes, the Laputans "had their ears adapted to hear the Musick of the Spheres" (157). Unmistakably, the Laputans in all their folly, like so many of the New Scientists, represent for Swift a curious throwback to the errors of an earlier generation of scientists — specifically, to the "mystical musicology of . . . thinkers" such as Johannes Kepler (1571–1630), the renowned German astronomer and "last great scientist to believe in [that same] literal music of the spheres the Laputans claim to hear" (Patey 818). The fate of the Laputans, isolated and incapable of living in the world, also foreshadows the fate of Lemuel Gulliver after the publication of his *Travels*.

Scientific and theatrical ideas of performance engage the reader throughout Gulliver's narrative. They occur in Gulliver's frequent reenactments of events within the narrative, such as his performance in his little boat for the queen of Brobdingnag (a reenactment of his actual voyaging), in the projects of the "artists" at the Grand Academy of Lagado (including the experimental conversations performed with *things* at the School of Languages), in the performances of the magicians in Glubbdubdrib, in the close scrutiny of human performance by the Houyhnhnms, and even in the disrobing Gulliver performs in chapter III of Part Four that confirms what the Houyhnhnms already believe:

> My Master observed the whole Performance with great Signs of Curiosity and Admiration. He took up all my Cloaths in his Pastern, one Piece after another and examined them diligently; he then stroaked my Body very gently, and looked round me several Times; after which he said, it was plain I must be a perfect *Yahoo;* but that I differed very much from the rest of my Species, in the Whiteness, and Smoothness of my Skin, my want of Hair in several Parts of my Body, the Shape and Shortness of my Claws behind and before, and my Affectation of walking continually on my two hinder Feet. He desired to see no more; and gave me leave to put on my Cloaths again, for I was shuddering with Cold. (218)

Gulliver reenacts this scene in chapter VIII when he strips himself "stark naked" to go swimming and attracts the attention of a "Female *Yahoo* standing behind a bank" (242). Her pursuit and passionate embrace of Gulliver convince him that he is "a real Yahoo, in every Limb and Feature" (242). In both of these episodes Gulliver's impulse to show off for his hosts results in some form of mortification. Gulliver characteristically seeks proof of his worth and wisdom in his "outworks," in his "powers" or his capacity to perform various "wonders" which, to his dismay, have the effect of diminishing his worth in the eyes of his hosts. This happens most dramatically in Part Two when Gulliver offers the king of Brobdingnag the formula for gunpowder — after giving a detailed account of its destructive powers. The king responds with horror and dismay, calling Gulliver an "impotent and groveling . . . Insect" (134).

The narrative frequently and ironically turns back on Gulliver in this way to comment on the tendency in society to make performance alone the most important measure of what the king of Brobdingnag sarcastically styles "human Grandeur." Performance, as the king recognizes, has nothing to do with truth or falsehood, and everything to do with desire and power. That such "Grandeur" can be performed or "mimicked" at all, the King tells Gulliver, makes it all the more "contemptible" (111). Swift's treatment of performance, then, relates directly to his satire on the spectacle of human pride and on what Thomas Hobbes calls that "general inclination of all mankind, a perpetual and restless desire of power after power, that ceaseth only in death" (64).

III

Swift's representations of the New Science in the context of different ideas of performance parallel Swift's ironic handling of Gulliver's narrative. Gulliver's intentions in writing his *Travels* change significantly after his return to England. Earlier, after leaving the Houyhnhnms, he says that he has chosen "to relate plain Matter of Fact in the simplest Manner . . . because [his] principal Design was to inform" his readers (262). This intention suits his aim as travel writer and reminds us, as well, of the associations the age made between travel books and science. John Locke, for example, uses "particulars" from the reports of travelers to frame general conclusions about human nature in his *Essay on Human Understanding* (Patey 825). And it's a commonplace that the eighteenth century revives the connections in Greek philosophy between travel, education, and science. Royal Society committees frequently scrutinized travel books, and in the public mind the figure of the traveler-scientist seemed nothing less than heroic.[6]

Jenny Mezciems points out, however, that for Swift the traveler-scientist is also a potentially "dangerous figure in a world where science takes responsibility for itself. The traveler becomes an authority by virtue of his unique personal experiences, presenting facts that cannot easily be questioned, telling tales that cannot be verified. . . . The traveler sets his own standards and creates his own horizons; he also begins to determine what is valuable . . . and to direct the requirements of society and the tastes of his readers" (276). Michael Adas, in his history of the "shifting views of non-western people," also comments on the power of travel authors over the reading public. He points out that the emphasis earlier writers placed on the gathering and communicating of information gives way in the eighteenth century to a new emphasis on the "interpretation and [application] of the accounts of overseas societies" to advance public policy or support a favored ideology. "Authors [now make] selective

---

[6] In *Establishing the New Science,* Michael Hunter refers to the preoccupation of the Society's Committee for Correspondence in 1664 with travel books. His reprint of the "Minutes and Reports of Committees of the Royal Society, 1663–5" includes a list of Books of Voyages consulted by the committee (118).

and often highly questionable use of materials on overseas societies to construct models for Europeans to emulate" (70). A similar shift in emphasis occurs in Gulliver's narrative. He cannot rest content with the intention simply to inform his readers; he also wants to determine the prerequisites of society, to make a model for people to emulate, and, in the case of his readers — I emphasize Gulliver's own words — to *convert, reform,* and *improve* them.

Gulliver's project to convert people and set standards for their behavior overturns his original intention to educate himself and his readers. The objective, empirical narrative we begin reading in Part One turns out to be another performance.[7] The narrative changes before our eyes into another incongruous mix of science and theatrics. And in the book's last pages, Swift distances himself from Gulliver by making *Gulliver's Travels* a parody of the kind of travel book (frequently published in this period) that uses its account of remote societies to shape public policy and influence people's behavior.

Swift also distances himself from Gulliver's project by fashioning unmistakable connections between Gulliver's performance as travel writer and storyteller and Gulliver's psychotic misanthropy. In performing the task of piecing together the story of his conversion to the perfection of the Houyhnhnms and then finding the world indifferent to his cause, Gulliver languishes. By the time he sits down to write his bill of complaint in "A Letter . . . to His Cousin Sympson" (27–31), he displays a profound sense of despair as well as signs of madness. Prior to the publication of his book, most readers would agree, his misanthropy falls short of the radical misanthropy Swift identified with Timon of Athens. But when he witnesses his book's failure to make any difference in the six months after its publication, Gulliver becomes a misanthrope in Timon's manner.[8] In this sense, in the language of J. L. Austin, Gulliver's story is not so much *constative,* representing the world as it is or describing "the way things are"; in a more important sense, his story

[7] Swift's earliest readers frequently call *Gulliver's Travels* a *performance,* at that time a common synonym for any written composition. The anonymous author of "A Letter from a Clergyman to his Friend, with an Account of Lemuel Gulliver" (1726) justifies his harsh attack on Swift's character and writing by calling the *Travels* a public "performance" and thus subject to the "various Opinions, Inclinations, Interests or Apprehensions" of its readers (5–6).

[8] In a letter dated September 29, 1725, from Swift to Alexander Pope, frequently cited by critics of *Gulliver's Travels,* Swift says: "I have got Materials Towards a Treatis proving the falsity of that Definition *animal rationale;* and to show it should be only *rationis capax.* Upon this great foundation of Misanthropy (though not Timon's manner) The Whole building of my Travels is erected" (*Corresp.* 3: 103).

is *performative:* its language, brilliantly joined by Swift to Gulliver's final expressions of misanthropy in the Sympson letter, "makes something happen" to Gulliver.[9] Storytelling leads Gulliver to look upon himself with loathing; it leads him to prefer the company of horses to the companionship of his wife, children, and neighbors and leads him to despair of the possibility of civilized life. He now spends at least four hours each day in the company of his horses, where he will remain fully convinced of the folly of his former "visionary Schemes [of reformation] for ever" (31).

Gulliver's Travels, therefore, turns out to be a story about the dangers and risks of telling stories to mend the world, and like so many of Swift's parodies of performative texts — sermons, proposals, projects, voyages, and arguments — this work also turns out to be a critique of its own creation.[10]

The risks writers take, of course, inevitably include the risk of rejection by their readers. Gulliver's "Letter to His Cousin Sympson" emphasizing what he considers to be errors in the production and reception of his book singles out, as well, the unsatisfactory responses of his reader. Throughout the body of his narrative, written months before his letter to Sympson, Gulliver had assumed a close, almost affectionate relationship with his reader, dramatizing the reader through words of polite regard such as "gentle," "curious," "judicious," "courteous," "indulgent," and "candid." The reader Gulliver cultivates and dramatizes in his text enjoys the author's gracious gestures of good will and shares the author's loyalty to England. This reader would also prefer not to be "trouble[d] . . . with the particular Account[s]" (84), accepts Gulliver's repeated claims that he *strictly adhere[s] to Truth* (262), and shows little patience with either difficulty or contradiction. Indeed, Gulliver repeatedly promises not to trouble or tax his reader with too many details. Unlike the divergent thinker, who cannot get *enough* detail and variety

[9] I take this formulation from J. Hillis Miller's comment on the "performative" aspect of literature in an interview conducted by Martin Heusser and Harold Schweizer and published in Miller, *Hawthorne & History.* Miller comments as follows: "As long as you see literature as purely constative, as doing no more than making statements about the world, about the way things are, then it's capable of being reduced to reflection or representation. But as soon as you see in literature the performative aspect, the way the writing, publication, reading of a work of literature by anyone at any time makes something happen, in however small a way, then it has escaped from the control of its context" (153).

[10] J. Hillis Miller makes a similar point about *Oedipus the King:* in "putting together" the facts of his life, Oedipus creates his tragedy. "*Oedipus the King* is a story about the awful danger of storytelling. Storytelling in this case makes something happen with a vengeance. It leads the storyteller to condemn, blind, and exile himself, and it leads his mother-wife, Jocasta, to kill herself." See Miller, "Narrative."

and who recognizes both similarity and difference within a single frame of reference,[11] Gulliver dramatizes a convergent reader who takes a single-minded view of the traveler's experience.

But Gulliver's feelings about this reader change just as his feelings about himself change after living with his beloved Houyhnhnms. Near the end of his stay with them he confesses that even the "Reflection of [his] own Form in a Lake or Fountain" fills him with "Horror and detestation" of himself (251). Six months after the publication of his *Travels*, Gulliver, still full of loathing for himself and his kind, considers his once gentle and friendly reader another Yahoo, a detestable creature totally resistant to performing the kinds of "Reformations, [Gulliver had] firmly counted upon" (29) after the publication of his book. He ends his "letter" to his Cousin Sympson by renouncing his reader and all "such visionary Schemes for ever" (31).

Swift also distances himself from Gulliver's dramatized reader. The actual text of the *Travels*, unlike the text Gulliver intends, implies a different kind of reader and a different idea of performance. I shall call this implied reader's behavior a *performance of understanding*,[12] a response to the text that reflects the reader's capacity to think divergently and to grasp the double perspectives Swift brings to Gulliver's experience.

Throughout my discussion of performance in *Gulliver's Travels* I have emphasized the ironic incongruities and duplicities in the connections Swift makes between performance in the sciences and performance on stages. Gulliver's mock-objective style frequently clashes with the theatrical content of his narrative; the technical and mathematical precision of the Lilliputians ironically goes hand-in-hand with their obsessive performances at court to win recognition, status, and power, and in Brobdingnag Gulliver becomes both carnival freak and scientific specimen. The flying island turns out to be both scientific wonder and stage machine. Even Gulliver's own travel book, despite its author's claim to

[11] Frederik N. Smith makes a similar distinction between, in his phrasing, the "characterized" and "implied" readers of Gulliver's text in "The Dangers of Reading Swift: The Double Binds of *Gulliver's Travels*." Janet E. Aikins infers from Gulliver's narrative three identities for the implied reader in "Reading 'with Conviction.'" For the distinction between convergent and divergent thinking, see J. P. Guilford, "Creativity: Its Measurement and Development." I discuss these terms in the context of reading eighteenth-century parody in "Teaching and Parody in Eighteenth-Century Poetry," in *Teaching Eighteenth-Century Poetry*, ed. Christopher Fox.

[12] I take this phrasing from Howard Gardner, *The Unschooled Mind* (9). In his discussion of how students learn, he distinguishes *performances of understanding* from "*rote, ritualistic, or conventional performances*," which occur when students simply take in and throw back "the particular facts, concepts, or problem sets they have been taught."

have written an objective, empirical document worthy of scrutiny by the Royal Society, turns out to be another performance, intended to convert readers to Gulliver's "mad" worship of the Houyhnhnms. Everything in *Gulliver's Travels,* as Swift's readers have repeatedly pointed out over the years, looks double.

Unlike Gulliver's dramatized, single-minded reader who grows impatient over particulars and complications, Swift's implied reader must move through a world full of vexations, questions, apprehensions, duplicities, and doubts. The actual text of the *Travels* resists the kind of convergent, unreflective reading Gulliver expects from his "gentle" reader. The perspectives of Part Four, for example, are always reversible and never decidable. This is not to say that any reading will do. It does mean that we will be frustrated, as countless readers in the past have been, if we insist on reducing Gulliver's experience to a single, fixed perspective. If we accept the argument that Gulliver is simply mad, we must accept our own world as sane, with all of its frightening parallels to the world of the Yahoos. But if we accept the view of our world as mad and corrupt in the way Gulliver sees it, we must contend with a Gulliver who "converse[s]" with his horses "at least four Hours every Day" (261).

Because the text of Swift's *Travels* never lets the implied reader rest with one angle of vision, because it relies so much on such devices of complication and indirection as irony, parody, oxymoron, and paradox, the implied reader must forego the comforts of fixed positions and final answers so typical in the history of opposing readings of Swift and characterized by the late James L. Clifford as the "hard" and "soft" schools of *Gulliver's Travels* criticism.[13] The implied reader must even give up, as Claude Rawson so aptly puts it, "the comforts of that author-reader complicity on which much satiric rhetoric depends," because even if we know that "Swift is making a more moderate attack on mankind than Gulliver, Gulliver's view hovers damagingly over it all." And even if "the book says we are better than the Yahoos," the book also "does not allow us to be too sure of the fact" (29).

If the analogy between reading books and reading people holds any merit, the proper counterpart to the implied, exemplary reader in Gulliver's story is the figure of Don Pedro de Mendez, the Portuguese

---

[13] Clifford used the terms "hard" and "soft" to describe the division between interpretations of Swift's "basic message" in *Gulliver's Travels.* By "hard" Clifford means "an interpretation that stresses the shock and difficulty of the work, with almost tragic overtone, while by 'soft' [he means] the tendency to find comic passages and compromise solutions." See his "Gulliver's Fourth Voyage" in Works Cited.

sea captain who rescues Gulliver after his banishment from the island of the Houyhnhnms. In spite of Gulliver's hostility and ingratitude, Mendez reads Gulliver's character with remarkable wisdom and understanding. While fully accepting Gulliver's "mad" and hostile behavior and taking sensible measures to prevent Gulliver from harming himself, Mendez returns Gulliver *gratis* to Lisbon, where he continues to care for him and arranges for Gulliver's final journey to England.

The name Mendez was closely associated with the community of Sephardic Jews in eighteenth-century London. And in the popular mind of Swift's age, a London Jew from Portugal named Mendez would have been thought of as an outsider and a member of a caste generally held in contempt.[14] But the name Mendez is derived from the Hebrew word *Menachem,* meaning *comforter,* and Swift's readers also would have identified Don Pedro de Mendez with the figure of the Good Samaritan in Luke 10:29 (Geracht 46). Just as the Sephardic Jew and the Good Samaritan are treated as outsiders, Gulliver treats Don Pedro as an outsider; he even looks upon him with contempt as another European Yahoo. But Gulliver also makes the concession that Don Pedro is a man of "very good *human* Understanding" (260), emphasis Swift's). This remark, together with Don Pedro's humane behavior, leaves the understanding reader with another double meaning: Don Pedro is both Yahoo and Samaritan, outsider and comforter, animal and angel. Swift's text, moreover, does not allow the reader to let go completely of either the beastlike or godlike side of this Mendez. To choose one or the other is to be caught in another convergent reading of the text. Rather, the text keeps the reader off balance and vexed about the nature of mankind, always, as Swift's friend Alexander Pope puts it in *An Essay on Man* (1733), "[i]n doubt to deem himself a God, or Beast" (Epistle II, 1.8).

Precarious counterbalances of this kind preclude notions of reading as simple rendition or rote performance, but they inspire the examples of discriminating, sensitive and divergent reading one finds in the history of readers' responses to *Gulliver's Travels,* responses so rich and varied as to command their own set of categories and to comprise a significant dimension of the book's larger meaning.[15]

---

[14] This conclusion owes much to the illuminating account of the significance of the name Mendez by Maurice A. Geracht in "Pedro De Mendez."

[15] Richard H. Rodino discusses the history of readers' responses to *Gulliver's Travels* as significant to its meaning in " 'Splendide Mendax': Authors, Characters, and Readers in *Gulliver's Travels.*"

WORKS CITED

Adas, Michael. *Machines as the Measure of Men: Science, Technology, and Ideologies of Western Dominance.* Ithaca: Cornell UP, 1989.

Aikins, Janet E. "Reading 'with Conviction': Trial by Satire." *The Genres of "Gulliver's Travels."* Ed. Frederik N. Smith. Newark: U of Delaware, 1990. 203–29.

Austin, J. L. *How to Do Things with Words.* Ed. J. O. Urmson and Marina Sbisa. 2nd ed. Cambridge, MA: Harvard UP, 1975.

Clifford, James L. "Gulliver's Fourth Voyage: 'Hard' and 'Soft' Schools of Interpretation." *Quick Springs of Sense: Studies in the Eighteenth Century.* Ed. Larry S. Champion. Athens: U of Georgia P, 1974. 33–49.

Conlon, Michael J. "Teaching and Parody in Eighteenth-Century Poetry." *Teaching Eighteenth-Century Poetry.* Ed. Christopher Fox. New York: AMS P, 1990. 47–59.

Fish, Stanley. "Literature in the Reader: Affective Stylistics." *New Literary History* 2 (1970): 123–62. Rpt. as ch. 1 of *Is There a Text in This Class?: The Authority of Interpretive Communities.* Cambridge, MA: Harvard UP, 1980. 21–67.

Gardner, Howard. *The Unschooled Mind: How Children Think and How Schools Should Teach.* New York: Basic Books, 1991.

Geracht, Maurice A. "Pedro De Mendez: Marrano Jew and Good Samaritan in Swift's *Voyages.*" *Swift Studies* 5 (1990): 38–52.

Gottlieb, Sidney. "The Emblematic Background of Swift's Flying Island." *Swift Studies* 1 (1986): 24–31.

Guilford, J. P. "Creativity: Its Measurement and Development." *A Creative Behavior Guidebook.* Ed. Sidney J. Parnes and Harold F. Harding. New York: Scribners, 1967. 151–68.

Hobbes, Thomas. *Leviathan or The matter, Forme and Power of A Commonwealth, Ecclesiastical and Civil.* Ed. Michael Oakeshott. Oxford: Basil Blackwell, [1946].

Hunter, Michael. *Establishing the New Science: The Experience of the Early Royal Society.* Woodbridge, Eng.: Boydell, 1989.

Kenner, Hugh. *Joyce's Voices.* Berkeley: U of California P, 1978.

Kronik, John. Editor's Note. *PMLA* 107 (1992): 425.

"A Letter from a Clergyman to his Friend, with an Account of Captain Lemuel Gulliver." 1726. Augustan Reprint Society Publication no. 143. Los Angeles: U of California P, 1970.

Maclean, Marie. *Narrative as Performance: The Baudelairean Experiment.* New York: Routledge, 1988.

Mezciems, Jenny. "Swift's Praise of Gulliver: Some Renaissance Background to the *Travels.*" *The Character of Swift's Satire: A Revised Focus.* Ed. Claude Rawson. Newark: U of Delaware P, 1983. 245–81.

Miller, J. Hillis. *Hawthorne & History: Defacing It.* Cambridge: Basil Blackwell, 1991.

———. "Narrative." *Critical Terms for Literary Study.* Ed. Frank Lentricchia and Thomas McLaughlin. Chicago: U of Chicago P, 1990. 66–79.

Mueller, Judith C. "The Reading Contract in Jonathan Swift's Political and Religious Satire." Diss. State U of New York at Binghamton, 1991. 1–25.

Nicolson, Marjorie, and Nora Mohler. "The Scientific Background of Swift's Voyage to Laputa." *Annals of Science* 2 (1937): 299–334.

Patey, Douglas Lane. "Swift's Satire on 'Science' and the Structure of *Gulliver's Travels.*" *ELH* 58 (1991): 809–39.

Pope, Alexander. *An Essay on Man.* Ed. Maynard Mack. London: Methuen, 1982. Vol. 3, pt. 1, of *The Poems of Alexander Pope.* The Twickenham Edition. Gen. ed. John Butt. 11 vols. 1938–68.

Rawson, Claude. *Gulliver and the Gentle Reader.* Atlantic Highlands, NJ: Humanities Press International, 1991.

Rodino, Richard H. " 'Splendide Mendax': Authors, Characters, and Readers in *Gulliver's Travels.*" *PMLA* 106 (Oct. 1991): 1054–70.

Rosenblatt, Louise. "A Performing Art." *English Journal* 55 (1966): 999–1005.

Schaffer, Simon. "Natural Philosophy and Public Spectacle in the Eighteenth Century." *History of Science* 21 (1983): 1–43.

Smith, Frederik N. "The Danger of Reading Swift: The Double Binds of *Gulliver's Travels.*" *Studies in the Literary Imagination* 17 (1984): 35–47.

———. "Scientific Discourse: *Gulliver's Travels* and *The Philosophical Transactions.*" 139–62. *The Genres of Gulliver's Travels.* Ed. Frederik N. Smith. Newark: U of Delaware P, 1990.

Swift, Jonathan. *The Correspondence.* Vol. 3. Ed. Harold Williams. Oxford: Clarendon, 1963–65.

———. *Gulliver's Travels.* Ed. Herbert Davis. Oxford: Basil Blackwell, 1965. Vol. 11 of *The Prose Works.* 14 Vols. 1939–68.

Taylor, Aline Mackenzie. "Sights and Monsters and Gulliver's Voyage to Brobdingnag." *Tulane Studies in English* 7 (1957): 29–82.

Todd, Dennis. "The Hairy Maid at the Harpsichord: Some Speculations on the Meaning of *Gulliver's Travels.*" *Texas Studies in Literature and Language* 34 (1992): 239–83.

Tompkins, Jane P., ed. *Reader-Response Criticism: From Formalism to Post-Structuralism.* Baltimore: Johns Hopkins UP, 1980.

Psychoanalytic Criticism
and
Gulliver's Travels

WHAT IS PSYCHOANALYTIC CRITICISM?

It seems natural to think about literature in terms of dreams. Like dreams, literary works are fictions, inventions of the mind that, although based on reality, are by definition not literally true. Like a literary work, a dream may have some truth to tell, but, like a literary work, it may need to be interpreted before that truth can be grasped. We can live vicariously through romantic fictions, much as we can through daydreams. Terrifying novels and nightmares affect us in much the same way, plunging us into an atmosphere that continues to cling, even after the last chapter has been read — or the alarm clock has sounded.

The notion that dreams allow such psychic explorations, of course, like the analogy between literary works and dreams, owes a great deal to the thinking of Sigmund Freud, the famous Austrian psychoanalyst who in 1900 published a seminal essay *The Interpretation of Dreams.* But is the reader who feels that Emily Brontë's *Wuthering Heights* is dreamlike — who feels that Mary Shelley's *Frankenstein* is nightmarish — necessarily a Freudian literary critic? To some extent the answer to both questions has to be yes. We are all Freudians, really, whether or not we have read a single work by Freud. At one time or another, most of us have referred to ego, libido, complexes, unconscious desires, and sexual repression. The premises of Freud's thought have changed the way the

Western world thinks about itself. Psychoanalytic criticism has influenced the teachers our teachers studied with, the works of scholarship and criticism they read, and the critical and creative writers *we* read as well.

What Freud did was develop a language that described, a model that explained, a theory that encompassed human psychology. Many of the elements of psychology he sought to describe and explain are present in the literary works of various ages and cultures, from Sophocles' *Oedipus Rex* to Shakespeare's *Hamlet* to works being written in our own day. When the great novel of the twenty-first century is written, many of these same elements of psychology will probably inform its discourse as well. If, by understanding human psychology according to Freud, we can appreciate literature on a new level, then we should acquaint ourselves with his insights.

Freud's theories are either directly or indirectly concerned with the nature of the unconscious mind. Freud didn't invent the notion of the unconscious; others before him had suggested that even the supposedly "sane" human mind was conscious and rational only at times, and even then at possibly only one level. But Freud went further, suggesting that the powers motivating men and women are *mainly* and *normally* unconscious.

Freud, then, powerfully developed an old idea: that the human mind is essentially dual in nature. He called the predominantly passional, irrational, unknown, and unconscious part of the psyche the *id*, or "it." The *ego*, or "I," was his term for the predominantly rational, logical, orderly, conscious part. Another aspect of the psyche, which he called the *superego*, is really a projection of the ego. The superego almost seems to be outside of the self, making moral judgments, telling us to make sacrifices for good causes even though self-sacrifice may not be quite logical or rational. And, in a sense, the superego *is* "outside," since much of what it tells us to do or think we have learned from our parents, our schools, or our religious institutions.

What the ego and superego tell us *not* to do or think is repressed, forced into the unconscious mind. One of Freud's most important contributions to the study of the psyche, the theory of repression, goes something like this: much of what lies in the unconscious mind has been put there by consciousness, which acts as a censor, driving underground unconscious or conscious thoughts or instincts that it deems unacceptable. Censored materials often involve infantile sexual desires, Freud postulated. Repressed to an unconscious state, they emerge only in disguised forms: in dreams, in language (so-called Freudian slips), in creative activity that may produce art (including literature), and in neurotic behavior.

According to Freud, all of us have repressed wishes and fears; we all have dreams in which repressed feelings and memories emerge disguised, and thus we are all potential candidates for dream analysis. One of the unconscious desires most commonly repressed is the childhood wish to displace the parent of our own sex and take his or her place in the affections of the parent of the opposite sex. This desire really involves a number of different but related wishes and fears. (A boy — and it should be remarked in passing that Freud here concerns himself mainly with the male — may fear that his father will castrate him, and he may wish that his mother would return to nursing him.) Freud referred to the whole complex of feelings by the word "oedipal," naming the complex after the Greek tragic hero Oedipus, who unwittingly killed his father and married his mother.

Why are oedipal wishes and fears repressed by the conscious side of the mind? And what happens to them after they have been censored? As Roy P. Basler puts it in *Sex, Symbolism, and Psychology in Literature* (1975), "from the beginning of recorded history such wishes have been restrained by the most powerful religious and social taboos, and as a result have come to be regarded as 'unnatural,'" even though "Freud found that such wishes are more or less characteristic of normal human development":

> In dreams, particularly, Freud found ample evidence that such wishes persisted. . . . Hence he conceived that natural urges, when identified as "wrong," may be repressed but not obliterated. . . . In the unconscious, these urges take on symbolic garb, regarded as nonsense by the waking mind that does not recognize their significance. (14)

Freud's belief in the significance of dreams, of course, was no more original than his belief that there is an unconscious side to the psyche. Again, it was the extent to which he developed a theory of how dreams work — and the extent to which that theory helped him, by analogy, to understand far more than just dreams — that made him unusual, important, and influential beyond the perimeters of medical schools and psychiatrists' offices.

The psychoanalytic approach to literature not only rests on the theories of Freud; it may even be said to have *begun* with Freud, who was interested in writers, especially those who relied heavily on symbols. Such writers regularly cloak or mystify ideas in figures that make sense only when interpreted, much as the unconscious mind of a neurotic disguises secret thoughts in dream stories or bizarre actions that need to be interpreted by an analyst. Freud's interest in literary artists led him to make some unfortunate generalizations about creativity; for example, in the twenty-third lecture in *Introductory Lectures on Psycho-Analysis* (1922), he defined the artist as "one urged on by instinctive needs that are too clamorous" (314). But it also led him to write creative literary criticism of his own, including an influential essay on "The Relation of a Poet to Daydreaming" (1908) and "The Uncanny" (1919), a provocative psychoanalytic reading of E. T. A. Hoffmann's supernatural tale "The Sandman."

Freud's application of psychoanalytic theory to literature quickly caught on. In 1909, only a year after Freud had published "The Relation of a Poet to Daydreaming," the psychoanalyst Otto Rank published *The Myth of the Birth of the Hero*. In that work, Rank subscribes to the notion that the artist turns a powerful, secret wish into a literary fantasy, and he uses Freud's notion about the "oedipal" complex to explain why the popular stories of so many heroes in literature are so similar. A year after Rank had published his psychoanalytic account of heroic texts, Ernest Jones, Freud's student and eventual biographer, turned his attention to a tragic text: Shakespeare's *Hamlet*. In an essay first published in the *American Journal of Psychology*, Jones, like Rank, makes use of the oedipal concept: he suggests that Hamlet is a victim of strong feelings toward his mother, the queen.

Between 1909 and 1949 numerous other critics decided that psychological and psychoanalytic theory could assist in the understanding of literature. I. A. Richards, Kenneth Burke, and Edmund Wilson were among the most influential to become interested in the new approach. Not all of the early critics were committed to the approach; neither were all of them Freudians. Some followed Alfred Adler, who believed that writers wrote out of inferiority complexes, and others applied the ideas of Carl Gustav Jung, who had broken with Freud over Freud's emphasis on sex and who had developed a theory of the *collective* unconscious. According to Jungian theory, a great work of literature is not a disguised expression of its author's personal, repressed wishes; rather, it is a manifestation of desires once held by the whole human race but now repressed because of the advent of civilization.

It is important to point out that among those who relied on Freud's models were a number of critics who were poets and novelists as well.

Conrad Aiken wrote a Freudian study of American literature, and poets such as Robert Graves and W. H. Auden applied Freudian insights when writing critical prose. William Faulkner, Henry James, James Joyce, D. H. Lawrence, Marcel Proust, and Toni Morrison are only a few of the novelists who have either written criticism influenced by Freud or who have written novels that conceive of character, conflict, and creative writing itself in Freudian terms. The poet H.D. (Hilda Doolittle) was actually a patient of Freud's and provided an account of her analysis in her book *Tribute to Freud*. By giving Freudian theory credibility among students of literature that only they could bestow, such writers helped to endow earlier psychoanalytic criticism with a largely Freudian orientation that has only begun to be challenged in the last two decades.

The willingness, even eagerness, of writers to use Freudian models in producing literature and criticism of their own consummated a relationship that, to Freud and other pioneering psychoanalytic theorists, had seemed fated from the beginning; after all, therapy involves the close analysis of language. René Wellek and Austin Warren included "psychological" criticism as one of the five "extrinsic" approaches to literature described in their influential book, *Theory of Literature* (1942). Psychological criticism, they suggest, typically attempts to do at least one of the following: provide a psychological study of an individual writer; explore the nature of the creative process; generalize about "types and laws present within works of literature"; or theorize about the psychological "effects of literature upon its readers" (81). Entire books on psychoanalytic criticism began to appear, such as Frederick J. Hoffman's *Freudianism and the Literary Mind* (1945).

Probably because of Freud's characterization of the creative mind as "clamorous" if not ill, psychoanalytic criticism written before 1950 tended to psychoanalyze the individual author. Poems were read as fantasies that allowed authors to indulge repressed wishes, to protect themselves from deep-seated anxieties, or both. A perfect example of author analysis would be Marie Bonaparte's 1933 study of Edgar Allan Poe. Bonaparte found Poe to be so fixated on his mother that his repressed longing emerges in his stories in images such as the white spot on a black cat's breast, said to represent mother's milk.

A later generation of psychoanalytic critics often paused to analyze the characters in novels and plays before proceeding to their authors. But not for long, since characters, both evil and good, tended to be seen by these critics as the author's potential selves or projections of various repressed aspects of his or her psyche. For instance, in *A Psychoanalytic*

Study of the Double in Literature (1970), Robert Rogers begins with the view that human beings are double or multiple in nature. Using this assumption, along with the psychoanalytic concept of "dissociation" (best known by its result, the dual or multiple personality), Rogers concludes that writers reveal instinctual or repressed selves in their books, often without realizing that they have done so.

In the view of critics attempting to arrive at more psychological insights into an author than biographical materials can provide, a work of literature is a fantasy or a dream — or at least so analogous to daydream or dream that Freudian analysis can help explain the nature of the mind that produced it. The author's purpose in writing is to gratify secretly some forbidden wish, in particular an infantile wish or desire that has been repressed into the unconscious mind. To discover what the wish is, the psychoanalytic critic employs many of the terms and procedures developed by Freud to analyze dreams.

The literal surface of a work is sometimes spoken of as its "manifest content" and treated as a "manifest dream" or "dream story" would be treated by a Freudian analyst. Just as the analyst tries to figure out the "dream thought" behind the dream story — that is, the latent or hidden content of the manifest dream — so the psychoanalytic literary critic tries to expose the latent, underlying content of a work. Freud used the words *condensation* and *displacement* to explain two of the mental processes whereby the mind disguises its wishes and fears in dream stories. In condensation several thoughts or persons may be condensed into a single manifestation or image in a dream story; in displacement, an anxiety, a wish, or a person may be displaced onto the image of another, with which or whom it is loosely connected through a string of associations that only an analyst can untangle. Psychoanalytic critics treat metaphors as if they were dream condensations; they treat metonyms — figures of speech based on extremely loose, arbitrary associations — as if they were dream displacements. Thus figurative literary language in general is treated as something that evolves as the writer's conscious mind resists what the unconscious tells it to picture or describe. A symbol is, in Daniel Weiss's words, "a meaningful concealment of truth as the truth promises to emerge as some frightening or forbidden idea" (20).

In a 1970 article entitled "The 'Unconscious' of Literature," Norman Holland, a literary critic trained in psychoanalysis, succinctly sums up the attitudes held by critics who would psychoanalyze authors, but without quite saying that it is the *author* that is being analyzed by the psychoanalytic critic. "When one looks at a poem psychoanalytically," he writes, "one considers it as though it were a dream or as though some ideal patient [were speaking] from the couch in iambic pentameter." One "looks for the general level or levels of fantasy associated with the language. By level I mean the familiar stages of childhood development — oral [when desires for nourishment and infantile sexual desires overlap], anal [when infants receive their primary pleasure from defecation], urethral [when urinary functions are the locus of sexual pleasure], phallic [when the penis or, in girls, some penis substitute is of primary interest], oedipal." Holland continues by analyzing not Robert Frost but Frost's poem "Mending Wall" as a specifically oral fantasy that is not unique to its author. "Mending Wall" is "about breaking down the wall which marks the separated or individuated self so as to return to a state of closeness to some Other" — including and perhaps essentially the nursing mother ("Unconscious" 136, 139).

While not denying the idea that the unconscious plays a role in creativity, psychoanalytic critics such as Holland began to focus more on the ways in which authors create works that appeal to *our* repressed wishes and fantasies. Consequently, they shifted their focus away from the psyche of the author and toward the psychology of the reader and the text. Holland's theories, which have concerned themselves more with the reader than with the text, have helped to establish another school of critical theory: reader-response criticism. Elizabeth Wright explains Holland's brand of modern psychoanalytic criticism in this way: "What draws us as readers to a text is the secret expression of what we desire to hear, much as we protest we do not. The disguise must be good enough to fool the censor into thinking that the text is respectable, but bad enough to allow the unconscious to glimpse the unrespectable" (117).

Holland is one of dozens of critics who have revised Freud significantly in the process of revitalizing psychoanalytic criticism. Another such critic is R. D. Laing, whose controversial and often poetical writings about personality, repression, masks, and the double or "schizoid" self have (re)blurred the boundary between creative writing and psychoanalytic discourse. Yet another is D. W. Winnicott, an "object relations" theorist who has had a significant impact on literary criticism. Critics influenced by Winnicott and his school have questioned the tendency to see reader/text as an either/or construct; instead, they have seen reader and text (or audience and play) in terms of a *relationship* taking place in what Winnicott calls a "transitional" or "potential space" — space in which binary terms like real and illusory, objective and subjective, have little or no meaning.

Psychoanalytic theorists influenced by Winnicott see the transitional or potential reader/text (or audience/play) space as being *like* the space entered into by psychoanalyst and patient. More important, they also see it as being similar to the space between mother and infant: a space characterized by trust in which categorizing terms such as *knowing* and *feeling* mix and merge and have little meaning apart from one another. Perhaps most characteristic of object-relations theory is the turn to an earlier period in life as the basis of psychic life. Whereas Freud emphasized the period of early childhood in which the child works through the oedipal complex, object-relations theorists such as Melanie Klein have stressed the primacy of a still earlier relationship, one dating as far back as the first stages of infancy.

Whereas Freud saw the mother-son relationship in terms of the son and his repressed oedipal complex (and saw the analyst-patient relationship in terms of the patient and the repressed "truth" that the analyst could scientifically extract), object-relations analysts see both relationships as *dyadic* — that is, as being dynamic in both directions. Consequently, they don't depersonalize analysis or their analyses. It is hardly surprising, therefore, that contemporary literary critics who apply object-relations theory to the texts they discuss don't depersonalize critics or categorize their interpretations as "truthful," at least, not in any objective or scientific sense. In the view of such critics, interpretations are made of language — itself a transitional object — and are themselves the mediating terms or transitional objects of a relationship.

Like critics of the Winnicottian School, the French structuralist theorist Jacques Lacan focuses on language and language-related issues. He treats the unconscious *as* a language and, consequently, views the dream not as Freud did (that is, as a form and symptom of repression) but rather as a form of discourse. Thus we may study dreams psychoanalytically in order to learn about literature, even as we may study literature in order to learn more about the unconscious. In Lacan's seminar on Poe's "The Purloined Letter," a pattern of repetition like that used by psychoanalysts in their analyses is used to arrive at a reading of the story. According to Wright, "the new psychoanalytic structural approach to literature" employs "analogies from psychoanalysis . . . to explain the workings of the text as distinct from the workings of a particular author's, character's, or even reader's mind" (125).

Lacan, however, did far more than extend Freud's theory of dreams, literature, and the interpretation of both. More significantly, he took Freud's whole theory of psyche and gender and added to it a crucial third term — that of language. In the process, he both used and significantly developed Freud's ideas about the oedipal stage and complex.

Lacan points out that the pre-oedipal stage, in which the child at first does not even recognize its independence from its mother, is also a pre*verbal* stage, one in which the child communicates without the medium of language, or — if we insist on calling the child's communications a language — in a language that can only be called *literal*. ("Coos," certainly, cannot be said to be figurative or symbolic.) Then, while still in the pre-oedipal stage, the child enters the *mirror* stage.

During the mirror period, the child comes to view itself and its mother, later other people as well, *as* independent selves. This is the stage in which the child is first able to fear the aggressions of another, to desire what is recognizably beyond the self (initially the mother), and, finally, to want to compete with another for the same, desired object. This is also the stage at which the child first becomes able to feel sympathy with another being who is being hurt by a third, to cry when another cries. All of these developments, of course, involve projecting beyond the self and, by extension, constructing one's own self (or "ego" or "I") as others view one — that is, as *another*. Such constructions, according to Lacan, are just that: constructs, products, artifacts — fictions of coherence that in fact hide what Lacan calls the "absence" or "lack" of being.

The mirror stage, which Lacan also refers to as the *imaginary* stage, is fairly quickly succeeded by the oedipal stage. As in Freud, this stage begins when the child, having come to view itself as self and the father and mother as separate selves, perceives gender and gender differences between its parents and between itself and one of its parents. For boys, gender awareness involves another, more powerful recognition, for the recognition of the father's phallus as the mark of his difference from the mother involves, at the same time, the recognition that his older and more powerful father is also his rival. That, in turn, leads to the understanding that what once seemed wholly his and even indistinguishable from himself is in fact someone else's: something properly desired only at a distance and in the form of socially acceptable *substitutes*.

The fact that the oedipal stage roughly coincides with the entry of the child into language is extremely important for Lacan. For the linguistic order is essentially a figurative or "Symbolic order"; words are not the things they stand for but are, rather, stand-ins or substitutes for those things. Hence boys, who in the most critical period of their development have had to submit to what Lacan calls the "Law of the Father" — a law that prohibits direct desire for and communicative intimacy with what has been the boy's whole world — enter more easily into the realm of language and the Symbolic order than do girls, who have never really had to renounce that which once seemed continuous with the self: the mother. The gap that has been opened up for boys, which includes the gap between signs and what they substitute — the gap marked by the phallus and encoded with the boy's sense of his maleness — has not opened up for girls, or has not opened up in the same way, to the same degree.

For Lacan, the father need not be present to trigger the oedipal stage; nor does his phallus have to be seen to catalyze the boy's (easier) transition into the Symbolic order. Rather, Lacan argues, a child's recognition of its gender is intricately tied up with a growing recognition of the system of names and naming, part of the larger system of substitutions we call language. A child has little doubt about who its mother is, but who is its father, and how would one know? The father's claim rests on the mother's *word* that he is in fact the father; the father's relationship to the child is thus established through language and a system of marriage and kinship — names — that in turn is basic to rules of everything from property to law. The name of the father (*nom du père*, which in French sounds like *non du père*) involves, in a sense, nothing of the father — nothing, that is, except his word or name.

Lacan's development of Freud has had several important results. First, his sexist-seeming association of maleness with the Symbolic order, together with his claim that women cannot therefore enter easily into the order, has prompted feminists not to reject his theory out of hand but, rather, to look more closely at the relation between language and gender, language and women's inequality. Some feminists have gone so far as to suggest that the social and political relationships between male and female will not be fundamentally altered until language itself has been radically changed. (That change might begin dialectically, with the development of some kind of "feminine language" grounded in the presymbolic, literal-to-imaginary, communication between mother and child.)

Second, Lacan's theory has proved of interest to deconstructors and other poststructuralists, in part because it holds that the ego (which in Freud's view is as necessary as it is natural) is a product or construct. The ego-artifact, produced during the mirror stage, *seems* at once unified, consistent, and organized around a determinate center. But the unified self, or ego, is a fiction, according to Lacan. The yoking together of fragments and destructively dissimilar elements takes its psychic toll, and it is the job of the Lacanian psychoanalyst to "deconstruct," as it were, the ego, to show its continuities to be contradictions as well.

In the essay that follows, Carol Barash views *Gulliver's Travels* as a novel that promotes a "*specularized* understanding of the female body," according to which "to be female is to be examined and to be male is to be the one who examines." This specular presentation — a product of Gulliver's tendency to examine women anatomically, thereby reducing them to "material" and "fluid" essences — exemplifies and at the same time satirizes an emerging eighteenth-century tendency to objectify and thereby control the female, in part by making the female body seem monstrous and thus in *need* of regulation. According to Barash, Swift's text "both enacts and criticizes two of the essential features of [the] new economy of sexuality: the fear of women physically reduced to but also culturally empowered as mothers, and the fear of men taking pleasure in playing the feminine role."

Suggesting that *Gulliver's Travels* was at once an agent of and an anxious reflection upon the broad cultural shifts of its time, Barash produces a psychoanalytic reading that nonetheless never veers far from the text's historical context, that of eighteenth-century England. Swift's culture, she argues, was in the process of constructing new, middle-class gender identities — and of attempting to universalize heterosexual norms. This was an age in which the female body and the maternal body (both of which stirred mixed feelings in the male-dominated society) came to be equated. Afraid of being seen as feminine while being both attracted to and repulsed by the female body, men sought to regulate that body even as they culturally empowered women as mothers. The 1720s in particular witnessed a crackdown on male homosexual and effeminate behavior as well as an increasing legal and cultural regulation of the female body.

Barash uses the theories of Freud to gain powerful insights into Swift's text. (She acknowledges, for instance, that classic psychoanalytic theory can account for Gulliver's simultaneous hatred of and pleasure in the female body.) At the same time, she views Freud as a writer who continued the cultural project of regulating the female body, equating the female and the maternal, and continuing the universalizing of heterosexuality that was begun in the eighteenth century by writers *like* Swift. Noting that Freud's account of the anal phase was anticipated in what psychoanalytic critic Norman O. Brown has referred to as Swift's "excremental vision," Barash summarizes Brown's argument that Swift anticipated Freud through his characterization of the Yahoos by associating the anal function with our (libidinous) animal nature. She then builds on Brown by showing that the "filthy" anal/animal Yahoos represent a double "sexual threat" to Gulliver: the threat of the female/maternal on one hand and the threat of homosexuality on the other.

In addition to Freudian theory, Jacques Lacan's concept of the "mirror stage" is put to use by Barash in her analysis. She also alludes to Melanie Klein's argument that a child's first consciousness of gender arises in the transition from the anal to the genital phase, during moments of sadistic rage against the maternal body. Barash writes that "it is in the relationship between maternal protection and violence against the symbolic mother that Gulliver desires but ultimately fails to be a male child" — to conquer the feminizing maternal body, complete with its "cavernous and cancerous breast," and, according to Melanie Klein, to achieve the oedipal "aim of *penetration* associated with the possession of the penis."

In the essay's one biographical passage, Barash points out that Swift's father died before his only son's birth, and that shortly after that birth Swift was kidnapped by his wet nurse and later "symbolically abandoned" by his mother. While Barash goes on to suggest that "there was certainly much in Swift's childhood that would suggest ambivalence about both his mother and things maternal," she should not be confused with the kind of old-fashioned psychoanalytic critic who used the text to psychoanalyze its author. Barash writes, "I do not rehearse the details of Swift's childhood in order to locate some primal moment in it." She argues instead that "*Gulliver's Travels* seems part of a much larger cultural shift that creates and privileges those very social divisions of gender and sexuality that Freud ultimately came to understand as biological imperatives."

Barash looks at *Gulliver's Travels* through the lens of psychoanalytic theory, and at psychoanalytic theory through the lens of Swift's age and text. Rather than equating Gulliver with Swift, she sees Gulliver as representative of the newly evolving discourses of his culture. These included an embryonic psychoanalytic discourse that "produces a universal(izing) account of heterosexual norms" and attempts to "render this model of gender *normative* by collapsing it onto sexual difference and the imperatives of heterosexual reproduction."

Ross C Murfin

PSYCHOANALYTIC CRITICISM: A SELECTED BIBLIOGRAPHY

Some Short Introductions to Psychological and Psychoanalytic Criticism

Holland, Norman N. "The 'Unconscious' of Literature." *Contemporary Criticism.* Ed. Norman Bradbury and David Palmer. Stratford-upon-Avon Series 12. New York: St. Martin's, 1970. 131–54.

Natoli, Joseph, and Frederik L. Rusch, comps. *Psychocriticism: An Annotated Bibliography.* Westport: Greenwood, 1984.

Scott, Wilbur. *Five Approaches of Literary Criticism.* New York: Collier, 1962.

Wellek, René, and Austin Warren. *Theory of Literature.* New York: Harcourt, 1949.

Wright, Elizabeth. "Modern Psychoanalytic Criticism." *Modern Literary Theory: A Comparative Introduction.* Ed. Ann Jefferson and David Robey. Totowa, NJ: Barnes, 1982. 113–33.

Freud, Lacan, and the Influence of Psychoanalysis

Basler, Roy P. *Sex, Symbolism, and Psychology in Literature.* New York: Octagon, 1967.

Clément, Catherine. *The Lives and Legends of Jacques Lacan.* Trans. Arthur Goldhammer. New York: Columbia UP, 1983.

Derrida, Jacques. "Freud and the Scene of Writing." *Writing and Difference.* Trans. Alan Bass. Chicago: U of Chicago P, 1978. 196–231.

Eagleton, Terry. *Literary Theory: An Introduction.* Minneapolis: U of Minnesota P, 1983. 151–93.

Felman, Shoshana, ed. *Literature and Psychoanalysis: The Question of Reading, Otherwise.* Baltimore: Johns Hopkins UP, 1982.

Freud, Sigmund. *Introductory Lectures of Psycho-Analysis.* Trans. Joan Riviere, London: Allen, 1922.

Gallop, Jane. *Reading Lacan.* Ithaca: Cornell UP, 1985.

Gay, Peter. *Freud: A Life for Our Time.* New York: Norton, 1988.

Hoffman, Frederick J. *Freudianism and the Literary Mind.* Baton Rouge: Louisiana State UP, 1945.

Hogan, Patrick Colm, and Lalita Pandit, eds. *Criticism and Lacan: Essays and Dialogue on Language, Structure, and the Unconscious.* Athens: U of Georgia P, 1990.

Kazin, Alfred. "Freud and His Consequences." *Contemporaries.* Boston: Little, 1962. 351–93.

Lacan, Jacques. *Écrits: A Selection.* Trans. Alan Sheridan. New York: Norton, 1977.

———. *Feminine Sexuality: Jacques Lacan and the école freudienne.* Ed. Juliet Mitchell and Jacqueline Rose. Trans. Rose. New York: Norton, 1982.

———. *The Four Fundamental Concepts of Psychoanalysis.* Trans. Alan Sheridan. New York: Norton, 1981.

Laplanche, Jean. *Life and Death in Psychoanalysis.* Trans. Jeffrey Mehlman. Baltimore: Johns Hopkins UP, 1976.

Laplanche, Jean, and J.-B. Pontalis. *The Language of Psycho-analysis.* New York and London: Norton, 1973.

MacCabe, Colin, ed. *The Talking Cure: Essays in Psychoanalysis and Language.* New York: St. Martin's, 1981.

Macey, David. *Lacan in Contexts.* New York: Verso, 1988.

Marcuse, Herbert. *Eros and Civilization.* Boston: Beacon, 1955.

Meisel, Perry, ed. *Freud: A Collection of Critical Essays.* Englewood Cliffs: Prentice, 1981.

Muller, John P., and William J. Richardson. *Lacan and Language: A Reader's Guide to "Ecrits."* New York: International UP, 1982.

Porter, Laurence M. *"The Interpretations of Dreams": Freud's Theories Revisited.* Twayne's Masterwork Studies Series. Boston: G. K. Hall, 1986.

Ragland Sullivan, Ellie. *Jacques Lacan and the Philosophy of Psychoanalysis.* Champaign: U of Illinois P, 1986.

Ragland Sullivan, Ellie, and Mark Bracher, eds. *Lacan and the Subject of Language.* New York: Routledge, 1991.

Reppen, Joseph, and Maurice Charney. *The Psychoanalytic Study of Literature.* Hillsdale: Analytic, 1985.

Ricoeur, Paul. *Freud and Philosophy.* New Haven: Yale UP, 1970.

Schneiderman, Stuart. *Jacques Lacan: The Death of an Intellectual Hero.* Cambridge, MA: Harvard UP, 1983.

———. *Returning to Freud: Clinical Psychoanalysis in the School of Lacan.* New Haven: Yale UP, 1980.

Selden, Raman. *A Reader's Guide to Contemporary Literary Theory.* 2nd ed. Lexington: U of Kentucky P, 1989. See "Jacques Lacan: Language and the Unconscious."

Trilling, Lionel. "Art and Neurosis." *The Liberal Imagination.* New York: Scribner's, 1950. 160–80.

Wilden, Anthony. "Lacan and the Discourse of the Other." *Speech and Language in Psychoanalysis.* Jacques Lacan. Trans. Wilden. Baltimore: Johns Hopkins UP, 1981. 159–311.

Psychoanalysis, Feminism, Gender, and Literature

Bernheimer, Charles, and Claire Kahane, eds. *In Dora's Case: Freud, Hysteria and Feminism.* New York: Columbia UP, 1985.

Chodorow, Nancy. *Feminism and Psychoanalytic Theory.* New Haven: Yale UP, 1989.

———. *The Reproduction of Mothering: Psychoanalysis and the Sociology of Gender.* Berkeley: U of California P, 1978.

———. "Women and Madness: The Critical Fallacy." *Diacritics* 5 (Winter 1975): 2–10.

Gallop, Jane. *The Daughter's Seduction: Feminism and Psychoanalysis.* Ithaca: Cornell UP, 1982.

Garner, Shirley Nelson, Claire Kahane, and Madelon Sprengnether, eds. *The (M)other Tongue: Essays in Feminist Psychoanalytic Interpretation.* Ithaca: Cornell UP, 1985.

Horney, Karen. *Feminine Psychology.* New York: Norton, 1967.

Ian, Marcia. *Remembering the Phallic Mother: Psychoanalysis, Modernism and the Fetish.* Ithaca: Cornell UP, 1993.

Irigaray, Luce. *The Speculum of the Other Woman.* Trans. Gillian C. Gill. Ithaca: Cornell UP, 1985.

———. *This Sex Which Is Not One.* Trans. Catherine Porter with Carolyn Burke. Ithaca: Cornell UP, 1985.

Jacobus, Mary. "Is There a Woman in This Text?" *New Literary History* 14 (1982): 117–54.

Kaplan, Cora. *Sea Changes: Essays on Culture and Feminism.* London: Verso, 1986.

Klein, Melanie. *Love, Guilt and Reparation and Other Works: 1921–1945.* New York: Macmillan, 1975.

Kofman, Sarah. *The Enigma of Woman: Woman in Freud's Writings.* Trans. Catherine Porter. Ithaca: Cornell UP, 1985.

Kristeva, Julia. *Desire in Language: A Semiotic Approach to Literature and Art.* Ed. Leon S. Roudiez. New York: Columbia UP, 1980.

———. *The Kristeva Reader.* Ed. Toril Moi. Trans. Thomas Gore. New York: Columbia UP, 1986.

m/f, 1 (1978), esp. essays by Adams, Cowie, and Montrelay.

Mitchell, Juliet. *Psychoanalysis and Feminism.* New York: Random House, 1974.

Mitchell, Juliet, and Jacqueline Rose. *Feminine Sexuality: Jacques Lacan and the école freudienne.* New York: Norton, 1982. 1–26, 26–57.

Sprengnether, Madelon. *The Spectral Mother: Freud, Feminism, and Psychoanalysis.* Ithaca: Cornell UP, 1990.

Young-Bruehl, Elisabeth, ed. *Freud on Women: A Reader.* New York: Norton, 1990.

Psychological and Psychoanalytic Studies of Literature

Bersani, Leo. *A Future for Astyanax: Character and Desire in Literature.* Boston: Little, Brown, 1976.

Bettelheim, Bruno. *The Uses of Enchantment: The Meaning and Importance of Fairy Tales.* New York: Vintage, 1976.

Crews, Frederick C. *Out of My System: Psychoanalysis, Ideology, and Critical Method.* New York: Oxford UP, 1975.

Diehl, Joanne Feit. "Re-Reading *The Letter:* Hawthorne, the Fetish, and the (Family) Romance." *Nathaniel Hawthorne, The Scarlet Letter.* Ed. Ross C Murfin. Case Studies in Contemporary Criticism Series. Ed. Ross C Murfin. Boston: Bedford–St. Martin's, 1991. 235–51.

Hallman, Ralph. *Psychology of Literature: A Study of Alienation and Tragedy.* New York: Philosophical Library, 1961.

Hartman, Geoffrey, ed. *Psychoanalysis and the Question of the Text.* Baltimore: Johns Hopkins UP, 1978.

Hertz, Neil. *The End of the Line: Essays on Psychoanalysis and the Sublime.* New York: Columbia UP, 1985.

Holland, Norman N. *Dynamics of Literary Response.* New York: Oxford UP, 1968.

———. *Poems in Persons: An Introduction to the Psychoanalysis of Literature.* New York: Norton, 1973.

Kris, Ernst. *Psychoanalytic Explorations in Art.* New York: International, 1952.

Lucas, F. L. *Literature and Psychology.* London: Cassell, 1951.

Natoli, Joseph, ed. *Psychological Perspectives on Literature: Freudian Dissidents and Non-Freudians: A Casebook.* Hamden: Archon Books-Shoe String, 1984.

Phillips, William, ed. *Art and Psychoanalysis.* New York: Criterion Books, 1957.

Rogers, Robert. *A Psychoanalytic Study of the Double in Literature.* Detroit: Wayne State UP, 1970.

Skura, Meredith. *The Literary Use of the Psychoanalytic Process.* New Haven: Yale UP, 1981.

Strelka, Joseph P. *Literary Criticism and Psychology.* University Park: Pennsylvania State UP, 1976.

Thorpe, James Ernest, ed. *Relations of Literary Study.* New York: MLA, 1967.

Weiss, Daniel. *The Critic Agonistes: Psychology, Myth, and the Art of Fiction.* Ed. Eric Solomon and Stephen Arkin. Seattle: U of Washington P, 1985.

Lacanian Psychoanalytic Studies of Literature

Collings, David. "The Monster and the Imaginary Mother: A Lacanian Reading of *Frankenstein.*" *Mary Shelley, Frankenstein.* Ed. Johanna M. Smith. Case Studies in Contemporary Criticism Series. Ed. Ross C Murfin. Boston: Bedford–St. Martin's, 1992. 245–58.

Davis, Robert Con, ed. *The Fictional Father: Lacanian Readings of the Text.* Amherst: U of Massachusetts P, 1981.

———. "Lacan and Narration." *Modern Language Notes* 5 (1983): 843–1063.

Felman, Shoshana, ed. *Jacques Lacan and the Adventure of Insight: Psychoanalysis in Contemporary Culture.* Cambridge, MA: Harvard UP, 1987.

Froula, Christine. "When Eve Reads Milton: Undoing the Canonical Economy." *Canons.* Ed. Robert von Hallberg. Chicago: U of Chicago P, 1984. 149–75.

Homans, Margaret. *Bearing the Word: Language and Female Experience in Nineteenth-Century Women's Writing.* Chicago: U of Chicago P, 1986.

Muller, John P., and William J. Richardson, eds. *The Purloined Poe: Lacan, Derrida, and Psychoanalytic Reading.* Baltimore: Johns Hopkins UP, 1988.

Psychoanalytic Readings of Swift and *Gulliver's Travels*

Brown, Norman O. "The Excremental Vision." *Life against Death: The Psychoanalytical Meaning of History.* Middletown, CT: Wesleyan UP, 1959. 179–201.

Bruce, Susan. "The Flying Island and Female Anatomy." *Genders* 2 (1988): 60–76.

Flynn, Carol Houlihan. *The Body in Swift and Defoe.* Cambridge: Cambridge UP, 1990.

Greenacre, Phyllis. *Swift and Carroll: A Psychoanalytic Study of Two Lives.* New York: International U Presses, 1955.

Pollak, Ellen. *The Poetics of Sexual Myth: Gender and Ideology in the Verse of Swift and Pope.* Chicago: U of Chicago P, 1985.

Salvaggio, Ruth. "Swift and Psychoanalysis, Language and Woman." *Women's Studies* 15 (1988): 417–434.

Stallybrass, Peter, and Allon White. *The Politics and Poetics of Transgression.* Ithaca: Cornell UP, 1986. 102–9.

Traugott, John. "The Yahoo in the Doll's House: *Gulliver's Travels* The Children's Classic." *English Satire and the Satiric Tradition.* Ed. Claude Rawson. Oxford: Basil Blackwell, 1984. 127–150.

A PSYCHOANALYTIC PERSPECTIVE

CAROL BARASH

Violence and the Maternal: Swift, Psychoanalysis, and the 1720s[1]

The poets were there before I was.

–SIGMUND FREUD

Freudian theory offers the one model of reading we have that can claim to make a text speak more than it knows.

–PETER HULME

In October 1726, the same month that *Gulliver's Travels* was published, Mary Toft of Godalming, in Surrey, shocked the English medical community by giving birth to a family of rabbits. Earlier that year, constables and their informants had raided London's "Molly Houses," centers of a homoerotic subculture where men danced and made love together, often by imitating heterosexual rituals of marriage and

[1] I would like to thank Christopher Fox, Jason Gieger, Ross Murfin, Ruth Perry, Supryia Ray, James Winn, and especially Marcia Ian, Wendy Motooka, and David Toise for reading and discussing drafts of this essay and suggesting ways to connect psychoanalytic and historical interpretations of the eighteenth-century novel.

childbirth. By the end of 1726 over twenty men had been tried and executed for their participation in the flamboyant, parodic world of the Molly Houses, and Toft was imprisoned for what proved to be a hoax. What do these *cultural narratives* — the well-publicized and widely contested stories of the "Rabbit Woman" and the busted Molly Houses — have to do with *Gulliver's Travels*? And, taken together, what do these stories tell us about the overlapping forms of gender, sexuality, and the novel in the 1720s?

Three overlapping cultural shifts — the construction of middle-class gender identity in the early English novel (Armstrong; McKeon), changing notions of women's role in reproduction (Laqueur; Perry 1991), and increasing regulation of male homosexuality (Bray; Trumbach 1977–78) — provide the historical ground for my reading of *Gulliver's Travels*. Responding to psychoanalytic and feminist interpretations of Swift's novel, I will argue that classic psychoanalytic theory produces a universal(izing) account of heterosexual norms from a much more unwieldy, historically specific set of sexual narratives. Regimes of knowledge about the (hetero)sexual self are produced *discursively*, through essentially literary practices of self-knowledge and self-regulation (Foucault). The novel is one of these new ways of reading, knowing, and regulating — of producing — modern gender and sexuality, and also one of the new practices by which women are given cultural authority as mothers (but by viewing their own bodies as both maternal and Other).

In the 1720s the novel participates in cultural debates around gender and sexuality, articulating new bourgeois norms (a way for middle-class men and women to think of themselves both in relation to one another and in relation to others) and remaining in tension with other possibilities, other available stories.[2] The preface to *Love Letters Between a Certain Late Nobleman and the Famous Mr. Wilson* (1723; rpt. 1990), an epistolary novel that straddles old and new forms of sexual ideology and sexual representation, explains to readers, "It is easy enough to take away all Offence of this Kind [that is, the "Vice" of love between men] by applying the Passion of these Letters to distinct Sexes" (14). In his important study of homosexuality in the early

---

[2] For the idea of the novel — as a genre — participating in larger cultural dialogues, see Bakhtin; the practice of "reading" various social texts against one another is shared by new historicism (e.g., Greenblatt) and the new cultural history (e.g., Walkowitz). Both Armstrong and McKeon read the rise of the novel as ideologically charged, crucial to new class and gender identities in the eighteenth century; Armstrong and Tennenhouse usefully discuss the changing relationship between literature and personal life in this period.

modern period, Alan Bray argues that increasing tolerance of male homosexuality, overall, was made possible by periodic raids on the Molly
Houses (88), and that what was being rooted out in these raids was not
love between men, but effeminacy: men acting like women (102). In
the context of the Molly House raids, the "distinct Sexes" of *Beau
Wilson*'s preface are a way of reading (and requiring) gender hierarchy
and heterosexuality at once.[3]

Enforcing these same sexual configurations, *Gulliver's Travels* oddly
anticipates the model of female sexual passivity that was generated over
the long eighteenth century and that was later theorized by Freud
(Laqueur). We can read Freud as both a late voice in the construction of
modern (hetero)sexuality and one that transforms cultural history into
a model of individual psychic and sexual development. In Freud's early
work, the female body is not naturally or essentially "maternal" but is
culturally constructed as such.[4] Historically, this construction of woman
as mother depends on new ways of reading and regulating the sexual
body in the eighteenth century (including attention to men and women
as anatomically distinct [Laqueur] and the regulation of male homoerotic subcultures like the Molly Houses). Using Lacanian terms historically, we might think of *Gulliver's Travels* as part of a new sexual *imaginary*, a world in which the sexual *symbolic* as we know it had not yet
crystallized (that is, the phallus and the breast did not yet symbolize
male and female forms of cultural power, but they were on their way to
those meanings).[5] Psychoanalysis thus imposes as a trajectory of human
psychological development what is really just one possible sexual history of our culture (that which privileges heterosexuality and reproduction).

Returning to the bizarre, dreamlike imaginary of the 1720s, Mary
Toft and Lemuel Gulliver (in both of whose names many people wrote)
become the subjects of socially meaningful texts in the history of gender
and sexuality. Although Toft's production of seventeen rabbits proved

[3]Epstein relates similar tensions in the early modern discourse around hermaphro-
dites.

[4]See *Three Essays* (1905) and "Femininity" (*New Introductory Lectures*, 1933) for
earlier and later versions of Freud's theory of how childhood bisexuality is transformed
into male and female adult sexuality. On the place of Freud in codifying the new sexual
paradigms, see Chauncey.

[5]For Lacan's notion of the *imaginary* and *symbolic*, see Laplanche and Pontalis; on
the *phallus* see Lacan (1977, 281–91); for the idea that the *breast* is analogous to the
phallus (i.e., symbolically central to the construction of female sexuality), see Gallop
(1994).

to be a hoax, her bodily contortions — rabbits jumping in her uterus, the pains of labor, and repeated stillbirths — were watched and recorded by several court physicians, including George I's surgeon and anatomist, Nathaniel St. André. Or so they claimed, much to their later horror.[6] Part of a long line of eighteenth-century medical hoaxes, Toft put herself grotesquely and convincingly on display. By forcing pieces of dead pig and rabbit flesh into her uterus, she created something resembling labor pains, which she then learned to imitate and exaggerate in order to feign the notorious birthing of rabbits.

Toft's story has been read in the context of shifting models of female anatomy and shifting narratives of female desire and human generation in the eighteenth century (see Bruce and Cody; for social context, Laqueur, Perry 1991, and Schiebinger). Early accounts of the "Rabbit Woman" reiterated her own elaborate story of having eaten rabbits during her pregnancy and then giving birth, on three separate occasions, to rabbits that died. When they initially examined her, local doctors, as well as those sent by George I's court, found pieces of rabbit flesh inside Toft's body and looked outside her to give meaning to the miraculous births. But as Toft was transported from Godalming to London, for further examination, the constant questioning and repeated explorations of her body (her breasts and tongue in addition to the more predictable vagina and uterus) seem to have broken her spirit as well as her story. Under the threat of "a very painful Experiment," Toft confessed to scheming with a neighbor woman (who had supplied her with the dead rabbits) and was sent to prison (Leslie 269–72).

Like the history of Mary Toft, *Gulliver's Travels* suggests an increasingly *specularized* understanding of the female body in the eighteenth century: new ways of describing women's bodies not as experienced or known from within, but as observed. In this specularized sexual economy, to be female is to be examined and to be male is to be the one who examines. Male sexual receptivity — men as sexual objects — thus becomes increasingly a cultural problem. Gulliver participates in this anatomical view of the female sexual body when he examines the women of Brobdingnag as if through a microscope. He travels metaphorically around and through the female body, arriving ultimately at a view of "humanity" that is markedly male and English but that he describes as universal. Several feminist discussions of *Gulliver's Travels* make

---

[6]I have relied on Leslie for published accounts of Toft's hoax, one of which was written by John Arbuthnot under the pseudonym "Lemuel Gulliver" (273).

connections between Gulliver's symbolic voyages through various parts of the female body, particularly in the Voyage to Laputa (from the Spanish *la puta*, "the whore"), and Swift's other descriptions of the female body as overwhelmingly material, and — like language — fluid and unstable (Bruce 69–73; Castle [in this volume]; Flynn 183–7; Salvaggio). According to Susan Bruce, Gulliver's Voyage to Laputa enacts men's ultimate inability to control women's bodies and desires (72). Gulliver's position as the consummate male spectator is thus satirized even as it is privileged by Swift.

Feminist critics have for the most part ignored the homoerotic play in these same encounters, the ways in which Swift's satiric narrator is himself subject to the gaze of the male author and reader. Furthermore, those parts of the *Travels* most fascinated with the details of female anatomy are also those moments in which Gulliver is himself most dependent and effeminized. Gulliver's dreamlike fascination with the female body as both grotesquely physical and powerfully maternal participates in much larger shifts in the meaning of sexual pleasure and the social roles of men and women in the eighteenth century. *Gulliver's Travels* both enacts and criticizes two of the essential features of this new economy of heterosexuality: the fear of women physically reduced to but also culturally empowered as mothers, and the fear of men taking pleasure in playing the feminine role. Toft's and Gulliver's stories are part of a near cultural obsession with monstrous births, monstrous mothers, and the possibility that maternity itself was something dangerous, excessive, and in need of public regulation. Freud's "anal phase" enacts a similar relationship to the maternal body as something that requires control and government.

PLEASURE, PUNISHMENT, AND ANALITY

In *Life against Death*, Norman O. Brown uses the phrase "excremental vision" to capture the central place of "scatalogical imagery" and "the anal function" in Swift's "anatomy of human nature" (Brown 179; Murry 432–48). Brown claims that Swift anticipates Freud in describing essential conflicts of human psychological and cultural development, particularly "the conflict between our animal body, appropriately epitomized in the anal function, and our pretentious sublimations, more specifically the pretensions of sublimated or romantic-Platonic love" (Brown 186). Central to Brown's argument is a leap from anal pleasure — and its potential to disrupt a narrative framed by the telos of heterosexual reproduction — to what he calls "romantic-Platonic love." In joining together *romantic* and *Platonic*, Brown both elides and calls attention to the male homoerotic origins of "Platonic" love (on Plato see Halperin).

Brown finds much evidence in *Gulliver's Travels* to confirm Freud's belief that our erotic desires are essentially bound up with our excretory demands. Brown reads the Yahoos as a "raw core of human bestiality," a crude animal filth that Swift finds both horrifying and, in its horror, bracingly — almost intoxicatingly — delicious and true. According to Brown, it is Gulliver who shrinks from this vision of primal physicality, not Swift: "The essence of Swift's vision and Gulliver's redemption is the recognition that the civilized man of Western Europe not only remains Yahoo but is worse than Yahoo — 'a Sort of Animals to whose share, by what Accident he could not conjecture, some small Pittance of *Reason* had fallen, whereof we made no other Use than by its Assistance to aggravate our *natural* Corruptions, and to acquire new ones which Nature had not given us'" (Brown 189; Swift 235).

Brown describes the Yahoos' excremental excess as "substantially identical with the psychoanalytical doctrine of the extensive role of anal eroticism" as the foundation of human culture:

> According to Freudian theory the human infant passes through a stage — the anal stage — as a result of which the libido, the life energy of the body, gets concentrated in the anal zone. This infantile stage of anal eroticism takes the essential form of attaching symbolic meaning to the anal product. As a result of these symbolic equations the anal product acquires for the child the significance of being his own child or creation, which he may use either to obtain narcissistic pleasure in play, or to obtain love from another (feces as gift), or to assert independence from another (feces as property), or to commit aggression (feces as weapon). Thus some of the most important categories of social behavior (play, gift, property, weapon) originate in the anal stage of infantile sexuality and — what is more important — never lose their connection with it. When infantile sexuality comes to its catastrophic end, nonbodily cultural objects inherit the symbolism originally attached to the anal product, but only as second-best substitutes for the original (sublimations). Sublimations are thus symbols of symbols. The category of property is not simply transferred from feces to money; on the contrary, money is feces, because the anal eroticism continues in the unconscious. The anal eroticism has not been renounced or abandoned but repressed. (191)

The human fascination with dirt and dung, for Brown as for Freud, is a central constituent of human culture, being the human infant's first attempt to control his universe through "defiance, mastery [and the] will to power" (Brown 192).

This symbolic manipulation of excrement and all its sublimations (dirt, money, weapons) is the basis not only of human reason, but also of human aggression: "The Yahoos' filthiness is manifested primarily in excremental aggression: psychoanalytic theory stresses the interconnection between anal organization and human aggression to the point of labeling this phase of infantile sexuality the anal-sadistic phase." Brown glosses over the connections between the Yahoos' pleasure in filth and physicality and their adult sexual practices, noting only that the female Yahoos' odors are heightened at mating time.

I have quoted Brown at length, in effect rolling with his argument, to show how its psychological trajectory works: anal pleasure leads to anal aggression leads to the will to power. The desire for symbolic imitation of the mother ("the anal product acquires for the child the significance of being his own child or creation") is turned into desire for control, desire for wealth. Brown's psychological narrative works ultimately by denying the mother's role as a sexual subject, making the child a subject and symbol-maker instead. The story is much less neatly resolved in Freud's "Character and Anal Erotism" (1908), which attends to residual conflicts from the anal stage:

> To relate obstinacy to an interest in defaecation would seem no
> · easy task; but it should be remembered that even babies can show
> self-will about parting with their stool . . . and that it is a general
> practice in children's upbringing to administer painful stimuli to
> the skin of the buttocks — which is linked up with the erotogenic
> anal zone — in order to break their obstinacy and make them
> more submissive. An invitation to a caress of the anal zone is still
> used to-day, as it was in ancient times, to express defiance or defi-
> ant scorn, and thus in reality signifies an act of tenderness that has
> been overtaken by repression. (173)

Unlike Brown, Freud is less concerned with the filth of the anus than with its pleasures. He notes that homosexual men, "who have retained the anal zone's erotogenic character in adult life" (175), tend not to exhibit the cluster of characteristics he associates with anality: "orderliness, parsimony and obstinacy" (171). For Freud the playful sexual dramas of the anal stage — excrement as pleasurable production and symbolic child, child as symbolic mother, masochism as both violence and game (not the shit itself, nor the repression, but what that process produces and what it means) — are at the foundation of human culture. But in Freud's account, like the Molly House raids, which seem to have allowed enough focused aggression against openly effeminate men to enable a homoerotic culture to survive, anal pleasures remain alive in the psyche even as they are transformed into culturally acceptable ends.

Whereas Brown was concerned with the Yahoos as embodiments of the base, animalistic side of humanity, I wish to emphasize the sexual threat they pose to Swift's narrator. In Gulliver's physical encounters with Yahoos, feces represents his vulnerability. Just before Gulliver arrives in Houyhnhnm-land, he is overtaken by his own sailors: "They all formed a Conspiracy to seize the Ship and secure me; which they did one Morning, rushing into my Cabbin, and binding me Hand and Foot, threatening to throw me overboard, if I offered to stir" (206). In Gulliver's first encounter with Yahoos, they look upon him as an "Object," one of them touching and staring at him "out of Curiosity or Mischief" (208). When he strikes out with his hanger and then runs up a tree to escape, "several of this cursed Brood [get] hold of the Branches behind, leap[t] up into the Tree, from whence they [begin] to discharge their Excrements on [his] Head" (208).

It is not touch by others that offends Gulliver, for he allows at least one Houyhnhnm to stroke his naked body (218), but rather the fear of being taken over, physically and sexually assaulted. Gulliver repeatedly incites Yahoos' aggression in the process of trying to control and separate himself from them:

> I once caught a young Male of three Years old, and endeavored by all Marks of Tenderness to make it quiet; but the little Imp fell a squalling, and scratching, and biting with such Violence, that I was forced to let it go. . . . I forgot another Circumstance (and perhaps I might have the Reader's Pardon, if it were wholly omitted) that while I held the odious Vermin in my Hands, it voided its filthy Excrements of a yellow liquid Substance, all over my Cloaths. (241)

Finally, Gulliver describes a ritual in which one court favorite symbolically replaces his predecessor:

> [The Favorite] continues in Office till a worse can be found; but the very Moment he is discarded, his Successor, at the Head of all the *Yahoos* in that District, Young and Old, Male and Female,

come in a Body, and discharge their Excrements upon him from Head to Foot. (238)

Gulliver's revulsion with Yahoo bodies is crucial to the lines he attempts to draw distinguishing Yahoos, Houyhnhnms, and humans, and excrement is central to that revulsion. But that response is not resolved as neatly as Brown would have it. Gulliver's description of the Yahoos' bodies distinguishes between male and female by attending to hair, breast, and anus:

> Their Heads and Breasts were covered with a thick Hair, some frizzled and others lank; they had Beards like Goats, and a Long Ridge of Hair down their Backs, and the fore Parts of their Legs and Feet; but the rest of their Bodies were bare, so that I might see their Skins, which were of a brown Buff Colour. They had no Tails, nor any Hair at all on their Buttocks, except about the *Anus.* . . . The Females . . . had long lank Hair on their Heads, and only a Sort of Down on the rest of their Bodies, except about the *Anus* and *Pudenda.* Their Dugs hung between their fore Feet, and often reached almost to the Ground as they walked. (207)

The male *anus* and female *pudenda* look alike, visually and symbolically linking sexual desire to anal pleasure. For the Yahoos, pleasure and aggression are linked through what Freud decorously and scientifically calls the "anal product." The Yahoos' excremental pleasures recall Freud's account of "an invitation to a caress of the anal zone . . . signif[ying] an act of tenderness that has been overtaken by repression" (that is, "kiss my butt" is — psychologically as well as historically speaking — a veiled come-on). The anal stage can only be molded into the sexually proscriptive story Brown relates by transforming pleasure *into* aggression, the desire to imitate the mother (feces as symbolic child) into power over the mother (violence and the will to power), and childhood bisexuality into a heterosexual imperative.

Brown's reading of Swift (and the homoerotically charged Freudian narrative it obscures) thus reinforces the cultural history at work between Swift and Freud. What remains to be elaborated is the extent to which Gulliver's negotiation of this web of perverse Yahoo desires requires hatred of the mother. Or, to put the problem another way: We cannot simply deny the *Travels'* essential misogyny by saying, as Brown does, that Gulliver hates all of mankind, not merely women (Brown 181). It is more accurate to say that Gulliver hates humanity through women, and more particularly and more violently through a primal revulsion with the maternal body. At the same time, Gulliver's revulsion obscures a related fear: that of wanting to become the mother — and the female — himself.

EXCREMENT AND THE MATERNAL

There is certainly much in Swift's childhood that would suggest ambivalence about both his own mother and things maternal. Swift's father, also named Jonathan, died eight months before the birth of his only son. Soon after Swift was born, his mother, Abigail, left him in the hands of a wet nurse, who kidnapped him and took him to England for several years. Swift claimed that his nurse was "extremely fond" of him and taught him to read and spell. On those occasions when Swift was returned to his mother, she symbolically abandoned him, most crucially at age six when she sent him to the Kilkenny grammar school, seventy miles from Dublin, and then left Ireland altogether with his older sister, Jane. Although Swift seems to have respected and often praised his mother, their relationship was distant, even by eighteenth-century standards (Ehrenpreis 1: 29–33). I do not rehearse the details of Swift's childhood in order to locate some primal moment in it that renders his literary imagination uniquely, personally perverse. Nor am I asserting that Swift's obsessions and the ways they overlap with psychoanalysis are universally true. Rather, *Gulliver's Travels* seems part of a much larger cultural shift that creates and privileges those very social divisions of gender and sexuality that Freud ultimately came to understand as biological imperatives. And, like Virginia Woolf's experience of childhood sexual abuse, Swift's life presents a compelling conjunction of an individual's psychological narrative and a larger, historically embedded cultural conflict.

If we return to those questions of sexual organization that Brown ignores, we find repeated references to the Yahoos' lasciviousness, their refusal to regulate their physical or sexual desires:

> those Animals [Yahoos], like other Brutes, had their Females in common; but in this they differed, that the She-*Yahoo* would admit the Male, while she was pregnant; and that the Hees would quarrel and fight with the Females as fiercely as with each other. (239)

In contrast to Yahoo promiscuity, the Houyhnhnms practice rigorous family planning; their females' desires are subordinated to the community's reproductive needs:

> When the Matron *Houyhnhnms* have produced one of each Sex, they no longer accompany with their Consorts, except they lose

one of their Issue by some Casualty, which very seldom happens: But in such a Case they meet again; or when the like Accident befalls a Person, whose Wife is past bearing, some other Couple bestows on him one of their own Colts, and then go together a second Time, until the Mother be pregnant. (243)

While the Houyhnhnm females are sexually modest and controlled, the Yahoo females are sexually aggressive, coquettish: "A Female *Yahoo* would often stand behind a Bank or a Bush, to gaze on the young Males . . . and then appear, and hide, using many antick Gestures and Grimaces . . . and when any of the Males advanced she would slowly retire, looking often back" (239). Finally, the she-Yahoos are sensually attracted to non-Yahoo women: "If a female Stranger came among them, three or four of her own Sex would get about her, and stare and chatter, and grin, and smell her all over" (240). Unlike Europeans, however, Yahoos draw the line at actually acting upon their homoerotic desires, which Gulliver describes as "unnatural Appetites in both Sexes."

Between his descriptions of Yahoo and Houyhnhnm sexual practices, Gulliver is assaulted by a female Yahoo:

Being one Day abroad with my Protector the Sorrel Nag, and the Weather exceeding hot, I entreated him to let me bathe in a River that was near. He consented, and I immediately stripped myself stark naked, and went down softly into the Stream. It happened that a young Female *Yahoo* standing behind a Bank, saw the whole Proceeding; and inflamed by Desire . . . came running with all Speed, and leaped into the Water within five Yards of the Place where I bathed. I was never in my Life so terribly frighted. . . . She embraced me after a most fulsome Manner; I roared as loud as I could, and the Nag came galloping towards me, whereupon she quitted her Grasp. (242)

The Yahoos' sexual aggressivity poses a physical as well as a moral threat. As a result of his shame and horror (an almost primal sexual assault that is not described further), when Gulliver returns from the land of the Houyhnhnms he can no longer tolerate the smells of his own wife and children. Gulliver explains, "When I began to consider, that by copulating with one of the *Yahoo*-Species, I had become a Parent of more; it struck me with the utmost Shame, Confusion and Horror" (261). In Gulliver's description of "copulating with one of the *Yahoo*-Species," the satiric distance between Gulliver and his story collapses; the boundaries between human and Yahoo become completely blurred. The Houyhnhnms' fierce regulation of all things sexual and familial — what

Gulliver calls the "Regulation of Children" (245)[7] — rescues him from the overwhelming threat of sexual anarchy, of being rendered a sexual object, a feminized man.

But the end of the novel is not the end of the story. Psychoanalysis suggests that one is profoundly attracted to what one most fears. Gulliver's overwhelming dread of sexual molestation as well as sexual pleasure — of being rendered a Yahoo or a "female Stranger" through sex — is the final chapter in what might be read as his career of male sexual initiation. Through psychoanalysis we can account, at once, for Gulliver's hatred of the female body, its smells and fluids and fleshiness, and his childlike pleasure in being engulfed by this same overwhelming and fleshy maternal otherness. In Lilliput, like the infant who knows himself and the world only through his bodily needs, Gulliver is grossly corporeal, his body monumentally compelling, both magically salvific and absurd. He remains in Lilliput "about nine Months" (63), calling his departure "the Issue of this great Adventure" (67).[8]

Gulliver becomes most elaborately conscious of his physical disgust with the female body as a tiny creature in Brobdingnag, where he is himself dependent on maternal figures. At the inaugural dinner, he describes a nurse soothing her young charge by nursing him:

> I must confess no Object ever disgusted me so much as the Sight of her monstrous Breast, which I cannot tell what to compare with, so as to give the curious Reader an Idea of its Bulk, Shape and Colour. It stood prominent six Foot, and could not be less than sixteen in circumference. The Nipple was about half the Bigness of my Head, and the Hue both of that and the Dug so varified with Spots, Pimples and Freckles, that nothing could appear more nauseaus. For I had a near sight of her, she sitting down the more conveniently to give Suck, and I standing on the table. (98)

The maids of honor do not think of Gulliver as a man, but a "creature who had no sort of consequence." Gulliver's nurse, Glumdalclitch, relates the story of his imminent danger (a story she learned from her own mother) with Gulliver "laid . . . on her Bosom" (102). When Gulliver says he takes the key to his cage from Glumdalclitch for fear that she will *lose* it, given their "great Affection" for one another, he is also covering

---

[7]Gulliver himself has fantasies of sexual regulation when, leaving Blefescu, he imagines taking "a Dozen of the Natives" with him, to breed them like sheep or cattle (87).

[8]According to the *Oxford English Dictionary*, the meaning of *issue* shifts in the eighteenth century from an earlier, more general usage to the modern, specifically legal, term for offspring.

his fear that she will *use* it, that she will not only nurture and dress him for public life (most significantly teaching him language from young girls' grammar books) but control him sexually (109). Most tellingly, in a passage that links fascination with the breast and anal eroticism, Gulliver describes another maid of honor as "a pleasant frolicsome Girl of sixteen," who "would sometimes set [him] astride one of her Nipples" (121).

In Brobdingnag, then, Gulliver is not only the clever and coddled darling, but also the sexual toy of so many maternal maids and their monstrously compelling bodies and breasts; like the infant who cannot control the source of his own food and pleasure, he both adores and detests the "monstrous Breast." Gulliver's ambivalence about the nurturing and engulfing aspects of all things maternal is epitomized in his fantasy about the beggar woman's cancerous breast, into which he imagines he "could have easily crept, and covered [his] whole Body" (115). For Gulliver, as for the subjects of a wide range of eighteenth-century cultural narratives, the constructs Woman and Mother come to be fused. Just as the range of actual women must be culturally mapped onto the new normative "Woman" (Wittig), the range of actual caregivers — wet nurses, siblings, fathers, other relatives — must be culturally remade into the new middle-class "Mother" to create the framework of the bourgeois family (Armstrong; Trumbach 1978). Such transformations, for the cultural subject as well as the culture, are by no means contained or final events: they always leave behind residue from what has been lost.

In a crucial moment in Brobdingnag, Gulliver goes through something like Lacan's *mirror stage* (Lacan 1977, 1–7), in which his imagined cultural mastery (such as taking the "stings" out of four wasps that he later gives to Gresham College, 113) is rendered insignificant in relation to his symbolic mother, the queen: "The Queen used to place me upon her Hand towards a Looking-Glass, by which both our persons appeared before me in full View together; and there could nothing be more ridiculous than the Comparison" (111). Gulliver's lack of physical mastery is imitated in his garbled syntax, "could nothing be" being grammatically incorrect. He is dressed and tended, ultimately, for the queen's amusement. Punningly anticipating the Yahoos' obsession with excrement, Glumdalclitch stands upon a "Stool on the Floor" to "take Care" of Gulliver. The mirror scene in Brobdingnag is recalled among the Houyhnhnms, when Gulliver describes his inability to look on his own form without disgust: "When I happened to behold the Reflection of my own Form in a Lake or Fountain, I turned away my Face in Horror and detestation of my self; and could better endure the Sight of a common *Yahoo*, than of my own Person" (251–52).

According to the psychoanalytic narrative of gender and sexuality, anal eroticism is a crucial part of the child's will to self-control and separation from the mother. The child's early attempts at self-mastery are also fantastic attempts to dismember and consume the overpowering mother, to destroy her through one's own bodily creations. Excrement is, in this sense, the child's first angry response to being controlled through food, to being dependent and a child (Klein 187). The child experiences the mother's rejection as punishment, and in the psychoanalytic account of childhood, pleasure and punishment, desire and guilt are always paired. Swift enacts this fear of punishment symbolically in Gulliver's description of the execution of a "Malefactor":

> The Malefactor was fixed in a Chair upon a Scaffold erected for the Purpose; and his Head cut off at one Blow with a Sword of about forty Foot long. The Veins and Arteries spouted up such a prodigious Quantity of Blood, and so high in the Air, that the great *Jet d'Eau* at *Versailles* was not equal for the Time it lasted; and the Head when it fell on the Scaffold Floor, gave such a Bounce, as made me start, although I were at least an *English* Mile distant. (121)

The jets of blood and water in this passage, like the bowl of cream in which Gulliver almost drowns (112), are also semen and milk, the glorious products of a "fixed" and mangled body that symbolically incarnates both mother and son.[9] Just as the breast in *Gulliver's Travels* is both horrifying and soothingly dreamlike, milk and water are similarly double, embodying playful tensions at work in childhood bisexuality.

Though later mapped onto the child's sense of inhabiting a male or a female body, the child's earliest sense of the fused cultural themes of pleasure and punishment is learned in relationship and in violent response to the mother. Even before the phallus — the cultural privilege that accrues to being male — rears its ugly head, the child is caught in a tension between self/maternal love and maternal/self punishment. To love himself, his body and his bodily productions, the child must mangle those productions and his attachment to the mother who is, like them, magically produced and enlarged by his visual and imaginative energies.

[9]In a very rigid psychoanalytic account of *Gulliver's Travels*, Rothman reads the execution as a castration scene.

Melanie Klein argues that in these first sadistic rages against the maternal body are also found the child's first consciousness of gender:

> The boy, when he finds himself impelled to abandon the oral and anal positions for the genital, passes on to the aim of *penetration* associated with the possession of the penis. Thus he changes not only his libido-position, but its *aim*, and this enables him to retain his original love-object. In the girl, on the other hand, the *receptive* aim is carried over from the oral to the genital position: she changes her libido-position, but retains its aim, which has already led to disappointment in relation to her mother. (186)

Whereas Norman Brown subordinates sexual difference (and indeed sexual pleasure) to the cultural productions and cultural violence associated with anality, it is for Klein the essentially sexual nature of the oral and anal phases that makes them early manifestations of gender difference. According to Lacan, these conflicts are structured like a language, in which they are symbolically resolved. Through language cultural laws of gender and sexuality are symbolically enforced in relation to one another; that is, masculinity and femininity make sense only as opposites, and only when mapped onto what Adrienne Rich calls "compulsory heterosexuality" (see Lacan 1977, 281–91; Mitchell and Rose 40–43 and 74–85; Wilden 186–88; also Abelove; Butler; Rich; Wittig). Boys come to associate their cultural authority with their masculinity, the phallus being the symbolic manifestation of sexual difference in language. So in the transition from the anal to the oedipal stage the male child learns his cultural position — his ability to wield the phallus as it were — through fantasies of violating the mother. The female child, on the other hand, learns to think of herself as the receptor for such violence, the one to be penetrated. And it is in the relationship between maternal protection and violence against the symbolic mother that Gulliver desires but ultimately fails to be a male child, one with a will to penetrate and master, to know and conquer through the colonizing eyes of science.

Psychoanalysis reverts in the extreme to a model of male sexual conquest, but it also suggests the fragile and disunified nature of male sexual subjectivity as a cultural construct (Chauncey; Sedgwick). And so too does Gulliver's return to the symbolic mother in Brobdingnag. Whenever Gulliver begins to experience a safely maternal relationship with his nurse, he is ripped out of his fantasies of conquest, and his elaborate ideas of self-control prove unequal to the demands of the queen and her maids. While the maids of honor repeatedly trivialize

Gulliver, rendering him physically and linguistically a "*Mannikin*" or "child-Man" (101), he is most horribly rendered not merely child, but not-even-human when he is "seized by a monkey" who holds him "as a Nurse doth a Child she is going to suckle" and "squeeze[s him] so hard" that he finds it "prudent to submit" (123). In retrospect Gulliver imagines he could have wounded the monkey with a knife, but at the time he did not. In contrast, when he is trapped by his mistress and attacked by two rats, he has the "good Fortune to rip up" the rat's "Belly" before he himself is eaten (100). Drawing on symbolic tensions at work in anal sadism, Gulliver's final adventure in Brobdingnag involves jumping into a pile of cow dung (bodily pleasure), yet he leaves Brobdingnag as the king attempts to find a woman to make him breed (forced reproduction as punishment). Once again like a child (or a pregnant woman), he travels for nine months (146) in a dark and womblike box, the ocean's uterine waves bringing occasional "faint Hopes of Relief" (141).

Gulliver imaginatively enters the female sexual body in Laputa; however, after time spent among the Houyhnhnms, he cannot distance himself far enough from the female body he has symbolically conquered and colonized. Gulliver's revulsion with the female body structures the fourth voyage. Gulliver leaves his wife, Mary, "big with Child" (205) at the beginning of the voyage and returns to find her "intolerable," the "very Smell" of his wife and children revolting (261). In the end, even marriage disgusts him, managed and regulated reproduction reminding him of his failure to conquer with reason, his inability to be sentient except through his body and its sticky, demanding bonds to other human bodies. To conquer the maternal body is always in some sense to be engulfed and feminized by it, to find comfort in the cavernous and cancerous breast. And, in Swift as in Freud, female desire must be culturally regulated in order to keep the overpowering aspects of the female body under male control. But why, finally, must mothers and feminized men be regulated? And how does this sexual regulation structure the early English novel?

THE NOVEL AND THE MATERNAL

Gulliver's Travels participates in cultural contests between female sexual agency and male subjectivity; between the voice of female desire and female authority associated with early-eighteenth-century women writers (Backscheider 71–104) and the essentially male political subject of liberal humanist discourse (Pateman).[10] As recent critics have shown, the containment of female desire is one of the major cultural projects of the eighteenth-century novel (Armstrong; Castle 1986). Psychoanalysis is a later cultural narrative that attempts to render this model of gender *normative* by collapsing it onto sexual difference and the imperatives of heterosexual reproduction.[11] But the residual tensions between female sexual agency and the disembodied but essentially male structures of domestic containment are crucial to the negotiation of class conflict and the consolidation of middle-class subjectivity at work in the eighteenth-century novel (Armstrong; McKeon).

Historically, *Gulliver's Travels* hearkens back to the early 1700s and the numerous women writers who invoked Queen Anne to grant symbolic authority to their literary productions.[12] Harold Williams suggests that Swift's initial work on *Gulliver's Travels* began in 1714, with the death of Queen Anne and the Tories' fall from power (Davis xii). Publicly pregnant some seventeen times yet unable to produce a child to succeed her on the throne of England, Queen Anne was a spectacle of failed maternity. Her propagandists were well aware of the cultural meanings and cultural uses of maternity, creating ways to translate the queen's bodily failure into political success. Swift evoked this historical moment in the prefatory "Letter from Capt. *Gulliver* to his Cousin *Sympson*" (27), and through public wrangling with printers over a chapter head about the ability of Queen Anne — Gulliver's "Political Mother" (133) — to govern, it became part of the ongoing popular discussion of the relationship between Swift and his satiric narrator.

The language of Swift's letter from the "Publisher to the Reader" suggests that in these public debates the author becomes like a mother, and the novel is his symbolic child.[13] Before Gulliver "quitted *Redriff*, he left the Custody of the following Papers" in the publisher's hands, "with the Liberty to dispose of them as [he] should think fit"; the pub-

---

[10]Other feminists have read Locke and liberal humanism as good for women; see, for example, Perry 1985.

[11]Freud, of course, did not begin by understanding male violence and female submission as biological in origin; his initial stories of childhood sexuality emphasized the cultural production of masculine and feminine sexuality. Freud later used the claims of biology to assert the scientific truth of psychoanalysis amidst fierce opposition from his medical colleagues (Gilman; Masson; Herman 17–19).

[12]See Barash in Grundy. *Gulliver's Travels* is, in its complicated relationship to early-eighteenth-century women writers and their symbolic affiliations with Queen Anne, linked to Pope's *Rape of the Lock* (1714) and *Dunciad* (1728) and Defoe's female-voiced novels, especially *Roxana* (1724).

[13]See Maus for the tradition of male author as symbolic mother.

lisher "by the Advice of several worthy Persons . . . now venture[s] to send them into the World" (31). Throughout the *Travels*, and especially in Brobdingnag, Gulliver is similarly dependent and helpless. The king of Brobdingnag does not believe that Gulliver is a living thing and calls him a "piece of Clock-work"; one of the male scholars describes him as "an abortive Birth" (107–08). Like Swift's novel at the mercy of English printers (and Swift himself dependent on Queen Anne), Gulliver in Brobdingnag is entirely in the queen's service, both at her beck and call and kept alive by her.

In *Gulliver's Travels*, then, Swift is both reentering the maternal political body of the early 1700s and subjecting that body to the new regulatory imperative of the 1720s. (With the phrase "regulatory imperative" I refer to a rash of new laws in the 1720s governing sexuality, women and colonials, and books.) In cultural narratives popular in the 1720s — not just the Toft stories and Gulliveriana, but such epistolary pseudomedical conduct books as *Onania; Or the Heinous Sin of Self-Pollution* (originally published in 1709, reprinted with sequels in the 1720s; see Fox) — discussions of monstrous mothers, feminized men and phallic women, and the dangers of reading sexual texts are often situated in relation to England's fears and fantasies about new colonial "others."[14] In these novels, popular tracts, and early conduct books, the regulation of homosexual desire and the regulation of sexual discourse (what can be written legitimately about desire) are overlapping concerns.[15] Together and over time, these two problems were crucial to new forms of class and national identity — to defining the middle class and their books in relation to all the things they were not permitted to be.

As a genre with roots in cultural rituals of shaming and exclusion (Elliott), satire is structurally analogous to anal sadism, in that its pleasures come from excluding and symbolically violating those who threaten to destroy the satirist's (and the community's) rules of order. The symbolic trajectory implicit in *Gulliver's Travels* (violating mothers to cover a dread of male passivity and the sexual anarchy it represents) finds its most extreme enactment in a later satiric novel, de Sade's *Philosophy in the Bedroom* (1795; rpt. 1965). In *Philosophy in the Bedroom* the daughter, Eugenie (literally "good-blood"), must watch as her

---

[14]See Nussbaum on how the maternal body is used to represent racial difference in works from a slightly later period.

[15]In *Before Novels*, J. Paul Hunter describes the range of popular narrative forms that evolved into the English novel.

mother (who represents all forms of sexual regulation) is violently raped by two bisexual men and then has her genitals sewn shut.[16] In effect, the more sodomy is allowed into a sexual text ("sodomy" being, in the legal sense that developed in the eighteenth century, all sexual acts not directed towards heterosexual reproduction), the more the fantastically controlling mother embodies the law of sexuality and must be punished for representing that law.

We should thus understand Gulliver's numerous close encounters with the stuff and junk of the female body not merely as gynophobic (or even matrophobic), nor merely as part of a new medical discourse that increasingly regulates in order to govern the female body. Rather, Gulliver is fascinated with the maternal body as essentially metamorphic: a body that is known in itself and through itself, but is never just itself; a maternal body that produces, governs, and regulates cultural difference because it is, at different times, different physical bodies. And, in this sense, the mother — like the effeminate man — represents a fundamentally new construction of gender, in which bodies are given meaning through social performance and exchange, rather than through class privilege. These metamorphic social bodies are in need of governance because they are bodies, potentially, that produce different sexual narratives, stories that undermine proscriptive accounts of gender and sexuality — including the account provided by traditional psychoanalysis.

WORKS CITED

Abelove, Henry. "Some Speculations on the History of Sexual Intercourse during the Long Eighteenth Century in England." *Genders* 6 (1989): 125–30.

Armstrong, Nancy. *Desire and Domestic Fiction: A Political History of the Novel*. New York: Oxford UP, 1987.

Armstrong, Nancy, and Tennenhouse, Leonard. *The Imaginary Puritan: Literature, Intellectual Labor, and the Origins of Personal Life*. Berkeley: U of California P, 1992.

Backscheider, Paula R. *Spectacular Politics: Theatrical Power and Mass Culture in Early Modern England*. Baltimore: Johns Hopkins UP, 1993.

[16]Hunt (17–35) suggests that modern pornography developed in those cultures and periods — seventeenth-century France; eighteenth-century England — in which the novel (and along with it women as authors and readers) also thrived.

Bakhtin, M. M. "Discourse in the Novel." *The Dialogic Imagination*. Trans. Caryl Emerson and Michael Holquist and ed. Holquist. Austin: U of Texas P, 1981. 259–422.

Barash, Carol. "'The Native Liberty . . . of the Subject': Configurations of Gender and Authority in the Works of Mary Chudleigh, Sarah Fyge Egerton, and Mary Astell." *Women, Writing, History 1640–1740*. Ed. Isobel Grundy and Susan Wiseman. Athens: U of Georgia P, 1992. 55–69.

Bray, Alan. *Homosexuality in Renaissance England*. London: Gay Men's Press, 1982.

Brown, Norman O. *Life against Death: The Psychoanalytic Meaning of History*. Middletown, CT: Wesleyan UP, 1959.

Bruce, Susan. "The Flying Island and Female Anatomy." *Genders* 2 (1988): 60–76.

Butler, Judith. *Gender Trouble: Feminism and the Subversion of Identity*. New York: Routledge, 1990.

Castle, Terry. *Masquerade and Civilization: The Carnivalesque in Eighteenth-Century English Culture and Fiction*. Stanford: Stanford UP, 1986.

———. "Why the Houyhnhnms Don't Write." *"Gulliver's Travels": A Case Study in Contemporary Criticism*. Ed. Christopher Fox. Boston: Bedford–St. Martin's, 1994. (379)

Chauncey, George. "From Sexual Inversion to Homosexuality: Medicine and the Changing Conceptualization of Female Deviance." *Salmagundi* 58–59 (1982–83): 114–46.

Cody, Lisa. "The Doctor's in Labour; or a New Whim Wham from Guildford." *Gender & History* 7 (1992): 175–96.

Davis, Herbert, ed. *Jonathan Swift's "Gulliver's Travels"*. Oxford: Basil Blackwell, 1965.

Elliott, Robert C. *The Power of Satire: Magic, Ritual, Art*. Princeton: Princeton UP, 1960.

Ehrenpreis, Irvin. *Swift: The Man, His Works, and the Age*. 3 vols. Cambridge, MA: Harvard UP, 1962–83.

Epstein, Julia. "Either/Or — Neither/Both: Sexual Ambiguity and the Ideology of Gender." *Genders* 7 (1990): 99–142.

Flynn, Carol Houlihan. *The Body in Swift and Defoe*. Cambridge: Cambridge UP, 1990.

Foucault, Michel. *The History of Sexuality. Volume I: An Introduction*. Trans. Robert Hurley. New York: Vintage, 1980.

Fox, Christopher. "The Myth of Narcissus in Swifts' *Travels*." *Eighteenth-Century Studies* 20 (1986–87): 17–33.

Foxon, David. *Libertine Literature in England, 1660–1745.* New Hyde, NY: University Books, 1965.

Freud, Sigmund. "Character and Anal Eroticism." Standard Edition, vol. IX. London: Hogarth, 1908.

——. "Femininity." *New Introductory Lectures on Psycho-Analysis.* Standard Edition, vol. XXII. London: Hogarth, 1933.

——. *Three Essays on the Theory of Sexuality.* 1905. Rpt. New York: Basic, 1962.

Gallop, Jane. "The Teacher's Breasts." *Pedagogy: The Question of Impersonation.* Ed. Jane Gallop. Bloomington: Indiana UP, 1994.

Gilman, Sandra. *Freud, Race and Gender.* Princeton: Princeton UP, 1993.

Greenblatt, Stephen. *Shakespearan Negotiations: The Circulation of Social Energy in Renaissance England.* Berkeley: U of California P, 1988.

Halperin, David M. *One Hundred Years of Homosexuality.* New York: Routledge, 1990.

Herman, Judith Lewis. *Trauma and Recovery.* New York: Basic, 1992.

Hulme, Peter. *Colonial Encounters: Europe and the Native Caribbean 1492–1797.* London: Methuen, 1986.

Hunt, Lynn, ed. *The Invention of Pornography: Obscenity and the Origins of Modernity, 1500–1800.* New York: Zone, 1993.

Hunter, J. Paul. *Before Novels: The Cultural Contexts of Eighteenth-Century English Fiction.* New York: Norton, 1990.

Klein, Melanie. *Love, Guilt and Reparation and Other Works, 1921–1945.* New York: Macmillan, 1975.

Lacan, Jacques. *Ecrits: A Selection.* Trans. Alan Sheridan. New York: Norton, 1977.

——. *Speech and Language in Psychoanalysis.* Ed. and trans. Anthony Wilden. Baltimore: Johns Hopkins UP, 1981.

Laplanche, J., and J.-B. Pontalis. *The Language of Psychoanalysis.* New York: Norton, 1973.

Laqueur, Thomas. *Making Sex: Body and Gender from the Greeks to Freud.* Cambridge, MA: Harvard UP, 1990.

Leslie, Glennda. "Cheat and Imposter: Debate Following the Case of the Rabbit Breeder." *The Eighteenth Century* 27.3 (1986): 269–86.

Love Letters Between a Certain Late Nobleman and the Famous Mr. Wilson. 1723. Ed. Michael S. Kimmel. New York: Rpt. Haworth, 1990.

Masson, Jeffrey. *The Assault on Truth: Freud's Suppression of the Seduction Theory*. New York: Farrar, 1984.

Maus, Katharine Eisaman. "A Womb of His Own: Male Renaissance Poets in the Female Body." *Sexuality and Gender in Early Modern Europe: Institutions, Texts, Images*. Ed. James Grantham Turner. Cambridge: Cambridge UP, 1993. 266–88.

McKeon, Michael. *The Origins of the English Novel, 1600–1740*. Baltimore: Johns Hopkins UP, 1987.

Mitchell, Juliet, and Jacqueline Rose. *Feminine Sexuality: Jacques Lacan and the école freudienne*. Trans. Rose. New York: Norton, 1982.

Murry, J. M. *Jonathan Swift: A Critical Biography*. London: Cape, 1954.

Nussbaum, Felicity. "The Other Woman: Polygamy, *Pamela* and the Prerogative of Empire." *Women, "Race," and Writing in the Early Modern Period*. Ed. Margot Hendricks and Patricia Parker. New York: Routledge, 1994. 138–159.

Pateman, Carol. *The Sexual Contract*. Stanford: Stanford UP, 1988.

Perry, Ruth. "Colonizing the Breast: Sexuality and Maternity in Eighteenth-Century England." *Journal of the History of Sexuality* 2.2 (1991): 204–34.

———. "Radical Doubt and the Liberation of Women." *Eighteenth-Century Studies* 18 (1985): 472–94.

Rich, Adrienne. "Compulsory Heterosexuality and Lesbian Existence." *Blood, Bread and Poetry: Selected Prose 1979–85*. New York: Norton, 1986. 23–75.

Rothman, Irving. "The Execution Scene in *Gulliver's Travels*." *Journal of Evolutionary Psychology* 3.1–2 (1982): 56–75.

Sade, Donatien Alphonse, marquis de. *La Philosophie dans le Boudoir (Philosophy in the Bedroom)*. 1795. Rpt. in *The Marquis de Sade: Justine, Philosophy in the Bedroom, and Other Writings*. Ed. Richard Seaver and Austryn Wainhouse. New York: Grove Weidenfeld, 1965. 179–367.

Salvaggio, Ruth. "Swift and Psychoanalysis, Language and Woman." *Women's Studies* 15.1 (1988): 417–34.

Schiebinger, Londa. *Nature's Body: Gender in the Making of Modern Science*. Boston: Beacon, 1993.

Sedgwick, Eve Kosofsky. *Epistemology of the Closet*. Berkeley: U of California P, 1990.

Trumbach, Randolph. "London's Sodomites: Homosexual Behavior and Western Culture in the eighteenth Century." *Journal of Social History* 11.1 (1977–78): 1–33.

————. *The Rise of the Egalitarian Family.* New York: Academic, 1978.

Walkowitz, Judith R. *City of Dreadful Delight: Narratives of Sexual Danger in Late-Victorian London.* Chicago: U of Chicago P, 1992.

Wilden, Anthony. "Lacan and the Discourse of the Other." *Speech and Language in Psychoanalysis.* Jacques Lacan. Trans. Wilden. Baltimore: Johns Hopkins UP, 1981. 159–311.

Wittig, Monique. "One Is Not Born a Woman." *The Straight Mind and Other Essays.* Boston: Beacon, 1992.

Glossary of Critical
and Theoretical Terms

Most terms have been glossed parenthetically where they first appear in the text. Mainly, the glossary lists terms that are too complex to define in a phrase or a sentence or two. A few of the terms listed are discussed at greater length elsewhere (feminist criticism, for instance); these terms are defined succinctly and a page reference to the longer discussion is provided.

AFFECTIVE FALLACY   First used by William K. Wimsatt and Monroe C. Beardsley to refer to what they regarded as the erroneous practice of interpreting texts according to the psychological responses of readers. "The Affective Fallacy," they wrote in a 1946 essay later republished in the *The Verbal Icon* (1954), "is a confusion between the poem and its *results* (what is *is* and what it *does*). . . . It begins by trying to derive the standards of criticism from the psychological effects of a poem and ends in impressionism and relativism." The affective fallacy, like the intentional fallacy (confusing the meaning of a work with the author's expressly intended meaning), was one of the main tenets of the New Criticism, or formalism. The affective fallacy has recently been contested by reader-response critics, who have deliberately dedicated their efforts to describing the way individual readers and "interpretive communities" go about "making sense" of texts.

See also: Authorial Intention, Formalism, Reader-Response Criticism.

AUTHORIAL INTENTION   Defined narrowly, an author's intention in writing a work, as expressed in letters, diaries, interviews, and conversations. Defined more broadly, "intentionality" involves unexpressed motivations, designs, and purposes, some of which may have remained unconscious.

The debate over whether critics should try to discern an author's intentions (conscious or otherwise) is an old one. William K. Wimsatt and Monroe C.

Beardsley, in an essay first published in the 1940s, coined the term "intentional fallacy" to refer to the practice of basing interpretations on the expressed or implied intentions of authors, a practice they judged to be erroneous. As proponents of the New Criticism, or formalism, they argued that a work of literature is an object in itself and should be studied as such. They believed that it is sometimes helpful to learn what an author intended, but the critic's real purpose is to show what is actually in the text, not what an author intended to put there.

See also: Affective Fallacy, Formalism.

BASE   *See* Marxist Criticism.

BINARY OPPOSITIONS   *See* Oppositions.

BLANKS   *See* Gaps.

CANON   Since the fourth century, used to refer to those books of the Bible that the Christian church accepts as being Holy Scripture. The term has come to be applied more generally to those literary works given special status, or "privileged," by a culture. Works we tend to think of as "classics" or the "Great Books" produced by Western culture — texts that are found in every anthology of American, British, and world literature — would be among those that constitute the canon.

Recently, Marxist, feminist, minority, and Third World critics have argued that, for political reasons, many excellent works never enter the canon. Canonized works, they claim, are those that reflect — and respect — the culture's dominant ideology and/or perform some socially acceptable or even necessary form of "cultural work." Attempts have been made to broaden or redefine the canon by discovering valuable texts, or versions of texts, that were repressed or ignored for political reasons. These have been published both in traditional and in nontraditional anthologies. The most outspoken critics of the canon, especially radical critics practicing cultural criticism, have called into question the whole concept of canon or "canonicity." Privileging no form of artistic expression that reflects and revises the culture, these critics treat cartoons, comics, and soap operas with the same cogency and respect they accord novels, poems, and plays.

See also: Cultural Criticism, Feminist Criticism, Ideology, Marxist Criticism.

CONFLICTS, CONTRADICTIONS   *See* Gaps.

CULTURAL CRITICISM   A critical approach that is sometimes referred to as "cultural studies" or "cultural critique." Practitioners of cultural criticism oppose "high" definitions of culture and take seriously popular cultural forms. Grounded in a variety of continental European influences, cultural criticism nonetheless gained institutional force in England, in 1964, with the founding of the Centre for Contemporary Cultural Studies at Birmingham University. Broadly interdisciplinary in its scope and approach, cultural criticism views the text as the locus and catalyst of a complex network of political and economic discourses. Cultural critics share with Marxist critics an interest in the ideological contexts of cultural forms.

DECONSTRUCTION   A poststructuralist approach to literature that is strongly influenced by the writings of the French philosopher Jacques Derrida.

Deconstruction, partly in response to structuralism and formalism, posits the undecidability of meaning for all texts. In fact, as the deconstructionist critic J. Hillis Miller points out, "deconstruction is not a dismantling of the structure of a text but a demonstration that it has already dismantled itself." See "What Is Deconstruction?" pp. 368–377.

DIALECTIC Originally developed by Greek philosophers, mainly Socrates and Plato, as a form and method of logical argumentation; the term later came to denote a philosophical notion of evolution. The German philosopher G. W. F. Hegel described dialectic as a process whereby a thesis, when countered by an antithesis, leads to the synthesis of a new idea. Karl Marx and Friedrich Engels, adapting Hegel's idealist theory, used the phrase "dialectical materialism" to discuss the way in which a revolutionary class war might lead to the synthesis of a new social economic order. The American Marxist critic Fredric Jameson has coined the phrase "dialectical criticism" to refer to a Marxist critical approach that synthesizes structuralist and poststructuralist methodologies.

See also: Marxist Criticism, Structuralism, Poststructuralism.

DIALOGIC *See* Discourse.

DISCOURSE Used specifically, can refer to (1) spoken or written discussion of a subject or area of knowledge; (2) the words in, or text of, a narrative as opposed to its story line; or (3) a "strand" within a given narrative that argues a certain point or defends a given value system.

More generally, "discourse" refers to the language in which a subject or area of knowledge is discussed or a certain kind of business is transacted. Human knowledge is collected and structured in discourses. Theology and medicine are defined by their discourses, as are politics, sexuality, and literary criticism.

A society is generally made up of a number of different discourses or "discourse communities," one or more of which may be dominant or serve the dominant ideology. Each discourse has its own vocabulary, concepts, and rules, knowledge of which constitutes power. The psychoanalyst and psychoanalytic critic Jacques Lacan has treated the unconscious as a form of discourse, the patterns of which are repeated in literature. Cultural critics, following Mikhail Bakhtin, use the word "dialogic" to discuss the dialogue *between* discourses that takes place within language or, more specifically, a literary text.

See also: Cultural Criticism, Ideology, Narrative, Psychoanalytic Criticism.

FEMINIST CRITICISM An aspect of the feminist movement whose primary goals include critiquing masculine-dominated language and literature by showing how they reflect a masculine ideology; writing the history of unknown or undervalued women writers, thereby earning them their rightful place in the literary canon; and helping create a climate in which women's creativity may be fully realized and appreciated. See "What Is Feminist Criticism?" pp. 307–314.

FIGURE *See* Metaphor, Metonymy, Symbol.

FORMALISM Also referred to as the New Criticism, formalism reached its height during the 1940s and 1950s but it is still practiced today. Formalists treat a work of literary art as if it were a self-contained, self-referential object. Rather than basing their interpretations of a text on the reader's response, the author's stated intentions, or parallels between the text and historical contexts (such as the author's life), formalists concentrate on the relationships *within* the text that give it its own distinctive character or form. Special attention is paid to repetition, particularly of images or symbols, but also of sound effects and rhythms in poetry.

Because of the importance placed on close analysis and the stress on the text as a carefully crafted, orderly object containing observable formal patterns, formalism has often been seen as an attack on Romanticism and impressionism, particularly impressionistic criticism. It has sometimes even been called an "objective" approach to literature. Formalists are more likely than certain other critics to believe and say that the meaning of a text can be known objectively. For instance, reader-response critics see meaning as a function either of each reader's experience or of the norms that govern a particular "interpretive community," and deconstructors argue that texts mean opposite things at the same time.

Formalism was originally based on essays written during the 1920s and 1930s by T. S. Eliot, I. A. Richards, and William Empson. It was significantly developed later by a group of American poets and critics, including R. P. Blackmur, Cleanth Brooks, John Crowe Ransom, Allen Tate, Robert Penn Warren, and William K. Wimsatt. Although we associate formalism with certain principles and terms (such as the "Affective Fallacy" and the "Intentional Fallacy" as defined by Wimsatt and Monroe C. Beardsley), formalists were trying to make a cultural statement rather than establish a critical dogma. Generally Southern, religious, and culturally conservative, they advocated the inherent value of literary works (particularly of literary works regarded as beautiful art objects) because they were sick of the growing ugliness of modern life and contemporary events. Some recent theorists even suggest that the rising popularity of formalism after World War II was a feature of American isolationism, the formalist tendency to isolate literature from biography and history being a manifestation of the American fatigue with wider involvements.

See also: Affective Fallacy, Authorial Intention, Deconstruction, Reader-Response Criticism, Symbol.

GAPS   When used by reader-response critics familiar with the theories of Wolfgang Iser, refers to "blanks" in texts that must be filled in by readers. A gap may be said to exist whenever and wherever a reader perceives something to be missing between words, sentences, paragraphs, stanzas, or chapters. Readers respond to gaps actively and creatively, explaining apparent inconsistencies in point of view, accounting for jumps in chronology, speculatively supplying information missing from plots, and resolving problems or issues left ambiguous or "indeterminate" in the text.

Reader-response critics sometimes speak as if a gap actually exists in a text; a gap is, of course, to some extent a product of readers' perceptions. Different readers may find gaps in different texts, and different gaps in the same text. Furthermore, they may fill these gaps in different ways, which is why, a reader-response critic might argue, works are interpreted in different ways.

Although the concept of the gap has been used mainly by reader-response critics, it has also been used by critics taking other theoretical approaches. Practitioners of deconstruction might use "gap" when speaking of the radical contradictoriness of a text. Marxists have used the term to speak of everything from the gap that opens up between economic base and cultural superstructure to the two kinds of conflicts or contradictions to be found in literary texts. The first of these, they would argue, results from the fact that texts reflect ideology, within which certain subjects cannot be covered, things that cannot be said, contradictory views that cannot be recognized as contradictory. The second kind of conflict, contradiction, or gap within a text results from the fact that works don't just reflect ideology: they are also fictions that, consciously or unconsciously, distance themselves from the same ideology.

See also: Deconstruction, Ideology, Marxist Criticism, Reader-Response Criticism.

GENRE A French word referring to a kind or type of literature. Individual works within a genre may exhibit a distinctive form, be governed by certain conventions, and/or represent characteristic subjects. Tragedy, epic, and romance are all genres.

Perhaps inevitably, the term "genre" is used loosely. Lyric poetry is a genre, but so are characteristic *types* of the lyric, such as the sonnet, the ode, and the elegy. Fiction is a genre, as are detective fiction and science fiction. The list of genres grows constantly as critics establish new lines of connection between individual works and discern new categories of works with common characteristics. Moreover, some writers form hybrid genres by combining the characteristics of several in a single work.

Knowledge of genres helps critics to understand and explain what is conventional and unconventional, borrowed and original, in a work.

HEGEMONY Given intellectual currency by the Italian communist Antonio Gramsci, the word (a translation of *egemonia*) refers to the pervasive system of assumptions, meanings, and values — the web of ideologies, in other words — that shapes the way things look, what they mean, and therefore what reality *is* for the majority of people within a given culture.

See also: Ideology, Marxist Criticism.

IDEOLOGY A set of beliefs underlying the customs, habits, and/or practices common to a given social group. To members of that group, the beliefs seem obviously true, natural, and even universally applicable. They may seem just as obviously arbitrary, idiosyncratic, and even false to outsiders or members of another group who adhere to another ideology. Within a society, several ideologies may coexist, or one or more may be dominant.

Ideologies may be forcefully imposed or willingly subscribed to. Their component beliefs may be held consciously or unconsciously. In either case, they come to form what Johanna M. Smith has called "the unexamined ground of our experience." Ideology governs our perceptions, judgments, and prejudices — our sense of what is acceptable, normal, and deviant. Ideology may cause a revolution; it may also allow discrimination and even exploitation.

Ideologies are of special interest to sociologically oriented critics of literature because of the way in which authors reflect or resist prevailing views in their texts. Some Marxist critics have argued that literary texts reflect and reproduce the ideologies that produced them; most, however, have shown how ideologies are riven with contradictions that works of literature manage to expose and widen. Still other Marxists have focused on the way in which texts themselves are characterized by gaps, conflicts, and contradictions between their ideological and anti-ideological functions.

Feminist critics have addressed the question of ideology by seeking to expose (and thereby call into question) the patriarchal ideology mirrored or inscribed in works written by men — even men who have sought to counter sexism and break down sexual stereotypes. New historicists have been interested in demonstrating the ideological underpinnings not only of literary representations but also of our interpretations of them. Fredric Jameson, an American Marxist critic, argues that all thought is ideological, but that ideological thought that knows itself as such stands the chance of seeing through and transcending ideology.

See also: Cultural Criticism, Feminist Criticism, Marxist Criticism, New Historicism.

IMAGINARY ORDER   One of the three essential orders of the psychoanalytic field (see Real and Symbolic Order), it is most closely associated with the senses (sight, sound, touch, taste, and smell). The infant, who by comparison to other animals is born premature and thus is wholly dependent on others for a prolonged period, enters the Imaginary order when it begins to experience a unity of body parts and motor control that is empowering. This usually occurs between six and eighteen months, and is called by Lacan the "mirror stage" or "mirror phase," in which the child anticipates mastery of its body. It does so by identifying with the *image* of wholeness (that is, seeing its own image in the mirror, experiencing its mother as a whole body, and so on). This sense of oneness, and also difference from others (especially the mother or primary caretaker), is established through an image or a vision of harmony that is both a mirroring and a "mirage of maturation" or false sense of individuality and independence. The Imaginary is a metaphor for unity, is related to the visual order, and is always part of human subjectivity. Because the subject is fundamentally separate from others and also internally divided (conscious/unconscious), the apparent coherence of the Imaginary, its fullness and grandiosity, is always false, a *mis*recognition that the ego (or "me") tries to deny by imagining itself as coherent and empowered. The Imaginary operates in conjunction with the Real and Symbolic and is not a "stage" of development equivalent to Freud's "preoedipal stage," nor is it pre-linguistic.

See also: Psychoanalytic Criticism, Real, Symbolic Order.

IMPLIED READER   A phrase used by reader-response critics in place of the phrase "the reader." Whereas "the reader" could refer to any idiosyncratic individual who happens to have read or to be reading the text, "the implied reader" is *the* reader intended, even created, by the text. Other reader-response critics seeking to describe this more generally conceived reader have spoken of the "informed reader" or the "narratee," who is "the necessary counterpart of a given narrator."

See Reader-Response Criticism.

INTENTIONAL FALLACY   *See* Authorial Intention.

INTENTIONALITY   *See* Authorial Intention.

INTERTEXTUALITY   The condition of interconnectedness among texts. Every author has been influenced by others, and every work contains explicit and implicit references to other works. Writers may consciously or unconsciously echo a predecessor or precursor; they may also consciously or unconsciously disguise their indebtedness, making intertextual relationships difficult for the critic to trace.

Reacting against the formalist tendency to view each work as a freestanding object, some poststructuralist critics suggested that the meaning of a work only emerges intertextually, that is, within the context provided by other works. But there has been a reaction, too, against this type of intertextual criticism. Some new historicist critics suggest that literary history is itself too narrow a context and that works should be interpreted in light of a larger set of cultural contexts.

There is, however, a broader definition of intertextuality, one that refers to the relationship between works of literature and a wide range of narratives and discourses that we don't usually consider literary. Thus defined, intertextuality could be used by a new historicist to refer to the significant interconnectedness between a literary text and nonliterary discussions of or discourses about contemporary culture. Or it could be used by a poststructuralist to suggest that a work can only be recognized and read within a vast field of signs and tropes that is *like* a text and that makes any single text self-contradictory and "undecidable."

See also: Discourse, Formalism, Narrative, New Historicism, Poststructuralism, Trope.

MARXIST CRITICISM   An approach that treats literary texts as material products, describing them in broadly historical terms. In Marxist criticism, the text is viewed in terms of its production and consumption, as a product *of* work that does identifiable cultural work of its own. Following Karl Marx, the founder of communism, Marxist critics have used the term "base" to refer to economic reality and "superstructure" to refer to the corresponding or "homologous" infrastructure consisting of politics, law, philosophy, religion, and the arts. Also following Marx, they have used the word "ideology" to refer to that set of cultural beliefs that literary works at once reproduce, resist, and revise.

METAPHOR   The representation of one thing by another related or similar thing. The image (or activity or concept) used to represent or "figure" something else is known as the "vehicle" of the metaphor; the thing represented is called the "tenor." In other words, the vehicle is what we substitute for the tenor. The relationship between vehicle and tenor can provide much additional meaning. Thus, instead of saying, "Last night I read a book," we might say, "Last night I plowed through a book." "Plowed through" (or the activity of plowing) is the vehicle of our metaphor; "read" (or the act of reading) is the tenor, the thing being figured. The increment in meaning through metaphor is fairly obvious. Our audience knows not only *that* we read but also *how* we read, because to read a book in the way that a plow rips through earth is surely to read in a relentless, unreflective way. Note that in the sentence above, a new metaphor — "rips through" — has been used to explain an old one. This serves (which is a metaphor) as an example of just how thick (another metaphor) language is with metaphors!

Metaphor is a kind of "trope" (literally, a "turning," that is, a figure that alters or "turns" the meaning of a word or phrase). Other tropes include allegory, conceit, metonymy, personification, simile, symbol, and synecdoche. Traditionally, metaphor and symbol have been viewed as the principal tropes; minor tropes have been categorized as *types* of these two major ones. Similes, for instance, are usually defined as simple metaphors that usually employ "like" or "as" and state the tenor outright, as in "My love is like a red, red rose." Synecdoche involves a vehicle that is a *part* of the tenor, as in "I see a sail" meaning "I see a boat." Metonymy is viewed as a metaphor involving two terms commonly if arbitrarily associated with (but not fundamentally or intrinsically related to) each other. Recently, however, deconstructors such as Paul de Man and J. Hillis Miller have questioned the "privilege" granted to metaphor and the metaphor/metonymy distinction or "opposition." They have suggested that all metaphors are really metonyms and that all figuration is arbitrary.

See also: Deconstruction, Metonymy, Oppositions, Symbol.

METONYMY The representation of one thing by another that is commonly and often physically associated with it. To refer to a writer's handwriting as his or her "hand" is to use a metonymic "figure" or "trope." The image or thing used to represent something else is known as the "vehicle" of the metonym; the thing represented is called the "tenor."

Like other tropes (such as metaphor), metonymy involves the replacement of one word or phrase by another. Liquor may be referred to as "the bottle," a monarch as "the crown." Narrowly defined, the vehicle of a metonym is arbitrarily, not intrinsically, associated with the tenor. In other words, the bottle just happens to be what liquor is stored in and poured from in our culture. The hand may be involved in the production of handwriting, but so are the brain and the pen. There is no special, intrinsic likeness between a crown and a monarch; it's just that crowns traditionally sit on monarchs' heads and not on the heads of university professors. More broadly, "metonym" and "metonymy" have been used by recent critics to refer to a wide range of figures and tropes. Deconstructors have questioned the distinction between metaphor and metonymy.

See also: Deconstruction, Metaphor, Trope.

NARRATIVE A story or a telling of a story, or an account of a situation or of events. A novel and a biography of a novelist are both narratives, as are Freud's case histories.

Some critics use the word "narrative" even more generally; Brook Thomas, a new historicist, has critiqued "narratives of human history that neglect the role human labor has played."

NEW CRITICISM *See* Formalism.

NEW HISTORICISM One of the most recent developments in contemporary critical theory, its practitioners share certain convictions, the major ones being that literary critics need to develop a high degree of historical consciousness and that literature should not be viewed apart from other human creations, artistic or otherwise. See "What Is the New Historicism?" pp. 337–346.

See also: Authorial Intention, Deconstruction, Formalism, Ideology, Poststructuralism, Psychoanalytic Criticism.

OPPOSITIONS A concept highly relevant to linguistics, since linguists maintain that words (such as "black" and "death") have meaning not in themselves, but in relation to other words ("white" and "life"). Jacques Derrida, a poststructuralist philosopher of language, has suggested that in the West we think in terms of these "binary oppositions" or dichotomies, which on examination turn out to be evaluative hierarchies. In other words, each opposition — beginning/end, presence/absence, or consciousness/unconsciousness — contains one term that our culture views as superior and one term that we view as negative or inferior.

Derrida has "deconstructed" a number of these binary oppositions, including two — speech/writing and signifier/signified — that he believes to be central to linguistics in particular and Western culture in general. He has concurrently critiqued the "law" of noncontradiction, which is fundamental to Western logic. He and other deconstructors have argued that a text can contain opposed strands of discourse and, therefore, mean opposite things: reason *and* passion, life *and* death, hope *and* despair, black *and* white. Traditionally, criticism has involved choosing between opposed or contradictory meanings and arguing that one is present in the text and the other absent.

French feminists have adopted the ideas of Derrida and other deconstructors, showing not only that we think in terms of such binary oppositions as male/female, reason/emotion, and active/passive, but that we also associate reason and activity with masculinity and emotion and passivity with femininity. Because of this, they have concluded that language is "phallocentric," or masculine-dominated.

See also: Deconstruction, Discourse, Feminist Criticism, Poststructuralism.

PHALLUS The symbolic value of the penis that organizes libidinal development and which Freud saw as a stage in the process of human subjectivity. Lacan viewed the Phallus as the representative of a fraudulent power (male over female) whose "law" is a principle of psychic division (conscious/unconscious) and sexual difference (masculine/feminine). The Symbolic order (see Symbolic) is ruled by the Phallus, which of itself has no inherent meaning *apart from* the power and meaning given to it by individual cultures and societies, and represented by the name of the father as lawgiver and namer.

POSTSTRUCTURALISM The general attempt to contest and subvert structuralism initiated by deconstructors and certain other critics associated with psychoanalytic, Marxist, and feminist theory. Structuralists, using linguistics as a model and employing semiotic (sign) theory, posit the possibility of knowing a text systematically and revealing the "grammar" behind its form and meaning. Poststructuralists argue against the possibility of such knowledge and description. They counter that texts can be shown to contradict not only structuralist accounts of them but also themselves. In making their adversarial claims, they rely on close readings of texts and on the work of theorists such as Jacques Derrida and Jacques Lacan.

Poststructuralists have suggested that structuralism rests on distinctions between "signifier" and "signified" (signs and the things they point toward), "self" and "language" (or "text"), texts and other texts, and text and world that are overly simplistic, if not patently inaccurate. Poststructuralists have shown how all signifieds are also signifiers, and they have treated texts as "intertexts." They have viewed the world as if it *were* a text (we desire a certain car because it *symbolizes* achievement) and the self as the subject, as well as the user, of language; for example, we may shape and speak through language, but it also shapes and speaks through us.

See also: Deconstruction, Feminist Criticism, Intertextuality, Psychoanalytic Criticism, Semiotics, Structuralism.

PSYCHOANALYTIC CRITICISM Grounded in the psychoanalytic theories of Sigmund Freud, it is one of the oldest critical methodologies still in use. Freud's view that works of literature, like dreams, express secret, unconscious desires led to criticism that interpreted literary works as manifestations of the authors' neuroses. More recently, psychoanalytic critics have come to see literary works as skillfully crafted artifacts that may appeal to *our* neuroses by tapping into our repressed wishes and fantasies. Other forms of psychological criticism that diverge from Freud, although they ultimately derive from his insights, include those based on the theories of Carl Jung and Jacques Lacan. See "What Is Psychoanalytic Criticism?" pp. 427–438.

READER-RESPONSE CRITICISM An approach to literature that, as its name implies, considers the way readers respond to texts, as they read. Stanley Fish describes the method by saying that it substitutes for one question, "What does this sentence mean?" a more operational question, "What does this sentence do?" Reader-response criticism shares with deconstruction a strong textual orientation and a reluctance to define a single meaning for a work. Along with psychoanalytic criticism, it shares an interest in the dynamics of mental response to textual cues. See "What Is Reader-Response Criticism?" pp. 398–406.

REAL One of the three orders of subjectivity (see Imaginary and Symbolic), the Real is the intractable and substantial world that resists and exceeds interpretation. The Real cannot be imagined, symbolized, or known directly. It constantly eludes our efforts to name it (death, gravity, the physicality of objects are examples of the Real), and thus challenges both the Imaginary and the Symbolic orders. The Real is fundamentally "Other," the mark of the divide between conscious and unconscious, and is signaled in language by gaps, slips, speechlessness, and the sense of the uncanny. The Real is not what we call "reality." It is the stumbling block of the Imaginary (which thinks it can "imagine" anything, including the Real) and of the Symbolic, which tries to bring the Real under its laws (the Real exposes the "phallacy" of the Law of the Phallus). The Real is frightening; we try to tame it with laws and language and call it "reality."

See also: Imaginary Order, Psychoanalytic Criticism, Symbolic Order.

SEMIOLOGY, SEMIOTIC *See* Semiotics.

SEMIOTICS The study of signs and sign systems and the way meaning is derived from them. Structuralist anthropologists, psychoanalysts, and literary critics developed semiotics during the decades following 1950, but much of the pioneering work had been done at the turn of the century by the founder of modern linguistics, Ferdinand de Saussure, and the American philosopher Charles Sanders Peirce.

Semiotics is based on several important distinctions, including the distinction between "signifier" and "signified" (the sign and what it points toward) and the distinction between "langue" and "parole." *Langue* (French for "tongue," as in "native tongue," meaning language) refers to the entire system within which individual utterances or usages of language have meaning; *parole*

(French for "word") refers to the particular utterances or usages. A principal tenet of semiotics is that signs, like words, are not significant in themselves, but instead have meaning only in relation to other signs and the entire system of signs, or langue.

The affinity between semiotics and structuralist literary criticism derives from this emphasis placed on langue, or system. Structuralist critics, after all, were reacting against formalists and their procedure of focusing on individual words as if meanings didn't depend on anything external to the text.

Poststructuralists have used semiotics but questioned some of its underlying assumptions, including the opposition between signifier and signified. The feminist poststructuralist Julia Kristeva, for instance, has used the word "semiotic" to describe feminine language, a highly figurative, fluid form of discourse that she sets in opposition to rigid, symbolic masculine language.

See also: Deconstruction, Feminist Criticism, Formalism, Poststructuralism, Oppositions, Structuralism, Symbol.

SIMILE *See* Metaphor.

SOCIOHISTORICAL CRITICISM *See* New Historicism.

STRUCTURALISM A science of humankind whose proponents attempted to show that all elements of human culture, including literature, may be understood as parts of a system of signs. Structuralism, according to Robert Scholes, was a reaction to "'modernist' alienation and despair."

Using Ferdinand de Saussure's linguistic theory, European structuralists such as Roman Jakobson, Claude Lévi-Strauss, and Roland Barthes (before his shift toward poststructuralism) attempted to develop a "semiology" or "semiotics" (science of signs). Barthes, among others, sought to recover literature and even language from the isolation in which they had been studied and to show that the laws that govern them govern all signs, from road signs to articles of clothing.

Particularly useful to structuralists were two of Saussure's concepts: the idea of "phoneme" in language and the idea that phonemes exist in two kinds of relationships: "synchronic" and "diachronic." A phoneme is the smallest consistently significant unit in language; thus, both "a" and "an" are phonemes, but "n" is not. A diachronic relationship is that which a phoneme has with those that have preceded it in time and those that will follow it. These "horizontal" relationships produce what we might call discourse or narrative and what Saussure called "parole." The synchronic relationship is the "vertical" one that a word has in a given instant with the entire system of language ("langue") in which it may generate meaning. "An" means what it means in English because those of us who speak the language are using it in the same way at a given time.

Following Saussure, Lévi-Strauss studied hundreds of myths, breaking them into their smallest meaningful units, which he called "mythemes." Removing each from its diachronic relations with other mythemes in a single myth (such as the myth of Oedipus and his mother), he vertically aligned those mythemes that he found to be homologous (structurally correspondent). He then studied the relationships within as well as between vertically aligned columns, in an attempt to understand scientifically, through ratios and proportions, those thoughts and processes that humankind has shared, both at one particular time and across time. One could say, then, that structuralists followed Saussure in preferring to think about the overriding langue or language of myth, in which each mytheme and mytheme-constituted myth fits meaningfully, rather than about isolated individual paroles or narratives. Structuralists followed Saussure's lead in believing what the poststructuralist Jacques Derrida later decided he could not subscribe to — that sign systems must be understood in terms of binary oppositions. In analyzing myths and texts to find basic structures, structuralists tended to find that opposite terms modulate until they are finally resolved or reconciled by some intermediary third term. Thus, a struturalist reading of *Paradise Lost* would show that the war between God and the bad angels becomes a rift between God and sinful, fallen man, the rift then being healed by the Son of God, the mediating third term.

See also: Deconstruction, Discourse, Narrative, Poststructuralism, Semiotics.

SUPERSTRUCTURE   *See* Marxist Criticism.

SYMBOL   A thing, image, or action that, although it is of interest in its own right, stands for or suggests something larger and more complex — often an idea or a range of interrelated ideas, attitudes, and practices.

Within a given culture, some things are understood to be symbols: the flag of the United States is an obvious example. More subtle cultural symbols might be the river as a symbol of time and the journey as a symbol of life and its manifold experiences.

Instead of appropriating symbols generally used and understood within their culture, writers often create symbols by setting up, in their works, a complex but identifiable web of associations. As a result, one object, image, or action suggests others, and often, ultimately, a range of ideas.

A symbol may thus be defined as a metaphor in which the "vehicle," the thing, image, or action used to represent something else, represents many related things (or "tenors") or is broadly suggestive. The urn in Keats's "Ode on a Grecian Urn" suggests many interrelated concepts, including art, truth, beauty, and timelessness.

Symbols have been of particular interest to formalists, who study how meanings emerge from the complex, patterned relationships between images in a work, and psychoanalytic critics, who are interested in how individual authors and the larger culture both disguise and reveal unconscious fears and desires through symbols. Recently, French feminists have also focused on the symbolic. They have suggested that, as wide-ranging as it seems, symbolic language is ultimately rigid and restrictive. They favor semiotic language and writing, which, they contend, is at once more rhythmic, unifying, and feminine.

See also: Feminist Criticism, Metaphor, Psychoanalytic Criticism, Trope.

SYMBOLIC ORDER   One of the three orders of subjectivity (see Imaginary Order and Real), it is the realm of law, language, and society; it is the repository of generally held cultural beliefs. Its symbolic system is language, whose agent is the father or lawgiver, the one who has the power of naming. The human subject is commanded into this preestablished order by language (a process that begins long before a child can speak) and must submit to its orders of communication (grammar, syntax, and so on). Entrance into the Symbolic order determines subjectivity according to a primary law of referentiality that takes the male sign (phallus, see Phallus) as its ordering principle. Lacan states that both sexes submit to the Law of the Phallus (the law of order, language, and differentiation) but their individual relation to the law determines whether they see themselves as — and are seen by others to be — either "masculine" or "feminine." The Symbolic institutes repression (of the Imaginary), thus creating the unconscious, which itself is structured like the language of the symbolic. The unconscious, a timeless realm, cannot be known directly, but it can be understood by a kind of translation that takes place in language — psychoanalysis is the "talking cure." The Symbolic is not a "stage" of development (as is Freud's "oedipal stage") nor is it set in place once and for all in human life. We constantly negotiate its threshold (in sleep, in drunkenness) and can "fall out" of it altogether in psychosis.

See also: Psychoanalytic Criticism, Imaginary Order, Real.

SYNECDOCHE   *See* Metaphor, Metonymy.

TENOR   *See* Metaphor, Metonymy, Symbol.

TROPE   A figure, as in "figure of speech." Literally a "turning," that is, a turning or twisting of a word or phrase to make it mean something else. Principal tropes include metaphor, metonymy, simile, personification, and synecdoche.

See also: Metaphor, Metonymy.

VEHICLE   *See* Metaphor, Metonymy, Symbol.

About the Contributors

THE VOLUME EDITOR

Christopher Fox chairs the Department of English at the University of Notre Dame. He is the author of *Locke and the Scriblerians: Identity and Consciousness in Early Eighteenth-Century Britain* (1988) and the editor or co-editor of several books, including *Psychology and Literature in the Eighteenth Century* (1987); *Teaching Eighteenth-Century Poetry* (1990); *Walking Naboth's Vineyard: New Studies of Swift* (1995); and *Inventing Human Science: Eighteenth-Century Domains* (forthcoming). He has lectured widely in the United States and abroad and is currently writing a book on Swift.

THE CRITICS

Carol Barash is professor of English at Rutgers University. She has published widely on Restoration and eighteenth-century women writers, including *English Women Poets, 1649–1714: Politics, Community and Linguistic Authority* (forthcoming). In addition to a study of shifting narratives of gender and sexuality in the early eighteenth century, of which her essay on *Gulliver's Travels* is a part, she is completing a new standard edition of the poetry of Anne Finch, Countess of Winchilsea.

Terry Castle teaches eighteenth-century literature at Stanford University. Her most recent books are *Masquerade and Civilization: The Carnivalesque in Eighteenth-Century English Culture and Fiction* (Stanford, 1986) and *The Apparitional Lesbian: Female Homosexuality and Modern Culture* (Columbia, 1993). An earlier essay, "The Female Thermometer," won the James L. Clifford Prize for the article of the year on an eighteenth-century topic.

Michael J. Conlon is professor of English and Master of College-in-the-Woods at Binghamton University. He has authored articles on Dryden, Swift, and eighteenth-century parody, and is currently writing a book on performance and spectacle in Swift. He received the 1994 national prize for teaching the eighteenth century, awarded by the American Society for Eighteenth-Century Studies.

Carole Fabricant teaches at the University of California, Riverside. She is the author of *Swift's Landscape* (1982) and numerous articles on eighteenth-century subjects. An earlier essay, "Binding and Dressing Nature's Loose Tresses: The Ideology of Augustan Landscape Design," won the James L. Clifford Prize for the article of the year on an eighteenth-century topic. She was a keynote speaker at Trinity College, Dublin's, Swift celebration in 1995, and is currently involved in a study of colonialism and historiography in the eighteenth century.

Felicity A. Nussbaum is professor of English and Women's Studies at Syracuse University. She is the author of *Torrid Zones: Maternity, Sexuality, and Empire in Eighteenth-Century Narrative*, forthcoming from Johns Hopkins University Press. Among her other books are *The Brink of All We Hate: Satires on Women, 1660–1750* (1984) and *The Autobiographical Subject: Gender and Ideology in Eighteenth-Century England* (1989), winner of the Louis Gottschalk Prize for the book of the year on an eighteenth-century subject.

THE SERIES EDITOR

Ross C Murfin, general editor of the Case Studies in Contemporary Criticism and volume editor of Joseph Conrad's *Heart of Darkness* and Nathaniel Hawthorne's *The Scarlet Letter* in the series, is provost and vice president for academic affairs at Southern Methodist University. He has taught at the University of Miami, Yale University, and the University of Virginia and has published scholarly studies of Joseph Conrad, Thomas Hardy, and D. H. Lawrence.